THE UNFINISHED NATION

A Concise History of
the American People

Volume I: To 1877

THE
UNFINISHED
NATION

A CONCISE HISTORY OF
THE AMERICAN PEOPLE

Volume I: To 1877

THIRD EDITION

ALAN BRINKLEY
Columbia University

Boston   Burr Ridge, IL   Dubuque, IA   Madison, WI   New York   San Francisco   St. Louis
Bangkok   Bogotá   Caracas   Lisbon   London   Madrid
Mexico City   Milan   New Delhi   Seoul   Singapore   Sydney   Taipei   Toronto

McGraw-Hill Higher Education

A Division of The **McGraw-Hill** Companies

THE UNFINISHED NATION: A CONCISE HISTORY OF THE AMERICAN PEOPLE, VOLUME ONE: TO 1877, THIRD EDITION

This book is printed on acid-free paper.

1 2 3 4 5 6 7 8 9 0 DOC/DOC 0 9 8 7 6 5 4 3 2 1 0

ISBN 0–07–229560–0

Editorial director: *Jane E. Vaicunas*
Senior sponsoring editor: *Lyn Uhl*
Developmental editors: *Kristen Mellitt/Jane Tufts*
Senior marketing manager: *Suzanne Daghlian*
Senior project manager: *Jayne Klein*
Production supervisor: *Sandy Ludovissy*
Designer: *Gino Cieslik*
Senior photo research coordinator: *Lori Hancock*
Supplement coordinator: *Tammy Juran*
Compositor: *Shepherd, Inc.*
Typeface: *10.5/13.5 Janson Text*
Printer: *R. R. Donnelley & Sons Company/Crawfordsville, IN*

Cover credit: *Steamboats on the Levee at New Orleans*, 1853, by Hippolyte V.V. Sebron. Tulane University Library, New Orleans.
Photo research: *Deborah Bull/PhotoSearch, Inc.*

The credits section for this book begins on page IC–1 and is considered an extension of the copyright page.

Library of Congress has cataloged the combined edition as follows:

Brinkley, Alan.
  The unfinished nation : a concise history of the American people / Alan Brinkley. — 3rd ed.
    p.   cm.
  Includes bibliographical references and index.
  ISBN 0–07–229559–7 (hc.)
  1. United States—History. I. Title.
E178.1.B827   2000
973—dc21   99–19682
                                                   CIP

www.mhhe.com

About the Author

Alan Brinkley is the Allan Nevins Professor of History at Columbia University in New York. He is the author of *Voices of Protest: Huey Long, Father Coughlin, and the Great Depression* (which won the 1983 American Book Award); *American History: A Survey; The End of Reform: New Deal Liberalism in Recession and War*; and *Liberalism and Its Discontents*. He was educated at Princeton and Harvard and has been a member of the faculties at M.I.T., Harvard (where he received the Joseph R. Levenson Memorial Teaching Prize), and the City University of New York Graduate School. He was the Harmsworth Professor of American History at Oxford University in 1998–1999, and has been a visiting professor at Princeton University, the Ecole des Haute Etudes en Sciences Sociales in Paris, and the University of Torino. His articles, essays, and reviews appear frequently in both scholarly and non-scholarly journals.

Contents

List of Illustrations   XV

List of Maps   XVIII

Preface   XX

CHAPTER ONE: The Meeting of Cultures   1

AMERICA BEFORE COLUMBUS   1
The Civilizations of the South 2   ~   *The Civilizations of the North 3*

EUROPE LOOKS WESTWARD   8
Commerce and Nationalism 8   ~   *Christopher Columbus 9*
The Spanish Empire 11   ~   *Northern Outposts 14*   ~   *Biological and*
Cultural Exchanges 15   ~   *Africa and America 17*

THE ARRIVAL OF THE ENGLISH   19
Incentives for Colonization 19   ~   *The French and the Dutch in America 22*
The First English Settlements 23

DEBATING THE PAST: THE AMERICAN POPULATION BEFORE COLUMBUS   6
CONCLUSION   25
FOR FURTHER REFERENCE   26

CHAPTER TWO: The English "Transplantations"   27

THE EARLY CHESAPEAKE   28
The Founding of Jamestown 28   ~   *Reorganization and Expansion 30*
Exchanges of Agricultural Technology 34   ~   *Maryland and the Calverts 35*
Bacon's Rebellion 36

CARIBBEAN COLONIZATION   38
The West Indies 38   ~   *Masters and Slaves 40*

THE GROWTH OF NEW ENGLAND   41
Plymouth Plantation 41   ~   *The Massachusetts Bay Experiment 43*
The Expansion of New England 45   ~   *Settlers and Natives 46*
The Pequot War and the Technology of Battle 47

THE RESTORATION COLONIES   49
The English Civil War 49   ~   *The Carolinas 50*   ~   *New Netherland,*
New York, and New Jersey 51   ~   *The Quaker Colonies 52*
The Founding of Georgia 54

THE DEVELOPMENT OF EMPIRE   55
The Dominion of New England 56   ～   The "Glorious Revolution" 57

CONCLUSION   58
FOR FURTHER REFERENCE   59

CHAPTER THREE: Society and Culture
                 in Provincial America   60

THE COLONIAL POPULATION   60
*Indentured Servitude 61   ～   Birth and Death 62   ～   Medicine in
the Colonies 63   ～   Women and Families in the Colonies 64
The Beginnings of Slavery in English North America 66   ～   Changing
Sources of European Immigration 70*

THE COLONIAL ECONOMIES   71
*The Southern Economy 71   ～   Northern Economic and
Technological Life 74   ～   The Extent and Limits of Technology 75
The Rise of Colonial Commerce 76*

PATTERNS OF SOCIETY   78
*Masters and Slaves on the Plantation 78   ～   The Puritan Community 79
Cities 82*

THE COLONIAL MIND   83
*The Pattern of Religions 83   ～   The Great Awakening 84
The Enlightenment 85   ～   Literacy and Technology 86   ～   Education 88
The Spread of Science 89   ～   Concepts of Law and Politics 90*

DEBATING THE PAST: THE ORIGINS OF SLAVERY   68
CONCLUSION   91
FOR FURTHER REFERENCE   92

CHAPTER FOUR: The Empire Under Strain   94

LOOSENING TIES   94
A Decentralized Empire 95   ～   The Colonies Divided 96

THE STRUGGLE FOR THE CONTINENT   96
*New France and the Iroquois Nation 97   ～   Anglo-French Conflicts 98
The Great War for the Empire 99*

THE NEW IMPERIALISM   102
*Burdens of Empire 102   ～   The British and the Tribes 103
Battles over Trade and Taxes 104*

STIRRINGS OF REVOLT   107
*The Stamp Act Crisis 107   ～   The Townshend Program 108
The Boston Massacre 109   ～   The Philosophy of Revolt 111
Sites of Resistance 113   ～   The Tea Excitement 115*

COOPERATION AND WAR   116
New Sources of Authority 117   ～   Lexington and Concord 118

CONCLUSION 120
FOR FURTHER REFERENCE 121

CHAPTER FIVE: The American Revolution 122

THE STATES UNITED 122
*Defining American War Aims 123 ～ The Declaration
of Independence 124 ～ Mobilizing for War 125*

THE WAR FOR INDEPENDENCE 128
*The First Phase: New England 128 ～ The Second Phase:
The Mid-Atlantic Region 130 ～ Securing Aid from Abroad 132
The Final Phase: The South 133 ～ Winning the Peace 136*

WAR AND SOCIETY 137
*Loyalists and Minorities 137 ～ Native Americans
and the Revolution 138 ～ Women's Rights and Women's Roles 139
The War Economy 140*

THE CREATION OF STATE GOVERNMENTS 141
*The Assumptions of Republicanism 141 ～ The First State
Constitutions 142 ～ Revising State Governments 143
Toleration and Slavery 143*

THE SEARCH FOR A NATIONAL GOVERNMENT 144
*The Confederation 144 ～ Diplomatic Failures 146 ～ The Confederation
and the Northwest 147 ～ Indians and the Western Lands 149
Debts, Taxes, and Daniel Shays 150*

DEBATING THE PAST: THE AMERICAN REVOLUTION 126
CONCLUSION 152
FOR FURTHER REFERENCE 153

CHAPTER SIX: The Constitution and the New Republic 155

FRAMING A NEW GOVERNMENT 155
*Advocates of Reform 156 ～ A Divided Convention 157
Compromise 159 ～ The Constitution of 1787 160*

ADOPTION AND ADAPTATION 161
Federalists and Antifederalists 161 ～ Completing the Structure 163

FEDERALISTS AND REPUBLICANS 165
*Hamilton and the Federalists 165 ～ Enacting the Federalist Program 167
The Republican Opposition 168*

ESTABLISHING NATIONAL SOVEREIGNTY 169
Securing the West 170 ～ Maintaining Neutrality 171

THE DOWNFALL OF THE FEDERALISTS 172
*The Election of 1796 173 ～ The Quasi War with France 173
Repression and Protest 174 ～ The "Revolution" of 1800 175*

CONCLUSION 177
FOR FURTHER REFERENCE 178

CHAPTER SEVEN: The Jeffersonian Era   180

THE RISE OF CULTURAL NATIONALISM   180
Educational and Literary Nationalism 181 ～ Medicine and Science 183
Cultural Aspirations of the New Nation 184 ～ Religion and Revivalism 185

STIRRINGS OF INDUSTRIALISM   188
Technology in America 188 ～ Transportation Innovations 191
Country and City 192

JEFFERSON THE PRESIDENT   193
The Federal City and the "People's President" 193
Dollars and Ships 195 ～ Conflict with the Courts 196

DOUBLING THE NATIONAL DOMAIN   198
Jefferson and Napoleon 198 ～ The Louisiana Purchase 199
Exploring the West 200 ～ The Burr Conspiracy 202

EXPANSION AND WAR   203
Conflict on the Seas 204 ～ Impressment 204 ～ "Peaceable Coercion" 205
The "Indian Problem" and the British 206 ～ Tecumseh and
the Prophet 207 ～ Florida and War Fever 209

THE WAR OF 1812   210
Battles with the Tribes 210 ～ Battles with the British 212
The Revolt of New England 214 ～ The Peace Settlement 214

CONCLUSION   215
FOR FURTHER REFERENCE   216

CHAPTER EIGHT: Varieties of American Nationalism   218

STABILIZING ECONOMIC GROWTH   218
The Government and Economic Growth 219 ～ Transportation 221

EXPANDING WESTWARD   222
The Great Migration 222 ～ White Settlers in the Old Northwest 223
The Plantation System in the Old Southwest 224 ～ Trade and Trapping
in the Far West 224 ～ Eastern Images of the West 226

THE "ERA OF GOOD FEELINGS"   226
The End of the First Party System 227 ～ John Quincy Adams
and Florida 228 ～ The Panic of 1819 230

SECTIONALISM AND NATIONALISM   230
The Missouri Compromise 230 ～ Marshall and the Court 232
The Court and the Tribes 234 ～ The Latin American Revolution
and the Monroe Doctrine 235

THE REVIVAL OF OPPOSITION   236
The "Corrupt Bargain" 237 ～ The Second President Adams 238
Jackson Triumphant 239

CONCLUSION   240
FOR FURTHER REFERENCE   240

CHAPTER NINE: Jacksonian America   242

THE RISE OF MASS POLITICS   242
The Expanding Electorate 243 ~ *The Legitimization of Party 245*
President of the Common Man 246

"OUR FEDERAL UNION"   250
Calhoun and Nullification 250 ~ *The Rise of Van Buren 251*
The Webster-Hayne Debate 251 ~ *The Nullification Crisis 252*

THE REMOVAL OF THE INDIANS   253
White Attitudes Toward the Tribes 253 ~ *The "Five Civilized Tribes" 254*
Trails of Tears 255 ~ *The Meaning of Removal 257*

JACKSON AND THE BANK WAR   258
Biddle's Institution 258 ~ *The "Monster" Destroyed 259*
The Taney Court 260

THE EMERGENCE OF THE SECOND PARTY SYSTEM   261
The Two Parties 261

POLITICS AFTER JACKSON   264
The Panic of 1837 264 ~ *The Van Buren Program 265*
The Log Cabin Campaign 266 ~ *The Frustration of the Whigs 268*
Whig Diplomacy 269

DEBATING THE PAST: JACKSONIAN DEMOCRACY   248
CONCLUSION   270
FOR FURTHER REFERENCE   271

CHAPTER TEN: America's Economic Revolution   272

THE CHANGING AMERICAN POPULATION   272
The American Population, 1820–1840 273 ~ *Immigration
and Urban Growth, 1840–1860 275* ~ *The Rise of Nativism 276*

TRANSPORTATION AND COMMUNICATIONS REVOLUTIONS   277
The Canal Age 277 ~ *The Early Railroads 280* ~ *The Triumph
of the Rails 281* ~ *The Telegraph 283* ~ *New Forms of Journalism 284*

COMMERCE AND INDUSTRY   285
The Expansion of Business, 1820–1840 285 ~ *The Emergence
of the Factory 286* ~ *Advances in Technology 286*
Innovations in Corporate Organization 289

MEN AND WOMEN AT WORK   289
Recruiting a Native Work Force 290 ~ *The Immigrant Work Force 292*
The Factory System and the Artisan Tradition 292 ~ *Fighting for Control 294*

PATTERNS OF SOCIETY   295
The Rich and the Poor 295 ~ *Social Mobility 296*
Middle-Class Life 297 ~ *The Changing Family 299*
The "Cult of Domesticity" 300 ~ *Leisure Activities 301*

THE AGRICULTURAL NORTH   303
Northeastern Agriculture 304 ∼ *The Old Northwest 304* ∼ *Rural Life 307*

CONCLUSION   308
FOR FURTHER REFERENCE   309

CHAPTER ELEVEN: Cotton, Slavery, and the Old South   310

THE COTTON ECONOMY   310
The Rise of King Cotton 311 ∼ *Southern Trade and Industry 314*
Sources of Southern Difference 315

SOUTHERN WHITE SOCIETY   317
The Planter Class 317 ∼ *The "Southern Lady" 318* ∼ *The Plain Folk 319*

THE "PECULIAR INSTITUTION"   321
Varieties of Slavery 323 ∼ *Life Under Slavery 324*
Slavery in the Cities 325 ∼ *Free Blacks 326* ∼ *Slave Resistance 326*

THE CULTURE OF SLAVERY   329
Slave Religion 329 ∼ *Language and Music 332* ∼ *The Slave Family 333*

DEBATING THE PAST: THE CHARACTER OF SLAVERY   330
CONCLUSION   334
FOR FURTHER REFERENCE   335

CHAPTER TWELVE: Antebellum Culture and Reform   337

THE ROMANTIC IMPULSE   338
Nationalism and Romanticism in American Painting 339 ∼ *An American
Literature 340* ∼ *Literature in the Antebellum South 341*
The Transcendentalists 342 ∼ *Visions of Utopia 344*
Redefining Gender Roles 345 ∼ *The Mormons 346*

REMAKING SOCIETY   347
Revivalism, Morality, and Order 348 ∼ *Health, Science,
and Phrenology 348* ∼ *Medical Science 351* ∼ *Education 352*
Rehabilitation 353 ∼ *The Rise of Feminism 355*

THE CRUSADE AGAINST SLAVERY   356
Early Opposition to Slavery 356 ∼ *Garrison and Abolitionism 357*
Black Abolitionists 357 ∼ *Anti-Abolitionism 359*
Abolitionism Divided 359

CONCLUSION   362
FOR FURTHER REFERENCE   362

CHAPTER THIRTEEN: The Impending Crisis   364

LOOKING WESTWARD   364
Manifest Destiny 365 ∼ *Americans in Texas 366* ∼ *Oregon 367*
The Westward Migration 369

EXPANSION AND WAR   372
The Democrats and Expansion 372 ∼ *The Southwest and California 373*
The Mexican War 374

THE SECTIONAL DEBATE 377
Slavery and the Territories 377 ~ *The California Gold Rush 379*
Rising Sectional Tensions 381 ~ *The Compromise of 1850 381*

THE CRISES OF THE 1850S 384
The Uneasy Truce 384 ~ *"Young America" 385* ~ *Slavery, Railroads, and
the West 386* ~ *The Kansas-Nebraska Controversy 387*
"Bleeding Kansas" 388 ~ *The Free-Soil Ideology 390* ~ *The Pro-Slavery
Argument 391* ~ *Buchanan and Depression 392* ~ *The* Dred Scott
Decision 393 ~ *Deadlock over Kansas 394* ~ *The Emergence
of Lincoln 395* ~ *John Brown's Raid 396* ~ *The Election of Lincoln 397*

CONCLUSION 398
FOR FURTHER REFERENCE 399

CHAPTER FOURTEEN: The Civil War 401

THE SECESSION CRISIS 401
The Withdrawal of the South 401 ~ *The Failure of Compromise 402*
The Opposing Sides 404

THE MOBILIZATION OF THE NORTH 405
Economic Nationalism 405 ~ *Raising the Union Armies 408*
Wartime Leadership and Politics 409 ~ *The Politics of Emancipation 410*
African Americans and the Union Cause 411 ~ *The War and
Economic Development 413* ~ *Women, Nursing, and the War 413*

THE MOBILIZATION OF THE SOUTH 414
Confederate Government 415 ~ *Money and Manpower 416*
Economic and Social Effects of the War 417

STRATEGY AND DIPLOMACY 418
The Commanders 418 ~ *The Role of Sea Power 420*
Europe and the Disunited States 421

CAMPAIGNS AND BATTLES 422
The Technology of War 423 ~ *The Opening Clashes, 1861 425*
The Western Theater, 1862 426 ~ *The Virginia Front, 1862 428*
1863: Year of Decision 431 ~ *The Last Stage, 1864–1865 435*

DEBATING THE PAST: THE CAUSES OF THE CIVIL WAR 406
CONCLUSION 439
FOR FURTHER REFERENCE 440

CHAPTER FIFTEEN: Reconstruction and
the New South 441

THE PROBLEMS OF PEACEMAKING 442
The Aftermath of War and Emancipation 443 ~ *Competing Notions
of Freedom 444* ~ *Plans for Reconstruction 446*
The Death of Lincoln 448 ~ *Johnson and "Restoration" 448*

RADICAL RECONSTRUCTION 449
The Black Codes 449 ~ *The Fourteenth Amendment 452*
The Congressional Plan 453 ~ *The Impeachment of the President 455*

THE SOUTH IN RECONSTRUCTION   455
The Reconstruction Governments 456   ~   Education 457
Landownership and Tenancy 458   ~   Incomes and Credit 459
The African-American Family in Freedom 460

THE GRANT ADMINISTRATION   462
The Soldier President 462   ~   The Grant Scandals 463
The Greenback Question 463   ~   Republican Diplomacy 464

THE ABANDONMENT OF RECONSTRUCTION   465
The Southern States "Redeemed" 465   ~   Waning Northern
Commitment 466   ~   The Compromise of 1877 466
The Legacy of Reconstruction 468

THE NEW SOUTH   469
The "Redeemers" 470   ~   Industrialization and the "New South" 471
Tenants and Sharecroppers 473   ~   African Americans and
the New South 473   ~   The Birth of Jim Crow 475

DEBATING THE PAST: RECONSTRUCTION   450
CONCLUSION   477
FOR FURTHER REFERENCE   479

APPENDIXES   A-1

MAPS

The United States in 1996   A-2

United States Territorial Expansion, 1783–1898   A-4

DOCUMENTS AND TABLES

The Declaration of Independence   A-5

The Constitution of the United States   A-10

Presidential Elections   A-30

Population of the United States, 1790–1998   A-37

Employment, 1870–1998   A-38

Production, Trade, and Federal Spending/Debt, 1790–1998   A-39

Illustration Credits   IC-1

Index   I-1

List of Illustrations

Indians Fishing   4

The Mexicans Strike Back   13

Roanoke   24

Recruiting for the Colonies, 1609   29

A Pequot Village Destroyed   48

Africans Bound for America   66

Selling Tobacco   73

A Study of Witchcraft   81

Town and Country-Man's Almanack   87

The Magnetic Dispensary   90

Recruiting for the French and Indian War   100

The Boston Massacre (1770), by Paul Revere   110

The Scales of Justis   114

Recruiting Patriots   117

Revolutionary Soldiers   128

Daniel Shays and Job Shattuck   151

The Convention at Philadelphia   158

Celebrating the Constitution   163

A Comment on the Whiskey Rebellion   170

Congressional Brawlers, 1798   176

Dr. William Gleason   183

The Camp Meeting   187

Slater's Mill   189

The Cotton Gin   190

Thomas Jefferson   194

The Burning of Washington   213

An Early Mill in New England   220

The Clermont's Engine   222

The Rendezvous   225

The Inauguration of James Monroe, 1816   227

Seminole Dance   229

John Marshall   233

Andrew Jackson En Route to Washington, 1829   244

Election Scene   247

Black Hawk and Whirling Thunder   254

The New York *Sun*   266

Whig Headquarters   267

An Appeal to Emigrants   274

Racing on the Railroad   280

The Early Sewing Machine   288

New England Textile Workers   290

A Toleware Maker, c. 1850   293

Nathan Hawley and Family   298

McCormick's Reaper   306

The New Orleans Cotton Exchange   314

De Bow's Commercial Review   316

Returning from the Cotton Field   322

Harriet Tubman with Escaped Slaves   328

The Old Plantation   333

Kindred Spirits   340

Plan for the Colony at New Harmony   345

The Drunkard's Progress   349

Phrenology   350

Frederick Douglass   358

Uncle Tom's Cabin   361

Crossing the Plains   371

Stephen Kearny in Santa Fe   377

Bleeding Kansas   389

John Brown   396

African-American Troops   412

The U.S. Sanitary Commission   414

Confederate Volunteers   417

Skirmish at Antietam   431

Ulysses S. Grant   435

Charleston, 1865   443

A Monument to the Confederate Dead   445

Abraham Lincoln   447

A Celebration of Reconstruction   453

After Slavery   457

African-American Work After Slavery   461

"Is This a Republican Form of Government?"   470

Tuskegee Institute, 1881   474

List of Maps

Principal Subsistence Patterns of Early Native Peoples of North America   5

European Journeys of Exploration and Conquest   10

Spanish America   12

Growth of the Chesapeake, 1607–1750   32

European Colonial Expansion in the Caribbean Basin, c. 1650   39

Growth of New England, 1620–1750   42

Dominant Immigrant Groups in Colonial America, c. 1760   72

Overseas Trade During the Colonial Period   77

The Thirteen Colonies in 1763   105

The First Battles of the Revolution   119

The Revolution in the North, 1775–1776   129

The Revolution in the Middle Colonies, 1776–1778   131

The Revolution in the South, 1778–1781   135

State Claims to Western Lands and Cessions to National Government, 1782–1802   145

Land Survey: Ordinance of 1785   148

Exploration of the Louisiana Purchase, 1803–1807   201

The War of 1812   211

The Missouri Compromise, 1820   231

The Expulsion of Indians from the South, 1830–1838   256

Canals in the Northeast, to 1860   278

The Growth of the Railroads, 1850–1860   282

Slavery and Cotton: The South in 1820 and 1860   313

Settlement of the Oregon Boundary Dispute, 1846   368

Western Trails, to 1860   370

The Mexican War, 1846–1848   375

American Expansion into the Southwest, 1845–1853   378

Slave and Free Territories According to the Compromise of 1850   382

Election of 1860   398

The Process of Secession   403

The War in the West, 1861–1863   427

The Virginia Theater, 1861–1863   429

Assault on Vicksburg, May 1862–July 1863   433

The Battle of Gettysburg, July 1–3, 1863   434

Virginia Campaigns, 1864–1865   437

Sherman's March to the Sea, 1864–1865   438

Election of 1876   467

The United States in 1996   A-2

United States Territorial Expansion, 1783–1898   A-4

Preface

T HE STORY OF the American past, which is the subject of this book, has undergone many transformations in recent decades. The past itself has not changed, of course, but the way Americans understand it has changed dramatically. And in the wake of those changes have come both new forms of presentation and bitter controversies.

In one sense, American history is thriving as almost never before through the workings of American popular culture. Historical museums and exhibitions have multiplied and have attracted large audiences. Popular writing on history—both nonfiction and novels—has grown in popularity. History is a continuing presence on television, in films, and increasingly on the Internet. The popular appetite for American history seems to be almost boundless. At the same time, however, historical scholarship has become the source of increasing debate—among historians themselves, among the various publics historians try to reach, and even among politicians, some of whom attack the historical profession for what they claim is an excessively critical view of the past.

Both the growing popularity of history and the growing controversies surrounding it reflect the character of our time. It is an era of rapid and bewildering change, which encourages people to look to the past for guidance and reassurance—for reminders of what many believe were simpler, stabler times. But the turbulence of our age has also encouraged historians to ask new questions of the past—and thus to reinterpret it—in an effort to understand the tensions and contests that preoccupy us today. As the population of the United States has become more diverse and as groups that once stood outside the view of scholarship have thrust themselves into its center, historians have labored to reveal the immense complexity of their country's past.

Historical narratives once recounted little beyond the experiences of great men and the unfolding of great public events. Today, they attempt to tell a more complicated story—one that includes private as well as public lives, ordinary people as well as celebrated ones, difference as well as unity. This newer history seems fragmented at times, because it attempts to embrace so many more areas of human experience than the older narratives. It is often disturbing, because it reveals failures and injustices as well as triumphs. But it is also richer, fuller, and better suited to helping us understand our own diverse and contentious world.

Threading one's way through the many, conflicting demands of contemporary scholars and contemporary readers is no easy task. But I have tried in this book to consider both the diversity and the unity that have characterized the American experience. The United States is, and has always been, a nation of many cultures. To understand its history, we must understand the experiences of the many groups who have shaped American society—the many worlds that have developed within it based on region, religion, class, ideology, race, gender, and ethnicity.

But the United States is not simply a collection of different cultures. It is also a great nation. And as important as understanding its diversity is understanding the forces that have drawn it together and allowed it to survive and flourish despite division. The United States has constructed a remarkably stable and enduring political system, which touches the lives of all Americans. It has developed an immense and highly productive national economy that affects the working and consuming lives of virtually everyone. It has created a mass popular culture that colors the experiences and assumptions of almost all Americans, and of the people of much of the rest of the world as well. One can admire these unifying forces for their contributions to America's considerable success as a nation, or condemn them for creating or failing to address injustices. But no one proposing to understand the history of the United States can afford to ignore them.

This third edition of *The Unfinished Nation*, like its predecessors, tries to tell the complicated and endlessly fascinating story of America for students of history and for general readers. Those familiar with earlier editions will notice some significant changes. Perhaps the most important is considerably expanded attention throughout the book to the history of science and technology, whose importance to American history has been incalculable. For example, chapter 1 contains new material on military technology to accompany the discussion of King Philip's War; and a new section on medical science, which discusses the discovery of anaesthesia and early steps toward the germ theory of disease has been added to chapter 12. I want to express my appreciation to the scholarly reviewers who helped to determine which science and technology topics the book should include: Edward J. Larson, University of Georgia; Sarah K. A. Pfatteicher, University of Wisconsin; Carroll Pursell, Case Western Reserve University; Bruce E. Seely, Michigan Technological University; Howard Segal, University of Maine; and Steven W. Usselman, Georgia Institute of Technology.

There is also a great deal of new material on the history of American culture, and on popular culture in particular. There is a new "Debating the Past" essay in chapter 1, examining the controversy over the pre-Columbian populations. There is a new summary conclusion at the end of each chapter, and new annotated bibliographies, which include references to relevant films and Internet sites.

The result of these and many other changes is, I hope, a book that will introduce readers to enough different aspects of American history to make them aware of its extraordinary richness and complexity. But I hope, too, that it will give readers some sense of the shared experiences of Americans and of the forces that have sustained the United States as a nation.

**

I am grateful to many people for their help on this book: Lyn Uhl, Kristen Mellitt, Suzanne Daghlian, and Jayne Klein at McGraw-Hill; Deborah Bull, for her expert photo research; and John Stoner and Thad Russell for their indispensable help with research. I also want to thank the various scholars who reviewed the second edition and its supplements, and offered suggestions and comments: Guy Alchon, *University of Delaware*; Paul Bethel, *American River College*; Thomas J. Brown, *University of South Carolina*; William R. Cario, *Concordia University Wisconsin*; Paul N. Chardoul, *Grand Rapids Community College*; J. H. DeBerry, *Somerset Community College*; David DiLeo, *Saddleback Community College*; William Dofflemyer, *San Joaquin Delta College*; Don Fisher, *Niagara County Community College*; Stephen E. Gooch, *Richland College*; Elizabeth A. Hachten, *University of Wisconsin–Whitewater*; Roger H. Hall, *Allan Hancock College*; Michael Haridopolos, *Brevard Community College*; Michael Mini, *Montgomery County Community College*; Ronald Petrin, *Oklahoma State University*; Jody Suhanek, *Lane Community College*; Roger Tate, *Somerset Community College*; Michael Welsh, *University of Northern Colorado*; and Nelson E.

Woodard, *California State University–Fullerton*. I am also grateful to those readers of the book who have offered me unsolicited comments, criticisms, and corrections. I hope they will continue to do so. Suggestions can be sent to me at the Department of History, Columbia University, New York, NY 10027, or by E-mail at ab65@columbia.edu.

Alan Brinkley

CHAPTER ONE

The Meeting of Cultures

America Before Columbus ~ *Europe Looks Westward*
The Arrival of the English

T HE DISCOVERY OF America did not begin with Christopher Columbus. It started many thousands of years earlier when human beings first crossed an ancient land bridge—over the Bering Strait into what is now Alaska—and almost certainly without realizing it began to people a new continent.

AMERICA BEFORE COLUMBUS

No one is certain when these migrations began; recent estimates suggest that they started between 14,000 and 16,000 years ago. They were probably a result of the development of stone-tipped spears and other hunting implements that made it possible for humans to pursue large animals from Asia into North America. Year after year, a few at a time, these nomadic peoples—probably drawn from a Mongolian stock similar to that of modern-day eastern Siberia—entered the new continent and moved deeper into its heart. Perhaps as early as 8,000 B.C., the migrations reached the southern tip of South America. By the end of the fifteenth century A.D., when the first important contact with Europeans occurred, America was the home of many millions of men and women. Scholars estimate that well over 50 million people—and perhaps as many as 75 million—lived in the Americas by 1500 and that perhaps 10 million lived in the territory that now constitutes the United States.

TIME LINE

16,000–14,000 B.C.		1492	1497	1502
Asians migrate to North America		Columbus discovers America	Cabot explores North America	African slaves arrive in Spanish America

1518–1530	1519–1522	1558	1565	1587
Smallpox ravages Indians	Magellan circumnavigates globe	Elizabeth I becomes English queen	St Augustine, Florida founded	"Lost Colony" established on Roanoke Island

1603	1607	1608	1609
James I becomes English king	Jamestown founded	French establish Quebec	Spanish found Santa Fe

The Civilizations of the South

The most elaborate of these societies emerged in South and Central America and in Mexico. In Peru, the Incas created a powerful empire of perhaps 6 million people. They developed a complex political system and a large network of paved roads that welded together the populations of many tribes under a single government. In Central America and on the Yucatan Peninsula of Mexico, the Mayas built a sophisticated culture with a written language, a numerical system similar to the Arabic, an accurate calendar, and an advanced agricultural system. They were succeeded by the Aztecs, a once-nomadic warrior tribe from the north. In the late thirteenth century, the Aztecs established a precarious rule over much of central and southern Mexico and built elaborate administrative, educational, and medical systems comparable to the most advanced in Europe at the time. The Aztecs also developed a harsh religion that required human sacrifice. Their Spanish conquerors discovered the skulls of 100,000 victims in one location when they arrived in 1519.

The economies of these societies were based primarily on agriculture, but there were also substantial cities. Tenochtitlán, the Aztec capital built on the site of present-day Mexico City, had a population of over 100,000 in 1500, which was comparable to some of the largest European cities of the time. The Mayas (at Mayapan and elsewhere) and the Incas (in such cities as Cuzco and Machu Picchu) produced elaborate settlements with striking religious and ceremonial structures. These civilizations accomplished all this without some of the important technologies that Asian and European civilizations possessed. As late as the sixteenth century, no American society had yet developed wheeled vehicles.

The Civilizations of the North

The peoples north of Mexico—in the lands that became the United States and Canada—developed less elaborate but still substantial civilizations. Inhabitants of the northern regions of the continent subsisted on some combination of hunting, gathering, and fishing. They included the Eskimos of the Arctic Circle, who fished and hunted seals and whose civilization spanned thousands of miles of largely frozen land; the big-game hunters of the northern forests, who led nomadic lives based on pursuit of moose and caribou; the tribes of the Pacific Northwest, whose principal occupation was salmon fishing and who created substantial permanent settlements along the coast; and a group of tribes spread through relatively arid regions of the Far West, who developed successful communities based on fishing, hunting small game, and gathering edible plants.

Other societies in North America were primarily agricultural. Among the most developed were those in the Southwest. The people of that arid region built large irrigation systems, and they constructed substantial towns of stone and adobe structures. In the Great Plains region, too, most tribes were engaged in sedentary farming (corn and other grains) and lived in large permanent settlements, although some small nomadic tribes subsisted by hunting buffalo.

The eastern third of what is now the United States—much of it covered with forests and inhabited by the Woodland Indians—had the greatest food resources of any area of the continent. Most of the many tribes of the region engaged in farming, hunting, gathering, and fishing simultaneously. In the South there were substantial permanent settlements and large trading networks based on the corn and other grains grown in the rich lands of the Mississippi River valley. Cahokia, a trading center located near present-day St. Louis, had a population of 40,000 at its peak in A.D. 1200.

The agricultural societies of the Northeast were less stationary. Farming techniques there were designed to exploit the land quickly rather than to develop permanent settlements. Many of the tribes living east of the Mississippi River were linked together loosely by common linguistic roots. The largest of these language groups consisted of the Algonquin tribes, which

INDIANS FISHING The English explorer John White visited areas of the Atlantic coast in the 1580s and created a series of watercolors of native life there—among them this scene of Woodland Indians fishing from a canoe.

lived along the Atlantic seaboard from Canada to Virginia; the Iroquois Confederacy, which was centered in what is now upstate New York; and the Muskogean tribes, which consisted of the tribes in the southernmost region of the eastern seaboard. Alliances among the various Indian societies (even among those with common languages) were fragile, since the peoples of the Americas did not think of themselves as members of a single civilization.

Religion was as important to Indian society as it was to most other cultures, and it was usually closely linked with the natural world on which the tribes depended. Native Americans worshipped many gods, whom they associated variously with crops, game, forests, rivers, and other elements of nature.

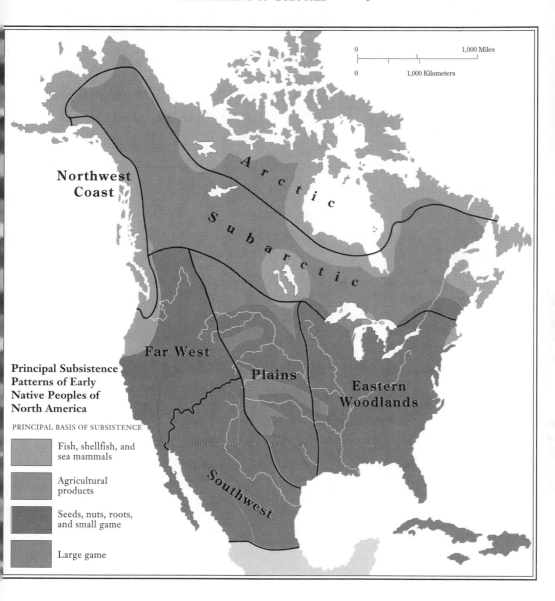

**Principal Subsistence
Patterns of Early
Native Peoples of
North America**

PRINCIPAL BASIS OF SUBSISTENCE

Fish, shellfish, and
sea mammals

Agricultural
products

Seeds, nuts, roots,
and small game

Large game

All tribes assigned women the jobs of caring for children, preparing
meals, and gathering certain foods. But the allocation of other tasks varied
from one society to another. Some tribal groups (notably the Pueblos of
the Southwest) reserved farming tasks almost entirely for men. Among
other groups (including the Algonquins, the Iroquois, and the Muskogean),
women tended the fields, while men engaged in hunting, warfare, or clearing land. Because women and children were often left alone for extended

D E B A T I N G   T H E   P A S T

The American Population Before Columbus

N O ONE knows how many people lived in the Americas in the centuries before Columbus. But scholars, and others, have spent more than a century, and have written many thousands of pages, debating the question nevertheless. Interest in this question survives, despite the near impossibility of answering it, because the debate over the pre-Columbian population is closely connected to the much larger debate over the consequences of European settlement of the Western Hemisphere.

Throughout the nineteenth century, Native Americans—drawing from their own rich tradition of oral history—spoke often of the great days before Columbus when there were many more people in their tribes. The painter and ethnographer George Catlin, who spent much time among the tribes in the 1830s, listened to these oral legends and estimated that there had been 16 million Indians in North America before the Europeans came. Other white Americans dismissed such claims as preposterous, insisting that Indian civilization was far too primitive ever to have sustained a population even as large as a million.

In 1928, James Mooney, an ethnologist at the Smithsonian Institution, drawing from early accounts of soldiers and missionaries in the sixteenth century, came up with the implausibly precise figure of 1.15 million natives who lived north of Mexico in the early sixteenth century. That was a larger figure than nineteenth-century writers had suggested, but still much smaller than the Indians themselves claimed. A few years later, the anthropologist Alfred Kroeber used some of Mooney's methods to come up with an estimate considerably larger than Mooney's, but much lower than Catlin's. He concluded in 1934 that there were 8.4 million people in the Americas in 1492, half in North America and half in the Caribbean and South America. His conclusions remained largely uncontested until the 1960s.

These low early estimates reflected an assumption that the arrival of the Europeans did not much reduce the native population. But in the 1960s and 1970s, scholars discovered that the early tribes had been catastrophically decimated by European plagues not long after the arrival of Columbus—that the numbers Europeans observed even in the late 1500s were already dramatically smaller than the numbers in 1492. Drawing on early work by anthropologists and others who discovered evidence of widespread deaths by disease, historians such as William McNeill in 1976 and Alfred Crosby a decade later produced powerful accounts of the near extinction of some tribes and the dramatic depopulation of others in a pestilential holocaust with few parallels in history.

The belief that the native population was much larger in 1492 than it was a few decades later has helped spur much larger estimates of how many people were in America before Columbus. Henry Dobyns, an anthropologist, claimed in 1966 that there were between 10 and 12 million people north of Mexico in 1492, and between 90 and 112 million in all of the Americas. No subsequent scholar has made so high a claim, but most subsequent estimates have been much closer to Dobyns's than to Kroeber's. The geographer William M. Denevan, for example, argued in 1976 that the American population in 1492 was around 55 million and that the population north of Mexico was under 4 million. These are among the lowest of modern estimates, but still dramatically higher than the nineteenth-century numbers.

The vehemence with which scholars, and at times the larger public, have debated these figures does not stem solely from the difficulty inherent in the effort to determine population size. It is also because the debate over the population is part of the debate over whether the arrival of Columbus—and the millions of Europeans who followed him—was a great advance in the history of civilization (as most Americans believed in 1892 when they ebulliently celebrated the 400th anniversary of Columbus's voyage) or an unparalleled catastrophe that virtually exterminated a large and flourishing native population (as some Americans and Europeans argued during the far more somber commemoration of the 500th anniversary in 1992). How to balance the many achievements of European civilization in the New World after 1492 against the terrible destruction of native peoples that accompanied it is, in the end, less a historical question, perhaps, than a moral one.

periods while men were away hunting or fighting, women in some tribes tended to control the social and economic organization of the settlements.

EUROPE LOOKS WESTWARD

Europeans were almost entirely unaware of the existence of the Americas before the fifteenth century. A few early wanderers—Leif Eriksson, an eleventh-century Norse seaman, and perhaps others—had glimpsed parts of the New World on their voyages. But even if their discoveries had become common knowledge (and they did not), there would have been little incentive for others to follow. Europe in the Middle Ages (roughly A.D. 500–1500) was too divided and decentralized, too limited in its commerce, and too lacking in powerful political leaders to inspire many great ventures. By the end of the fifteenth century, however, conditions in Europe had changed, and the incentive for overseas exploration had grown.

Commerce and Nationalism

Two changes in particular encouraged Europeans to look toward new lands. One was a result of the significant growth in Europe's population in the fifteenth century. The Black Death, a catastrophic epidemic of the bubonic plague that began in Constantinople in 1347, had killed (according to some estimates) as many as half the people of the continent. But a century and a half later, the population had rebounded. With that growth came a reawakening of commerce and a general increase in prosperity. A new merchant class was emerging to meet the rising demand for goods from abroad. As trade increased, and as advances in navigation and shipbuilding made long-distance sea travel more feasible, interest in expanding trade even further grew quickly.

The second change was the emergence of new governments that were more united and powerful than the feeble political entities of the feudal past. In the western areas of Europe in particular, strong new monarchs were emerging, creating centralized nation-states and growing eager to enhance the commercial development of their nations.

Ever since the early fourteenth century, when Marco Polo and other adventurers had returned from Asia bearing exotic spices, cloths, and dyes, and even more exotic tales, Europeans who craved commercial glory had dreamed above all of trade with the East. For two centuries, that trade had been limited by the difficulties of the long overland journey to the Asian courts. But in the fourteenth century, as the maritime talents of several western European societies increased, talk of finding a faster, safer sea route to East Asia began. In the late fifteenth century, some of the new monarchs were ready to finance daring voyages to find it.

The Portuguese were the preeminent maritime power in the fifteenth century largely because of Prince Henry the Navigator, who devoted much of his life to the promotion of exploration. In 1486, after Henry's death, the Portuguese explorer Bartholomeu Dias rounded the southern tip of Africa (the Cape of Good Hope); and in 1497–1498, Vasco da Gama proceeded all the way around the cape to India. But the Portuguese were not the first to encounter the New World.

Christopher Columbus

Christopher Columbus was born and reared in Genoa, Italy, and spent his early seafaring years in the service of the Portuguese. By the time he was a young man, he had developed great ambitions. He believed he could reach East Asia by sailing west, across the Atlantic, rather than east, around Africa. Columbus's optimism rested on several basic misconceptions. He thought the world was far smaller than it actually is. He also believed that the Asian continent extended farther eastward than it actually does. Most important, he did not realize that anything lay to the west between Europe and the lands of Asia.

Columbus failed to enlist the leaders of Portugal behind his plan, so he turned instead to Spain. The marriage of Spain's two most powerful regional rulers, Ferdinand of Aragon and Isabella of Castile, had produced the strongest monarchy in Europe, one that was eager to demonstrate its strength by sponsoring new commercial ventures. Columbus appealed to Queen Isabella for support for his proposed westward voyage, and in 1492, she agreed. Commanding ninety men and three ships—the *Niña*, the *Pinta*, and the *Santa María*—Columbus left Spain in August 1492 and sailed west into the Atlantic. Ten weeks later, he sighted land and assumed he had reached an island off Asia. In fact, he had landed in the Bahamas. When he pushed on and encountered Cuba, he assumed he had reached China. He returned to Spain, bringing with him several captured natives as evidence of his achievement. (He called the natives "Indians" because he believed they were from the East Indies in the Pacific.)

But Columbus did not, of course, bring back news of the great khan's court in China or any samples of the fabled wealth of the Indies. And so a year later, he tried again, this time with a much larger expedition. As before, he headed into the Caribbean, discovering several other islands and leaving a small and short-lived colony on Hispaniola. On a third voyage,

European Journeys of Exploration and Conquest

SPANISH VOYAGES

- ◄•••••••• Columbus, 1492
- ◄— — — Columbus, 1493
- ◄- - - - - Columbus, 1498
- ◄-·-·-·- Columbus, 1502
- ◄——— Other Spanish routes

OTHER EUROPEAN VOYAGES

- ◄——— French
- ◄——— English

Native American empires

FROBISHER 1576–1578
HUDSON 1610
GILBERT 1583
CABOT 1497
LABRADOR
CARTIER 1534, 1535
CARTIER 1535
HUDSON 1610
Hudson Bay
James Bay
CARTIER 1535
VERRAZANO 1524
Gulf of St. Lawrence
St. Lawrence R.
Sagadahoc
Drake's Bay
Missouri R.
Ohio R.
ATLANTIC OCEAN
VERRAZANO 1524
Arkansas R.
CORONADO 1540–1542
Red R.
DE SOTO
DE SOTO 1539–1542
Rio Grande
Pecos R.
Mississippi R.
HAWKINS 1580
St. Augustine
PONCE DE LEÓN 1513
COLUMBUS 1492
Gulf of Mexico
PONCE DE LEÓN
Havana
Tenochtitlan (Mexico City)
CORTÉS 1518–1521
Mayapan
Chichen Itza
Santiago de Cuba
San Juan
AZTEC EMPIRE
MAYAN EMPIRE
YUCATÁN PENINSULA
COLUMBUS 1493
DRAKE 1577–1580
HAWKINS 1580
Caribbean Sea
1493
COLUMBUS 1502
PACIFIC OCEAN
BALBOA 1513
COLUMBUS 1498
1502
Orinoco River
ISTHMUS OF PANAMA
PIZARRO 1531–1533
INCA EMPIRE

0   500 Miles
0   500 Kilometers

45°
41°
34°
38°
34°
41°
45°

in 1498, he finally reached the mainland and cruised along the northern coast of South America. He then realized, for the first time, that he had encountered not a part of Asia but a separate continent. Still, he remained convinced that Asia was only a short distance away.

Columbus's celebrated accomplishments made him a popular hero for a time, but he ended his life in obscurity. Ultimately, he was even unable to give his name to the land he had revealed to the Europeans. That distinction went instead to a Florentine merchant, Amerigo Vespucci, a passenger on a later Portuguese expedition to the New World, who wrote a series of vivid descriptions of the lands he visited and helped popularize the idea that the Americas were new continents.

Partly as a result of Columbus's initiative, Spain began to devote greater resources and energy to maritime exploration and gradually replaced Portugal as the foremost seafaring nation. In 1513 the Spaniard Vasco de Balboa crossed the Isthmus of Panama and became the first known European to gaze westward upon the great ocean that separated America from China. Seeking access to that ocean, Ferdinand Magellan, a Portuguese in Spanish employ, found the strait that now bears his name at the southern end of South America, struggled through the stormy narrows and into the ocean (so calm by contrast that he christened it the *Pacific*), and then proceeded to the Philippines. There Magellan died in a conflict with the natives, but his expedition went on to complete the first known circumnavigation of the globe (1519–1522). By 1550, Spaniards had explored the coasts of North America as far north as Oregon in the west and Labrador in the east.

The Spanish Empire

In time, Spanish explorers in the New World stopped thinking of America simply as an obstacle to their search for a route to the East and began instead to consider it a possible source of wealth in itself. The Spanish claimed for themselves the whole of the New World, except for a piece of it (today's Brazil) that was reserved by a papal decree for the Portuguese; and by the mid-sixteenth century, they were establishing a substantial American empire.

The early Spanish colonists, beginning with those Columbus brought on his second voyage, settled on the islands of the Caribbean. But then, in 1518, Hernando Cortés, who had been an unsuccessful Spanish government official in Cuba for fourteen years, decided to lead a small military expedition (about 600 men) against the Aztecs in Mexico and their powerful emperor, Montezuma, after hearing stories of great treasures there. His

San Francisco (1776)
Monterey (1770)
San Luis Obispo (1772)
Los Angeles (1781)
San Juan Capistrano (1776)
San Diego de Alcala (1769)
Tucson (1709)
Taos (1609)
Santa Fe (1607)

LOUISIANA
(Spanish 1763-1800)

UNITED STATES
(from 1783)

Red R.

Mississippi R.

Rio Grande

SPANISH FLORIDA
(to 1819)

St. Augustine (1565)

Gulf of Mexico

Bahamas
(to Britain 1646)

ATLANTIC OCEAN

World divided into Spanish and Portuguese hemispheres: Treaty of Tordesillas (1494)

Culiacán (1531)

Tampico

VICEROYALTY OF

La Habana (1515)

Mexico City (Tenochtitlán) (1325)
Veracruz (1519)

Yucatan Peninsula

Cuba (1492)
Santiago (1514)

Espanola (1492)

Puerto Rico (1502)

NEW SPAIN

Jamaica
(to Britain 1655)

HAITI
(French after 1697)

Santo Domingo (1496)

Guatemala (1519)

Caribbean Sea

Panama (1519)

Caracas (1567)

Orinoco R.

Trinidad (1498)

FRENCH GUIANA (1626)

PACIFIC OCEAN

VICEROYALTY OF
NEW GRANADA

Santa Fe de Bogotá (1538)

SURINAM
(Dutch) (1625)

Quito (1534)

Amazon River

Guayaquil (1535)

Ciudad de los Reyes (Lima) (1535)

Cuzco (1535)

VICEROYALTY OF
NEW CASTILIA
(Peru)

La Paz (1548)

VICEROYALTY OF
LA PLATA

Parana R.

Rio de Janeiro (1567)

São Paulo (1554)

Valparaiso (1544)

Santiago (1541)

Buenos Aires (1580)

Montevideo (1724)

Rio de la Plata

PORTUGUESE BRAZIL

Straits of Magellan
Tierra del Fuego

Spanish America

Colonial boundaries and provincial names are for the late 18th century

Aztec Empire at the time of Spanish conquest

Inca Empire at the time of Spanish conquest

OUTPOSTS ON THE NORTHERN FRONTIER OF NEW SPAIN
(Not simultaneous; through the 18th century)

• Missions

○ Forts (sometimes with missions)

• Settlements

0   1,000 Miles
0   1,000 Kilometers

THE MEXICANS STRIKE BACK In this vivid scene from the Duran Codex, Mexican artists illustrate a rare moment in which Mexican warriors gained the upper hand over the Spanish invaders. Driven back by native fighters, the Spanish have taken refuge in a room in the royal palace in Tenochtitlán while brightly attired Mexican warriors besiege them. Although the Mexicans gained a temporary advantage in this battle, the drawing illustrates one of the reasons for their inability to withstand the Spanish in the longer term. The Spanish soldiers are armed with rifles and crossbows, while the Indians carry only spears and shields.

first assault on Tenochtitlán, the Aztec capital, failed. But Cortés and his army had, unknowingly, unleashed an assault on the Aztecs far more devastating than military attack: they had exposed the natives to smallpox. An epidemic of that deadly disease decimated the Aztec population and made it possible for the Spanish to triumph in their second attempt at conquest. Through his ruthless suppression of the surviving natives, Cortés established himself as one of the most brutal of the Spanish "conquistadores" (conquerors). Twenty years later, Francisco Pizarro conquered the Incas in Peru and opened the way for other advances into South America.

The conquistadores—through their daring and their terrible brutality—had cleared the way for the first Spanish settlers in America. They were interested only in exploiting the American stores of gold and silver, and they were fabulously successful. For 300 years, beginning in the sixteenth century, the mines of Spanish America yielded more than ten times as much gold and silver as the rest of the world's mines together. After the first wave of conquest, however, most Spanish settlers in America traveled to the New World for other reasons. Many went in hopes of profiting from agriculture, and they helped establish elements of European civilization permanently in America. Other Spaniards—priests, friars, and other missionaries—went to America to spread the Christian religion; through their efforts, the influence of the Catholic Church ultimately extended throughout South and Central America and Mexico.

By the end of the sixteenth century, the Spanish Empire had become one of the largest in the history of the world. It included the Caribbean islands, Mexico, and southern North America. The Spanish Empire also spread into South America and included what is now Chile, Argentina, and Peru. In 1580, when the Spanish and Portuguese monarchies temporarily united, Brazil came under Spanish jurisdiction as well.

Northern Outposts

The Spanish fort of St. Augustine, established in Florida in 1565, became the first permanent European settlement in the present-day United States. But it was little more than a small military outpost. A more substantial colonizing venture began in the Southwest in 1598, when Don Juan de Onate traveled north from Mexico with a party of 500, claimed for Spain some of the lands of the Pueblo Indians in what is now New Mexico, and began to establish a colony. Onate granted *encomiendas* (the right to exact tribute and labor from the natives on large tracts of land) to favored Spaniards. In 1609, Spanish colonists founded Santa Fe. By 1680, there were over 2,000 Spanish colonists living among about 30,000 Pueblos. The economic heart of the colony was cattle and sheep, raised on the *ranchos* that stretched out around the small towns Spanish settlers established.

In 1680, the colony was nearly destroyed when the Pueblos rose in revolt. Despite widespread conversions to Catholicism, most natives (including the converts) continued also to practice their own religious rituals. In 1680, Spanish priests and the colonial government were trying to suppress these rituals. In response, Pope, an Indian religious leader, led an uprising that killed hundreds of European settlers (including twenty-one priests), captured Santa Fe, and drove the Spanish temporarily from the region. Twelve years later the Spanish returned, resumed seizing Pueblo lands, and crushed a last revolt in 1696.

After the revolts, many Spanish colonists seemed to understand that they could not hope to prosper in New Mexico in constant conflict with a native population that greatly outnumbered them. On the one hand, the Spanish intensified their efforts to assimilate the Indians—baptizing Indian children at birth and enforcing observance of Catholic rituals. On the other hand, they now permitted the Pueblos to own land; they stopped commandeering Indian labor; and they tacitly tolerated the survival of tribal religious rituals. There was significant intermarriage between Europeans and Indians. And increasingly, the Pueblos came to consider the Spanish their allies in the continuing battles with the Apaches and Navajos. By 1750, the Spanish population had grown modestly to about 4,000. The Pueblo population had declined (through disease, war, and migration) to about 13,000—less than half what it had been in 1680. New Mexico had by then become a reasonably stable but still weak and isolated outpost of the Spanish Empire.

Biological and Cultural Exchanges

European and native cultures never entirely merged in the Spanish Empire. Indeed, significant differences remain today between European and Indian cultures throughout South and Central America. Nevertheless, the arrival of whites launched a process of interaction between different peoples that left no one unchanged.

That Europeans were exploring the Americas at all was a result of their early contacts with the natives, from whom they had learned of the rich deposits of gold and silver. From then on, the history of the Americas became one of increasing levels of exchanges—some beneficial, some catastrophic—among different peoples and cultures. The first and perhaps most profound result of this exchange was the importation of European diseases to the New World. It would be difficult to exaggerate the consequences of the exposure of Native Americans to such illnesses as influenza, measles, typhus, and above all smallpox—diseases to which Europeans had, over time, developed at least a partial immunity but to which Americans were tragically vulnerable. Millions died. In some areas, native populations were virtually wiped out within a few decades of their first contact with whites. On Hispaniola—where the Dominican Republic and Haiti are today, and where Columbus landed and established a small, short-lived colony in the 1490s—the native population quickly declined from approximately 1 million to about 500. In the Mayan areas of Mexico, as much as 95 percent of the population perished within a few years of the natives' first contact with the Spanish. Many (although not all) of the tribes north of Mexico, whose contact with European settlers came later and was often less intimate, were spared the worst of the epidemics. But for other areas of the New World, this was a catastrophe at least as grave as, and in some places far worse than, the Black Death that had killed as much as half the population of Europe two centuries before.

The decimation of native populations in the southern regions of the Americas was not, however, purely a result of exposure to infection. It was also a result of the conquistadores' deliberate policy of subjugation and extermination. Their brutality was in part a reflection of the ruthlessness with which Europeans waged war in all parts of the world. It was also a result of their conviction that the natives were "savages"—uncivilized peoples who could be treated as somehow not fully human. By the 1540s, the combined effects of European diseases and European military brutality had all but destroyed the empires of Mexico and South America and allowed the Spanish to exert their authority with few organized challenges from the natives.

Not all aspects of the exchange were so disastrous to the Indians. The Europeans introduced to America important new crops (among them sugar and bananas), domestic livestock (cattle, pigs, and sheep), and, perhaps most significant, the horse, which gradually became central to the lives of many natives and transformed their societies.

The exchange was at least as important (and more beneficial) to the Europeans. In both North and South America, the arriving white peoples learned from the natives new agricultural techniques appropriate to the demands of the new land. They discovered new crops—above all maize (corn), which Columbus took back to Europe from his first trip to America. Such foods as squash, pumpkins, beans, sweet potatoes, tomatoes, peppers, and potatoes all found their way into European diets by way of the natives of the Americas.

In South America, Central America, and Mexico, a society in which Europeans and natives lived in intimate, if unequal, contact with one another emerged. Many natives gradually came to speak Spanish or Portuguese, but they created a range of dialects fusing the European languages with elements of their own. Gradually, Europeans spread Catholicism through most areas of the Spanish Empire. But native Christians combined the new religion with features of their old religions. European men outnumbered European women by at least ten to one. As a result, male Spanish immigrants had substantial sexual contact with native women. Intermarriage—often forcible—became frequent. Before long, the population of the colonies came to be dominated (numerically, at least) by people of mixed race, or mestizos.

Virtually all the enterprises of the Spanish and Portuguese colonists depended on an Indian work force. In some places, Indians were sold into slavery. More often, colonists used a coercive (or "indentured") wage system, under which Indians worked in the mines and on the plantations under duress for fixed periods. That was not, in the end, enough to meet the labor needs of the colonists—particularly since the native population had declined (and in some places virtually vanished) because of disease and war. As early as 1502, therefore, European settlers began importing slaves from Africa.

Africa and America

Over half of all the immigrants to the New World between 1500 and 1800 were Africans, virtually all of them sent to America against their will. Most came from a large region in west Africa below the Sahara Desert, known as Guinea.

Europeans and white Americans came to portray African society as primitive and uncivilized (in part to justify the enslavement of Africa's people). But most Africans were, in fact, civilized peoples with well-developed economies and political systems. The residents of upper Guinea had substantial commercial contact with the Mediterranean world—trading ivory, gold, and slaves for finished goods—and, largely as a result, became early converts to Islam. After the collapse of the ancient kingdom of Ghana around A.D. 1100, they created the even larger empire of Mali, which survived into the fifteenth century and whose trading center at Timbuktu became fabled as a center of education and a meeting place of the peoples of many lands.

Farther south, Africans were more isolated from Europe and the Mediterranean and were more politically fragmented. The central social unit was the village, which usually consisted of members of an extended family group. Some groups of villages united in small kingdoms. But no large empires emerged in the south. Nevertheless, these southern societies developed extensive trade—in woven fabrics, ceramics, wooden and iron goods, as well as crops and livestock—both among themselves and, to a lesser degree, with the outside world.

African civilizations developed economies that reflected the climates and resources of their lands. In upper Guinea, fishing and rice cultivation, supplemented by the extensive trade with Mediterranean lands, were the foundation of the economy. Farther south, Africans grew wheat and other food crops, raised livestock, and fished. There were some more nomadic tribes in the interior, who subsisted largely on hunting and gathering and had less elaborate social systems. But most Africans were sedentary, farming people.

As in many Indian societies in America, but unlike societies in Europe, African families tended to be matrilineal. This means that people traced their heredity through and inherited property from their mothers. Women played a major role, often the dominant role, in trade. In many areas, they were the principal farmers (while the men hunted, fished, and raised livestock), and everywhere, they managed child care and food preparation. Most tribes also divided political power by gender, with men choosing leaders and systems for managing male affairs and women choosing parallel leaders to handle female matters.

In those areas of west Africa where indigenous religions had survived the spread of Islam (which included most of the lands south of the empire of Mali), people worshiped many gods, whom they associated with various aspects of the natural world and whose spirits they believed lived in trees, rocks, forests, and streams. Most Africans also developed forms of ancestor worship and took great care in tracing family lineage; the most revered priests were generally the oldest people.

Small elites of priests and nobles stood at the top of many African societies. Most people belonged to a large middle group of farmers, traders, crafts workers, and others. At the bottom of society were slaves—men and women who were put into bondage after being captured in wars, because of criminal behavior, or as a result of unpaid debts. Slavery was not usually permanent; African people were generally in bondage for a fixed term, and in the meantime retained certain legal protections (including the right to marry). Children did not inherit their parents' condition of bondage.

The African slave trade long preceded European settlement in the New World. As early as the eighth century, west Africans began selling small numbers of slaves to traders from the Mediterranean and later to the Portuguese. In the sixteenth century, however, the market for slaves increased dramatically as a result of the growing European demand for sugar cane. The small areas of sugar cultivation in the Mediterranean could not meet the demand, and production soon spread to new areas: to the island of Madeira off the African coast, which became a Portuguese colony, and not long thereafter (still in the sixteenth century) to the Caribbean islands and Brazil. Sugar was a labor-intensive crop, and the demand for African workers in these new areas of cultivation was high. At first the slave traders were overwhelmingly Portuguese and, to a lesser extent, Spanish. By the seventeenth century, the Dutch had won control of most of the market. In the eighteenth century, the English dominated it. By then, slavery had spread well beyond its original locations in the Caribbean and South America and into the English colonies to the north.

THE ARRIVAL OF THE ENGLISH

England's first documented contact with the New World came only five years after Spain's. In 1497, John Cabot (like Columbus, a native of Genoa) sailed to the northeastern coast of North America on an expedition sponsored by King Henry VII, in an unsuccessful search for a northwest passage through the New World to the Orient. But nearly a century passed before the English made any serious efforts to establish colonies in America. Like other European nations, England had to experience an internal transformation before it could begin settling new lands.

Incentives for Colonization

Interest in colonization grew in part as a response to social and economic problems in sixteenth-century England. The English people suffered from frequent and costly European wars, and they suffered from almost constant religious strife within their own land. Many suffered, too, from harsh economic changes in their countryside. Because the worldwide demand for wool was growing rapidly, landowners were converting their land from fields for crops to pastures for sheep. The result was a significant growth in the wool trade but a reduction in the amount of land available for growing food. Many of the displaced farmers became beggars or criminals. England's food supply declined at the same time that the English population was growing—from 3 million in 1485 to 4 million in 1603. To some of the English, the New World began to seem attractive because it offered something that was growing scarce in England: land.

At the same time, new merchant capitalists were prospering by selling the products of England's growing wool-cloth industry abroad. At first, most exporters did business almost entirely as individuals. In time, however, merchants formed companies, whose charters from the king gave them monopolies for trading in particular regions. Investors in these companies often made fantastic profits, and they were eager to expand their trade.

Central to this trading drive was the emergence of a new concept of economic life known as mercantilism. Mercantilism rested on the belief that the world's wealth was finite, that one person or nation could grow rich only at the expense of another, and that a nation's economic health depended, therefore, on selling as much as possible to foreign lands and buying as little as possible from them. The principles of mercantilism spread throughout Europe in the sixteenth and seventeenth centuries and increased the competition among nations. One result was the increased attractiveness of acquiring colonies, which could become the source of raw materials and a market for the colonizing power's goods.

In England, the mercantilistic program thrived at first on the basis of the flourishing wool trade with the European continent, and particularly with the great cloth market in Antwerp. In the 1550s, however, that glutted market began to collapse, and English merchants had to look elsewhere for overseas trade. The establishment of colonies seemed to be an answer to their problems. Some English also believed colonies would help alleviate poverty and unemployment by siphoning off the surplus population. Perhaps most important, colonial commerce would allow England to acquire products for which the nation had previously been dependent on foreigners—products such as lumber, naval stores, and silver and gold.

There were also religious motives for colonization. The Protestant Reformation began in Germany in 1517, when Martin Luther challenged some of the basic practices and beliefs of the Roman Catholic Church, which had been, until then, the supreme religious authority. Luther quickly won a wide following among ordinary men and women in northern Europe. When the pope excommunicated him in 1520, Luther began leading his followers out of the Catholic Church entirely.

As the spirit of the Reformation spread rapidly throughout Europe, other dissidents began offering other alternatives to Catholicism. The Swiss theologian John Calvin went even further than Luther had in rejecting the Catholic belief that human behavior could affect an individual's prospects for salvation. Calvin introduced the doctrine of predestination. God "elected" some people to be saved and condemned others to damnation; each person's destiny was determined before birth, and no one could change that predetermined fate. But those who accepted Calvin's teachings came to believe that the way they led their lives might reveal to them their chances of salvation. A wicked or useless existence would be a sign of damnation; saintliness, diligence, and success could be signs of grace. Calvinism created anxieties among its followers, but it also produced a strong incentive to lead virtuous, productive lives. The new creed spread rapidly throughout northern Europe and produced (among other groups) the Huguenots in France and the Puritans in England.

The English Reformation, however, was more a result of a political dispute between the king and the pope than of these doctrinal revolts. In 1529 King Henry VIII, angered by the refusal of the pope to grant him a divorce from his Spanish wife, broke England's ties with the Catholic

Church and established himself as the head of the Christian faith in his country. After Henry's death, his Catholic daughter, Queen Mary, restored England's allegiance to Rome and persecuted those who resisted. But when Mary died in 1558, her half-sister, Elizabeth I, became England's sovereign and once again severed the nation's connection with the Catholic Church, this time for good.

To many English people, however, the new Church of England—which differed little at first from the Catholic Church—was not reformed enough. Some had been affected by the teachings of the European Reformation, and they complained that theirs was a church that had abandoned Rome without abandoning Rome's offensive beliefs and practices. They clamored for reforms that would "purify" the church, and thus they became known as Puritans.

The most radical Puritans, known as Separatists, were determined to worship as they pleased in their own independent congregations, despite English laws that required all subjects to attend regular Anglican services. But most Puritans did not wish to leave the Church of England. They wanted, rather, to simplify Anglican forms of worship and reform the leadership of the church. Like the Separatists, they grew increasingly frustrated by the refusal of political and ecclesiastical authorities to respond to their demands.

Puritan discontent grew rapidly after the death of Elizabeth, the last of the Tudors, and the accession of James I, the first of the Stuarts, in 1603. Convinced that kings ruled by divine right, James quickly antagonized the Puritans, a group that included most of the rising businessmen, by resorting to illegal and arbitrary taxation, by favoring English Catholics in the granting of charters and other favors, and by supporting "high-church" forms of ceremony. By the early seventeenth century, some religious nonconformists were beginning to look for places of refuge outside the kingdom.

England's first experience with colonization came not in the New World but in neighboring Ireland. The English had long laid claim to the island, but only in the late sixteenth century did serious efforts at colonization begin. The long, brutal process by which the English attempted (never entirely successfully) to subdue the Irish led to an important assumption about colonization that the English would take with them to America: the belief that settlements in foreign lands must retain a rigid separation from the native populations. Unlike the Spanish in America, the English in Ireland tried to build a separate society of their own, peopled with emigrants from England itself. They would take that concept with them to the New World.

The French and the Dutch in America

English settlers in North America were to encounter not only natives but also other Europeans who were, like them, driven by mercantilist ideas. There were scattered North American outposts of the Spanish Empire, whose residents looked on the English as intruders. And, more important, there were French and Dutch settlers who were also vying for a stake in the New World.

France founded its first permanent settlement in America at Quebec in 1608, less than a year after the English started their first at Jamestown. The colony's population grew very slowly, but the French exercised an influence in the New World disproportionate to their numbers, because of their relationships with Native Americans. Unlike the early English settlers, who hugged the coastline and traded with the Indians of the interior mostly through intermediaries, the French forged close ties with natives deep inside the continent. French Jesuit missionaries established some of the first contacts between the two peoples. More important were the *coureurs de bois*— adventurous fur traders and trappers—who also penetrated far into the wilderness and developed an extensive trade that became one of the underpinnings of the French colonial economy. The French traders formed partnerships with the Indians and often became virtually a part of native society, living among the natives and at times marrying Indian women. The fur trade helped open the way for French agricultural estates (or *seigneuries*) along the St. Lawrence River and for the development of trade and military centers at Quebec and Montreal.

The English also faced competition from the Dutch in North America. Holland in the early seventeenth century was one of the leading trading nations of the world. In 1609 an English explorer in the employ of the Dutch, Henry Hudson, sailed up the river that was to be named for him in what is now New York State. His explorations led to a Dutch claim on that territory. In 1624, not long after the first two permanent English colonies took root in Jamestown and Plymouth, the Dutch created a wedge between them when the Dutch West India Company established a series of permanent trading posts on the Hudson, Delaware, and Connecticut Rivers that soon became the colony of New Netherland. Its principal town, New Amsterdam, was on Manhattan Island. The Dutch population remained relatively small.

The First English Settlements

The first permanent English settlement in the New World was established at Jamestown, in Virginia, in 1607. But for nearly thirty years before that, English merchants and adventurers had been engaged in a series of failed efforts to create colonies in America.

Through much of the sixteenth century, the English had harbored mixed feelings about the New World. They were intrigued by its possibilities, but they were also leery of Spain, which remained the dominant force in America and the dominant naval power in Europe. In 1588, however, King Philip II of Spain sent one of the largest military fleets in the history of warfare—the Spanish Armada—across the English Channel to attack England itself. The smaller English fleet, taking advantage of its greater maneuverability, defeated the armada and, in a single stroke, ended Spain's domination of the Atlantic. This great shift in naval power caused interest in colonizing the New World to grow quickly.

The pioneers of English colonization were Sir Humphrey Gilbert and his half-brother Sir Walter Raleigh—both friends of Queen Elizabeth, and both veterans of earlier colonial efforts in Ireland. In 1578 Gilbert obtained from Elizabeth a six-year patent granting him the exclusive right "to inhabit and possess any remote and heathen lands not already in the possession of any Christian prince." Five years later, after several setbacks, he led an expedition to Newfoundland and proceeded south looking for a good place to build a profitable colony. But a storm sank his ship, and he was lost at sea. The next year, Sir Walter Raleigh secured his own six-year grant from the queen and sent a small group of men on an expedition to explore the North American coast. When they returned, Raleigh named the region they had explored Virginia, in honor of Elizabeth, who was unmarried and was known as the "Virgin Queen."

In 1585 Raleigh recruited his cousin, Sir Richard Grenville, to lead a group of men to the island of Roanoke, off the coast of what is now North Carolina, to establish a colony. Grenville deposited the settlers on the island, antagonized the natives by destroying an Indian village as retaliation for a minor theft, and returned to England. The following spring, with expected supplies and reinforcements from England long overdue, Sir Francis Drake unexpectedly arrived in Roanoke. The dispirited colonists boarded his ships and left.

Raleigh tried again in 1587, sending an expedition to Roanoke carrying ninety-one men, seventeen women (two of them pregnant), and nine children. The settlers attempted to take up where the first group of colonists

ROANOKE A drawing by one of the English colonists in the ill-fated Roanoke expedition of 1585 became the basis for this engraving by Theodore DeBry, published in England in 1590. A small European ship carrying settlers approaches the island of Roanoke, at left. The wreckage of several larger vessels farther out to sea and the presence of Indian settlements on the mainland and on Roanoke itself suggest some of the perils the settlers encountered.

had left off. (Shortly after arriving, one of the women—the daughter of the commander of the expedition, John White—gave birth to a daughter, Virginia Dare, the first American-born child of English parents.) White returned to England after several weeks, in search of supplies and additional settlers, leaving his daughter and granddaughter behind. Because of a war with Spain, he was unable to return to Roanoke for three years. When he did, in 1590, he found the island utterly deserted, with no clue to the fate of the settlers other than the cryptic inscription "Croatoan" carved on a post. No solution to the mystery of the "Lost Colony" has ever been found.

The Roanoke disaster marked the end of Sir Walter Raleigh's involvement in English colonization of the New World. No later colonizer would receive grants of land in America as vast or undefined as those Raleigh and Gilbert had acquired. But despite the discouraging example of these first experiences, the colonizing impulse remained very much alive. In the early years of the seventeenth century, a group of London merchants to whom Raleigh had assigned his charter rights decided to renew the attempt at colonization in Virginia. A rival group of merchants, from the area around Plymouth, was also interested in American ventures and was sponsoring voyages of exploration farther north. In 1606 James I issued a new charter, which divided North America between the two groups. The London group got the exclusive right to colonize in the south, and the Plymouth merchants received the same right in the north. Through the efforts of these and other companies, the first enduring English colonies would be established in America.

CONCLUSION

The lands that Europeans eventually named the Americas were the home of many millions of people before the arrival of Columbus. Having migrated from Asia thousands of years earlier, the pre-Columbian Americans spread throughout the Western Hemisphere and eventually created great civilizations. Among the most notable of them were the Incas in Peru, and the Mayas and Aztecs in Mexico. In the regions north of what was later named the Rio Grande, the human population was smaller and the civilizations less advanced than they were further south. Even so, North American natives created a cluster of civilizations that thrived and expanded. There may have been as many as 10 million people living north of Mexico by the time Columbus arrived.

In the century after European contact, these native populations suffered a series of catastrophes that all but destroyed the civilizations they had built: brutal invasions by Spanish and Portuguese conquistadore and, even more devastating, a series of plagues inadvertently imported by Europeans that decimated native populations. By the middle of the sixteenth century, the Spanish and Portuguese—no longer faced with effective resistance from the native populations—had established colonial control over all of South America and much of North America, creating one of the largest empires in the world.

In the parts of North America that would eventually become the United States, the European presence was for a time much less powerful. The Spanish established an important northern outpost in what is now New Mexico, a society in which Europeans and Indians lived together intimately, if unequally. They created a fort at St. Augustine, Florida. On the whole, however, the North American Indians remained largely undisturbed by Europeans until the English, French, and Dutch migrations began in the early seventeenth century.

FOR FURTHER REFERENCE

Suggested Readings

Alvin M. Josephy, ed., *America in 1492: The World of the Indian Peoples Before the Arrival of Columbus* (1993) provides a strong introduction to pre-Columbian history. Francis Jennings, *The Founders of America* (1993) and *The Invasion of America: Indians, Colonialism, and the Cant of Conquest* (1975) are important histories of the native populations both before and after European contact. William M. Denevan, ed., *The Native Population of the Americas in 1492* (1976) is an important contribution to the debate over the size and character of the American population before Columbus. Alfred Crosby, *The Columbian Exchange: Biological and Cultural Consequences of 1492* (1972) explores the results of European-Indian contact both in the Americas and Europe. D. W. Meinig, *The Shaping of America, Vol I: Atlantic America, 1492–1800* (1986) is an account of the early contacts between Europeans and the New World. James H. Merrell, *The Indians' New World* (1989) is an excellent social history of native adaptation to the arrival of Europeans. James Axtell, *Beyond 1492: Encounters in Colonial North America* (1992) examines the early interaction between Europeans and Indians. Patrick Manning, *Slavery and African Life* (1990) is a good introduction to the early slave trade with the New World. Peter Laslett, *The World We Have Lost* (1965) is a classic study of Britain around the time of colonization. Karen Kupperman, *Roanoke: The Abandoned Colony* (1984) is a fine study of the first English settlement in the New World.

Films

(The best source for information on how to find these and other films is *Bowker's Complete Video Directory*—three volumes.)

Columbus & the Age of Discovery (1991) is a seven-volume documentary series on Christopher Columbus, his era, and his legacy. *Native American History, Pt. 1: Wilderness* (1993) explores the history of pre-Columbian American peoples, based on recent assessments by historians and archaeologists, and reveals the extent to which the European arrival altered life for Native Americans. *Early American Civilizations* (1988) documents the story of the Olmecs, Mayas, Toltecs, Aztecs, and Incas. *Slavery in the Americas & the Triangular Trade* (1992) looks at the Africans, Europeans, and Americans who participated in the Atlantic slave trade. *Roanoke* (1986) recreates the dress and setting for both settlers and Indians in the doomed English settlement.

Internet Resources

Internet websites containing historical material relevant to the subjects discussed in this chapter can be reached through the McGraw-Hill history site at www.mhhe.com/socscience/history/usa/link/linktop.htm.

CHAPTER TWO

The English "Transplantations"

The Early Chesapeake ~ Caribbean Colonization
The Growth of New England ~ The Restoration Colonies
The Development of Empire

T HE ROANOKE FIASCO dampened colonization enthusiasm in England for a time. But the lures of the New World—the presumably vast riches, the abundant land, the promise of religious freedom, the chance to begin anew—were too strong to be suppressed for very long. By the early seventeenth century, the effort to establish permanent English colonies in the New World had resumed.

The new efforts were much like the earlier, failed ones: private ventures, with little planning or direction from the English government; small, fragile enterprises led by people unprepared for the hardships they were to face. Unlike the Roanoke experiment, they survived, but not before experiencing a series of disastrous setbacks.

Four things in particular shaped the character of these English settlements. First, the colonies were business enterprises, and one of their principal concerns was to produce a profit for their corporate sponsors. Second, because the colonies were tied only indirectly to the crown, they began from the start to develop their own political and social institutions. Third, as in Ireland, there were few efforts to blend English society with the society of the natives. The Europeans tried to isolate themselves from the Indians and created communities that would be entirely their own: "transplantations" of societies from the Old World to the New. And fourth, almost nothing worked out as they had planned.

TIME LINE

1607	1619	1620	1622	1624	1630
Jamestown founded	First African workers in Virginia	Pilgrims found Plymouth Colony	Powhatan Indians attack Virginia	Dutch settle Manhattan	Puritans establish Massachusetts Bay Colony
	Virginia House of Burgesses meets				

1634	1636	1637		1663	1664
Maryland founded	Roger Williams founds Rhode Island	Anne Hutchinson expelled from Massachusetts Bay Colony		Carolina chartered	English capture New Netherlands
		Pequot War			

1675	1676	1681	1686	1689	1732
King Philip's War	Bacon's Rebellion	Pennsylvania chartered	Dominion of New England	Glorious Revolution in America	Georgia chartered

THE EARLY CHESAPEAKE

Once James I had issued his 1606 charters to the London and Plymouth Companies, the Plymouth group floundered and largely abandoned its efforts at settling the northern regions of British America. But the London Company moved quickly and decisively to launch a colonizing expedition headed for Virginia—a party of 144 men aboard three ships, the *Godspeed*, the *Discovery*, and the *Susan Constant*, which set sail for America early in 1607.

The Founding of Jamestown

Only 104 men survived the journey. They reached the American coast in the spring of 1607, sailed into Chesapeake Bay and up a river they named the James, and established their colony on a peninsula. They called it Jamestown.

They chose an inland setting that they believed would offer them security from the natives. But they chose poorly. The site was low and

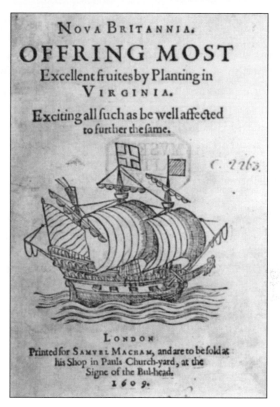

NOVA BRITANNIA.
OFFRING MOST
Excellent fruites by Planting in
VIRGINIA.

Exciting all such as be well affected
to further the same.

C. 2263.

LONDON
Printed for SAMVEL MACHAM, and are to be sold at
his Shop in Pauls Church-yard, at the
Signe of the Bul-head.
1609.

RECRUITING FOR THE COLONIES, 1609 This is the title page for a pamphlet that describes the attractions of settlement in the New World. Most accounts of the "excellent fruites" of life in Virginia were, like this one, written by people who had never seen America but who shared the excitement that the colonies inspired among the early-seventeenth-century English.

swampy and subject to outbreaks of malaria. It was surrounded by thick woods, which were difficult to clear for cultivation. And it bordered the territories of powerful local Indians. The result could hardly have been more disastrous. For seventeen years, one wave of settlers after another attempted to make Jamestown a habitable and profitable colony. Every effort failed. The town became instead a place of misery and death, and the London Company found itself saddled with endless losses. All that could be said of Jamestown at the end of this first period of its existence was that it had survived.

The initial colonists ran into serious difficulties from the moment they landed. They had no prior exposure to the infections of the new land and were highly vulnerable to local diseases, particularly malaria. The promoters in London demanded a quick return on their investment and diverted the colonists' energies into futile searches for gold and only slightly more successful efforts to pile up lumber, tar, pitch, and iron for export. These energies would have been better spent on growing food. The promoters also had little interest in creating a family-centered community, and they sent virtually no women to Jamestown. Hence, settlers could not establish real households and had difficulty feeling any sense of a permanent stake in the community.

By January 1608, when ships appeared with additional men and supplies, all but 38 of the first 104 colonists were dead. Jamestown, now facing extinction, survived largely as a result of the efforts of Captain John Smith, who at age twenty-seven was already a famous world traveler. Leadership in the colony had been bitterly divided until the fall of 1608, when Smith took control. He imposed work and order on the community. He also organized raids on neighboring Indian villages to steal food and kidnap natives. During the colony's second winter, fewer than a dozen (in a population of about 200) died. By the summer of 1609, when Smith returned to England, the colony was showing promise of survival. But Jamestown's ordeal was not over yet.

Reorganization and Expansion

As Jamestown struggled to survive, the London Company (now renamed the Virginia Company) was already dreaming of bigger things. In 1609, it obtained a new charter from the king, which increased its power and enlarged its territory; and it sent Lord De La Warr to be the colony's first governor. The company raised money by selling additional stock. It offered stock in the company to planters who were willing to migrate at their own expense. And it provided free passage to Virginia for poorer people who would agree to serve the company for seven years. In the spring of 1609, confident that it was now poised to transform Jamestown into a vibrant, successful venture, the Virginia Company dispatched a fleet of nine vessels with about 600 people aboard (including some women and children) to Virginia.

Disaster followed. One of the Virginia-bound ships was lost at sea in a hurricane. Another ran aground on one of the Bermuda islands and was unable to free itself for months. Many of those who reached Jamestown, still weak from their long and stormy voyage, succumbed to fevers before winter came. The winter of 1609–1610 became known as the "starving time," a period worse than anything before. The local Indians, antagonized by hostile actions by the early English settlers, killed off the livestock in the woods and kept the colonists barricaded within their palisade. The Europeans lived on what they could find: "dogs, cats, rats, snakes, toadstools, horsehides," and even the "corpses of dead men," as one survivor recalled. When the migrants who had run aground in Bermuda finally arrived in Jamestown the following May, they found only about 60 emaciated people (out of 500 residents the previous summer) still alive. The new arrivals took the survivors onto their ship, abandoned the settlement, and sailed for home. But as the refugees proceeded down the James, they met an English ship coming up the river—part of a fleet bringing supplies and the colony's first governor, Lord De La Warr. The departing settlers agreed to return to Jamestown. New relief expeditions with hundreds of colonists soon began to arrive, and the effort to turn a profit in Jamestown resumed.

Under the leadership of its first governors, Virginia survived and even expanded. New settlements began lining the river above and below Jamestown. That was partly because of the order and discipline the governors at times managed to impose and because of increased military assaults on the local Indian tribes to protect the new settlements. But it was also because the colonists had at last discovered a marketable crop: tobacco.

Europeans had become aware of tobacco soon after Columbus's first return from the West Indies, where he had seen the Cuban natives smoking small cigars (tabacos), which they inserted in the nostril. By the early seventeenth century, tobacco from the Spanish colonies was already in wide use in Europe. Then in 1612, the Jamestown planter John Rolfe, noting that local Indians were growing a strain of tobacco, began trying to cultivate the crop in Virginia. Tobacco planting soon spread up and down the James.

Almost immediately, tobacco cultivation created great pressure for territorial expansion. Tobacco growers needed large areas of farmland to grow their profitable crops; and because tobacco exhausted the soil very quickly, the demand for land increased rapidly. As a result, English farmers began establishing plantations deeper and deeper in the interior, isolating themselves from the center of European settlement, Jamestown, and penetrating farther into the territory of the native tribes.

Growth of the Chesapeake, 1607–1750

The tobacco economy also created a heavy demand for labor. To entice new workers to the colony, the Virginia Company established what it called the "headright" system. Headrights were fifty-acre grants of land. Those who already lived in the colony received two headrights (100 acres) apiece. Each new settler received a single headright for himself or herself. This system encouraged family groups to migrate together, since the more family members who traveled to America, the more land the family would receive. In addition, anyone who paid for the passage of immigrants to Virginia would receive an extra headright for each arrival, an encouragement to the prosperous to import new laborers. As a result, some colonists were able to assemble large plantations.

The company also transported ironworkers and other skilled craftsmen to Virginia to diversify the economy. In 1619, it sent 100 Englishwomen to the colony (which was still overwhelmingly male) to become the wives of male colonists. It promised the male colonists the full rights of Englishmen (as provided in the original charter of 1606), an end to strict and arbitrary rule, and even a share in self-government. On July 30, 1619, delegates from the various communities met as the House of Burgesses. It was the first meeting of an elected legislature within what was to become the United States.

A month later, Virginia established another important precedent. As John Rolfe recorded, "about the latter end of August" a Dutch ship brought in "20 and odd Negroes." There is some reason to believe that the colonists did not consider these first Africans in Virginia slaves, that they thought of them rather as servants to be held for a term of years and then freed, like the white servants with whom the planters were already familiar. For a time, moreover, the use of black labor remained limited. Although Africans trickled steadily into the colony, planters continued to prefer European indentured servants until at least the 1670s, when white servants began to become scarce and expensive. But the small group of blacks who arrived in 1619 marked the first step toward the enslavement of Africans within what was to be the American republic.

The European settlers in Virginia built their society not only on the coerced labor of imported Africans but also on the effective suppression of the local Indians. For two years in the 1610s, Sir Thomas Dale, De La Warr's successor as governor, led unrelenting assaults against the Powhatan Indians, led by (and named for) their formidable chief, Powhatan. In the process, Dale kidnapped Powhatan's young daughter Pocahontas. Several years earlier, Pocahontas had played a role in mediating differences between her people and the Europeans and, according to legend, once intervened with her father to spare John Smith from execution. But now, Powhatan refused to ransom her. Living among the English, Pocahontas gradually adapted to many of their ways. She converted to Christianity and in 1614 married John Rolfe and visited England with him. As a Christian convert and a gracious woman, she stirred interest among many English in projects to "civilize" the Indians. She died shortly before her planned return to Virginia.

By the time of Pocahontas's marriage, Powhatan had ceased his attacks on the English in the face of overwhelming odds. But after his death several years later, his brother, Opechancanough began secretly to plan the elimination of the English intruders. On a March morning in 1622, tribesmen called on the white settlements as if to offer goods for sale; then they suddenly attacked. Not until 347 whites of both sexes and all ages (including

John Rolfe) lay dead were the Indian warriors finally forced to retreat. And not until over twenty years later were the Powhatans finally defeated.

By then, however, the Virginia Company in London was defunct. The company had poured virtually all its funds into its profitless Jamestown venture and in the aftermath of the 1622 Indian uprising faced imminent bankruptcy. In 1624, James I revoked the company's charter, and the colony at last came under the control of the crown where it would remain until 1776. The colony, if not the company, had survived—but at a terrible cost. In Virginia's first seventeen years, more than 8,500 white settlers had arrived in the colony, and nearly eighty percent of them had died.

Exchanges of Agricultural Technology

The hostility the early English settlers expressed toward their Indian neighbors was in part a result of their conviction that their own civilization was greatly superior to that of the natives—and perhaps above all that they were more technologically advanced. The English, after all, had great ocean-going vessels, muskets and other advanced implements of weaponry, and many other tools that the Indians had not developed. Indeed, when John Smith and other early Jamestown residents grew frustrated at their inability to find gold and other precious commodities, they often blamed the backwardness of the natives. The Spanish in South America, Smith once wrote, had grown rich because the natives there had built advanced civilizations and mined much gold and silver. If Mexico and Peru had been as "ill peopled, as little planted, laboured and manured as Virginia," he added, the Spanish would have found no more wealth than the English did.

Yet the survival of Jamestown was, in the end, largely a result of agricultural technologies developed by Indians and borrowed by the English. Native agriculture was far better adapted to the soil and climate of Virginia than the agricultural traditions the English settlers brought with them. The Indians of Virginia were not nomadic hunters, but settled farmers whose villages were surrounded by neatly ordered fields in which grew a variety of crops—beans, pumpkins, vegetables, and above all maize (known to us as corn), which had been previously unknown to the English. Some of the Indian farmlands stretched over hundreds of acres and supported substantial populations.

The English settlers did not adopt all the Indian agricultural techniques. Natives cleared fields not, as the English did, by cutting down and uprooting all the trees. Instead they killed trees in place by "girdling" them (that is, making deep incisions around the base) in the areas in which they planted or setting fire to their roots; and they planted crops not in long, straight rows, but in curving patterns around the dead tree trunks. But in other respects, the English learned a great deal from the Indians about how to grow food in the New World. In particular, they quickly recognized the great value of corn, which proved to be easier to cultivate and to produce much greater yields than any of the European grains the English had known at home. Corn was also attractive to the settlers because its stalks could be a source of sugar and it spoiled less easily than other grains. The English also learned the advantages of growing beans alongside corn to enrich the soil. An early settler in New England (where the English also learned how to cultivate corn from the natives) wrote that the Indians had taught the settlers "to cull out the finest seede, to observe the fittest season, to keepe distance for holes, and fit measure for hills, to worme it, and weede it; to prune it, and dresse it as occasion shall require."

Like the natives, the English quickly learned to combine the foods they grew with food for which they hunted and fished, and here, too, Indian techniques proved of great value. Particularly valuable was the canoe, which was much better at navigating the rivers and streams of Virginia (and later New England) than were any English vessels, and which proved especially useful for fishing and for reaching hunting areas as agricultural cultivation of the coastal region drove many animals inland. Canoes could be made by hollowing them out from a single log (dugouts) or sewing birchbark around a simple frame and sealing it with resin (birchbark canoes, some of which could hold as many as eighty people). John Smith was a particular admirer of the Indian canoes, and compared them unfavorably to the large and cumbersome river vessels that the Virginia Company sent to Jamestown from England. The "primitive" civilizations of the natives in fact provided the early settlers with some of their most vital agricultural techniques and technologies.

Maryland and the Calverts

The Maryland colony ultimately came to look much like Virginia, but its origins were very different from those of its southern neighbor. George Calvert, the first Lord Baltimore, was a recent convert to Catholicism and a shrewd businessman, and he envisioned establishing a colony in America both as a great speculative venture in real estate and as a retreat for English Catholics oppressed by the Anglican establishment at home. Calvert died while still negotiating with the king for a charter to establish a colony in the Chesapeake region. But in 1632 his son Cecilius, the second Lord Baltimore, finally received the charter.

Lord Baltimore named his brother, Leonard Calvert, as governor of the colony. In March 1634, two ships—the *Ark* and the *Dove*—bearing Calvert along with 200 or 300 other colonists, entered the Potomac River, turned into one of its eastern tributaries, and established the village of St. Mary's on a high, dry bluff. Neighboring Indians befriended the settlers and provided them with temporary shelter and with stocks of corn. The early Marylanders experienced no Indian assaults, no plagues, no starving time.

The Calverts needed to attract thousands of settlers to Maryland if their expensive colonial venture was to pay. As a result, they had to encourage the immigration of Protestants as well as their fellow English Catholics. The Calverts soon realized that Catholics would always be a minority in the colony, and so they adopted a policy of religious toleration, embodied in the 1649 "Act Concerning Religion," which ensured freedom of worship for all Christians. Nevertheless, politics in Maryland remained plagued for years by tensions, and at times violence, between the Catholic minority and the Protestant majority.

At the insistence of the first settlers, the Calverts agreed in 1635 to the calling of a representative assembly—the House of Delegates—whose proceedings were based on the rules of Parliament. But the proprietor retained absolute authority to distribute land as he wished; and since Lord Baltimore granted large estates to his relatives and to other English aristocrats, a distinct upper class soon established itself. By 1640, a severe labor shortage forced a modification of the land-grant procedure; and Maryland, like Virginia, adopted a headright system—a grant of 100 acres to each male settler, another 100 for his wife and each servant, and 50 for each of his children. But the great landlords of the colony's earliest years remained powerful even as the population grew larger and more diverse. Like Virginia, Maryland became a center of tobacco cultivation; and as in Virginia, planters worked their land with the aid, first, of indentured servants imported from England and then, beginning late in the seventeenth century, of slaves imported from Africa.

Bacon's Rebellion

For more than thirty years, one man—Sir William Berkeley, the royal governor of Virginia—dominated the politics of the colony. He took office in 1642 at the age of thirty-six and with but one brief interruption remained in control of the government until the 1670s. In his first years as governor, he helped open up the interior of Virginia by sending explorers across the Blue Ridge Mountains and crushing a 1644 Indian uprising. The defeated Indians agreed to a treaty ceding to England most of the territory east of the mountains and establishing a boundary west of which white settlement would be prohibited. But the rapid growth of the Virginia population made this agreement difficult to sustain. Between 1640 and 1660, Virginia's population rose from 8,000 to over 40,000. By 1652, English settlers had established three counties in the territory set aside by the treaty for the Indians. Unsurprisingly, there were frequent clashes between natives and whites.

In the meantime, Berkeley was expanding his own powers. By 1670, the vote for delegates to the House of Burgesses, once open to all white men, was restricted to landowners. Elections were rare, and the same burgesses, representing the established planters of the eastern (or tidewater) region of the colony and subservient to the governor, remained in office year after year. The more recent settlers on the frontier were underrepresented in the assembly or not represented at all.

Resentment of the power of the governor and the tidewater aristocrats grew steadily in the newly settled lands of the west (often known as the "backcountry"). In 1676, this resentment helped create a major conflict, led by Nathaniel Bacon, a young, handsome aristocrat who had arrived in Virginia in 1673. Bacon had a good farm in the west and a seat on the governor's council. But like other members of the new backcountry gentry, he chafed at the governor's attempts to hold the line of settlement steady so as to avoid antagonizing the Indians. Bacon's rift with Berkeley was also a result of resentment that he was not part of the inner circle of the governor's council and that Berkeley refused to allow him a piece of the Indian fur trade, which the governor himself controlled.

In 1675, a major conflict erupted in the west between whites and natives. As the fighting escalated, Bacon and other concerned landholders demanded that the governor send the militia. When Berkeley refused, Bacon responded by offering to organize a volunteer army of backcountry men who would do their own fighting. Berkeley, who saw Bacon as a potential rival and feared a needless slaughter of the natives, rejected the offer. Bacon ignored him and launched a series of vicious but unsuccessful pursuits of the Indian challengers. When Berkeley heard of the unauthorized military effort, he dismissed Bacon from the governor's council and proclaimed him and his men to be rebels. Bacon now turned his army against the governor and, in what became known as Bacon's Rebellion, twice led his troops east to Jamestown. The first time he won a temporary pardon from the governor; the second time, after the governor repudiated the agreement, Bacon burned much of the city and drove the governor into exile. But then Bacon died suddenly of dysentery; and Berkeley, his position bolstered by the arrival of British troops, soon regained control. In 1677, the Indians (aware of their inability to defeat the white forces militarily) reluctantly signed a new treaty that opened new lands to white settlement.

Bacon's Rebellion was evidence of the continuing struggle to define the Indian and white spheres of influence in Virginia. It also revealed the bitterness of the competition among rival elites and between easterners and westerners in particular, and it demonstrated the potential for instability in the colony's large population of free, landless men. One result was that landed elites in both eastern and western Virginia began to recognize a common interest in quelling social unrest from below. That was among the reasons that they turned increasingly to the African slave trade to fulfill their need for labor. African slaves, unlike white indentured servants, did not need to be released after a fixed term and hence did not threaten to become an unstable, landless class.

CARIBBEAN COLONIZATION

The Chesapeake was the site of the first permanent English settlements in the New World. But throughout the first half of the seventeenth century, the most important destinations for English immigrants were the islands of the Caribbean and the northern way station of Bermuda. These Caribbean societies had close ties to English North America and influenced the development of the mainland colonies in many ways.

The West Indies

Before the arrival of the Europeans, most of the Caribbean islands had substantial native populations. But beginning with Christopher Columbus's first visit in 1492, and accelerating after 1496, when the Spanish established their first colony on Hispaniola, the native population was all but wiped out by European epidemics.

The Spanish claimed all the Caribbean islands, but they created substantial settlements only on the largest of them: Cuba, Hispaniola, and Puerto Rico. English, French, and Dutch traders began settling on some of the smaller islands early in the sixteenth century, despite the Spanish

European Colonial Expansion in the Caribbean Basin, c. 1650

European Claims in the Lesser Antilles, c. 1650

ATLANTIC OCEAN

Anguilla 1640
St. Maarten/St. Martin 1638; with France after 1646
St. Barthelemy 1640
Barbuda 1627
Antigua 1632
Saba 1640
St. Eustatius 1634
Guadeloupe 1635
St. Kitts 1623; with France after 1625
Marie Galante
Nevis 1628
Montserrat 1632
Dominica
Martinique 1635

■ Carib
■ Spanish
■ British
■ French
■ Dutch

Dates indicate formal claim; note that ownership changed frequently throughout the colonial period.

Caribbean Sea

St. Lucia
St. Vincent
Barbados 1627
Grenada
Tobago
Trinidad 1498

SPANISH ORGANIZATION OF THE VICEROYALTY OF NEW SPAIN
(see map below)

Audencia of Guadalajara
Audencia of Santo Domingo
Audencia of Guatemala
Audencia of Mexico

SPANISH TRADE ROUTES
(routes of the treasure *flota*)
- - -► To Spain
——— From Spain

St. Augustine

Gulf of Mexico

Monterrey
Tampico
Mexico City
Veracruz

Havana
BAHAMAS

ATLANTIC OCEAN

Santiago
Hispaniola
Santo Domingo
Puerto Rico
San Juan

Jamaica
(Br. after 1655)

Caribbean Sea

VICEROYALTY OF NEW SPAIN

Guatemala City
AUDENCIA OF GUATEMALA (1543)
Granada

PACIFIC OCEAN

Cartagena
Caracas

Panama City

VICEROYALTY OF PERU

0   400 Miles
0   400 Kilometers

39

claim to them. These fledgling colonies were always vulnerable to Spanish attack. But after Spain and the Netherlands went to war in 1621 (distracting the Spanish navy and leaving the English in the Caribbean relatively unmolested), the pace of English colonization increased. By midcentury, there were several important English settlements on the islands, the most important of them on Antigua, St. Kitts, Jamaica, and Barbados.

In their first years in the Caribbean, English settlers experimented unsuccessfully with tobacco and cotton. But they soon discovered that the most lucrative export crop was sugar, for which there was a substantial and growing market in Europe. Because raising sugar required a great deal of labor, and because the native population was too small to provide a work force, English planters quickly found it necessary to import laborers. As in the Chesapeake, they began by bringing indentured servants from England. But the arduous work and the tropical climate discouraged white laborers. By midcentury, therefore, the English planters in the Caribbean (like the Spanish colonists) were relying more and more heavily on an enslaved African work force, which soon substantially outnumbered them.

On Barbados and other islands where a flourishing sugar economy developed, the English planters were a tough, aggressive, and ambitious breed. Some of them grew enormously wealthy; and since their livelihoods depended on their work forces, they created a rigid slave system remarkably quickly. By the late seventeenth century, African slaves outnumbered white settlers by better than four to one.

Masters and Slaves

A small white population, much of it enjoying great economic success, and a large African population, all of it in bondage, were a potentially explosive combination. Fearful of slave revolts, whites in the Caribbean monitored their labor forces closely and often harshly, and the English West Indians devised a rigid set of laws and practices to ensure control over their black laborers. Planters paid little attention to the welfare of their workers. Many concluded it was cheaper to buy new slaves periodically than to protect the well-being of those they already owned, and it was not uncommon for masters literally to work their slaves to death. Few African workers survived more than a decade in the brutal Caribbean working environment. Even whites, who worked far less strenuously, often succumbed to the harsh climate and the local diseases; most died before the age of forty.

Establishing a stable society and culture was extremely difficult for people living in such harsh and even deadly conditions. Those whites who could returned to England with their fortunes and left their estates in the hands of overseers, and the white population remained a distinct minority on the islands. The society of Europeans in the Caribbean lacked many of the institutions that gave stability to the North American settlements: church, family, community.

Africans in the Caribbean faced much greater difficulties than the white settlers, but because they had no chance of leaving, they created what was in many ways a more elaborate culture than did the white settlers. They started families (although many of them were broken up by death or the slave trade); they sustained African religious and social traditions (and resisted Christianity); and within the rigidly controlled world of the sugar plantations, they established patterns of resistance.

The Caribbean settlements became an important part of the Atlantic trading nexus in which many Americans became involved. They were the principal source of African slaves for the mainland colonies. And because Caribbean planters established an elaborate plantation system earlier than planters in North America, they provided models that many mainland people emulated.

THE GROWTH OF NEW ENGLAND

The northern regions of British North America were slow to attract settlers, in part because the Plymouth Company was never able to mount a successful colonizing expedition after receiving its charter in 1606. It did, however, sponsor explorations of the region. Captain John Smith, after his departure from Jamestown, made an exploratory journey for the Plymouth merchants, wrote an enthusiastic pamphlet about the lands he had seen, and called them New England.

Plymouth Plantation

A discontented congregation of Puritan Separatists in England, not the Plymouth Company, established the first enduring European settlement in New England. In 1608, after years of persecution for attempting to practice their own religion, a congregation of Separatists from the hamlet of Scrooby began emigrating quietly (and illegally), a few at a time, to

Growth of New England, 1620–1750

(1639) Date settlement founded

GRANTS

To Mason and Gorges, 1622

To Massachusetts Bay, 1629

To Plymouth Colony, 1630

To New Haven Colony, 1636

To Hartford Colony, 1662

To Duke of York, 1664

To Rhode Island, 1663

Leyden, Holland, where they could enjoy freedom of worship. But as foreigners in Holland, they had to work at unskilled and poorly paid jobs. They also watched with alarm as their children began to adapt to Dutch society and drift away from their church. Finally, some of the Separatists decided to move again, across the Atlantic, where they hoped to create a stable, protected community where they could spread "the gospel of the Kingdom of Christ in those remote parts of the world."

In 1620, leaders of the Scrooby group obtained permission from the Virginia Company to settle in Virginia. Several English merchants advanced the necessary funds for the venture. The "Pilgrims," as they saw themselves, sailed from Plymouth, England, in September 1620 on the *Mayflower*; thirty-five "saints" (Puritan Separatists) and sixty-seven "strangers" (people who were not part of the congregation) were aboard. In November, after a long and difficult voyage, they sighted land—the shore of what is now known as Cape Cod. That had not been their destination, but it was too late in the year to sail farther south. So the Pilgrims chose a site for their settlement in the area just north of the cape, a place John Smith had labeled "Plymouth" on a map he had drawn during an earlier exploration of New England. Because Plymouth lay outside the London Company's territory, the settlers were not bound by the company's rules. While still aboard ship, the "saints" in the group drew up an agreement, the Mayflower Compact, to establish a government for themselves. Then, on December 21, 1620, they stepped ashore at Plymouth Rock.

The Pilgrims' first winter was a difficult one. Half the colonists perished from malnutrition, disease, and exposure. But the colony survived, in large part because of crucial assistance from local Indians, who showed them how to gather seafood and cultivate corn. Trade and other exchanges with the Indians were critical to the settlers and attractive to the natives. The tribes provided the colonists with furs (contributing to a rapid depletion of the fur-bearing animal population of the region). They also showed the settlers how to cultivate corn and how to hunt wild animals for meat. After the first autumn harvest, the settlers invited the natives to join them in a festival, the original Thanksgiving. But the relationship between the settlers and the local Indians was not a happy one for long. Thirteen years after the Pilgrims arrived, a devastating smallpox epidemic—a result of natives' exposure to Europeans carrying the disease—wiped out much of the Indian population around Plymouth.

The Pilgrims could not create rich farms on the sandy and marshy soil around Plymouth, but they developed a profitable trade in fish and furs. New colonists arrived from England, and in a decade the population reached 300. The people of Plymouth Plantation chose as their governor the remarkable William Bradford, who governed successfully for many years without any serious interference from London. The Pilgrims were always poor. As late as the 1640s, they had only one plow among them. But they were, on the whole, content to be left alone to live their lives in what they considered godly ways.

The Massachusetts Bay Experiment

Events in England encouraged other Puritans to migrate to the New World. King James I had pursued harsh, repressive policies toward Puritans for years. When he died in 1653, his son and successor, Charles I, was even more hostile to Puritans than his father had been and imprisoned many of them for their beliefs. The king dissolved Parliament in 1629 (it was not to be recalled until 1640), ensuring that there would be no one in a position to oppose him.

In the midst of this turmoil, a group of Puritan merchants began organizing a new colonial venture in America. They obtained a grant of land in New England for most of the area now comprising Massachusetts and New Hampshire, and they acquired a charter from the king (who was evidently unaware of their religious inclinations) allowing them to create the Massachusetts Bay Company and to establish a colony in the New World. Some members of the Massachusetts Bay Company saw the enterprise as more than a business venture. They wanted to create a refuge in New England for Puritans. They bought out the interests of company members who preferred to stay in England, and owners elected a governor, John Winthrop. They then sailed for New England in 1630. With 17 ships and 1,000 people, mostly family groups, it was the largest single migration of its kind in the seventeenth century. Winthrop carried with him the charter of the Massachusetts Bay Company, which meant that the colonists would be responsible to no company officials in England.

The Massachusetts migration quickly produced several settlements. The port of Boston, at the mouth of the Charles River, became the capital, but in the course of the next decade colonists established several other towns in eastern Massachusetts: Charlestown, Newtown (later renamed Cambridge), Roxbury, Dorchester, Watertown, Ipswich, Concord, Sudbury, and others.

The Massachusetts Puritans were not grim or joyless, as many critics would later come to believe, but they were serious and pious. They strove to lead useful, conscientious lives of thrift and hard work, and they honored material success as evidence of God's favor. Winthrop and the other founders of Massachusetts believed they were founding a holy commonwealth, a model—a "city upon a hill"—for the corrupt world to see and emulate. To that end, the ministers and the officers of the government worked closely together. Colonial Massachusetts was a "theocracy," a society in which the church was almost indistinguishable from the state. Residents had no more freedom of worship than the Puritans themselves had had in England.

Like other new settlements, the Massachusetts Bay colony had early difficulties. During the first winter (1629–1630), nearly 200 people died and many others decided to leave. But, more rapidly than Jamestown, the colony grew and prospered. The nearby Pilgrims and neighboring Indians helped with food and advice. Incoming settlers, many of them affluent, brought needed tools and other goods. The dominance of families in the colony (a sharp contrast to the early years at Jamestown) helped ensure a feeling of commitment to the community and a sense of order among the settlers, and it also ensured that the population would reproduce itself.

The Expansion of New England

It did not take long for English settlement to begin moving outward from Massachusetts Bay to other parts of New England and beyond. Some people migrated in search of soil more productive than that the stony land around Boston provided. Others left because of the oppressiveness of the church-dominated government of Massachusetts.

The Connecticut River valley, about 100 miles west of Boston, began attracting English families as early as the 1630s—despite the presence of powerful native tribes and despite claims to those lands by the Dutch—because of the valley's fertile lands and its isolation from Massachusetts Bay. In 1635, Thomas Hooker, a minister of Newtown (Cambridge), defied the Massachusetts government, led his congregation west, and established the town of Hartford. Four years later, the people of Hartford and of two other newly founded towns nearby established a colonial government of their own and adopted a constitution known as the Fundamental Orders of Connecticut, which created a government similar to that of Massachusetts Bay but gave a larger proportion of the men the right to vote and hold office. (Women were barred from voting virtually everywhere.)

Another Connecticut colony grew up around New Haven on the Connecticut coast. Unlike Hartford, it reflected unhappiness with what its founders considered the increasing religious laxity in Boston. The Fundamental Articles of New Haven (1639) established a Bible-based government even stricter than that of Massachusetts Bay. New Haven remained independent until 1662, when a royal charter officially gave the Hartford colony jurisdiction over the New Haven settlements.

European settlement in what is now Rhode Island was a result of the religious and political dissent of Roger Williams, an engaging but controversial young minister who lived for a time in Salem, Massachusetts. Williams was a confirmed Separatist who argued that the Massachusetts church should abandon all allegiance to the Church of England. He was also friendly with the neighboring Indians and proclaimed that the land the colonists were occupying belonged to the natives and not to the king or to the Massachusetts Bay Company. The colonial government voted to deport him, but he escaped before they could do so. During the winter of 1635–1636, he took refuge with Narragansett tribesmen; the following spring he bought a tract of land from them, and with a few followers, created the town of Providence. In 1644, after obtaining a charter from Parliament, he established a government for Providence and the surrounding settlements—a government similar to that of Massachusetts but without any ties to the church. For a time, Rhode Island was the only colony in which all faiths (including Judaism) could worship without interference.

Another challenge to the established religious order in Massachusetts Bay came from Anne Hutchinson, an intelligent and charismatic woman from a substantial Boston family. She argued that many clergy (including her own uninspiring minister) were not among the "elect" and were, therefore, entitled to no spiritual authority. Such teachings (known as the Antinomian heresy) were a serious threat to the spiritual authority of the established clergy. Hutchinson also challenged prevailing assumptions about the proper role of women in Puritan society. She was not a retiring, deferential wife and mother but a powerful religious figure in her own right. As Hutchinson's influence grew, and as she began to deliver open attacks on members of the clergy, the Massachusetts hierarchy mobilized to stop her. In 1638, she was convicted of heresy and sedition and was banished. With her family and some of her followers, she moved to a point on Narragansett Bay not far from Providence. Later she moved south into New York, where in 1643 she and her family died during an Indian uprising.

The Hutchinson affair had an important impact on the settlement of the areas north of Massachusetts Bay. New Hampshire and Maine were established in 1629 by two English proprietors. But few settlers moved into these northern regions until the religious disruptions in Massachusetts Bay. In 1639, John Wheelwright, a disciple of Anne Hutchinson, led some of his fellow dissenters to Exeter, New Hampshire. Others soon followed. The Massachusetts Bay Company tried to extend its authority over this entire northern territory, but with only partial success. New Hampshire became a separate colony in 1679. Maine remained a part of Massachusetts until 1820.

Settlers and Natives

The first white settlers in New England had generally friendly relations with the natives. Indians taught whites how to grow vital food crops such as corn, beans, pumpkins, and potatoes; they also taught them new agricultural techniques, such as annual burning for fertilization and planting beans to replenish exhausted soil. European farmers also benefited from the extensive lands Indians had already cleared (and either abandoned or sold). White traders used Indians as partners in some of their most important trading activities (and particularly in the creation of the thriving North American fur trade). Indeed, commerce with the Indians was responsible for the creation of some of the first great fortunes in British North America.

Other white settlers attempted to educate the Indians in European religion and culture. Protestant missionaries converted some natives to Christianity, and a few Indians became at least partially assimilated into white society.

But as in other areas of white settlement, tensions soon developed—primarily as a result of the white colonists' insatiable appetite for land. The particular character of those conflicts—and the brutality with which whites assaulted their Indian foes—emerged as well out of Puritan attitudes toward the natives. The religious leaders of New England came to consider the tribes a threat to their hopes of creating a godly community in the New World. Gradually, the image of Indians as helpful neighbors came to be replaced by the image of Indians as "heathens" and barbarians.

The Pequot War and the Technology of Battle

In 1637, hostilities broke out between English settlers in the Connecticut Valley and the Pequot Indians of the region, a conflict (known as the Pequot War) that ended disastrously for the natives. The Pequot tribe was almost wiped out. But the bloodiest and most prolonged encounter between whites and Indians in the seventeenth century began in 1675, a conflict that whites called King Philip's War. As in the Pequot War, an Indian tribe—the Wampanoags, under the leadership of a chieftain known to the white settlers as King Philip and among his own people as Metacomet—rose up to resist the English. For three years, the natives inflicted terror on a string of Massachusetts towns, killing over a thousand people. But beginning in 1676, the white settlers gradually prevailed, and with the help of a group of Mohawk allies who ambushed Metacomet, shot and killed him. Without Metacomet, the fragile alliance among the tribes collapsed, and the white settlers were soon able to crush the uprising.

The character of the Pequot War, King Philip's War, and many other conflicts between natives and settlers in the years that followed was crucially affected by earlier exchanges of technology between the English and the tribes. In particular, the Indians made effective use of a relatively new weapon introduced to New England by Myles Standish and others: the flintlock rifle. It replaced the earlier staple of colonial musketry; the matchlock rifle, which proved too heavy, cumbersome, and inaccurate to be useful in the kind of combat characteristic of Anglo-Indian struggles. The matchlock had to be steadied on a fixed object and ignited with a match before firing; the flintlock could be held up without support and fired without a match. (Indians using bows and arrows often outmatched settlers using the clumsy matchlocks.)

A PEQUOT VILLAGE DESTROYED An English artist drew this view of a fortified
Pequot village in Connecticut surrounded by English soldiers and their allies
from other tribes during the Pequot War in 1637. The invaders massacred more
than 600 residents of the settlement.

Many English settlers were slow to give up their cumbersome
matchlocks for the lighter flintlocks. But the Indians recognized the advantages of the newer rifles right away and began purchasing them in
large quantities as part of their regular trade with the colonists. Despite
rules forbidding colonists to instruct natives on how to use and repair the
weapons, the natives learned to handle the rifles, and even to repair them,
very effectively on their own. They even built a substantial forge for shaping and repairing rifle parts. In King Philip's War, the very high casualties
on both sides were a result of the use of these more advanced rifles.

Indians also used more traditional military technologies in their conflicts with the English—especially the construction of forts. The Narragansetts, allies of the Wampanoags in King Philip's War, built an enormous
fort in the Great Swamp of Rhode Island in 1675, which became the site of

one of the bloodiest battles of the war before English attackers burned it down. After that, a band of Narragansetts set out to build a large stone fort, with the help of a member of the tribe who had learned masonry while working with the English. When English soldiers discovered the stone fort in 1676, after the end of King Philip's War, they killed most of its occupants and destroyed it. In the end, the technological skills of the Indians (both those they borrowed from the English and those they drew from their own traditions) were no match for the overwhelming advantages of the English settlers in both numbers and firepower.

THE RESTORATION COLONIES

For nearly thirty years after Lord Baltimore received the charter for Maryland in 1632, no new English colonies were established in America. England had to deal with troubles of its own at home before it could resume its colonizing ventures.

The English Civil War

After Charles I dissolved Parliament in 1629 and began ruling as an absolute monarch, he steadily alienated a growing number of his subjects—and the members of the powerful Puritan community, above all. Finally, desperately in need of money, Charles called Parliament back into session in 1640 and asked it to levy new taxes. But he antagonized the members by dismissing them twice in two years; and in 1642, they organized a military force, thus beginning the English Civil War.

The conflict between the Cavaliers (the supporters of the king) and the Roundheads (the forces of Parliament, who were largely Puritans) lasted seven years. In 1649, the Roundheads defeated the king's forces, captured Charles himself, and beheaded the monarch. The stern Roundhead leader Oliver Cromwell replaced the king and assumed the position of "protector." But when Cromwell died in 1658, his son and heir proved unable to maintain his authority. Two years later, King Charles II, son of the beheaded monarch, returned from exile and seized the throne, in what became known as the Restoration.

Among the results of the Restoration was the resumption of colonization in America. Charles II rewarded faithful courtiers with grants of land in the New World, and in the twenty-five years of his reign he issued charters for four additional colonies: Carolina, New York, New Jersey, and Pennsylvania.

The Carolinas

In successive charters issued in 1663 and 1665, Charles II awarded eight proprietors joint title to a vast territory stretching south from Virginia to the Florida peninsula and west to the Pacific Ocean. Like Lord Baltimore, they received almost kingly powers over their grant, which they prudently called Carolina (a name derived from the Latin word for "Charles"). They reserved tremendous estates for themselves and distributed the rest through a headright system similar to those in Virginia and Maryland, after which they collected annual payments from the settlers. Although committed Anglicans themselves, the proprietors guaranteed religious freedom to all Christian faiths. They also created a representative assembly to make laws. They hoped to attract settlers from the existing American colonies and to avoid the expense of financing expeditions from England.

But their initial efforts to profit from settlement in Carolina failed dismally. A few early attempts at colonization were quickly abandoned, and most of the original proprietors soon gave up the project. Anthony Ashley Cooper, however, persisted. He convinced the other proprietors to give up on attracting settlers from other colonies and to finance expeditions to Carolina from England, the first of which set sail with 300 people in the spring of 1670. Only 100 people survived the difficult voyage; those who did established a settlement at Port Royal on the Carolina coast. Ten years later they founded a city at the junction of the Ashley and Cooper Rivers, which in 1690 became the colonial capital. They called it Charles Town (it was later renamed Charleston).

With the aid of the English philosopher John Locke, Cooper (now the earl of Shaftesbury) drew up the Fundamental Constitution for Carolina in 1669 in an attempt to create a highly ordered society. It divided the colony into counties of equal size and divided each county into equal parcels. It also envisioned an elaborate social hierarchy of the proprietors themselves (who were to be known as "seigneurs"), a local aristocracy (consisting of lesser nobles known as "landgraves" or "caciques"), and ordinary settlers ("leetmen"). At the bottom of this stratified society would be poor whites, who would have few political rights, and African slaves, whose subjection would be complete. Proprietors, nobles, and other landholders would have a voice in the colonial parliament in proportion to the size of their landholdings.

In reality, Carolina developed along lines quite different from the carefully ordered vision of Shaftesbury and Locke. For one thing, the colony was never really united in anything more than name. The northern and southern regions of settlement were widely separated and socially and economically distinct from one another. The northern settlers were mainly backwoods farmers, scratching out a meager existence at subsistence agriculture. In the south, fertile lands and the good harbor at Charles Town promoted a more prosperous economy and a more stratified, aristocratic society. Settlements grew up rapidly along the Ashley and Cooper Rivers, and colonists established a flourishing trade, particularly (beginning in the 1660s) in rice—which was to become the colony's principal commercial crop.

Southern Carolina very early developed close commercial ties to the large (and overpopulated) European colony on the Caribbean island of Barbados (see pp. 38–41). During the first ten years of settlement, in fact, most of the new residents in Carolina were Barbadians, some of whom arrived with large groups of black workers and established themselves as substantial landlords. African slavery had taken root on Barbados earlier than in any of the mainland colonies, and the white Caribbean migrants—tough, uncompromising profit seekers—established a similar slave-based plantation society in Carolina.

Carolina was one of the most divided English colonies in America. There were tensions between the small farmers of the Albemarle region in the north and the wealthy planters in the south. And there were conflicts between the rich Barbadians in southern Carolina and the smaller landowners around them. After Lord Shaftesbury's death, the proprietors proved unable to establish order. In 1719, the colonists seized control of the colony from them. Ten years later, the king divided the region into two royal colonies, North Carolina and South Carolina.

New Netherland, New York, and New Jersey

In 1664, Charles II granted his brother James, the duke of York, all the territory lying between the Connecticut and Delaware Rivers. But the grant faced a major challenge from the Dutch, who claimed the entire area and controlled settlements at New Amsterdam and other strategic points.

England and the Netherlands were already commercial rivals in Europe, and that rivalry now extended to America, where the Dutch served as a wedge between the northern and southern English colonies. In 1664, vessels of the English navy, under the command of Richard Nicolls, put in at New Amsterdam, the capital of the Dutch colony of New Netherland, and extracted a surrender from the arbitrary and unpopular Dutch governor, Peter Stuyvesant. Several years later, in 1673, the Dutch reconquered and briefly held their old provincial capital. But they lost it again, this time for good, in 1674.

The duke of York, now firmly in possession of his territory, renamed it New York and set out to govern the diverse region. New York contained not only Dutch and English but Scandinavians, Germans, French, and a large number of Africans (imported as slaves by the Dutch West India Company), as well as members of several different Indian tribes. James wisely made no effort to impose his own Roman Catholicism on the colony. He delegated powers to a governor and a council but made no provision for representative assemblies.

Property holding and political power remained highly divided and highly unequal in New York. In addition to confirming the great Dutch "patroonships" already in existence, James granted large estates to some of his own political supporters. Power in the colony thus remained widely dispersed among wealthy English landlords, Dutch patroons, fur traders, and the duke's political appointees. By 1685, when the duke of York ascended the English throne as James II, New York contained about four times as many people (around 30,000) as it had twenty years before, and it was one of the most turbulent colonies in America.

Shortly after James received his charter, he gave a large part of the land south of New York to a pair of political allies, both Carolina proprietors, Sir John Berkeley and Sir George Carteret. Carteret named the territory New Jersey, after the island in the English Channel on which he had been born. But the venture in New Jersey generated few profits, and in 1674, Berkeley sold his half interest. The colony was divided into two jurisdictions, East Jersey and West Jersey, which squabbled with one another until 1702, when the two halves of the colony were again joined and became a single royal colony. New Jersey, like New York (from which much of its population came), was a colony of enormous ethnic and religious diversity, and the weak colonial government made few efforts to impose strict control over the fragmented society. But unlike New York, New Jersey developed no important class of large landowners (most of its residents remained small farmers) and nor did New Jersey produce any single important city.

The Quaker Colonies

Pennsylvania was born out of the efforts of a dissenting English Protestant sect, the Society of Friends, to find a home for their own distinctive social order. The society began in the mid-seventeenth century under the leadership of George Fox, a Nottingham shoemaker, and Margaret Fell. Their followers came to be known as Quakers (from Fox's instruction to them to "tremble at the name of the Lord"). Unlike the Puritans, Quakers rejected the concept of predestination and original sin. All people, they believed, had divinity within themselves and need only learn to cultivate it; all could attain salvation. Also unlike the Puritans, Quakers granted women a position within the church generally equal to that of men.

The Quakers had no formal church government and no traditional church buildings, only meetinghouses. They had no paid clergy, and in their worship they spoke up one by one as the spirit moved them. Disregarding distinctions of gender and class, they addressed one another with the terms "thee" and "thou," words commonly used in other parts of English society only in speaking to servants and social inferiors. As confirmed pacifists, they would not take part in wars. Unpopular in England both with the government and with members of other religious orders (whose services Quakers occasionally disrupted), the Quakers began looking to America for asylum. A few migrated to New England or Carolina, but most Quakers wanted a colony of their own. As members of a despised sect, however, they could not get the necessary royal grant without the aid of someone influential at the court.

Fortunately for the Quaker cause, a number of wealthy and prominent men had converted to the faith. One of them was William Penn, son of an admiral in the Royal Navy who was also a landlord of valuable Irish estates. Over his father's objections, the younger Penn converted to Quakerism, took up evangelism, and was sent repeatedly to prison. He soon began working with George Fox to create a Quaker colony in America. When his father died in 1681, Charles II paid a large debt he had owed to the older Penn with an enormous grant to the son of territory between New York and Maryland. Penn was to control it as both landlord and ruler. At the king's insistence, the territory was to be named Pennsylvania, after Penn's late father.

Through his informative and honest advertising, Penn soon made Pennsylvania the best-known and most cosmopolitan of all the English colonies in America, a place to which settlers flocked from England and the Continent. More than any other English colony, Pennsylvania prospered from the outset, because of Penn's successful recruiting, his careful planning, and the region's mild climate and fertile soil. Penn sailed to Pennsylvania in 1682 to oversee the laying out, between the Delaware and Schuylkill Rivers, of the city he named Philadelphia ("Brotherly Love"), which, with its rectangular streets, helped set the pattern for most later cities in America. Penn recognized Indians' claims to the land in the province, and he was scrupulous about reimbursing them for it. The Indians generally respected Penn, and during his lifetime the colony had no major battles with the natives.

But the colony was not without conflict. By the late 1690s, some residents of Pennsylvania were beginning to resist the nearly absolute power of the proprietor. Residents of the southern areas of the colony, in particular, complained that the government in Philadelphia was unresponsive to their needs. Pressure from these groups grew to the point that in 1701, shortly before he departed for England for the last time, Penn agreed to a Charter of Liberties for the colony. The charter established a representative assembly (consisting, alone among the English colonies, of only one house) that greatly limited the authority of the proprietor. The charter also permitted "the lower counties" of the colony to establish their own representative assembly. The three counties did so in 1703 and as a result became, in effect, a separate colony—Delaware—although until the American Revolution it continued to have the same governor as Pennsylvania.

The Founding of Georgia

Not until 1733, decades after the founding of the Restoration colonies, did another new English settlement emerge in America: Georgia, the last English colony to be established in what would become the United States. Georgia was unlike any other colony. It was founded neither by a corporation nor by a wealthy proprietor. Its guiding purpose was neither the pursuit of profit nor the desire for a religious refuge. The founders of Georgia, led by General James Oglethorpe, were driven primarily by military and philanthropic motives. They wanted to erect a military barrier between the Spanish lands to the south and the established English colonies to the north, and they wanted to provide a refuge for the impoverished, a place where English men and women without prospects at home could begin a new life.

The need for a military buffer between South Carolina and the Spanish settlements in Florida seemed urgent in the 1730s because of tense relations between England and Spain that made new wars between them seem imminent. Oglethorpe, a hero of Queen Anne's War (a conflict between England and Spain that lasted from 1701 to 1713), was aware of the military advantages of the new colony. But his own interests were primarily philanthropic. As head of a parliamentary committee investigating English prisons, he was moved by the plight of honest debtors rotting in confinement. Such prisoners, and other poor people in danger of succumbing to a similar fate, could, he believed, become the farmer-soldiers of the new colony in America.

In 1732, a charter from King George II transferred the land between the Savannah and Altamaha Rivers to Oglethorpe and his fellow trustees. Oglethorpe himself led the first colonial expedition to Georgia, which built a fortified town at the mouth of the Savannah River in 1733 and later constructed additional forts south of the Altamaha. The trustees organized the colony in part to make it militarily defensible. They limited the size of landholdings to make the settlement compact and easily defended against Spanish and Indian attacks. Blacks—free or slave—and Roman Catholics were excluded; rum was prohibited; trade with the Indians was strictly regulated—all to limit the possibility of wartime insurrection or collusion with future enemies. Only a few debtors were released from jail and sent to Georgia, but the trustees brought hundreds of needy tradesmen and artisans from England and Scotland and many religious refugees from Switzerland and Germany.

The strict rules governing life in the new colony stifled its development and created dissent in its early years. Settlers in Georgia needed a work force and almost from the start demanded the right to buy slaves. Some opposed the restrictions on the size of individual property holdings. Many resented the nearly absolute political power of Oglethorpe and the trustees. As a result, newcomers to the region generally preferred to settle in South Carolina, where there were fewer restrictive laws. Eventually, the trustees removed the limitation on individual landholdings and later the ban on slavery and the prohibition of rum. In 1751, they returned control of the colony to the king, who permitted the election of a representative assembly. Georgia continued to grow more slowly than the other southern colonies, but it now developed along lines roughly similar to those of South Carolina.

THE DEVELOPMENT OF EMPIRE

The English colonies in America had begun as separate projects, and for the most part they grew up independent of one another and subject to little more than nominal control from London. Yet by the mid-seventeenth century, the growing commercial success of the colonial ventures was producing pressure in England for a more rational, uniform structure to the empire.

The English government began trying to regulate colonial trade in the 1650s, when Parliament passed laws to keep Dutch ships out of the English colonies. Later, Parliament passed three important Navigation Acts. The first of them, in 1660, closed the colonies to all trade except that carried by English ships, and it required that tobacco and other items be exported from the colonies only to England or to English possessions. The second act, in 1663, required that all goods sent from Europe to the colonies pass through England on the way, where they would be subject to English taxation. The third act, in 1673, imposed duties on the coastal trade among the English colonies, and it provided for the appointment of customs officials to enforce the Navigation Acts. These acts, and later additions to them, formed the legal basis of England's regulation of the colonies for a century.

The Dominion of New England

Before the Navigation Acts, all the colonial governments (except that of Virginia, a royal colony with a governor appointed by the king) had operated largely independently of the crown, with governors chosen by the proprietors or by the colonists themselves and with powerful representative assemblies. Officials in London recognized that to increase their control over their colonies they would have to create a center of authority less tied to the independent-minded colonial governments, which were unlikely to enforce the new laws.

In 1675, the king created a new body, the Lords of Trade, to make recommendations for imperial reform. In 1679, following their advice, he moved to increase his control over Massachusetts, the most defiant of the colonies. He stripped it of its authority over New Hampshire and chartered a separate, royal colony there whose governor he would himself appoint. And in 1684, citing the colonial assembly's defiance of the Navigation Acts, he revoked the Massachusetts charter.

Charles II's brother James II, who succeeded him to the throne in 1685, went further. He created a single Dominion of New England, which combined the government of Massachusetts with the governments of the rest of the New England colonies and later with those of New York and New Jersey as well. He eliminated the existing assemblies within the new Dominion and appointed a single governor, Sir Edmund Andros, to supervise the entire region from Boston. Andros's rigid enforcement of the Navigation Acts and his brusque dismissal of the colonists' claims to the "rights of Englishmen" made him quickly and thoroughly unpopular.

The "Glorious Revolution"

James II was not only losing friends in America; he was making powerful enemies in England by attempting to control Parliament and the courts and by appointing his fellow Catholics to high office. By 1688, his popular support had all but vanished, and Parliament invited his Protestant daughter Mary and her husband, William of Orange, ruler of the Netherlands, to assume the throne. James II (perhaps remembering what had happened to his father, Charles I) offered no resistance and fled to France. As a result of this bloodless coup, which the English called the "Glorious Revolution," William and Mary became joint sovereigns.

When Bostonians heard of the overthrow of James II, they arrested and imprisoned the unpopular Andros. The new sovereigns in England accepted the toppling of Andros, abolished the Dominion of New England, and restored separate colonial governments. They did not, however, re-create them as they had been. In 1691, they combined Massachusetts with Plymouth and made it a single, royal colony. The new charter restored the General Court, but it gave the crown the right to appoint the governor. It also replaced church membership with property ownership as the basis for voting and officeholding.

Andros had been governing New York through a lieutenant governor, Captain Francis Nicholson, who enjoyed the support of the wealthy merchants and fur traders of the province. Other, less favored colonists—farmers, mechanics, small traders, and shopkeepers—had a long accumulation of grievances against Nicholson and his allies. The leader of the New York dissidents was Jacob Leisler, a German immigrant and a prosperous merchant who had never won acceptance as one of the colony's ruling class. In May 1689, when news of the Glorious Revolution in England and the fall of Andros in Boston reached New York, Leisler raised a militia, captured the city fort, drove Nicholson into exile, and proclaimed himself the new head of government in New York. For two years, he tried in vain to stabilize his power in the colony amid fierce factional rivalry. In 1691, when William and Mary appointed a new governor, Leisler briefly resisted. He was convicted of treason and executed. Fierce rivalry between what became known as the "Leislerians" and the "anti-Leislerians" dominated the politics of the colony for many years thereafter.

In Maryland, many people erroneously assumed when they heard news of the Glorious Revolution that their proprietor, the Catholic Lord Baltimore, who was living in England, had sided with the Catholic James II and opposed William and Mary. So in 1689, an old opponent of the proprietor's government, the Protestant John Coode, led a revolt that drove out Lord Baltimore's officials and led to Maryland's establishment as a royal colony in 1691. The colonial assembly then established the Church of England as the colony's official religion and excluded Catholics from public office. Maryland became a proprietary colony again in 1715, after the fifth Lord Baltimore joined the Anglican Church.

The Glorious Revolution of 1688 in England touched off revolutions, mostly bloodless ones, in several colonies. Under the new king and queen, the representative assemblies that had been abolished were revived, and the scheme for colonial unification from above was abandoned. But the Glorious Revolution in America did not stop the reorganization of the empire. Its ultimate results, in fact, were governments that actually increased the crown's potential authority. As the first century of English settlement in America came to its end, the colonists were becoming more a part of the imperial system than ever before.

CONCLUSION

The English colonization of North America—which began with several unsuccessful attempts at settlement in the late sixteenth century and started its permanent life in Virginia in 1607—was part of a larger effort by England and other European nations to expand the reach of their increasingly commercial societies. Although some English settlers came to the New World to escape religious or political persecution, most came in hopes of finding opportunities to prosper by serving the needs of the emerging market economies of Europe.

In the South, civilization grew rapidly once the settlers discovered a European market for tobacco. Land was plentiful and cheap, but labor was scarce. So the early settlers relied heavily on indentured white laborers from England. Gradually, however, they turned instead to another source of labor: men and women captured in Africa, carried forcibly to the Americas, and sold into bondage. The white recruitment of African labor gradually evolved into a rigid system of absolute white ownership of blacks—slavery.

In the northern colonies, the economies and the European populations were more diverse—and composed in much greater numbers of religious refugees from England and of immigrants from other European nations as well. There an even more vigorously commercial economy developed that relied heavily on trade with Europe and the Caribbean.

By the early eighteenth century, English settlement had spread from northern New England (in what is now Maine) south into Georgia, while a substantial French empire had developed to the north in Canada. Most of the colonists considered themselves English subjects, with the same rights and privileges as those who lived in England itself. But as time went on, they began to develop social and political traditions very different from those in England—traditions that led to increasing of tension and conflict.

FOR FURTHER REFERENCE

Suggested Readings

William Cronon, *Changes in the Land: Indians, Colonists, and the Ecology of New England* (1983) examines the social and environmental effects of English settlement in colonial America. Perry Miller, *The New England Mind: From Colony to Province* (1953) and Edmund Morgan, *The Puritan Dilemma: The Story of John Winthrop* (1958) are classic expositions of the Puritan intellectual milieu. David Hall, *Worlds of Wonder, Days of Judgment* (1989) is a reconsideration of Puritan theology. Michael Kammen, *Colonial New York* (1975) illuminates the diversity and pluralism of New York under the Dutch and the English. Edmund Morgan, *American Slavery, American Freedom* (1975) is an excellent narrative of political and social development in early Virginia, as is T. H. Breen, *Tobacco Culture* (1985). Peter H. Wood, *Black Majority* (1974) describes the early importance of slavery in the founding of South Carolina. Richard S. Dunn, *Sugar and Slaves: The Rise of the Planter Class in the English West Indies, 1624–1713* (1972) is important for understanding the origins of British colonial slavery. Gary Nash, *Red, White and Black: The Peoples of Early America* (1982) provides a brief survey of the cultural and racial mixture of peoples in early America. Philip Curtin, *The Atlantic Slave Trade: A Census* (1969) has become the indispensable starting point for understanding African forced migration to the Americas. An outstanding collection of essays that summarizes recent scholarship on colonial America is Jack P. Greene and J. R. Pole, eds., *Colonial British America: Essays in the New History of the Early Modern Era* (1984).

Films

(The best source for information on how to find these and other films is *Bowker's Complete Video Directory*—three volumes.) *The Era of Colonization*, Vol. 2 (1996) explores European settlement from New England to Virginia, and relations between Europeans and Indians from the late sixteenth century through the Seven Years' War. *The Puritan Experience: Forsaking England*, and *The Puritan Experience: Making of a New World* (1975) follow the Higgins family from England to Massachusetts in the 1630s. *Jamestown: The Beginning* (1992) tells the story of Virginia's first permanent English settlement from the viewpoint of John Leydon, one of the few settlers who managed to survive the first few decades of settlement. *Slavery & Freedom*, Vol. 3 (1996) examines the rise of slavery in the New World. *The Southern Colonies* (1987) analyzes the origins of slavery in colonial Virginia.

Internet Resources

Internet websites containing historical material relevant to the subjects discussed in this chapter can be reached through the McGraw-Hill history site at www.mhhe.com/socscience/history/usa/link/linktop.htm.

CHAPTER THREE

Society and Culture in Provincial America

The Colonial Population ～ *The Colonial Economies*
Patterns of Society ～ *The Colonial Mind*

A S THE EXTENT of settlement in North America grew, and as the economies of the colonies began to flourish, several distinctive ways of life emerged. The new American societies differed considerably from the society that most had attempted to re-create in the New World—the society of England. They differed as well from one another. Indeed, the pattern of society in some areas of North America seemed to resemble that of others scarcely at all. Americans would eventually decide that they had enough in common to enable them to join together and form a single nation. But regional differences would continue to shape their society throughout their history.

THE COLONIAL POPULATION

After uncertain beginnings at Jamestown and Plymouth, the non-Indian population of English North America grew rapidly and substantially, through continued immigration and through natural increase. By the late seventeenth century European and African immigrants outnumbered the natives along the Atlantic coast.

A few of the early settlers were members of the English upper classes, but the dominant element was English laborers. Some came independently, such as the religious dissenters in early New England, who paid their own way and settled on their own land. But in the Chesapeake, at

TIME LINE				
1636	**1662**	**1685**	**1692**	**1697**
Harvard founded	Halfway Covenant	Huguenots migrate to America	Salem witchcraft trials	Slave importations increase

1720	**1734**	**1739**	**1740s**	
Cotton Mather starts smallpox inoculations	Great Awakening begins Zenger Trial	George Whitefield arrives in America Great Awakening intensifies Stono Slave rebellion	Indigo production begins	

least three-fourths of the immigrants in the seventeenth century arrived as indentured servants.

Indentured Servitude

The system of temporary servitude developed out of practices in England. Young men and women bound themselves to masters for fixed terms of servitude (usually four to five years) in exchange for passage to America, food, and shelter. Male indentures were supposed to receive clothing, tools, and occasionally land upon completion of their service. In reality, however, many left service with nothing. Most women indentures—who constituted roughly one-fourth of the total in the Chesapeake—worked as domestic servants and were expected to marry when their terms of servitude expired. Since men greatly outnumbered women in the region, most of them did.

By the late seventeenth century, the indentured servant population had become one of the largest elements of the colonial population and was creating serious social problems. Some former indentures managed to establish themselves successfully as farmers, tradespeople, or artisans, and some of the women married propertied men. Others (mostly males) found themselves without land, without employment, without families, and without prospects; and there grew up in some areas, particularly the Chesapeake, a large floating population of young single men—such as those who supported Bacon's Rebellion—who served as a potential (and at times actual) source of social unrest.

Beginning in the 1670s, a decrease in the birth rate in England and an improvement in economic conditions there reduced the pressures on laboring men and women to emigrate, and the flow of indentured servants declined. Those who did travel to America as indentures now generally avoided the southern colonies, where working conditions were arduous and prospects for advancement were slim. In the Chesapeake, therefore, landowners began to rely much more heavily on African slavery as their principal source of labor.

Birth and Death

Although immigration remained for a time the greatest source of population growth, the most important long-range factor in the increase of the colonial population was its ability to reproduce itself. Marked improvement in the reproduction rate began in New England and the mid-Atlantic colonies in the second half of the seventeenth century, and after the 1650s natural increase became the most important source of population growth in those areas. The New England population more than quadrupled through reproduction alone in the second half of the seventeenth century. This rise was a result not only of families having large numbers of children. It was also because life expectancy in New England was unusually high, both in comparison to that of other colonies and in comparison to that of England.

Conditions improved much more slowly in the South. The high death rates in the Chesapeake region did not begin to decline to the levels of those elsewhere until the mid-eighteenth century. Throughout the seventeenth century, the average life expectancy for European men in the region was just over forty years, and for women slightly less. (In New England, life expectancy was up to thirty years longer.) One in four white children died in infancy, and half died before the age of twenty. Children who survived infancy often lost one or both of their parents before reaching maturity. Widows, widowers, and orphans thus formed a substantial proportion of the white Chesapeake population. Only after settlers developed immunity to local diseases (particularly malaria) did life expectancy increase significantly. Population growth was substantial in the region, but it was largely a result of immigration.

The natural increases in the population in the seventeenth century were in large part a result of steady improvement in the balance between men and women in the colonies. In the early years of settlement, more than three-quarters of the white population of the Chesapeake consisted of men. And even in New England, which from the beginning had attracted more families (and thus more women) than the southern colonies, 60 percent of the inhabitants were male in 1650. Gradually, however, more women began to arrive in the colonies; and increasing birth rates, which of course produced roughly equal numbers of males and females, contributed to shifting the sex ratio (the balance between men and women) as well. Throughout the colonial period, the population almost doubled every twenty-five years. By 1775, the non-Indian population of the colonies was over 2 million—a nearly tenfold increase since the beginning of the century.

Medicine in the Colonies

The very high death rates of women who bore children illustrate the primitive nature of medical knowledge and practice in the colonies. Seventeenth- and eighteenth-century physicians had little or no understanding of infection and sterilization. As a result, many people died from infections contracted during childbirth or surgery. Because communities were unaware of bacteria, many were plagued with infectious diseases transmitted by garbage or unclean water.

One result of the limited extent of medical knowledge was that it was relatively easy for people to enter the field, even without any professional training. The biggest beneficiaries of this ease of access were women, who established themselves in considerable numbers as midwives. Midwives assisted women in childbirth, but they also dispensed other medical advice—usually urging their patients to use herbs or other natural remedies. Midwives were popular because they were usually friends and neighbors of the people they treated, unlike physicians, who were few and therefore not often well known to their patients. Male doctors felt threatened by the midwives and struggled continually to drive them from the field, although they did not make substantial progress in doing so until the nineteenth century.

Midwives and doctors alike practiced medicine on the basis of the prevailing assumptions of their time, most of them derived from the theory of "humoralism" popularized by the great second-century Roman physican Galen. Galen argued that the human body was governed by four "humors" that were lodged in four bodily fluids: yellow bile (or "choler"), black bile ("melancholy"), blood, and phlegm. In a healthy body, the four humors existed in balance. Illness represented an imbalance and suggested the need for removing from the body the excesses of whatever fluid was causing the imbalance. That was the rationale that lay behind the principal medical techniques of the seventeenth century: purging, expulsion, and bleeding. Bleeding was the most extreme of the treatments (and the most destructive), and it was practiced mostly by male physicians. Midwives preferred more homeopathic treatments and favored "pukes" and laxatives. The great majority of early Americans, however, had little contact with physicians, or even midwives, and sought instead to deal with illness on their own, confident that their own abilities were equal to those of educated physicians. The assumption that treating illness was the exclusive province of trained professionals, so much a part of the twentieth century, lay far in the distance in the colonial era.

That seventeenth-century medicine rested so much on ideas produced 1,400 years before is evidence of how little support there was for the scientific method—which rests on experimentation and observation rather than on inherited faiths—in England and America at the time. Bleeding, for example, had been in use for hundreds of years, during which time there had been no evidence at all that it helped people recover from illness; indeed, if anyone had chosen to look for it, there was considerable evidence that bleeding could do great harm. But what would seem in later eras to be the simple process of testing scientific assumptions was not yet a common part of Western thought. That was one reason that the birth of the Enlightenment in the late seventeenth century—with its faith in human reason and its belief in the capacity of individuals and societies to create better lives— was important not just to politics but to science.

Women and Families in the Colonies

Because there were many more men than women in colonial America, few women remained unmarried for long. The average European woman in America married for the first time at twenty or twenty-one years of age, considerably earlier than in England. Because of the large numbers of indentured servants who were forbidden to marry until their terms of service expired, premarital sexual relationships were frequent. Over a third of Chesapeake marriages occurred with the bride already pregnant. Children born out of wedlock to indentured women were often taken from their mothers at a young age and themselves bound out as indentured servants.

Women in the Chesapeake could anticipate a life consumed with childbearing. The average wife experienced pregnancies every two years. Those who lived long enough bore an average of eight children apiece (up to five of whom typically died in infancy or early childhood). Since childbirth was one of the most frequent causes of female death, many women did not survive to see their children grow to maturity. Those who did, however, were often widowed, since they were usually much younger than their husbands. By the early eighteenth century, however, the demographic character of the Chesapeake was beginning to change, and with it the nature and structure of the typical family. Life expectancy was increasing, and indentured servitude was in decline. Natural reproduction was becoming the principal source of white population growth.

In New England, where many more immigrants arrived with family members and where death rates declined far more quickly, family structure was much more stable than in the Chesapeake and hence more traditional. The sex ratio was more balanced than in the Chesapeake, so most men could expect to marry. As in the Chesapeake, women married young, began producing children early, and continued to do so well into their thirties. In contrast to the situation in the South, however, northern children were more likely to survive (the average family raised six to eight children to maturity), and their families were more likely to remain intact. Fewer New England women became widows, and those who did generally lost their husbands later in life. Hence women were less often cast in roles independent of their husbands. Young women, moreover, had less control over the conditions of marriage, both because there were fewer unmarried men vying for them than in the South and because their fathers were more likely to be alive and able to exercise control over their choices.

The longer lives in New England meant that parents continued to control their children longer than did parents in the South. Few sons and daughters could choose a spouse entirely independently of their parents' wishes. Men tended to rely on their fathers for land to cultivate—generally a prerequisite for beginning families of their own. Women needed dowries from their parents if they were to attract desirable husbands. Stricter parental supervision of children meant, too, that fewer women became pregnant before marriage than was the case in the South (although even in Puritan New England the premarital pregnancy rate was as high as 20 percent in some communities).

Puritanism placed a high value on the family, and the position of wife and mother was highly valued in Puritan culture. At the same time, however, Puritanism served to reinforce the idea of nearly absolute male authority and the assumption of female weakness and inferiority. Women were expected to be modest and submissive. A wife was expected to devote herself almost entirely to serving the needs of her husband. Women were vital to the family economy, and they continuously engaged in tasks crucial to the functioning of the farm—gardening, raising poultry, tending cattle, spinning, and weaving, as well as cooking, cleaning, and washing.

The Beginnings of Slavery in English North America

The demand for African servants to supplement the scarce southern labor force existed almost from the first moments of settlement. For a time, however, black workers were hard to find. Not until the mid-seventeenth century, when a substantial commerce in slaves grew up between the Caribbean islands and the southern colonies, did black workers become generally available in North America.

The demand for slaves in North America helped expand the transatlantic slave trade. And as slave trading grew more extensive and more sophisticated, it also grew more horrible. Before it ended in the nineteenth century, it was responsible for the forced immigration of as many as 11 million Africans to North and South America and the Caribbean. Indeed, through much of the eighteenth century, the number of African immigrants to the Americas was higher than that of Europeans. In the flourishing slave marts

AFRICANS BOUND FOR AMERICA Shown here are the below-deck slave quarters of a Spanish vessel en route to the West Indies. A British warship captured the slaver, and a young English naval officer (Lt. Francis Meynell) made this watercolor sketch on the spot. The Africans seen in this picture appear somewhat more comfortable than prisoners on other slave ships, some of whom were chained and packed together so tightly that they had no room to stand or even sit.

on the African coast, native chieftains brought captured members of rival tribes to the ports. The terrified victims were then packed into the dark, filthy holds of ships for the horrors of the "middle passage"—the long journey to the Americas, during which the prisoners were usually kept chained in the bowels of the slave ships and supplied with only minimal food and water. Women were often victims of rape and other sexual abuse. Many slave traders tried to cram as many Africans as possible into their ships to ensure that enough would survive to yield a profit at journey's end. Those who died en route, and many did, were simply thrown overboard. Upon arrival in the New World, slaves were auctioned off to white landowners and transported, frightened and bewildered, to their new homes.

North America was a less important direct destination for African slaves than were such other parts of the New World as the Caribbean islands and Brazil; fewer than 5 percent of the Africans imported to the Americas arrived first in the English colonies. Through most of the seventeenth century, those blacks who were transported to what became the United States came not directly from Africa but from the West Indies. Not until the 1670s did traders start importing blacks directly from Africa to North America. Even then the flow remained small for a time, mainly because a single group, the Royal African Company of England, monopolized the trade and kept prices high and supplies low.

A turning point in the history of the black population in North America was 1697, the year rival traders broke the Royal African Company's monopoly. With the trade now open to competition, prices fell and the number of Africans greatly increased. By 1700, about 25,000 African slaves lived in English North America. That was only 10 percent of the total non-Indian population, but because blacks were so heavily concentrated in a few southern colonies, they were already beginning to outnumber whites in some areas. There were perhaps twice as many black men as black women in most areas, but in some places the African-American population grew by natural increase nevertheless. In the Chesapeake more new slaves were being born than were being imported from Africa. In South Carolina, by contrast, the arduous conditions of rice cultivation ensured that the black population would barely be able to sustain itself through natural increase until much later. By 1760, the number of Africans in the colonies had increased to approximately a quarter of a million. A few (16,000 in 1763) lived in New England; slightly more (29,000) lived in the middle colonies. The vast majority, however, lived in the South. By then blacks had almost wholly replaced white indentured servants as the basis of the southern work force.

D E B A T I N G T H E P A S T

The Origins of Slavery

HE DEBATE among historians over how and why white Americans created a system of slave labor in the seventeenth century—and how and why they determined that African Americans and no others should populate that system—has been an unusually lively one. At its center is a debate over whether slavery was a result of white racism, or whether racism was a result of slavery.

In 1950, Oscar and Mary Handlin published an influential article comparing slavery to other systems of "unfreedom" in the colonies. What separated slavery from other conditions of servitude, they argued, was that it was restricted to people of African descent, that it was permanent, and that it passed from one generation to the next. The unique characteristics of slavery, the Handlins argued, were part of an effort by colonial legislatures to increase the available labor force. White laborers needed an incentive to come to America; black laborers, forcibly imported from Africa, did not. The distinction between the conditions of white workers and the conditions of black workers was, therefore, based on legal and economic motives, not on racism.

Winthrop Jordan was one of a number of historians who later challenged the Handlins' thesis and argued that white racism, more than economic interests, produced African slavery. In *White Over Black* (1968) and other works, Jordan argued that Europeans had long viewed people of color—and black Africans in particular—as inferior beings appropriate for serving whites. Those attitudes migrated with white Europeans to the New World, and white racism shaped the treatment of Africans in America—and the nature of the slave labor system—from the beginning. Even without the economic incentives the Handlins described, in other words, whites would have been likely to oppress blacks in the New World.

Peter Wood's *Black Majority* (1974), a study of seventeenth-century South Carolina, was one of a number of works that moved the debate back toward social and economic conditions. Wood demonstrated that blacks and whites often worked together on relatively equal terms in the early years of settlement; that racism, in other words, did not inevitably shape the relationships between the blacks and whites. But as rice cultivation expanded, it became more difficult to find white laborers willing to do the arduous work. The increase in the forcible importation of African workers, and the creation of a system of permanent bondage, was a response to this growing demand for labor. It was also a response to fears among whites that without slavery it would be difficult to control a labor force brought to America against its will. Edmund Morgan's *American Slavery, American Freedom* (1975) argued similarly that the southern labor system was at first relatively flexible and later grew more rigid. In colonial Virginia, he claimed, white settlers did not at first intend to create a system of permanent bondage for blacks or whites. But as the tobacco economy grew and created a high demand for cheap labor, white landowners began to feel uneasy about their dependence on a large group of dependent white workers. Such workers were difficult to recruit and control. Slavery, therefore, was less a result of racism than of the desire for whites to find a reliable and stable labor force.

Robin Blackburn's *The Making of New World Slavery* (1996) argues particularly strenuously that, while race was a factor in making the enslavement of Africans easier for whites to justify to themselves, the real reasons for the emergence of slavery were hardheaded economic decisions by ambitious entrepreneurs who realized very early that a slave-labor system in the labor-intensive agricultural world of the American South and the Caribbean was more profitable than a free-labor system. Slavery served the interests of a powerful combination of groups: planters, merchants, industrialists, and consumers. The most important reason for the creation and continuation of the system, therefore, was not racism, but the pursuit of profit—and the success of the system in producing it. Slavery was not, Blackburn concludes, an antiquated remnant of an older world. It was a recognizably modern labor system that, however horrible, served the needs of an emerging market economy.

For a time, the legal and social status of the African laborers remained somewhat fluid. In some areas—South Carolina, for example, where the number of black arrivals grew more quickly than anywhere else—white and black laborers worked together at first on terms of relative equality. Some blacks were treated much like white hired servants, and some were freed after a fixed term of servitude. By the late seventeenth century, however, a rigid distinction was emerging between blacks and whites. Gradually, the assumption spread that blacks would remain in service permanently and that black children would inherit their parents' bondage. White beliefs about the inferiority of the black race reinforced the growing rigidity of the system. Whites had long ago defined themselves as a superior race in their relations with the native Indian population; the idea of subordinating an "inferior" race was, therefore, already part of European thinking by the time substantial numbers of Africans appeared in their midst.

The system of permanent servitude—American slavery—became legal in the early eighteenth century when colonial assemblies began to pass "slave codes" granting white masters almost absolute authority over their slaves. Only one factor determined whether a person was subject to the slave codes: color. In the colonial societies of Spanish America, people of mixed race were granted a different (and higher) status than pure Africans. English America recognized no such distinctions. Any African ancestry was enough to classify a person as black.

Changing Sources of European Immigration

The most distinctive and enduring feature of the American population was that it brought together peoples of many different races, ethnic groups, and nationalities. North America was home to a substantial population of natives, to a growing number of English immigrants, to forcibly imported Africans, and to substantial non-English groups from Europe.

The earliest of these non-English European immigrants were about 300,000 French Calvinists, or Huguenots, who left Roman Catholic France for the English colonies of North America after the Edict of Nantes, which had guaranteed them substantial liberties, was revoked in 1685. Many German Protestants emigrated to America to escape similarly arbitrary religious policies and the frequent wars between their principalities and France. The Rhineland of southwestern Germany, known as the Palatinate, was exposed to frequent invasion; more than 12,000 Palitinate Germans fled to England early in the eighteenth century, and approximately 3,000 of them found their way to America. Most settled in Pennsylvania, where they ultimately became known to English settlers as the "Pennsylvania Dutch" (a corruption of the German term for their nationality, *Deutsch*). Other, later German immigrants headed to Pennsylvania as well, among them the Moravians and Mennonites, whose religious views were similar to those of the Quakers.

The most numerous of the newcomers were the so-called Scotch-Irish—Scotch Presbyterians who had settled in northern Ireland (in the province of Ulster) in the early seventeenth century. Most of the Scotch-Irish in America pushed out to the edges of European settlement and occupied land without much regard for who actually claimed to own it. They were as ruthless in their displacement and suppression of the Indians as they had been with the native Irish Catholics in Ireland.

There were also immigrants from Scotland itself and from southern Ireland. Scottish Highlanders, some of them Roman Catholics, mainly immigrated into North Carolina. Scottish Presbyterian Lowlanders, fleeing high rents and unemployment, left for America in large numbers shortly before the American Revolution. The Irish migrated steadily over a long period and by the time of the Revolution were almost as numerous as the Scots. Many of them abandoned their Roman Catholic religion and much of their ethnic identity after they arrived in America.

THE COLONIAL ECONOMIES

Farming dominated almost all areas of European and African settlement in North America throughout the seventeenth and eighteenth centuries. Even so, the economies of the different regions varied markedly from one another.

The Southern Economy

A strong European demand for tobacco enabled some planters in the Chesapeake (Maryland and Virginia) to become enormously wealthy and at times allowed the region as a whole to prosper. But throughout the seventeenth and eighteenth centuries, production of tobacco frequently exceeded demand, and as a result the price of the crop sometimes suffered severe declines. The result was a boom-and-bust cycle in the Chesapeake economy, with the first major bust occurring in 1640.

South Carolina and Georgia relied on rice production, since the low-lying coastline with its many tidal rivers made it possible to create rice

Lake Huron

Lake Ontario

Lake Erie

Lake Champlain

St. Lawrence R.

Mohawk R.

Connecticut R.

MAINE (Mass.) ● Augusta

● Portland

NEW HAMPSHIRE

● Portsmouth

MASSACHUSETTS ● Boston

● Providence
Hartford ● Newport
CONNECTICUT
RHODE ISLAND
New Haven ●

NEW ENGLAND

PENNSYLVANIA

Delaware R.

Hudson R.

Susquehanna R.

Ohio R.

Potomac R.

New York ●
NEW JERSEY
Philadelphia ●

Baltimore ●

DELAWARE

MARYLAND

MIDDLE COLONIES

ATLANTIC OCEAN

VIRGINIA

James R.

Roanoke R.

Norfolk ●

Cape Fear R.

NORTH CAROLINA

New Bern ●

SOUTH CAROLINA

Pee Dee R.

Wilmington ●

SOUTHERN COLONIES

Santee R.

Savannah R.

GEORGIA

Altamaha R.

Charleston ●

Savannah ●

Dominant Immigrant Groups in Colonial America, c. 1760

English

Scotch-Irish

German

Dutch

African

0   200 Miles
0   200 Kilometers

SELLING TOBACCO This late-seventeenth-century label was used in the sale of American tobacco in England. The drawing depicts Virginia as a land of bright sunshine, energetic slaves, and prosperous, pipe-smoking planters.

paddies that could be flooded and drained. Rice cultivation was arduous work performed standing knee-deep in malarial swamps—a task so difficult and unhealthy that white laborers generally refused to perform it. Hence planters in South Carolina and Georgia were much more dependent on slaves than were their northern counterparts. African workers were adept at rice cultivation, in part because some of them had come from rice-producing regions of west Africa and in part because they were generally more accustomed to the hot, humid climate than were Europeans.

Because of their dependence on large-scale cash crops, the southern colonies developed less of a commercial or industrial economy than the colonies of the North. The trading in tobacco and rice was handled largely by merchants based in London and, later, in the northern colonies. Few cities of more than modest size developed in the South.

Northern Economic and Technological Life

In the North, as in the South, agriculture continued to dominate, but it was agriculture of a more diverse kind. Agriculture, however, did not remain the only major economic activity in the North because conditions for farming were less favorable there than in the South. In northern New England, in particular, colder weather and hard, rocky soil made it difficult for colonists to develop the kind of large-scale commercial farming system that southerners were creating. Conditions for agriculture were better in southern New England and the middle colonies, where the soil was fertile and the weather more temperate. New York, Pennsylvania, and the Connecticut River valley were the chief suppliers of wheat to much of New England and to parts of the South. Even there, however, a substantial commercial economy emerged alongside the agricultural one.

Almost every colonist engaged in a certain amount of industry at home. Occasionally these home industries provided families with surplus goods they could trade or sell. Beyond these domestic efforts, craftsmen and artisans established themselves in colonial towns as cobblers, blacksmiths, riflemakers, cabinetmakers, silversmiths, and printers. In some areas, entrepreneurs harnessed water power to run small mills for grinding grain, processing cloth, or milling lumber. And in several places, large-scale shipbuilding operations began to flourish.

The first effort to establish a significant metals industry in the colonies was an ironworks established in Saugus, Massachusetts, in the 1640s after iron ore deposits had been discovered in the region. Iron technology was already advancing rapidly in England, and the colonists attempted to transfer those skills to America. The Saugus works used water power to drive a bellows, which controlled the heat in a charcoal furnace. The carbon from the burning charcoal helped remove the oxygen from the ore and thus reduced its melting temperature. As the ore melted, it trickled down into molds or was taken in the form of simple "sow bars" to a nearby forge to be shaped into iron objects such as pots and anvils. There was also a mill suitable for turning the "sow bars" into narrow rods that blacksmiths could cut into nails. The Saugus works was a technological success; indeed, it could boast technological capabilities equal to any ironworks in Europe at the time. But it was a financial failure. It began operations in 1646; in 1668, its financial problems forced it to close its doors.

Metal works, however, gradually became an important part of the colonial economy. The largest industrial enterprise anywhere in English North America was the ironworks of the German ironmaster Peter

Hasenclever in northern New Jersey. Founded in 1764 with British capital, it employed several hundred laborers, many of them imported from ironworks in Germany. There were other, smaller ironmaking enterprises in every northern colony (with particular concentrations in Massachusetts, New Jersey, and Pennsylvania), and there were ironworks as well in several of the southern colonies. Even so, these and other growing industries did not become the basis for the kind of explosive industrial growth that Great Britain experienced in the late eighteenth century—in part because English parliamentary regulations such as the Iron Act of 1750 restricted metal processing in the colonies. Similar prohibitions limited the manufacture of woolens, hats, and other goods. But the biggest obstacles to industrialization in America were an inadequate labor supply, a small domestic market, and inadequate transportation facilities and energy supplies.

More important than manufacturing were industries that exploited the natural resources of the continent. By the mid-seventeenth century, the flourishing fur trade of earlier years was in decline. Taking its place were lumbering, mining, and fishing, particularly in the waters off the New England coast. These industries provided commodities that could be exported to England in exchange for manufactured goods. And they helped produce the most distinctive feature of the northern economy: a thriving commercial class.

The Extent and Limits of Technology

Despite the technological progress that was occurring in some parts of America in the seventeenth and eighteenth centuries, much of colonial society was conspicuously lacking in even very basic technological capacities. Up to half the farmers in the colonies were so primitively equipped that they did not even own a plow. Substantial numbers of households owned no pots or kettles for cooking. And only about half the households in the colonies owned guns or rifles—with rural people almost as unlikely to have firearms as urban people. The relatively low levels of ownership of these and other elementary tools was not because such things were difficult to make, but because most Americans remained too poor or too isolated to be able to afford them. Many households had few if any candles, because they were unable to afford candle molds or tallow (wax), or because they had no access to commercially produced candles. In the early eighteenth century, very few farmers owned wagons. Most made do with two-wheeled carts, which could be hauled by hand (or by horse) around the farm but which were not very efficient for transporting crops to market. The most commonly-owned tool on American farms was the axe, which suggests how much time most farmers had to spend clearing land.

Even so, few colonists were self-sufficient in the late seventeenth and early eighteenth centuries. The popular image of early American households is of people who had little connection to the market, who grew their own food, made their own clothes, and bought little from anyone else. In fact, relatively few colonial families owned spinning wheels or looms, which suggests that most people purchased whatever yarn and cloth they needed, or could afford, from merchants. Most farmers who grew grain took it to centralized facilities for processing.

In general, unsurprisingly, people who lived in isolated or poor areas owned fewer tools and had less access to advanced technologies than did those in more populous or affluent areas. But throughout the colonies, the ability of people to acquire manufactured implements lagged far behind the economy's capacity to produce them.

The Rise of Colonial Commerce

Perhaps the most remarkable feature of colonial commerce in the seventeenth century was that it was able to survive at all. American merchants faced such bewildering and intimidating obstacles, and lacked so many of the basic institutions of trade, that they managed to stay afloat only with great difficulty. The colonies had almost no gold or silver, and their paper currency was not acceptable as payment for goods from abroad. For many years, colonial merchants had to rely on barter or on money substitutes such as beaver skins.

A second obstacle was lack of information about supply and demand. Traders had no way of knowing what they would find in foreign ports; vessels sometimes stayed at sea for years, journeying from one port to another, trading one commodity for another, attempting to find some way to turn a profit. There was also an enormous number of small, fiercely competitive companies, which made the problem of rationalizing the system even more acute.

Nevertheless, commerce in the colonies survived and grew. There was elaborate trade among the colonies themselves and with the West Indies. The mainland colonies offered their Caribbean trading partners rum, agricultural products, meat, and fish. The islands offered sugar, molasses, and at times slaves in return. There was also trade with England, continental Europe, and the west coast of Africa. This commerce has often

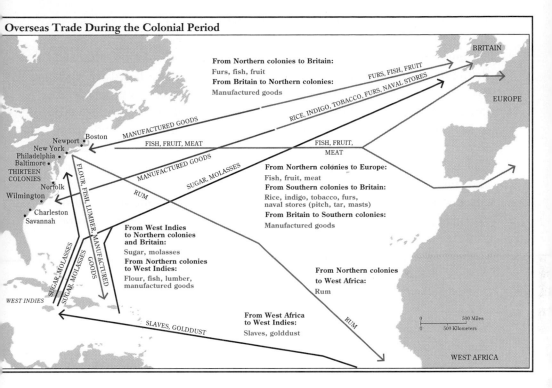

Overseas Trade During the Colonial Period

From Northern colonies to Britain:
Furs, fish, fruit
From Britain to Northern colonies:
Manufactured goods

From Northern colonies to Europe:
Fish, fruit, meat
From Southern colonies to Britain:
Rice, indigo, tobacco, furs,
naval stores (pitch, tar, masts)
From Britain to Southern colonies:
Manufactured goods

From West Indies
to Northern colonies
and Britain:
Sugar, molasses
From Northern colonies
to West Indies:
Flour, fish, lumber,
manufactured goods

From Northern colonies
to West Africa:
Rum

From West Africa
to West Indies:
Slaves, golddust

been described, somewhat inaccurately, as the "triangular trade," suggesting a neat process by which merchants carried rum and other goods from New England to Africa, exchanged their merchandise for slaves, whom they then transported to the West Indies (hence the term "middle passage" for the dreaded journey—it was the second of the three legs of the voyage), and then exchanged the slaves for sugar and molasses, which they shipped back to New England to be distilled into rum. In reality, the so-called triangular trade in rum, slaves, and sugar was a complicated maze of highly diverse trade routes. Out of this risky trade emerged a group of adventurous entrepreneurs who by the mid-eighteenth century were beginning to constitute a distinct merchant class concentrated in the port cities of the North. The British Navigation Acts protected them from foreign competition in the colonies. They had ready access to the market in England for such colonial products as furs, timber, and American-built ships. But they also developed markets illegally outside the British Empire—in the French, Spanish, and Dutch West Indies—where they could often get higher prices for their goods than in the British colonies.

PATTERNS OF SOCIETY

Although there were sharp social distinctions in the colonies, the well-defined and deeply entrenched class system of England failed to reproduce itself in America. In England, land was scarce and the population large, and the relatively few landowners had enormous power over the landless. In colonial America, in contrast, land was abundant and people were scarce. Aristocracies emerged there, to be sure; but they tended to rely less on landownership than on control of a substantial work force, and they were generally less secure and less powerful than their English counterparts. More than in England, white people in America faced opportunities for social mobility—both up and down. There were also new forms of community in America, and they varied greatly from one region to another.

Masters and Slaves on the Plantation

The plantation system of the American South produced one form of community. The first plantations emerged in the tobacco-growing areas of Virginia and Maryland. Some of the early planters became established aristocrats with vast estates. On the whole, however, seventeenth-century colonial plantations were rough and relatively small. In the early days in Virginia, they were little more than crude clearings where landowners and indentured servants worked side by side in conditions so harsh that death was an everyday occurrence. Even in later years, when the death rate declined and the landholdings became more established, plantation work forces seldom exceeded thirty people. Most landowners lived in rough cabins or houses, with their servants or slaves nearby. The economy of the plantation was a precarious one. Planters could not control their markets, so even the largest of them were constantly at risk. When prices fell—as tobacco prices did, for example, in the 1660s—planters faced the prospect of ruin. The plantation economy created many new wealthy landowners, but it also destroyed many.

The enslaved African Americans, of course, lived very differently. On the smaller farms with only a handful of slaves, it was not always possible for a rigid separation to develop between whites and blacks. But by the early eighteenth century, over three-fourths of all blacks lived on plantations of at least ten slaves, and nearly half lived in communities of fifty slaves or more. In those settings, they were able to develop a society and culture of their own. Although whites seldom encouraged formal marriages among slaves, blacks themselves developed a strong and elaborate family structure, even though slave families were always precarious because any member could be sold at any time to another planter, even to one in another colony. There was also a distinctive slave religion, which blended Christianity with African folklore and which became a central element in the emergence of an independent black culture.

Nevertheless, black society was subject to constant intrusions from and interaction with white society. Black house servants, for example, were isolated from their own community and were under constant surveillance from whites. Black women were subject to usually unwanted sexual advances from owners and overseers and hence to bearing mulatto children, who were rarely recognized by their white fathers but were generally accepted as members of the slave community. On some plantations, black workers were treated with kindness and sometimes responded to their owners with genuine devotion. On others, they encountered physical brutality and occasionally even sadism, against which they were virtually powerless.

Slaves often resisted their masters, in large ways and small. The most serious example in the colonial period was the Stono Rebellion in South Carolina in 1739, during which about 100 blacks rose up, seized weapons, killed several whites, and attempted to escape south to Florida. The uprising was quickly crushed, and most participants were executed. A more frequent form of resistance was simply running away, but that provided no real solution either. There was nowhere to go. So for most slaves, resistance took the form of subtle, and often undetected, defiance or evasion of their masters' wishes.

Most slaves, male and female, worked as field hands (with the women shouldering the additional burdens of cooking and child rearing). But on the larger plantations that aspired to genuine self-sufficiency, some slaves learned trades and crafts: blacksmithing, carpentry, shoemaking, spinning, weaving, sewing, midwifery, and others. These skilled crafts workers were at times hired out to other planters. Some set up their own establishments in towns or cities and shared their profits with their owners. A few were able to buy their freedom. There was a small free black population living in southern cities by the time of the Revolution.

The Puritan Community

The characteristic social unit in New England was not the isolated farm but the Puritan town, which was both an economic and a religious unit. In the early years of colonization, each new settlement drew up a "covenant" binding all residents tightly together both religiously and socially.

Colonists laid out a village, with houses and a meetinghouse arranged around a central pasture, or "common." Thus families generally lived with their neighbors close by, reinforcing a strong sense of community. They divided up the outlying fields and woodlands among the residents; the size and location of a family's field depended on the family's numbers, wealth, and social station.

Once a town was established, residents held a yearly "town meeting" to decide important questions and to choose a group of "selectmen," who ran the town's affairs. Participation in the meeting was generally restricted to adult males who were members of the church. Only those who could give evidence of being among the elect assured of salvation (the "visible saints") were admitted to full church membership, although other residents of the town were required to attend church services.

New Englanders did not adopt the English system of primogeniture—the passing of all property to the firstborn son. Instead, a father divided up his land among all his sons. His control of this inheritance gave him great power over the family. Often a son would reach his late twenties before his father would allow him to move into his own household and work his own land. Even then, sons would usually continue to live in close proximity to their fathers. Young women were generally more mobile than their brothers, since they did not stand to inherit land.

The early Puritan community was a tightly knit organism. Yet as the years passed and the communities grew, this communal structure experienced strains. This was partly because of the increasing commercialization of New England society, which introduced new forces and new tensions into the communities of the region. It was also partly because of population growth. As towns grew larger, residents tended to cultivate lands farther and farther from the community center and, by necessity, to live at increasing distances from the church. The control of land by fathers also created strains. In the first generations, fathers generally controlled enough land to satisfy the needs of all their sons. After several generations, however, when such lands were being subdivided for the third or fourth time, there was often too little to go around, particularly in communities surrounded by other towns, with no room to expand outward. The result was that in many communities, groups of younger residents broke off and moved elsewhere—at times far away—to form towns of their own.

The tensions building in Puritan communities could produce bizarre and disastrous events. One example was the widespread hysteria in the 1680s and 1690s over accusations of witchcraft (the human exercise of satanic powers) in New England. The most famous outbreak (although by no means the only one) was in Salem, Massachusetts, where adolescent girls began to exhibit strange behavior and leveled charges of witchcraft against several West Indian servants steeped in voodoo lore. Hysteria spread throughout the town, and hundreds of people (most of them women) were accused of witchcraft. Nineteen residents of Salem were put to death before the trials finally ended in 1692; the girls who had been the original accusers later recanted and admitted that their story had been fabricated.

The Salem experience was not unique. Accusations of witchcraft spread through many New England towns in the early 1690s (and indeed had emerged regularly in Puritan society for many years before) and centered

A STUDY OF WITCHCRAFT This pamphlet, originally written in 1697 near the height of the witchcraft phenomenon in New England, was one of many contemporary studies to take the idea of witchcraft seriously. Belief in witches was widespread in early New England society, and many of the charges that seem preposterous to twentieth-century eyes appeared entirely plausible even to educated people of the time.

mostly on women. Research into the background of accused witches reveals that most were middle-aged women, often widowed, with few or no children. Many accused witches were of low social position, were often involved in domestic conflicts, had frequently been accused of other crimes, and were considered abrasive by their neighbors. Others were women who, through inheritance or hard work, had come into possession of substantial property of their own and thus challenged the gender norms of the community.

The witchcraft controversies were also a reflection of the highly religious character of New England societies. New Englanders believed in the power of Satan and his ability to assert his power in the world. Belief in witchcraft was not a marginal superstition rejected by the mainstream. It was a common feature of Puritan religious conviction.

Cities

In the 1770s the two largest colonial ports—Philadelphia and New York—had populations of 28,000 and 25,000, respectively, which made them larger than most English urban centers of their time. Boston (16,000), Charles Town (later Charleston), South Carolina (12,000), and Newport, Rhode Island (11,000), were also substantial communities by the standards of the day.

Colonial cities served as trading centers for the farmers of their regions and as marts for international commerce. Their leaders were generally merchants who had acquired substantial wealth. Class divisions in American cities were not as sharp as those in Europe. But more than in any other area of colonial life (except, of course, in the relationship between masters and slaves), social distinctions were real and visible in urban areas.

Cities were the centers of much of what industry there was in the colonies, such as distilleries for turning imported molasses into exportable rum. They were the locations of the most advanced schools and sophisticated cultural activities and of shops where imported goods could be bought. In addition, they were communities with urban social problems: crime, vice, pollution, traffic. Unlike smaller towns, cities needed to set up constables' offices and fire departments and develop systems for supporting the urban poor, whose numbers became especially large in times of economic crisis—to which cities were particularly vulnerable.

Finally, cities were places where new ideas could circulate and be discussed. There were newspapers, books, and other publications from abroad, and hence new intellectual influences. The taverns and coffeehouses of cities provided forums in which people could gather and debate the issues of the day. That is one reason why the Revolutionary crisis, when it began to build in the 1760s and 1770s, began first in the cities.

THE COLONIAL MIND

Intellectual life in colonial America revolved around the conflict between the traditional outlook of the sixteenth and seventeenth centuries, with its emphasis on a personal God deeply involved in individual lives, and the new spirit of the Enlightenment, which was sweeping both Europe and America and which stressed the importance of science and human reason. The old views placed a high value on a stern moral code in which intellect was less important than faith. The Enlightenment suggested that people had substantial control over their own lives and societies.

The Pattern of Religions

Religious toleration flourished in America to a degree unmatched in any European nation, not because Americans deliberately sought to produce it but because conditions virtually required it. Settlers in America brought with them so many different religious practices that it proved impossible to impose a single religious code on any large area.

The Church of England was established as the official faith in Virginia, Maryland, New York, the Carolinas, and Georgia. Except in Virginia and Maryland, however, the laws establishing the Church of England as the official colonial religion were largely ignored. Even in New England, where the Puritans had originally believed that they were all part of a single faith, there was a growing tendency in the eighteenth century for different congregations to affiliate with different denominations, especially Congregationalism and Presbyterianism. In parts of New York and New Jersey, Dutch settlers had established their own Calvinist denomination, Dutch Reformed, which survived after the colonies became part of the British Empire. American Baptists (of whom Roger Williams is considered the first) developed a great variety of sects. All Baptists shared the belief that rebaptism, usually by total immersion, was necessary when believers reached maturity. But while some Baptists remained Calvinists (believers in predestination) others came to believe in salvation by free will.

Protestants extended toleration to one another more readily than they did to Roman Catholics. Many Protestants in America, like many in England, feared and hated the pope. New Englanders, in particular, viewed their Catholic neighbors in New France (Canada) not only as commercial and military rivals but also as dangerous agents of Rome. In most of the English colonies, however, Roman Catholics were too few to cause serious conflict. They were most numerous in Maryland, and even there they numbered no more than 3,000. Perhaps for that reason they suffered their worst persecution in that colony. After the overthrow of the original proprietors in 1691, Catholics in Maryland not only lost their political rights but also were forbidden to hold religious services except in private houses.

Jews in provincial America totaled no more than about 2,000 at any time. The largest community lived in New York City. Smaller groups settled in Newport and Charleston, and there were scattered Jewish families in all the colonies. Nowhere could they vote or hold office. Only in Rhode Island could they practice their religion openly.

By the beginning of the eighteenth century, some Americans were growing troubled by the apparent decline in religious piety in their society. The movement of the population westward and the wide scattering of settlements had caused many communities to lose touch with organized religion. The rise of commercial prosperity created a more secular outlook in urban areas. The progress of science and free thought in Europe—and the importation of Enlightenment ideas to America—caused at least some colonists to doubt traditional religious beliefs.

Concerns about weakening piety surfaced as early as the 1660s in New England, where the Puritan oligarchy warned of a decline in the power of the church. Sabbath after Sabbath, ministers preached sermons of despair (known as "jeremiads"), deploring the signs of waning piety. By the standards of other societies or other eras, the Puritan faith remained remarkably strong. But New Englanders measured their faith by their own standards, and to them the "declension" of religious piety seemed a serious problem.

The Great Awakening

By the early eighteenth century, similar concerns were emerging in other regions and among members of other faiths. Everywhere, colonists were coming to believe, religious piety was in decline and opportunities for spiritual regeneration were dwindling. The result was the first great American revival: the Great Awakening.

The Great Awakening began in earnest in the 1730s, reached its climax in the 1740s, and brought a new spirit of religious fervor that many Americans believed was reversing the trend away from piety. The revival had particular appeal to women (who constituted the majority of converts) and to younger sons of the third or fourth generation of settlers—those who stood to inherit the least land and who faced the most uncertain futures. The rhetoric of the revival emphasized the potential for every person to break away from the constraints of the past and start anew in his or her relationship with God. Such beliefs may have reflected the desires of many people to break away from their families or communities and start a new life.

Powerful evangelists from England helped spread the revival. John and Charles Wesley, the founders of Methodism, visited Georgia and other colonies in the 1730s. George Whitefield, a powerful open-air preacher and for a time an associate of the Wesleys', made several evangelizing tours through the colonies and drew tremendous crowds. But the outstanding preacher of the Great Awakening was the New England Congregationalist Jonathan Edwards, a deeply orthodox Puritan but a highly original theologian. From his pulpit in Northampton, Massachusetts, Edwards attacked the new doctrines of easy salvation for all. He preached anew the traditional Puritan ideas of the absolute sovereignty of God, predestination, and salvation by God's grace alone. His vivid descriptions of hell could terrify his listeners.

The Great Awakening led to the division of existing congregations (between "New Light" revivalists and "Old Light" traditionalists) and to the founding of new ones. It also affected areas of society outside the churches. Some of the revivalists denounced book learning as a hindrance to salvation, and some communities repudiated secular education altogether. But other evangelists saw education as a means of furthering religion, and they founded or led schools for the training of New Light ministers.

The Enlightenment

The Great Awakening caused one great cultural upheaval in the colonies. The Enlightenment caused another, very different one. The Enlightenment was the product of some of the great scientific and intellectual discoveries in Europe in the seventeenth century—discoveries that revealed what scientists and others considered the "natural laws" that regulated the workings of nature. The new scientific knowledge encouraged many thinkers to begin celebrating the power of human reason and scientific inquiry, and to argue that rational thought, not just religious faith, could create progress and advance knowledge in the world.

In celebrating reason, the Enlightenment slowly undermined the power of traditional religious authority. It encouraged men and women to look to themselves and their own intellect—not just to God—for guidance as to how to live their lives and shape their societies. It helped produce a growing interest in education and a heightened concern with politics and government.

In the early seventeenth century, Enlightenment ideas in America were largely borrowed from Europe—from such great thinkers as Francis Bacon and John Locke of England, Baruch Spinoza of Amsterdam, and René Descartes of France. Later, however, such Americans as Benjamin Franklin, Thomas Paine, Thomas Jefferson, and James Madison made their own important contributions to Enlightenment thought.

Literacy and Technology

White male Americans achieved a high degree of literacy in the eighteenth century. By the time of the Revolution, well over half of all white men could read and write, a rate substantially higher than that in most European countries. The literacy rate for women lagged behind the rate for men until the nineteenth century. While opportunities for education beyond the primary level were scarce for men, they were almost nonexistent for women. Nevertheless, the literacy rate for American females was also substantially higher than that of their European counterparts.

The large number of colonists who could read created a market for the first widely circulated publications in America other than the Bible: almanacs. They appeared first in the 1630s in Massachusetts. By 1700, there were dozens, perhaps hundreds, of almanacs circulating throughout the colonies and even in the sparsely settled lands to the west. Most families had at least one, and they appeared in many languages to serve the various ethnic communities in the colonies. Almanacs provided medical advice, navigational and agricultural information, practical wisdom, humor, and predictions about the future—most famously, predictions about weather patterns for the coming year, which many farmers used as the basis of decisions about crops even though the predictions were notoriously unreliable. The most famous almanac in eighteenth-century America was *Poor Richard's Almanac*, published by Benjamin Franklin in Philadelphia.

The wide availability of reading material in colonial America by the eighteenth century was a result of both improvements in and the spread of printing technology. The first printing press began operating in the colonies in 1639, and by 1695 there were more towns in America with printers than there were in England. At first, many of these presses did not get very much use. Over time, however, the rising literacy of the society created a demand for books, pamphlets, and almanacs that the presses rushed to fill.

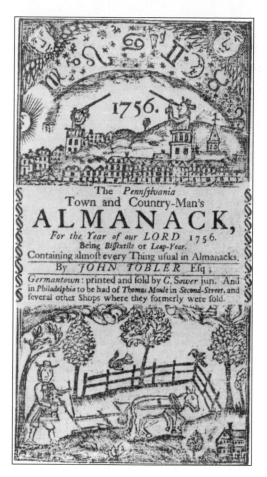

TOWN AND COUNTRY-MAN'S ALMANACK As the population of colonial cities and towns grew, almanacs—originally targeted mainly at farmers—began to appeal to townspeople as well.

The first newspaper in the colonies, *Publick Occurrences*, was published in Boston in 1690 using a relatively advanced printing facility there. It lasted only one issue, but it was the first step toward what would eventually become a large newspaper industry in America. One reason the Stamp Act of 1765, which imposed a tax on printed materials, created such a furor in the colonies (see pp. 107–108) was because printing technology—and thus print itself—had by then become central to colonial life.

Education

Even before Enlightenment ideas penetrated America, colonists placed a high value on formal education, despite the difficulties they confronted in gaining access to it. Some families tried to teach their children to read and write at home, although the heavy burden of work in most agricultural households limited the time available for schooling. In Massachusetts, a 1647 law required that every town support a school; and even though many communities failed to comply, a modest network of public schools emerged as a result. The Quakers and other sects operated church schools, and in some communities widows or unmarried women conducted "dame schools" by holding private classes in their homes. In cities, master craftsmen set up evening schools for their apprentices.

African Americans, most of whom were enslaved, had virtually no access to education. Occasionally a master or mistress would teach slave children to read and write; but as the slave system became more firmly entrenched, strong social (and ultimately legal) sanctions developed to discourage such efforts because of fears that literacy might encourage slaves to question their stations. Indians, too, remained largely outside the white educational system—to a large degree by choice: most tribes preferred to educate their children in their own way. Some white missionaries and philanthropists established schools for Native Americans and helped create a small population of Indians literate in spoken and written English.

Harvard, the first American college, was established in 1636 by Puritan theologians who wanted to create a training center for ministers. (The college was named for a Charlestown minister, John Harvard, who had left it his library and half his estate). In 1693, William and Mary College (named for the English king and queen) was established in Williamsburg, Virginia, by Anglicans; like Harvard, it was conceived as an academy to train clergymen. And in 1701, conservative Congregationalists, dissatisfied with the growing religious liberalism of Harvard, founded Yale (named for one of its first benefactors, Elihu Yale) in New Haven, Connecticut. Out of the Great Awakening emerged the College of New Jersey, founded in 1746 and known later as Princeton (after the town in which it was located); one of its first presidents was Jonathan Edwards. Despite the religious basis of these colleges, most of them offered curricula that included not only theology but logic, ethics, physics, geometry, astronomy, rhetoric, Latin, Hebrew, and Greek. King's College, founded in New York in 1754 and later renamed Columbia, was specifically devoted to the spread of secular knowledge; it had no theological faculty and was interdenominational from the start. The Academy and College of Philadelphia, founded in 1755 and later renamed the University of Pennsylvania, was also a completely secular institution, established by a group of laymen under the inspiration of Benjamin Franklin.

After 1700, most colonial leaders received their entire educations in America (rather than attending university in England, as had once been the case). But higher education remained available only to relatively affluent white men.

The Spread of Science

The clearest indication of the spreading influence of the Enlightenment in America was an increasing interest in scientific knowledge. Most of the early colleges established chairs in the natural sciences and introduced some of the advanced scientific theories of Europe, including Copernican astronomy and Newtonian physics, to their students. But the most vigorous promotion of science in these years occurred outside the colleges, through the private efforts of amateurs and the activities of scientific societies. Leading merchants, planters, and even theologians became corresponding members of the Royal Society of London, the leading English scientific organization. Benjamin Franklin, the most celebrated amateur scientist in America, won international fame through his experiments with electricity. Particularly notable was his 1747 theory and his 1752 demonstration, using a kite, that lightning and electricity were the same. Previously, most scientists had believed that there were several distinct types of electricity; Franklin's discovery that there was only one represented a major advance in knowledge about electricity. His research on the way in which electricity could be "grounded" led to the development of the lightning rod, which greatly reduced fires and other damage to buildings during thunderstorms.

The high value that influential Americans were beginning to place on scientific knowledge was clearly demonstrated by the most daring and controversial scientific experiment of the eighteenth century: inoculation against smallpox. The Puritan theologian Cotton Mather had learned of experiments in England by which people had been deliberately infected with mild cases of smallpox in order to immunize them against the deadly disease. Despite strong opposition from many of his neighbors, he urged inoculation on his fellow Bostonians during an epidemic in the 1720s. The results confirmed the effectiveness of the technique. Other theologians (including Jonathan Edwards) took up the cause, along with many physicians. By the mid-eighteenth century, inoculation had become a common medical procedure in America.

THE MAGNETIC DISPENSARY In this 1790 painting, artist Samuel Collings caricatured the popular enthusiasm that Benjamin Franklin and others had produced for scientific experiments. The men and women shown here are rubbing iron rods with silk cloth to produce static electricity. A popular pastime was to place the charged rods over people's heads to watch their hair stand on end.

Concepts of Law and Politics

In law and politics, as in other parts of their lives, Americans in the seventeenth and eighteenth centuries believed that they were re-creating in the New World the practices and institutions of the Old. But as in other areas, they in fact created something very different.

Changes in the law in America resulted in part from the scarcity of English-trained lawyers, who were almost unknown in the colonies until after 1700. Although the American legal system adopted most of the essential elements of the English system, including such ancient rights as trial by jury, significant differences developed in court procedures, punishments, and the definition of crimes. In England, for example, a printed attack on a public official, whether true or false, was considered libelous. At the 1734 trial of the New York publisher John Peter Zenger, who was powerfully defended by the Philadelphia lawyer Andrew Hamilton, the courts ruled that criticisms of the government were not libelous if factually true—a verdict that removed some colonial restrictions on the freedom of the press.

More significant for the future of the relationship between the colonies and England were differences emerging between the American and British political systems. Because the royal government—in theory the ultimate authority over the colonies—was so far away, Americans created a group of institutions of their own that gave them a large measure of self-government. In most colonies, local communities grew accustomed to running their own affairs with minimal interference from higher authorities. The colonial assemblies came to exercise many of the powers that Parliament exercised in England. Provincial governors (appointed by the king after the 1690s) had broad powers on paper, but their actual influence was limited. Control over appointments and contracts resided largely in England or with local colonial leaders.

The result of all this was that colonial politics had a largely local focus. The provincial governments became accustomed to acting more or less independently of Parliament, and a set of assumptions and expectations about the rights of the colonists took hold in America that was not shared by policymakers in England. These differences caused few problems before the 1760s, because the British did little to exert the authority they believed they possessed. But when, beginning in 1763, the English government began attempting to tighten its control over the American colonies, a historic crisis resulted.

CONCLUSION

What began as a few small, isolated, precarious settlements in the wilderness had evolved by the mid-eighteenth century into a large and complex society. The English colonies in America grew steadily between the 1650s and the 1750s: in population, in the size of their economies, and in the sophistication—and diversity—of their cultures. Although most white Americans in the 1750s still believed that they were fully a part of the British Empire, they were in fact living in a world that had become very different from that of England.

Many distinct societies developed in the colonies, but the greatest distinction was between the colonies of the North and those of the South. In the North, society was dominated by relatively small family farms and by towns and cities of growing size. A thriving commercial class was developing, and with it an increasingly elaborate urban culture. In the South, there were many family farms as well. But there were also large plantations cultivating tobacco, rice, indigo, and cotton for export. By the late seventeenth century, these plantations were relying heavily on African workers who had been brought to the colonies forcibly as slaves. There were few significant towns and cities in the South, and little commerce other than the marketing of crops.

The colonies did, however, also have much in common. Most white Americans accepted common assumptions about racial inequality. That enabled them to tolerate (and at times celebrate) the enslavement of African men and women and to justify a campaign of displacement and often violence against Native Americans that would continue for two centuries. Most white Americans (and, in different ways, most nonwhite Americans as well) were deeply religious. The Great Awakening, therefore, had a powerful impact throughout the colonies, North and South. And most white colonists shared a belief in certain basic principles of law and politics, which they considered embedded in the English constitution, and which in the years after the 1750s would lead to a great imperial crisis.

FOR FURTHER REFERENCE

Suggested Readings

Bernard Bailyn, *Voyagers to the West: A Passage in the Peopling of America on the Eve of the Revolution* (1986) reveals the complexity and scope of European emigration to North America. Bailyn's *The Origin of American Politics* (1968) remains an excellent introduction to colonial politics. David Hackett Fischer, *Albion's Seed* (1989) offers a provocative argument that four major folkways shaped English settlement in America. Laurel Thatcher Ulrich, *Good Wives: Image and Reality in the Lives of Women in Northern New England, 1650–1750* (1982) offers a typology of women's roles in colonial New England. Kathleen M. Brown, *Good Wives, Nasty Wenches, and Anxious Patriarchs: Gender, Race and Power in Colonial Virginia* (1996) places gender at the center of the development of slavery in the Chesapeake. Rhys Isaac, *The Transformation of Virginia, 1740–1790* (1982) uses the methods of cultural anthropology in an influential study of the world of the colonial Virginia gentry. Richard Bushman, *The Refinement of America: Persons, Houses, Cities* (1992) traces the growing interest of Americans in material comfort and display. John Putnam Demos, *Entertaining Satan: Witchcraft and the Culture of Early New England* (1982); Paul Boyer and Stephen Nissenbaum, *Salem Possessed* (1974); and Carol Karlsen, *The Devil in the Shape of a Woman: Witchcraft in Colonial New England* (1987) are three important studies of witchcraft in New England.

Films

(The best source for information on how to find these and other films is *Bowker's Complete Video Directory*—3 volumes.) *The Roots of Democracy: The 1700s* studies the economic forces and political beliefs that shaped the British colonies. *Colonial America: Life in the Maturing Colonies* (1991) looks at the lives of New World settlers and explores their attitudes toward Indians, slaves, and women. *Benjamin Franklin* (1987) looks at the life of one of the leading figures of American colonial history. *Religion in the Colonies* (1994) explores the diversity of religious sects transported from Europe to the American colonies. *Anne Hutchinson* (1983) narrates the life and struggles of an important dissident woman in the Massachusetts Bay colony. *The Salem Witch Trials* introduces the accused "witches," judges, and girls involved in a tragic episode in the history of colonial Massachusetts.

Internet Resources

Internet websites containing historical material relevant to the subjects discussed in this chapter can be reached through the McGraw-Hill history site at www.mhhe.com/socscience/history/usa/link/linktop.htm.

CHAPTER FOUR

The Empire Under Strain

Loosening Ties ∼ *The Struggle for the Continent*
The New Imperialism ∼ *Stirrings of Revolt*
Cooperation and War

S LATE AS the 1750s, few Americans objected to their membership in the British Empire. The imperial system provided many
commercial and political benefits to the Americans, and it had few costs,
because for the most part the English government left the colonies alone.
By the mid-1770s, however, the relationship between the American
colonies and their British rulers had become so strained, so poisoned, so
characterized by suspicion and resentment that the empire was on the
verge of unraveling. And in the spring of 1775, the first shots were fired in
a war that would ultimately win America its independence. How had it
happened? And why so quickly?

LOOSENING TIES

In one sense, it had not happened quickly at all. Ever since the first days of
English settlement in North America, the ideas and institutions of the
colonies had been diverging from those in Britain in countless ways. In
another sense, however, the Revolutionary crisis emerged in response to
important and relatively sudden changes in the administration of the empire. In 1763 the English government began to enforce a series of policies
toward its colonies that brought the differences between the two societies
into sharp focus.

TIME LINE				
1754	**1756**	**1760**	**1763**	**1764**
Beginning of French and Indian War	Seven Years' War begins	George III becomes king	Peace of Paris Proclamation of 1763	Sugar Act
1765	**1766**	**1767**	**1770**	
Stamp Act	Stamp Act repealed Declaratory Act	Townshend Duties	Boston Massacre Most Townshend Duties repealed	
1771	**1772**	**1773**	**1774**	**1775**
Regulator movement in North Carolina	Committees of correspondence in Boston Gaspée incident	Tea Act, Boston Tea Party	Intolerable Acts First Continental Congress in Philadelphia	Battles of Lexingon and Concord American Revolution begins

A Decentralized Empire

In the fifty years after the Glorious Revolution, the English Parliament (which became the British Parliament after the union of England and Scotland in 1707) established a growing supremacy over the king. Under Kings George I (1714–1727) and George II (1727–1760), both of whom were German-born and unaccustomed to English ways, the prime minister and his cabinet became the nation's real executives. Because they depended politically on the great merchants and landholders of England, who had a great stake in the colonial trade, they were less inclined than the seventeenth-century monarchs had been to try to tighten control over the empire, which many merchants feared would disrupt the profitable commerce with the colonies. As a result, administration of the colonies remained loose, decentralized, and inefficient, with no single office or agency responsible for colonial affairs.

The character of the royal officials in America—the governors and other officers of the royal colonies and (in all the colonies) the naval officers and collectors of customs—contributed further to the looseness of the imperial system. Few governors were able men. Many, perhaps most, had used bribery to obtain their offices and continued to accept bribes once they assumed their offices. Some appointees remained in England and hired substitutes to take their places in America.

The colonial assemblies, taking advantage of the weak imperial administration, had asserted their own authority to levy taxes, make appropriations, approve appointments, and pass laws for their respective colonies. The assemblies came to look upon themselves as little parliaments, each practically as sovereign within its colony as Parliament itself was in England.

The Colonies Divided

Even so, the colonists continued to think of themselves as loyal English subjects. Many felt stronger ties to England than they did to the other American colonies because the differences among the colonial societies were so great. Although the colonies had slowly learned to cooperate with one another on such practical matters as intercolonial trade, road construction, and the creation of a colonial postal service, they remained reluctant to cooperate in larger ways, even when, in 1754, they faced a common threat from their old rivals, the French, and France's Indian allies. Delegates from Pennsylvania, Maryland, New York, and New England met in Albany in that year to negotiate a treaty with the Iroquois and tentatively approved a proposal by Benjamin Franklin to set up a "general government" in America to manage relations with the Indians on behalf of all the colonies. War with the French and Indians was already beginning when the Albany Plan was presented to the colonial assemblies. None approved it.

THE STRUGGLE FOR THE CONTINENT

The war that raged in North America through the late 1750s and early 1760s was part of a larger struggle between England and France for dominance in world trade and naval power. The British victory in that struggle, known in Europe as the Seven Years' War, confirmed England's commercial supremacy and cemented its control of the settled regions of North America. In America, however, the conflict was also the final stage in a long struggle among the three principal powers in northeastern North America: the English, the French, and the Iroquois.

New France and the Iroquois Nation

By the end of the seventeenth century, the French Empire in America had come to possess a vast territory: the whole length of the Mississippi River and its delta (which they named Louisiana, after their king), and the continental interior as far west as the Rocky Mountains and as far south as the Rio Grande. France claimed, in effect, the entire interior of the continent.

To secure their hold on these enormous claims, they founded a string of widely separated communities, strategically located fortresses, and far-flung missions and trading posts. Would-be feudal lords established large estates (*seigneuries*) along the banks of the St. Lawrence River. On a high bluff above the river stood the fortified city of Quebec, the center of the French Empire in America. Montreal to the south and Sault Sainte Marie and Detroit to the west marked the northern boundaries of French settlement. On the lower Mississippi emerged plantations much like those in the southern colonies of English America, worked by black slaves and owned by "Creoles" (white immigrants of French descent). New Orleans, founded in 1718 to service the French plantation economy, was soon as big as some of the larger cities of the Atlantic seaboard; Biloxi and Mobile to the east completed the string of French settlement.

But the French shared the continental interior with a large and powerful Indian population. Both the French and the English were aware that the battle for control of North America would be determined in part by which group could best win the allegiance of native tribes—as trading partners and, at times, as military allies. The English—with their more advanced commercial economy—could usually offer the Indians better and more plentiful goods. But the French offered tolerance. Unlike the English, the French settlers in the interior generally adjusted their own behavior to Indian patterns. French fur traders frequently married Indian women and adopted tribal ways; Jesuit missionaries interacted comfortably with the natives and converted them to Catholicism by the thousands without challenging most of their social customs. By the mid-eighteenth century, therefore, the French had better and closer relations with most of the Indians of the interior than did the English.

The most powerful native group, however, had remained aloof from both the British and the French. The Iroquois Confederacy—five Indian nations (Mohawk, Seneca, Cayuga, Onondaga, and Oneida) that had formed a defensive alliance in the fifteenth century—had been the most powerful native presence in the Ohio Valley and a large surrounding region since the 1640s, unchallenged by either the French or the English. The Iroquois maintained their autonomy by avoiding too close a relationship with either group. They traded successfully with both the English and the French and astutely played the two groups against each other. As a result, they maintained an uneasy balance of power in the Great Lakes region.

Anglo-French Conflicts

As long as England and France remained at peace and as long as the precarious balance in the North American interior survived, English and French colonists coexisted without serious difficulty. But after the Glorious Revolution in England, a series of Anglo-French wars erupted in Europe and continued intermittently for nearly eighty years, creating important repercussions in America.

King William's War (1689–1697) produced only a few, indecisive clashes between the English and the French in northern New England. Queen Anne's War, which began in 1701 and continued for nearly twelve years, generated more substantial conflicts: border fighting with the Spaniards in the South as well as with the French and their Indian allies in the North. The Treaty of Utrecht, which brought the conflict to a close in 1713, transferred substantial territory from the French to the English in North America, including Acadia (Nova Scotia) and Newfoundland. Two decades later, disputes over British trading rights in the Spanish colonies produced a conflict between England and Spain that soon grew into a much larger European war, in which England and France lined up on opposite sides. The English colonists in America were drawn into the struggle, which they called King George's War; and between 1744 and 1748 they engaged in a series of conflicts with the French. New Englanders captured the French bastion at Louisbourg on Cape Breton Island, but the peace treaty that finally ended the conflict forced them to abandon it.

In the aftermath of King George's War, relations among the English, French, and Iroquois in North America quickly deteriorated. The Iroquois (in what appears to have been a major blunder) granted trading concessions in the interior to English merchants for the first time. The French, fearful (probably correctly) that the English were using the concessions as a first step toward expansion into French lands, began in 1749 to construct new fortresses in the Ohio Valley. The English interpreted the French activity as a threat to their western settlements, protested, and began building up their military forces and building fortresses of their own. The balance of power that the Iroquois had carefully and successfully maintained for so long rapidly disintegrated.

For the next five years, tensions between the English and the French increased. In the summer of 1754 the governor of Virginia sent a militia force (under the command of an inexperienced young colonel, George Washington) into the Ohio Valley to challenge French expansion. Washington built a crude stockade (Fort Necessity) not far from Fort Duquesne, the larger outpost the French were building on the site of what is now Pittsburgh. After the Virginians staged an unsuccessful attack on a French detachment, the French countered with an assault on Fort Necessity, trapping Washington and his soldiers inside. After a third of them died in the fighting, Washington surrendered. The clash marked the beginning of the French and Indian War.

The Great War for the Empire

The French and Indian War lasted nearly nine years, and it moved through three distinct phases. During the first of these phases, from the Fort Necessity debacle in 1754 until the expansion of the war to Europe in 1756, it was primarily a local, North American conflict. Virtually all the tribes except the Iroquois were now allied with the French; they had interpreted the defeat of the Virginians at Fort Duquesne as evidence of British weakness and launched a series of raids on western English settlements. The English colonists fought largely alone to defend themselves against those raids. The Iroquois, although nominally allied with the British, feared antagonizing the French and remained largely passive in the conflict. By late 1755, many English settlers along the frontier had withdrawn to the east of the Allegheny Mountains to escape the hostilities.

The second phase of the struggle began in 1756, when the governments of France and England formally opened hostilities and a truly international conflict (the Seven Years' War) began. The fighting now spread to the West Indies, India, and Europe itself. But the principal struggle remained the one in North America, where so far England had suffered nothing but frustration and defeat. Beginning in 1757, William Pitt, the English secretary of state (and future prime minister), brought the war for the first time fully under British control. Pitt himself planned military strategy, appointed commanders, and issued orders to the colonists. Military recruitment had slowed dramatically in America, and to replenish the army British commanders began forcibly enlisting colonists (a practice known as "impressment"). Officers also seized supplies from local farmers

ALL those who prefer the Glory of bearing Arms to any servile mean Employ, and have Spirit to stand forth in Defence of their King and Country, against the treacherous Designs of *France* and *Spain*, in the

Suffex Light Dragoons,

Commanded by

Lt. Col. John Baker Holroyd,

Let them repair to

Where they shall be handsomely Cloathed, most compleatly Accoutred, mounted on noble Hunters. and treated with Kindness and Generosity.

RECUITING FOR THE FRENCH AND INDIAN WAR The extravagant promises in this recruiting poster, distributed to colonists during the French and Indian War, suggest how difficult it sometimes was to persuade Americans to fight in the British army.

and tradesmen and compelled colonists to offer shelter to British troops—all generally without compensation. The Americans resented these new impositions and firmly resisted them—at times, as in a 1757 riot in New York City, violently. By early 1758, the friction between the British authorities and the colonists was threatening to bring the war effort to a halt.

Beginning in 1758, therefore, Pitt initiated the third and final phase of the war by relaxing many of the policies that Americans had found obnoxious. He agreed to reimburse the colonists for all supplies requisitioned by the army. He returned control over recruitment to the colonial assemblies (which resulted in an immediate and dramatic increase in enlistments). And he dispatched large numbers of additional British troops to America. Finally, the tide of battle began to turn in England's favor. The French had always been outnumbered by the British colonists. After 1756, more-over, they suffered from a series of poor harvests. As a result, they were unable to sustain their early military successes. By mid-1758, the British regulars in America (who did the bulk of the actual fighting) and the colo-nial militias were seizing one French stronghold after another. Two bril-liant English generals, Jeffrey Amherst and James Wolfe, captured the fortress at Louisbourg in July 1758; a few months later Fort Duquesne fell without a fight. The next year, at the end of a siege of Quebec, supposedly impregnable atop its towering cliff, the army of General Wolfe struggled up a hidden ravine under cover of darkness, surprised the larger forces of the Marquis de Montcalm, and defeated them in a battle in which both commanders were killed. The dramatic fall of Quebec on September 13, 1759, marked the beginning of the end of the American phase of the war. A year later, in September 1760, the French army formally surrendered to Amherst in Montreal. Peace finally came in 1763, with the Peace of Paris, by which the French ceded to Great Britain some of their West Indian is-lands, most of their colonies in India and Canada, and all other French territory in North America east of the Mississippi. They ceded New Or-leans and their claims west of the Mississippi to Spain, thus surrendering all title to the mainland of North America.

The French and Indian War had profound effects on the British Em-pire and the American colonies. It greatly expanded England's territorial claims in the New World. At the same time, the cost of the war greatly enlarged Britain's debt and substantially increased British resentment of the Americans. English leaders were contemptuous of the colonists for what they considered American military ineptitude during the war; they were angry that the colonists had made so few financial contributions to a struggle waged, they believed, largely for American benefit; they were particularly bitter that some colonial merchants had been selling food and other goods to the French in the West Indies throughout the conflict. All these factors combined to persuade many English leaders that a major re-organization of the empire giving London increased authority over the colonies would be necessary in the aftermath of the war.

The war had an equally profound but very different effect on the American colonists. It was an experience that forced them, for the first time, to act in concert against a common foe. And the friction of 1756–1757 over British requisition and impressment policies and the 1758 return of authority to the colonial assemblies seemed to many Americans to confirm the illegitimacy of English interference in local affairs.

For the Indians of the Ohio Valley, the third major party in the French and Indian War, the British victory was disastrous. Those tribes that had allied themselves with the French had earned the enmity of the victorious English. The Iroquois Confederacy, which had allied itself with Britain, fared only slightly better. English officials saw the passivity of the Iroquois during the war (a result of their effort to hedge their bets and avoid antagonizing the French) as evidence of duplicity. In the aftermath of the peace settlement, the Iroquois alliance with the British quickly unraveled, and the Iroquois Confederacy itself began to crumble from within. The tribes would continue to contest the English for control of the Ohio Valley for another fifty years; but increasingly divided and increasingly outnumbered, they would seldom again be in a position to deal with their European rivals on terms of military or political equality.

THE NEW IMPERIALISM

With the treaty of 1763, England found itself truly at peace for the first time in more than fifty years. As a result, the British government could now turn its attention to the organization of its empire. Saddled with enormous debts from the many years of fighting, England was desperately in need of new revenues from its empire. Responsible for vast new lands in the New World that had doubled the size of the British Empire, the imperial government believed it must increase its administrative capacities in America. The result was a dramatic and, for England, disastrous redefinition of the colonial relationship.

Burdens of Empire

The experience of the French and Indian War should have suggested that increasing imperial control over the colonies would not be easy. Not only had the colonists proved so resistant to British control that Pitt had been forced to relax his policies in 1758, but the colonial assemblies had continued after that to chart a course different from, and often in conflict with, the desires of the government in London. Defiance of imperial trade regulations and other British demands continued. The American colonial governments were already claiming jurisdiction over much of the western territories, although many officials in London wanted authority over the new lands to remain in England. But the most immediate problem for London was its staggering war debt. Landlords and merchants in England were objecting strenuously to any further tax increases, and the colonial assemblies had repeatedly demonstrated their unwillingness to pay for the war effort. Many officials in England believed that only by taxing the Americans directly from London could the empire effectively meet its financial needs.

At this crucial moment in Anglo-American relations, with the imperial system in need of redefinition, the government of England was thrown into turmoil by the accession to the throne of a new king, George III, who assumed power in 1760. He brought two particularly unfortunate qualities to the office. First, he was determined, unlike his two predecessors, to reassert the authority of the monarchy. He removed from power the relatively stable coalition of Whigs that had governed the empire for much of the century and replaced it with a new and very unstable coalition of his own, assembled through patronage and bribes. The new ministries that emerged as a result of this change each lasted in office an average of only about two years.

The king also had serious intellectual and psychological limitations. He suffered, apparently, from a rare mental disease that produced intermittent bouts of insanity. (Indeed, in the last years of his long reign he was, according to most accounts, a virtual lunatic, confined to the palace and unable to perform any official functions.) Yet even when George III was lucid and rational, which was most of the time in the 1760s and 1770s, he was painfully immature (he was only twenty two when he ascended the throne) and insecure. The king's personality, therefore, contributed both to the instability and to the rigidity of the British government during these critical years.

More directly responsible for the problems that soon emerged with the colonies, however, was George Grenville, whom the king made prime minister in 1763. Grenville shared the prevailing opinion within Britain that the colonists had been too long indulged and that they should be compelled to obey the laws and to pay a part of the cost of defending and administering the empire.

The British and the Tribes

With the defeat of the French, frontiersmen from the English colonies had begun immediately to move over the mountains and into tribal lands in the upper Ohio Valley. An alliance of Indian tribes, under the Ottawa chieftain Pontiac, struck back. Fearing that an escalation of the fighting might threaten western trade, the British government—in the Proclamation of

1763—forbade settlers to advance beyond the mountains that divided the Atlantic coast from the interior. Slower western settlement, London believed, would limit costly wars with the Indians.

Although Native Americans had few illusions about the Proclamation, many Indian groups supported the agreement as the best bargain available to them. The Cherokee, in particular, worked actively to hasten the drawing of the boundary, hoping finally to put an end to white movements into their lands. Relations between the western tribes and the British improved for a time in at least some areas after the Proclamation, partly as a result of the work of the Indian superintendents the British appointed, who were sympathetic to tribal needs.

In the end, however, the Proclamation of 1763 failed to meet even the modest expectations of the Indians, because on the crucial point of the line of settlement it was almost completely ineffective. White settlers continued to swarm across the boundary and continued to claim lands farther and farther into the Ohio Valley. The British authorities failed repeatedly to enforce limits to the expansion. In 1768, new agreements with the western tribes pushed the boundary further west in another effort to create a permanent western boundary for European settlement. But these treaties (signed respectively at Hard Labor Creek, South Carolina, and Fort Stanwix, New York) also failed to stop the white advance. Within a few years, the 1768 agreements were replaced with new ones, which pushed the line of settlement still farther west.

Battles over Trade and Taxes

The Grenville ministry increased its authority in the colonies in other ways as well. Regular British troops were stationed permanently in America, and under the Mutiny Act of 1765 the colonists were required to help provision and maintain the army. Ships of the British navy patrolled American waters to search for smugglers. The customs service was reorganized and enlarged. Royal officials were required to take up their colonial posts in person instead of sending substitutes. Colonial manufacturing was restricted, so that it would not compete with rapidly expanding industries in Great Britain.

The Sugar Act of 1764, designed in part to eliminate the illegal sugar trade between the continental colonies and the French and Spanish West Indies, raised the duty on sugar (while lowering the duty on molasses, further damaging the market for sugar grown in the colonies). It also established new vice-admiralty courts in America to try accused smugglers—thus

HUDSON'S BAY COMPANY

QUÉBEC

MAINE
(Mass.)

Lake Superior

Fort Michilimackinac

Lake Huron

Fort
Frontenac

Québec

Montreal

BRITISH   TERRITORY

La Baye

Lake Michigan

Lake Ontario

Fort
Stanwix

Falmouth

Portsmouth

N.H.

Gloucester

Boston

Fort Niagara

Bennington

Albany

MASS.

Plymouth

Fort Detroit

Lake Erie

NEW YORK

Kingston

CONN.

Providence

St. Joseph

Maumee R.

Allegheny R.

PENNSYLVANIA

Poughkeepsie

Hartford

R.I.

Newport

New Haven

Southampton

Illinois R.

Ohio R.

Fort
Duquesne

Susquehanna R.

Reading

Mountains

New York

Perth Amboy

Trenton

NEW JERSEY

Delaware R.

Philadelphia

Burlington

New Castle

Baltimore

Dover

St. Louis

Vincennes

Ohio R.

Wabash R.

Shenandoah R.

Potomac R.

Annapolis

DELAWARE

MARYLAND

SPANISH
LOUISIANA

VIRGINIA

Richmond

Williamsburg

James R.

Petersburg

Norfolk

Roanoke R.

Appalachian

Cumberland R.

Edenton

ATLANTIC OCEAN

NORTH CAROLINA

Greensville

Mississippi R.

New Bern

Tennessee R.

Fayetteville

Cape Fear R.

Portsmouth

Wilmington

DISPUTED TERRITORY
(Claimed by Spain and Britain)

Camden

Columbia

Augusta

Savannah R.

Santee R.

Kingston

SOUTH
CAROLINA

Ashley R.

Cooper R.

Charleston

GEORGIA

Altamaha R.

Savannah

The Thirteen Colonies
in 1763

NON-INDIAN SETTLEMENT

Before 1700

1700–1763

Frontier line
in 1763

WEST FLORIDA

Proclamation line
of 1763

Mobile

Pensacola

Provincial capital

New Orleans

Gulf of Mexico

EAST FLORIDA

St. Augustine

0   150 Miles

0   200 Kilometers

cutting them off from sympathetic local juries. The Currency Act of 1764 required that the colonial assemblies stop issuing paper money. Most momentously, the Stamp Act of 1765 imposed a tax on every printed document in the colonies: newspapers, almanacs, pamphlets, deeds, wills, licenses. British officials were soon collecting more than ten times as much annual revenue in America as they had been before 1763. But the new policies created many more problems than they solved.

It was difficult for the colonists to resist these unpopular new laws. For one thing, Americans continued to harbor as many grievances against one another as they did against the authorities in London. In 1763, for example, a band of Pennsylvania frontiersmen known as the Paxton Boys descended on Philadelphia to demand tax relief and financial support for their defense against Indians. Bloodshed was averted only by concessions from the colonial assembly. In 1771, a small-scale civil war broke out in North Carolina when the Regulators, farmers of the Carolina upcountry, organized and armed themselves to resist the high taxes that local sheriffs (appointed by the colonial governor) collected. An army of militiamen, most of them from the eastern counties, crushed the revolt in the Battle of Alamance.

But the Grenville program helped the colonists overcome their internal conflicts and recognize that the policies from London were a threat to all Americans. Northern merchants would suffer from restraints on their commerce, from the closing of the West to land speculation and fur trading, and from the restriction of opportunities for manufacturing. Southern planters, in debt to English merchants, would be unable to ease their debts by speculating in western land. Small farmers, the largest group in the colonies, would suffer from the abolition of paper money, which had been the source of most of their loans. Workers in towns faced the prospect of narrowing opportunities, particularly because of the restraints on manufacturing and currency. Everyone stood to suffer from increased taxes. The new restrictions came, moreover, at the beginning of a postwar economic depression in America.

In reality, most Americans soon found ways to live with (or circumvent) the new British laws without terrible hardship. But their political grievances remained. Americans were accustomed (and deeply attached) to wide latitude in self-government. They believed that colonial assemblies had the sole right to control appropriations for the costs of government within the colonies. By attempting to circumvent the assemblies and raise extensive revenues directly from the public, the British government was challenging the basis of colonial political power.

STIRRINGS OF REVOLT

By the mid-1760s, a hardening of positions had begun in both England and America that would bring the colonies into increasing conflict with the mother country. The result was a progression of events that, more rapidly than imagined, destroyed the British Empire in America.

The Stamp Act Crisis

Grenville could not have devised a better method for antagonizing and unifying the colonies than the Stamp Act of 1765 if he had tried. Unlike the Sugar Act of a year earlier, which affected only a few New England merchants, the tax on printed documents fell on everyone. More alarming than the relatively light taxes, however, was the precedent they seemed to create. In the past, taxes and duties on colonial trade had always been designed to regulate commerce, not raise money. The Stamp Act, however, was clearly an attempt by England to raise revenue in the colonies without the consent of the colonial assemblies.

Few colonists believed that they could do anything more than grumble until the Virginia House of Burgesses aroused Americans to action. Patrick Henry made a dramatic speech to the House in May 1765, concluding with a vague prediction that if present policies were not revised, George III, like earlier tyrants, might lose his head. There were shocked cries of "Treason!" and, according to one witness, an immediate apology from Henry (although many years later he was quoted as having made the defiant reply: "If this be treason, make the most of it"). But Henry introduced a set of resolutions (only some of which the assembly passed) declaring that Americans possessed the same rights as the English, especially the right to be taxed only by their own representatives; that Virginians should pay no taxes except those voted by the Virginia assembly; and that anyone advocating the right of Parliament to tax Virginians should be deemed an enemy of the colony. Henry's resolutions were printed and circulated as the "Virginia Resolves."

In Massachusetts at about the same time, James Otis persuaded his fellow members of the colonial assembly to call an intercolonial congress to take action against the new tax. And in October 1765, the Stamp Act Congress, as it was called, met in New York with delegates from nine colonies. In a petition to the British government, the congress denied that the colonies could rightfully be taxed except through their own provincial assemblies.

In the summer of 1765, meanwhile, mobs were rising up in several colonial cities against the Stamp Act. The largest of them was in Boston, where men belonging to the newly organized Sons of Liberty terrorized stamp agents and burned stamps. The agents, themselves Americans, hastily resigned. In Boston, the mob also attacked such supposedly pro-British "aristocrats" as the lieutenant governor, Thomas Hutchinson (who had privately opposed passage of the Stamp Act but who felt obliged to support it once it became law). Hutchinson's elegant house was pillaged and virtually destroyed.

The crisis finally subsided largely because England backed down. The authorities in London were less affected by the political protests than by economic pressure. Many New Englanders had stopped buying English goods to protest the Sugar Act of 1764, and the Stamp Act caused the boycott to spread, particularly once the Sons of Liberty intimidated reluctant colonists into participating in it. Under pressure from English merchants concerned about the loss of much of their colonial market, Parliament—under a new prime minister, the Marquis of Rockingham—repealed the unpopular law on March 18, 1766. To satisfy his strong and vociferous opponents, Rockingham also pushed through the Declaratory Act, which confirmed parliamentary authority over the colonies "in all cases whatsoever." In their rejoicing over the Stamp Act repeal, most Americans paid little attention to this ominous declaration of Parliament's power.

The Townshend Program

When the Rockingham government's policy of appeasement met substantial opposition in England, the king dismissed the Rockingham ministry and replaced it with a new government led by the aging but still powerful William Pitt, who was now Lord Chatham. Chatham had been a critic of the Stamp Act and had in the past been sympathetic toward American interests. Once in office, however, he was so hobbled by gout and at times so incapacitated by mental illness that the actual leadership of his administration fell to the chancellor of the exchequer, Charles Townshend.

Townshend had to deal with colonial grievances left over from the Grenville ministry. With the Stamp Act repealed, the greatest American grievance involved the Mutiny (or Quartering) Act of 1765, which required the colonists to provide shelter and supplies for British troops in America. The colonists objected not so much to quartering or supplying the troops but to being required by London to do so. It was, they believed, another form of taxation without their consent. The Massachusetts and New York assemblies went so far as to refuse to vote the mandated supplies to the troops.

Townshend responded in 1767 by disbanding the New York Assembly until the colonists agreed to obey the Mutiny Act. By singling out New York, he believed, he would avoid antagonizing all the colonies at once. He also imposed new taxes (known as the Townshend Duties) on various goods imported to the colonies from England—lead, paint, paper, and tea. Townshend assumed that since these were taxes purely on "external" transactions (imports from overseas), as opposed to the internal transactions the Stamp Act had taxed, the colonists would not object. But all the colonies resented the suspension of the New York Assembly, believing it to be a threat to every colonial government. And all the colonies rejected Townshend's careful distinction between external and internal taxation. The purpose of the new duties, they claimed, was the same as that of the Stamp Act: to raise revenue from the colonists without their consent.

Townshend also established a board of customs commissioners in America to stop the rampant corruption in the colonial customs houses. To some extent the plan worked. The new commissioners virtually ended smuggling in Boston, where they established their headquarters, although smugglers continued to carry on a busy trade in other colonial seaports. The Boston merchants—accustomed to loose enforcement of the Navigation Acts and angry that the new commission was diverting the lucrative smuggling trade elsewhere—helped organize a boycott of British goods that were subject to the Townshend Duties. Merchants in Philadelphia and New York joined them in a nonimportation agreement in 1768, and later some southern merchants and planters also agreed to cooperate. Throughout the colonies, American homespun and other domestic products became suddenly fashionable, while English luxuries fell from favor.

Late in 1767, Charles Townshend died—before the consequences of his ill-conceived program had become fully apparent. In March 1770, the new prime minister, Lord North, hoping to end the American boycott, repealed all the Townshend Duties except the tea tax.

The Boston Massacre

Before news of the repeal reached America, an event in Massachusetts electrified colonial opinion. The harassment of the new customs commissioners in Boston had grown so intense that the British government had placed four regiments of regular troops in the city—a constant affront to the colonists' sense of independence. Many of the poorly paid British soldiers looked for

THE BOSTON MASSACRE (1770), BY PAUL REVERE This is one of many engravings, by Revere and others, of the conflict between British troops and Boston laborers that became important as propaganda for the Patriot cause in the 1770s. Among the victims of the massacre listed by Revere was Crispus Attucks, probably the first black man to die in the struggle for American independence.

jobs in their off-duty hours and thus competed with local workers in an already difficult labor market. Clashes between the two groups were frequent.

On the night of March 5, 1770, a few days after a particularly intense skirmish between workers at a ship-rigging factory and British soldiers who were trying to find jobs there, a mob of dockworkers, "liberty boys," and others began pelting the sentries at the customs house with rocks and snowballs. Hastily, Captain Thomas Preston of the British regiment lined up several of his men in front of the building to protect it. There was some scuffling; one of the soldiers was knocked down; and in the midst of it all, apparently, several British soldiers fired into the crowd, killing five people (among them a mulatto sailor, Crispus Attucks).

This murky incident, almost certainly the result of panic and confusion, was quickly transformed by local resistance leaders into the "Boston Massacre"—a graphic symbol of British oppression and brutality. The victims became popular martyrs; the event became the subject of such lurid (and inaccurate) accounts as the widely circulated pamphlet *Innocent Blood Crying to God from the Streets of Boston.* A famous engraving by Paul Revere portrayed the massacre as a calculated assault on a peaceful crowd. The British soldiers, tried before a jury of Bostonians, were found guilty only of manslaughter and given token punishment. But colonial pamphlets and newspapers convinced many Americans that the soldiers were guilty of official murder. Year after year, resistance leaders marked the anniversary of the massacre with demonstrations and speeches.

The leading figure in fomenting public outrage over the Boston Massacre was Samuel Adams, the most effective radical in the colonies. England, he argued, had become a morass of sin and corruption; only in America did public virtue survive. In 1772, he proposed the creation of a "committee of correspondence" in Boston to publicize the grievances against England throughout the colony. Other colonies followed Massachusetts's lead, and a loose intercolonial network of political organizations was soon established that kept the spirit of dissent alive through the 1770s.

The Philosophy of Revolt

Although a superficial calm settled on the colonies for approximately three years after the Boston Massacre, the crises of the 1760s had helped arouse enduring ideological challenges to England and had produced powerful instruments for publicizing colonial grievances. Gradually a political outlook gained a following in America that would ultimately serve to justify revolt.

The ideas that would support the Revolution emerged from many sources. Some were drawn from religious (particularly Puritan) sources or from the political experiences of the colonies. Others came from abroad. Most important, perhaps, were the "radical" ideas of those in Great Britain who stood in opposition to their government. Some were Scots, who considered the English state tyrannical. Others were embittered "country Whigs," who felt excluded from power and considered the existing system corrupt and oppressive. Drawing from some of the great philosophical minds of earlier generations—most notably John Locke—these English dissidents framed a powerful argument against their government.

Central to this emerging ideology was a new concept of what government should be. Because humans were inherently corrupt and selfish, government was necessary to protect individuals from the evil in one another. But because any government was run by corruptible people, the people needed safeguards against its possible abuses of power. Most people in both England and America considered the English constitution the best system ever devised to meet these necessities. By distributing power among the three elements of society—the monarchy, the aristocracy, and the common people—the English political system ensured that no individual or group could exercise authority unchecked by another. Yet by the mid-seventeenth century, dissidents in both England and America had become convinced that the constitution was in danger. A single center of power—the king and his ministers—was becoming so powerful that it could not be effectively checked, and the system was becoming a corrupt and dangerous tyranny.

Such arguments found little sympathy in most of England. The English constitution was not a written document or a fixed set of unchangeable rules. It was a general sense of the "way things are done," and most people in England were willing to accept changes in it. Americans, by contrast, drew from their experience with colonial charters, in which the shape and powers of government were permanently inscribed on paper. They resisted the idea of a flexible, changing set of basic principles.

One basic principle, Americans believed, was the right of people to be taxed only with their own consent—a belief that gradually took shape in the widely repeated slogan, "No taxation without representation." Whatever the nature of a tax—whether internal or external, whether designed to raise revenue or to control trade—it could not be levied without the consent of the colonists themselves.

This clamor about "representation" made little sense to the English. According to English constitutional theory, members of Parliament did not represent individuals or particular geographical areas. Instead, each member represented the interests of the whole nation and indeed the whole empire, no matter where the member happened to come from. The many boroughs of England that had no representative in Parliament, the whole of Ireland, and the colonies thousands of miles away—all were thus represented in the Parliament at London, even though they elected no representatives of their own. This was the theory of "virtual" representation. But Americans, drawing from their experiences with their town meetings and their colonial assemblies, believed in "actual" representation. Every community was entitled to its own representative, elected by the people of that community and directly responsible to them. Since the colonists had none of their own representatives in Parliament, it followed that they were not represented there. Americans believed that the colonial assemblies played the same role within the colonies that Parliament did within England. The empire, the Americans argued, was a sort of federation of commonwealths, each with its own legislative body, all tied together by common loyalty to the king.

Such ideas illustrated a fundamental difference of opinion between England and America over the nature of sovereignty—over the question of where ultimate power lay. By arguing that Parliament had the right to legislate for England and for the empire as a whole, but that only the provincial assemblies could legislate for the individual colonies, Americans were in effect arguing for a division of sovereignty. Parliament would be sovereign in some matters; the assemblies would be sovereign in others. To the British, such an argument was absurd. In any system of government there must be a single, ultimate authority. And since the empire was, in their view, a single, undivided unit, there could be only one authority within it: the English government of king and Parliament.

Sites of Resistance

The apparent calm in America in the first years of the 1770s hid a growing sense of frustration and resentment about the continued and increasingly heavy-handed enforcement of the Navigation Acts. Popular anger was visible in occasional acts of rebellion. At one point, colonists seized a British revenue ship on the lower Delaware River. In 1772, angry residents of Rhode Island boarded the British schooner *Gaspée*, set it afire, and sank it in Narragansett Bay.

Colonists kept the growing spirit of resistance alive in many ways, but most of all through writing and talking. Dissenting leaflets, pamphlets, and books circulated widely through the colonies. In towns and cities, men gathered in churches, schools, town squares, and above all in taverns to discuss politics. Indeed, the tavern culture of the colonies was crucial to the growth of Revolutionary sentiment. Taverns were appealing, of course, because they provided alcoholic drinks in a culture where the craving for alcohol—and the extent of drunkenness—was very high. But taverns were also among the few public spaces were people could meet and talk openly, and to many colonists the life of the tavern was the only vaguely democratic experience open to them. The tavern was a mostly male institution, just as politics was considered a mostly male concern. The combination of male companionship and political conversation emerged naturally out of the tavern culture.

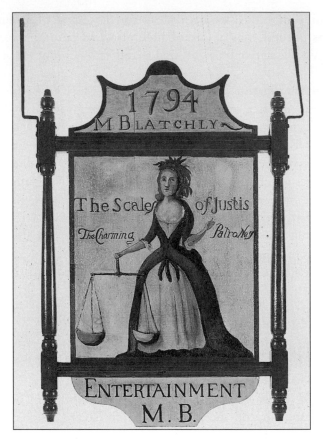

THE SCALES OF JUSTIS This sign for a Hartford tavern promises hospitality (from "the charming Patroness") and "entertainment" as well as food and drink.

As the Revolutionary crisis deepened, taverns and pubs became the central meeting places for discussions of ideas about resistance—and the sites of elaborate celebrations of the anniversaries of resistance to the Stamp Act. Taverns were also places were resistance pamphlets and leaflets could be distributed, and the settings for meetings for the planning of protests and demonstrations. Massachusetts had the most elaborately developed tavern culture, which was perhaps one reason why the spirit of resistance grew more quickly there than anywhere else. Almost all politicians in Boston found it necessary to visit taverns if they wanted any real contact with the public.

The Tea Excitement

The Revolutionary fervor of the 1760s revived, finally, as a result of a new act of Parliament—one that the English government had expected to be relatively uncontroversial. It involved the business of selling tea. In 1773, Britain's East India Company (which possessed an official monopoly on trade with the Far East) was sitting on large stocks of tea that it could not sell in England. It was on the verge of bankruptcy. In an effort to save it, the government passed the Tea Act of 1773, which gave the company the right to export its merchandise directly to the colonies without paying any of the regular taxes that were imposed on the colonial merchants, who had traditionally served as the middlemen in such transactions. With these privileges, the company could undersell American merchants and monopolize the colonial tea trade.

The act proved inflammatory for several reasons. First, it angered influential colonial merchants, who feared being replaced and bankrupted by a powerful monopoly. More important, however, the Tea Act revived American passions about the issue of taxation without representation. The law provided no new tax on tea. But the original Townshend duty on the commodity—the only one of the original duties that had not been repealed—survived; and the East India Company was now exempt from paying it. Lord North had assumed that most colonists would welcome the new law because it would reduce the price of tea to consumers by removing the middlemen. But resistance leaders in America argued that the law, in effect, represented an unconstitutional tax. The colonists responded by boycotting tea.

Unlike earlier protests, most of which had involved relatively small numbers of people, the tea boycott mobilized large segments of the population. It also helped link the colonies together in a common experience of mass popular protest. Particularly important to the movement were the activities of colonial women, who were among the principal consumers of tea and who became the leaders of the effort to boycott it. The Daughters of Liberty—a women's patriotic organization which, like the Sons of Liberty, was committed to agitating against British policies—proclaimed, "rather than Freedom, we'll part with our Tea."

In the last weeks of 1773, with strong popular support, leaders in various colonies made plans to prevent the East India Company from landing its cargoes in colonial ports. In Philadelphia and New York, determined colonists kept the tea from leaving the company's ships, and in

Charleston, they stored it away in a public warehouse. In Boston, after failing to turn three ships away from the harbor, local patriots staged a spectacular drama. On the evening of December 16, 1773, three companies of fifty men each, masquerading as Mohawk Indians, passed through a crowd of spectators, went aboard the three ships, broke open the tea chests, and heaved them into the harbor. As the electrifying news of the Boston "tea party" spread, colonists in other seaports staged similar acts of resistance.

Parliament retaliated in four acts of 1774: closing the port of Boston, drastically reducing the powers of self-government in Massachusetts, permitting royal officers in America to be tried in other colonies or in England when accused of crimes, and providing for the quartering of troops by the colonists. These Coercive Acts—or, as they were more widely known in America, "Intolerable Acts"—were followed by the Quebec Act, which was unrelated to them but also provocative to English Americans. The law extended the boundaries of Quebec to include the French communities between the Ohio and Mississippi Rivers. It also granted political rights to Roman Catholics and recognized the legality of the Roman Catholic Church within the enlarged province. Many colonists feared that a plot was afoot in London to subject Americans to the authority of the pope. Those interested in western lands, moreover, believed that the act would hinder westward expansion.

The Coercive Acts, far from isolating Massachusetts, made it a martyr in the eyes of residents of other colonies and sparked new resistance up and down the coast. Colonial legislatures passed a series of resolves supporting Massachusetts. Women's groups throughout the colonies mobilized to extend the boycotts of British goods and to create substitutes for the tea, textiles, and other commodities they were shunning. In Edenton, North Carolina, fifty-one women signed an agreement in October 1774 declaring their "sincere adherence" to the anti-British resolutions of their provincial assembly and proclaiming their duty to do "every thing as far as lies in our power" to support the "publick good."

COOPERATION AND WAR

Beginning in 1765, colonial leaders developed a variety of organizations for converting popular discontent into action—organizations that in time formed the basis for an independent government.

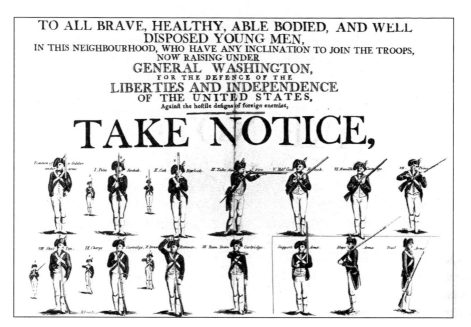

RECRUITING PATRIOTS This Revolutionary War recruiting poster tries to attract recruits by appealing to their patriotism (asking them to defend "the liberties and independence of the United States"), their vanity (by showing the "handsome clothing" and impressive bearing of soldiers), and their greed (by offering them "a bounty of twelve dollars" and "sixty dollars a year").

New Sources of Authority

The passage of authority from the royal government to the colonists themselves began on the local level. In colony after colony, local institutions responded to the resistance movement by simply seizing authority on their own. At times, entirely new institutions emerged and began to perform some of the functions of government.

The most effective of these new groups were the committees of correspondence that Samuel Adams had inaugurated in Massachusetts in 1772. Virginia later established the first intercolonial committees of correspondence, which helped make possible continuous cooperation among the colonies, and later took the greatest step of all toward united action. After the royal governor dissolved the assembly in 1774, a rump session met in the Raleigh Tavern at Williamsburg, declared that the Intolerable Acts menaced the liberties of every colony, and issued a call for a Continental Congress.

Delegates from all thirteen colonies except Georgia were present when, in September 1774, the First Continental Congress convened in Philadelphia. They made five major decisions. First, they rejected a plan for a colonial union under British authority. Second, they endorsed a relatively moderate statement of grievances, which seemed to concede Parliament's right to regulate colonial trade by addressing the king as "Most Gracious Sovereign," but which also included a demand for the repeal of all oppressive legislation passed since 1763. Third, they approved a series of resolutions from a Massachusetts convention recommending that military preparations be made for defense against possible attack by the British troops in Boston. Fourth, they agreed to a series of boycotts that they hoped would stop all trade with Great Britain, and they formed a "Continental Association" to see that these agreements were enforced. Finally, the delegates agreed to meet again the following spring, evidence that they saw the Continental Congress as a continuing organization.

During the winter, the Parliament in London debated proposals for conciliating the colonists, and early in 1775 Lord North finally won approval for a series of measures known as the Conciliatory Propositions. Parliament proposed that the colonies, instead of being taxed directly by Parliament, would tax themselves at Parliament's demand. With this offer, Lord North hoped to separate the American moderates, whom he believed represented the views of the majority, from the extremist minority. But his offer was too little and too late. It did not reach America until after the first shots of war had been fired.

Lexington and Concord

For months, the farmers and townspeople of Massachusetts had been gathering arms and ammunition and training as "minutemen," preparing to fight on a minute's notice. The Continental Congress had approved preparations for a defensive war, and the citizen-soldiers waited only for an aggressive move by the British regulars in Boston.

In Boston, General Thomas Gage, commanding the British garrison, considered his army too small to do anything without reinforcements. He resisted the advice of less cautious officers, who assured him that the Americans would never dare actually to fight, that they would back down quickly before any show of British force. When General Gage received orders to arrest the rebel leaders Sam Adams and John Hancock, known to be in the vicinity of Lexington, he still hesitated. But when he heard that the minutemen had stored a large supply of gunpowder in Concord

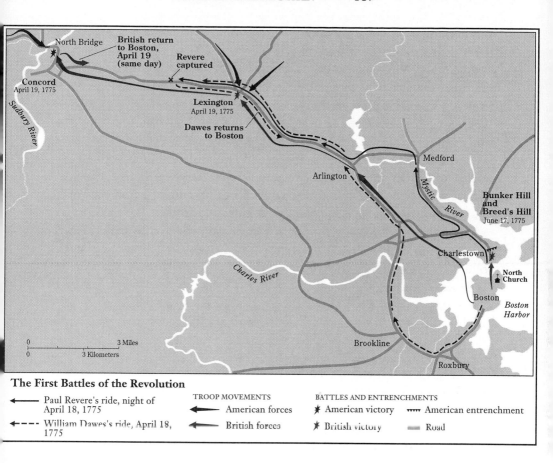

The First Battles of the Revolution

◄—— Paul Revere's ride, night of
April 18, 1775

◄- - - - William Dawes's ride, April 18,
1775

TROOP MOVEMENTS

◄—— American forces

◄—— British forces

BATTLES AND ENTRENCHMENTS

✳ American victory　　wwww American entrenchment

✳ British victory　　　▬▬▬ Road

(eighteen miles from Boston), he decided to act. On the night of April 18, 1775, he sent a detachment of about 1,000 men out from Boston on the road to Lexington and Concord. He hoped to surprise the colonials and seize the illegal supplies without bloodshed.

But patriots in Boston were watching the British movements closely, and during the night two horsemen, William Dawes and Paul Revere, rode out to warn the villages and farms. When the redcoats arrived in Lexington the next day, several dozen minutemen awaited them on the town common. Shots were fired and minutemen fell; eight of them were killed and ten more were wounded. Advancing to Concord, the British discovered that the Americans had hastily removed most of the powder supply, but the redcoats burned what was left of it. All along the road from Concord back to Boston, the British were harassed by the gunfire of farmers hiding behind trees, rocks, and stone walls. By the end of the day, the British had lost almost three times as many men as the Americans.

The first shots—the "shots heard 'round the world," as Americans later called them—had been fired. But who had fired them first? According to one of the minutemen at Lexington, the British commander, Major Thomas Pitcairn, had shouted to the colonists on his arrival, "Disperse, ye rebels!" When they ignored him, he ordered his troops to fire. British officers and soldiers claimed that the minutemen had fired first and that only after seeing the flash of American guns had they begun to shoot. Whatever the truth, the rebels succeeded in circulating their account well ahead of the British version, adorning it with tales of British atrocities. The effect was to rally to the rebel cause thousands of colonists, North and South, who previously had little enthusiasm for it.

It was not immediately clear to the British, or even to many Americans, that the skirmishes at Lexington and Concord were the first battles of a war. But whether they recognized it at the time or not, the War for Independence had begun.

CONCLUSION

When the French and Indian War ended in 1763, it might have seemed reasonable to expect that relations between the English colonists in America and Great Britain itself would have been cemented more firmly than ever. America and Britain had fought together in a great war against the French and their Indian allies. They had won impressive victories. They had vastly expanded the size of the British Empire.

But in fact the end of the French and Indian War altered the imperial relationship forever, in ways that ultimately drove Americans to rebel against English rule and begin a war for independence. To the British, the lesson of the war was that the colonies in America needed firmer control from London. The empire was now much bigger, and it needed better administration. The war had produced great debts, and the Americans—among the principal beneficiaries of the war—should help pay them. And so for more than a decade after the end of the fighting, the British tried one strategy after another to tighten control over and extract money from the colonies, all of them in the end failures.

To the colonists, this effort to tighten imperial rule appeared both a betrayal of the sacrifices they had made in the war and a challenge to their long-developing assumptions about the rights of English people to rule themselves. Gradually, white Americans came to see in the British policies evidence of a conspiracy to establish tyranny in the New World. And so throughout the 1760s and 1770s, the colonists developed ever more overt and effective forms of resistance. By the time the first shots were fired in the American Revolution in 1775, Britain and America—not long before bonded so closely to one another that most white Americans considered themselves as English as any resident of London—had come to view each other as two very different societies. Their differences, which came to seem irreconcilable, propelled them into a war that would change the course of both countries' history.

FOR FURTHER REFERENCE

Suggested Readings

Richard White, *The Middle Ground: Indians, Empires, and Republics in the Great Lakes Region, 1650–1815* (1991) argues that Indians in the Great Lakes region were able to take advantage of European rivalries for much of the eighteenth century. Francis Jennings, *The Ambiguous Iroquois Empire* (1984) makes a similar point. Richard Bushman, *King and People in Colonial Massachusetts* (1987) traces the fracture between Massachusetts colonists and the imperial government. Fred Anderson, *A People's Army: Massachusetts Soldiers and Society in the Seven Years' War* (1984) describes the ideological impact of the French and Indian War on the colonists who fought in it. Gary Nash, *The Urban Crucible: The Northern Seaports and the Origins of the American Revolution* (1979) argues that increasing class stratification in northern cities contributed to the coming of the American Revolution. Robert R. Palmer, *The Age of Democratic Revolution: Vol. 1, The Challenge* (1959) and J. G. A. Pocock, *The Machiavellian Moment* (1975) both place the American Revolution in the context of a transatlantic political culture. Bernard Bailyn, *The Ideological Origins of the American Revolution* (1967) was one of the first works by an American historian to emphasize the importance of English republican political thought to the Revolutionary ideology of the American colonists.

Films

(The best source for information on how to find these and other films is *Bowker's Complete Video Directory*—3 volumes.) *The American Story, No. 1: Road to Revolution* (1985) reviews the events, beginning with the Stamp Act crisis, that led the American colonies to the brink of open rebellion. *Colonial America in the Seventeen Sixties* (1967) examines the conflicts between the colonies and Britain in the crucial years after 1763. *Colonial America: The Roots of Revolution, 1607–1775* (1979) uses full-costume re-creations to help explain the economic, cultural, and religious reasons for revolution. *Paul Revere* (1996) is a biography of one of America's most celebrated patriots. *Lexington, Concord, & Independence* (1967) narrates the first battles of the American Revolution. *Patrick Henry: Virginia Patriot* (1990) documents the life and achievements of the man whose words "Give Me Liberty or Give Me Death" became a rallying cry of the Revolution.

Internet Resources

Internet websites containing historical material relevant to the subjects discussed in this chapter can be reached through the McGraw-Hill history site at www.mhhe.com/socscience/history/usa/link/linktop.htm.

CHAPTER FIVE

The American Revolution

The States United ～ *The War for Independence*
War and Society ～ *The Creation of State Governments*
The Search for a National Government

WO STRUGGLES OCCURRED simultaneously during the seven years of war that began in April of 1775. One was the military conflict with Great Britain. The second was a political conflict within America.

The military conflict was, by the standards of later wars, a relatively modest one. By the standards of its own day, however, it was an unusually savage conflict, pitting not only army against army but the civilian population against a powerful external force. The shift of the war from a traditional, conventional struggle to a new kind of conflict—a revolutionary war for liberation—is what made it possible for the United States to defeat the more powerful British.

At the same time, Americans were wrestling with the great political questions that the conflict necessarily produced: first, whether to demand independence from Britain; then, how to structure the new nation they had proclaimed. Only the first of these questions had been resolved by the time of the British surrender at Yorktown in 1781.

THE STATES UNITED

Although many Americans had been expecting a military conflict with Britain for months, even years, the actual beginning of hostilities in 1775 found the colonies generally unprepared for war against the world's greatest armed power.

122

TIME LINE				
1775	**1776**	**1777**	**1778**	**1781**
Second Continental Congress	Paine's *Common Sense*	Articles of Confederation adopted	French-America alliance	Articles of Confederation ratified
Washigton commands American forces	Declaration of Independence Battle of Trenton	British defeat at Saratoga		Cornwallis surrenders at Yorktown

1783	**1784**		**1786**	**1787**
Treaty of Paris	Postwar depression begins		Shays's Rebellion	Northwest Ordinance

Defining American War Aims

Three weeks after the battles of Lexington and Concord, when the Second Continental Congress met in Philadelphia, delegates from every colony (except Georgia, which had not yet sent a representative) agreed to support the war. But they disagreed about its purpose. At one extreme was a group led by the Adams cousins (John and Samuel), Richard Henry Lee of Virginia, and others, who already favored independence; at the other extreme was a group led by such moderates as John Dickinson of Pennsylvania, who hoped for a quick reconciliation with Great Britain. Most of the delegates tried to find some middle ground between these positions.

Like the moderates in Congress, most Americans believed at first that they were fighting not for independence but for a redress of grievances within the British Empire. During the first year of fighting, however, many of them began to change their minds. The costs of the war—human and financial—were so high that the original war aims began to seem too modest to justify them. Many colonists were enraged when the British began trying to recruit Indians, African slaves, and German mercenaries (the hated "Hessians") against them. When the British government blockaded the colonial ports to cut off overseas trade and rejected all efforts at conciliation, many colonists concluded that independence was the only remaining option.

An impassioned pamphlet crystallized these feelings in January 1776: Thomas Paine's *Common Sense*. Paine, who had emigrated from England to

America less than two years before, wanted to turn the anger of Americans away from particular parliamentary measures and toward what he considered the root of the problem—the English constitution itself. It was simple common sense, he wrote, for Americans to break completely with a political system that could produce so corrupt a monarch as George III and could inflict such brutality on its own people. *Common Sense* sold more than 100,000 copies (an astonishing number given the size of the colonial population) in only a few months. It helped create a rapid growth of support for the idea of independence in the early months of 1776.

The Declaration of Independence

In the meantime, the Continental Congress in Philadelphia was moving toward a complete break with England. At the beginning of the summer, it appointed a committee to draft a formal declaration of independence; and on July 2, 1776, it adopted a resolution: "That these United Colonies are, and, of right, ought to be, free and independent states; that they are absolved from all allegiance to the British crown, and that all political connexion between them and the state of Great Britain is, and ought to be, totally dissolved." Two days later, on July 4, Congress approved the Declaration of Independence itself, which provided formal justifications for the actions the delegates had taken two days earlier.

Thomas Jefferson, a thirty-three-year-old Virginian, wrote most of the Declaration, with help from Benjamin Franklin and John Adams. As Adams later observed, Jefferson said little in the document that was new, but brought to its familiar ideas a compelling eloquence. The Declaration expressed concepts that had been circulating throughout the colonies over the previous few months in the form of at least ninety other, local "declarations of independence"—declarations drafted up and down the coast by town meetings, artisan and militia organizations, county officials, grand juries, Sons of Liberty, and colonial assemblies. Jefferson borrowed heavily from these texts, both for the ideas he expressed and even, to some extent, for the precise language he used.

The final document was in two parts. In the first, the Declaration restated the familiar contract theory of John Locke: the theory that governments were formed to protect what Jefferson called "life, liberty and the pursuit of happiness." In the second part, it listed the alleged crimes of the king, who, with the backing of Parliament, had violated his contract with the colonists and thus had forfeited all claim to their loyalty.

The Declaration launched a period of energetic political innovation, as one colony after another reconstituted itself as a "state." By 1781, most states had produced written constitutions for themselves that established republican governments. At the national level, however, the process was more uncertain. In November 1777, finally, Congress adopted a plan for union, the Articles of Confederation. The document confirmed the existing weak, decentralized system, which proved ill-suited for managing a continental war.

Mobilizing for War

Financing the war was particularly difficult, because Congress lacked the authority and the states generally lacked the inclination to impose taxes on the public. Congress had no authority to levy taxes on its own, and when it requisitioned money from the state governments, none contributed more than a small part of its expected share. Congress had little success borrowing from the public, since few Americans could afford to buy bonds and those who could preferred to invest in more profitable ventures, such as privateering. In the end, there was no alternative but to issue paper money. Printing presses turned out enormous amounts of "Continental currency," and the states printed currencies of their own. The result, predictably, was soaring inflation. Unable to stop the inflation, Congress soon found that the Continental currency was virtually worthless. Ultimately, it financed the war mostly by borrowing from other nations.

After a first surge of patriotism in 1775, volunteer soldiers were scarce. States had to pay bounties or use a draft to recruit the needed men. At first, the militiamen remained under the control of their respective states. But Congress recognized the need for a centralized military command, and it created a Continental army with a single commander in chief: George Washington. A forty-three-year-old Virginia planter-aristocrat who had commanded colonial forces during the French and Indian War, Washington had considerable military experience and was an early advocate of independence; he was admired, respected, and trusted by nearly all Patriots. He took command of the new army in June 1775. With the aid of foreign military experts such as the Marquis de Lafayette from France and the Baron von Steuben from Prussia, he built a force that prevailed against the mightiest power in the world. Even more important, perhaps, Washington's steadiness, courage, and dedication to his cause provided the army—and the people—with a symbol of stability around which they could rally.

D E B A T I N G   T H E   P A S T

The American Revolution

T HE LONGSTANDING debate over the origins of the American Revolution has intended to reflect two broad schools of interpretation. One sees the Revolution largely as a political and intellectual event and argues that the revolt against Britain was part of a defence of ideals and principles. The other views the Revolution as a social and economic phenomenon and contends that material interests were at the heart of the rebellion.

The Revolutionary generation itself portrayed the conflict as a struggle over ideals, and this interpretation prevailed through most of the nineteenth century. But in the early twentieth century, historians influenced by the reform currents of the progressive era began to identify social and economic forces that they believed had contributed to the rebellion. Carl Becker, for example, wrote in a 1909 study of New York that two questions had shaped the Revolution: "The first was the question of home rule; the second was the question . . . of who should rule at home." The colonists were not only fighting the British; they were also engaged in a kind of civil war, a contest between radicals and conservatives that led to the "democratization of American politics and society."

Other "progressive" historians elaborated on Becker's thesis. J. Franklin Jameson, writing in 1926, argued, "Many economic desires, many social aspirations, were set free by the political struggle, many aspects of society profoundly altered by the forces thus let loose." Arthur M. Schlesinger maintained a 1917 book that colonial merchants, motivated by their own interest in escaping the restrictive policies of Bitish mercantilism, aroused American resistance in the 1760s and 1770s.

Beginning in the 1950s, a new generation of scholars began to reemphasize the role of ideology and de-emphasize the role of economic interests. Robert E. Brown (in 1955) and Edmund S. Morgan (in 1956) both argued that most eighteenth-century Americans shared common political principles and that the social and economic conflicts the progressives had identified were not severe. The rhetoric of the Revolution, they suggested, was not propaganda but a real reflection of the ideas of the colonists. Bernard Bailyn, in *The Ideological Origins of the American Revolution* (1967), demonstrated the complex roots of the ideas behind the Revolution and argued that this carefully constructed political stance was not a disguise for economic interests but a genuine ideology, rooted in deeply held convictions about rights and power, that itself motivated the colonists to act. The Revolution, he exclaimed, "was above all an ideological, constitutional, political struggle and not primarily a controversy between social groups undertaken to force changes in the organization of the society or the economy."

By the late 1960s, a new generation of historians—many influenced by the New Left—were reviving economic interpretations of the Revolution by exploring the social and economic tensions that they claimed shaped the Revolutionary struggle. Historians cited the actions of mobs in colonial cities, the economic pressures on colonial merchants, the growing climate of economic distress in colonial cities, and other changes in the character of American culture and society as critical prerequisites for the growth of the Revolutionary movement. Gary Nash, attempting to reconcile the emphasis on economic interests with the role of ideology, argued that the two things were not incompatible. "Everyone has economic interests," he claimed, "and everyone . . . has an ideology." Exploring the relationship between the two, he argues, is critical to historians' ability to understand either. Also, as Linda Kerber and others have argued, the newer social interpretations have raised increasing interest in the experience of workers, slaves, women, Native Americans, and other groups previously considered marginal to public life as part of the explanation of the Revolutionary struggle.

Finally, Gordon Wood, in *The Radicalism of the American Revolution* (1992) revived an idea once popular and recently unfashionable: that the Revolution was a genuinely radical event that led to the breakdown of such longstanding characteristics of society as deference, patriarchy, and traditional gender relations. Class conflict may not have caused the Revolution, he argues, but the Revolution had a profound, even radical, effect on society nevertheless.

REVOLUTIONARY SOLDIERS Jean Baptist de Verger, a French officer serving in America during the Revolution, kept an illustrated journal of his experiences. Here he portrays four American soldiers carrying different kinds of arms: a black infantryman with a light rifle, a musketman, a rifleman, and an artilleryman.

THE WAR FOR INDEPENDENCE

The British seemed to have overwhelming advantages as the War for Independence began: the greatest navy and the best-equipped army in the world, the resources of an empire, a coherent structure of command. Yet the United States had advantages, too. Americans were fighting on their own ground. They were more committed to the conflict than were the British. And, beginning in 1777, they received substantial aid from abroad.

But the American victory was also a result of a series of blunders and miscalculations by the British in the early stages of the fighting, when England could (and probably should) have won. And it was, finally, a result of the transformation of the war—through three distinct phases—into a new kind of conflict that the British military, for all its strength, was unable to win.

The First Phase: New England

For the first year of the conflict—from the spring of 1775 to the spring of 1776—many English authorities thought that British forces were not fighting a real war, but simply quelling pockets of rebellion in the contentious area around Boston. After the redcoats withdrew from Lexington and Concord in

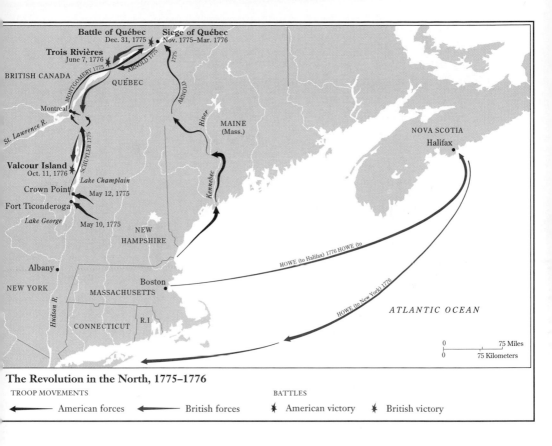

The Revolution in the North, 1775–1776

TROOP MOVEMENTS   BATTLES

← American forces   ← British forces   ✳ American victory   ✳ British victory

April, American forces besieged them in Boston. In the Battle of Bunker Hill (actually fought on Breed's Hill) on June 17, 1775, the Patriots suffered severe casualties and withdrew. But they inflicted even greater losses on the enemy (indeed, the heaviest casualties the British were to suffer in the entire war). The siege continued. Early in 1776, finally, the British decided that Boston was a poor place from which to fight. It was in the center of the most anti-British part of America and tactically difficult to defend because it was easily isolated and surrounded. And so, on March 17, 1776, the redcoats evacuated Boston for Halifax, Nova Scotia, with hundreds of Loyalist refugees.

In the meantime, a band of southern Patriots, at Moore's Creek Bridge in North Carolina, crushed an uprising of Loyalists (Americans still loyal to England and its king) on February 27, 1776, and discouraged a British plan to invade the southern states. And to the north, the Americans began an invasion of Canada. Generals Benedict Arnold and Richard Montgomery unsuccessfully threatened Quebec in late 1775 and early 1776 in a battle in which Montgomery was killed and Arnold wounded.

With the defeat at Quebec died any American hopes that Canada would join the Revolution.

By the spring of 1776, it had become clear to the British that the conflict was not just a local phenomenon in the area around Boston. The American campaigns in Canada, the agitation in the South, and the growing evidence of colonial unity all suggested that England must prepare to fight a much larger conflict.

The Second Phase: The Mid-Atlantic Region

During the next phase of the war, which lasted from 1776 until early 1778, the British were in a good position to win. Indeed, had it not been for a series of blunders and misfortunes, they probably would have crushed the rebellion.

The British regrouped quickly after their retreat from Boston. During the summer of 1776, hundreds of British ships and 32,000 British soldiers arrived in New York, under the command of General William Howe, who hoped simply to awe the Americans into submission. He offered Congress a choice between surrender with royal pardon and a battle against apparently overwhelming odds. To oppose Howe's great force, Washington could muster only about 19,000 inadequately armed and poorly trained soldiers; he had no navy at all. Even so, the Americans rejected Howe's offer and suffered a succession of major defeats. The British pushed the Patriot forces off Long Island, forced them to abandon Manhattan, and then drove them in slow retreat over the plains of New Jersey, across the Delaware River, and into Pennsylvania.

The British settled down for the winter in northern and central New Jersey, with an outpost of Hessians at Trenton, on the Delaware River. But Washington did not sit still. On Christmas night 1776, he daringly recrossed the icy Delaware River, surprised and scattered the Hessians, and occupied Trenton. Then he advanced to Princeton and drove a force of redcoats from their base in the college there. But Washington was unable to hold either Princeton or Trenton and finally took refuge for the rest of the winter in the hills around Morristown. The campaign of 1776 came to an end with the Americans having triumphed in two minor battles and with their main army still intact. The British were no nearer than before to a decisive triumph.

For the campaigns of 1777 the British devised a strategy to divide the United States in two. Howe would move from New York up the Hudson to Albany, while another force would come down from Canada to meet

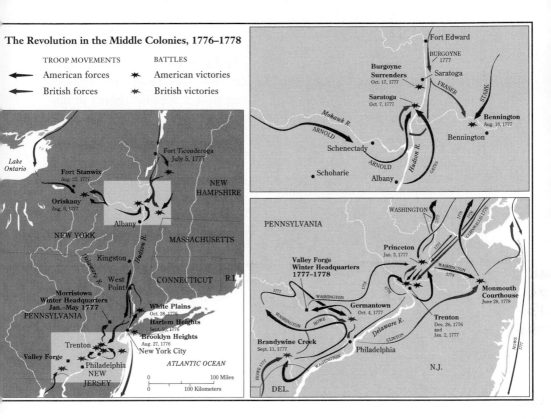

The Revolution in the Middle Colonies, 1776–1778

TROOP MOVEMENTS

← American forces

← British forces

BATTLES

✳ American victories

✳ British victories

him. John Burgoyne, commander of the northern force, began a two-pronged attack to the south along both the Mohawk and the upper Hudson approaches to Albany. But having set the plan in motion, Howe abandoned his part of it. Instead of moving north to meet Burgoyne, he went south and captured Philadelphia, hoping that his seizure of the rebel capital would discourage the Patriots, rally the Loyalists, and bring the war to a speedy conclusion. Philadelphia fell with little resistance—and the Continental Congress moved into exile in York, Pennsylvania. After launching an unsuccessful Patriot attack against the British on October 4 at Germantown (just outside Philadelphia), Washington went into winter quarters at Valley Forge.

Howe's move to Philadelphia left Burgoyne to carry out the campaign in the north alone. He sent Colonel Barry St. Leger up the St. Lawrence River toward Lake Ontario. Burgoyne himself advanced directly down the upper Hudson Valley and easily seized Fort Ticonderoga, with its large store of powder and supplies. But Burgoyne soon experienced two staggering defeats.

In one of them—at Oriskany, New York, on August 6—Patriots held off a force of Indians and Tories commanded by St. Leger. That allowed Benedict Arnold to close off the Mohawk Valley to St. Leger's advance. In the other battle—at Bennington, Vermont, on August 16—New England militiamen mauled a detachment that Burgoyne had sent to seek supplies. Short of materials, with all help cut off, Burgoyne fought several costly engagements and then withdrew to Saratoga, where General Horatio Gates surrounded him. On October 17, 1777, Burgoyne surrendered—an event that became a major turning point in the war.

The campaign in upstate New York was not just a British defeat. It was a setback for the ambitious efforts of several Iroquois leaders. Although the Iroquois Confederacy had declared its neutrality in the Revolutionary War in 1776, some of its members allied themselves with the British, among them a Mohawk brother and sister, Joseph and Mary Brant. This ill-fated alliance further divided the already weakened Iroquois Confederacy, because only three of the Iroquois nations (the Mohawk, the Seneca, and the Cayuga) followed the Brants in support of the British. A year after the defeat at Oriskany, Iroquois forces joined British troops in a series of raids on white settlements in upstate New York. Patriot forces under the command of General John Sullivan harshly retaliated, wreaking such destruction on Indian settlements that large groups of Iroquois fled north into Canada to seek refuge. Many never returned.

Securing Aid from Abroad

The leaders of the American effort knew that victory would not be likely without aid from abroad. And their most promising allies, they realized, were the French, who believed they had much to gain from seeing Britain lose a crucial part of its empire. At first, France provided the United States with badly needed supplies but remained reluctant to grant formal diplomatic recognition to the United States. After the Declaration of Independence, Benjamin Franklin himself went to France to lobby for aid and diplomatic recognition. Franklin quickly became a hero to the French, but France's foreign minister, the Count de Vergennes, wanted evidence that the Americans had a real chance of winning before supporting open French intervention. The British defeat at Saratoga, he believed, offered that evidence.

When the news from Saratoga arrived in London and Paris in early December 1777, a shaken Lord North made a new peace offer: complete home rule within the empire for Americans if they would quit the war.

Vergennes feared the Americans might accept the offer and thus destroy France's opportunity to weaken Britain. Encouraged by Franklin, he agreed on February 6, 1778, to give formal recognition to the United States as a sovereign nation and to provide it with greatly expanded military assistance.

France's entry into the war made it an international conflict, which over the year pitted France, Spain, and the Netherlands against Great Britain. That helped reduce the resources available for the English effort in America. All three of Britain's foes offered assistance to the Patriots, but France was always America's most important ally. It furnished the new nation with most of its money and munitions, and it provided a navy and an expeditionary force that were vital to the final, successful phase of the Revolutionary conflict.

The Final Phase: The South

The American victory at Saratoga and the intervention of the French transformed the war and began its final phase. Instead of mounting a full-scale military struggle against the American army, the British now tried to enlist the support of those elements of the American population—a majority, they continued to believe—who were still loyal to the crown. And since Loyalist sentiment was thought to be strongest in the South, and since the English also hoped slaves would rally to their cause, the main focus of the British effort shifted there.

The new strategy was a dismal failure. British forces spent three years (from 1778 to 1781) moving through the South, fighting small battles and large. But they had badly overestimated the extent of Loyalist sentiment. And they had underestimated the logistical problems they would face. Patriot forces could move at will throughout the region, living off the resources of the countryside, blending in with the civilian population, and leaving the British unable to distinguish friend from foe. The British, by contrast, suffered all the disadvantages of an army in hostile territory.

It was this phase of the conflict that made the war "revolutionary"—not only because it introduced a new kind of warfare, but because it had the effect of mobilizing and politicizing large groups of the population who had until then remained aloof from the struggle. With the war expanding into previously isolated communities, with many civilians forced to involve themselves whether they liked it or not, the political climate of the United States grew more heated than ever. And support for independence, far from being crushed as the British had hoped, greatly increased.

In the North, where significant numbers of British troops remained, the fighting settled into a stalemate. Sir Henry Clinton replaced the unsuccessful William Howe in May 1778 and moved what had been Howe's army from Philadelphia back to New York. There the British troops stayed for more than a year, with Washington and his army keeping watch around them. In the meantime, George Rogers Clark led a Patriot expedition over the Green Mountains and captured settlements in the Illinois country from the British and their Indian allies. On the whole, however, there was relatively little military activity in the North after 1778. There was, however, considerable intrigue. In the fall of 1789, American forces were shocked by the exposure of treason on the part of General Benedict Arnold. Arnold had been one of the early heroes of the war, but now, convinced that the American cause was hopeless, he conspired with British agents to betray the Patriot stronghold at West Point on the Hudson River. When the scheme was exposed and foiled, Arnold fled to the safety of the British camp, where he spent the rest of the war.

The British did have some significant military successes during this period. On December 29, 1778, they captured Savannah, Georgia. On May 12, 1780, they took the port of Charleston, South Carolina, and inspired some Loyalists to take up arms and advance with them into the interior. But although the British were able to win conventional battles, they were constantly harassed as they moved through the countryside by Patriot guerrillas led by such resourceful fighters as Thomas Sumter, Andrew Pickens, and Francis Marion, the "Swamp Fox." Penetrating to Camden, South Carolina, Lord Cornwallis (whom Clinton named British commander in the South) met and crushed a Patriot force under Horatio Gates on August 16, 1780. Congress recalled Gates, and Washington replaced him with Nathanael Greene, one of the ablest of all the American generals of the time.

Even before Greene arrived in the South, the tide of battle had begun to turn against Cornwallis. At King's Mountain (near the North Carolina–South Carolina border) on October 7, 1780, a band of Patriot riflemen from the backwoods killed, wounded, or captured every man in a force of 1,100 New York and South Carolina Tories, upon whom Cornwallis had depended as auxiliaries. Once Greene arrived, he confused and exasperated Cornwallis by dividing the American forces into fast-moving contingents while avoiding open, conventional battles. One of the contingents inflicted what Cornwallis admitted was "a very unexpected and severe blow" at Cowpens on January 17, 1781. Finally, after receiving reinforcements, Greene combined all his forces and maneuvered to meet the British at Guilford Court House, North

PENNSYLVANIA

MARYLAND

NEW JERSEY

DELAWARE

VIRGINIA

Potomac R.

Chesapeake Bay

Charlottesville

LAFAYETTE

WASHINGTON & ROCHAMBEAU

HOOD & GRAVES

Yorktown
AUG. 30–OCT. 19,
1781

Richmond

James R.

Cape
Charles

GREENE

CORNWALLIS

Guilford Court House
MAR. 15, 1781

NORTH CAROLINA

CORNWALLIS
MAY 1781

Cowpens
JAN. 17, 1781

New Bern

Cape
Hatteras

DE GRASSE

GREENE

King's Mountain
OCT. 7, 1780

MORGAN

TARLETON

GATES

Pee Dee R.

Cape Fear R.

Cape
Lookout

Camden
AUG. 16, 1780

Wilmington

Kettle Creek
FEB. 14, 1779

Savannah R.

SOUTH   CAROLINA

Augusta
OCC. BY BRITISH
JAN. 29, 1779

GEORGIA

Eutaw Springs
SEPT. 8, 1781

CLINTON & CORNWALLIS

MARCH 1780

ATLANTIC OCEAN

Charleston
MAY 12, 1780

Briar Creek
MAR. 3, 1779

CAMPBELL 1778

0   100 Miles

0   100 Kilometers

Savannah
OCC. BY BRITISH
DEC. 29, 1778

PREVOST

D'ESTAING
SEPT.–OCT. 1779

The Revolution in the South, 1778–1781

TROOP MOVEMENTS

← American forces   ← French fleet   ← British forces

BATTLES

✳ American victory

✳ British victory

Carolina. After a hard-fought battle there on March 15, 1781, Greene was driven from the field; but Cornwallis had lost so many men that he decided to abandon the Carolina campaign. Instead, he moved north, hoping to carry on raids in the interior of Virginia. But Clinton, fearful that the southern army might be destroyed, ordered him to take up a defensive position on the peninsula between the York and James Rivers and wait for transport to New York or Charleston. Cornwallis retreated to Yorktown and began to build fortifications there.

At that point, American and French forces descended on Yorktown in an effort to trap Cornwallis. Washington and the Count de Rochambeau marched a French-American army from New York to join the Marquis de Lafayette in Virginia, while Admiral de Grasse took a French fleet with additional troops up Chesapeake Bay to the York River. These joint operations caught Cornwallis between land and sea. After a few shows of resistance, he surrendered on October 17, 1781. Two days later, as a military band played the old tune "The World Turn'd Upside Down," he surrendered his whole army of more than 7,000.

Winning the Peace

Cornwallis's defeat provoked outcries in England against continuing the war. Lord North resigned as prime minister; Lord Shelburne emerged from the political wreckage to succeed him; and British emissaries appeared in France to talk informally with the American diplomats there, of whom the three principals were Benjamin Franklin, John Adams, and John Jay.

The Americans were under instructions to cooperate with France in their negotiations with England. But Vergennes, the French foreign minister, insisted that France could not agree to any settlement of the war with England until its ally Spain had achieved its principal war aim: winning back Gibraltar from the British. There was no real prospect of that happening soon, and the Americans began to fear that the alliance with France might keep them at war indefinitely. As a result, Franklin, Jay, and Adams began proceeding on their own, without informing Vergennes, and soon drew up a preliminary treaty with Great Britain, which was signed on November 30, 1782. Franklin, in the meantime, skillfully pacified Vergennes and avoided an immediate rift in the French-American alliance.

The final treaty was signed September 3, 1783, after both Spain and France agreed to end hostilities against Britain. The agreement was, on the whole, remarkably favorable to the United States. It provided a clear-cut recognition of independence and a large, though ambiguous, cession of territory to the new nation—from the southern boundary of Canada to the northern boundary of Florida and from the Atlantic to the Mississippi. The American people had good reason to celebrate as the last of the British occupation forces embarked from New York and General Washington, at the head of his troops, rode triumphantly into the city.

WAR AND SOCIETY

Historians have long debated whether the American Revolution was a social as well as a political revolution. But whatever the intention of those who launched and fought the war, the conflict had important effects on the nature of American society.

Loyalists and Minorities

Estimates differ as to how many Americans remained loyal to England during the Revolution, but it is clear that there were many—at least a fifth (and some estimate as much as a third) of the white population. Some were officeholders in the imperial government. Others were merchants whose trade was closely tied to the imperial system (although most merchants supported the Revolution). Still others were people who lived in relative isolation and had simply retained their traditional loyalties. And there were those who, expecting the British to win the war, were simply currying favor with the anticipated victors.

Many of these Loyalists were hounded by Patriots in their communities and harassed by legislative and judicial actions. Up to 100,000 fled the country. Those who could afford to—for example, the hated Tory governor of Massachusetts, Thomas Hutchinson—fled to England. Others of more modest means moved to Canada, establishing the first English-speaking community in the province of Quebec. Some returned to America after the war and gradually managed to reenter the life of the nation. Others remained abroad for the rest of their lives.

The war weakened other groups as well. The Anglican Church, many of whose members were Loyalist, lost its status as the official religion of Virginia and Maryland, as well as the economic aid they were accustomed to receiving from Britain. By the time the fighting ended, many Anglican parishes could no longer even afford clergymen. Also weakened were the Quakers, whose pacifism won them widespread unpopularity when they refused to support the war.

Other Protestant denominations, however, grew stronger as a result of their enthusiastic support for the war. Presbyterian, Congregational, and Baptist churches successfully tied themselves to the Patriot cause. And most American Catholics also supported the Patriots during the war and won increased (although far from universal) popularity as a result. Shortly after the peace treaty was signed, the Vatican provided the United States with its own hierarchy and, in 1789, its first bishop.

For the largest of America's minorities—the African-American population—the war had limited effects. For some, the Revolution meant freedom. Because so much of the fighting occurred in the South during the last years of the war, many slaves came into contact with the British army, which—in the interests of disrupting and weakening the American cause—emancipated thousands of them and took them out of the country. For most African Americans, however, the Revolution meant exposure to the idea, although not the reality, of liberty.

Native Americans and the Revolution

Indians viewed the American Revolution with considerable uncertainty. Most tribes ultimately chose to stay out of the war. But many Indians feared that the Revolution would replace a ruling group in which they had developed at least some measure of trust (the British, who had tried to limit the expansion of white settlement into tribal land) with one they considered generally hostile to them (the Patriots, who had spearheaded the expansion). Thus some Indians, among them the Iroquois who participated in the Burgoyne campaign in upper New York, chose to join the English cause. Still others took advantage of the conflict to launch attacks of their own.

In the western Carolinas and Virginia, Cherokee led by Chief Dragging Canoe launched a series of attacks on outlying white settlements in the summer of 1776. Patriot militias responded in great force, ravaging Cherokee lands and forcing the chief and many of his followers to flee west across the Tennessee River. Those Cherokee who remained behind agreed to a new treaty by which they gave up still more land. Some Iroquois, despite the setbacks at Oriskany, continued to wage war against Americans in the West and caused widespread destruction in agricultural areas of New York and Pennsylvania whose crops were of crucial importance to the Patriot cause. The retaliating American armies inflicted heavy losses on the Indians, but the attacks continued throughout the war.

In the end, the Revolution generally weakened the position of Native Americans in several ways. The Patriot victory increased white demand for western lands. Many whites resented the assistance such nations as the Mohawk had given the British and insisted on treating them as conquered people. Others drew from the Revolution a paternalistic view of the tribes that was only slightly less dangerous to the Native Americans than open hostility. Thomas Jefferson, for example, came to view the Indians as "noble savages," uncivilized in their present state but redeemable if they were willing to adapt to the norms of white society.

Women's Rights and Women's Roles

The long Revolutionary War had a profound effect on American women. The departure of so many men to fight in the Patriot armies left wives, mothers, sisters, and daughters in charge of farms and businesses. Often, women handled these tasks with great success. But in other cases, inexperience, inflation, the unavailability of male labor, or the threat of enemy troops led to failure. Some women whose husbands or fathers were called away to war did not have even a farm or shop to fall back on. Cities and towns had significant populations of impoverished women, who on occasion led protests against price increases or rioted and looted for food. On several other occasions (in New Jersey and Staten Island), women launched attacks on occupying British troops, whom they were required to house and feed at considerable expense.

Not all women stayed behind when the men went off to war. Sometimes by choice, more often by necessity, women flocked to the camps of the Patriot armies to join their male relatives. These female "camp followers" increased army morale and provided a ready source of volunteers to do cooking, laundry, nursing, and other necessary tasks. In the rough environment of the camps, traditional gender distinctions proved difficult to maintain. Considerable numbers of women became involved, at least intermittently, in combat—including the legendary "Molly Pitcher" (so named because she carried pitchers of water to soldiers on the battlefield), who watched her husband fall during one encounter and immediately took his place at a gun. A few women even disguised themselves as men so as to be able to fight.

The emphasis on liberty and the "rights of man" led some women to begin to question their own position in society. "By the way," Abigail Adams wrote to her husband John Adams in 1776, "in the new code of laws which I suppose it will be necessary for you to make, I desire you would remember the ladies and be more generous and favorable to them than your ancestors. Do not put such unlimited power into the hands of the Husbands." Adams was calling for a relatively modest expansion of women's rights: for new protections against abusive and tyrannical men. A few women, however, went further. Judith Sargent Murray, one of the leading essayists of the late eighteenth century, wrote in 1779 that women's minds were as good as those of men and that girls as well as boys therefore deserved access to education.

But little changed as a result. Under English common law, an unmarried woman had some legal rights, but a married woman had virtually no rights at all. Everything she owned and everything she earned belonged to her husband. Because she had no property rights, she could not engage in any legal transactions on her own (buying or selling, suing or being sued, writing wills). She could not vote. She had no legal authority over her children. Nor could she initiate a divorce; that, too, was a right reserved almost exclusively to men. After the Revolution, it did become easier for women to obtain divorces in a few states. In New Jersey, women obtained the right to vote (although that right was repealed in 1807). Otherwise, there were few advances and some setbacks—including the loss of the right of widows to regain their dowries from their husbands' estates. The Revolution, in other words, did not really challenge, but actually confirmed and strengthened, the patriarchal legal system. Abigail Adams, in the same letter in which she asked her husband to "remember the ladies," also urged him to "regard us then as Beings placed by providence under your protection and in imitation of the Supreme Being make use of that power only for our happiness."

But the Revolution did encourage people of both sexes to reevaluate the contribution of women to the family and society. As the new republic searched for a cultural identity for itself, it attributed a higher value to the role of women as mothers. The new nation was, many Americans liked to believe, producing a new kind of citizen, steeped in the principles of liberty. Mothers had a particularly important task, therefore, in instructing their children in the virtues that the republican citizenry now was expected to possess.

The War Economy

The Revolution also produced important changes in the structure of the American economy. After more than a century of dependence on the British imperial system, American commerce suddenly found itself on its own. English ships no longer protected American vessels, but tried to drive them from the seas. British imperial ports—including those in England itself—were closed to American trade. But this disruption in traditional economic patterns served in the long run to strengthen the American economy. The restrictive rules of empire had inhibited American exploration of many markets. Now, enterprising merchants in New England and elsewhere began to develop new commerce in the Caribbean and South America. By the mid-1780s, American merchants were also developing an important trade with Asia. There was also a substantial increase in trade among the American states.

When English imports to America were cut off—first by the prewar boycott, then by the war itself—there were desperate efforts throughout the states to stimulate domestic manufacturing of certain necessities. No great industrial expansion resulted, but there was a modest increase in production and an even greater increase in expectations.

THE CREATION OF STATE GOVERNMENTS

At the same time that Americans were struggling to win their independence on the battlefield, they were also struggling to create new institutions of government to replace the British system they had repudiated. That struggle continued for more than fifteen years, but its most important phase occurred during the war itself, at the state level.

The Assumptions of Republicanism

If Americans agreed on nothing else when they began to build new governments for themselves, they agreed that those governments would be republican. To them, that meant a political system in which all power came from the people, rather than from some supreme authority (such as a king). The success of such a government depended on the nature of its citizenry. If the population consisted of sturdy, independent property owners imbued with civic virtue, then the republic could survive. If it consisted of a few powerful aristocrats and a great mass of dependent workers, then it would be in danger. From the beginning, therefore, the ideal of the small freeholder (the independent landowner) was basic to American political ideology.

Another crucial part of that ideology was the concept of equality. The Declaration of Independence had given voice to that idea in its most ringing phrase: "All men are created equal." It was a belief that stood in direct contrast to the old European assumption of an inherited aristocracy. The innate talents and energies of individuals, not their positions at birth, would determine their roles in society. Some people would inevitably be wealthier and more powerful than others. But all people would have to earn their success. There would be no equality of condition, but there would be equality of opportunity.

In reality, of course, the United States was never a nation in which all citizens were independent property holders. From the beginning, there was a sizable dependent labor force—the white members of which were allowed many of the privileges of citizenship, the black members of which were allowed virtually none. American women remained both politically and economically subordinate. Native Americans were systematically exploited and displaced. Nor was there ever full equality of opportunity. American society was more open and more fluid than that of most European nations, but the condition of a person's birth was almost always a crucial determinant of success.

Nevertheless, in embracing the assumptions of republicanism, Americans were adopting a powerful, even revolutionary, ideology, and their experiment in statecraft became a model for many other countries. It made the United States for a time the most admired and studied nation on earth.

The First State Constitutions

Two states—Connecticut and Rhode Island—already had governments that were republican in all but name even before the Revolution. They simply deleted references to England and the king from their charters and adopted them as constitutions. The other eleven states, however, produced new documents.

The first and perhaps most basic decision was that the constitutions were to be written down, because Americans believed the vagueness of England's unwritten constitution had produced corruption. The second decision was that the power of the executive, which Americans believed had grown too great in England, must be limited. Pennsylvania eliminated the executive altogether. Most other states inserted provisions limiting the power of governors over appointments, reducing or eliminating their right to veto bills, and preventing them from dismissing the legislature. Most important, every state forbade the governor or any other executive officer from holding a seat in the legislature, thus ensuring that, unlike in England, the two branches of government would remain wholly separate.

But the new constitutions did not embrace direct popular rule. In Georgia and Pennsylvania, the legislature consisted of one popularly elected house. But in every other state, there was an upper and a lower chamber, and in most cases, the upper chamber was designed to represent the "higher orders" of society. There were property requirements for voters—some modest, some substantial—in all states.

Revising State Governments

By the late 1770s, Americans were growing concerned about the apparent divisiveness and instability of their new state governments, which were having trouble accomplishing anything at all. Many believed the problem was one of too much democracy. As a result, most of the states began to revise their constitutions to limit popular power. Massachusetts was the first to act on the new concerns. By waiting until 1780 to ratify its first constitution, Massachusetts allowed these changing ideas to shape its government, and the state produced a constitution that served as a model for others.

Two changes in particular differentiated the Massachusetts and later constitutions from the earlier ones. The first was a change in the process of constitution writing itself. Most of the first documents had been written by state legislatures and thus could easily be amended (or violated) by them. Massachusetts, and later other states, sought a way to protect the constitutions from ordinary politics and created the constitutional convention: a special assembly of the people that would meet only for the purpose of writing the constitution and that would never (except under extraordinary circumstances) meet again.

The second change was a significant strengthening of the executive, a reaction to what many believed was the instability of the original state governments that had weak governors. The 1780 Massachusetts constitution made the governor one of the strongest in any state. He was to be elected directly by the people; he was to have a fixed salary (in other words, he would not be dependent on the good will of the legislature each year for his wages); he would have significant appointment powers and a veto over legislation. Other states followed. Those with weak or nonexistent upper houses strengthened or created them. Most increased the powers of the governor. Pennsylvania, which had no executive at all at first, now produced a strong one. By the late 1780s, almost every state had either revised its constitution or drawn up an entirely new one in an effort to produce stability in government.

Toleration and Slavery

The new states moved far in the direction of complete religious freedom. Most Americans continued to believe that religion should play some role in government, but they did not wish to give special privileges to any particular denomination. The privileges that churches had once enjoyed were now largely stripped away. In 1786, Virginia enacted the Statute of Religious Liberty, written by Thomas Jefferson, which called for the complete separation of church and state.

More difficult to resolve was the question of slavery. In areas where slavery was already weak—in New England, where there had never been many slaves, and in Pennsylvania, where the Quakers opposed slavery—it was abolished. Even in the South, there were some pressures to amend or even eliminate the institution; every state but South Carolina and Georgia prohibited further importation of slaves from abroad, and South Carolina banned the slave trade during the war. Virginia passed a law encouraging manumission (the freeing of slaves).

Nevertheless, slavery survived in all the southern and border states. There were several reasons: racist assumptions among whites about the inferiority of blacks; the enormous economic investments many white southerners had in their slaves; and the inability of even such men as Washington and Jefferson, who had moral misgivings about slavery, to envision any alternative to it. If slavery were abolished, what would happen to the black people in America? Few whites believed blacks could be integrated into American society as equals. In maintaining slavery, Jefferson once remarked, Americans were holding a "wolf by the ears." However unappealing it was to hold on to it, letting go would be even worse.

THE SEARCH FOR A NATIONAL GOVERNMENT

Americans were much quicker to agree on state institutions than they were on the structure of their national government. At first, most believed that the central government should remain a relatively weak and unimportant force and that each state would be virtually a sovereign nation. It was in response to such ideas that the Articles of Confederation emerged.

The Confederation

The Articles of Confederation, which the Continental Congress had adopted in 1777, provided for a national government much like the one already in place. Congress remained the central—indeed the only— institution of national authority. Its powers expanded to give it authority to conduct wars and foreign relations and to appropriate, borrow, and issue money. But it did not have power to regulate trade, draft troops, or levy taxes directly on the people. For troops and taxes it had to make

Border disputed until 1842

BRITISH POSSESSIONS

Border disputed until 1842

Lake Superior

Claimed by N.Y. and N.H.
Made a state 1791

MAINE (Mass.)

Lake Huron

VT.

N.H.

Lake Ontario

NEW YORK

MASSACHUSETTS

Ceded 1786

CONN.   R.I.

Lake Erie

Massachusetts claim ceded 1785

Ceded 1782

Connecticut claim ceded 1786

Ceded 1800

PENNSYLVANIA

N.J.

River

Missouri R.

New York claim ceded 1782

MD.

DEL.

Virginia claim ceded 1784

Ohio River

VIRGINIA

LOUISIANA
Ceded by Spain to France 1800
Sold by France to United States
1803

Mississippi

North Carolina claim ceded 1790

NORTH CAROLINA

South Carolina claim ceded 1787

Savannah R.

SOUTH CAROLINA

Georgia claim ceded 1802

GEORGIA

Spanish claim ceded 1795
Georgia claim ceded 1802

ATLANTIC OCEAN

SPANISH POSSESSIONS

SPANISH FLORIDA

0   200 Miles
0   200 Kilometers

Gulf of Mexico

State Claims to Western Lands and Cessions to National Government, 1782–1802

States with claims to Western lands	Virginia (1784)	South Carolina (1787)	Georgia (1802)
WESTERN CLAIMS (date of cession)	Massachusetts (1785, 1786)	North Carolina (1790)	Disputed
New York (1782)	Connecticut (1782, 1786, 1800)		

145

formal requests to the state legislatures, which could—and often did—
refuse them. There was no separate executive; the "president of the
United States" was merely the presiding officer at the sessions of Congress. Each state had a single vote in Congress, and at least nine of the
states had to approve any important measure. All thirteen state legislatures had to approve any amendment of the Articles.

During the process of ratifying the Articles of Confederation (which
required approval by all thirteen states), broad disagreements over the
plan became evident. The small states had insisted on equal state representation, but the larger states wanted representation to be based on population. The smaller states prevailed on that issue. More important, the
states claiming western lands wished to keep them, but the rest of the
states demanded that all such territory be turned over to the national government. New York and Virginia had to give up their western claims before the Articles were finally approved. They went into effect in 1781.

The Confederation, which existed from 1781 until 1789, was not a
complete failure, but it was far from a success. It lacked adequate powers
to deal with interstate issues or to enforce its will on the states, and it had
little stature in the eyes of the world.

Diplomatic Failures

Evidence of the low esteem in which the rest of the world held the Confederation was its difficulty in persuading Great Britain (and to a lesser extent Spain) to live up to the terms of the peace treaty of 1783.

The British had promised to evacuate American territory, but British
forces continued to occupy a string of frontier posts along the Great
Lakes within the United States. Nor did the British honor their agreement to make restitution to slaveowners whose slaves the British army had
confiscated. There were also disputes over the northeastern boundary of
the new nation and over the border between the United States and
Florida, which Britain had ceded back to Spain in the treaty. Most American trade remained within the British Empire, and Americans wanted full
access to British markets; England, however, placed sharp restrictions on
that access.

In 1784, Congress sent John Adams as minister to London to resolve
these differences, but Adams made no headway with the English, who
were never sure whether he represented a single nation or thirteen different ones. Throughout the 1780s, the British government refused even to
send a diplomatic minister to the American capital.

Confederation diplomats agreed to a treaty with Spain in 1786. The Spanish accepted the American interpretation of the Florida boundary. In return the Americans recognized the Spanish possessions in North America and accepted limits on the right of United States vessels to navigate the Mississippi for twenty years. Southern states, incensed at the idea of giving up their access to the Mississippi, blocked ratification, further weakening the government's standing in world diplomacy.

The Confederation and the Northwest

The Confederation's most important accomplishment was its resolution of some of the controversies involving the western lands. When the Revolution began, only a few thousand whites lived west of the Appalachian divide; by 1790 their numbers had increased to 120,000. The Confederation had to find a way to include these new settlements in the political structure of the new nation. The landed states began to yield their claims to the national government in 1781, and by 1784 the Confederation controlled enough land to permit Congress to begin making policy for the national domain.

The Ordinance of 1784, based on a proposal by Thomas Jefferson, divided the western territory into ten self-governing districts, each of which could petition Congress for statehood when its population equaled the number of free inhabitants of the smallest existing state. Then, in the Ordinance of 1785, Congress created a system for surveying and selling the western lands. The territory north of the Ohio River was to be surveyed and marked off into neat rectangular townships, each divided into thirty-six identical sections. In every township four sections were to be set aside for the United States; the revenue from the sale of one of the other sections was to support creation of a public school. Sections were to be sold at auction for no less than one dollar an acre.

The organization of the western territories established a pattern that would dominate much of the landscape of the United States for centuries to come: the grid. The precise rectangular pattern imposed on the Northwest Territory became a model for all subsequent land policies of the federal government and for many other planning decisions in states and localities. The grid also became characteristic of the layout of many American cities, among them New York and Philadelphia. The grid had many advantages. It eliminated the uncertainty about property borders that earlier, more informal land systems had produced. It sped the development of the western lands by making land ownership simple and

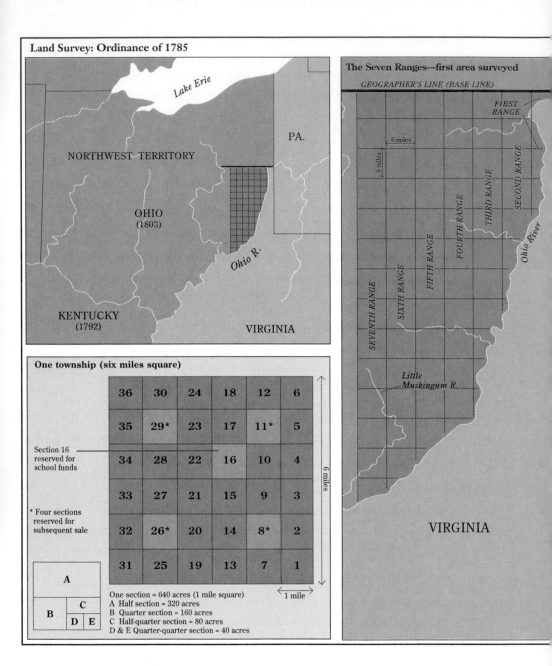

Land Survey: Ordinance of 1785

Lake Erie

PA.

NORTHWEST TERRITORY

OHIO
(1803)

Ohio R.

KENTUCKY
(1792)

VIRGINIA

The Seven Ranges—first area surveyed

GEOGRAPHER'S LINE (BASE LINE)

FIRST RANGE

SECOND RANGE

THIRD RANGE

FOURTH RANGE

FIFTH RANGE

SIXTH RANGE

SEVENTH RANGE

6 miles

6 miles

Ohio River

Little Muskingum R.

VIRGINIA

One township (six miles square)

36	30	24	18	12	6
35	29*	23	17	11*	5
34	28	22	16	10	4
33	27	21	15	9	3
32	26*	20	14	8*	2
31	25	19	13	7	1

Section 16 reserved for school funds

* Four sections reserved for subsequent sale

6 miles

1 mile

A	
B	C
	D	E

One section = 640 acres (1 mile square)
A Half section = 320 acres
B Quarter section = 160 acres
C Half-quarter section = 80 acres
D & E Quarter-quarter section = 40 acres

understandable. But it also encouraged a dispersed form of settlement—with each farm family separated from its neighbors—that made the formation of community more difficult; and it led farmers to arrange their fields in ways that did not necessarily make the best use of the local topography. Whatever its consequences, however, the 1785 Ordinance made a dramatic and indelible mark on the American landscape.

The original ordinances proved highly favorable to land speculators and less so to ordinary settlers, many of whom could not afford the price of the land. Congress compounded the problem by selling much of the best land to the Ohio and Scioto Companies before making it available to anyone else. Criticism of these policies led to the passage in 1787 of another law governing western settlement—legislation that became known as the "Northwest Ordinance." The 1787 Ordinance abandoned the ten districts established in 1784 and created a single Northwest Territory out of the lands north of the Ohio; the territory could be divided subsequently into between three and five territories. It also specified a population of 60,000 as a minimum for statehood, guaranteed freedom of religion and the right to trial by jury to residents of the Northwest, and prohibited slavery throughout the territory.

The western lands south of the Ohio River received less attention from Congress, and development was more chaotic there. The region that became Kentucky and Tennessee developed rapidly in the late 1770s, and in the 1780s speculators and settlers began setting up governments and asking for recognition as states. The Confederation Congress was never able to resolve the conflicting claims in that region successfully.

Indians and the Western Lands

On paper at least, the western land policies of the Confederation created a system that brought order and stability to the process of white settlement in the Northwest. But in reality, order and stability came slowly and at great cost, because much of the land the Confederation was neatly subdividing and offering for sale consisted of territory claimed by the Indians of the region. Congress tried to resolve that problem in 1784, 1785, and 1786 by persuading Iroquois, Choctaw, Chickasaw, and Cherokee leaders to sign treaties ceding substantial western lands in the North and South to the United States. But those agreements proved ineffective. In 1786, the leadership of the Iroquois Confederacy repudiated the treaty it had signed two years earlier and threatened to attack white settlements in the disputed lands. Other tribes had never really accepted the treaties affecting them and continued to resist white movement into their lands.

Violence between whites and Indians on the Northwest frontier reached a crescendo in the early 1790s. In 1790 and again in 1791, the Miami, led by the famed warrior Little Turtle, defeated United States forces in two major battles near what is now the western border of Ohio; in the second of those battles, on November 4, 1791, 630 white Americans died in fighting at the Wabash River (the greatest military victory Indians had ever or would ever achieve in their battles with whites). Efforts to negotiate a settlement failed because of the Miami's insistence that no treaty was possible unless it forbade white settlement west of the Ohio River. Negotiations did not resume until after General Anthony Wayne led 4,000 soldiers into the Ohio Valley in 1794 and defeated the Indians in the Battle of Fallen Timbers.

A year later, the Miami signed the Treaty of Greenville, ceding substantial new lands to the United States (which was now operating under the Constitution of 1789) in exchange for a formal acknowledgment of their claim to the territory they had managed to retain. This was the first time the new federal government recognized the sovereignty of Indian nations; in doing so, the United States was affirming that Indian lands could be ceded only by the tribes themselves. That hard-won assurance, however, proved a frail protection against the pressure of white expansion westward in later years.

Debts, Taxes, and Daniel Shays

The postwar depression, which lasted from 1784 to 1787, increased the perennial American problem of an inadequate money supply, a problem that weighed particularly heavily on debtors. In dealing with this problem, Congress most clearly demonstrated its weakness.

The Confederation itself had an enormous outstanding debt that it had accumulated during the Revolutionary War, and few means with which to pay it. It had sold war bonds that were now due to be repaid; it owed money to its soldiers; it had substantial debts abroad. But it had no power to tax. It could only make requisitions of the states, and it received only about one-sixth of the money it requisitioned. The fragile new nation was faced with the grim prospect of defaulting on its obligations.

This alarming possibility brought to the fore a group of leaders who would play a crucial role in the shaping of the republic for several decades. Committed nationalists, they sought ways to increase the powers of the central government and to meet its financial obligations. Robert Morris, the head of the Confederation's treasury; Alexander Hamilton, his young

DANIEL SHAYS AND JOB SHATTUCK Shays and Shattuck were the principal leaders of the 1786 uprising of poor Massachusetts farmers demanding relief from their indebtedness. Shattuck led an insurrection in the east, which collapsed when he was captured on November 30. Shays organized the rebellion in the west, which continued until it was finally dispersed by state militia in late February 1787. The following year, state authorities pardoned Shays; even before that, the legislature responded to the rebellion by providing some relief to the impoverished farmers. This drawing is part of a hostile account of the rebellion published in 1787 in a Boston almanac.

protégé; James Madison of Virginia; and others called for a "continental impost"—a 5 percent duty on imported goods to be levied by Congress and used to fund the debt. Many Americans, however, feared that the impost plan would concentrate too much financial power in the hands of Morris and his allies in Philadelphia. Congress failed to approve the impost in 1781 and again in 1783. Angry and discouraged, the nationalists largely withdrew from any active involvement in the Confederation.

The states had war debts, too, and they generally relied on increased taxation to pay them. But poor farmers, already burdened by debt and now burdened again by new taxes, considered such policies unfair, even tyrannical. They demanded that the state governments issue paper currency to increase the money supply and make it easier for them to meet their obligations. Resentment was especially high among farmers in New England, who felt that the states were squeezing them to enrich already wealthy bondholders in Boston and other towns.

Throughout the late 1780s, therefore, mobs of distressed farmers rioted periodically in various parts of New England. Dissidents in the Connecticut Valley and the Berkshire Hills of Massachusetts, many of them Revolutionary veterans, rallied behind Daniel Shays, a former captain in the Continental army. Shays issued a set of demands that included paper money, tax relief, a moratorium on debts, the relocation of the state capital from Boston to the interior, and the abolition of imprisonment for debt. During the summer of 1786, the Shaysites concentrated on preventing the collection of debts, private or public, and used force to keep courts from sitting and sheriffs from selling confiscated property. In Boston, members of the legislature, including Samuel Adams, denounced Shays and his men as rebels and traitors. When winter came, the rebels advanced on Springfield, hoping to seize weapons from the arsenal there. An army of state militiamen, financed by a loan from wealthy merchants, set out from Boston to confront them. In January 1787, this army met Shays's band and dispersed his ragged troops.

As a military enterprise, Shays's Rebellion was a failure, although it produced some concessions to the aggrieved farmers. Shays and his lieutenants, at first sentenced to death, were later pardoned, and Massachusetts offered the protesters some tax relief and a postponement of debt payments. The rebellion had more important consequences for the future of the United States, for it added urgency to a movement already gathering support throughout the new nation—the movement to produce a new, national constitution.

CONCLUSION

Between a small, inconclusive battle on a village green in New England in 1775 and a momentous surrender at Yorktown in 1781, the American people fought a great and terrible war against the mightiest military nation in the world. No one outside America, and few within it, would have predicted in 1775 that the makeshift armies of the colonies could withstand the armies and navies of the British empire. But a combination of luck, brilliance, determination, and timely aid from abroad allowed the patriots, as they began to call themselves, to make full use of the advantages of fighting on their home soil and to frustrate British designs time and again.

The war was not just a historic military event. It was also a great political one, for it propelled the colonies to unite, to organize, and—in July 1776—to declare their independence. Having done so, they fought with even greater determination, defending now not just a set of principles, but an actual, fledgling nation. By the end of the war, they had created new governments at both the state and national level and had begun experimenting with new political forms that would distinguish the United States from any previous nation in history.

The war was also important for its effects on American society—for the way it shook (although never overturned) the existing social order; for the way it caused women to question (although seldom openly to challenge) their place in society; and for the way it spread notions of liberty and freedom throughout a society that in the past had often been rigidly hierarchiacal and highly deferential. Even African-American slaves absorbed some of the ideas of the Revolution, although it would be many years before they would be in any position to make very much use of them.

Victory in the American Revolution solved many of the problems of the new nation, but it also produced others. What should the United States do about its relations with the Indians and with its neighbors to the north and south? What should it do about the distribution of western lands? What should it do about slavery? How should it balance its commitment to liberty with its need for order? These questions bedeviled the new national government in its first years of existence and ultimately led Americans to create a new polical order.

FOR FURTHER REFERENCE

Suggested Readings

Robert Middlekauff, *The Glorious Cause: The American Revolution, 1763-1789* (1985) and Edward Countryman, *The American Revolution* (1985) are useful overviews. Gordon Wood, *The Radicalism of the American Revolution* (1992) emphasizes the profound political change that the Revolution entailed. Charles Royster, *A Revolutionary People at War: The Continental Army and American Character* (1979) suggests the importance of the military service for American men. Mary Beth Norton, *Libertys Daughters: The Revolutionary Experience of American Women, 1750–1800* (1980) demonstrates that the Revolution had a significant impact on the lives of American women as well, and Linda K. Kerber, *Women of the Republic: Intellect and Ideology in Revolutionary America* (1980) shows the impact of the Revolutionary era on the assumptions and roles of women. Eric Foner, *Tom Paine and Revolutionary America* (1976) connects the leading pamphleteer of the Revolution with urban radicalism in Philadelphia. Pauline Maier, *American Scripture* (1997) is a penetratng study of the making of the Declaration of Independence, and of its impact on subsequent generations of Americans. Collin Calloway, *The American Revolution in Indian Country* (1995) is a new and important study on an often neglected aspect of the war. Sylvia R. Frey, *Water from the Rock: Black Resistance in a Revolutionary Age* (1991) argues that the American Revolution was a major turning point in the history of slavery in the American South. John Shy, *A People Numerous and Armed* (1976) and *The American Revolution* (1973) are excellent military histories. Bernard Bailyn, *The Ordeal of Thomas Hutchinson* (1974) is a classic study of a Loyalist before and during the Revolution. Jack N. Rakove, *The Beginning of National Politics* (1979) is a fine study of the United States before the Constitution.

Films

(The best source for information on how to find these and other films is *Bowker's Complete Video Directory*—3 volumes.) *Liberty* (1997) is a compelling six-hour documentary history of the American Revolution from its early origins in the 1760s. *The American Revolution Collector's Edition* is a comprehensive (300 minutes) and riveting documentary produced by the Art & Entertainment Network. *The American Story, No. 2: Declaring Independence* (1985) features the writing, consequences, and significance of the Declaration of Independence. *The Early Campaigns of Francis Marion and the Loyalists in the South* explores key battles of the American Revolution in the southern colonies. *Thomas Jefferson: Philosopher of Freedom* (1996) is a biography of America's leading Revolutionary from the Arts & Entertainment Network. *The Battle of Yorktown* (1983) examines the climactic battles of the American Revolution.

Internet Resources

Internet websites containing historical material relevant to the subjects discussed in this chapter can be reached through the McGraw-Hill history site at www.mhhe.com/socscience/history/usa/link/linktop.htm.

CHAPTER SIX

The Constitution and the New Republic

Framing a New Government ∼ *Adoption and Adaptation*
Federalists and Republicans ∼ *Establishing National Sovereignty*
The Downfall of the Federalists

B Y THE LATE 1780s, many Americans had grown dissatisfied with the Confederation. It was ridden with factions, unable to deal effectively with economic problems, and frighteningly powerless in the face of Shays's Rebellion. A decade earlier, Americans had deliberately avoided creating a strong national government. Now they reconsidered. In 1787, in a burst of great political creativity, the nation produced a new constitution and a new, much more powerful government with three independent branches. The government the Constitution produced has survived for more than two centuries as one of the stablest and most successful in the world. Yet the adoption of the Constitution did not complete the creation of the republic. For, while most Americans agreed that the Constitution was a nearly perfect document, they disagreed—at times fundamentally—on what that document meant.

FRAMING A NEW GOVERNMENT

The Confederation Congress had become so unpopular and ineffectual by the mid-1780s that it began to lead an almost waiflike existence. In 1783, its members timidly withdrew from Philadelphia to escape army veterans demanding their back pay. They took refuge for a while in Princeton, New Jersey, then moved on to Annapolis, and in 1785 settled in New York. Delegates were often scarce. Only with great difficulty could Congress produce a quorum to ratify the treaty with Great Britain ending the Revolutionary

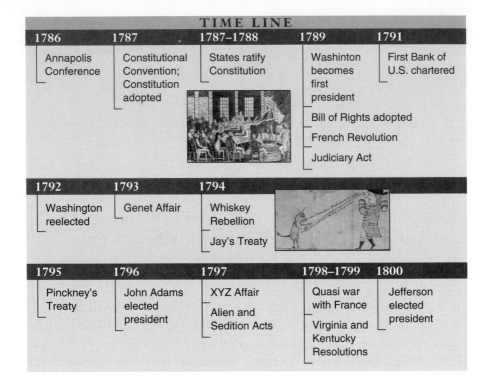

TIME LINE

1786	1787	1787–1788	1789	1791
Annapolis Conference	Constitutional Convention; Constitution adopted	States ratify Constitution	Washinton becomes first president	First Bank of U.S. chartered
			Bill of Rights adopted	
			French Revolution	
			Judiciary Act	

1792	1793	1794
Washington reelected	Genet Affair	Whiskey Rebellion
		Jay's Treaty

1795	1796	1797	1798–1799	1800
Pinckney's Treaty	John Adams elected president	XYZ Affair	Quasi war with France	Jefferson elected president
		Alien and Sedition Acts	Virginia and Kentucky Resolutions	

War. Only eight state delegations voted on the Confederation's most important piece of legislation, the Northwest Ordinance.

Advocates of Reform

In the 1780s, some of the wealthiest and most powerful groups in the population began to clamor for a genuinely national government capable of dealing more effectively with the country's problems. By 1786, such demands had grown so intense that even defenders of the existing system reluctantly agreed that the government needed strengthening at its weakest point—its lack of power to tax.

The most resourceful advocate of a stronger national government was Alexander Hamilton, the illegitimate son of a Scottish merchant in the West Indies, who had become a successful New York lawyer and had once served as an aide to George Washington. Hamilton now called for a national convention to overhaul the Articles of Confederation. He found an important ally in James Madison of Virginia, who persuaded the Virginia legislature to convene an interstate conference on commercial questions.

Only five states sent delegates to the meeting, which took place at Annapolis, Maryland, in 1786; but the conference approved a proposal drafted by Hamilton for a convention of special delegates from all the states to meet in Philadelphia the next year and consider ways to "render the constitution of the Federal government adequate to the exigencies of the union."

At first there seemed little reason to believe the Philadelphia convention would attract any more delegates than had the Annapolis meeting. Then, early in 1787, the news of Shays's Rebellion spread throughout the nation, alarming many previously apathetic leaders. Most important of all, the rebellion aroused George Washington, who promptly made plans to travel to Philadelphia for the Constitutional Convention. His support gave the meeting wide credibility.

A Divided Convention

Fifty-five men, representing all the states except Rhode Island, attended one or more sessions of the convention that sat in the Philadelphia State House from May to September 1787. These "Founding Fathers," as they became known much later, were relatively young men; the average age was forty-four, and only one delegate (Benjamin Franklin, then eighty-one) was genuinely aged. They were well educated by the standards of their time. Most were relatively wealthy property owners, and many feared what one of them called the "turbulence and follies" of democracy. Yet all were also products of the American Revolution and retained the Revolutionary suspicion of concentrated power.

The convention unanimously chose Washington to preside over its sessions and then closed its business to the public and the press. (If James Madison had not kept a private diary chronicling the proceedings, historians might know little about what happened in Philadelphia.) It then ruled that each state delegation would have a single vote and that major decisions would require not unanimity, as they did in Congress, but a simple majority. Almost all the delegates agreed that the United States needed a stronger central government. But there agreement ended.

Virginia, the largest state in population, sent a well-prepared delegation to Philadelphia led by James Madison (thirty-six years old), who had devised in some detail a plan for a new "national" government. The Virginia Plan shaped the agenda of the convention from the moment Edmund Randolph of Virginia opened the debate by proposing "a national government ought to be established, consisting of a supreme Legislative, Executive, and Judiciary." Even that brief description outlined a government very

THE CONVENTION AT PHILADELPHIA This engraving of delegates at work, created in 1823, is one of countless efforts in the early nineteenth century to imaginatively re-create the great Constitutional Convention in Philadelphia in 1787. It appeared in an early *History of the United States of America* by Rev. Charles A. Goodrich.

different from the Confederation, which had no executive and no independent judiciary. But the delegates were so committed to fundamental reform that they approved the resolution after only brief debate.

There was less agreement about the details of Madison's Virginia Plan. It called for a national legislature of two houses. In the lower house, states would be represented in proportion to their population; thus the largest state (Virginia) would have about ten times as many representatives as the smallest (Delaware). Members of the upper house were to be elected by the lower house under no rigid system of representation; thus some of the smaller states might at times have no members at all in the upper house.

The proposal aroused immediate opposition among delegates from the smaller states. William Paterson of New Jersey offered an alternative (the New Jersey Plan) that would have retained the essence of the existing system with its one-house legislature in which all states had equal representation, but which would have given Congress expanded powers to tax and to regulate commerce. The convention rejected Paterson's proposal, but supporters of the Virginia Plan now realized they would have to make concessions to the small states if the delegations were ever to agree. They agreed to permit members of the upper house to be elected by the state legislatures, ensuring that every state would be represented.

Many questions remained unresolved. Among the most important was the question of slavery. There was no serious discussion of abolishing slavery during the convention. But other issues were debated heatedly. Would slaves be counted as part of the population in determining representation in Congress? Or would they be considered property, not entitled to representation? Delegates from the states with large slave populations wanted to have it both ways. They argued that slaves should be considered persons in determining representation but as property if the new government levied taxes on the states on the basis of population. Representatives from states where slavery had disappeared or was expected soon to disappear argued that slaves should be included in calculating taxation but not representation.

Compromise

The delegates argued for weeks. By the end of June, as both temperature and tempers rose to uncomfortable heights, the convention seemed in danger of collapsing. But the delegates refused to give up (partly because of the patient urging of Benjamin Franklin). Finally, on July 2, the convention created a "grand committee," chaired by Franklin and with one delegate from each state, which produced a proposal that became the basis of the "Great Compromise." It called for a two-house legislature. In the lower house, the states would be represented on the basis of population; each slave would be counted as three-fifths of a free person in determining the basis for both representation and direct taxation. In the upper house, the states would be represented equally with two members apiece. On July 16, 1787, the convention voted to accept the compromise.

In the next few weeks, the convention agreed to another important compromise on the explosive issue of slavery. To placate southern delegates, who feared the new government would interfere with slavery, the convention agreed to bar the new government from stopping the slave trade for twenty years.

Some significant issues remained unaddressed. Most important was the absence of a list of individual rights, which would restrain the powers of the national government in the way that bills of rights restrained the state governments. Madison opposed the idea, arguing that specifying rights that were reserved to the people would, in effect, limit those rights. Others, however, feared that without such protections the national government might abuse its new authority.

The Constitution of 1787

Many people contributed to the creation of the American Constitution, but the most important person in the process was James Madison. Madison had devised the Virginia Plan, from which the final document ultimately emerged, and he did most of the drafting of the Constitution itself. Madison's most important achievement, however, was in helping resolve two important philosophical questions that had served as obstacles to the creation of an effective national government: the question of sovereignty and the question of limiting power.

How could a national government exercise sovereignty concurrently with state governments? Where did ultimate sovereignty lie? The answer, Madison and his contemporaries decided, was that all power, at all levels of government, flowed ultimately from the people. Thus neither the federal government nor the state governments were truly sovereign. All of them derived their authority from below. The opening phrase of the Constitution—"We the people of the United States of America"—is an expression of that belief. The resolution of the problem of sovereignty made possible one of the distinctive features of the Constitution—its division of powers between the national and state governments. The Constitution and the government it created were to be the "supreme law" of the land; no state would have the authority to defy it. At the same time, however, the Constitution left important powers in the hands of the states.

In addition to solving the question of sovereignty, the Constitution produced a distinctive solution to the problem of concentrated authority, which many Americans feared would produce tyranny. Drawing from the ideas of the French philosopher Baron de Montesquieu, most Americans had long believed that the best way to avoid tyranny was to keep government close to the people. A republic must remain confined to a relatively small area; a large nation would breed corruption and despotism because the rulers would be so distant from most of the people that there would be no way to control them.

Madison, however, helped break the grip of these assumptions by arguing that a large republic would be less, not more, likely to produce tyranny because it would contain so many different factions that no single group would ever be able to dominate it. This idea of many centers of power "checking each other" and preventing any single, despotic authority from emerging also helped shape the internal structure of the federal government. The Constitution's most distinctive feature was its "separation of powers" within the government, its creation of "checks and balances" among the legislative, executive, and judicial branches. The forces within the government would constantly compete with (and often frustrate) one another. Congress would have two chambers, each checking the other, since both would have to agree before any law could be passed. The president would have the power to veto acts of Congress. The federal courts would be protected from both the executive and the legislature, because judges, once appointed by the president and confirmed by the Senate, would serve for life.

The "federal" structure of the government was designed to protect the United States from the kind of despotism that Americans believed had emerged in England. But it was also designed to protect the nation from another kind of despotism: the tyranny of the people. Shays's Rebellion, most of the founders believed, had been only one example of what could happen if a nation did not defend itself against the unchecked exercise of popular will. Thus in the new government, only the members of the House of Representatives would be elected directly by the people. Senators, the president, federal judges—all would be insulated in varying degrees from the public.

On September 17, 1787, thirty-nine delegates signed the Constitution. Benjamin Franklin expressed the feelings of many of them at the end when he said: "Thus I consent, Sir, to this Constitution, because I expect no better, and because I am not sure that it is not the best."

ADOPTION AND ADAPTATION

The delegates at Philadelphia had greatly exceeded their instructions from Congress and the states. Instead of making simple revisions in the Articles of Confederation, they had produced a plan for a completely different form of government. They feared that the Constitution would not be ratified under the rules of the Articles of Confederation, which required unanimous approval by the state legislatures. So the convention changed the rules, proposing that the new government come into being when nine of the thirteen states ratified the Constitution and recommending that state conventions, not state legislatures, be called to ratify it.

Federalists and Antifederalists

The Congress in New York, demoralized and overshadowed by the events in Philadelphia, passively accepted the convention's work and submitted it to the states for approval. All the state legislatures except Rhode Island elected delegates to ratifying conventions, most of which began meeting in early 1788. Even before the ratifying conventions adjourned, however, a great national debate on the new Constitution had begun—in the state legislatures, in public meetings, in newspapers, and in ordinary conversations.

Supporters of the Constitution had a number of advantages. They were better organized. They had the support of the two most eminent men in America, Franklin and Washington. And they seized an appealing label for themselves: "Federalists"—a term that opponents of centralization had once used to describe themselves—thus implying that they were less committed to a "nationalist" government than in fact they were. The Federalists also had the support of the ablest political philosophers of their time: Alexander Hamilton, James Madison, and John Jay. Those three men, under the joint pseudonym "Publius," wrote a series of essays—widely published in newspapers throughout the nation—explaining the meaning and virtues of the Constitution. The essays were later issued as a book, and they are known today as *The Federalist Papers.* They are among the greatest American contributions to political theory.

The Federalists called their critics "Antifederalists," which suggested that their rivals had nothing to offer except opposition. But the Antifederalists, too, were represented by distinguished leaders of the Revolution, among them Patrick Henry and Samuel Adams. And they had serious and intelligent arguments of their own. They saw themselves as the defenders of the true principles of the Revolution. The Constitution, they believed, would betray those principles by establishing a strong, potentially tyrannical, center of power in the new national government. The new government, they claimed, would increase taxes, weaken the states, wield dictatorial powers, favor the "well-born" over the common people, and abolish individual liberty. But their biggest complaint was that the Constitution lacked a bill of rights. No government could be trusted to protect the liberties of its citizens, they argued. Only by enumerating the natural rights of the people could there be any certainty that those rights would be protected.

Despite the efforts of the Antifederalists, ratification proceeded quickly during the winter of 1787–1788. The Delaware convention was the first to act. It ratified the Constitution unanimously, as did New Jersey and Georgia. New Hampshire ratified the document in June 1788—the ninth state to do so. It was now theoretically possible for the Constitution to go into effect. A new government could not hope to succeed, however, without Virginia and New York, whose conventions remained closely divided. But by the end of June, first Virginia and then New York had consented to the Constitution by narrow margins—on the assumption that a bill of rights would be added in the form of amendments to the Constitu-

CELEBRATING THE CONSITUTION Perhaps because opposition to the Constitution had been so intense, its champions staged elaborate celebrations at the time of ratification in an effort to enhance its legitimacy. In 1788, supporters of the constitution organized an elaborate parade down Wall Street, which included the ship on wheels (representing the "ship of state") pictured here. Alexander Hamilton, whose name is emblazoned on the ship's banners, was New York's leading advocate of the Constitution.

tion. North Carolina's convention adjourned without taking action, waiting to see what happened to the amendments. Rhode Island did not even consider ratification.

Completing the Structure

The first elections under the Constitution were held in the early months of 1789. Almost all the newly elected members of Congress had favored ratification, and many had served as delegates to the Philadelphia convention. There was never any doubt about who would be the first president. George Washington had presided at the Constitutional Convention, and many who had favored ratification did so only because they expected him to preside over the new government as well. Washington received the votes of all the presidential electors. John Adams, a leading Federalist, became vice president. After a journey from his estate at Mount Vernon, Virginia, marked by elaborate celebrations along the way, Washington was inaugurated in New York on April 30, 1789.

The first Congress served in many ways as a continuation of the Constitutional Convention, because its principal responsibility was filling in the various gaps in the Constitution. Its most important task was drafting a bill of rights. By early 1789, even Madison had come to agree that some sort of bill of rights would be essential to legitimize the new government in the eyes of its opponents. On September 25, 1789, Congress approved twelve amendments, ten of which were ratified by the states by the end of 1791. These first ten amendments to the Constitution comprise what we know as the Bill of Rights. Nine of them placed limitations on Congress by forbidding it to infringe on certain fundamental rights: freedom of religion, speech, and the press; immunity from arbitrary arrest; trial by jury; and others. The Tenth Amendment reserved to the states all powers except those specifically withheld from them or delegated to the federal government.

On the subject of federal courts, the Constitution said only: "The judicial power of the United States shall be vested in one Supreme Court, and in such inferior courts as the Congress may from time to time ordain and establish." It was left to Congress to determine the number of Supreme Court judges to be appointed and the kinds of lower courts to be organized. In the Judiciary Act of 1789, Congress provided for a Supreme Court of six members and a system of lower district courts and courts of appeal. In the same act, Congress gave the Supreme Court the power to make the final decision in cases involving the constitutionality of state laws.

The Constitution referred indirectly to executive departments but did not specify which ones or how many there should be. The first Congress created three such departments—state, treasury, and war—and also established the offices of the attorney general and postmaster general. To the office of secretary of the treasury Washington appointed Alexander Hamilton of New York, who at age thirty-two was an acknowledged expert in public finance. For secretary of war he chose a Massachusetts Federalist, General Henry Knox. As attorney general he named Edmund Randolph of Virginia, sponsor of the plan on which the Constitution had been based. As secretary of state he chose another Virginian, Thomas Jefferson.

FEDERALISTS AND REPUBLICANS

The resolution of these initial issues, however, did not resolve the disagreements about the nature of the new government. The framers of the Constitution had dealt with many controversies not by solving them but by papering them over with a series of vague compromises; as a result, the disagreements survived to plague the new government, and the first twelve years under the Constitution produced a politics of unusual acrimony.

At the heart of the controversies of the 1790s was the same basic difference in philosophy that had been at the heart of the debate over the Constitution. On one side stood a powerful group who believed that America required a strong, national government. They envisioned that the country's mission was to become a genuine nation-state, with centralized authority, a complex commercial economy, and a proud standing in world affairs. On the other side stood another group—a minority at first, but one that gained strength during the decade—whose members envisioned a more modest national government. The United States should not, this group believed, aspire to be a highly commercial or urban nation. It should remain predominantly rural and agrarian. The centralizers became known as the Federalists and gravitated to the leadership of Alexander Hamilton. Their opponents acquired the name Republicans and gathered under the leadership of Thomas Jefferson and James Madison.

Hamilton and the Federalists

For twelve years, the Federalists retained firm control of the new government. That was in part because George Washington had always envisioned a strong national government and as president did little to stop those attempting to create one. But the president, Washington believed, should stand above political controversies, and so he avoided personal involvement in the deliberations of Congress. As a result, the dominant figure in his administration became Alexander Hamilton, who exerted more influence than anyone else on domestic and foreign policy. Of all the national leaders of his time, Hamilton was one of the most aristocratic in personal tastes and political philosophy; he believed that a stable and effective government required an elite ruling class. Thus the new government needed the support of the wealthy and powerful; and to get that, it needed to give elites a stake in its success. Hamilton proposed, therefore, that the existing public debt be "funded": that the various certificates of indebtedness that the old Congress had issued during and after the Revolution—many of them now in the possession of wealthy speculators—be called in and exchanged for interest-bearing bonds. He also recommended that the States' Revolutionary debts be "assumed" (taken over by the federal government) to cause state bondholders also to look to the central government for eventual payment. Hamilton did not envision paying off and thus eliminating the debt; he wanted to create a permanent national debt, with new bonds being issued as old ones were paid off. The result, he believed, would be that the wealthy classes, who were the most likely to lend money to the government, would always have a reason to want the government to survive.

Hamilton also wanted to create a national bank. It would provide loans and currency to businesses. It would give the government a safe place for the deposit of federal funds. It would facilitate the collection of taxes and the disbursement of the government's expenditures. And it would provide a stable center to the nation's small and feeble banking system. The bank would be chartered by the federal government and would have a monopoly of the government's own banking business, but much of its capital would come from private investors.

The funding and assumption of debts would require new sources of revenue for the national government. Hamilton recommended two kinds of taxes to complement the receipts anticipated from the sales of public land. One was an excise tax on alcoholic beverages, a tax that would be most burdensome to the whiskey distillers of the backcountry, especially those in Pennsylvania, Virginia, and North Carolina—small farmers who converted part of their corn and rye crops into whiskey. The other was a tariff on imports, which Hamilton saw not only as a way to raise money but as a way to protect domestic industries from foreign competition. In his famous "Report on Manufactures" of 1791, he outlined a plan for stimulating the growth of industry in the United States and spoke glowingly of the advantages to society of a healthy manufacturing sector.

The Federalists, in short, offered more than a vision of a stable new government. They offered a vision of the sort of nation America should become—a nation with a wealthy, enlightened ruling class, a vigorous, independent commercial economy, and a thriving manufacturing sector; a country able to play a prominent role in world economic affairs.

Enacting the Federalist Program

Few members of Congress objected to Hamilton's plan for funding the national debt, but many did oppose his proposal to exchange new bonds for old certificates of indebtedness on a dollar-for-dollar basis. Many of the original holders—farmers and merchants who had sold goods to the Continental army, soldiers who had received bonds as payment for their service—had been forced to sell during the hard times of the 1780s to speculators, who had bought them at a fraction of their face value. James Madison, now a representative from Virginia, argued for a plan by which the new bonds would be divided between the original purchasers and the speculators. But Hamilton's allies insisted that such a plan was both impractical and dangerous, that the honor of the government required a literal fulfillment of its earlier promises to pay whoever held the bonds. Congress finally passed the funding bill Hamilton wanted.

Hamilton's proposal that the federal government assume the state debts encountered greater difficulty. Its opponents argued that if the federal government took over the state debts, the states with few debts would have to pay taxes to service the states with large ones. Massachusetts, for example, owed much more money than did Virginia. Only by striking a bargain with the Virginians were Hamilton and his supporters able to win passage of the assumption bill.

The deal involved the location of the national capital. The Virginians wanted to create a new capital near them in the South. Hamilton and Jefferson met and agreed to exchange northern support for placing the capital in the South for Virginia's votes for the assumption bill. The bargain called for the construction of a new capital city on the banks of the Potomac River, which divided Maryland and Virginia, on land to be selected by George Washington. The government would move its operations there by the beginning of the new century.

Hamilton's bank bill produced the most heated debates. Madison, Jefferson, Randolph, and others argued that because the Constitution made no provision for a national bank (or for Congress's issuing of articles of incorporation), Congress had no authority to create one. But Congress agreed to Hamilton's bill despite these objections, and Washington, although he had some apparent reservations, signed it. The Bank of the United States began operations in 1791, under a twenty-year charter.

Hamilton also had his way with the excise tax, although protests from farmers later forced revisions to reduce the burden on the smaller distillers. He failed to win passage of a tariff as highly protective as he had hoped for, but the tariff law of 1792 did raise the rates somewhat.

Once enacted, Hamilton's program won the support of manufacturers, creditors, and other influential segments of the population, as he had hoped. But others found the Hamilton program less appealing. Small farmers, who formed the majority of the population, complained that they were being taxed excessively. They and others began to argue that the Federalist program served the interests not of the people but of small, wealthy elites. Out of this feeling an organized political opposition arose.

The Republican Opposition

The Constitution made no reference to political parties, and the omission was not an oversight. Most of the framers—and George Washington in particular—believed that organized parties were dangerous and to be avoided. Disagreement was inevitable on particular issues, but most of the founders believed that such disagreements need not and should not lead to the formation of permanent factions.

Yet not many years had passed after the ratification of the Constitution before Madison and others became convinced that Hamilton and his followers had become a dangerous, self-interested faction. The Federalists had used the powers of their offices to reward their supporters and win additional allies. They had encouraged the formation of local associations— largely aristocratic in nature—to strengthen their standing in local communities. They were doing many of the same things, their opponents believed, that the corrupt British governments of the early eighteenth century had done.

Because the Federalists appeared to their critics to be creating such a menacing and tyrannical structure of power, there was no alternative but to organize a vigorous opposition. The result was the emergence of an alternative political organization, whose members called themselves "Republicans." (These first Republicans are not institutionally related to the modern Republican Party, which was born in the 1850s.) By the late 1790s, the Republicans were going to even greater lengths than the Federalists to create vehicles of partisan influence. In every state they had formed committees, societies, and caucuses; Republican groups were corresponding with one another across state lines; they were banding to-gether to influence state and local elections. And they were justifying their actions by claiming, just as Hamilton and his supporters claimed, that they and they alone represented the true interests of the nation. Neither side was willing to admit that it was acting as a party, nor would either concede the right of the other to exist. This institutionalized factionalism is known to historians as the "first party system."

From the beginning, the preeminent figures among the Republicans were Thomas Jefferson and James Madison. Jefferson, the more politically magnetic of the two, became the most prominent spokesman for the cause. He promoted a vision of an agrarian republic, in which most citizens would farm their own land. Jefferson did not scorn commercial or industrial activity. But he believed that the nation should be wary of too much urbanization and industrialization.

Although both parties had supporters in all parts of the country and among all classes, there were regional and economic differences. The Federalists were most numerous in the commercial centers of the Northeast and in such southern seaports as Charleston; the Republicans were most numerous in the rural areas of the South and the West. The difference in their philosophies was visible in, among other things, their reactions to the progress of the French Revolution. As that revolution grew increasingly radical in the 1790s, with its attacks on organized religion, the overthrow of the monarchy, and eventually the execution of the king and queen, the Federalists expressed horror. But the Republicans applauded the democratic, antiaristocratic spirit they believed the French Revolution displayed.

When the time came for the nation's second presidential election, in 1792, both Jefferson and Hamilton urged Washington to run for a second term. The president reluctantly agreed. But while Washington had the respect of both factions, he was, in reality, more in sympathy with the Federalists than with the Republicans. And during his presidency, Hamilton remained the dominant figure in government.

ESTABLISHING NATIONAL SOVEREIGNTY

The Federalists consolidated their position—and attracted wide public support for the new national government—by acting effectively in two areas in which the old Confederation had not always been successful: the western territories and diplomacy.

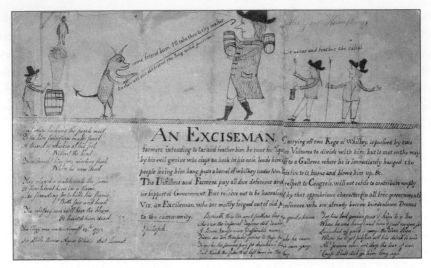

A COMMENT ON THE WHISKEY REBELLION Although Thomas Jefferson and other Republicans claimed to welcome occasional popular uprisings, the Federalists were horrified by such insurgencies as Shays's Rebellion in Massachusetts and, later, the Whiskey Rebellion in Pennsylvania. This Federalist cartoon portrays the rebels as demons who pursue and eventually hang an unfortunate "exciseman" (tax collector) who has confiscated two kegs of rum.

Securing the West

Despite the Northwest Ordinance, the old Congress had largely failed to tie the outlying western areas of the country firmly to the national government. Farmers in western Massachusetts had rebelled; settlers in Vermont, Kentucky, and Tennessee had flirted with seceding from the Union. At first, the new government under the Constitution faced similar problems.

In 1794, farmers in western Pennsylvania raised a major challenge to federal authority when they refused to pay the new whiskey excise tax and began terrorizing tax collectors in the region. But the federal government did not leave settlement of the so-called Whiskey Rebellion to the authorities of Pennsylvania as Congress had left the task of quelling Shays's Rebellion to the authorities of Massachusetts. At Hamilton's urging, Washington called out the militias of three states and assembled an army of nearly 15,000—a larger force than he had commanded against the British during most of the Revolution—and he personally accompanied the troops into Pennsylvania. At the approach of the militiamen, the rebellion quickly collapsed.

The federal government won the allegiance of the whiskey rebels through intimidation. It won the loyalties of other western people by accepting new states as members of the Union. The last two of the original thirteen colonies joined the Union once the Bill of Rights had been appended to the Constitution—North Carolina in 1789 and Rhode Island in 1790. Vermont became the fourteenth state in 1791 after New York and New Hampshire agreed to give up their claims to it. Next came Kentucky, in 1792, when Virginia gave up its claim to that region. After North Carolina ceded its western lands to the Union, Tennessee became a state in 1796.

The new government faced a greater challenge in more distant areas of the Northwest and the Southwest. The ordinances of 1784–1787, establishing the terms of white settlement in the West, had produced a series of border conflicts with Indian tribes that were resisting white settlement in their lands. The new government inherited these clashes, which continued with few interruptions for nearly a decade.

These clashes revealed another issue the Constitution had done little to resolve: the place of the Indian nations within the new federal structure. The Constitution made almost no mention of Native Americans. It gave Congress power to "regulate Commerce . . . with the Indian tribes." And it bound the new government to respect treaties negotiated by the Confederation, most of which had been with the tribes. But none of this did very much to clarify the precise legal standing of Indians or Indian nations within the United States. The tribes received no direct representation in the new government. Above all, the Constitution did not address the major issue that would govern relations between whites and Indians: land. Indian nations lived within the boundaries of the United States, yet they claimed (and the white government at times agreed) that they had some measure of sovereignty over their own land. But neither the Constitution nor common law offered any clear guide to the rights of a "nation within a nation" or to the precise nature of tribal sovereignty, which ultimately depended on control of land.

Maintaining Neutrality

Not until 1791 did Great Britain send a minister to the United States, and then only because Madison and the Republicans were threatening to place special trade restrictions on British ships. A new crisis in Anglo-American relations emerged in 1793 when the new French government established after the revolution of 1789 went to war with Great Britain. Both the president and Congress took steps to establish American neutrality in the conflict, but that neutrality was severely tested.

Early in 1794, the Royal Navy began seizing hundreds of American ships engaged in trade in the French West Indies, outraging public opinion in the United States. Hamilton was deeply concerned. War would mean an end to imports from England, and most of the revenue for maintaining his financial system came from duties on those imports.

Hamilton and the Federalists did not trust the State Department, now in the hands of the ardently pro-French Edmund Randolph, to find a solution to the crisis. So they persuaded Washington to name a special commissioner to go to England and negotiate a solution: the staunch New York Federalist and chief justice of the Supreme Court, John Jay. Jay was instructed to secure compensation for the recent British assaults on American shipping, to demand withdrawal of British forces from their posts on the frontier of the United States, and to negotiate a commercial treaty with Britain compatible with America's 1778 treaty with France.

The long and complex treaty Jay negotiated in 1794 failed to achieve these goals. But it was not without merit. It settled the conflict with Britain, avoiding a likely war. It provided for undisputed American sovereignty over the entire Northwest. It produced a reasonably satisfactory commercial relationship with a nation whose trade was important to the United States. Nevertheless, when the terms became known in America, criticism was intense and Jay was burned in effigy in some places. Opponents of the treaty—who included almost all the Republicans and even many Federalists—went to great lengths to defeat it in the Senate, cheered on by agents of France. But in the end the Senate ratified what was by then known as Jay's Treaty.

Jay's Treaty paved the way for a settlement of important American disputes with Spain. Under Pinckney's Treaty (negotiated by Thomas Pinckney and signed in 1795), Spain recognized the right of Americans to navigate the Mississippi to its mouth and to deposit goods at New Orleans for reloading on oceangoing ships; agreed to fix the northern boundary of Florida where Americans always had insisted it should be, along the 31st parallel; and commanded its authorities to prevent the Indians in Florida from launching raids north across the border.

THE DOWNFALL OF THE FEDERALISTS

Since almost everyone in the 1790s agreed that there was no place in a stable republic for organized parties, the emergence of the Republicans as a powerful and apparently permanent opposition seemed to the Federalists a grave threat to national stability. And so when major international perils confronted the government in the 1790s, the temptation to move force-fully against this "illegitimate" opposition was strong.

The Election of 1796

George Washington refused to run for a third term as president in 1796, thus removing the last obstacle to the open expression of the partisan rivalries that had been building over the previous eight years. Jefferson was the obvious presidential candidate of the Republicans that year, but the Federalists faced a more difficult choice. Hamilton had created too many enemies to be a credible candidate. Vice President John Adams, who was directly associated with none of the controversial Federalist achievements, received the party's nomination for president at a caucus of the Federalists in Congress.

The Federalists were still clearly the dominant party. But without Washington to mediate, they fell victim to fierce factional rivalries. Adams defeated Jefferson by only three electoral votes and assumed the presidency as head of a divided party facing a powerful opposition. Jefferson became vice president as a result of finishing second. (Not until the adoption of the Twelfth Amendment in 1804 did electors vote separately for president and vice president.)

The Quasi War with France

American relations with Great Britain and Spain improved as a result of Jay's and Pinckney's Treaties. But the nation's relations with revolutionary France quickly deteriorated. French vessels captured American ships on the high seas and at times imprisoned the crews. The French government refused to receive Charles Cotesworth Pinckney when he arrived in Paris as the new American minister. In an effort to stabilize relations, Adams appointed a bipartisan commission to negotiate with France. When the Americans arrived in Paris in 1797, three agents of the French foreign minister, Prince Talleyrand, demanded a loan for France and a bribe for French officials before any negotiations could begin. Pinckney, a member of the commission, responded succinctly and angrily: "No! No! Not a sixpence!"

When Adams heard of the incident, he sent a message to Congress denouncing French insults and urging preparations for war. Before giving the commissioners' report to Congress, he deleted the names of the three French agents and designated them only as Messrs. X, Y, and Z. When the report was published, the "XYZ Affair," as it quickly became known, provoked widespread popular outrage at France's actions and strong popular support for the Federalists' response. For nearly two years, 1798 and 1799, the United States found itself engaged in an undeclared war with France.

Adams persuaded Congress to cut off all trade with France, to abrogate the treaties of 1778, and to authorize American vessels to capture French armed ships on the high seas. In 1798, Congress created the Department of the Navy and appropriated money for the construction of new warships. The navy soon won a number of duels and captured a total of eighty-five French ships, including armed merchantmen. The United States also began cooperating so closely with the British as to be virtually a cobelligerent in England's war with France. In response, the French began trying to conciliate the United States. Adams sent another commission to Paris in 1800, and the new French government (headed now by "First Consul" Napoleon Bonaparte) agreed to a treaty with the United States that canceled the old agreements of 1778 and established new commercial arrangements. As a result, the "quasi war" came to a reasonably peaceful end, and the United States freed itself from the entanglements and embarrassments of its alliance with France.

Repression and Protest

The conflict with France helped the Federalists increase their majorities in Congress in 1798. Armed with this new strength, they began to consider ways to silence the Republican opposition. The result was some of the most controversial legislation in American history: the Alien and Sedition Acts.

The Alien Act placed new obstacles in the way of foreigners who wished to become American citizens, and it strengthened the president's hand in dealing with aliens. The Sedition Act allowed the government to prosecute those who engaged in "sedition" against the government. In theory, only libelous or treasonous activities were subject to prosecution; but since such activities had no clear definition, the law, in effect, gave the government authority to stifle virtually any opposition. The Republicans interpreted the new laws as part of a Federalist campaign to destroy them and fought back.

President Adams signed the new laws but was cautious in implementing them. He did not deport any aliens, and he prevented the government from launching a broad crusade against the Republicans. But the legislation did have a significant repressive effect. The Alien Act discouraged immigration and encouraged some foreigners already in the country to leave. And the administration used the Sedition Act to arrest and convict ten men, most of them Republican newspaper editors whose only crime had been criticism of the Federalists in government.

Republican leaders began to look for ways to reverse the Alien and Sedition Acts. The Supreme Court had not yet established its right to nullify congressional legislation, so some Republicans looked to the state legislatures for help. They developed a theory to justify action by the states against the federal government in two sets of resolutions of 1798–1799, one written (anonymously) by Jefferson and adopted by the Kentucky legislature and the other drafted by Madison and approved by the Virginia legislature. The Virginia and Kentucky Resolutions, as they were known, used the ideas of John Locke and the Tenth Amendment to the Constitution to argue that the federal government had been formed by a "compact" or contract among the states and possessed only certain delegated powers. Whenever a party to the contract, a state, decided that the central government had exceeded those powers, it had the right to "nullify" the appropriate laws.

The Republicans did not win wide support for the nullification idea; only Virginia and Kentucky declared the congressional statutes void. They did, however, succeed in elevating their dispute with the Federalists to the level of a national crisis. By the late 1790s, the entire nation was as deeply and bitterly politicized as at any time in its history. State legislatures at times resembled battlegrounds. Even the United States Congress was plagued with violent disagreements. In one celebrated incident in the chamber of the House of Representatives, Matthew Lyon, a Republican from Vermont, responded to an insult from Roger Griswold, a Federalist from Connecticut, by spitting in Griswold's eye. Griswold attacked Lyon with his cane, Lyon fought back with a pair of fire tongs, and soon the two men were wrestling on the floor.

The "Revolution" of 1800

These bitter controversies shaped the presidential election of 1800. The presidential candidates were the same as four years earlier: Adams for the Federalists, Jefferson for the Republicans. But the campaign of 1800 was very different from the one preceding it. Indeed, it was probably the ugliest in American history. Adams and Jefferson themselves displayed reasonable dignity, but their supporters showed no such restraint. The Federalists accused Jefferson of being a dangerous radical and his followers of being wild men who, if they should come to power, would bring on a reign of terror

CONGRESSIONAL BRAWLERS, 1798 This savage cartoon was inspired by the celebrated fight on the floor of the House of Representatives between Matthew Lyon, a Republican representative from Vermont, and Roger Griswold, a Federalist from Connecticut. Griswold (at right) attacks Lyon with his cane, and Lyon retaliates with fire tongs. Other members of Congress are portrayed enjoying the battle.

comparable to that of the French Revolution. The Republicans portrayed Adams as a tyrant conspiring to become king, and they accused the Federalists of plotting to subvert human liberty and impose slavery on the people. There was considerable personal invective as well. (It was during this campaign that the story of Jefferson's alleged romantic involvement with Sally Hemmings, a slave woman on his plantation, was first widely aired.) The election was close, and the crucial contest was in New York. There, Aaron Burr mobilized an organization of Revolutionary War veterans, the Tammany Society, to serve as a Republican political machine. Through Tammany's efforts, the party carried the city by a large majority, and with it the state. Jefferson was, apparently, elected.

But an unexpected complication soon jeopardized the Republican victory. The Constitution called for each elector to "vote by ballot for two persons." The normal practice was that an elector would cast one vote for his party's presidential candidate and another for the vice presidential candidate. To avoid a tie, the Republicans had intended that one elector would refrain from voting for the party's vice-presidential candidate,

Aaron Burr. But the plan went awry. When the votes were counted, Jefferson and Burr each had 73. No candidate had a majority, and—in accordance with the Constitution—the House of Representatives had to choose between the two top candidates, Jefferson and Burr. Each state delegation would cast a single vote.

The new Congress, elected in 1800 with a Republican majority, was not to convene until after the inauguration of the president, so it was the Federalist Congress that had to decide the question. Some Federalists hoped to use the situation to salvage the election for their party; others wanted to strike a bargain with Burr and elect him. But after a long deadlock, several leading Federalists, most prominent among them Alexander Hamilton, concluded that Burr (whom many suspected of having engineered the deadlock in the first place) was too unreliable to trust with the presidency. On the thirty-sixth ballot, Jefferson was elected.

After the election of 1800, the only branch of the federal government left in Federalist hands was the judiciary. The Adams administration spent its last months in office taking steps to make the party's hold on the courts secure. With the Judiciary Act of 1801, passed by the lame duck Congress, the Federalists reduced the number of Supreme Court justiceships by one but greatly increased the number of federal judgeships as a whole. Adams quickly appointed Federalists to the newly created positions. Indeed, there were charges that he stayed up until midnight on his last day in office to finish signing the new judges' commissions. These officeholders became known as the "midnight appointments."

Even so, the Republicans viewed their victory as almost complete. The nation had, they believed, been saved from tyranny. A new era could now begin, one in which the true principles of America would once again govern the land. The exuberance with which the victors viewed the future—and the importance they ascribed to the defeat of the Federalists—was evident in the phrase Jefferson himself later used to describe his election. He called it the "Revolution of 1800."

CONCLUSION

The writing of the Constitution of 1787 was the single most important political event in the history of the United States, and a notable event in the political history of the modern world. In creating a "federal" system of dispersed authority—authority divided among national and state governments, authority divided among an executive, a legislature, and a judiciary—the young nation sought to balance its need for an effective central government against its fear of concentrated and despotic power. The ability of the delegates to the Constitutional Convention to compromise again and again to produce the ultimate structure gave evidence of the deep yearning among them for a stable political system. The same willingness to compromise allowed the greatest challenge to the ideals of the new democracy—slavery—to survive intact.

The writing and ratifying of the Constitution settled some questions about the shape of the new nation. The first twelve years under the government created by the Constitution solved others. And yet by the year 1800, a basic disagreement about the future of the nation—a disagreement personified by the differences between committed nationalist Alexander Hamilton and the self-proclaimed champion of democracy Thomas Jefferson—remained unresolved and was creating bitter divisions and conflicts within the political world. The election of Thomas Jefferson to the presidency that year opened a new chapter in the nation's public history. It also brought to a close, at least temporarily, savage political conflicts that had seemed to threaten the nation's future.

FOR FURTHER REFERENCE

Suggested Readings

Charles Beard, *An Economic Interpretation of the Constitution of the United States* (1913), a seminal work of modern American historical inquiry, offers a class-centered interpretation of the origins of the Constitution. Gordon Wood, *The Creation of the American Republic* (1969) is the leading analysis of the intellectual path from the Declaration of Independence to the American Constitution. Jack Rakove, *Original Meanings: Politics and Ideas in the Making of the Constitution* (1996) connects the politics of the 1780s with the political ideas embedded in the Constitution. Michael Kammen, *A Machine that Would Go of Itself: The Constitution in American Culture* (1986) discusses the ways in which different generations of Americans have viewed the Constitution. Max Farrand, ed., *Records of the Federal Convention of 1787*, 4 vols. (1911–1937) is an excellent documentary source. Stanley Elkins and Eric McKitrick, *The Age of Federalism* (1993) provides a lengthy overview of political and economic development in the 1790s. Joyce Appleby, *Capitalism and a New Social Order: The Republican Vision of the 1790s* (1984) highlights liberal and capitalist impulses unleashed after the ratification of the Constitution. Dumas Malone, *Jefferson and His Time*, 6 vols. (1948–1981) is a magisterial biography of one of the greatest of the nation's founders.

Films

(The best source for information on how to find these and other films is *Bowker's Complete Video Directory*—3 volumes.) *The American Story, No. 3: Creating a Republic; No. 4: Experiment in Government; No. 5: The Federalist Era* (1985) cover the years from the American Revolution to 1800. *The Constitution: An American Adventure* explores the development of the Constitution from colonial dissent in the 1760s through the Articles of Confederation. *The Background of the United States Constitution* (1982) explains the calling of the Constitutional Convention as well as the compromises hammered out to produce the Constitution and get it ratified. *The Constitution of the United States* (1982) is a dramatized version of the Constitutional Convention, seen through the eyes of James Madison. *George Washington—The Man Who Wouldn't Be King* (1992) explores the life of America's first president. *George Washington & the Whiskey Rebellion* (1975) illustrates an important episode in Washington's presidency, one of the first challenges to the authority of the federal government.

Internet Resources

Internet websites containing historical material relevant to the subjects discussed in this chapter can be reached through the McGraw-Hill history site at www.mhhe.com/socscience/history/usa/link/linktop.htm.

CHAPTER SEVEN

The Jeffersonian Era

The Rise of Cultural Nationalism ～ *Stirrings of Industrialism*
Jefferson the President ～ *Doubling the National Domain*
Expansion and War ～ *The War of 1812*

THOMAS JEFFERSON AND his followers assumed control of the national government in 1801 as the champions of a distinctive vision of America. They favored a society of sturdy, independent farmers, happily free from the workshops, the industrial towns, and the city mobs of Europe. They celebrated localism and republican simplicity. Above all, they proposed a federal government of sharply limited power, with most public authority remaining at the level of the states.

Almost nothing worked out as they had planned, for during their years in power the young republic was developing in ways that made much of their vision obsolete. The American economy in the period of Republican ascendancy became steadily more diversified and complex, making the ideal of a simple, agrarian society impossible to maintain. American cultural life was dominated by a vigorous and ambitious nationalism reminiscent of (and often encouraged by) the Federalists. And Jefferson himself contributed to the changes by exercising strong national authority at times, and by arranging the greatest single increase in the size of the United States in its history.

THE RISE OF CULTURAL NATIONALISM

In many respects, American cultural life in the early nineteenth century reflected the Republican vision of the nation's future. Opportunities for education increased, the nation's literary and artistic life began to free itself from European influences, and American religion began to adjust to

180

TIME LINE

1793	1800	1801	1803	1804–1806
Eli Whitney invents cotton gin	U.S. capital moves to Washington	Second Great Awakening begins Marshall chief justice of Supreme Court	Louisiana Purchase *Marbury* v. *Madison*	Lewis and Clark expedition

1804	1807	1808	1809	1810
Jefferson reelected	Embargo	Madison elected president	Non-Intercourse Act Tecumseh Confederacy formed	Macon's Bill No. 2

1811	1812	1814	1815
Battle of Tippecanoe	U.S. declares war on Great Britain Madison reelected	Hartford Convention Treaty of Ghent	Battle of New Orleans

the spread of Enlightenment rationalism. In other respects, however, the new culture was posing a serious challenge to Republican ideals.

Educational and Literary Nationalism

Central to the Republican vision of America was the concept of a virtuous and enlightened citizenry. Republicans believed, therefore, in the creation of a nationwide system of public schools in which all male citizens would receive free education. Such hopes were not fulfilled. As late as 1815, no state had actually created an effective system of free schools (although several had endorsed the idea). Instead, schooling remained primarily the responsibility of private institutions, most of which were open only to those who could afford to pay for them. In the South and in the mid-Atlantic states, most schools were run by religious groups. In New England, private academies were often more secular, many of them modeled on those founded by the Phillips family at Andover, Massachusetts, in 1778, and at Exeter, New Hampshire, three years later. Many were frankly aristocratic in outlook, training their students to become members of the nation's elite. There were a few educational institutions open to the poor, but not nearly enough to accommodate everyone, and the education they offered was usually clearly inferior to that provided for more prosperous students.

Private secondary schools such as those in New England generally accepted only male students; even many public schools excluded females from the classroom. Yet the late eighteenth and early nineteenth centuries did see some important advances in education for women. As Americans began to place a higher value on the importance of the "republican mother" who would help train the new generation, they began to ask how mothers could raise their children to be enlightened if the mothers themselves were uneducated. Such concerns helped speed the creation of female academies throughout the nation (usually for the daughters of affluent families). In 1789, Massachusetts required that its public schools serve females as well as males. Other states, although not all, soon followed.

Some women aspired to more. In 1784, Judith Sargent Murray published an essay defending the right of women to education, and defending it in terms very different from those used by most men. Men and women were equal in intellect and equal in potential, Murray argued. Women, therefore, should have precisely the same educational opportunities as men. What was more, they should have opportunities to earn their own livings and to establish roles for themselves in society apart from their husbands and families. Murray's ideas attracted relatively little support at the time from men or women.

Many early-nineteenth-century reformers believed in the power of education to reform and redeem "backward" people, and they took an interest, therefore, in Indian education. Because Jefferson and his followers liked to think of Native Americans as "noble savages" (uncivilized but not necessarily uncivilizable) they hoped that schooling the Indians in white culture would "uplift" the tribes. Missionaries and mission schools proliferated among the tribes. There were no comparable efforts to educate enslaved African Americans, largely because their owners preferred that they remain ignorant and thus presumably less likely to rebel.

Higher education similarly diverged from Republican ideals. The number of colleges and universities in America grew substantially, from nine at the time of the Revolution to twenty-two in 1800, and the number increased steadily thereafter. None of the new schools, however, was truly public. Even universities established by state legislatures (in Georgia, North Carolina, Vermont, Ohio, and South Carolina, for example) relied on private contributions and tuition fees to survive. Scarcely more than one white man in a thousand (and virtually no women, blacks, or Indians) had access to any college education, and those few who did attend universities were, almost without exception, members of prosperous, propertied families.

"DR. WILLIAM GLEASON" This 1780 painting by the American artist Winthrop Chandler shows a male physician treating a female patient. Obviously reluctant to see a woman reclining in her bed, he takes her pulse by holding the wrist she discreetly extends from behind a curtain.

Medicine and Science

Medicine and science were not always closely connected to one another in the early nineteenth century, but many physicians were working hard to strengthen the link. The University of Pennsylvania created the first American medical school early in the nineteenth century, under the leadership of Benjamin Rush. Most doctors, however, studied medicine by working with an established practitioner, who might or might not have had any scientific training himself. Some American physicians believed in applying new scientific methods to medicine, but they had to struggle against age-old prejudices and superstitions. Efforts to teach anatomy, for example, encountered strong public hostility because of the dissection of cadavers that the study required. Municipal authorities had virtually no understanding of medical science and almost no idea of what to do in the face of the severe epidemics that so often swept their populations; only slowly did they respond to the warnings of Rush and others that lack of adequate sanitation programs was to blame for much disease.

Individual patients often had more to fear from their doctors than from their illnesses. Even the leading advocates of scientific medicine often embraced useless and dangerous treatments. Benjamin Rush, for example, was an advocate of the new and supposedly scientific techniques of bleeding and purging. Many of his patients died. George Washington's death in 1799 was probably less a result of the minor throat infection that had afflicted him than of his physicians' efforts to cure him by bleeding and purging.

The medical profession also used its newfound commitment to the "scientific" method to justify expanding its control over kinds of care that had traditionally been outside its domain. Most childbirths, for example, had been attended by female midwives. In the early nineteenth century, physicians began to handle deliveries themselves and to demand restrictions on the role of midwives. Among the results of that change was a narrowing of opportunities for women (midwifery was an important female occupation) and a restriction of access to childbirth care for poor mothers (who could have afforded midwives, but who could not pay the higher physicians' fees).

Cultural Aspirations of the New Nation

Many Americans—Federalists and Republicans alike—dreamed of an American literary and artistic life that would rival the greatest achievements of Europe. The 1772 "Poem on the Rising Glory of America" predicted that America was destined to become the "seat of empire" and the "final stage" of civilization, with "glorious works of high invention and of wond'rous art." The Connecticut schoolmaster and lawyer Noah Webster (author of widely used American spellers and dictionaries) echoed such sentiments, arguing that the American schoolboy should be educated as a nationalist. "As soon as he opens his lips," Webster wrote, "he should rehearse the history of his own country; he should lisp the praise of liberty, and of those illustrious heroes and statesmen who have wrought a revolution in her favor."

American writers had great difficulty getting their work published. Even so, a growing number of native authors began working to create a strong American literature. Among the most ambitious was the Philadelphia writer Charles Brockden Brown. But his fascination with horror and deviance kept him from developing a popular audience. More successful was Washington Irving of New York, whose popular folk tales, recounting the adventures of such American rustics as Ichabod Crane and Rip Van Winkle, made him the widely acknowledged leader of American literary life in the early eighteenth century.

Religion and Revivalism

The American Revolution had weakened traditional forms of religious practice. It had detached established churches from government, and it had elevated ideas of individual liberty and reason that challenged many ecclesiastical traditions. By the 1790s, only a small proportion of white Americans (perhaps as few as 10 percent) were members of formal churches, and ministers were complaining about the "decay of vital piety."

Religious traditionalists were particularly alarmed about the emergence of new, "rational" religious doctrines—theologies that reflected modern, scientific attitudes and sharply de-emphasized the role of God in the world. "Deism," which had originated among Enlightenment philosophers in France, attracted such educated Americans as Jefferson and Franklin and by 1800 was reaching a moderately broad popular audience. Deists accepted the existence of God, but they considered Him a remote being who, after having created the universe, had withdrawn from direct involvement with the human race and its sins. Religious skepticism also produced the philosophies of "universalism" and "unitarianism." Disciples of these new ideas rejected the traditional Calvinist belief in predestination, arguing that salvation was available to all. They rejected, too, the idea of the Trinity. Jesus was only a great religious teacher, they claimed, not the son of God. But religious skepticism appeared more powerful than it actually was, in part because those who clung to more traditional faiths were for a time confused and disorganized, unable to react effectively. Beginning in 1801, however, traditional religion staged a dramatic comeback in the form of a wave of revivalism known as the Second Great Awakening.

The origins of the Awakening lay in the efforts of conservative theologians of the 1790s to fight the spread of religious rationalism and in the efforts of church establishments to revitalize their organizations. Presbyterians expanded their efforts on the western fringes of white settlement. The Methodists, whose denomination had been founded in England by John Wesley and had spread to America in the 1770s, sent itinerant preachers throughout the nation to win recruits for the new church, which soon became the fastest-growing denomination in America. Almost as successful were the Baptists, who were themselves relatively new to America; they found an especially fervent following in the South.

By 1800, the revivalist energies of all these denominations were combining to create the greatest surge of evangelical fervor since the first Great Awakening sixty years before. In only a few years, the revivalists mobilized a large proportion of the American people, and membership in those churches embracing revivalism—most prominently the Methodist, Baptist, and Presbyterian—was mushrooming. At Cane Ridge, Kentucky, in the summer of 1801, a group of evangelical ministers presided over the nation's first "camp meeting"—an extraordinary revival that lasted several days and impressed all who saw it with its size (some estimated that 25,000 people attended) and its fervor. Such events became common in subsequent years, as the Methodists in particular came to rely on them as a way to "harvest" new members.

The basic message of the Second Great Awakening was that individuals must readmit God and Christ into their daily lives; must embrace a fervent, active piety; and must reject the skeptical rationalism that threatened traditional beliefs. Yet the wave of revivalism did not restore the religion of the past. Few denominations any longer accepted the idea of predestination, and the belief that a person could affect his or her own chances for salvation, rather than encouraging irreligion as many had feared, added intensity to the individual's search for salvation. The Awakening, in short, combined a more active piety with a belief in a God whose grace could be attained through faith and good works.

One of the striking features of the Awakening was the preponderance of women, particularly young women, within it. Female converts far outnumbered males. That may have been in part because of the movement of industrial work out of the home (where women had often contributed to the family economy through spinning and weaving) and into the factory. That process, which was making rapid strides in the early nineteenth century, robbed women of one of their most important social roles. Religious enthusiasm provided, among other things, access to a new range of activities associated with the churches—charitable societies ministering to orphans and the poor, missionary organizations, and others—in which women came to play important roles.

THE CAMP MEETING Camp meetings became a popular feature of evangelical
religion in America beginning around 1800. By the 1820s, there were about
1,000 such meetings a year, most of them in the South and the West. This
lithograph, which dates from the 1830s, illustrates the central role of women in
the religious revivals of the time.

In some areas of the country, revival meetings were open to people of
all races. From these revivals emerged a group of black preachers who became important figures within the slave community. Some of them trans-
lated the apparently egalitarian religious message of the Awakening—that
salvation was available to all—into a similarly egalitarian message for
blacks in the present world. Out of black revival meetings in Virginia, for
example, arose an elaborate plan in 1800 (devised by Gabriel Prosser, the
brother of a black preacher) for a slave rebellion and an attack on Richmond. The plan was discovered and foiled in advance by whites, but revivalism continued in subsequent years to create occasional racial unrest in
the South.

The spirit of revivalism was particularly strong in these years among
Native Americans, although its origins and the forms it took were very
different from those in white or black society. Presbyterian and Baptist
missionaries were active among the southern tribes and sparked a wave of
conversions. But the most important revivalism came from the efforts of a
great Indian prophet: Handsome Lake, a Seneca whose seemingly miracu-
lous "rebirth" after years of alcoholism helped give him a special stature

within his tribe. Handsome Lake, like the earlier Indian prophet Neolin, who had been active in the 1760s, called for a revival of traditional Indian ways. That meant repudiating the individualism of white society and restoring the communal quality of the Indian world. Handsome Lake's message spread through the scattered Iroquois communities that had survived the military and political setbacks of previous decades and inspired many Indians to give up whiskey, gambling, and other destructive customs derived from white society. But Handsome Lake also encouraged Christian missionaries to become active within the tribes, and he urged Iroquois men to abandon their roles as hunters (partly because so much of their hunting land had been seized by whites) and become sedentary farmers instead. Iroquois women, who had traditionally done the farming, were to move into more domestic roles.

STIRRINGS OF INDUSTRIALISM

It was not only culturally and religiously that the nation was developing in ways unforeseen by Jefferson and his followers. Economically, the United States was taking the first, tentative steps toward a transformation that would ultimately shatter forever the vision of a simple, agrarian republic.

Technology in America

While Americans were engaged in a revolution to win their independence, an even more important revolution was in progress in England: the emergence of modern industrialism. Power-driven machines were taking the place of hand-operated tools and were permitting manufacturing to become more rapid and extensive—with profound social and economic consequences. Not since the agrarian revolution thousands of years earlier, when humans had turned from hunting to farming for sustenance, had there been an economic change of a magnitude comparable to the industrial revolution. Centuries of traditions, of social patterns, of cultural and religious assumptions were challenged and often shattered.

Nothing even remotely comparable to the English industrial revolution occurred in America in the first two decades of the nineteenth century. Yet even while Jeffersonians warned of the dangers of rapid economic change, they were witnessing a series of technological advances that would ultimately help ensure that the United States too would be transformed. Some of these technological advances were imported from

SLATER'S MILL   Slater served as an apprentice in England in the 1780s to Richard Arkwright, an inventor of machinery for the new cotton mills that were driving the English industrial revolution. In 1790 Slater, having immigrated to America, designed the first successful cotton-spinning mill in the United States at Pawtucket, Rhode Island. This drawing shows the Pawtucket bridge, falls, and mill as they appeared sometime between 1810 and 1819.

England. Despite efforts by the British government to prevent the export of textile machinery or the emigration of skilled mechanics, a number of immigrants with advanced knowledge of English technology arrived in the United States eager to introduce the new machines to America. Samuel Slater, for example, used the knowledge he had acquired before leaving England to build a spinning mill in Pawtucket, Rhode Island, for the Quaker merchant Moses Brown in 1790. It was generally recognized as the first modern factory in America.

America in the early nineteenth century also produced notable inventors of its own. In 1793, Eli Whitney, a New Englander who was working as a tutor on a Georgia plantation, invented a machine that performed the arduous task of removing the seeds from short-staple cotton quickly and efficiently. It was dubbed the cotton gin ("gin" was a derivative of "engine"). With the device a single operator could clean as much cotton in a few hours as a group of workers had once needed a whole day to do. The results were profound. Soon cotton growing spread throughout the South.

THE COTTON GIN Eli Whitney's cotton gin revolutionized the cotton economy of the South by making the processing of short-staple cotton simple and economical. These 1794 drawings are part of Whitney's application for a federal patent on his device.

(Previously it had been restricted largely to the coast and the Sea Islands, the only places where long-staple cotton—easily cleaned without the cotton gin—could be grown.) Within a decade, the total cotton crop increased eightfold. African-American slavery, which with the decline of tobacco production had seemed for a time to be a dwindling institution, expanded and firmly fixed itself upon the South. The large supply of domestically produced fiber also served as a strong incentive to entrepreneurs in New England and elsewhere to develop a native textile industry.

Whitney was an important figure in the history of American technology for another reason as well—as a major figure in introducing the concept of interchangeable parts to the United States. As machines such as the cotton gin began to be widely used, it became increasingly important that owners of such machines have access to spare parts—and that the parts be made so that they would fit the machines properly. Whitney not only designed the cotton gin, therefore, but designed machine tools that could manufacture its component parts to exact specifications. Thus a cotton gin in Alabama would be identical to one in Georgia, and could use the same parts. The U.S. government later commissioned Whitney to manufacture 1,000 muskets for the army. Each part of the gun had to be interchangeable with the equivalent part in every other gun.

Interchangeability was of great importance in the United States because of the vast size of the nation, the great distances many people had to travel to reach towns or cities, and the relatively limited transportation systems available to them. Many people, farmers in particular, lived far from skilled toolmakers and other craftsmen. Interchangeable parts meant that a farmer could repair a machine himself rather than transport it over great distances to a machine shop or armory. But the interchangeability that Whitney championed was not easy to achieve. In theory, many parts were designed to be interchangeable. In reality, the actual manufacturing of such parts was for many years not nearly as precise as it was supposed to be. Farmers and others often had to do considerable fitting before the parts would work in their equipment. Not until later in the nineteenth century would machine tools be developed to the point that parts could be made truly interchangeable.

Transportation Innovations

One of the prerequisites for industrialization is a transportation system that allows the efficient movement of raw materials to factories and of finished goods to markets. The United States had no such system in the early years of the republic, and thus it had no domestic market extensive enough to justify large-scale production. But projects were under way that would ultimately remove the transportation obstacle.

One such project was the development of the steamboat. England had pioneered steam power, and even steam navigation, in the eighteenth century, and there had been experiments in America in the 1780s and 1790s in various forms of steam-powered transportation. John Fitch attached a small steam engine to a series of oars on a boat in 1787. Two years later, Oliver Evans received the first U.S. patent for a steam-powered boat. A major advance over these early efforts emerged out of the efforts of the inventor Robert Fulton and the promoter Robert R. Livingston, who made significant advances in steam-powered navigation that made possible the launching of a steamboat large enough to carry passengers. Their *Clermont*, equipped with paddle wheels and an English-built engine, sailed up the Hudson in the summer of 1807.

Meanwhile, what was to become known as the "turnpike era" had begun. There was no public sentiment on behalf of using government funds to build roads, so Americans turned to a method that had been introduced to England in the 1660s: allowing private companies to build roads and then to charge a fee to those who used them. In 1794, a corporation constructed a toll road running the sixty miles from Philadelphia to Lancaster, Pennsylvania, with a hard-packed surface of crushed stone, which provided a good year-round surface with effective drainage (but was very expensive to use). The Pennsylvania venture proved so successful that similar turnpikes (so named from the kind of tollgate frequently used) were laid out from other cities to neighboring towns.

The process of building the turnpikes was a difficult one. Companies had to survey their routes with many things in mind, particularly elevation. Horse-drawn vehicles had great difficulty traveling along roads with more than a five-degree incline, which required many roads to take very circuitous routes to avoid climbing straight up steep hills. Building roads over mountains was an almost insurmountable task, and no company was successful in doing so until governments began to participate in the financing of the projects.

Country and City

Despite all the changes, America remained in the early nineteenth century an overwhelmingly rural and agrarian nation. Only 3 percent of the population lived in towns of more than 8,000 in 1800. Even the nation's largest cities could not begin to compare, either in size or in cultural sophistication, with such European capitals as London and Paris (although Philadelphia, with 70,000 residents, New York, with 60,000, and others were becoming centers of commerce, learning, and urban culture comparable to many of the secondary cities of Europe).

People who lived in cities and towns lived differently from the vast majority of Americans who continued to work as farmers. Among other things, urban life produced affluence, and affluent people sought amenities that would not have entered the imaginings of all but the wealthiest farmers. They sought increasing elegance and refinement in their homes, their grounds, and their dress. They also looked for diversions—music, theater, dancing, and, for many people, one of the most popular entertainments of all, horse racing. It was natural that horse racing would appeal to Americans in this era, when horses were a daily part of life and virtually the only means of transportation other than walking for most people. Informal horse racing had begun as early as the 1620s, and the first formal race course opened near New York City in 1665. By the early nineteenth century, horse racing was a popular activity in most areas of the country, and many cities had heavily attended race tracks. Many of the best jockeys were African Americans (some of them young male slaves trained to race the masters' horses). The crowds that gathered at horse races were an early sign of the vast appetite for popular, public entertainments that would be an enduring part of American culture—and a powerful force unifying an otherwise fragmented nation.

It was still possible for some to believe in the early eighteenth century that this small, half-formed nation might not become a complex modern society. But the forces already at work would soon lastingly transform the United States. And Thomas Jefferson, for all his commitment to the agrarian ideal, found himself, as president, obliged to confront and accommodate them.

JEFFERSON THE PRESIDENT

Privately, Thomas Jefferson may well have considered his victory over John Adams in 1800 to be what he later termed it: a revolution "as real . . . as that of 1776." Publicly, however, he was restrained and conciliatory, attempting to minimize the differences between the two parties and calm the passions that the bitter campaign had aroused. There was no complete repudiation of Federalist policies, no true "revolution." Indeed, at times Jefferson seemed to outdo the Federalists at their own work—most notably in overseeing a remarkable expansion of the territory of the United States.

The Federal City and the "People's President"

The relative unimportance of the federal government during the Jeffersonian era was symbolized by the character of the newly founded national capital, the city of Washington. John Adams had moved to the new seat of government during the last year of his administration. And there were many at that time who envisioned that the raw, uncompleted town would soon emerge as a great and majestic city. The French architect Pierre

THOMAS JEFFERSON This 1805 portrait by the noted American painter Rembrandt Peale shows Jefferson at the beginning of his second term as president. It also conveys (through the simplicity of dress and the slightly unkempt hair) the image of democratic simplicity that Jefferson liked to project as the champion of the "common man."

L'Enfant had designed the capital on a grand scale. Many Americans believed Washington would become the Paris of the United States.

In reality, throughout Jefferson's presidency—indeed, throughout most of the nineteenth century—Washington remained little more than a straggling, provincial village. Although the population increased steadily from the 3,200 counted in the 1800 census, it never rivaled that of New York, Philadelphia, or the other major cities of the nation. The city remained a raw, inhospitable community, with few public buildings of any consequence. Members of Congress viewed Washington not as a home but as a place to visit briefly during sessions of the legislature and leave as quickly as possible. Most lived in a cluster of simple boardinghouses in the vicinity of the Capitol. It was not unusual for a member of Congress to resign his seat in the midst of a session to return home if he had an opportunity to accept the more prestigious post of member of his state legislature.

Jefferson was a wealthy and aristocratic planter by background, but as president he conveyed to the public an image of plain, almost crude disdain for pretension. He walked like an ordinary citizen to and from his inauguration at the Capitol, instead of riding in a coach at the head of a procession. In the presidential mansion, which had not yet acquired the name "White House," he disregarded the courtly etiquette of his predecessors. He did not always bother to dress up, prompting the British ambassador to complain on one occasion of being received by the president in clothes that were "indicative of utter slovenliness and indifference to appearances."

Yet Jefferson managed nevertheless to impress most of those who knew him. He was a brilliant conversationalist, a gifted writer, and one of the nation's most intelligent and creative men, with a wider range of interests and accomplishments than any major public figure in American history with the possible exception of Benjamin Franklin. In addition to politics and diplomacy, he was an active architect, educator, inventor, scientific farmer, and philosopher-scientist.

Jefferson was, above all, a shrewd and practical politician. He went to great lengths to eliminate the aura of majesty surrounding the presidency that he believed his predecessors had created. But he also worked hard to exert influence as the leader of his party, giving direction to Republicans in Congress by quiet and sometimes even devious means. Although the Republicans had objected strenuously to the efforts of their Federalist predecessors to build a network of influence through patronage, Jefferson used his powers of appointment as an effective political weapon. Like Washington before him, he believed that federal offices should be filled with men loyal to the principles and policies of the administration. By the end of his second term practically all federal jobs were held by loyal Republicans. Jefferson was a popular president during his first term and had little difficulty winning reelection against the Federalist Charles C. Pinckney in 1804. The Republican ticket carried even the New England states (except Connecticut), and Jefferson won by the overwhelming electoral majority of 162 to 14. Republican membership of both houses of Congress increased.

Dollars and Ships

Under Washington and Adams, the Republicans believed, the government had been needlessly extravagant. Yearly federal expenditures had nearly tripled between 1793 and 1800. The public debt had also risen, as Hamilton had intended. And an extensive system of internal taxation, including the hated whiskey excise tax, had been erected.

The Jefferson administration moved deliberately to reverse these trends. In 1802, the president persuaded Congress to abolish all internal taxes, leaving customs duties and the sale of western lands as the only sources of revenue for the government. Meanwhile, Secretary of the Treasury Albert Gallatin drastically reduced government spending, cutting the already small staffs of the executive departments to minuscule levels. Although Jefferson was unable entirely to retire the national debt as he had hoped, he did cut it almost in half (from $83 million to $45 million).

Jefferson also scaled down the armed forces. He reduced the already tiny army of 4,000 men to 2,500. He pared down the navy from twenty-five ships in commission to seven, cutting the number of officers and sailors accordingly. Anything but the smallest of standing armies, he argued, might menace civil liberties and civilian control of government. And a large navy, he feared, might be misused to promote overseas commerce, which Jefferson believed should remain secondary to agriculture. Yet Jefferson was not a pacifist. At the same time that he was reducing the size of the army and navy, he helped establish the United States Military Academy at West Point, founded in 1802. And when trouble started brewing overseas, he began again to build up the fleet. Such trouble appeared first in the Mediterranean, off the coast of northern Africa. For years the Barbary states of North Africa—Morocco, Algiers, Tunis, and Tripoli—had been demanding protection money, paid to avoid piracy, from all nations whose ships sailed the Mediterranean. Even Great Britain gave regular contributions to the pirates. During the 1780s and 1790s the United States, too, had agreed to treaties providing for annual tribute to the Barbary states, but Jefferson showed reluctance to continue this policy of appeasement.

In 1801, the pasha of Tripoli forced Jefferson's hand. Unhappy with American responses to his demands, he ordered the flagpole of the American consulate chopped down—a symbolic declaration of war. Jefferson responded cautiously and built up American naval forces in the area over the next several years. Finally, in 1805, he agreed to terms by which the United States ended the payment of tribute to Tripoli but paid a substantial (and humiliating) ransom for the release of American prisoners.

Conflict with the Courts

Having won control of the executive and legislative branches of government, the Republicans looked with suspicion on the judiciary, which remained largely in the hands of Federalist judges. Soon after Jefferson's first inauguration, his followers in Congress launched an attack on this last preserve of the opposition. Their first step was the repeal of the Judiciary Act of 1801, thus eliminating the judgeships to which Adams had made his "midnight appointments."

The debate over the courts led to one of the most important judicial decisions in the history of the nation. Federalists had long maintained that the Supreme Court had the authority to nullify acts of Congress (although the Constitution said nothing specifically to support the claim), and the Court itself had actually exercised the power of judicial review in 1796 when it upheld the validity of a law passed by Congress. But the Court's authority in this area would not be secure, it was clear, until it actually declared a congressional act unconstitutional. In 1803, in the case of *Marbury* v. *Madison*, it did so. William Marbury, one of Adams's "midnight appointments," had been named a justice of the peace in the District of Columbia. But his commission, although signed and sealed, had not been delivered to him before Adams left office. When Jefferson took office, his secretary of state, James Madison, refused to hand over the commission. Marbury asked the Supreme Court to direct Madison to perform his official duty. But the Court ruled that while Marbury had a right to his commission, the Court had no authority to order Madison to deliver it. On the surface, therefore, the decision was a victory for the administration. But of much greater importance than the relatively insignificant matter of Marbury's commission was the Court's reasoning in the decision.

The original Judiciary Act of 1789 had given the Court the power to compel executive officials to act in such matters as the delivery of commissions, and it was on that basis that Marbury had filed his suit. But the Court ruled that Congress had exceeded its authority, that the Constitution defined the powers of the judiciary, and that the legislature had no right to expand them. The relevant section of the 1789 act was, therefore, void. In seeming to deny its own authority, the Court was in fact radically enlarging it. The justices had repudiated a relatively minor power (the power to force the delivery of a commission) by asserting a vastly greater one (the power to nullify an act of Congress).

The chief justice of the United States at the time of the ruling (and until 1835) was John Marshall, one of the towering figures in the history of American law. A leading Federalist and prominent Virginia lawyer, he had served John Adams as secretary of state. (It was Marshall, ironically, who had neglected to deliver Marbury's commission in the closing hours of the administration.) In 1801, just before leaving office, Adams had appointed him chief justice, and almost immediately Marshall established himself as the dominant figure of the Court, shaping virtually all its most important rulings—including, of course, *Marbury* v. *Madison*. Through a succession of Republican presidents, he battled to give the federal government unity and strength. And in so doing, he established the judiciary as a coequal branch of government with the executive and the legislature—a position that the founders of the republic had never clearly indicated it should occupy.

DOUBLING THE NATIONAL DOMAIN

In the same year Jefferson was elected president of the United States, Napoleon Bonaparte made himself ruler of France with the title of first consul. In the year Jefferson was reelected, Napoleon named himself emperor. The two men had little in common. Yet for a time they were of great assistance to each other in international politics—until Napoleon's ambitions moved from Europe to America and created conflict and estrangement.

Jefferson and Napoleon

Having failed in a grandiose plan to seize India from the British Empire, Napoleon began to dream of restoring French power in the New World. The territory east of the Mississippi, which France had ceded to Great Britain in 1763, was now part of the United States and lost forever. But Napoleon hoped to regain the lands west of the Mississippi, which belonged to Spain. In 1800, under the secret Treaty of San Ildefonso, France regained title to Louisiana, which included almost the whole of the Mississippi Valley to the west of the river, plus New Orleans near the river's mouth. The Louisiana Territory would, Napoleon hoped, become the heart of a great French empire in America.

Jefferson was unaware at first of Napoleon's imperial ambitions in America, and for a time he pursued a foreign policy that reflected his well-known admiration for France. But he began to reassess American relations with the French when he heard rumors of the secret transfer of Louisiana. Particularly troubling to Jefferson was French control of New Orleans, the outlet through which the produce of the fast-growing western regions of the United States was shipped to the markets of the world. If France should actually take and hold New Orleans, Jefferson said, then "we must marry ourselves to the British fleet and nation."

Jefferson was even more alarmed when, in the fall of 1802, he learned that the Spanish intendant at New Orleans (who still governed the city, since the French had not yet taken formal possession of the region) had announced a disturbing new regulation. American ships sailing the Mississippi River had for many years been accustomed to depositing their cargoes in New Orleans for transfer to oceangoing vessels. The intendant now forbade the practice, even though Spain had guaranteed Americans that right in the Pinckney Treaty of 1795; the prohibition effectively closed the lower Mississippi to American shippers.

Westerners demanded that the federal government do something to reopen the river, and the president faced a dilemma. If he yielded to the frontier clamor and tried to change the policy by force, he would run the risk of a major war with France. If he ignored the westerners' demands, he might lose political support. But Jefferson saw another solution. He instructed Robert Livingston, the American ambassador in Paris, to negotiate for the purchase of New Orleans. Livingston, on his own authority, proposed that the French sell the United States the rest of Louisiana as well.

In the meantime, Jefferson persuaded Congress to appropriate funds for an expansion of the army and the construction of a river fleet, and he hinted that American forces might soon descend on New Orleans and that the United States might form an alliance with Great Britain if the problems with France were not resolved. Perhaps in response, Napoleon suddenly decided to offer the United States the entire Louisiana Territory.

Napoleon had good reasons for the decision. His plans for an empire in America had already gone seriously awry, partly because a yellow fever epidemic had wiped out much of the French army in the New World and partly because the expeditionary force he wished to send to reinforce the troops and take possession of Louisiana had been icebound in a Dutch harbor through the winter of 1802–1803. By the time the harbor thawed in the spring of 1803, Napoleon was preparing for a renewed war in Europe. He would not, he realized, have the resources to secure an empire in America.

The Louisiana Purchase

Faced with Napoleon's sudden proposal, Livingston and James Monroe, whom Jefferson had sent to Paris to assist in the negotiations, had to decide whether they should accept it even if they had no authorization from their government to do so. But fearful that Napoleon might withdraw the offer, they decided to proceed without further instructions from home. After some haggling over the price, Livingston and Monroe signed an agreement with Napoleon on April 30, 1803.

By the terms of the treaty, the United States was to pay a total of 80 million francs ($15 million) to the French government. The United States was also to grant certain exclusive commercial privileges to France in the port of New Orleans and was to incorporate the residents of Louisiana into the Union with the same rights and privileges as other citizens. The boundaries of the purchase were not clearly defined; the treaty simply specified that Louisiana would consist of the same territory France and Spain had claimed.

In Washington, the president was both pleased and embarrassed when he received the treaty. He was pleased with the terms of the bargain; but because he believed the Constitution should be strictly observed, he was uncertain about his authority to accept it, since the Constitution said nothing about the acquisition of new territory. But Jefferson's advisers persuaded him that his treaty-making power under the Constitution would justify the purchase of Louisiana, and Congress promptly approved the treaty and appropriated money to implement it. Finally, late in 1803, General James Wilkinson, commissioner of the United States and the commander of a small occupation force, took formal control of the territory on behalf of the United States. In New Orleans, beneath a bright December sun, the French tricolor was lowered and the American flag raised.

Before long, the Louisiana Territory was organized on the general pattern of the Northwest Territory, with the assumption that it would be divided eventually into states. The first of these was admitted to the Union as the state of Louisiana in 1812.

Exploring the West

Meanwhile, a series of explorations was revealing the geography of the far-flung new territory to white Americans. In 1803, even before Napoleon's offer to sell Louisiana, Jefferson helped plan an expedition that was to cross the continent to the Pacific Ocean, gather geographical facts, and investigate prospects for trade with the Indians. He named as its leader his private secretary and Virginia neighbor, the thirty-two-year-old Meriwether Lewis, a veteran of Indian wars who was skilled in the ways of the wilderness. Lewis chose as a colleague the twenty-eight-year-old William Clark, who—like George Rogers Clark, his older brother—was an experienced frontiersman and Indian fighter. In the spring of 1804, Lewis and Clark, with a company of four dozen men, started up the Missouri River from St. Louis. With the Shoshone woman Sacajawea as their interpreter, they eventually crossed the Rocky Mountains, descended

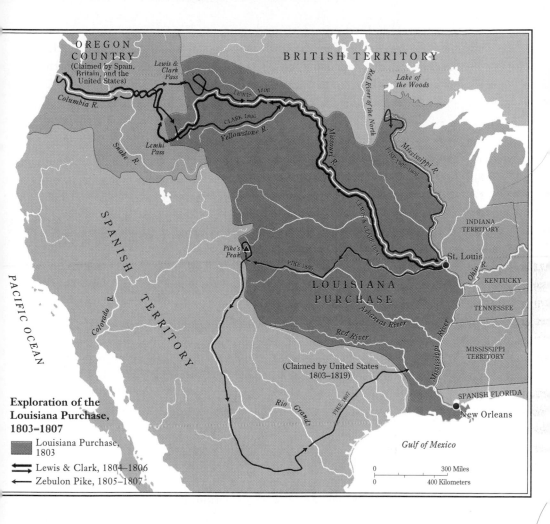

Exploration of the Louisiana Purchase, 1803–1807

Louisiana Purchase, 1803

Lewis & Clark, 1804–1806

Zebulon Pike, 1805–1807

along the Snake and Columbia Rivers, and in the late autumn of 1805 camped on the Pacific coast. In September 1806, they were back in St. Louis with elaborate records of the geography and the Indian civilizations they had observed along the way.

While Lewis and Clark were on their journey, Jefferson dispatched other explorers to other parts of the Louisiana Territory. Lieutenant Zebulon Montgomery Pike, twenty-six years old, led an expedition in the fall of 1805 from St. Louis into the upper Mississippi Valley. In the summer of 1806, he set out again, proceeding up the valley of the Arkansas River and into what later became Colorado, where he encountered, but failed in his attempt to climb, the peak that now bears his name. His account of his western travels helped create an enduring (and inaccurate) impression among most Americans that the land between the Missouri and the Rockies was a desert that farmers could never cultivate and that would be left forever to the nomadic Indian tribes.

The Burr Conspiracy

Jefferson's triumphant reelection in 1804 suggested that most of the nation approved the new territorial acquisition. But some New England Federalists raged against it. They realized that the more the West grew and the more new states joined the Union, the less power the Federalists and their region would retain. In Massachusetts, a group of the most extreme Federalists, known as the Essex Junto, concluded that the only recourse for New England was to secede from the Union and form a separate "northern confederacy." If a northern confederacy was to have any hope for lasting success as a separate nation, the Federalists believed, it would have to include New York and New Jersey as well as New England. But the leading Federalist in New York, Alexander Hamilton, refused to support the secessionist scheme.

Federalists in New York then turned to Hamilton's greatest political rival: Vice President Aaron Burr, a politician without prospects in his own party, because Jefferson had never forgiven him for the 1800 election deadlock. Burr accepted a Federalist proposal that he become their candidate for governor of New York in 1804, and there were rumors (unsupported by any evidence) that he had also agreed to support the Federalist plans for secession. Hamilton accused Burr of plotting treason and made numerous private remarks, widely reported in the press, about Burr's "despicable" character. When Burr lost the election, he blamed his defeat on Hamilton's malevolence and challenged him to a duel. Hamilton feared that refusing Burr's challenge would brand him a coward. And so, on a July morning in 1804, the two men met at Weehawken, New Jersey. Hamilton was mortally wounded; he died the next day.

The resourceful and charismatic Burr was now a political outcast, who had to flee New York to avoid an indictment for murder. He found new outlets for his ambitions in the West. Even before the duel, he had begun corresponding with prominent white settlers in the Southwest, especially with General James Wilkinson, now governor of the Louisiana Territory. Burr and Wilkinson, it seems clear, hoped to lead an expedition that would capture Mexico from the Spanish. But there were also rumors that they wanted to separate the Southwest from the Union and create a western empire that Burr would rule. There is little evidence that these rumors were true.

Whether true or not, many of Burr's opponents chose to believe the rumors—including, ultimately, Jefferson himself. When Burr led a group of armed followers down the Ohio River by boat in 1806, disturbing reports flowed into Washington (the most alarming from Wilkinson, who had suddenly turned against Burr and who now informed the president that treason was afoot) that an attack on New Orleans was imminent. Jefferson ordered the arrest of Burr and his men as traitors. Burr was brought to Richmond for trial. Jefferson carefully managed the government's case from Washington. But Chief Justice Marshall, presiding over the case on circuit duty, limited the evidence the government could present and defined the charge in such a way that the jury had little choice but to acquit Burr.

The Burr conspiracy was in part the story of a single man's soaring ambitions and flamboyant personality. But it was also a symbol of the larger perils still facing the new nation. With a central government that remained deliberately weak, with vast tracts of land only nominally controlled by the United States, with ambitious political leaders willing, if necessary, to circumvent normal channels in their search for power, the legitimacy of the federal government—and indeed the existence of the United States as a stable and united nation—remained to be fully established.

EXPANSION AND WAR

Two very different conflicts were taking shape in the last years of Jefferson's presidency that would, together, draw the United States into a difficult and frustrating war. One was the continuing tension in Europe, which in 1803 escalated once again into a full-scale conflict (the Napoleonic Wars). As fighting between the British and the French increased, each side took steps to prevent the United States from trading with (and thus assisting) the other. The other conflict occurred in North America itself, a result of the ceaseless westward expansion of white settlement, which was now stretching to the Mississippi River and beyond, colliding again with a native population committed to protecting its lands from intruders. In both the North and the South, the threatened tribes mobilized to resist white encroachments. They began as well to forge connections with British forces in Canada and Spanish forces in Florida. The Indian conflict on land, therefore, became intertwined with the European conflict on the seas, and ultimately helped cause the War of 1812, an unpopular conflict with ambiguous results.

Conflict on the Seas

Politicians at the time, and historians since, have argued over whether the conflict in the West or the conflict on the seas was the real cause of the War of 1812. In fact, the war was a result of both.

In 1805, at the Battle of Trafalgar, a British fleet virtually destroyed what was left of the French navy. Because France could no longer challenge the British at sea, Napoleon now chose to pressure England in other ways. The result was what he called the Continental System, designed to close the European continent to British trade. Napoleon issued a series of decrees (one in Berlin in 1806 and another in Milan in 1807) barring British ships and neutral ships touching at British ports from landing their cargoes at any European port controlled by France or its allies. The British government replied to Napoleon's decrees by establishing—through a series of "orders in council"—a blockade of the European coast. The blockade required that any goods being shipped to Napoleon's Europe be carried either in British vessels or in neutral vessels stopping at British ports—precisely what Napoleon's policies forbade.

In the early nineteenth century, the United States had developed one of the most important merchant marines in the world, one that soon controlled a large proportion of the trade between Europe and the West Indies. But the events in Europe now challenged that control, because American ships were caught between Napoleon's Berlin and Milan decrees and Britain's orders in council. If they sailed directly for the European continent, they risked being captured by the British navy. If they sailed by way of a British port, they ran the risk of seizure by the French. Both of the warring powers were violating America's rights as a neutral nation. But most Americans considered the British, with their greater sea power, the worse offender—especially since British vessels frequently stopped American ships on the high seas and seized sailors off the decks, making them victims of "impressment."

Impressment

British sailors called their navy—with its floggings, its low pay, and its terrible shipboard conditions—a "floating hell." Few volunteered. Most had had to be "impressed" (forced) into the service. At every opportunity they deserted. By 1807, many of these deserters had emigrated to the United States and joined the American merchant marine or the American navy. To check this loss of manpower, the British claimed the right to stop and search

American merchantmen (although not naval vessels) and reimpress deserters. They did not claim the right to take native-born Americans, but they did insist on the right to seize naturalized Americans born on British soil. In practice, the British navy often made no careful distinctions, impressing British deserters and native-born Americans alike into their service.

In the summer of 1807, the British went to more provocative extremes in an incident involving a vessel of the American navy. Sailing from Norfolk, with several alleged deserters from the British navy among the crew, the American naval frigate *Chesapeake* was hailed by the British ship *Leopard*. When the American commander, James Barron, refused to allow the British to search the *Chesapeake*, the *Leopard* opened fire. Barron had no choice but to surrender, and a boarding party from the *Leopard* dragged four men off the American frigate.

When news of the *Chesapeake-Leopard* incident reached the United States, there was a great popular clamor for revenge. But Jefferson and Madison tried to maintain the peace. Jefferson expelled all British warships from American waters to lessen the likelihood of future incidents. Then he sent instructions to his minister in England, James Monroe, to demand from the British government an end to impressment. The British government disavowed the actions of the *Leopard's* commanding officer and recalled him; it offered compensation for those killed and wounded in the incident; and it promised to return three of the captured sailors (one of the original four had been hanged). But the British cabinet refused to renounce impressment and instead reasserted its right to recover deserting seamen.

"Peaceable Coercion"

In an effort to prevent future incidents that might bring the nation again to the brink of war, Jefferson persuaded Congress to pass a drastic measure late in 1807. It was known as the Embargo, and it prohibited American ships from leaving the United States for any foreign port anywhere in the world. (If it had specified only British and French ports, Jefferson reasoned, it could have been evaded with false clearance papers.)

The law was widely evaded, but it was effective enough to create a serious depression throughout most of the nation. Hardest hit were the merchants and shipowners of the Northeast, most of them Federalists. Their once-lucrative shipping business came to a virtual standstill. They became convinced that Jefferson had acted unconstitutionally.

The presidential election of 1808 came in the midst of this Embargo-induced depression. James Madison, Jefferson's secretary of state and political ally, was elected president, but the Federalist candidate, Charles Pinckney again, ran much more strongly than he had in 1804. The Federalists gained seats in Congress, although the Republicans still controlled both houses. The Embargo was clearly a growing political liability, and Jefferson decided to back down. A few days before leaving office, he approved a bill ending his experiment with what he called "peaceable coercion."

To replace the Embargo, Congress passed the Non-Intercourse Act just before Madison took office. It reopened trade with all nations but Great Britain and France. A year later, in 1810, the Non-Intercourse Act expired and was replaced by Macon's Bill No. 2, which reopened free commercial relations with Britain and France but authorized the president to prohibit commerce with either belligerent if it should continue violating neutral shipping after the other had stopped. Napoleon, in an effort to induce the United States to reimpose the Embargo against Britain, announced that France would no longer interfere with American shipping. Madison announced that an embargo against Great Britain alone would automatically go into effect early in 1811 unless Britain renounced its restrictions on American shipping.

In time, this new, limited embargo persuaded England to repeal its blockade of Europe. But the repeal came too late to prevent war. In any case, naval policies were only part of the reason for tensions between Britain and the United States.

The "Indian Problem" and the British

Given the ruthlessness with which white settlers in North America had dislodged Indian tribes to make room for expanding settlement, it was hardly surprising that ever since the Revolution most Indians had continued to look to England—which had historically attempted to limit western expansion—for protection. The British in Canada, for their part, had relied on the Indians as partners in the lucrative fur trade and as potential military allies. There had been relative peace in the Northwest for over a decade after Jay's Treaty and Anthony Wayne's victory over the tribes at Fallen Timbers in 1794. But the 1807 war crisis following the *Chesapeake-Leopard* incident revived the conflict between Indians and white settlers. Two important (and very different) men emerged to lead it: William Henry Harrison and Tecumseh.

The Virginia-born Harrison, already a veteran Indian fighter at age twenty-six, went to Washington as the congressional delegate from the

Northwest Territory in 1799. He was a committed advocate of growth and development in the western lands, and he was largely responsible for the passage in 1800 of the so-called Harrison Land Law, which enabled white settlers to acquire farms from the public domain on much easier terms than before.

In 1801, Jefferson appointed Harrison governor of Indiana Territory to administer the president's proposed solution to the "Indian problem." Jefferson offered the Indians a choice: they could convert themselves into settled farmers and become a part of white society, or they could migrate west of the Mississippi. In either case, they would have to give up their claims to their tribal lands in the Northwest.

Jefferson considered the assimilation policy a benign alternative to the continuing conflict between Indians and white settlers, a conflict he assumed the tribes were destined to lose. But to the tribes, the new policy seemed far from benign, especially given the bludgeonlike efficiency with which Harrison set out to implement it. He played one tribe against another and used threats, bribes, trickery, and whatever other tactics he felt would help him. By 1807, the United States had extracted treaty rights to eastern Michigan, southern Indiana, and most of Illinois from reluctant tribal leaders.

Meanwhile, in the Southwest, white Americans were taking millions of acres from other tribes in Georgia, Tennessee, and Mississippi. The Indians wanted desperately to resist, but the separate tribes were helpless by themselves against the power of the United States. They might have accepted their fate passively but for the emergence of two new factors.

One factor was the policy of British authorities in Canada. After the *Chesapeake* incident and the surge of anti-British feeling throughout the United States, the British colonial authorities began to expect an American invasion of Canada and took desperate measures for their own defense. Among those measures were efforts to renew friendship with the Indians and provide them with increased supplies.

Tecumseh and the Prophet

The second, and more important, factor intensifying the border conflict was the rise of two remarkable native leaders. One was Tenskwatawa, a charismatic religious leader and orator known as "the Prophet." He had experienced a mystical awakening in the process of recovering from alcoholism. Having freed himself from what he considered the evil effects of white culture, he began to speak to his people of the superior virtues of

Indian civilization and the sinfulness and corruption of the white world. In the process, he inspired a religious revival that spread through numerous tribes and helped unite them. The Prophet's headquarters at the meeting of Tippecanoe Creek and the Wabash River (known as Prophetstown) became a sacred place for people of many tribes and attracted thousands of Indians from throughout the Midwest. Out of their common religious experiences, they began to consider joint political and military efforts as well.

The Prophet's brother Tecumseh—"the Shooting Star," chief of the Shawnees—emerged as the leader of these more secular efforts. Tecumseh understood, as few other Indian leaders had, that only through united action could the tribes hope to resist the steady advance of white civilization. Beginning in 1809, he set out to unite all the tribes of the Mississippi Valley, north and south into what became known as the Tecumseh Confederacy. Together, he promised, they would halt white expansion, recover the whole Northwest, and make the Ohio River the boundary between the United States and Indian country. He maintained that Harrison and others, by negotiating treaties with individual tribes, had obtained no real title to land. The land belonged to all the tribes; none of them could rightfully cede any of it without the consent of the others. In 1811, Tecumseh left Prophetstown and traveled down the Mississippi to visit the tribes of the South and persuade them to join the alliance.

During Tecumseh's absence, Governor Harrison saw a chance to destroy the growing influence of the two Indian leaders. With 1,000 soldiers he camped near Prophetstown, and on November 7, 1811, he provoked an armed conflict. Although the white forces suffered losses as heavy as those of the natives, Harrison drove off the Indians and burned the town. The Battle of Tippecanoe (named for the creek near which it was fought) disillusioned many of the Prophet's followers, who had believed that his magic would protect them; and Tecumseh returned to find the confederacy in disarray. But there were still warriors eager for combat, and by spring of 1812 they were active along the frontier, from Michigan to Mississippi, raiding white settlements and terrifying settlers.

The bloodshed along the western borders was largely a result of the Indians' own initiative, but Britain's agents in Canada had encouraged and helped to supply the uprising. To Harrison and most white residents of the regions, there seemed only one way to make the West safe for Americans: to drive the British out of Canada and annex that province to the

United States—a goal that many westerners had long cherished for other reasons as well.

Florida and War Fever

While white "frontiersmen" in the North demanded the conquest of Canada, those in the South looked to the acquisition of Spanish Florida (a territory that included the present state of Florida and the southern areas of what are now Alabama, Mississippi, and Louisiana). The territory was a continuing threat to whites in the southern United States. Slaves escaped across the Florida border; Indians in Florida launched frequent raids north into white settlements along the border. But white southerners also coveted Florida because through it ran rivers that could provide residents of the Southwest with access to valuable ports on the Gulf of Mexico.

In 1810, American settlers in West Florida (the area presently part of Mississippi and Louisiana) seized the Spanish fort at Baton Rouge and asked the federal government to annex the territory to the United States. President Madison happily agreed and then began planning to get the rest of Florida, too. The desire for Florida became yet another motivation for war with Britain. Spain was Britain's ally, and a war with England might provide an excuse for taking Spanish as well as British territory.

By 1812, therefore, war fever was raging on both the northern and southern borders of the United States. The demands of the residents of these areas found substantial support in Washington among a group of determined young congressmen who soon earned the name "War Hawks."

In the congressional elections of 1810, voters elected a large number of representatives of both parties eager for war with Britain. These congressmen represented a new generation, aggressive and impatient. The most influential of them came from the new states in the West or from the backcountry of the old states in the South. Two of their leaders, both recently elected to the House of Representatives, were Henry Clay of Kentucky and John C. Calhoun of South Carolina, men of great intellect, magnetism, and ambition who would play a large role in national politics for nearly forty years. Both were supporters of war with Great Britain.

Clay was elected Speaker of the House in 1811, and he appointed Calhoun to the crucial Committee on Foreign Affairs. Both men began agitating for the conquest of Canada. Madison still preferred peace but was losing control of Congress. On June 18, 1812, he approved a declaration of war against Britain.

THE WAR OF 1812

Preoccupied with their struggle against Napoleon in Europe, the British were not eager for an open conflict with the United States. Even after the Americans declared war, Britain largely ignored them for a time. But in the fall of 1812, Napoleon launched a catastrophic campaign against Russia that left his army in disarray and his power in Europe diminished. By late 1813, with the French empire on its way to final defeat, Britain was able to turn its military attention to America.

Battles with the Tribes

Americans entered the War of 1812 with great enthusiasm, but events on the battlefield soon cooled their ardor. In the summer of 1812, American forces invaded Canada through Detroit. They soon had to retreat back to Detroit and in August surrendered the fort there. Other invasion efforts also failed. In the meantime, Fort Dearborn (later Chicago) fell before an Indian attack.

Things went only slightly better for the United States on the seas. At first, American frigates won some spectacular victories over British warships. But by 1813, the British navy was counterattacking effectively, driving the American frigates to cover and imposing a blockade on the United States.

The United States did, however, achieve significant early military successes on the Great Lakes. First, the Americans took command of Lake Ontario; this permitted them to raid and burn York (now Toronto), the capital of Canada. American forces then seized control of Lake Erie, mainly through the work of the young Oliver Hazard Perry, who engaged and dispersed a British fleet at Put-in Bay on September 10, 1813. This made possible, at last, an invasion of Canada by way of Detroit, which Americans could now reach easily by water. William Henry Harrison, the American commander in the West, pushed up the river Thames into upper Canada and on October 5, 1813, won a victory notable for the death of Tecumseh, who was serving as a brigadier general in the British army. The Battle of the Thames resulted in no lasting occupation of Canada, but it weakened and disheartened the Indians of the Northwest and greatly diminished their ability to defend their claims to the region.

In the meantime, another white military leader was striking an even harder blow at the Indians of the Southwest. The Creeks, aroused by Tecumseh on a southern visit and supplied by the Spaniards in Florida, had been attacking white settlers near the Florida border. Andrew Jackson, a

The War of 1812

NAVAL AND TROOP MOVEMENTS
⬅ American forces
⬅ British forces
◣◣◣ British blockade

BATTLES
✷ American victory
✸ British victory
✩ Indian battles

Lake Superior

BRITISH AMERICA

Quebec

MAINE (Mass.)

Eastport

Halifax

Montreal

Machias

Bangor

Waterville

Castine
Sept. 1814

Fort Mackinac
surrendered to British
July 1812

Lake Huron

Kingston

Sackett's Harbor

VT.

N.H.

Portland

MICHIGAN TERRITORY

Lake Michigan

Lake Ontario

Fort Ticonderoga

NEW YORK

MASS.

Boston

Lake Erie

CONN.

R.I.

Fort Dearborn
surrendered to British
Aug. 1812

INDIANA TERR.

PENNSYLVANIA

N.J.

New York

ILLINOIS TERRITORY

OHIO

Pittsburgh

Philadelphia

Tippecanoe
Nov. 7, 1811

HARRISON 1811

MD.

DEL.

Wabash R.

MISSOURI TERRITORY

KENTUCKY

VIRGINIA

Norfolk

1814

TENNESSEE

NORTH CAROLINA

Wilmington

MISSISSIPPI TERRITORY

Talladega
Nov. 9, 1813

GEORGIA

SOUTH CAROLINA

Charleston

Fort Jackson

Horseshoe Bend
Mar. 05, 1814

LA.

Vicksburg

JACKSON 1813

Savannah

Fort Mims Massacre
Aug. 30, 1813

Natchez

JACKSON 1814–1815

Pensacola
Nov. 7, 1814

Fort Bowyer
Sept. 15, 1814

ATLANTIC OCEAN

New Orleans
Jan. 8, 1815

Gulf of Mexico

1814

SPANISH FLORIDA

0   200 Miles
0   200 Kilometers

PENNSYLVANIA

MARYLAND

Godly Wood
Sept. 12, 1814

Baltimore

Fort McHenry
bombardment
Sept. 13–14, 1814

DELAWARE

Washington
burned
Aug. 24, 1814

Chesapeake Bay

VIRGINIA

Lake Michigan

Lake Huron

St. Lawrence R.

PREVOST–DOWNIE 1814

Châteaugay
Oct. 23, 1813

Chrysler's Farm
Nov. 11, 1813

LaColle Mill
March 1814

MICHIGAN TERRITORY

HARRISON 1813

York (Toronto)
April 27, 1813

MAINE (Mass.)

Fort Detroit
surrendered to British
July 1812

Battle of the Thames
Oct. 5, 1813

DEARBORN 1813

Plattsburgh
Sept. 11, 1814

Lake Ontario

Frenchtown
Jan. 22, 1813

BROCK 1812

Lundy's Lane
July 25, 1814

VT.

WINCHESTER 1812–1813

Lake Erie

Stoney Creek
June 6, 1813

The Chippewa
July 5, 1814

N.H.

INDIANA TERR.

Fort Stephenson

Put-in Bay
Sept. 10, 1813

NEW YORK

MASS.

ATLANTIC OCEAN

OHIO

PENNSYLVANIA

wealthy Tennessee planter and a general in the state militia, temporarily abandoned plans for an invasion of Florida and set off in pursuit of the Creeks. On March 27, 1814, in the Battle of Horseshoe Bend, Jackson's men took terrible revenge on the Indians—slaughtering women and children along with warriors—and broke the resistance of the Creeks. The tribe agreed to cede most of its lands to the United States and retreated westward, farther into the interior. The battle also won Jackson a commission as major general in the United States Army, and in that capacity he led his men farther south into Florida. On November 7, 1814, he seized the Spanish fort at Pensacola.

Battles with the British

But the victories over the tribes were not enough to win the war. After the surrender of Napoleon in 1814, England prepared to invade the United States. A British armada sailed up the Patuxent River from Chesapeake Bay and landed an army that marched to nearby Bladensburg, on the outskirts of Washington, where it dispersed a poorly trained force of American militiamen. On August 24, 1814, the British troops entered Washington and put the government to flight. Then they set fire to several public buildings, including the White House, in retaliation for the earlier American burning of the Canadian capital at York. This was the low point of American fortunes in the war.

Leaving Washington in partial ruins, the invading army proceeded up the bay toward Baltimore. But Baltimore, guarded by Fort McHenry, was prepared. To block the approaching fleet, the American garrison had sunk several ships in the Patapsco River (the entry to Baltimore's harbor), thus forcing the British to bombard the fort from a distance. Through the night of September 13, Francis Scott Key (a Washington lawyer on board one of the British ships, where he was trying to secure the release of an American prisoner) watched the bombardment. The next morning, "by the dawn's early light," he could see the flag on the fort still flying; he recorded his pride in the moment by writing a poem—"The Star-Spangled Banner." The British withdrew from Baltimore, and Key's words were soon set to the tune of an old English drinking song. (In 1931 "The Star-Spangled Banner" became the official national anthem.)

Meanwhile, American forces repelled another British invasion in northern New York; at the Battle of Plattsburgh, on September 11, 1814, they turned back a much more numerous British naval and land force and secured the northern border of the United States. In the South, a formi-

THE BURNING OF WASHINGTON This dramatic engraving somewhat exaggerates the extent of the blazes in Washington when the British occupied the city in August 1814. But the invaders did set fire to the Capitol, the White House, and other public buildings in retaliation for the American burning of the Canadian capital at York.

dable array of battle-hardened British veterans, fresh from the campaign against the French in Spain, landed below New Orleans and prepared to advance north up the Mississippi. Awaiting the British was Andrew Jackson with a motley collection of Tennesseans, Kentuckians, Creoles, blacks, pirates, and regular army troops drawn up behind earthen breastworks. On January 8, 1815, the redcoats advanced on the American fortifications, but the exposed British forces were no match for Jackson's well-protected men. After the Americans had repulsed several waves of attackers, the British finally retreated, leaving behind 700 dead (including their commander, Sir Edward Pakenham), 1,400 wounded, and 500 prisoners. Jackson's losses: 8 killed, 13 wounded. Only later did news reach North America that the United States and Britain had signed a peace treaty several weeks before the Battle of New Orleans.

The Revolt of New England

With a few notable exceptions, such as the Battles of Put-in Bay and New Orleans, the military efforts of the United States between 1812 and 1815 consisted of a series of humiliating failures. As a result, the American government faced increasing popular opposition as the contest dragged on. In New England, opposition both to the war and to the Republican government that was waging it was so extreme that some Federalists celebrated British victories. In Congress, in the meantime, the Republicans had continual trouble with the Federalist opposition, led by a young congressman from New Hampshire, Daniel Webster, who missed no opportunity to embarrass the administration.

By now the Federalists were very much in the minority in the country as a whole, but they were still the majority party in New England. Some of them began to dream of creating a separate nation in that region, which they could dominate and in which they could escape what they saw as the tyranny of slaveholders and backwoodsmen. Talk of secession reached a climax in the winter of 1814–1815.

On December 15, 1814, delegates from the New England states met in Hartford, Connecticut, to discuss their grievances against the Madison administration. The would-be seceders at the Hartford Convention were outnumbered by a comparatively moderate majority. But while the convention's report only hinted at secession, it reasserted the right of nullification and proposed seven amendments to the Constitution (presumably as the condition of New England's remaining in the Union)—amendments designed to protect New England from the growing influence of the South and the West.

Because the war was going so badly, the New Englanders assumed that the Republicans would have to agree to their demands. Soon after the convention adjourned, however, the news of Jackson's victory at New Orleans reached the cities of the Northeast. A day or two later, reports of a peace treaty arrived from abroad. In the changed atmosphere these apparent triumphs produced, the Hartford Convention and the Federalist party came to seem futile, irrelevant, even treasonable.

The Peace Settlement

Serious negotiations between the United States and Britain began in August 1814, when American and British diplomats met in Ghent, Belgium. John Quincy Adams, Henry Clay, and Albert Gallatin led the American delegation. Although both sides began with extravagant demands, the final treaty did very little except end the fighting itself. The Americans gave up their demand for a British renunciation of impressment and for the cession of Canada to the United States. The British abandoned their call for creation of an Indian buffer state in the Northwest and made other, minor territorial concessions. The negotiators referred other disputes to arbitration. Hastily drawn up, the treaty was signed on Christmas Eve 1814.

Both sides had reason to accept this skimpy agreement. The British, exhausted and in debt from their prolonged conflict with Napoleon, were eager to settle the lesser dispute in North America. The Americans realized that with the defeat of Napoleon in Europe, the British would no longer have much incentive to interfere with American commerce. Indeed, by the end of 1815, impressment had all but ceased.

Other settlements followed the Treaty of Ghent and contributed to a long-term improvement in Anglo-American relations. A commercial treaty in 1815 gave Americans the right to trade freely with England and much of the British Empire. The Rush-Bagot agreement of 1817 provided for mutual disarmament on the Great Lakes; eventually (although not until 1872) the Canadian-American boundary became the longest "unguarded frontier" in the world.

For the other parties to the War of 1812—the Indian tribes east of the Mississippi—the conflict proved another disastrous blow to the capacity of Indians to resist white expansion. Tecumseh, their most important leader, was dead. The British, their most important allies, were gone from the Northwest. The intertribal alliance that Tecumseh and the Prophet had forged was in disarray. The end of the war served to spur white movement westward, into land the Indians were less than ever able to defend.

CONCLUSION

Thomas Jefferson called his election to the presidency the "Revolution of 1800," and his supporters believed that his victory would bring a dramatic change in the character of the nation—a retreat from Hamilton's dreams of a powerful, developing nation with great stature in the world; a return to an ideal of simple agrarian republic happily isolated from the corruption and intrigue of Europe.

But American society was changing rapidly in the early nineteenth century, making it virtually impossible for the Jeffersonian dream to prevail. The nation's population was expanding and diversifying. Its cities were growing, and its commercial life was becoming ever more important. In 1803, Jefferson himself made one of the most important contributions to the growth of the United States: the Louisiana Purchase, which dramatically expanded the physical boundaries of the nation—and which began extending white settlement deeper into the continent. In the process, it greatly widened the battles between Europeans and Native Americans.

The growing national pride and commercial ambitions of the United States gradually created another serious conflict with Great Britain: the War of 1812, a war that went badly for the Americans on the whole, but that was settled finally in 1814 on terms at least mildly favorable to the United States. By then, the bitter party rivalries that had characterized the first years of the republic had to some degree subsided, and the nation was poised to enter what became known as the "Era of Good Feelings." It was to be an era in which good feelings did not last for very long.

FOR FURTHER REFERENCE

Suggested Readings

Charles Mayfield, *The New Nation* (1981) is a useful survey of the period. Henry Adams, *History of the United States During the Administration of Jefferson and Adams*, 9 vols. (1889–1891) is one of the great literary achievements of early American historiography. Thomas C. Cochran, *Frontiers of Change: Early Industrialization in America* (1981) summarizes economic development in the early republic. Jeanne Boydston, *Home and Work: Housework, Wages, and the Ideology of Labor in the Early Republic* (1990) argues that the cultural status of women declined as the market revolution began to transform the American economy. Joseph J. Ellis, *American Sphinx: The Character of Thomas Jefferson* (1997) is an excellent inquiry into the roots of Jefferson's beliefs and actions. Drew McCoy, *The Elusive Republic: Political Economy in Jeffersonian America* (1980) traces the Jeffersonian struggle to keep the United States free from European-style corruption and decay. Paul Finkleman, *Slavery and the Founders: Race and Liberty in the Age of Jefferson* (1996) reflects on the problem of slavery in the early republic. James Henretta and Gregory Nobles, *The Evolution of American Society, 1700–1815* (rev. ed. 1987) examines the economic growth of the United States in the early nineteenth century. Richard White, *The Roots of Dependency* (1983) examines the tangled relationship between Native Americans and the white citizens of the early United States. J. C. A. Stagg, *Mr. Madison's War: Politics, Diplomacy, and Warfare in the Early American Republic, 1783–1830* (1983) argues that James Madison led the United States to war against Great Britain in order to preserve vital American commercial interests, but that he underestimated New England opposition to his policies.

Films

(The best source for information on how to find these and other films is *Bowker's Complete Video Directory*—3 volumes.) *An Age of Revolutions* (1978) traces early American diplomacy from the Revolution through the early federal period, including the Louisiana Purchase and the War of 1812. *The Louisiana Purchase: Moving West of the Mississippi* (1990) highlights the political events that led to the Louisiana Purchase and links the settlement of the region with the era of "Manifest Destiny." *The War of 1812* (1982) introduces students to an important but poorly understood event in American history. *The American Story, No. 6: Nationalism* and *No. 7: The Emerging Nation* (1985) detail American political and economic development after the War of 1812, through the Era of Good Feelings. *Sea of Honor: The U.S. Navy Story, Vol. 3: The War of 1812* explores one of the formative moments for the American military.

Internet Resources

Internet websites containing historical material relevant to the subjects discussed in this chapter can be reached through the McGraw-Hill history site at www.mhhe.com/socscience/history/usa/link/linktop.htm.

CHAPTER EIGHT

Varieties of American Nationalism

Stabilizing Economic Growth ～ *Expanding Westward*
The "Era of Good Feelings" ～ *Sectionalism and Nationalism*
The Revival of Opposition

L IKE A "FIRE BELL in the night," as Thomas Jefferson put it, the issue of slavery arose after the War of 1812 to threaten the unity of the nation. The debate began when the territory of Missouri applied for admission to the Union, raising the question of whether it would be a free or a slaveholding state. But the larger issue, one that would arise again and again to plague the republic, was whether the vast new western regions of the United States would ultimately move into the orbit of the North or the South.

The Missouri crisis, which Congress settled by compromise in 1820, was significant because it was a sign of the sectional crises to come. But at the time, it was also significant because it stood in such sharp contrast to the rising American nationalism of the years following the war. Whatever forces might be working to pull the nation apart, stronger ones were acting for the moment to draw it together.

STABILIZING ECONOMIC GROWTH

The end of the War of 1812 allowed the United States to resume the economic growth and territorial expansion that had characterized the first decade of the nineteenth century. A vigorous postwar boom led to a disastrous bust in 1819. Brief though it was, the collapse was evidence that the United States continued to lack some of the basic institutions necessary to sustain long-term growth.

TIME LINE			
1815	**1816**	**1818**	**1819**
U.S. takes western lands from Indians	Second Bank of U.S. Monroe elected president	Seminole War ends	Panic and depression *Dartmouth College* v. *Woodward*; *McCulloch* v. *Maryland*

1820	**1823**	**1824**	**1828**
Missouri Compromise Monroe reelected	Monroe Doctrine	John Quincy Adams elected	Tariff of abominations Jackson elected president

The Government and Economic Growth

The War of 1812 may have stimulated the growth of manufactures. But it also produced chaos in shipping and banking, and it exposed dramatically the inadequacy of the existing transportation and financial systems. The aftermath of the war, therefore, saw the emergence of a series of political issues connected with national economic development.

The wartime experience underlined the need for another national bank. After the expiration of the first Bank's charter, a large number of state banks had issued vast quantities of bank notes, creating a confusing variety of currency of widely differing value in circulation at the same time. Honest business was difficult since it was difficult to tell what any bank note was really worth, and counterfeiting was easy. In response to these problems, Congress chartered a second Bank of the United States in 1816, much like its predecessor of 1791 but with more capital. The national bank could not forbid state banks from issuing notes, but its size and power enabled it to compel the state banks to issue only sound notes or risk being forced out of business.

Congress also acted to promote manufacturing, which the war (by cutting off imports) had already greatly stimulated. The American textile industry had experienced a particularly dramatic growth. Between 1807 and 1815, the total number of cotton spindles in the country increased more than fifteenfold, from 8,000 to 130,000. Until 1814, the textile factories—most of them in New England—produced only yarn and thread;

families operating hand looms at home did the actual weaving of cloth. Then the Boston merchant Francis Cabot Lowell, after examining textile machinery in England, developed a power loom better than its English counterpart. In 1813, in Waltham, Massachusetts, Lowell founded the first mill in America to carry on the processes of spinning and weaving under a single roof. His company was an important step in revolutionizing American manufacturing.

But the end of the war suddenly dimmed the prospects for American industry. British ships—determined to recapture their lost markets—swarmed into American ports and unloaded cargoes of manufactured goods, many priced below cost. In 1816, protectionists in Congress passed a tariff law that effectively limited competition from abroad on a wide range of items, including cotton cloth, despite objections from agricultural interests, who stood to pay higher prices for manufactured goods.

AN EARLY MILL IN NEW ENGLAND This early folk painting, dating around 1814, shows the small town of East Chelmford, Massachusetts—still primarily agrarian, with its rural houses, open fields, and grazing livestock, but with a small textile mill already operating along the stream, at right. A little more than a decade later, the town had been transformed into a major manufacturing center and renamed for the family that owned the mills: Lowell.

Transportation

The nation's most pressing economic need was for improvements in its transportation system that would give manufacturers access to raw materials and markets. An old debate resumed: Should the federal government help to finance roads and other "internal improvements"? The idea of using government funds to finance road building was not a new one. When Ohio entered the Union in 1803, the federal government agreed that part of the proceeds from the sale of public lands there should finance road construction. And in 1807, Congress enacted a law proposed by the Jefferson administration that permitted using revenues from Ohio land sales to finance a National Road from the Potomac River to the Ohio. By 1818, the highway ran as far as Wheeling, Virginia, on the Ohio River; and the Lancaster Pike, financed in part by the state of Pennsylvania, extended westward to Pittsburgh. The roads were heavily traveled and helped lower shipping costs across the mountains.

At the same time, on the rivers and the Great Lakes, steam-powered shipping was expanding rapidly. By 1816, river steamers were beginning to journey up and down the Mississippi to the Ohio River, and up the Ohio as far as Pittsburgh. Steamboats were soon carrying more cargo on the Mississippi than all the earlier forms of river transport—flatboats, barges, and others—combined. They stimulated the agricultural economy of the West and the South by providing access to markets at greatly reduced cost, and they enabled eastern manufacturers to send their finished goods west much more readily.

But despite the progress with steamboats and turnpikes, serious gaps in the nation's transportation network remained, as experience during the War of 1812 had shown. Once the British blockade had cut off Atlantic shipping, the coastal roads had become choked by the unaccustomed volume of north-south traffic. Merchants and consumers experienced long delays and serious shortages. Congress passed a bill introduced by Representative John C. Calhoun that allowed the use of government funds to finance internal improvements, but Madison, on his last day in office, vetoed it. He supported the purpose of the bill, he explained, but he believed that Congress lacked authority to fund the improvements without a constitutional amendment. For a time, state governments and private enterprise were left on their own to build the transportation network necessary for the growing American economy.

THE CLERMONT'S ENGINE Robert Fulton's Clermont became the first steamboat to travel from New York to Albany (in 32 hours) in 1809. Its great paddle was driven by a powerful piston, which was driven in turn by power generated by a steam boiler. This is Fulton's own drawing of the engine system.

EXPANDING WESTWARD

One reason for the growing interest in internal improvements was the sudden and dramatic surge in westward expansion in the years following the War of 1812. By the time of the census of 1820, white settlers had pushed well beyond the Mississippi River, and the population of the western regions was increasing more rapidly than that of the nation as a whole.

The Great Migration

The westward movement of the white American population was one of the most important developments of the century. There were several major reasons for this expansion.

One reason was population growth, which drove many white Americans out of the East. Between 1800 and 1820, the population nearly doubled—from 5.3 million to 9.6 million. Most Americans were still farmers, and the agricultural lands of the East were by now largely occupied or exhausted. In the South, the spread of the plantation system and its slave labor force limited opportunities for new settlers. Another reason was that the West itself was becoming increasingly attractive to white settlers. Land there was much more plentiful than it was in the East. And in the aftermath of the War of 1812, the federal government continued its policy of pushing the Indian tribes farther and farther west, making the fertile regions beyond the Mississippi safer for white settlement. Migrants from throughout the East flocked in increasing numbers to what was then known as the Old Northwest (now part of the Midwest), most of them via the Ohio and Monongahela Rivers. Once on the Ohio, most floated downstream on flatboats, then left the river (often at Cincinnati, which was becoming one of the region's—and the nation's—principal cities) and traveled overland with wagons, handcarts, packhorses, cattle, and hogs.

White Settlers in the Old Northwest

Having arrived at their destination, most settlers built lean-tos or cabins and then hewed clearings out of the forest and planted crops of corn to supplement the wild game they caught and the domestic animals they had brought with them. It was a rough and lonely existence. Men, women, and children worked side by side in the fields—and at times had virtually no contact for weeks or months with anyone outside their own families.

Life in the western territories was not, however, entirely solitary or individualistic. Migrants often journeyed westward in groups, stayed together, and built new communities with schools, churches, stores, and other institutions. The labor shortage in the interior led neighbors to develop systems of mutual aid. They gathered periodically to raise a barn, clear land, harvest crops, or make quilts.

Another common feature of life in the Northwest (and indeed in much of early-nineteenth-century America) was mobility. Individuals and families were constantly on the move, settling for a few years in one place and then selling their land (often at a significant profit, given the rapidly rising prices in the region) and resettling somewhere else. When new areas for settlement opened farther to the west, it was often the people already on the western edges of white settlement—rather than those who remained in the East—who flocked to them first.

The Plantation System in the Old Southwest

In the Old Southwest (now generally known as the Deep South), the new agricultural economy emerged along different lines. The market for cotton continued to grow, and the Southwest contained a broad zone where cotton could thrive. That zone included what was to become known as the Black Belt of central Alabama and Mississippi, a vast prairie with a dark, productive soil.

The first arrivals in the uncultivated regions of the Old Southwest were usually ordinary people like the settlers farther north, small farmers who made rough clearings in the forest. But wealthier planters soon followed. They bought up the cleared or partially cleared land, and the original settlers moved farther west and started over again. Success in the wilderness was by no means assured, even for the wealthiest settlers. But many planters soon expanded small clearings into vast cotton fields. They replaced the cabins of the early pioneers with more sumptuous log dwellings and ultimately with imposing mansions that demonstrated the rise of a newly wealthy class. They also built up large slave work forces.

The rapid growth of the Old Northwest and Southwest resulted in the admission of four new states to the Union in the immediate aftermath of the War of 1812: Indiana in 1816, Mississippi in 1817, Illinois in 1818, and Alabama in 1819.

Trade and Trapping in the Far West

Not many Anglo-Americans yet knew much about or were much interested in the far western areas of the continent. But a significant trade nevertheless began to develop between these western regions and the United States early in the nineteenth century, and it grew steadily for decades.

Mexico, which continued to control Texas, California, and much of the rest of the far Southwest, won its independence from Spain in 1821. Almost immediately, it opened its northern territories to trade with the United States, hoping to revive their stagnant economy. American traders poured into the region—overland into Texas and New Mexico, by sea into California. Merchants from the United States quickly displaced Indian and Mexican traders. In New Mexico, for example, the Missouri trader William Becknell began in 1821 to offer American manufactured goods for sale, priced considerably below the inferior Mexican goods that had dominated the market in the past. Mexico effectively lost its markets in its own colony as a steady traffic of commercial wagon trains began moving back and forth along the Santa Fe Trail between Missouri and New Mexico.

Becknell and those who followed him diverted an established trade from Mexico to the United States. But fur traders created a wholly new kind of commerce. After the War of 1812, John Jacob Astor's American Fur Company and others extended their operations from the Great Lakes area westward to the Rockies. At first, fur traders did most of their business by purchasing pelts from the Indians. But increasingly, white trappers entered the region and joined the Iroquois and other Indians in pursuit of beaver and other furs.

The trappers, or "mountain men," who began trading in and exploring the Far West were small in number. But they developed important relationships with the existing residents of the West—Indian and Mexican—and altered the character of society there. White trappers were mostly young, single men. Perhaps unsurprisingly, many of them entered into sexual relationships with Indian and Mexican women. They also recruited the women as helpers in the difficult work of preparing furs and skins for trading. Perhaps two-thirds of the white trappers married Indian or Hispanic women.

In 1822, Andrew and William Ashley founded the Rocky Mountain Fur Company and recruited white trappers to move permanently into the Rockies in search of furs, which were becoming scarce farther east. The Ashleys dispatched supplies annually to their trappers in exchange for furs and skins. The arrival of the supply train became the occasion for a gathering of scores

THE RENDEZVOUS The annual rendezvous of fur trappers and traders was a major event in the lives of the lonely men who made their livelihoods gathering furs. It was also a gathering of representatives of the many cultures that mingled in the Far West, among them Anglo-Americans, French Canadians, Indians, and Hispanics.

of mountain men, some of whom lived much of the year in considerable isolation.

But however isolated their daily lives, these mountain men were closely bound up with the expanding market economy of the United States. Some were employees of the Rocky Mountain Fur Company (or some other, similar business enterprise), earning a salary in return for providing a steady supply of furs. Others trapped on their own and simply sold their furs for cash, but they too depended on merchants from the East for their livelihoods. Whatever the character of the transactions, the bulk of the profits from the trade flowed to the merchants, not the trappers.

Eastern Images of the West

Americans in the East were only dimly aware of the world the trappers were entering and helping to reshape, and the trappers themselves, who did not often write of their lives or draw maps of the lands they explored, did little to enlighten others. More important in increasing eastern awareness of the West were explorers, many of them dispatched by the United States government with instructions to chart the territories they visited. In 1819 and 1820, with instructions from the War Department to find the source of the Red River, Stephen H. Long led nineteen soldiers on a journey up the Platte and South Platte Rivers through what is now Nebraska and eastern Colorado (where he discovered the peak that would be named for him), and then returned eastward along the Arkansas River through what is now Kansas. He failed to find the headwaters of the Red River. But he wrote an influential report on his trip, which echoed the dismissive conclusions of Zebulon Pike fifteen years before. The region "between the Missouri River and the Rocky Mountains," Long wrote, "is almost wholly unfit for cultivation, and of course uninhabitable by a people depending upon agriculture for their subsistence." On the published map of his expedition, he labeled the Great Plains the "Great American Desert."

THE "ERA OF GOOD FEELINGS"

The expansion of the economy, the growth of white settlement and trade in the West, the creation of new states—all reflected the rising spirit of nationalism that was permeating the United States in the years following the War of 1812. That spirit found reflection for a time in the character of national politics.

The End of the First Party System

Ever since 1800, the presidency seemed to have been the special possession of Virginians. After two terms in office Jefferson chose his secretary
of state, James Madison of Virginia, to succeed him, and after two more
terms, Madison secured the presidential nomination for his secretary of
state, James Monroe, also of Virginia. Many in the North were expressing
impatience with the so-called Virginia Dynasty, but the Republicans had
no difficulty electing their candidate in the listless campaign of 1816.
Monroe received 183 ballots in the electoral college; his Federalist opponent, Rufus King of New York, received only 34—from Massachusetts,
Connecticut, and Delaware.

Monroe was sixty-one years old when he became president. In the
course of his long career, he had served as a soldier in the Revolution, as a
diplomat, and most recently as a cabinet officer. He entered office under
what seemed to be remarkably favorable circumstances. With the decline
of the Federalists, his party faced no serious opposition. With the conclusion of the War of 1812, the nation faced no important international
threats. American politicians had dreamed since the first days of the republic of a time in which partisan divisions and factional disputes might
come to an end. In the prosperous postwar years, Monroe attempted to
use his office to realize that dream.

THE INAUGURATION OF JAMES MONROE, 1816 The ruins of part of the United States
Capitol, burned by the British two years earlier late in the War of 1812, provided
a bleak backdrop for James Monroe's first inauguration in 1816.

He made that clear, above all, in the selection of his cabinet. For secretary of state, he chose the New Englander and former Federalist John Quincy Adams. Jefferson, Madison, and Monroe had all served as secretary of state before becoming president; Adams, therefore, immediately became the heir apparent, suggesting that the "Virginia Dynasty" would soon come to an end. Speaker of the House Henry Clay declined an offer to be secretary of war, so Monroe named John C. Calhoun instead. In his other appointments, too, Monroe took pains to include both northerners and southerners, easterners and westerners, Federalists and Republicans.

Soon after his inauguration, Monroe did what no president since Washington had done: he made a good-will tour through the country. In New England, so recently the scene of rabid Federalist discontent, he was greeted everywhere with enthusiastic demonstrations. The *Columbian Centinel*, a Federalist newspaper in Boston, commenting on the "Presidential Jubilee" in that city, observed that an "era of good feelings" had arrived. And on the surface, at least, the years of Monroe's presidency did appear to be an "era of good feelings." In 1820, Monroe was reelected without opposition. For all practical purposes, the Federalist Party had now ceased to exist.

John Quincy Adams and Florida

Like his father, the second president of the United States, John Quincy Adams had spent much of his life in diplomatic service. And even before becoming secretary of state, he had become one of the great diplomats in American history. He was also a committed nationalist, and he considered his most important task to be the promotion of American expansion.

His first challenge was Florida. The United States had already annexed West Florida, but that claim was in dispute. Most Americans, moreover, still believed the nation should gain possession of the entire peninsula. In 1817, Adams began negotiations with the Spanish minister, Luis de Onís, in hopes of resolving the dispute and gaining the entire territory for the United States.

In the meantime, however, events were taking their own course in Florida itself. Andrew Jackson, now in command of American troops along the Florida frontier, had orders from Secretary of War Calhoun to "adopt the necessary measures" to stop continuing raids on American territory by Seminole Indians south of the border. Jackson used those orders as an excuse to invade Florida, seize the Spanish forts at St. Marks and Pensacola, and order the hanging of two British subjects on the charge of

SEMINOLE DANCE This 1838 drawing by a U.S. military officer portrays a dance by Seminole Indians near Fort Butler in Florida. It was made in the midst of the prolonged Second Seminole War, which ended in 1842 with the removal of most of the tribe from Florida to reservations west of the Mississippi.

supplying and inciting the Indians. The operation became known as the Seminole War.

Instead of condemning Jackson's raid, Adams urged the government to assume responsibility for it. The United States, he told the Spanish, had the right under international law to defend itself against threats from across its borders. Since Spain was unwilling or unable to curb those threats, America had simply done what was necessary. Jackson's raid demonstrated to the Spanish that the United States could easily take Florida by force. Adams implied that the nation might consider doing so.

Onís realized, therefore, that he had little choice but to come to terms with the Americans. Under the provisions of the Adams-Onís Treaty of 1819, Spain ceded all of Florida to the United States and gave up its claim to territory north of the 42nd parallel in the Pacific Northwest. In return, the American government gave up its claims to Texas.

The Panic of 1819

But the Monroe administration had little time to revel in its diplomatic successes, for the nation was falling victim to a serious economic crisis: the Panic of 1819. It followed a period of high foreign demand for American farm goods and thus of exceptionally high prices for American farmers (all as a result of the disruption of European agriculture caused by the Napoleonic Wars). The rising prices for farm goods had stimulated a land boom in the western United States. Fueled by speculative investments, land prices soared.

The availability of easy credit to settlers and speculators—from the government (under the land acts of 1800 and 1804), from state banks and wildcat banks, even for a time from the rechartered Bank of the United States—fueled the land boom. Beginning in 1819, however, new management at the national bank began tightening credit, calling in loans, and foreclosing mortgages. This precipitated a series of failures by state banks, and the result was a financial panic, which many Americans, particularly those in the West, blamed on the national bank. Thus began a process that would eventually make the Bank's existence one of the nation's most burning political issues. Six years of depression followed.

Some Americans saw the Panic of 1819 and the widespread distress that followed as a warning that rapid economic growth and territorial expansion would destabilize the nation and threaten its survival. But by 1820 most Americans were irrevocably committed to the idea of growth and expansion. Public debate in the future would revolve less around whether growth was good or bad than around how to encourage and control it.

SECTIONALISM AND NATIONALISM

For a brief but alarming moment in 1819–1820, the increasing differences between the North and the South threatened the unity of the United States—until the Missouri Compromise averted a sectional crisis for a time. The forces of nationalism continued to assert themselves, and the federal government began to assume the role of promoter of economic growth.

The Missouri Compromise

When Missouri applied for admission to the Union as a state in 1819, slavery was already well established there. Even so, Representative James Tallmadge, Jr. of New York proposed an amendment to the Missouri statehood bill that would prohibit the further introduction of slaves into

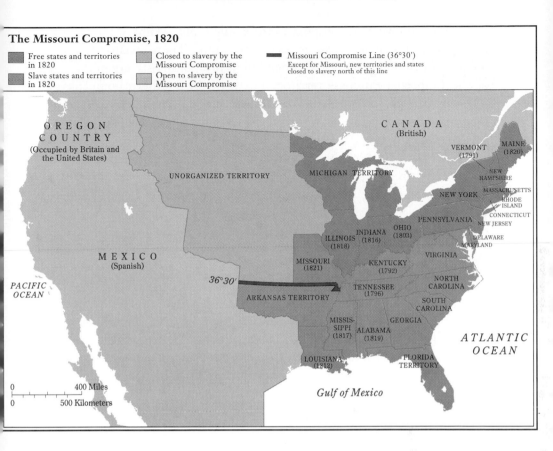

The Missouri Compromise, 1820

Free states and territories in 1820

Slave states and territories in 1820

Closed to slavery by the Missouri Compromise

Open to slavery by the Missouri Compromise

Missouri Compromise Line (36°30')
Except for Missouri, new territories and states closed to slavery north of this line

OREGON COUNTRY
(Occupied by Britain and the United States)

CANADA (British)

VERMONT (1791)

MAINE (1820)

UNORGANIZED TERRITORY

MICHIGAN TERRITORY

NEW HAMPSHIRE

NEW YORK

MASSACHUSETTS

RHODE ISLAND

CONNECTICUT

NEW JERSEY

PENNSYLVANIA

MEXICO (Spanish)

ILLINOIS (1818)

INDIANA (1816)

OHIO (1803)

DELAWARE

MARYLAND

PACIFIC OCEAN

36°30'

MISSOURI (1821)

KENTUCKY (1792)

VIRGINIA

NORTH CAROLINA

ARKANSAS TERRITORY

TENNESSEE (1796)

SOUTH CAROLINA

MISSIS-SIPPI (1817)

ALABAMA (1819)

GEORGIA

ATLANTIC OCEAN

LOUISIANA (1812)

FLORIDA TERRITORY

0   400 Miles

0   500 Kilometers

Gulf of Mexico

Missouri and provide for the gradual emancipation of those already there. The Tallmadge Amendment provoked a controversy that was to rage for the next two years.

Since the beginning of the republic, partly by chance and partly by design, new states had come into the Union more or less in pairs, one from the North, another from the South. In 1819, there were eleven free states and eleven slave states; the admission of Missouri would upset that balance and increase the political power of the North over the South. Hence the controversy over slavery and freedom in Missouri.

Complicating the Missouri question was the application of Maine (previously the northern part of Massachusetts) for admission as a new (and free) state. Speaker of the House Henry Clay informed northern members that if they blocked Missouri from entering the Union as a slave state, southerners would block the admission of Maine. But Maine ultimately offered a way out of the impasse, as the Senate agreed to combine the Maine and Missouri proposals into a single bill. Maine would be admitted as a free state, Missouri as a slave state. Then Senator Jesse B. Thomas of Illinois proposed an amendment prohibiting slavery in the rest of the Louisiana Purchase territory north of the southern boundary of Missouri (the 36° 30′ parallel). The Senate adopted the Thomas Amendment, and Speaker Clay, with great difficulty, guided the amended Maine-Missouri bill through the House.

Nationalists in both North and South hailed this settlement—which became known as the Missouri Compromise—as a happy resolution of a danger to the Union. But the debate over it had revealed a strong undercurrent of sectionalism that was competing with—although at the moment failing to derail—the powerful tides of nationalism.

Marshall and the Court

John Marshall served as chief justice of the United States for almost thirty-five years, from 1801 to 1835, and he dominated the Court more fully than anyone else before or since. More than anyone but the framers themselves, he molded the development of the Constitution: strengthening the judicial branch at the expense of the executive and legislative branches, increasing the power of the federal government at the expense of the states, and advancing the interests of the propertied and commercial classes.

Committed to promoting commerce, the Marshall Court staunchly defended the inviolability of contracts. In *Fletcher v. Peck* (1810), which arose out of a series of notorious land frauds in Georgia, the Court had to decide whether the Georgia legislature of 1796 could repeal the act of the previous legislature granting lands under shady circumstances to the Yazoo Land Companies. In a unanimous decision, Marshall held that a land grant was a valid contract and could not be repealed even if corruption was involved.

Dartmouth College v. Woodward (1819) further expanded the meaning of the contract clause of the Constitution. Having gained control of the New Hampshire state government, Republicans tried to revise Dartmouth College's charter (granted by King George III in 1769) to convert the private college into a state university. Daniel Webster, a Dartmouth graduate and brilliant orator, argued the college's case. The Dartmouth charter, he insisted, was a contract, protected by the same doctrine that the Court had already upheld in *Fletcher v. Peck.* Then, according to legend, he brought some of the justices to tears with an irrelevant passage that concluded: "It is, sir, . . . a small college. And yet there are those who love it." The Court ruled for Dartmouth, proclaiming that corporation charters such as

JOHN MARSHALL Marshall became Chief Justice of the United States Supreme Court in 1801 after establishing himself as one of the leaders of the Federalist Party. He served as Chief Justice for thirty-five years, longer than anyone else in American history. And despite the frequent opposition of a series of Republican presidents, he used his position to make the judiciary a vigorous instrument for asserting and strengthening American nationalism.

the one the colonial legislature had granted the college were contracts and thus inviolable. The decision placed important restrictions on the ability of state governments to control corporations.

In overturning the act of the legislature and the decisions of the New Hampshire courts, the justices also implicitly claimed for themselves the right to override the decisions of state courts. But advocates of states' rights, especially in the South, continued to challenge its right to do so. In *Cohens* v. *Virginia* (1821), Marshall explicitly affirmed the constitutionality of federal review of state court decisions. The states had given up part of their sovereignty in ratifying the Constitution, he explained, and their courts must submit to federal jurisdiction; otherwise, the federal government would be prostrated "at the feet of every state in the Union."

Meanwhile, in *McCulloch* v. *Maryland* (1819), Marshall confirmed the "implied powers" of Congress by upholding the constitutionality of the Bank of the United States. The Bank had become so unpopular in the South and the West that several of the states tried to drive branches out of business by outright prohibition or by confiscatory taxes. This case presented two constitutional questions to the Supreme Court: Could Congress charter a bank? And if so, could individual states ban it or tax it? Daniel Webster, one of the Bank's attorneys, argued that establishing such an institution came within the "necessary and proper" clause of the Constitution and that the power to tax involved a "power to destroy." If the states could tax the Bank at all, they could tax it to death. Marshall adopted Webster's words in deciding for the Bank.

In the case of *Gibbons* v. *Ogden* (1824), the Court strengthened Congress's power to regulate interstate commerce. The state of New York had granted the steamboat company of Robert Fulton and Robert Livingston the exclusive right to carry passengers on the Hudson River to New York City. Fulton and Livingston then gave Aaron Ogden the business of carrying passengers across the river between New York and New Jersey. But Thomas Gibbons, with a license granted under an act of Congress, began competing with Ogden for the ferry traffic. Ogden brought suit against him and won in the New York courts. Gibbons appealed to the Supreme Court. The most important question facing the justices was whether Congress's power to give Gibbons a license to operate his ferry superseded the state of New York's power to grant Ogden a monopoly. Marshall claimed that the power of Congress to regulate interstate commerce (which, he said, included navigation) was "complete in itself" and might be "exercised to its utmost extent." Ogden's state-granted monopoly, therefore, was void.

The decisions of the Marshall Court established the primacy of the federal government over the states in regulating the economy and opened the way for an increased federal role in promoting economic growth. They protected corporations and other private economic institutions from local government interference. They were, in short, highly nationalistic decisions, designed to promote the growth of a strong, unified, and economically developed United States.

The Court and the Tribes

The nationalist inclinations of the Marshall Court were visible as well in a series of decisions concerning the legal status of Indian tribes within the United States. But these decisions did not simply affirm the supremacy of the United States; they also carved out a distinctive position for Native Americans within the constitutional structure.

The first of the crucial Indian decisions was in the case of *Johnson* v. *McIntosh* (1823). Leaders of the Illinois and Pinakeshaw tribes had sold parcels of their land to a group of white settlers (including Johnson) but had later signed a treaty with the federal government ceding territory that included those same parcels to the United States. The government proceeded to grant homestead rights to new white settlers (among them McIntosh) on the land claimed by Johnson. The Court was asked to decide which claim had precedence. Marshall's ruling, not surprisingly, favored the United States. But in explaining it, he offered a preliminary definition of the place of Indians within the nation. The tribes had a basic right to their tribal lands, he said, that preceded all other American law. Individual American citizens could not buy or take land from the tribes; only the federal government—the supreme authority—could do that.

Even more important was the Court's 1832 decision in *Worcester* v. *Georgia*, in which the Court invalidated a Georgia law that attempted to regulate access by U.S. citizens to Cherokee country. Only the federal government could do that, Marshall claimed, thus taking another important step in consolidating federal authority over the states (and over the tribes). In doing so, he further defined the nature of the Indian nations. The tribes, he explained, were sovereign entities in much the same way Georgia was a sovereign entity—"distinct political communities, having territorial boundaries within which their authority is exclusive." In defending the power of the federal government, he was also affirming, indeed expanding, the rights of the tribes to remain free from the authority of state governments.

The Marshall decisions, therefore, did what the Constitution itself had not done: they defined a place for Indian tribes within the American political system. The tribes had basic property rights. They were sovereign entities not subject to the authority of state governments. But the federal government, like a "guardian" governing its "ward," had ultimate authority over tribal affairs—even if that authority was, according to the Court, limited by the government's obligation to protect Indian welfare. These provisions were seldom enough to defend Indians from the steady westward march of white civilization, but they formed the basis of what legal protections they had.

The Latin American Revolution and the Monroe Doctrine

Just as the Supreme Court was asserting American nationalism in the shaping of the country's economic life, so the Monroe administration was asserting nationalism in foreign policy. As always, American diplomacy was principally concerned with Europe. But in the 1820s, dealing with Europe forced the United States to develop a policy toward Latin America.

Americans looking southward in the years following the War of 1812 beheld a gigantic spectacle: the Spanish Empire in its death throes, a whole continent in revolt, new nations in the making. Already the United States had developed a profitable trade with Latin America and was rivaling Great Britain as the principal trading nation there. Many believed the success of the anti-Spanish revolutions would further strengthen America's position in the region.

In 1815, the United States proclaimed neutrality in the wars between Spain and its rebellious colonies, implying a partial recognition of the rebels' status as nations. Moreover, the United States sold ships and supplies to the revolutionaries, a clear indication that it was not genuinely neutral but was trying to help the insurgents. Finally, in 1822, President Monroe established diplomatic relations with five new nations—La Plata (later Argentina), Chile, Peru, Colombia, and Mexico—making the United States the first country to recognize them.

In 1823, Monroe went further and announced a policy that would ultimately be known (beginning some thirty years later) as the "Monroe Doctrine," even though it was primarily the work of John Quincy Adams. "The American continents," Monroe declared, ". . . are henceforth not to be considered as subjects for future colonization by any European powers." The United States would consider any foreign challenge to the sovereignty of existing American nations an unfriendly act. At the same time, he proclaimed, "Our policy in regard to Europe . . . is not to interfere in the internal concerns of any of its powers."

The Monroe Doctrine emerged directly out of America's relations with Europe in the 1820s. Many Americans feared that Spain's European allies (notably France) would assist Spain in an effort to retake its lost empire. Even more troubling to Adams (and many other Americans) was the fear that Great Britain had designs on Cuba. Adams wanted to keep Cuba in Spanish hands until it fell (as he believed it ultimately would) to the Americans.

The Monroe Doctrine had few immediate effects, but it was important as an expression of the growing spirit of nationalism in the United States in the 1820s. And it established the idea of the United States as the dominant power in the Western Hemisphere.

THE REVIVAL OF OPPOSITION

After 1816, the Federalist Party offered no presidential candidate and soon ceased to exist as a national political force. The Republican Party (which considered itself not a party at all but an organization representing the whole of the population) was the only organized force in national politics.

By the late 1820s, however, partisan divisions were emerging once again. In some respects, the division mirrored the schism that had produced the first party system in the 1790s. The Republicans had in many ways come to resemble the early Federalist regimes in their promotion of economic growth and centralization. And the opposition, like the opposition in the 1790s, objected to the federal government's expanding role in the economy. There was, however, a crucial difference. At the beginning of the century, the opponents of centralization had also often been opponents of economic growth. Now, in the 1820s, the controversy involved not whether but how the nation should continue to expand.

The "Corrupt Bargain"

Until 1820, when the Federalist Party effectively ceased operations and James Monroe ran for reelection unopposed, presidential candidates were nominated by caucuses of the two parties in Congress. But in 1824, "King Caucus" was overthrown. The Republican caucus nominated William H. Crawford of Georgia, the secretary of the treasury and the favorite of the extreme states' rights faction of the party. But other candidates received nominations from state legislatures and won endorsements from irregular mass meetings throughout the country.

One of them was Secretary of State John Quincy Adams, who held the office that was the traditional stepping-stone to the presidency. But as he himself ruefully understood, he was a man of cold and forbidding manners, with little popular appeal. Another contender was Henry Clay, the Speaker of the House. He had a devoted personal following and a definite and coherent program: the "American System," which proposed creating a great home market for factory and farm producers by raising the protective tariff, strengthening the national bank, and financing internal improvements. Andrew Jackson, the fourth major candidate, had no significant political record—even though he had served briefly as a representative in Congress and was now a new member of the United States Senate. But he was a military hero and had the help of shrewd political allies from his home state of Tennessee.

Jackson received more popular and electoral votes than any other candidate, but not a majority. He had 99 electoral votes to Adams's 84, Crawford's 41, and Clay's 37. The Twelfth Amendment to the Constitution (passed in the aftermath of the contested 1800 election) required the House of Representatives to choose among the three candidates with the largest numbers of electoral votes. Crawford was seriously ill and not a plausible candidate. Clay was out of the running, but he was in a strong position to influence the result. Jackson was Clay's most dangerous political rival in the West, so Clay supported Adams, in part because, alone among the candidates, he was an ardent nationalist and a likely supporter of the American System. With Clay's endorsement, Adams won election in the House.

The Jacksonians believed their large popular and electoral pluralities entitled their candidate to the presidency, and they were enraged when he lost. But they grew angrier still when Adams named Clay his secretary of state. The State Department was the well-established route to the presidency, and Adams thus appeared to be naming Clay as his own successor. The outrage the Jacksonians expressed at what they called a "corrupt bargain" haunted Adams throughout his presidency.

The Second President Adams

Throughout Adams's term in the White House, the political bitterness arising from the "corrupt bargain" charges thoroughly frustrated his policies. Adams proposed an ambitiously nationalist program reminiscent of Clay's American System. But Jacksonians in Congress blocked most of it.

Adams also experienced diplomatic frustrations. He appointed delegates to an international conference that the Venezuelan liberator, Simón Bolívar, had called in Panama in 1826. But Haiti was one of the participating nations, and southerners in Congress opposed the idea of white Americans mingling with the black delegates. Congress delayed approving the Panama mission so long that the American delegation did not arrive until after the conference was over.

Adams also lost a contest with the state of Georgia, which wished to remove the remaining Creek and Cherokee Indians from the state to gain additional soil for cotton planters. The United States government, in a 1791 treaty, had guaranteed that land to the Creeks; but in 1825, white Georgians had extracted a new treaty from William McIntosh, the leader of one faction in the tribe and a longtime advocate of Indian cooperation with the United States. Adams believed the new treaty had no legal force, since McIntosh clearly did not represent the wishes of the tribe; and he refused to enforce the treaty, setting up a direct conflict between the president and the state. The governor of Georgia defied the president and proceeded with plans for Indian removal. Adams found no way to stop him.

Even more damaging to the administration was its support for a new tariff on imported goods in 1828. This measure originated with the demands of Massachusetts and Rhode Island woolen manufacturers, who complained that the British were dumping textiles on the American market at artificially low prices. But to win support from middle and western states, the administration had to accept duties on other items. In the process, it antagonized the original New England supporters of the bill; the benefits of protecting their manufactured goods from foreign competition now had to be weighed against the prospects of having to pay more for raw materials. Adams signed the bill, earning the animosity of southerners, who cursed it as the "tariff of abominations."

Jackson Triumphant

By the time of the 1828 presidential election, a new two-party system had begun to emerge out of the divisions among the Republicans. On one side stood the supporters of John Quincy Adams, who called themselves the National Republicans and who supported the economic nationalism of the preceding years. Opposing them were the followers of Andrew Jackson, who took the name Democratic Republicans and who called for an assault on privilege and a widening of opportunity. Adams attracted the support of most of the remaining Federalists; Jackson appealed to a broad coalition that opposed the "economic aristocracy."

But issues seemed to count for little in the end, as the campaign degenerated into a war of personal invective. The Jacksonians charged that Adams as president had been guilty of gross waste and extravagance and had used public funds to buy gambling devices (a chess set and a billiard table) for the White House. Adams's supporters hurled even worse accusations at Jackson. They called him a murderer and distributed a "coffin handbill," which listed, within coffin-shaped outlines, the names of militiamen whom Jackson was said to have shot in cold blood during the War of 1812. (The men had been deserters who were legally executed after sentence by a court-martial.) And they called his wife a bigamist. Jackson had married his beloved Rachel at a time when the pair incorrectly believed her first husband had divorced her. (When Jackson's wife first read of the accusations against her shortly after the election, she collapsed, and a few weeks later, died; not without reason, Jackson blamed his opponents for her death.)

Jackson's victory was decisive, but sectional. He won 56 percent of the popular vote and an electoral majority of 178 votes to 83. Adams swept virtually all of New England and showed significant strength in the mid-Atlantic region. Nevertheless, the Jacksonians considered their victory as complete and as important as Jefferson's in 1800. Once again, the forces of privilege had been driven from Washington. Once again, a champion of democracy would occupy the White House and restore liberty to the people and to the economy. America had entered, some Jacksonians claimed, a new era of democracy, the "era of the common man."

CONCLUSION

In the aftermath of the War of 1812, a vigorous nationalism came increasingly to characterize the political and popular culture of the United States. In all regions of the country, white men and women celebrated the achievements of the early leaders of the republic, the genius of the Constitution, and the success of the nation in withstanding serious challenges both from without and within. Party divisions faded to the point that James Monroe, the fifth president, won reelection in 1820 without opposition.

But the broad nationalism of the so-called era of good feelings disguised some deep divisions within the United States. Indeed, the character of American nationalism differed substantially from one region, and one group, to another. Battles continued between those who favored a strong central government committed to advancing the economic development of the nation and those who wanted a decentralization of power to open opportunity to more people. Battles continued as well over the role of slavery in American life—and in particular over the place of slavery in the new western territories that the United States was rapidly populating (and wresting from the tribes). The Missouri Compromise of 1820 postponed the day of reckoning on that issue—but only for a time, as Andrew Jackson would discover soon after becoming president in 1829.

FOR FURTHER REFERENCE

Suggested Readings

Frederick Jackson Turner, *The Frontier in American History* (1920) is the classic statement of American exceptionalism. Turner argued that the western frontier endowed the United States with a distinctive, individualist and democratic national character. John Mack Faragher, *Women and Men on the Overland Trail* (1979) was an early and influential book in the "new western history" that challenged Turner. Robert V. Remini, *Andrew Jackson and the Course of American Empire: 1767–1821* (1977) emphasizes Andrew Jackson's importance in American territorial expansion in the South prior to 1821 and in the development of American nationalism. Morton J. Horwitz, *The Transformation of American Law, 1780–1865* (1977), an important work in American legal history, connects changes in the law to changes in the American economy. Ernest R.

May, *The Making of the Monroe Doctrine* (1975) describes the creation of a leading principle of American foreign policy.

Films

(The best source for information on how to find these and other films is *Bowker's Complete Video Directory*—3 volumes.) *Expansionism, Vol. 6* (1996) discusses American expansion from the Louisiana Purchase to the California gold rush. *Expansion & Growth: Nineteenth-Century America* explores similar themes. *Lewis & Clark*, an A&E Biography, traces the historic expedition that mapped the Louisiana Purchase. *Daniel Boone's Final Frontier* (1995) reenacts Daniel Boone's last years in the Louisiana Territory, based on the journals of Nathan and Jemima Boone. *Marbury v. Madison* (1977) dramatizes the 1803 Supreme Court case that established the legitimacy of judicial review. *John Marshall* (1983) focuses on the 1807 treason trial of Aaron Burr. *McCulloch v. Maryland* (1977) examines the case that helped to establish federal supremacy over the states.

Internet Resources

Internet websites containing historical material relevant to the subjects discussed in this chapter can be reached through the McGraw-Hill history site at www.mhhe.com/socscience/history/usa/link/linktop.htm

CHAPTER NINE

Jacksonian America

The Rise of Mass Politics ∼ *"Our Federal Union"*
The Removal of the Indians ∼ *Jackson and the Bank War*
The Emergence of the Second Party System ∼ *Politics After Jackson*

MANY AMERICANS WERE growing apprehensive about the future of their republic in the 1820s and 1830s, as the nation expanded both economically and territorially. Some feared that the rapid growth of the United States would produce social chaos; they insisted that the country's first priority must be to establish order and a clear system of authority. Others argued that the greatest danger facing the nation was the growth of inequality and privilege; they believed that society's goal should be to eliminate the favored status of powerful elites and make opportunity more widely available. Advocates of this latter vision seized control of the federal government in 1829 with the inauguration of Andrew Jackson.

THE RISE OF MASS POLITICS

On March 4, 1829, thousands of Americans from all regions of the country—including many farmers, laborers, and other ordinary men and women—crowded before the United States Capitol to watch the inauguration of Andrew Jackson. After the ceremonies, the crowd poured into a public reception at the White House, where, in their eagerness to shake the new president's hand, they filled the state rooms to overflowing, trampled one another, soiled the carpets, and damaged the upholstery. "It was a proud day for the people," wrote Amos Kendall, one of Jackson's closest political associates. Supreme Court justice Joseph Story, a

242

TIME LINE

1830	1830–1838	1831	1832	
Webster and Hayne debate	Indians expelled from Southeast	Anti-Mason Party holds first convention	Jackson vetoes recharter of Bank of U.S.	
			Jackson reelected	

1832–1833	1833	1835	1835–1842
Nullification crisis	Jackson removes deposits from Bank of U.S.	Taney named chief justice of Supreme Court	Seminole War
	Commercial panic		

1836	1837–1844	1840	1841
Specie Circular	Panic and depression	William Henry Harrison elected president	Harrison dies; Tyler becomes president
Van Buren elected president		Independent Treasury Act	

friend and colleague of John Marshall, looked on the inaugural levee, as it was called, and remarked with disgust: "The reign of King 'Mob' seems triumphant."

In fact, the "age of Jackson" was much less a triumph of the common people than Kendall hoped and Story feared. But it did mark a transformation of American politics that extended power widely to new groups. Once restricted to a relatively small elite of property owners, politics now became open to virtually all the nation's white male citizens. In a political sense at least, the era had some claim to the title the Jacksonians gave it: the "era of the common man."

The Expanding Electorate

Until the 1820s, relatively few Americans had been permitted to vote; most states restricted the franchise to white male property owners or taxpayers or both, effectively removing a great mass of the less affluent from

ANDREW JACKSON EN ROUTE TO WASHINGTON, 1829 Only a few weeks after Andrew Jackson's wife died (a result, he believed, of vicious attacks on her by his political enemies), the president-elect began a slow, triumphal procession from Tennessee to Washington, greeted by throngs of admirers in every town through which he passed.

the voting lists. But even before Jackson's election, the franchise began to expand. Change came first in Ohio and other new states of the West, which, on joining the Union, adopted constitutions that guaranteed all adult white males—not just property owners or taxpayers—the right to vote and permitted all voters the right to hold public office. Older states, concerned about the loss of their population to the West, began to drop or reduce their own property ownership or taxpaying requirements. Eventually, every state democratized its electorate to at least some degree.

The wave of state reforms was generally peaceful, but in Rhode Island democratization efforts created considerable instability. The Rhode Island constitution barred more than half the adult males in the state from voting in the 1830s. In 1840, the lawyer and activist Thomas L. Dorr and a group of his followers formed a "People's party," held a convention, drafted a new constitution, and submitted it to a popular vote. It was overwhelmingly approved, and the Dorrites began to set up a new government, with Dorr as governor. The existing legislature, however, rejected the legitimacy of Dorr's constitution. And so, in 1842, two governments were claiming to be the real power in Rhode Island. The old state government proclaimed that Dorr and his followers were rebels and began to imprison them. The Dorrites, meanwhile, made an ineffectual effort to capture the state arsenal. The Dorr Rebellion, as it was known, quickly failed; Dorr himself surrendered and was briefly imprisoned. But the episode helped spur the old guard to draft a new constitution that greatly expanded the suffrage.

The democratization process was far from complete. In much of the South, of course, no slaves could vote. In addition, southern election laws continued to favor the planters and politicians of the older counties and to limit the influence of white residents of more newly settled western areas. Free blacks could not vote anywhere in the South and hardly anywhere in the North. Pennsylvania, in fact, amended its state constitution in 1838 to strip blacks of the right to vote, which they had previously held. In no state could women vote. Nowhere was the ballot secret, and often it was cast as a spoken vote rather than a written one, which meant that voters could be, and often were, bribed or intimidated. Despite the persisting limitations, however, the number of voters increased much more rapidly than did the population as a whole.

One of the most striking political trends of the early nineteenth century was the change in the method of choosing presidential electors and the dramatic increase in popular participation in the process. In 1800, the legislatures had chosen the presidential electors in ten states, and the people in only six. By 1828, electors were chosen by popular vote in every state but South Carolina. In the presidential election of 1824, fewer than 27 percent of adult white males had voted. In the election of 1828, the figure was 58 percent; and in 1840, 80 percent.

The high level of voter participation was only in part the result of an expanded electorate. It was also the result of a growing popular interest in politics and a strengthening of party organization.

The Legitimization of Party

Although factional competition was part of American politics almost from the beginning of the republic, acceptance of the idea of party was not. But in the 1820s and 1830s, most Americans gradually came to consider permanent, institutionalized parties to be a desirable part of the political process, indeed essential to democracy.

The elevation of the idea of party occurred first at the state level, most prominently in New York. There, Martin Van Buren led a dissident political faction (known as the "Bucktails" or the "Albany Regency"). In the years after the War of 1812 this group began to challenge the established political elite—led by the aristocratic governor, De Witt Clinton—that had dominated the state for years. Refuting the traditional view of political parties as undemocratic, they argued that only an institutionalized party, based in the populace, could ensure genuine democracy. The alternative was the sort of closed elite that Clinton had created. For a party to survive, moreover, it must have a permanent opposition. Competing parties would force politicians to remain continually sensitive to the will of the people; they would check and balance each other in much the same way that the different branches of government checked and balanced one another.

By the late 1820s, this new idea of party had spread beyond New York. The election of Jackson in 1828, the result of a popular movement that stood apart from the usual political elites, seemed further to legitimize it. In the 1830s, finally, a fully formed two-party system began to operate at the national level, with each party committed to its own existence as an institution and willing to accept the legitimacy of its opposition. The anti-Jackson forces began to call themselves the Whigs. Jackson's followers called themselves Democrats, thus giving a permanent name to what is now the nation's oldest political party.

President of the Common Man

Andrew Jackson embraced a distinct and simple theory of democracy. Government, he said, should offer "equal protection and equal benefits" to all its white male citizens and favor no one region or class over another. In practice, that meant launching an assault on what Jackson and his associates considered the citadels of the eastern aristocracy and making an effort to extend opportunities to the rising classes of the West and the South.

Jackson's first target was the entrenched officeholders in the federal government, many of whom had been in place for a generation or more. Jackson bitterly denounced what he considered a class of permanent officeholders. Offices, he said, belonged to the people, not to a self-serving bureaucracy. Equally important, a large turnover in the bureaucracy would allow him to reward his own supporters with offices.

ELECTION SCENE Frequent and often boisterous campaign rallies were characteristic of electoral politics in the 1840s, when party loyalties were high and political passions intense—as this 1845 drawing by Alfred Jacob Miller of a rally in Catonsville, Maryland suggests.

One of Jackson's allies, William L. Marcy of New York, once explained, "To the victors belong the spoils"; and patronage, the process of giving out jobs as political rewards, became known as the "spoils system." Although Jackson removed no more than one-fifth of the existing federal officeholders, his embrace of the spoils system helped cement its place in party politics.

Jackson's supporters also worked to transform the process by which presidential candidates were selected. In 1832, the president's followers staged a national convention to renominate him. Through the convention, its founders believed, power in the party would arise directly from the people in a great democratic conclave rather than from such elite political institutions as the congressional caucus.

Debating the Past

Jacksonian Democracy

To many Americans in the 1820s and 1830s, Andrew Jackson was a champion of democracy, a symbol of the spirit of antielitism and egalitarianism that was sweeping American life. Historians, however, have disagreed sharply not only in their assessments of Jackson himself but in their portrayal of American society in his era.

The "progressive" historians of the early twentieth century tended to see Jacksonian politics as a forebear of their own battles against economic privilege and political corruption. Frederick Jackson Turner encouraged scholars to see Jacksonianism as the product of the democratic West: a protest by the people of the frontier against the conservative aristocracy of the East, which they believed restricted their own freedom and opportunity. Jackson represented those who wanted to make government responsive to the will of the people rather than to the power of special interests. The culmination of this progressive interpretation of Jacksonianism was the publication in 1945 of Arthur M. Schlesinger, Jr.'s *The Age of Jackson.* Schlesinger was less interested in the regional basis of Jacksonianism than the disciples of Turner had been. Jacksonian Democracy, he argued, was the effort "to control the power of the capitalist groups, mainly Eastern, for the benefit of non-capitalist groups, farmers and laboring men, East, West, and South." He portrayed Jacksonianism as an early version of modern reform efforts (in the progressive era and the New Deal) to "restrain the power of the business community."

Richard Hofstadter, in an influential 1948 essay, sharply disagreed. Jackson, he argued, was the spokesman of rising entrepreneurs—aspiring businessmen who saw the road to opportunity blocked by the monopolistic power of Eastern aristocrats. The Jacksonians opposed special privileges only to the extent that those privileges blocked their own road to success. They were less sympathetic to the aspirations of those below them. Bray Hammond, writing in 1957, argued similarly that the Jacksonian cause was "one of enterpriser against capitalist," of rising elites against entrenched ones. Other historians, exploring the ideological origins of the movement, saw Jacksonianism less as a democratic reform movement than as a nostalgic effort to restore a lost (and largely imagined) past. Marvin Meyers's *The Jacksonian Persuasion* (1957) argued that Jackson and his followers looked with misgivings on the new industrial society emerging around them and yearned instead for a restoration of the agrarian, republican virtues of an earlier time.

In the 1960s, historians began taking less interest in Jackson and his supporters and more in the social and cultural bases of American politics in the time of Jackson. Lee Benson's *The Concept of Jacksonian Democracy* (1961) used quantitative techniques to demonstrate the role of religion and ethnicity in shaping party divisions. Edward Pessen's *Jacksonian America* (1969) portrayed America in the Jacksonian era as an increasingly stratified, and increasingly unequal, society. This inclination to look more closely at society than at formal "Jacksonianism" has continued into the 1980s and 1990s. Sean Wilentz, in *Chants Democratic* (1984), examined the rise of a powerful class identification among workers in New York, who were attracted less to Jackson than to an artisanal notion of democracy.

Gradually, this attention to the nature of society has led to reassessments of Jackson himself and the nature of his regime. In *Father and Children* (1975), Michael Rogin portrays Jackson as a leader determined to secure the supremacy of white men in the United States, a commitment illustrated by his almost pathological violence toward Indians. Alexander Saxton, in *The Rise and Fall of the White Republic* (1990) makes the related argument that "Jacksonian Democracy" was explicitly a white man's democracy that rested on the subjugation of slaves, women, and Native Americans. But the portrayal of Jackson as a champion of the common man has not vanished from scholarship entirely. The most renowned postwar biographer of Jackson, Robert V. Remini, argues that, despite the flaws in his democratic vision, he was—within the context of his time—a genuine "man of the people."

"OUR FEDERAL UNION"

Jackson's commitment to extending power beyond entrenched elites led him to want to reduce the functions of the federal government. A concentration of power in Washington would, he believed, restrict opportunity to people with political connections. But Jackson also believed in forceful presidential leadership and was strongly committed to the preservation of the Union. Thus at the same time that Jackson was promoting an economic program to reduce the power of the national government, he was asserting the supremacy of the Union in the face of a potent challenge. For no sooner had he entered office than his own vice president—John C. Calhoun— began to champion a controversial (and, in Jackson's view, dangerous) constitutional theory: nullification.

Calhoun and Nullification

Calhoun was forty-six years old in 1828, with a distinguished past and an apparently promising future. But the smoldering issue of the tariff created a dilemma for him. Once he had been an outspoken protectionist and had strongly supported the tariff of 1816. But by the late 1820s, many South Carolinians had come to believe that the "tariff of abominations" was responsible for the stagnation of their state's economy—even though the stagnation was largely a result of the exhaustion of South Carolina's farmland, which could no longer compete effectively with the newly opened and fertile lands of the Southwest. Some exasperated Carolinians were ready to consider a drastic remedy—secession.

Calhoun's future political hopes rested on how he met this challenge in his home state. He did so by developing a theory that he believed offered a more moderate alternative to secession: the theory of nullification. Drawing from the ideas of Madison and Jefferson and their Virginia and Kentucky Resolutions of 1798–1799 and citing the Tenth Amendment to the Constitution, Calhoun argued that since the federal government was a creation of the states, the states—not the courts or Congress—were the final arbiters of the constitutionality of federal laws. If a state concluded that Congress had passed an unconstitutional law, then it could hold a special convention and declare the federal law null and void within the state. The nullification doctrine—and the idea of using it to nullify the 1828 tariff—quickly attracted broad support in South Carolina. But it did nothing to help Calhoun's standing within the new administration, in part because he had a powerful rival in Martin Van Buren.

The Rise of Van Buren

Van Buren was about the same age as Calhoun and equally ambitious. He had won election to the governorship of New York in 1828 and then resigned in 1829 when Jackson appointed him secretary of state. Alone among the figures in the Jackson administration, Van Buren soon established himself as a member both of the official cabinet and of the president's unofficial circle of political allies, known as the "Kitchen Cabinet" (which included such Democratic newspaper editors as Isaac Hill of New Hampshire and Amos Kendall and Francis P. Blair of Kentucky). Van Buren's influence with the president was unmatched and grew stronger still as a result of a quarrel over etiquette that drove a wedge between the president and Calhoun.

Peggy O'Neale was the attractive daughter of a Washington tavern keeper with whom both Andrew Jackson and his friend John H. Eaton had taken lodgings while serving as senators from Tennessee. O'Neale was married, but rumors circulated in Washington in the mid-1820s that she and Senator Eaton were having an affair. O'Neale's husband died in 1828, and she and Eaton were soon married. A few weeks later, Jackson named Eaton secretary of war and thus made the new Mrs. Eaton a cabinet wife. The rest of the administration wives, led by Mrs. Calhoun, refused to receive her. Jackson (remembering the effects of public slander directed against his own late wife) was furious and demanded that the members of the cabinet accept her into their social world. Calhoun, under pressure from his wife, refused. Van Buren, a widower, befriended the Eatons and thus ingratiated himself with Jackson. By 1831, partly as a result of the Peggy Eaton affair, Jackson had chosen Van Buren to succeed him in the White House, apparently ending Calhoun's dreams of the presidency.

The Webster-Hayne Debate

In January 1830, as the controversy over nullification grew more intense, a great debate occurred in the United States Senate over another sectional controversy. In the midst of a routine debate over federal policy toward western lands, a senator from Connecticut suggested that all land sales and surveys be temporarily discontinued. Robert Y. Hayne, a young senator from South Carolina, responded, charging that slowing down the growth of the West was a way for the East to retain its political and economic power. Although he had no real interest in western lands, he hoped his stance would attract support from westerners in Congress for South

Carolina's drive to lower the tariff. Both the South and the West, he argued, were victims of the tyranny of the Northeast. He hinted that the two regions might combine to defend themselves against that tyranny.

Daniel Webster, now a senator from Massachusetts and a nationalistic Whig, answered Hayne the next day. He attacked Hayne, and through him Calhoun, for what he considered their challenge to the integrity of the Union—in effect, challenging Hayne to a debate not on public lands and the tariff but on the issue of states' rights versus national power. Hayne, coached by Calhoun, responded with a defense of the theory of nullification. Webster then spent two full afternoons delivering what became known as his "Second Reply to Hayne," a speech that northerners quoted and revered for years to come. He concluded with the ringing appeal: "Liberty and Union, now and for ever, one and inseparable!"

Both sides now waited to hear what President Jackson thought of the argument. The answer became clear at the annual Democratic Party banquet in honor of Thomas Jefferson. After dinner, guests delivered a series of toasts. The president arrived with a written text in which he had underscored certain words: "Our Federal Union—It must be preserved." While he spoke, he looked directly at Calhoun. The diminutive Van Buren, who stood on his chair to see better, thought he saw Calhoun's hand shake and a trickle of wine run down his glass as he responded to the president's toast with his own: "The Union, next to our liberty most dear." Sharp lines were being drawn.

The Nullification Crisis

In 1832, finally, the controversy over nullification produced a crisis when South Carolinians responded angrily to a congressional tariff bill that offered them no relief from the 1828 "tariff of abominations." Almost immediately, the legislature summoned a state convention, which voted to nullify the tariffs of 1828 and 1832 and to forbid the collection of duties within the state. At the same time, South Carolina elected Hayne to serve as governor and Calhoun (who resigned as vice president) to replace Hayne as senator.

Jackson insisted that nullification was treason and that those implementing it were traitors. He strengthened the federal forts in South Carolina and ordered a warship and several revenue ships to Charleston. When Congress convened early in 1833, Jackson proposed a force bill authorizing the president to use the military to see that acts of Congress were obeyed. Violence seemed a real possibility.

Calhoun faced a predicament as he took his place in the Senate. Not a single state had come to South Carolina's support. Even South Carolina itself was divided and could not hope to prevail in a showdown with the federal government. But the timely intervention of Henry Clay, newly elected to the Senate, averted a crisis. Clay devised a compromise by which the tariff would be lowered gradually so that, by 1842, it would reach approximately the same level as in 1816. The compromise and the force bill were passed on the same day, March 1, 1833. Jackson signed them both. In South Carolina, the convention reassembled and repealed its nullification of the tariffs. But unwilling to allow Congress to have the last word, the convention nullified the force act—a purely symbolic act, since the tariff toward which the force act was directed had already been repealed. Calhoun and his followers claimed a victory for nullification, which had, they insisted, forced the revision of the tariff. But the episode taught Calhoun and his allies that no state could defy the federal government alone.

THE REMOVAL OF THE INDIANS

Andrew Jackson's attitude toward the Indian tribes that remained in the eastern United States was simple and clear. He wanted them to move west, out of the way of expanding white settlement. Jackson harbored a deep hostility toward the Indians drawn from his earlier experiences leading military campaigns against the tribes. In embracing these prejudices, he was little different from most white Americans.

White Attitudes Toward the Tribes

In the eighteenth century, many whites had shared Thomas Jefferson's view of the Indians as "noble savages," peoples without real civilization but with an inherent dignity that made civilization possible among them. By the first decades of the nineteenth century, however, this vaguely philanthropic attitude was fading, particularly among the whites in the West. They were coming to view Native Americans simply as "savages," not only uncivilized but uncivilizable. That was one reason for the growing white commitment to removing the Indians from all the lands east of the Mississippi: the belief that whites could not be expected to live in close proximity to "savages." But white westerners also favored removal to put an end to violence and conflict in the western areas of white settlement. Most of all, however, they wanted valuable land that the tribes still possessed.

BLACK HAWK AND WHIRLING THUNDER After his defeat by white settlers in Illinois in 1832, the famed Sauk warrior Black Hawk and his son, Whirling Thunder, were captured and sent on a tour by Andrew Jackson, displayed to the public as trophies of war. They showed such dignity through the ordeal that much of the white public quickly began to sympathize with them. This portrait, by John Wesley Jarvis, was painted on the tour's final stop, in New York City. Black Hawk wears the European-style suit, while Whirling Thunder wears native costume to emphasize his commitment to his tribal roots. Soon thereafter, Black Hawk returned to his tribe, wrote a celebrated autobiography, and died in 1838.

Events in the Northwest added urgency to the issue of removal. In Illinois, an alliance of Sauk (or Sac) and Fox Indians under the fabled and now aged warrior Black Hawk fought white settlers in 1831–1832 in an effort to overturn what Black Hawk considered an illegal treaty ceding tribal lands in that state to the United States. The Black Hawk War was a major defeat for the Indians, and was notable for the viciousness of the white military efforts. White forces attacked the Indians even when they attempted to surrender, pursued them as they retreated, and slaughtered many of them. But its real impact was to reinforce the determination of whites to remove all the tribes to the West.

The "Five Civilized Tribes"

Even more troubling to the government in the 1830s were the remaining Indian tribes of the South. In western Georgia, Alabama, Mississippi, and Florida lived what were known as the "Five Civilized Tribes"—the Cherokee, Creek, Seminole, Chickasaw, and Choctaw—most of whom were part of settled agricultural societies. In 1830, both the federal government and several southern states were accelerating efforts to remove the tribes to the West. Most were too weak to resist, but some fought back.

The Cherokees tried to stop the state of Georgia from taking their lands through an appeal in the Supreme Court, and the Court's rulings in *Cherokee Nation* v. *Georgia* and *Worcester* v. *Georgia* supported the tribe's contention that the state had no authority to negotiate with tribal representatives. But Jackson repudiated the decisions, reportedly responding to news of the rulings with the contemptuous statement: "John Marshall has made his decision. Now let him enforce it." Then, in 1835, the United States government extracted a treaty from a minority faction of the Cherokees that ceded to Georgia the tribe's land in that state in return for $5 million and a reservation west of the Mississippi. The great majority of the 17,000 Cherokees did not recognize the treaty as legitimate and refused to leave their homes. But Jackson sent an army of 7,000 under General Winfield Scott to round them up and drive them westward.

Trails of Tears

About 1,000 Cherokee fled to North Carolina, where eventually the federal government provided them with a small reservation in the Smoky Mountains that survives today. But most of the rest made a long, forced trek to "Indian Territory" (formally created by the Indian Intercourse Act of 1834), what later became Oklahoma, beginning in the winter of 1838. Thousands, perhaps a quarter or more of the émigrés, perished before reaching their unwanted destination. In the harsh new reservations in which they were now forced to live, the survivors remembered the terrible journey as "The Trail Where They Cried," the Trail of Tears.

Between 1830 and 1838, virtually all the Five Civilized Tribes were expelled from the southern states and forced to travel along their own Trails of Tears to Indian Territory. The Choctaws of Mississippi and western Alabama were the first to make the trek, beginning in 1830. The army moved out the Creeks of eastern Alabama and western Georgia in 1836. The Chickasaws in northern Mississippi began the long march westward a year later, and the Cherokees, finally, a year after that.

Only the Seminoles in Florida were able to resist the pressures, and even their success was limited. Like other tribes, the Seminoles had

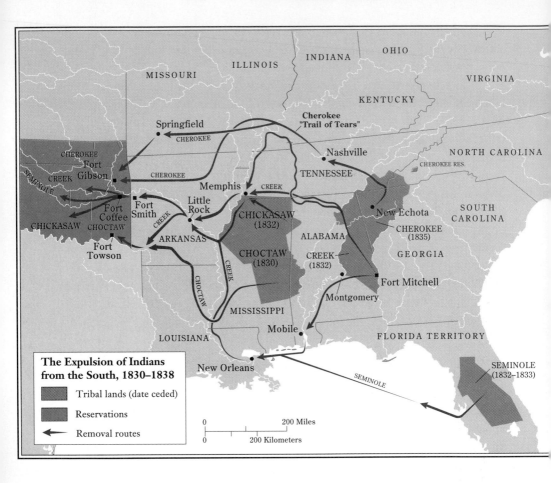

The Expulsion of Indians
from the South, 1830–1838

- Tribal lands (date ceded)
- Reservations
- ← Removal routes

0 — 200 Miles
0 — 200 Kilometers

agreed under pressure to a settlement (the 1832–1833 treaties of Payne's
Landing) by which they ceded their lands to the United States and
agreed to move to Indian Territory within three years. Most did move
west, but a substantial minority, under the leadership of the chieftain
Osceola, balked and staged an uprising beginning in 1835 to defend their
lands. (Joining the Indians in their struggle was a group of runaway black
slaves, who had been living with the tribe.) The Seminole War dragged
on for years. Jackson sent troops to Florida, but the Seminoles and their
black allies were masters of guerrilla warfare in the junglelike Everglades.
Finally, in 1842, the government abandoned the war. By then, many of
the Seminoles had been either killed or forced westward. But the reloca-

tion of the Seminoles, unlike the relocation of most of the other tribes, was never complete.

The Meaning of Removal

By the end of the 1830s, virtually all the important Indian societies east of the Mississippi (with a few exceptions such as remnants of the Seminoles and Cherokees) had been removed to the West. The tribes had ceded over 100 million acres of eastern land to the federal government; they had received in return about $68 million and 32 million acres in the far less hospitable lands west of the Mississippi. There they lived, divided by tribe into a series of separate reservations, in a territory surrounded by a string of United States forts to keep them in (and to keep most whites out), in a region whose climate and topography bore little relation to anything they had known before. Eventually, even this forlorn enclave would face pressures from white civilization.

What were the alternatives to the removal of the eastern Indians? There was probably never any realistic possibility that the government could stop white expansion westward. White people had already been penetrating the West for nearly two centuries, and such penetrations were certain to continue. But there were, in theory at least, alternatives to the brutal removal policy. The West was filled with examples of white settlers and native tribes living side by side and creating a shared (if not necessarily equal) world. In the pueblos of New Mexico, in the fur trading posts of the Pacific Northwest, in parts of Texas and California, settlers from Mexico, Canada, and the United States had created societies in which Indians and whites were in intimate contact with each other. Even the Lewis and Clark expedition, during its famous explorations, had lived with western Indians on terms of such intimacy that many of its members contracted venereal disease from Indian sexual partners. Sometimes these close contacts between whites and Indians were beneficial to both sides, even reasonably equal. Often they were cruel and exploitive. But the early multiracial societies of the West did not separate whites and Indians. They demonstrated ways in which the two cultures could interact, each shaping the other.

By the mid-nineteenth century, however, white Americans had adopted a different model as they contemplated westward expansion. Much as the early British settlers along the Atlantic coast had established "plantations," from which natives were, in theory, to be excluded, so the western whites of later years believed that Indians could not be partners—either equal or subordinate—in the creation of new societies in the West. They were obstacles to be removed and, as far as possible, isolated.

JACKSON AND THE BANK WAR

Jackson was quite willing to use federal power against the Indian tribes. Where white Americans were concerned, however, he was more reluctant. An early example of that was his 1830 veto of a congressional measure providing a subsidy to the proposed Maysville Road in Kentucky. The bill was unconstitutional, Jackson argued, because the road in question lay entirely within Kentucky and was not, therefore, a part of "interstate commerce." But the bill was also unwise because it committed the government to what Jackson considered extravagant expenditures. A similar resistance to federal power lay behind the most celebrated episode of Jackson's presidency: the war against the Bank of the United States.

Biddle's Institution

The Bank of the United States had a monopoly on the deposits of the federal government, which owned one-fifth of the Bank's stock; it also did a tremendous business in general banking. It provided credit to growing enterprises; it issued bank notes that served as a dependable medium of exchange throughout the country; and it exercised a restraining effect on the less well-managed state banks. Nicholas Biddle, who ran the Bank from 1823 on from its imposing headquarters in Philadelphia, had done much to put the institution on a sound and prosperous basis. Nevertheless, many Americans—among them Andrew Jackson—were determined to destroy it.

Opposition to the Bank came from two very different groups: the "soft-money" faction and the "hard-money" faction. Advocates of soft money consisted largely of state bankers and their allies. They objected to the Bank of the United States because it restrained the state banks from issuing notes freely. The hard-money supporters believed that coin was the only safe currency, and they condemned all banks that issued bank notes, including the Bank of the United States. The soft-money advocates were believers in rapid economic growth and speculation; the hard-money forces embraced older ideas of "public virtue" and looked with suspicion on expansion and speculation. Jackson himself supported the hard-money position, but he was also sensitive to the complaints of his many soft-money supporters in the West and the South. He made it clear that he would not favor renewing the charter of the Bank of the United States, which was due to expire in 1836.

Biddle was a Philadelphia aristocrat, unaccustomed to politics. But in his efforts to save the Bank, he began granting banking favors to influential men. In particular, he relied on Daniel Webster, whom he named the Bank's legal counsel and director of the Boston branch. Webster was also a frequent, heavy borrower. He helped Biddle enlist the support of Henry Clay as well. Clay, Webster, and other advisers persuaded Biddle to apply to Congress for a recharter bill in 1832, four years ahead of the expiration date. Congress passed the recharter bill; Jackson vetoed it; and the Bank's supporters in Congress failed to override the veto. The Bank question then emerged as the paramount issue of the 1832 election, just as Clay had hoped.

In 1832, Clay ran for president as the unanimous choice of the National Republicans. But the "Bank War" failed to provide Clay with the winning issue for which he had hoped. Jackson, with Van Buren as his running mate, won an overwhelming victory with 55 percent of the popular vote and 219 electoral votes.

The "Monster" Destroyed

Jackson was now more determined than ever to destroy the "monster." He could not legally abolish the Bank before the expiration of its charter. But he weakened it by removing the government's deposits from it. His secretary of the treasury believed that such an action would destabilize the financial system and refused to give the order. Jackson fired him and appointed a replacement. When the new secretary similarly procrastinated, Jackson fired him, too, and named a third: Roger B. Taney, the attorney general, a close friend and loyal ally of the president.

Taney soon began taking the government's deposits out of the Bank of the United States and putting them in a number of state banks (which Jackson's enemies called "pet banks"). In response, Biddle called in loans and raised interest rates, explaining that without the government deposits the Bank's resources were stretched too thin. His actions precipitated a short recession, which Biddle thought would pressure Congress to recharter the Bank.

As financial conditions worsened in the winter of 1833–1834, sup-porters of the Bank organized meetings around the country and sent petitions to Washington urging a rechartering of the Bank. But the Jacksonians blamed the recession on Biddle and refused. The banker fi-nally carried his contraction of credit too far and had to reverse himself to appease the business community. His hopes of winning a recharter of the Bank died in the process. Jackson had won a considerable political victory. But when the Bank of the United States died in 1836, the coun-try lost an important financial institution and was left with a frag-mented and chronically unstable banking system that would plague the economy for many years.

The Taney Court

In the aftermath of the Bank War, Jackson moved against the most power-ful remaining institution of economic nationalism: the Supreme Court. In 1835, when John Marshall died, the president appointed as the new chief justice his trusted ally Roger B. Taney. Taney did not bring a sharp break in constitutional interpretation, but he did help modify Marshall's vigor-ous nationalism.

Perhaps the clearest indication of the new judicial climate was the celebrated case of *Charles River Bridge* v. *Warren Bridge* of 1837. The case involved a dispute between two Massachusetts companies over the right to build a bridge across the Charles River between Boston and Cam-bridge. One company had a longstanding charter from the state to oper-ate a toll bridge, a charter that the firm claimed guaranteed it a monopoly of the bridge traffic. Another company had applied to the legislature for authorization to construct a second, competing bridge that would—since it would be toll-free—greatly reduce the value of the first company's charter. The first company contended that in granting the second char-ter, the legislature was engaging in a breach of contract; and it noted that the Marshall Court, in the *Dartmouth College* case and other decisions, had ruled that states had no right to abrogate contracts. But now Taney, speaking for the Democratic majority on the Court, supported the right of Massachusetts to award the second charter. The object of government, Taney maintained, was to promote the general happiness, an object that took precedence over the rights of property. A state, therefore, had the right to amend or abrogate a contract if such action was necessary to ad-vance the well-being of the community. The decision reflected one of the cornerstones of the Jacksonian idea: that the key to democracy was an expansion of economic opportunity, which would not occur if older corporations could maintain monopolies and choke off competition from newer companies.

THE EMERGENCE OF THE SECOND PARTY SYSTEM

Jackson's forceful—some claimed tyrannical—tactics in crushing first the nullification movement and then the Bank of the United States helped galvanize a growing opposition coalition that by the mid-1830s was ready to assert itself in national politics. It began as a gathering of national political leaders opposed to Jackson's use of power. Denouncing the president as "King Andrew I," they began to refer to themselves as Whigs, after the party in England that traditionally worked to limit the power of the king. With the emergence of the Whigs, the nation once again had two competing political parties. What scholars now call the "second party system" had begun what would turn out to be its relatively brief life.

The Two Parties

The philosophy of the Democratic Party in the 1830s bore the stamp of Andrew Jackson. The federal government, the Democrats believed, should be limited in power, except to the degree that it worked to eliminate social and economic arrangements that entrenched privilege and stifled opportunity. The rights of states should be protected except to the extent that state governments interfered with social and economic mobility. Jacksonian Democrats celebrated "honest workers," "simple farmers," and "forthright businessmen" and contrasted them to the corrupt, monopolistic, aristocratic forces of established wealth. Democrats were more likely than Whigs to support territorial expansion, which would, they believed, widen opportunities for aspiring Americans. Among the most radical members of the party—the so-called Locofocos, mainly workingmen and small businessmen and professionals in the Northeast—sentiment was strong for a vigorous, perhaps even violent, assault on monopoly and privilege far in advance of anything Jackson himself ever contemplated.

The political philosophy that became known as Whiggery favored expanding the power of the federal government, encouraging industrial and commercial development, and knitting the country together into a consolidated economic system. Whigs were cautious about westward expansion, fearful that rapid territorial growth would produce instability. Their vision of America was of a nation embracing the industrial future and rising to greatness as a commercial and manufacturing power. And although Whigs insisted that their vision would result in increasing opportunities for all Americans, they tended to attribute particular value to the elites they considered the productive, modernizing forces in society—the entrepreneurs and institutions that most effectively promoted economic growth.

The Whigs were strongest among the more substantial merchants and manufacturers of the Northeast; the wealthier planters of the South (those who favored commercial development and the strengthening of ties with the North); and the ambitious farmers and rising commercial class of the West—usually migrants from the Northeast—who advocated internal improvements, expanding trade, and rapid economic progress. The Democrats drew more support from smaller merchants and the workingmen of the Northeast; from Southern planters suspicious of industrial growth; and from westerners—usually with Southern roots—who favored a predominantly agrarian economy and opposed the development of powerful economic institutions in their region. Whigs tended to be wealthier than Democrats, tended to have more aristocratic backgrounds, and tended to be more commercially ambitious. But Whigs and Democrats alike were more interested in winning elections than in maintaining philosophical purity. And both parties made adjustments from region to region in order to attract the largest possible number of voters, often at the sacrifice of party philosophy.

In New York, for example, the Whigs developed a popular following through a movement known as Anti-Masonry. The Anti-Mason Party had emerged in the 1820s in response to widespread resentment against the secret and exclusive, hence supposedly undemocratic, Society of Freemasons. Such resentment increased in 1826 when a former Mason, William Morgan, mysteriously disappeared from his home in Batavia, New York, shortly before he was scheduled to publish a book that would allegedly expose the secrets of Freemasonry. The assumption was widespread that Morgan had been abducted and murdered by the vengeful Masons. Whigs seized on the Anti-Mason frenzy to launch spirited attacks on Jackson and Van Buren (both Freemasons), implying that the Democrats were connected with the antidemocratic conspiracy. By embracing Anti-Masonry, Whigs were attacking the Democrats with the Democrats' own issues.

Religious and ethnic divisions also played an important role in determining the constituencies of the two parties. Irish and German Catholics, among the largest of the recent immigrant groups, tended to support the

Democrats, who appeared to share their own vague aversion to commercial development and entrepreneurial progress and who seemed to respect and protect their cultural values and habits. Evangelical Protestants gravitated toward the Whigs because they associated the party with constant development and improvement, goals their own religion embraced. They envisioned a society progressing steadily toward unity and order, and they looked on the new immigrant communities as a threat to that progress— as groups that needed to be disciplined and taught "American" ways.

The Whig Party was more successful at defining its positions and attracting a constituency than it was in uniting behind a national leader. No one person was ever able to command the loyalties of the party in the way Jackson commanded the loyalties of the Democrats. Instead, Whigs tended to divide their allegiance among three major figures: Henry Clay, Daniel Webster, and John C. Calhoun.

Clay won support from many of those who favored internal improvements and economic development, what he called the American System; such improvements were especially important to people living in the western states, where the absence of good transportation routes to the markets of the east often proved crippling to commerce. But Clay's image as a devious political operator and his identification with the West proved an insuperable liability. He ran for president three times and never won. Daniel Webster, the greatest orator of his era, won broad support among the Whigs with his passionate speeches in defense of the Constitution and the Union; but his close connection with the Bank of the United States and the protective tariff, his reliance on rich men for financial support, and his excessive fondness for brandy prevented him from developing enough of a national constituency to win him the office he so desperately wanted. John C. Calhoun, the third member of what became known as the Great Triumvirate, never considered himself a true Whig, and his identification with the nullification controversy in effect disqualified him from national leadership in any case. Yet, he sided with Clay and Webster on the issue of the national bank, and he shared with them a strong animosity toward Andrew Jackson.

The Whigs competed relatively evenly with the Democrats in congressional, state, and local races, but they managed to win only two presidential elections in the more than twenty years of their history. Their problems became particularly clear in 1836. The Democrats were united behind Andrew Jackson's personal choice for president, Martin Van Buren. The Whigs could not even agree on a single candidate. Instead, they ran several candidates, hoping to profit from the regional strength of each: Webster in New England; Hugh Lawson White of Tennessee in the South; and the former Indian fighter and hero of the War of 1812, William Henry Harrison of Ohio, in the middle states and the West. Whig leaders hoped they might separately draw enough votes from Van Buren to prevent his getting a majority and throw the election to the House of Representatives, where the Whigs might be better able to elect one of their candidates. In the end, however, the three Whigs were no match for the one Democrat. Van Buren won easily, with 170 electoral votes to 124 for all his opponents.

POLITICS AFTER JACKSON

Andrew Jackson retired from public life in 1837, the most beloved political figure of his age. Martin Van Buren was less fortunate. He could not match Jackson's personal magnetism, and his administration suffered from economic difficulties that hurt both him and his party.

The Panic of 1837

Van Buren's success in the 1836 election was a result in part of a nationwide economic boom that was then reaching its height. Canal and railroad builders were at a peak of activity. Prices were rising, and credit was plentiful. The land business, in particular, was booming. Between 1835 and 1837, the government sold nearly 40 million acres of public land, nearly three-fourths of it to speculators who purchased large tracts in hopes of reselling them at a profit. These land sales, along with revenues the government received from the tariff of 1833, created a series of substantial federal budget surpluses and made possible a steady reduction of the national debt (something Jackson had always advocated). From 1835 to 1837, the government for the first and only time in its history was out of debt, with a substantial surplus in the Treasury.

Congress and the administration now faced the question of what to do with the Treasury surplus. Support soon grew for returning the federal surplus to the states. An 1836 "distribution" act required the federal government to pay its surplus funds to the states each year in four quarterly installments as interest-free, unsecured loans. No one expected the "loans" to be repaid. The states spent the money quickly, mainly to promote the construction of highways, railroads, and canals. The distribution of the surplus thus gave further stimulus to the economic boom. At the same time, the withdrawal of federal funds strained the state (or "pet") banks in which they had been deposited by the government; the banks had to call in their own loans to make the transfer of funds to the state governments.

Congress did nothing to check the speculative fever, with which many congressmen themselves were badly infected. But Jackson, always suspicious of paper currency, feared that the government was selling land for state bank notes of questionable value. In 1836, not long before leaving office, he issued an executive order, the "specie circular." It provided that in payment for public lands, the government would accept only gold or silver coins or currency backed by gold or silver. The specie circular produced a financial panic that began in the first months of Van Buren's presidency. Hundreds of banks and hundreds of businesses failed. Unemployment grew. There were bread riots in some of the larger cities. Prices fell, especially the price of land. Many railroad and canal projects failed; several of the debt-burdened state governments ceased to pay interest on their bonds, and a few repudiated their debts, at least temporarily. It was the worst depression in American history to that point, and it lasted for five years. It was a political catastrophe for Van Buren and the Democrats.

The Van Buren Program

The Van Buren administration, which strongly opposed government intervention in the economy, did little to fight the depression. Some of the steps it took—borrowing money to pay government debts and accepting only specie for payment of taxes—may have made things worse. Other efforts failed in Congress: a "preemption" bill that would have given settlers the right to buy government land near them before it was opened for public sale, and another bill that would have lowered the price of land. Van Buren did succeed in establishing a ten-hour workday on all federal projects by issuing a presidential order, but he had few legislative achievements.

The most important and controversial measure in the president's program was a proposal for a new financial system to replace the Bank of the United States. Under Van Buren's plan, known as the "independent treasury" or "subtreasury" system, government funds would be placed in an independent treasury in Washington and in subtreasuries in other cities. No private banks would have the government's money or name to use as a basis for speculation; the government and the banks would be "divorced." Van Buren called a special session of Congress in 1837 to consider the proposal, which failed in the House. In 1840, the administration finally succeeded in driving the measure through both houses of Congress.

The Log Cabin Campaign

As the campaign of 1840 approached, the Whigs realized that they would have to settle on one candidate for president. In December 1839, they held their first nomination convention. Passing over Henry Clay, they chose William Henry Harrison—a descendant of the Virginia aristocracy who had spent his adult life in the Northwest. He was a renowned soldier and a popular national figure. The Democrats again nominated Van Buren.

The 1840 campaign was the first in which the new and popular "penny press" carried news of the candidates to large audiences of workers and tradespeople. Newspapers of the "penny press" were deliberately livelier and even more sensationalistic than the newspapers of the past, which had been almost entirely directed at the upper classes. The New York *Sun*, the first of the new breed, began publishing in 1833 and was from the beginning self-

THE NEW YORK *SUN* This 1834 front page of the *Sun*, which had begun publication a year earlier, contains advertisements, light stories, a description of a slave auction in Charleston, South Carolina, and homespun advice: "Life is short. The poor pittance of several years is not worth being a villain for."

consciously egalitarian, eager to tweak and embarrass the rich and powerful. It soon had the largest circulation in New York. Other, similar papers soon began appearing in other cities—reinforcing the increasingly democratic character of political culture and validating the inclination of both parties to try to appeal to ordinary voters as they planned their campaigns.

The campaign of 1840 also illustrated how fully the spirit of party competition had established itself in America. The Whigs—who had emerged as a party largely because of their opposition to Andrew Jackson's common-man democracy, who in most regions represented the

WHIG HEADQUARTERS The Whig Party managed in 1840 to disguise its relatively elitist roots by portraying its presidential candidate, the patrician General William Henry Harrison, as a product of a log cabin who enjoyed drinking hard cider from a jug. Pictures of log cabins abounded in Whig campaign posters, as seen in this drawing of a Harrison rally in Philadelphia.

more affluent elements of the population, who favored government policies that would aid business—presented themselves in 1840 as the party
of the common people. So, of course, did the Democrats. Both parties
used the same techniques of mass voter appeal, the same evocation of
simple, rustic values. What mattered was not the philosophical purity of
the party but its ability to win votes. The Whig campaign was particularly effective in portraying William Henry Harrison, a wealthy member
of the frontier elite with a considerable estate, as a simple man of the
people who loved log cabins and hard cider. The Democrats, already
weakened by the depression, had no effective defense against such tactics.
Harrison won the election with 234 electoral votes to 60 for Van Buren
and with a popular majority of 53 percent.

The Frustration of the Whigs

But the Whigs found the four years after their resounding victory frustrating and divisive. In large part, that was because their appealing new president died of pneumonia one month after taking office. Vice President John
Tyler of Virginia succeeded him. Control of the administration thus fell to
a man with whom the Whig Party leadership had relatively weak ties.

Tyler was a former Democrat who had left the party in reaction to
what he considered Jackson's excessively egalitarian program and his im-
perious methods. But his approach to public policy still showed signs of
his Democratic past. The president did agree to bills abolishing Van
Buren's independent-treasury system and raising tariff rates. But he refused to support Clay's attempt to recharter the Bank of the United States.
And he vetoed several internal improvement bills sponsored by Clay and
other congressional Whigs. Finally, a conference of congressional Whigs
(many of whom referred scornfully to the new president as "His Acci-
dency") read Tyler out of the party. Every cabinet member but Webster,
who was serving as secretary of state, resigned; five former Democrats
took their places. When Webster, too, left the cabinet, Tyler appointed
Calhoun, who had rejoined the Democratic Party, to replace him.

A new political alignment was taking shape. Tyler and a small band of
conservative southern Whigs were preparing to rejoin the Democrats.
Into the common man's party of Jackson and Van Buren was arriving a
faction with decidedly aristocratic political ideas, men who thought that
government had an obligation to protect and even expand the institution
of slavery and who believed in states' rights with almost fanatical devotion.

Whig Diplomacy

In the midst of these domestic controversies, a series of incidents brought Great Britain and the United States to the brink of war in the late 1830s.

Anti-British factions in Canada launched an unsuccessful rebellion against the colonial government there in 1837. When the insurrection failed, some of the rebels took refuge near the United States border and chartered an American steamship, the *Caroline*, to ship them supplies across the Niagara River from New York. British authorities in Canada seized the *Caroline* and burned it, killing one American in the process. The British government refused either to disavow the attack or to provide compensation for it, and resentment in the United States grew rapidly.

At the same time, tensions flared over the boundary between Canada and Maine, which had been in dispute since the treaty of 1783. In 1838, rival groups of Americans and Canadians, mostly lumberjacks, began moving into the Aroostook River region in the disputed area, precipitating a violent brawl between them that became known as the "Aroostook War." Several years later, there were yet more Anglo-American problems. In 1841, an American ship, the *Creole*, sailed from Virginia for New Orleans with more than 100 slaves aboard. En route the slaves mutinied, seized possession of the ship, and took it to the Bahamas. British officials there declared the slaves free, and the English government refused to overrule them. Many Americans, especially southerners, were furious.

At this critical juncture a new government eager to reduce tensions with the United States came to power in Great Britain. It sent Lord Ashburton, an admirer of America, to negotiate an agreement on the Maine boundary and other matters. The result was the Webster-Ashburton Treaty of 1842, under which the United States received slightly more than half the disputed area and agreed to a revised northern boundary as far west as the Rocky Mountains. Ashburton also eased the memory of the *Caroline* and *Creole* affairs by expressing regret and promising no future "officious interference" with American ships. The Webster-Ashburton Treaty was popular in America, and Anglo-American relations improved significantly as a result.

During the Tyler administration, the United States established its first diplomatic relations with China as part of an effort to win a share in the newly emerging China trade. In the Treaty of Wang Hya, concluded in 1844, American diplomats secured the same trading privileges as the English. In the next ten years, American trade with China steadily increased.

In their diplomatic efforts, at least, the Whigs were able to secure some important successes. But by the end of the Tyler administration, the party could look back on few other victories. In the election of 1844, the Whigs lost the White House. They were to win only one more national election in their history.

CONCLUSION

The election of Andrew Jackson to the presidency in 1828 marked not only the triumph of a particular vision of government and democracy. It represented as well the emergence of a new political world. Throughout the American nation, the laws governing political participation were loosening and the number of people permitted to vote (which eventually included most white males, but almost no one else) was increasing. Along with this expansion of the electorate was emerging a new spirit of party politics. Parties had once been reviled by American leaders as contributing to the spirit of faction. Now a new set of ideas was emerging that saw institutionalized parties not as a challenge, but as a contribution to democracy. Party competition would be a way of containing and muting disagreements that might otherwise run amok. It would be another of the healthy restraints—another part of the system of checks and balances—that made American government work.

Andrew Jackson was a party man, and he set out as president to entrench his party, the Democrats, in power. He was also a fierce defender of his region, the West, and a sharp critic of what he considered the stranglehold of the aristocratic East on the nation's economic life. He sought to limit the role of the federal government in economic affairs, fearful that it would serve to entrench existing patterns of wealth and power. He worked to destroy the Bank of the United States, which he considered a corrupt vehicle of aristocratic influence. Jackson was, finally, a nationalist. And he confronted the greatest challenge to American unity yet to have emerged in the young nation—the nullification crisis of 1832–1833—with a strong assertion of the power and importance of the Union. These positions won him broad popularity and ensured his reelection in 1832 and the election of his designated successor, Martin Van Buren, in 1836.

But the Democrats were not the only ones to have learned the lessons of the age of parties. A new coalition of anti-Jacksonians, who called themselves the Whigs, launched a powerful new party that used much of the same anti-elitist rhetoric the Democrats had used to win support for their own much more nationalist program. Their emergence culminated in the campaign of 1840 with the election of the first Whig president.

FOR FURTHER REFERENCE

Suggested Readings

Harry L. Watson, *Liberty and Power: The Politics of Jacksonian America* (1990) and Charles Sellers, *The Market Revolution: Jacksonian America, 1815–1846* (1991) are good recent syntheses of the Jacksonian era. Arthur M. Schlesinger, Jr., *The Age of Jackson* (1945) is a classic study, which represents Jacksonian politics as an eastern, urban democratic movement. Bray Hammond, *Banks and Politics in America from the Revolution to the Civil War* (1957) challenged Schlesinger by arguing that the Bank War was essentially a struggle between different groups of capitalist elites. Daniel Walker Howe, *The Political Culture of the American Whigs* (1979) analyzes the careers of several leading Whig politicians, including the Whig triumvirate of Calhoun, Clay, and Webster. William V. Freehling, *Prelude to Civil War: The Nullification Controversy in South Carolina* (1966) argues that South Carolina planters' anxiety over the fate of slavery was at the heart of the nullification crisis. Francis P. Prucha, *American Indian Policy in the Formative Years* (1962) is an overview of early Indian policy by the leading scholar of the subject. Michael Rogin, *Fathers and Children: Andrew Jackson and the Destruction of American Indians* (1975) offers a more radical and idiosyncratic perspective on Jackson's career as an Indian-fighter using the methods of psychoanalysis. Sean Wilentz, *Chants Democratic: New York City and the Rise of the American Working Class, 1788–1850* (1984) is an important study of the working-class ideology during the Jacksonian period. Robert V. Remini, the leading modern biographer of Jackson, is the author of *Andrew Jackson and the Course of American Empire: 1767–1821* (1977); *Andrew Jackson and the Course of American Freedom: 1822–1832* (1981); *Andrew Jackson and the Course of American Democracy* (1984); and *The Life of Andrew Jackson* (1988).

Films

Andrew Jackson: A Man for the People is part of the Arts & Entertainment Network biography series. *The Jackson Years: The New Americans* (1971) dramatizes episodes in Jackson's life. *The Jackson Years: Toward Civil War* (1971) focuses on Jackson's dominant personality in an analysis of the major events of Jackson's presidential administration. *The Jacksonian Persuasion* uses the example of a country store in the West and Charleston, South Carolina, to illustrate themes in Jacksonian politics from Indian removal to nullification. *The American Story, No. 8: Expansion and Removal* (1985) examines the removal of Indians from their lands east of the Mississippi and the expansion of United States settlement to the west. *Trail of Tears* (1973) follows the forced removal of the Cherokee Indians to the West, and the subsequent Cherokee struggle to retain a sense of identity and heritage. See also *The Seminole* (1993).

Internet Resources

Internet websites containing historical material relevant to the subjects discussed in this chapter can be reached through the McGraw-Hill history site at www.mhhe.com/socscience/history/usa/link/linktop.htm.

CHAPTER TEN

America's Economic Revolution

The Changing American Population

Transportation and Commucications Revolutions

Commerce and Industry ∼ *Men and Women at Work*

Patterns of Society ∼ *The Agricultural North*

HEN THE UNITED States entered the War of 1812, it was still an essentially agrarian nation. There were, to be sure, some substantial cities in America. There was also modest but growing manufacturing, mainly in the Northeast. But the overwhelming majority of Americans were farmers and tradespeople, working within an economy that was still mainly local.

By the time the Civil War began in 1861, the United States had transformed itself. Most Americans were still rural people. But even American farmers were, with few exceptions, now part of a national, and even international, market economy. Equally important, the United States had developed a major manufacturing sector and was beginning to challenge the industrial nations of Europe for supremacy. The nation had experienced the beginning of its industrial revolution.

THE CHANGING AMERICAN POPULATION

The American industrial revolution was a result of many factors: population growth, advances in transportation and communications, the growth of manufacturing technology, and the development of new systems of business organization. By 1860, the northern regions of the nation had acquired at least the beginnings of all those things.

TIME LINE				
1817–1825	**1830**	**1830s**	**1834**	**1837**
Erie Canal constructed	Baltimore and Ohio Railroad begins operation	Immigration from southern Ireland begins	Lowell mills women strike McCormick patents mechanical reaper	Native American Association fights immigration
1844	**1845**	**1846**	**1847**	**1852**
Morse sends first telegraph message	Native American Party formed	Rotary press invented	John Deere manufactures steel plows	American Party (Know Nothings) formed

The American Population, 1820–1840

Three trends characterized the American population between 1820 and 1840, all of them contributing in various ways to economic growth. The population was increasing rapidly. Much of it was moving westward. And much of it was becoming concentrated in towns and cities, where the new residents provided a work force for industry.

The American population had stood at only 4 million in 1790. By 1820, it had reached 10 million; and by 1840, 17 million. The United States was growing much more rapidly in population than Britain or Europe. One reason for the growth was improvements in public health; the number and ferocity of epidemics (such as the great cholera plague of 1832) slowly declined, as did the mortality rate as a whole. But the population increase was also a result of a high birth rate. In 1840, white women bore an average of 6.14 children each.

The African-American population increased more slowly than the white population. After 1808, when the importation of slaves became illegal, the proportion of blacks to whites in the nation as a whole steadily declined. In 1820, there was one African American to every four whites; in 1840, one to every five. The slower increase of the black population was a result of its comparatively high death rate. Slave mothers had large families, but life was shorter for both slaves and free blacks than for whites—a result of the enforced poverty in which virtually all African Americans lived.

Immigration, choked off by wars in Europe and economic crises in America, contributed little to the American population in the first three decades of the nineteenth century. Of the total 1830 population of nearly 13 million, the foreign-born numbered fewer than 500,000. Soon, however, immigration began to grow once again. Reduced transportation costs and increasing economic opportunities in America helped stimulate the immigration boom, as did deteriorating economic conditions in some areas of Europe. The migrations introduced new groups to the United

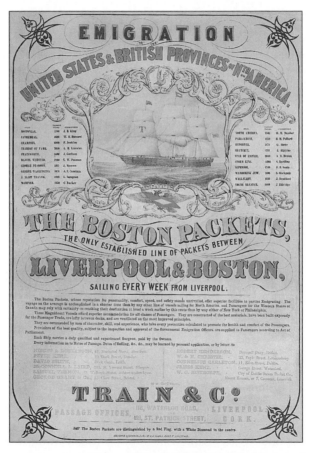

AN APPEAL TO EMIGRANTS This widely-distributed advertising card was one of many such appeals to potential English and Irish travelers to America in the 1830s and 1840s. Like many such companies, this shipping line tried to appeal both to affluent passengers (by boasting of "superior accommodations") and working-class people of modest means.

States. In particular, the number of immigrants arriving from the southern (Catholic) counties of Ireland began to grow.

Much of this new European immigration flowed into the rapidly growing cities of the Northeast. But urban growth was a result of substantial internal migration as well. As the agricultural regions of New England and other areas grew less profitable, more and more people picked up stakes and moved—some to promising agricultural regions in the West, but many to eastern cities. In 1790, one person in thirty had lived in a city (defined as a community of 8,000 or more); in 1820, one in twenty; and in 1840, one in twelve. The largest such cities were in the Northeast.

The rise of New York City was particularly dramatic. By 1810 it was the largest city in the United States, partly a result of its excellent natural harbor. It was also a result of the Erie Canal (completed in 1825), which gave the city unrivaled access to the interior. And it was a result, too, of liberal state laws that made the city attractive for both foreign and domestic commerce.

Immigration and Urban Growth, 1840–1860

The growth of cities accelerated dramatically between 1840 and 1860. The population of New York, for example, rose from 312,000 to 805,000. Philadelphia's population grew over the same twenty-year period from 220,000 to 565,000; Boston's, from 93,000 to 177,000. By 1860, 26 percent of the population of the free states was living in towns (places of 2,500 people or more) or cities, up from 14 percent in 1840. In the South, by contrast, the increase of urban residents was only from 6 percent in 1840 to 10 percent in 1860.

The booming agricultural economy of the western regions of the nation produced significant urban growth as well. Between 1820 and 1840, communities that had once been small villages or trading posts became major cities: St. Louis, Pittsburgh, Cincinnati, Louisville. Each of them benefited from a strategic position on the Mississippi River or one of its major tributaries. All of them became centers of the growing carrying trade that connected the farmers of the Midwest with New Orleans and, through it, the cities of the Northeast. After 1830, however, an increasing proportion of this shipping moved from the river to the Great Lakes and created major new urban centers that gradually superseded the river ports. Among them were Buffalo, Detroit, Milwaukee, Cleveland, and—most important in the end—Chicago.

The enlarged urban population was to a large degree a result of the flow of two major groups of people into cities: the native farmers of the Northeast, who were being forced off the land by competition from the West; and, even more significantly by the 1850s, immigrants from Europe. Only 500,000 foreigners had arrived in the United States in the depression years of the 1830s, but between 1840 and 1850, more than 1.5 million Europeans moved to America. In the 1850s, the number rose to 2.5 million. Almost half the residents of New York City in the 1850s were recent immigrants. In St. Louis, Chicago, and Milwaukee, the foreign-born outnumbered those of native birth. Few immigrants settled in the South. Only 500,000 lived in the slave states in 1860, a third of them in Missouri.

The newcomers came from many different countries, but the overwhelming majority came from Ireland and Germany, where widespread poverty and political upheavals were driving many people out. By 1860, there were more than 1.5 million Irish-born and approximately 1 million German-born people in the United States. Most of the Irish stayed in the eastern cities where they landed and became part of the unskilled labor force. The largest single group of Irish immigrants were young, single women, who worked in factories or in domestic service. Germans, who— unlike the Irish—usually arrived with at least some money and often came in family groups, generally moved on to the Northwest, where they became farmers or went into business in the western towns.

The Rise of Nativism

The new foreign-born population almost immediately became a major factor in American political life. Many politicians eagerly courted the support of the new arrivals. Others, however, viewed the growing foreign population with alarm. Some argued that the immigrants were racially inferior or that they corrupted politics by selling their votes. Others complained that because the foreign-born were willing to work for low wages, they were stealing jobs from the native work force. Protestants worried that the growing Irish population would increase the power of the Catholic Church in America. Older-stock Americans feared that immigrants would become a radical force in politics. Out of these fears and prejudices emerged a number of secret societies to combat the "alien menace."

The first was the Native American Association, founded in 1837, which in 1845 became the Native American Party. In 1850, it joined with other nativist groups to form the Supreme Order of the Star-Spangled Banner, whose demands included banning Catholics or aliens from holding public office, enacting more restrictive naturalization laws, and establishing literacy tests for voting. The order adopted a strict code of secrecy, which included a secret password, used in lodges across the country: "I know nothing." Ultimately, members of the movement came to be known as the "Know-Nothings."

After the 1852 elections, the Know-Nothings created a new political organization that they called the American Party. It scored an immediate and astonishing success in the elections of 1854. The Know-Nothings did well in Pennsylvania and New York and actually won control of the state government in Massachusetts. Outside the Northeast, however, their progress was more modest. After 1854, the strength of the Know-Nothings declined and the party soon disappeared.

TRANSPORTATION AND COMMUNICATIONS REVOLUTIONS

Just as the industrial revolution required an expanding population, it also required an efficient and effective system of transportation and communications. The first half of the nineteenth century saw dramatic changes in both.

The Canal Age

From 1790 until the 1820s, the so-called turnpike era, the United States had relied largely on roads for internal transportation. But roads alone were not adequate for the nation's expanding needs. And so, in the 1820s and 1830s, Americans began to turn to other means of transportation as well.

The larger rivers, especially the Mississippi and the Ohio, became increasingly important as steamboats replaced the slow barges that had previously dominated water traffic. The new riverboats carried the corn and wheat of northwestern farmers and the cotton and tobacco of southwestern planters to New Orleans. From New Orleans, oceangoing ships took the cargoes on to eastern ports.

But this roundabout river-sea route satisfied neither western farmers nor eastern merchants, who wanted a way to ship goods directly to the urban markets of the Atlantic coast. New highways across the mountains provided a partial solution to the problem. But the costs of hauling goods overland, although lower than before, were still too high for anything except the most compact and valuable merchandise. And so interest grew in

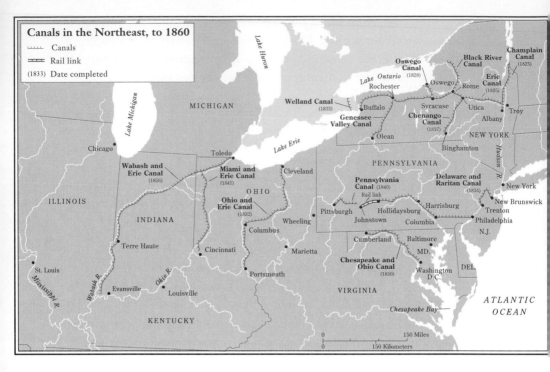

Canals in the Northeast, to 1860

⊔⊔⊔⊔ Canals
═══ Rail link
(1833) Date completed

building inland waterways. On a turnpike, four horses could haul one and a half tons eighteen miles in a day. But the same four horses could draw a boatload of a hundred tons twenty-four miles a day on a canal.

Canal building was too expensive for private enterprise, and the job of financing canals fell largely to the states. New York was the first to act. It had the natural advantage of a good land route between the Hudson River and Lake Erie through the only break in the Appalachian chain. But the engineering tasks were still imposing. The distance was more than 350 miles, several times as long as any of the existing canals in America. The route was interrupted by high ridges and thick woods. After a long public debate, canal advocates prevailed when De Witt Clinton, a late but ardent convert to the cause, became governor in 1817. Digging began on July 4, 1817.

The building of the Erie Canal was the greatest construction project Americans had ever undertaken. The canal itself was basically a simple ditch forty feet wide and four feet deep, with towpaths along the banks for the horses or mules that were to draw the canal boats. But its construction involved hundreds of difficult cuts and fills to enable the canal to pass through hills and over valleys, stone aqueducts to carry it across streams, and eighty-eight locks, of heavy masonry with great wooden gates, to permit ascents and descents. The Erie Canal was not just an engineering triumph but an immediate financial success. It opened in October 1825, amid elaborate ceremonies and celebrations, and traffic was soon so heavy that within about seven years tolls had repaid the entire cost of construction. By providing a route to the Great Lakes, the canal gave New York access to Chicago and the growing markets of the West and established the city as the greatest metropolitan center in the nation. The Erie Canal also contributed to the decline of agriculture in New England. Now that it was so much cheaper for western farmers to ship their crops east, people farming marginal land in the Northeast found themselves unable to compete.

The system of water transportation extended farther when the states of Ohio and Indiana, inspired by the success of the Erie Canal, provided water connections between Lake Erie and the Ohio River. These canals made it possible to ship goods by inland waterways all the way from New York to New Orleans, although it was still necessary to transfer cargoes several times between canal, lake, and river craft.

One of the immediate results of these new transportation routes was increased white settlement in the Northwest, because it was now easier for migrants to make the westward journey and to ship their goods back to eastern markets. Much of the western produce continued to go downriver to New Orleans, but an increasing proportion (including most of the wheat of the Northwest) went east to New York. And manufactured goods from throughout the East now moved in growing volume through New York and then to the West via the new water routes.

Rival cities along the Atlantic seaboard took alarm at the prospect of New York's acquiring access to (and control over) so vast a market, largely at their expense. But they had limited success in catching up. Boston, its way to the Hudson River blocked by the Berkshire Mountains, did not even try to connect itself to the West by canal. Philadelphia, Baltimore, Richmond, and Charleston all aspired to build water routes to the Ohio Valley, but never completed them.

Canals did not provide a satisfactory way to the West for any of New York's rivals. Some cities, however, saw opportunities in a different and newer means of transportation. Even before the canal age had reached its height, the era of the railroad was beginning.

The Early Railroads

Railroads played a relatively small role in the nation's transportation system in the 1820s and 1830s, but railroad pioneers laid the groundwork in those years for the great surge of railroad building in midcentury that would link the nation together as never before. Eventually, railroads became the primary transportation system for the United States, and they remained so until the construction of the interstate highway system in the mid-twentieth century. They also eventually became critical sites of development for innovations in technology and corporate organization.

Railroads emerged from a combination of technological and entrepreneurial innovations: the invention of tracks, the creation of steam-powered locomotives, and the development of trains as public carriers of passengers and freight. By 1804, both English and American inventors had experimented with steam engines for propelling land vehicles. In 1820, John Stevens ran a locomotive and cars around a circular track on his New Jersey estate. And in 1825, the Stockton and Darlington Railroad in England opened a short length of track and became the first line to carry general traffic.

American entrepreneurs, especially in those northeastern cities that sought better communication with the West, quickly grew interested in the English experiment. The first company to begin actual operations was the Baltimore and Ohio, which opened a thirteen-mile stretch of

RACING ON THE RAILROAD Peter Cooper designed and built the first steam-powered locomotives in America in 1830 for the Baltimore and Ohio railroad. On August 28 of that year, he raced his locomotive (the "Tom Thumb") against a horse-drawn railroad car. This sketch depicts the moment when Cooper's engine overtook the horse-car.

track in 1830. In New York, the Mohawk and Hudson began running trains along the sixteen miles between Schenectady and Albany in 1831. By 1836, more than a thousand miles of track had been laid in eleven states.

But there was not yet a true railroad system. Even the longest of the lines was comparatively short in the 1830s, and most of them served simply to connect water routes, not to link one railroad to another. When two lines did connect, the tracks often differed in gauge (width), so cars from one line could not fit onto the tracks of another. Schedules were erratic, and wrecks were frequent. But railroads made some important advances in the 1830s and 1840s. The introduction of heavier iron rails improved the roadbeds. Steam locomotives became more flexible and powerful. Redesigned passenger cars became stabler, more comfortable, and larger.

The Triumph of the Rails

After 1840, railroads gradually supplanted canals and all other forms of transport. In 1840, the total railroad trackage of the country was under 3,000 miles. By 1860, it was over 27,000 miles. The Northeast developed the most comprehensive and efficient system, with twice as much trackage per square mile as the Northwest and four times as much as the South. Railroads even crossed the Mississippi at several points by great iron bridges. Chicago eventually became the rail center of the West, served by fifteen lines and more than a hundred daily trains.

The emergence of the great train lines diverted traffic from the main water routes—the Erie Canal and the Mississippi River. By lessening the dependence of the West on the Mississippi, the railroads also helped weaken further the connection between the Northwest and the South.

Railroad construction required massive amounts of capital. Some of it came from private sources, but much of it came from government funding. State and local governments invested in railroads, but even greater assistance came from the federal government in the form of public land grants. By 1860, Congress had allotted over 30 million acres to eleven states to assist railroad construction.

It would be difficult to exaggerate the impact of the rails on the American economy, on American society, even on American culture. It was, some claimed, a "magic wand" that transformed everything in its path. It was, according to one writer, "the resistless chariot of civilization with

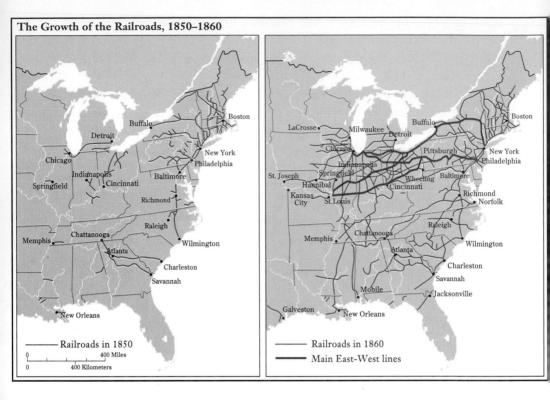

The Growth of the Railroads, 1850–1860

Railroads in 1850
0   400 Miles
0   400 Kilometers

Railroads in 1860
Main East-West lines

scythed axles mowing down ignorance and prejudice as it whirls along
. . . [driving] the shadows of the past . . . into the dim woods." Where
railroads went, towns, ranches, and farms grew up rapidly along their
routes. Areas once cut off from markets during winter and other spells of
bad weather found that the railroad could transport goods to and from
them at any time of year. Most of all, the railroads cut the time of ship-
ment and travel. In the 1830s, traveling from New York to Chicago by
lake and canal took roughly three weeks. By railroad in the 1850s, the
same trip took less than two days. A team of horses could haul a wag-
onload of grain a dozen miles on a good day; a railroad could carry it hundreds of miles in the same amount of time.

The railroads were much more than a fast and economically attractive
form of transportation. As the nation's largest enterprises in the second
half of the nineteenth century, railroads were the breeding ground for several generations of technological advances; a key to the nation's economic
growth; and the birthplace of the modern corporate form of organization.

They also became a symbol to many Americans of the nation's technological prowess, and as such turned into something close to a national obsession. To many people, railroads were the most visible sign of the country's progress and greatness. Many Americans expressed great pride, for example, when Russia asked for help from railroad engineers in the United States when they built the rail line connecting Moscow and St. Petersburg in the 1840s.

The Telegraph

What the railroad was to transportation the telegraph was to communication—a dramatic advance over traditional methods and a symbol of national progress and technological expertise.

Before the invention of the telegraph, communication over great distances on land—a particular challenge in the increasingly vast United States—could be achieved only by direct, physical contact. That meant that virtually all long-distance communication relied on the mail, which traveled first on horseback and coach, and later by railroad. There were obvious disadvantages to this system, not the least of which was the difficulty in coordinating the necessarily precise schedules of railroads. By the 1830s, experiments with many methods of improving long-distance communication had been conducted, among them using the sun and reflective devices to send light signals as far as 187 miles (although only, of course, in sunny weather).

In 1832, Samuel F. B. Morse—a professor of art at New York University with an essentially amateur interest in science—began experimenting with a different system. Fascinated with the possibilities of electricity, which still had found few wide utilities despite the great enthusiasm that had greeted its discovery a half-century earlier, Morse set out to find a way to send signals along an electrical cable. Technology did not yet permit the use of electrical wiring to send reproductions of the human voice or any complex information. But Morse realized that electricity itself could serve as a communication device—that pulses of electricity could themselves become a kind of language. He experimented at first with a numerical code, in which each number would represent a word on a list available to recipients. Gradually, however, he became convinced of the need to find a more universal telegraphic "language," and he developed what became the Morse Code, in which alternating long and short bursts of electrical current would represent individual letters.

By 1835, Morse had developed his idea for telegraphic communication to the point that he was ready to promote it. Eight years later, Congress appropriated $30,000 for the construction of an experimental telegraph line between Baltimore and Washington; in May 1844, it was complete, and Morse succeeded in transmitting the news of James K. Polk's nomination for the presidency over the wires from Baltimore to Washington. By 1860, more than 50,000 miles of wire connected most parts of the country; a year later, the Pacific Telegraph, with 3,595 miles of wire, opened between New York and San Francisco. By then, nearly all the independent lines had joined in one organization, the Western Union Telegraph Company. The telegraph spread rapidly across Europe as well, and in 1866, the first transatlantic cable was laid across the Atlantic, permitting telegraphic communication between the United States and Europe.

One of the first beneficiaries of the telegraph was the growing system of rails in the United States. Telegraph wires often ran alongside railroad tracks, and telegraph offices were often located in railroad stations—which suggests how closely connected the two technologies were. The telegraph allowed railroad operators to communicate directly with stations in cities, small towns, and even rural hamlets—to alert them to schedule changes, warn them about delays and breakdowns, and convey other information about the movement of the trains. Among other things, this new form of communication helped prevent accidents on the rails by alerting stations to problems that in the past engineers had to discover for themselves.

New Forms of Journalism

Another beneficiary of the telegraph was American journalism, which used the wires to get news from around the country—and eventually, the world—that had once taken days, weeks, and even months to reach them, in the space of a few hours. Where once the exchange of national and international news relied on the cumbersome exchange of newspapers by mail, now it was possible for papers to share their reporting with one another. In 1846, newspaper publishers from around the nation formed the Associated Press to promote cooperative news gathering by wire.

Other technological advances spurred the development of the American press. In 1846, Richard Hoe invented the steam cylinder rotary press, making it possible to print newspapers much more rapidly and cheaply than had been possible in the past. Among other things, the rotary press spurred the dramatic growth of mass-circulation newspapers, such as the penny press, which had emerged over a decade earlier. The New York *Sun*, the most widely circulated paper in the nation, had 8,000 readers in 1834. By 1860, its succesful rival the *New York Herald*—benefitting from the speed and economies of production the rotary press made possible, had a circulation of 77,000.

COMMERCE AND INDUSTRY

By the middle years of the nineteenth century, aided by population growth and improvements in transportation and communications, the United States had developed the beginnings of a modern capitalist economy and an advanced industrial capacity. But the economy had developed along highly unequal lines—benefiting some classes and some regions far more than others.

The Expansion of Business, 1820–1840

American business grew rapidly in the 1820s and 1830s in part because of important innovations in business management. Individuals or limited partnerships continued to operate most businesses, and the dominating figures were still the great merchant capitalists, who generally had sole ownership of their enterprises. In some larger businesses, however, the individual merchant capitalist was giving way to the corporation. Corporations had the advantage of combining the resources of a large number of shareholders, and they began to develop particularly rapidly in the 1830s, when some legal obstacles to their formation were removed. Previously, a corporation could obtain a charter only by a special act of a state legislature; by the 1830s, states were beginning to pass general incorporation laws, under which a group could secure a charter merely by paying a fee. The laws also permitted a system of limited liability, in which individual stockholders risked losing only the value of their own investment if a corporation should fail; they were not liable (as they had been in the past) for the corporation's larger losses. These changes made possible the accumulation of much greater amounts of capital and hence made possible much larger manufacturing and business enterprises.

The Emergence of the Factory

The most profound economic development in mid-nineteenth-century America was the rise of the factory. Before the War of 1812, most of what manufacturing there was in the United States took place within households or in small, individually operated workshops. Early in the nineteenth century, however, New England textile manufacturers began using new machines driven by water power that allowed them to bring their operations together under a single roof. This "factory system," as it came to be known, spread rapidly in the 1820s and soon penetrated the shoe industry and other industries as well. Machine technology advanced more rapidly in the United States in the mid-nineteenth century than in any other country in the world. By the end of the 1830s, American technology had become so advanced—particularly in textile manufacturing—that industrialists in Britain and Europe were beginning to travel to the United States to learn new techniques, instead of the other way around.

Between 1840 and 1860, American industry—spurred on by the factory system—experienced particularly dramatic growth. In 1840, the total value of manufactured goods produced in the United States stood at $483 million; by 1860 it had climbed to nearly $2 billion. For the first time, the value of manufactured goods was roughly equal to that of agricultural products. More than half of the approximately 140,000 manufacturing establishments in the country in 1860 were located in the Northeast, and they included most of the larger enterprises. The Northeast thus produced more than two-thirds of the manufactured goods and employed nearly three-quarters of the men and women working in manufacturing.

Advances in Technology

Even the most highly developed industries were still relatively immature. American cotton manufacturers, for example, produced goods of coarse grade; fine items continued to come from England. But by the 1840s, significant advances were in progress.

Among the most important was in the manufacturing of machine tools—the tools used to make machinery parts. The government supported much of the research and development of machine tools, often in connection with supplying the military. For example, a government armory in Springfield, Massachusetts, developed two important tools—the turret lathe (used for cutting screws and other metal parts) and the universal milling machine (which replaced the hand chiseling of complicated parts and dies with a machine process that could ensure that all milling would be identical)—early in the nineteenth century. The precision grinding machine (which became critical to, among other things, the construction of sewing machines) was designed in the 1850s to help the United States Army produce standardized rifle parts. The federal armories such as those at Springfield and Harpers Ferry, Virginia, where these and other tools were developed, became the breeding ground for many technological discoveries, and a magnet for craftsmen and factory owners looking for ideas that could be of use to them. By the 1840s, the machine tools used in the factories of the Northeast were already better than those in most European factories.

One of the principal results of the creation of better machine tools was that the principle of interchangeable parts, which Eli Whitney and Simeon North had tried to introduce into gun factories they had designed decades earlier, now found its way into many industries. Eventually, interchangeability would revolutionize watch and clock making, the manufacturing of locomotives, the creation of steam engines, and the making of many farm tools. It would also help make possible such newer devices as bicycles, sewing machines, typewriters, cash registers, and eventually the automobile.

Industrialization was also profiting from the introduction of new sources of energy. Coal was replacing wood and water power as fuel for many factories. The production of coal, most of it mined around Pittsburgh in western Pennsylvania, leaped from 50,000 tons in 1820 to 14 million tons in 1860. The new power source made it possible to locate mills away from running streams and thus permitted industry to expand still more widely.

The great technological advances in American industry owed much to American inventors, as the patent records of the time make clear. In 1830, the number of inventions patented was 544; by 1850, the figure had risen to 993; and in 1860, it stood at 4,778. Several industries provide particularly vivid examples of how a technological innovation could produce a major economic change. In 1839, Charles Goodyear, a New England hardware merchant, discovered a method of vulcanizing rubber (treating it to give it greater strength and elasticity); by 1860, his process had found over 500 uses and had helped create a major American rubber

THE EARLY SEWING MACHINE *Scientific America*, which reported American scientific and technological achievements, was a popular journal in the mid-nineteenth century. Here it gives front-page attention to the design and construction of Isaac Singer's sewing machine, alongside articles trumpeting news of the progess of the railroads and urging the invention of a ballpoint pen.

industry. In 1846, Elias Howe of Massachusetts constructed a sewing machine; Isaac Singer made improvements on it, and the Howe-Singer machine was soon being used in the manufacture of ready-to-wear clothing. A few years later, during the Civil War, it would supply the Northern troops with uniforms.

Innovations in Corporate Organization

The merchant capitalists—entrepreneurs who were engaged primarily in foreign and domestic trade and who at times invested some of their profits in small-scale manufacturing ventures—remained figures of importance in the 1840s. In such cities as New York, Philadelphia, and Boston, influential mercantile groups operated shipping lines to southern ports—carrying off cotton, rice, and sugar—or dispatched fleets of trading vessels to the ports of Europe and Asia. Among their vessels were the famous clippers, the fastest (and most beautiful) sailing ships afloat. In their heyday in the late 1840s and early 1850s, the clippers could average 300 miles a day, which compared favorably with the best time of contemporary steamships.

But merchant capitalism was declining by the middle of the century. This was partly because British competitors were stealing much of America's export trade. But the more important reason for the decline was the discovery by the merchants themselves that there were greater opportunities for profit in manufacturing than in trade. That was one reason why industries developed first in the Northeast: an affluent merchant class already existed there and had the money and the will to finance them.

By the 1840s, the corporate form of organization was spreading rapidly, particularly in the textile industry. Ownership of American enterprise was gradually moving away from individuals and families and toward its highly dispersed modern form: many stockholders, each owning a relatively small proportion of the total. But whatever the form of business organization—and there continued to be many different forms—industrial capitalists soon became the new ruling class, the aristocrats of the Northeast, with far-reaching economic and political influence.

MEN AND WOMEN AT WORK

However advanced industrial firms became technologically and administratively, manufacturers still relied above all on a supply of labor. In the 1820s and 1830s, factory labor came primarily from the native-born population. After 1840, the growing immigrant population became the most important new source of workers.

Recruiting a Native Work Force

Recruiting a labor force was not an easy task in the early years of the factory system. Ninety percent of the American people in the 1820s still lived and worked on farms. Many of the relatively small number of urban residents were skilled artisans who owned and managed their own shops. The available unskilled workers were not numerous enough to form a reservoir from which the new industries could draw. But the transformation of American agriculture in the nineteenth century gradually created a supply of industrial workers. Dramatic improvements in agricultural production, particularly in the Midwest, meant that each region no longer had to feed itself; it could import the food it needed. As a result, some of the relatively unprofitable farming areas of the East began to decline, and rural people began leaving the land to work in the factories.

Two systems of recruitment emerged to bring this new labor supply to the expanding textile mills. One, common in the mid-Atlantic states (especially in New York and Philadelphia), brought whole families from the farm to work together in the mill—parents working alongside children, some of whom were no more than four or five years old. The second sys-

NEW ENGLAND TEXTILE WORKERS Women continued to constitute the majority of the work force in the cotton mills of New England even after the carefully monitored life of the "Lowell girls" became a thing of the past—as this 1868 engraving by Winslow Homer suggests.

tem, common in Massachusetts, enlisted young women, mostly farmers' daughters in their late teens and early twenties. It was known as the Lowell or Waltham system, after the towns in which it first emerged. Many of these women worked for several years in the factories, saved their wages, and then returned home to marry and raise children. Others married men they met in the factories or in town and remained part of the industrial world. Most eventually stopped working in the mills and took up domestic roles instead.

Labor conditions in these early years of the factory system, hard as they often were, remained significantly better than they would later become. The Lowell workers, for example, lived in clean boardinghouses and dormitories, which the factory owners maintained for them. They were well fed and carefully supervised. Employers quickly dismissed women suspected of immoral conduct. Wages for the Lowell workers were relatively generous by the standards of the time. The women even published a monthly magazine, the *Lowell Offering*.

Yet even these relatively well-treated workers found the transition from farm life to factory work difficult, even traumatic. Uprooted from everything familiar, forced to live among strangers in a regimented environment, many women had difficulty adjusting to the nature of factory work—the repetition of fixed tasks hour after hour, day after day. However uncomfortable women may have found factory work, they had few other options. Work in the mills was in many cases virtually the only alternative to returning to farms that could no longer support them.

The paternalistic factory system of Lowell did not, in any case, survive for long. In the competitive textile market as it developed in the 1830s and 1840s—a market prey to booms and busts—manufacturers found it difficult to maintain the high living standards and reasonably attractive working conditions with which they had begun. Wages declined; the hours of work lengthened; the conditions of the boardinghouses deteriorated as buildings decayed and overcrowding increased. In 1834, mill workers in Lowell organized a union—the Factory Girls Association—which staged a strike to protest a 25 percent wage cut. Two years later, the association struck again—against a rent increase in the boardinghouses. Both strikes failed, and a recession in 1837 virtually destroyed the organization. Eight years later the Lowell women, led by the militant Sarah Bagley, created the Female Labor Reform Association and began agitating for a ten-hour day and for improvements in conditions in the mills. The new association not only made demands of management; it turned to state government and asked for legislative investigation of conditions in the mills. By then, however, the character of the factory work force was changing again. Many mill girls were gradually moving into other occupations: teaching, domestic service, or marriage. And textile manufacturers were turning to a less demanding labor supply: immigrants.

The Immigrant Work Force

The increasing supply of immigrant workers after 1840 was a boon to manufacturers and other entrepreneurs. At last they had access to a cheap and plentiful source of labor. These new workers, because of their growing numbers and their unfamiliarity with their new country, had even less leverage than the women they at times displaced, and thus they often encountered far worse working conditions. Poorly paid construction gangs, made up increasingly of Irish immigrants, performed the heavy, unskilled work on turnpikes, canals, and railroads under often intolerable conditions. Many of them lived in flimsy shanties, in grim conditions that endangered the health of their families (and reinforced native prejudices toward the "shanty Irish"). Irish workers began to predominate in the New England textile mills as well in the 1840s, and their arrival accelerated the deterioration of working conditions there. Employers began paying piece rates rather than a daily wage and used other devices to speed up production and exploit the labor force more efficiently. The factories themselves were becoming large, noisy, unsanitary, and often dangerous places to work; the average workday was extending to twelve, often fourteen hours; and wages were declining. Women and children, whatever their skills, earned less than most men.

The Factory System and the Artisan Tradition

Mill workers were not the only group who suffered from the transition to the modern factory system. Factories were also displacing the trades of skilled artisans. The artisan tradition was as much a part of the older, republican vision of America as the tradition of sturdy yeoman farmers. Independent craftsmen clung to a vision of economic life that was in some ways very different from the one the new capitalist class was promoting. It was a vision based not just on the idea of individual, acquisitive success but also on a sense of a "moral community." Skilled artisans valued their independence; they also valued the stability and relative equality within their economic world.

The factory system threatened that world with obsolescence. Some artisans made successful transitions into small-scale industry. But others found themselves unable to compete with the new factory-made goods that sold for a fraction of the artisans' prices. In the face of this competition from industrial capitalists, skilled workers in cities such as Philadelphia, Baltimore, Boston, and New York formed societies for mutual aid. During the 1820s and 1830s, these craft societies began to combine on a

A TOLEWARE MAKER, C. 1850 By the middle of the nineteenth century, skilled artisans—such as this maker of handcrafted kitchenware—were rapidly being replaced by semiskilled workers producing similar goods in factories. The craftsman pictured here conveys some of the important elements of the vanishing artisanal world: formal dress in the workplace, to suggest his status as a highly skilled craftsman; pride in his workmanship; and a middle-class sensibility that, in the end, made it difficult for artisans to fight the forces driving them toward obsolescence.

citywide basis and set up central organizations known as trade unions. In 1834, delegates from six cities founded the National Trades' Union, and in 1836, printers and cordwainers (makers of high-quality shoes and boots) set up their own national craft unions.

This early craft union movement fared poorly. Hostile laws and hostile courts handicapped the unions. The Panic of 1837 and the depression that followed weakened the movement further. But the failure of these first organizations did not end the efforts by workers—artisans and factory operatives alike—to gain some control over their productive lives.

Fighting for Control

Workers at all levels of the emerging industrial economy made continuous efforts to improve their lots. They tried, with little success, to persuade state legislatures to pass laws setting a maximum workday and regulating child labor. The greatest legal victory of industrial workers came in Massachusetts in 1842, when the state supreme court, in *Commonwealth* v. *Hunt*, declared that unions were lawful organizations and that the strike was a lawful weapon. Other state courts gradually accepted the principles of the Massachusetts decision. But on the whole, the union movement of the 1830s and 1840s remained generally ineffective.

Virtually all the early craft unions excluded women, even though female workers were numerous in almost every industry. As a result, women began establishing their own protective unions by the 1850s, often with the support of middle-class female reformers. Like the male craft unions, the female protective unions had little power in dealing with employers. They did, however, serve an important role as mutual aid societies for women workers.

Many factors combined to inhibit the growth of effective labor resistance. Among the most important was the flood of immigrant laborers into the country. The newcomers were usually willing to work for lower wages than native workers; and because they were so numerous, manufacturers had little difficulty replacing disgruntled or striking workers with eager immigrants. Ethnic divisions and tensions—both between natives and immigrants and among the various immigrant groups themselves—often led workers to channel their resentments into internal bickering rather than into their shared grievances against employers. Another obstacle was the sheer strength of the industrial capitalists, who had not only economic but political and social power and could usually triumph over even the most militant challenges.

PATTERNS OF SOCIETY

The industrial revolution was making the United States—and particularly its more economically developed regions—dramatically wealthier by the year. It was also making society more unequal, and it was transforming social relationships at almost every level—from the workplace to the family.

The Rich and the Poor

The commercial and industrial growth of the United States greatly elevated the average income of the American people. But this increasing wealth was being distributed highly unequally. Substantial groups of the population, of course, shared hardly at all in the economic growth: slaves, Indians, landless farmers, and many of the unskilled workers on the fringes of the manufacturing system. But even among the rest of the population, disparities of income were increasingly marked. Among the American people overall in 1860, according to scholarly estimates, 5 percent of the families possessed more than 50 percent of the wealth. Merchants and industrialists were accumulating enormous fortunes; and because there was now a significant number of rich people living in cities, a distinctive culture of wealth began to emerge.

In large cities, people of great wealth gathered together in neighborhoods of astonishing opulence. They founded clubs and developed elaborate social rituals. They looked increasingly for ways to display their wealth—in the great mansions they built, the showy carriages in which they rode, the lavish household goods they accumulated, the clothes they wore, the elegant social establishments they patronized. New York, which had more wealthy families than anywhere else, developed a particularly elaborate high society. The construction of the city's great Central Park, which began in the 1850s, was in part a result of pressure from the members of high society, who wanted an elegant setting for their daily carriage rides.

There was also a significant population of genuinely destitute people emerging in the growing urban centers of the nation. These were people who were not merely poor, in the sense of having to struggle to sustain themselves—most Americans were poor in that sense. They were almost entirely without resources, often homeless, dependent on charity or crime or both for survival. Substantial numbers of people actually starved to death or died of exposure. Some of these "paupers," as contemporaries called them, were recent immigrants who had failed to find work or to adjust to life in the New World. Some were widows and orphans, stripped of the family structures that allowed most working-class Americans to survive. Some were people suffering from alcoholism or mental illness, unable to work. Others were victims of native prejudice—barred from all but the most menial employment because of race or ethnicity. The Irish were particular victims of such prejudice.

Among the worst victims were free blacks. African-American communities in antebellum northern cities were small by later standards, but most major urban areas had significant black populations. Some of these African Americans were descendants of families that had lived in the North for generations. Others were former slaves who had escaped or been released by their masters. In material terms, at least, life was not always much better for them in the North than it had been in slavery. Most had access to very menial jobs at best. In most parts of the North, blacks could not vote, could not attend public schools, indeed could not use any of the public services available to white residents. Even so, most blacks preferred life in the North, however arduous, to life in the South, because it permitted them at least some level of freedom.

Social Mobility

Despite the contrasts between conspicuous wealth and conspicuous poverty in antebellum America, there was relatively little overt class conflict. For one thing, life, in material terms at least, was better for most factory workers than it had been on the farms or in the European societies from which they had migrated. They ate better, they were often better clothed and housed, and they had greater access to consumer goods.

There was also a significant amount of mobility within the working class, which helped limit discontent. A few workers managed to move from poverty to riches by dint of work, ingenuity, and luck—a very small number, but enough to support the dreams of those who watched them. And a much larger number of workers managed to move at least one notch up the ladder—for example, becoming in the course of a lifetime a skilled, rather than an unskilled, laborer. Such people could envision their children and grandchildren moving up even further.

More important than social mobility was geographical mobility. Some workers saved money, bought land, and moved west to farm it. But few urban workers, and even fewer poor ones, could afford to make such a move. Much more common was the movement of laborers from one industrial town to another. These migratory workers were often the victims of layoffs, looking for better opportunities elsewhere. Their search may seldom have led to a marked improvement in their circumstances, but the rootlessness of this large segment of the work force—one of the most distressed segments—made effective organization and protest more difficult.

Middle-Class Life

For all the visibility of the very rich and the very poor in antebellum society, the fastest-growing group in America was the middle class. The expansion of the middle class was in part a result of the growth of the industrial economy, and the increasing commercial life that accompanied it. Economic development opened many more opportunities for people to own or work in businesses, to own shops, to engage in trade, to enter professions, and to administer organizations. In earlier times, when ownership of land had been the only real basis of wealth, society had been divided between people with little or no land (people Europeans generally called peasants) and a landed gentry (which in Europe usually became an inherited aristocracy). Once commerce and industry became a source of wealth, these rigid distinctions broke down; many people could become prosperous without owning land, but by providing valuable services to the new economy.

Middle-class life in the years before the Civil War rapidly established itself as the most influential cultural form of urban America. Middle-class families lived in solid and often substantial homes. Their houses lined city streets, larger in size and more elaborate in design than the cramped, functional rowhouses in working-class neighborhoods—but also far less lavish than the great houses of the very rich. Like the wealthy, middle-class people tended to own their homes. Workers and artisans were increasingly becoming renters—a relatively new phenomenon in American cities that spread widely in the early nineteenth century.

Middle-class women usually remained in the home and cared for their children and the household, although increasingly they were also able to hire servants—usually young, unmarried immigrant women who put in long hours of arduous work for very little money. One of the aspirations of middle-class women in an age when doing the family's laundry could take an entire day was to escape from some of the drudgery of housework.

New household inventions altered, and greatly improved, the character of life in middle-class homes. Perhaps the most important was the invention of the cast-iron stove, which began to replace fireplaces as the principal vehicle for cooking in the 1840s and also became an important source of heat. These wood- or coal-burning devices were hot, clumsy,

NATHAN HAWLEY AND FAMILY Nathan Hawley, seated at center in this 1801
painting, was typical of many early-nineteenth-century middle-class fathers in
having a very large family. Nine members are visible here. Hawley at the time was
the warden of the Albany County jail in New York, and the painting was by
William Wilkie, one of the inmates there. The painting suggests that Hawley was
a man of modest but not great means. His family is fashionably dressed, and there
are paintings on the walls—signs of style and affluence. But the house is very
simply furnished, without drapes for the windows, and with a simple painted floor
cloth in the front room and a bare floor in the back.

and dirty by the standards of the twentieth century; but compared to the
inconvenience and danger of cooking on an open hearth, they seemed a
great luxury to nineteenth-century families. Stoves gave cooks more control over the preparation of food and allowed them to cook several things
at once.

Middle-class diets were changing rapidly in the antebellum years, and
not just because of the wider range of cooking the stove made possible.
The expansion and diversification of American agriculture and the ability
of farmers to ship goods to urban markets by rail from distant regions
greatly increased the variety of food available in cities. Fruits and vegetables were difficult to ship over long distances in an age with little refriger-

ation, but families had access to a greater variety of meats, grains, and dairy products than they had had in the past. A few households acquired iceboxes in the years before the Civil War, and the sight of wagons delivering large chunks of ice to wealthy and middle-class homes began to become a familiar part of urban life. Iceboxes allowed some families to keep fresh meat and dairy products for as long as several days without spoilage. Most families, however, did not yet have any kind of refrigeration. For them, preserving food meant curing meat with salt and preserving fruits in sugar. Diets were generally much heavier and starchier than they are today, and middle-class people tended to be considerably stouter than would be considered healthy or fashionable in the twentieth century.

Middle-class homes came to differentiate themselves from those of workers and artisans in other ways as well. They were more elaborately decorated and furnished, with items made available for the first time through factory production of household goods. Houses that had once had bare walls and floors now had carpeting, wallpaper, and curtains. The spare, simple styles of eighteenth-century homes gave way to the much more elaborate, even baroque household styles of the Victorian era— styles increasingly characterized by crowded, even cluttered rooms, dark colors, lush fabrics, and heavy furniture and draperies. Middle-class homes also became larger. It became less common for children to share beds and for all members of families to sleep in the same room. Parlors and dining rooms separate from the kitchen—once a luxury reserved largely for the wealthy—became the norm now for the middle class as well. Some urban middle-class homes had indoor plumbing and indoor toilets by the 1850s—a significant advance over the outdoor wells and privies that had been virtually universal only a few years earlier (and that remained common among working-class people).

The Changing Family

The new industrializing society of the northern regions of the United States produced profound changes in the nature and function of the family. At the heart of the transformation was the movement of families from farms to urban areas, where jobs, not land, were the most valued commodities. The family patterns of the countryside, where powerful fathers controlled their children's futures by controlling the distribution of land to them, could not survive the move to a city or town. Sons and daughters in urban households were much more likely to leave the family in search of work than they had been in the rural world.

Another important change was the shift of income-earning work out of the home and into the shop, mill, or factory. In the early decades of the nineteenth century (and for many years before that), the family itself had been the principal unit of economic activity. Now most income earners left home each day to work elsewhere. A sharp distinction began to emerge between the public world of the workplace—the world of commerce and industry—and the private world of the family. The world of the family was now dominated not by production but by housekeeping, child rearing, and other primarily domestic concerns.

Accompanying (and perhaps in part caused by) the changing economic function of the family was a decline in the birth rate. In 1800, the average American woman could be expected to give birth to approximately seven children during her childbearing years. By 1860, the average woman bore five children. The birth rate fell most quickly in urban areas and among middle-class women.

The "Cult of Domesticity"

The growing separation between the public and private worlds, between the workplace and the home, helped cause increasingly sharp distinctions between the social roles of men and women. Those distinctions affected not only factory workers and farmers but members of the growing middle class as well.

Traditional inequalities remained. Women had many fewer legal and political rights than did men, and within the family they remained under the virtually absolute authority of their husbands. Women were seldom encouraged—and in most cases were effectively barred—from pursuing education above the primary level. Not until 1837 did any college or university accept women students: Oberlin in Ohio, which educated both women and men; and Mt. Holyoke in Massachusetts, founded by Mary Lyon as an academy for women. Not until much later in the century were there more than a handful of others.

However unequal the positions of men and women in the preindustrial era, those positions had generally been defined within the context of a household in which all members played important economic roles. In the middle-class family of the new industrial society, by contrast, the husband was assumed to be the principal, usually the only, income producer. The wife was now expected to remain in the home and to engage in largely domestic activities. The image of women changed from one of contributors to the family economy to one of guardians of the "domestic virtues." Middle-class women, no longer producers, now became more important as consumers. They learned to place a higher value on keeping a clean, comfortable, and well-appointed home; on entertaining; on dressing elegantly and stylishly.

Within their own separate sphere, middle-class women began to develop a distinctive female culture. A "lady's" literature began to emerge to meet the demands of middle-class women. There were romantic novels (many of them by female writers), which focused on the private sphere that middle-class women now inhabited. There were women's magazines, which focused on fashions, shopping, homemaking, and other purely domestic concerns.

This "cult of domesticity," as some scholars have called it, gave many women greater material comfort than they had enjoyed in the past and placed a higher value on their "female virtues" and on their roles as wives and mothers. At the same time, it left women increasingly detached from the public world, with few outlets for their interests and energies. Except for teaching and nursing—the favored occupations of unmarried middle-class women—work by women outside the household gradually came to be seen as a lower-class preserve.

Working-class women continued to work in factories and mills, but under conditions far worse than those that the original, more "respectable" women workers of Lowell and Waltham had experienced. Domestic service became another frequent source of female employment. Now that production had moved outside the household, women who needed to earn money had to move outside their own homes to do so.

Leisure Activities

Leisure time was scarce for all but the wealthiest Americans in the mid-nineteenth century. Most people worked long hours. Saturday was a normal working day. Vacations—paid or unpaid—were rare. For most people, Sunday was the only respite from work; and Sundays were generally reserved for religion and rest. For many working-class and middle-class people, therefore, holidays took on a special importance. That was one reason for the strikingly elaborate celebrations of the Fourth of July throughout the country in the nineteenth century. The celebrations were not just expressions of patriotism. They were a way of enjoying one of the few non-religious holidays from work available to most Americans.

In rural America, where most people still lived, the erratic pattern of farmwork gave many people some relief from the relentless working schedules of city residents. For urban people, however, leisure was something to be seized in what few free moments they had. Men gravitated to taverns for drinking, talking, and game-playing after work. Women gathered in one another's homes for conversation and card games, or to share work on such household tasks as sewing. For educated people, whose numbers were rapidly expanding, reading became one of the principal leisure activities. Newspapers and magazines proliferated rapidly, and books—novels, histories, autobiographies, biographies, travelogues, and others—became staples of affluent homes. Women were particularly avid readers, and women writers created a new genre of fiction specifically for females—the "sentimental novel," which often offered idealized visions of women's lives and romances.

There was also a vigorous culture of public leisure, even if many families had to struggle to find time to participate in it. In larger cities, theaters were becoming increasingly popular; and while some of them catered to particular social groups, others attracted audiences that crossed class lines. Wealthy people, middle-class people, workers and their families—all could sometimes be found together watching a performance. Much of the popular theater of the time consisted of melodrama based on popular novels or American myths. But much of it reflected the great love of Shakespeare that extended through all levels of the theater-going population.

By the 1830s, when theater was the single most popular entertainment in America, Shakespeare was the single most popular playwright. American performances of his work tended to be lively, irreverent, and highly inaccurate. Tragedies had happy endings. Texts included American dialect. Plays were abbreviated and sandwiched into programs containing other popular works. So familiar were many Shakespearean plots that parodies of them were staples of regional theater, through productions of such comedies as *Hamlet and Egglet* or *Julius Sneezer*. American audiences were noisy and rambunctious, and at times crowded onto the stage to participate in battle or crowd scenes. The love of Shakespeare among many ordinary people of all classes was so intense, and their loyalties to their favorite actors so strong, that in 1849 there was a major riot at New York's Astor Place Opera House when supporters of a popular American Shakespearean actor, Edwin Forrest, gathered to protest a visit from an eminent English Shakespearean, Charles Macready. More than twenty people died.

Minstrel shows—in which white actors wearing blackface mimicked (and ridiculed) African-American culture—became increasingly popular. Public sporting events—boxing, horse racing, cockfighting (already becoming controversial), and others—often attracted considerable audiences. Baseball—not yet organized into professional leagues—was beginning to attract large crowds when played in city parks or fields on the edges of towns. A particularly exciting event in many communities was the arrival of the circus—a traveling entertainment with roots in the middle ages that continued to entertain, delight, and bamboozle children and adults alike.

Popular tastes in public spectacle tended toward the bizarre and the fantastic. Most men and women lived in a constricted world of familiar things. Relatively few people traveled; and in the absence of film, radio, television, or even much photography, they hungered for visions of unusual phenomena that contrasted with their normal experiences. People going to the theater or the circus or the museum wanted to see things that amazed and even frightened them. Perhaps the most celebrated provider of such experiences was the famous and unscrupulous showman P. T. Barnum, who opened the American Museum in New York in 1842—not a showcase for art or nature, but a great freak show populated by midgets (the most famous named Tom Thumb), Siamese twins, magicians, and ventriloquists. Barnum was a genius in publicizing his ventures with garish posters and elaborate newspaper announcements. Later, in the 1870s, he launched the famous circus for which he is still best remembered. He was a pioneer in exploiting public tastes for the wild and exotic.

One of the ways Barnum tried to draw visitors to his museum was by engaging lecturers. He did so because he understood that the lecture was one of the most popular forms of entertainment in nineteenth-century America. Men and women flocked in enormous numbers to lyceums, churches, schools, and auditoriums to hear lecturers explain the latest advances in science, describe their visits to exotic places, provide vivid historical narratives, or rail against the evils of alcohol or slavery. Messages of social uplift and reform attracted rapt audiences, particularly among women eager for guidance as they adjusted to the often jarring changes in the character of family life in the industrializing world.

THE AGRICULTURAL NORTH

Even in the rapidly urbanizing and industrializing Northeast, and more so in what nineteenth-century Americans called the Northwest (what Americans today call the Midwest), most people remained tied to the agricultural world. But agriculture, like industry and commerce, was becoming increasingly a part of the new capitalist economy, linked to the national and international market.

Northeastern Agriculture

The story of agriculture in the Northeast after 1840 is one of decline and transformation. The reason for the decline was simple: the farmers of the section could no longer compete with the new and richer soil of the Northwest. In 1840, the leading wheat-growing states were New York, Pennsylvania, Ohio, and Virginia; in 1860 they were Illinois, Indiana, Wisconsin, Ohio, and Michigan. In raising corn, Illinois, Ohio, and Missouri supplanted New York, Pennsylvania, and Virginia. In 1840 the most important cattle-raising areas in the country were New York, Pennsylvania, and New England; but by the 1850s the leading cattle states were Illinois, Indiana, Ohio, and Iowa in the West and Texas in the South.

Some eastern farmers responded to these changes by moving west themselves and establishing new farms. Still others moved to mill towns and became laborers. Some farmers, however, remained on the land and turned to the task of supplying food to the growing cities of the East; they raised vegetables (truck farming) or fruit and sold their produce in nearby towns. New York, for example, led all other states in apple production. Supplying milk, butter, and cheese to local urban markets also attracted many farmers in central New York, southeastern Pennsylvania, and various parts of New England.

The Old Northwest

Life was different in the states of the Northwest in the mid-nineteenth century. There was some industry in this region (more than in the South), and in the two decades before the Civil War the section experienced steady industrial growth. There were flourishing industrial and commercial areas in and around Cleveland (on Lake Erie) and Cincinnati, the center of meatpacking in the Ohio Valley. Farther west, the rising city of Chicago, destined to become the great metropolis of the section, was emerging as the national center of the agricultural machinery and meatpacking industries. Most of the major industrial activities of the West either served agriculture (as in the case of farm machinery) or relied on agricultural products (as in flour milling, meatpacking, whiskey distilling, and the making of leather goods).

Some areas of the Northwest were not yet dominated by whites. Indians remained the most numerous inhabitants of large portions of the upper third of the Great Lakes states until after the Civil War. In those areas, hunting and fishing, along with some sedentary agriculture, remained the principal economic activities. But the tribes did not become integrated into the new commercialized economy that was emerging else-where in the Northwest.

For the white (and occasionally black) settlers who populated the lands farther south that they had by now largely wrested from the natives, the Northwest was primarily an agricultural region. Its rich and plentiful lands made farming a lucrative and expanding activity there, in contrast to the de-clining agrarian Northeast. Thus the typical citizen of the Northwest was not the industrial worker or poor, marginal farmer but the owner of a reasonably prosperous family farm. The average size of western farms was 200 acres, the great majority of them owned by the people who worked them.

Industrialization, in both the United States and Europe, provided the greatest boost to agriculture. With the growth of factories and cities in the Northeast, the domestic market for farm goods increased dramatically. The growing national and worldwide demand for farm products resulted in steadily rising farm prices. For most farmers, the 1840s and early 1850s were years of increasing prosperity.

The expansion of agricultural markets had profound effects on sec-tional alignments in the United States. The Northwest sold most of its products to the Northeast and became an important market for the prod-ucts of eastern industry. A strong economic relationship was emerging be-tween the two sections that was profitable to both—and that was increas-ing the isolation of the South within the Union.

By 1850, the growing western white population was moving into the prairie regions on both sides of the Mississippi: areas of Indiana, Michi-gan, Illinois, Missouri, Iowa, and Minnesota. These farmers cleared forest lands or made use of fields the Indians had cleared many years earlier. And they began to develop a timber industry to make use of the forests that re-mained. Wheat was the staple crop of the region, but other crops—corn, potatoes, and oats—and livestock were also important.

The Northwest also increased production by adopting new agricul-tural techniques that greatly reduced the labor necessary for producing a crop. Farmers began to cultivate new varieties of seed, notably Mediter-ranean wheat, which was hardier than the native type; and they imported better breeds of animals, such as hogs and sheep from England and Spain, to take the place of native stock. Most important were improved tools and farm machines. The cast-iron plow, an earlier innovation, remained popu-lar because its parts could be replaced when broken. An even better tool appeared in 1847, when John Deere established at Moline, Illinois, a fac-tory to manufacture plows with steel moldboards, which were more durable than those made of iron.

Two new machines heralded a coming revolution in grain production. The most important was the automatic reaper, the invention of Cyrus H. McCormick of Virginia. The reaper took the place of sickle, cradle, and hand labor. Pulled by a team of horses, it had a row of horizontal knives on one side for cutting wheat; the wheels drove a paddle that bent the stalks over the knives, which then fell onto a moving belt that carried it into the back of the vehicle. The reaper enabled a crew of six or seven men to harvest in a day as much wheat (or any other small grain) as fifteen men could harvest using the older methods. McCormick, who had patented his device in 1834, established a factory at Chicago, in the heart of the grain belt, in 1847. By 1860, more than 100,000 reapers were in use on western farms. Almost as important to the grain grower was the thresher—a machine that separated the grain from the wheat stalks. Threshers appeared in large numbers after 1840. Before that, farmers generally flailed grain by hand (seven bushels a day was a good average for a farm) or used farm animals to tread it (twenty bushels a day on the average). A threshing machine could thresh twenty-five bushels or more in an hour. The Jerome I. Case factory in Racine, Wisconsin, manufactured most of the threshers. (Modern "harvesters" later combined the functions of the reaper and the thresher.)

MCCORMICK'S REAPER This 1850 advertisement for the automatic reaper created by Cyrus McCormick was aimed at farmers in Ohio and Illinois. But the reaper's greatest impact was to be in the vast grain-growing regions farther west, which were already attracting large numbers of white settlers and would attract many more in the decades to come.

The Northwest was the most self-consciously democratic section of the country. But its democracy was of a relatively conservative type—capitalistic, property-conscious, middle-class. Abraham Lincoln, an Illinois Whig, voiced the economic opinions of many of the people of his section. "I take it that it is best for all to leave each man free to acquire property as fast as he can," said Lincoln. "Some will get wealthy. I don't believe in a law to prevent a man from getting rich; it would do more harm than good. . . . When one starts poor, as most do in the race of life, free society is such that he knows he can better his condition; he knows that there is no fixed condition of labor for his whole life."

Rural Life

Life for farming people was very different from life for people in towns and cities. It also varied greatly from one farming region to another. In the more densely populated farm areas east of the Appalachians and in the easternmost areas of the Northwest, farmers were usually part of relatively vibrant communities and made extensive use of the institutions of those communities—the churches, schools, stores, and taverns. As white settlement moved further west, farmers became more isolated and had to struggle to find any occasions for contact with people outside their own families.

Although the extent of social interaction differed from one area to another, the forms of interaction—outside the South at least—were usually very similar. Religion drew farm communities together perhaps more than any other force, particularly since so many farm areas were populated by people of common ethnic (and therefore religious) backgrounds. Town or village churches were popular meeting places, both for services and for social events—most of them dominated by women. Even in areas with no organized churches, farm families—and, again, women in particular—gathered in one another's homes for prayer meetings, Bible readings, and other religious activities. Weddings, baptisms, and funerals also brought communities together in celebration or mourning.

But religion was only one of many reasons for interaction. Farm people joined together frequently to share tasks that a single family would have difficulty performing on their own; barn raisings were among the most frequent. On those occasions, families would gather and create a festive atmosphere of celebration. Women prepared large suppers while the men worked on the barn and the children played. Large numbers of families gathered together at harvest time as well to help bring in crops, husk corn, or thresh wheat. Women came together to share domestic tasks as well, holding "bees" in which groups of women joined together to make quilts, baked goods, preserves, and other products.

Rural life was not always as isolating as it was sometimes portrayed. But despite the many social gatherings farm families managed to create, they lived in a world with much less contact with popular culture and public social life than people who lived in towns and cities. Rural people, often even more than urban ones, treasured their links to the outside world—letters from relatives and friends in distant places, newspapers and magazines from cities they had never seen, catalogs advertising merchandise that their local stores never had. Yet many also valued their separation from urban culture and cherished the relative autonomy that a farm life gave them. One reason many rural Americans looked back nostalgically on country life once they moved to the city was that they sensed that in the urban world they did not have as much control over the patterns of their daily lives as they had once known.

CONCLUSION

Between the 1820s and the 1850s, the American economy experienced the beginnings of an industrial revolution—a change so profound that in the United States, as in Europe, it transformed almost every area of life in fundamental ways.

The American industrial revolution was a result of many things: population growth (through both natural increase and immigration), advances in transportation and communication, new technologies that spurred the development of factories capable of mass producing goods, the recruiting of a large industrial labor force, and the creation of corporate bodies capable of managing large enterprises. The new economy created great wealth, expanding the ranks of the wealthy and helping to create a large new middle class. It also created high levels of inequality.

Culture in the industrializing areas of the North changed, too, and there were important changes in the structure and behavior of the family, in the role of women, and in the way people used their leisure time and encountered popular culture. The changes were often alluring, often disorienting, and often both. They helped widen the gap in experience and understanding between the generation of the Revolution and the generation of the mid-nineteenth century. They also helped widen the gap between North and South.

FOR FURTHER REFERENCE

Suggested Readings

George R. Taylor, *The Transportation Revolution* (1951) is an authoritative account of economic development in the antebellum period. Charles G. Sellers, *The Market Revolution: Jacksonian America, 1815–1846* (1991) demonstrates the overwhelming impact of the market revolution on American social and political development, but from a pessimistic perspective. Daniel Feller, *The Jacksonian Promise: America, 1815–1840* (1995) challenges Sellers by suggesting a more optimistic portrait of the impact of economic change. Sean Wilentz, *Chants Democratic: New York City and the Rise of the American Working Class, 1788–1850* (1984) is an influential account of the impact of early industrialization on mostly male artisans in the most industrialized city of the era. David R. Roediger, *The Wages of Whiteness: Race and the Making of the American Working Class* (1991) is a provocative and controversial history of labor and race in early America. Alice Kessler-Harris, *Out to Work: A History of Wage-Earning Women in the United States* (1982), in contrast, reminds readers that women were a substantial part of the early wage labor force. Christine Stansell, *City of Women: Sex and Class in New York, 1789–1860* (1986) examines the social and cultural milieu in which women lived and worked. Mary Ryan, *Cradle of the Middle Class: The Family in Oneida County, New York, 1790–1865* (1981) demonstrates the relationship between the market revolution and the changing character of middle-class family structure. John Bodnar, *The Transplanted: A History of Immigrants in America* (1985) is an excellent survey.

Films

(The best source for information on how to find these and other films is *Bowker's Complete Video Directory*—3 volumes.) *The Industrial Revolution: Beginnings in the United States* (1968) traces the explosive growth of American industry beginning in the 1790s. *Samuel Slater & the Industrial Revolution* (1981) sketches the biography of a pioneer in early American textile manufacturing. *Irish Americans* (1993) celebrates the history and culture of Irish Americans. *Her Own Words: Pioneer Women's Diaries* (1986) brings to life the observations of pioneer women in the upper Midwest in the 1830s, 1840s, and 1850s. *In Search of the Oregon Trail* (1996) focuses on the role of women in the epic migration on the Oregon Trail. *California Gold: Stories of Two Women* (1985) traces the lives of two women who lived through the gold rush.

Internet Resources

Internet websites containing historical material relevant to the subjects discussed in this chapter can be reached through the McGraw-Hill history site at www.mhhe.com/socscience/history/usa/link/linktop.htm.

CHAPTER ELEVEN

Cotton, Slavery, and the Old South

The Cotton Economy ∽ *Southern White Society*
The "Peculiar Institution" ∽ *The Culture of Slavery*

T HE SOUTH, LIKE the North, experienced dramatic growth in the middle years of the nineteen century. Southerners fanned out into the Southwest and established new communities, new states, and new markets. The southern agricultural economy grew increasingly productive and increasingly prosperous. Trade in such staples as sugar, rice, tobacco, and above all cotton made the South a major force in international commerce and created substantial new wealth within the region. It also tied the South securely to the emerging capitalist world of the United States and its European trading partners.

Yet for all the changes, the South experienced a much less fundamental transformation in these years than did the North. It had begun the nineteenth century a primarily agricultural region; it remained overwhelmingly agrarian in 1860. It had begun the century with few important cities and little industry; and so it remained sixty years later. In 1800, a plantation system dependent on slave labor had dominated the southern economy; by 1860, that system had only strengthened its grip on the region. As one historian has written, "The South grew, but it did not develop." And as a result, it became increasingly unlike the North and increasingly sensitive to what it considered to be threats to its distinctive way of life.

THE COTTON ECONOMY

The most important economic development in the mid-nineteenth-century South was the shift of economic power from the "upper South," the original

TIME LINE				
1800	**1808**	**1820s**	**1822**	**1831**
Gabriel Prosser's unsuccessful slave revolt	Slave importation banned	Depression in tobacco prices begins High cotton production in Southwest	Denmark Vesey's conspiracy	Nat Turner slave rebellion

1833	**1837**	**1846**	**1849**	
John Randolph frees 400 slaves	Cotton prices plummet	*De Bow's Review* founded	Cotton Production boom	

southern states along the Atlantic coast, to the "lower South," the expanding agricultural regions in the new states of the Southwest. That shift reflected above all the growing dominance of cotton in the southern economy.

The Rise of King Cotton

Much of the upper South continued in the nineteenth century to rely, as it always had, on the cultivation of tobacco. But the market for that crop was notoriously unstable, and tobacco rapidly exhausted the land on which it grew. By the 1830s, therefore, many farmers in the old tobacco-growing regions of Virginia, Maryland, and North Carolina were shifting to other crops—notably wheat—while the center of tobacco cultivation was moving westward, into the Piedmont area.

The southern regions of the coastal South—South Carolina, Georgia, and parts of Florida—continued to rely on the cultivation of rice, a more stable and lucrative crop. But rice demanded substantial irrigation and needed an exceptionally long growing season (nine months), so cultivation of that staple remained restricted to a relatively small area. Sugar growers along the Gulf Coast, similarly, enjoyed a reasonably profitable market for their crop. But sugar cultivation required intensive (and debilitating) labor and a long growing time; only relatively wealthy planters could afford to engage in it. In addition, producers faced major competition from the great sugar plantations of the Caribbean. Sugar cultivation, therefore, did not spread much beyond a small area in southern Louisiana and eastern Texas. Long-staple (Sea Island) cotton was another lucrative crop, but like rice and sugar, it could grow only in a limited area—the coastal regions of the Southeast.

The decline of the tobacco economy in the upper South, and the inherent limits of the sugar, rice, and long-staple cotton economies farther
south, might have forced the region to shift its attention in the nineteenth
century to other, nonagricultural pursuits had it not been for the growing
importance of a new product that soon overshadowed all else: short-staple
cotton. This was a hardier and coarser strain of cotton that could grow
successfully in a variety of climates and in a variety of soils. It was harder
to process than the long-staple variety because its seeds were difficult to
remove from the fiber. But the invention of the cotton gin (see p. 189) had
largely solved that problem.

Demand for cotton increased rapidly in the nineteenth century with
the growth of the textile industry in Britain in the 1820s and 1830s and in
New England in the 1840s and 1850s. In response to that demand, beginning in the 1820s, cotton production spread rapidly. From the western
areas of South Carolina and Georgia, production moved into Alabama and
Mississippi and then into northern Louisiana, Texas, and Arkansas. By the
1850s, cotton had become the linchpin of the southern economy. In 1820,
the South had produced only about 500,000 bales of cotton. By 1860 it
was producing nearly 5 million bales a year. There were periodic booms
and busts, but the cotton economy continued to grow, even if in fits and
starts. By the time of the Civil War, cotton constituted nearly two-thirds
of the total export trade of the United States. It was little wonder that
southern politicians now proclaimed: "Cotton is king!"

Cotton production boomed in the relatively recently settled areas of
what came to be known as the "lower South" (or, in a later era, the "Deep
South"). Some began to call it the "Cotton Kingdom." The prospect of
tremendous profits drew settlers to the lower South by the thousands.
Some were wealthy planters from the older states who transferred their
assets and slaves to new and larger plantations. Most were small slaveholders or slaveless farmers who hoped to move into the planter class.

A similar shift, if an involuntary one, occurred in the slave population. In the period from 1820 to 1860, the number of slaves in Alabama
leaped from 41,000 to 435,000, and in Mississippi from 32,000 to
436,000. Between 1840 and 1860, according to some estimates, 410,000
slaves moved from the upper South to the cotton states—either accompanying masters who were themselves migrating to the Southwest or
(more often) sold to planters already there. The sale of slaves to the
Southwest became an important economic activity in the upper South

Slavery and Cotton: The South in 1820 and 1860

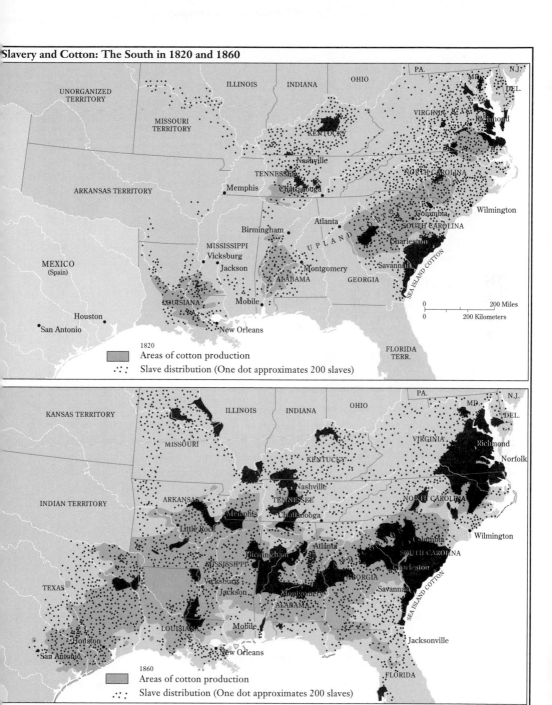

1820
Areas of cotton production
Slave distribution (One dot approximates 200 slaves)

1860
Areas of cotton production
Slave distribution (One dot approximates 200 slaves)

THE NEW ORLEANS COTTON EXCHANGE Edgar Degas, the great French impressionist, painted this scene of cotton traders examining samples in the New Orleans cotton exchange in 1873. By that time the cotton trade was producing less impressive profits than those that had made it the driving force of the booming southern economy of the 1850s. Degas's mother came from a Creole family of cotton brokers in New Orleans, and two of the artist's brothers (depicted here reading a newspaper and leaning against a window) joined the business in America.

and helped the troubled planters of that region compensate for the declining value of their crops.

Southern Trade and Industry

In the face of this booming agricultural expansion, other forms of economic activity developed slowly in the South. There was growing activity in flour milling and in textile and iron manufacturing, particularly in the upper South. The Tredegar Iron Works in Richmond, for example, compared favorably with the best iron mills in the Northeast. But industry remained an insignificant force in comparison with the agricultural economy. The total value of southern textile manufactures in 1860 was $4.5 million—a threefold increase over the value of those goods twenty years before, but only about 2 percent of the value of the cotton exported that year.

The limited nonfarm commercial sector that did develop in the South was largely intended to serve the needs of the plantation economy. Particularly important were the brokers, or "factors," who marketed the planters' crops. The South had only a very rudimentary financial system, and the factors often also served the planters as bankers, providing them with credit. Other obstacles to economic development included the South's inadequate transportation system. In the North in the antebellum period, governments and entrepreneurs were investing enormous sums in roads, canals, and above all railroads to knit the region together into an integrated market. In the South there were few such investments. Canals were almost nonexistent; most roads were crude and unsuitable for heavy transport; and railroads, although they expanded substantially in the 1840s and 1850s, failed to tie the region together effectively. The principal means of transportation was water. Planters generally shipped their crops to market along rivers or by sea; most manufacturing was in or near port towns.

The South was, therefore, becoming more and more dependent on the manufacturers, merchants, and professionals of the North. Some southerners began to advocate economic independence for the region, among them James B. D. De Bow of New Orleans, whose magazine *De Bow's Commercial Review*, published from 1846 to 1860, called for southern commercial and agricultural expansion and economic independence from the North. Yet even *De Bow's Commercial Review* was filled with advertisements from northern manufacturing firms; and its circulation was far smaller in the South than such northern magazines as *Harper's Weekly*.

Sources of Southern Difference

Despite this growing concern about what De Bow called the region's "colonial dependency," the South made few serious efforts to build an economy that might challenge that dependency. An important question about antebellum southern history, therefore, is why the region did so little

DE BOW'S COMMERCIAL REVIEW J. D. B. De Bow, owner and editor of the South's leading magazine, presented his *Review* as a commercial publication—designed for those committed to commerce. But it also contained essays and articles promoting the South's way of life and what many white southerners considered the region's distinctive (and superior) culture.

to develop a larger industrial and commercial economy of its own. Why did it remain so different from the North?

Part of the reason was the great profitability of the region's agricultural system, and particularly of cotton production. In the Northeast, many people had turned to manufacturing as the agricultural economy of the region declined. In the South, the agricultural economy was booming, and ambitious people eager to profit from the emerging capitalist economy had little incentive to look elsewhere. Another reason was that wealthy southerners had so much capital invested in their land and their slaves that they had little left for other investments. Some historians have suggested that the southern climate—with its long, hot, steamy summers—was less suitable for industrial development than the climate of the North.

But the southern failure to create a flourishing commercial or industrial economy was also in part the result of a set of values distinctive to the South. Many white southerners liked to think of themselves as representatives of a special way of life. Southerners were, they argued, people happily free from the base, acquisitive instincts of northerners; they were more concerned with a refined and gracious way of life than with rapid growth and development. But appealing as this image was to southern whites, it conformed to the reality of southern society in very limited ways.

SOUTHERN WHITE SOCIETY

Only a small minority of southern whites owned slaves. In 1860, when the white population was just above 8 million, the number of slaveholders was only 383,637. Even with all members of slaveowning families included in the figures, those living in slaveowning households still amounted to perhaps no more than one-quarter of the white population. And only a small proportion of this relatively small number of slaveowners owned slaves in substantial numbers.

The Planter Class

How, then, did the South come to be seen—both by the outside world and by many southerners themselves—as a society dominated by great plantations and wealthy landowning planters? In large part, it was because the planter aristocracy exercised power and influence far in excess of their numbers. They became a class to which all others deferred.

White southerners liked to compare their planter class to the old upper classes of England and Europe: true aristocracies, long entrenched, "cavaliers." In fact, most of the southern upper class was in most cases not at all similar to the landed aristocracies of the Old World. In some areas of the upper South—the tidewater region of Virginia, for example—some of the great aristocrats were indeed people whose families had occupied positions of wealth and power for generations. In most of the South, however, there was no longstanding landed aristocracy. As late as the 1850s, many of the great landowners in the lower South were still first-generation settlers, who had arrived with only modest resources, struggled for many years, and only relatively recently started to live in the comfort and luxury for which they became famous. Large areas of the South had been settled and cultivated for less than two decades at the time of the Civil War.

Nor was the world of the planter nearly as leisured and genteel as the "cavalier" myth would suggest. Growing staple crops was a business—often a big and highly profitable business. Planters were, in many respects, just as much competitive capitalists as the industrialists of the North whose lifestyles they claimed to hold in contempt. Even many affluent planters lived rather modestly, their wealth so heavily invested in land and slaves that there was little left for personal comfort. And white planters, including some substantial ones, tended to move frequently as new and presumably more productive areas opened up to cultivation.

Wealthy southern whites sustained their image of themselves as aristocrats in many ways. They adopted an elaborate code of "chivalry," which obligated white men to defend their "honor," often through dueling—which survived in the South long after it had largely vanished in the North. They avoided such "coarse" occupations as trade and commerce; those who did not become planters often gravitated toward the military. The aristocratic ideal also found reflection in the definition of a special role for southern white women.

The "Southern Lady"

In some respects, affluent white women in the South occupied roles very similar to those of middle-class white women in the North. Their lives generally centered in the home, where (according to the South's social ideal) they served as companions to and hostesses for their husbands and as nurturing mothers for their children. Even less frequently than in the North did "genteel" southern white women engage in public activities or find income-producing employment.

But the life of the "southern lady" was also in many ways very different from that of her northern counterpart. For one thing, the cult of honor in the region meant that southern white men gave particular importance to the defense of women. In practice, this generally meant that white men were even more dominant and white women even more subordinate in southern culture than they were in the North. George Fitzhugh, one of the South's most important social theorists, wrote in the 1850s: "Women, like children, have but one right, and that is the right to protection. The right to protection involves the obligation to obey."

More important in determining the role of southern white women, however, was that the vast majority of them lived on farms, relatively isolated from people outside their own families, with little access to the "public world" and thus few opportunities to look beyond their roles as wives and mothers. For many white women, living on farms of modest size meant a fuller engagement in the economic life of the family than was becoming typical for middle-class women in the North. These women engaged in spinning, weaving, and other production; they participated in agricultural tasks; they helped supervise the slave work force. On the larger plantations, however, even these limited roles were often considered unsuitable for white women, and the "plantation mistress" became, in some cases, more an ornament for her husband than an active part of the economy or the society. Southern white women also had less access to education than their northern counterparts. Nearly a quarter of all white women over twenty were completely illiterate; relatively few women had more than a rudimentary education. The few female "academies" in the South trained women primarily to be suitable wives.

Southern white women had other special burdens as well. The southern white birth rate remained nearly 20 percent higher than that of the nation as a whole, and infant mortality in the region remained higher than elsewhere. The slave labor system also had a mixed impact on white women. It helped spare many of them from certain kinds of arduous labor, but it also damaged their relationships with their husbands. Male slaveowners had frequent sexual relationships with the female slaves on their plantations; the children of those unions became part of the plantation labor force and served as a constant reminder to white women of their husbands' infidelities. Black women (and men) were obviously the most important victims of such practices, but white women suffered, too.

The Plain Folk

The typical white southerner was not a great planter and slaveholder but a modest yeoman farmer. Some of these "plain folk," as they became known, owned a few slaves, with whom they worked and lived more closely than did the larger planters. Most owned no slaves at all. Some plain folk, most of whom owned their own land, devoted themselves largely to subsistence farming; others grew cotton or other crops for the market, but usually could not produce enough to allow them to expand their operations or even get out of debt. Most yeomen knew that they had little prospect of substantially bettering their lot.

One reason was the southern educational system. For the sons of wealthy planters, the region provided ample opportunities to gain an education. In 1860 there were 260 southern colleges and universities, public and private, with 25,000 students enrolled in them—more than half the total number of students in the United States. But as in the rest of the United States, universities were only within the reach of the upper class. The elementary and secondary schools of the South were not only fewer than but also inferior to those of the Northeast (although not much worse than the crude schools of the Northwest). The South had more than 500,000 illiterate whites, or over half the country's total.

The subordination of the plain folk to the planter class raises an important question: Why did lower-class whites not oppose the aristocratic social system from which they benefited so little? Why did they not resent the system of slavery, from which they generally did not profit?

Some nonslaveowning whites did oppose the planter elite, but for the most part in limited ways and in relatively few, isolated areas. These were mainly the southern highlanders, the "hill people," who lived in the Appalachian ranges east of the Mississippi, in the Ozarks to the west of the river, and in other "hill country" or "backcountry" areas cut off from the more commercial world of the plantation system. Of all southern whites, they were the most isolated from the mainstream of the region's life. They practiced a simple form of subsistence agriculture and owned practically no slaves. They were, in most respects, unconnected to the new commercial economy that dominated the great cotton-planting region of the South.

Such whites frequently expressed animosity toward the planter aristocracy of the other regions of the South. The mountain region was the only part of the South to defy the trend toward sectional conformity, and it was the only part to resist the movement toward secession when it finally developed. Even during the Civil War itself, many refused to support the Confederacy; some went so far as to fight for the Union.

Far greater in number, however, were the nonslaveowning whites who lived in the midst of the plantation system. Many, perhaps most of them, accepted that system because they were tied to it in important ways. Small farmers depended on the local plantation aristocracy for many things: access to cotton gins, markets for their modest crops and their livestock, credit or other financial assistance in time of need. In many areas, moreover, the poorest resident of a county might easily be a cousin of the richest aristocrat. In the 1850s, the boom in the cotton economy allowed many small farmers to improve their economic fortunes. Some bought more land, became slaveowners, and moved into at least the fringes of plantation society. Others simply felt more secure in their positions as independent yeomen and hence more likely to embrace the fierce regional loyalty that was spreading throughout the white South in these years.

There were other white southerners, however, who shared almost not at all in the plantation economy and yet continued to accept its premises. These were the members of a degraded class—numbering perhaps a half-million in 1850—known variously as "crackers," "sand hillers," or "poor white trash." Occupying the infertile lands of the pine barrens, the red hills, and the swamps, they lived in genuine squalor. Many owned no land (or owned land on which virtually nothing could be grown) and supported themselves by foraging or hunting. Others worked at times as common laborers for their neighbors, although the slave system limited their opportunities to do so. Their degradation resulted partly from dietary deficiencies and disease. They resorted at times to eating clay (hence the tendency of more affluent whites to refer to them disparagingly as "clay eaters"), and they suffered from pellagra, hookworm, and malaria. Planters and small farmers alike held them in contempt. In some material respects, their plight was worse than that of the black slaves (who themselves often looked down on the poor whites).

Even among these southerners— the true outcasts of white society in the region—there was no real opposition to the plantation system or slavery. In part, undoubtedly, this was because these men and women were so benumbed by poverty that they had little strength to protest. But it resulted also from perhaps the single greatest unifying factor among the southern white population: their perception of race. However poor and miserable white southerners might be, they could still consider themselves members of a ruling race; they could still look down on the black population of the region and feel a bond with their fellow whites born of a determination to maintain their racial supremacy.

THE "PECULIAR INSTITUTION"

White southerners often referred to slavery as the "peculiar institution." By that they meant not that the institution was odd but that it was distinctive, special. American slavery was indeed distinctive. The South in the

RETURNING FROM THE COTTON FIELD In this photograph, South Carolina field workers return after a day of picking cotton, some of their harvest carried in bundles on their heads. A black slave driver leads the way.

mid-nineteenth century was the only area in the Western world—except for Brazil, Cuba, and Puerto Rico—where slavery still existed. Slavery, more than any other single factor, isolated the South from the rest of American society. And as that isolation increased, so did the commitment of southerners to defend the institution.

Within the South itself, the institution of slavery had paradoxical results. On the one hand, it isolated blacks from whites, drawing a sharp and inviolable racial line dividing one group of southerners from another. As a result, African Americans under slavery began to develop a society and culture of their own. On the other hand, slavery created a unique bond between blacks and whites—masters and slaves—in the South. The two groups may have maintained separate spheres, but each sphere was deeply influenced by, indeed dependent on, the other.

Varieties of Slavery

Slavery was an institution established and regulated in detail by law. The slave codes of the southern states forbade slaves to hold property, to leave their masters' premises without permission, to be out after dark, to congregate with other slaves except at church, to carry firearms, or to strike a white person even in self-defense. The codes prohibited whites from teaching slaves to read or write and denied slaves the right to testify in court against white people. The laws contained no provisions to legalize slave marriages or divorces. If an owner killed a slave while punishing him, the act was generally not considered a crime. Slaves, however, faced the death penalty for killing or even resisting a white person and for inciting revolt. The codes also contained extraordinarily rigid provisions for defining a person's race. Anyone with a trace (or often even a rumor) of African ancestry was defined as black.

Enforcement of the laws, however, was spotty and uneven. Some slaves did acquire property, did learn to read and write, and did assemble with other slaves, in spite of laws to the contrary. White owners handled most transgressions by their slaves and inflicted widely varying punishments. In other words, despite the rigid provisions of law, there was in reality considerable variety within the slave system. Some slaves lived in almost prisonlike conditions, rigidly and harshly controlled by their masters. Many (probably most) others enjoyed considerable flexibility and autonomy.

The nature of the relationship between masters and slaves depended in part on the size of the plantation. White farmers with few slaves generally supervised their workers directly and often worked closely alongside them. On such farms, blacks and whites developed a form of intimacy unknown on larger plantations. The paternal relationship between such masters and their slaves could, like relationships between fathers and children, be warm and benevolent. It could also be tyrannical and cruel. In general, African Americans themselves preferred to live on larger plantations, where they had more privacy and a chance for a social world of their own.

Although the majority of slaveowners were small farmers, the majority of slaves lived on plantations of medium or large size, with substantial slave work forces. Thus the relationship between master and slave was much less intimate for the typical slave than for the typical slaveowner. Substantial planters often hired overseers and even assistant overseers to represent them. "Head drivers," trusted and responsible slaves often assisted by several subdrivers, acted under the overseer as foremen.

Life Under Slavery

Slaves generally received an adequate yet simple diet, consisting mainly of cornmeal, salt pork, molasses, and on special occasions fresh meat or poultry. Many slaves cultivated gardens for their own use. Their masters provided them with cheap clothing and shoes. They lived in rough cabins, called slave quarters, usually clustered together in a complex near the master's house. The plantation mistress or a doctor retained by the owner provided some medical care, but slave women themselves—as "healers" and midwives, or simply as mothers—were the more important source.

Slaves worked hard, beginning with light tasks as children; their workdays were longest at harvest time. Slave women worked particularly hard. They generally labored in the fields with the men, and they also handled cooking, cleaning, and child rearing. Many slave families were divided. Husbands and fathers often lived on neighboring plantations; at times, one spouse (usually the male) would be sold to a plantation owner far away. As a result, black women often found themselves acting in effect as single parents. Within the slave family, therefore, women had special burdens but also a special authority.

Slaves were, as a group, much less healthy than southern whites. After 1808, when the importation of slaves became illegal, the proportion of blacks to whites in the nation as a whole steadily declined. The slower increase of the black population was a result of its comparatively high death rate. Slave mothers had large families, but the enforced poverty in which virtually all African Americans lived ensured that fewer of their children would survive to adulthood than the children of white parents. Even those who did survive typically died at a younger age than the average white person.

Household servants had a somewhat easier life—physically at least—than did field hands. On a small plantation, the same slaves might do both field work and housework. But on a large estate, there would generally be a separate domestic staff: nursemaids, housemaids, cooks, butlers, coachmen. These people lived close to the master and his family, eating the leftovers from the family table and in some cases even sleeping in the "big house." Between the blacks and whites of such households affectionate, almost familial relationships might develop. More often, however, house servants resented their isolation from their fellow slaves and the lack of privacy that came with living in such close proximity to the master's family. Among other things, that proximity meant that their transgressions were more visible than those of field hands, and so they received punishments more often than did other slaves. When emancipation came after the Civil War, it was often the house servants who were the first to leave the plantations of their former owners.

Female household servants were especially vulnerable to sexual abuse by their masters and white overseers, who often pressured them into sexual relationships and sometimes literally raped them. In addition to being subjected to unwanted sexual attention from white men, female slaves often received vindictive treatment from white women. Plantation mistresses naturally resented the sexual liaisons between their husbands and female slaves. Punishing their husbands was not usually possible, so they often punished the slaves instead—with arbitrary beatings, increased workloads, and various forms of psychological torment.

Slavery in the Cities

The conditions of slavery in the cities differed significantly from those in the countryside. On the relatively isolated plantations, slaves had little contact with free blacks and lower-class whites, and masters maintained a fairly direct and effective control; a deep and seemingly unbridgeable chasm yawned between slavery and freedom. In the city, however, a master often could not supervise his slaves closely and at the same time use them profitably. Even if they slept at night in carefully watched backyard barracks, they moved about during the day alone, performing errands of various kinds.

There was a considerable market in the South for common laborers, particularly since, unlike in the North, there were few European immigrants to perform menial chores. As a result, masters often hired out slaves for such tasks. Slaves on contract worked in mining and lumbering (often far from cities), but others worked on the docks and on construction sites, drove wagons, and performed other unskilled jobs in cities and towns. Slave women and children worked in the region's few textile mills. Particularly skilled workers such as blacksmiths or carpenters were also often hired out. After regular working hours, many of them fended for themselves; neither their owners nor their employers bothered to supervise them. Thus urban slaves gained numerous opportunities to mingle with free blacks and with whites. In the cities, the line between slavery and freedom was less distinct than on the plantation.

Free Blacks

There were about 250,000 free blacks in the slaveholding states by the start of the Civil War, more than half of them in Virginia and Maryland. In some cases, they were slaves who had somehow earned money with which they managed to buy their own and their families' freedom, usually by developing a skill they could market independently of their masters. It was most often urban blacks, with their greater freedom of movement and activity, who could take that route. One example was Elizabeth Keckley, a slave woman who bought freedom for herself and her son with proceeds from sewing. She later became a seamstress, personal servant, and companion to Mary Todd Lincoln in the White House. But few masters had any incentive, or inclination, to give up their slaves, so this route was open to relatively few people.

Some slaves were set free by a master who had moral qualms about slavery, or by a master's will after his death—for example, the more than 400 slaves belonging to John Randolph of Roanoke, freed in 1833. From the 1830s on, however, state laws governing slavery became more rigid. That was in part a response to the fears Nat Turner's revolt (see pp. 330-331) created among white southerners: free blacks, removed from close supervision by whites, might generate more violence and rebellion than would slaves. The new laws made it more and more difficult, and in some cases practically impossible, for owners to set free (or "manumit") their slaves.

A few free blacks (generally those on the northern fringes of the slaveholding regions) attained wealth and prominence. Some owned slaves themselves, usually relatives whom they had bought in order to ensure their ultimate emancipation. In a few cities—New Orleans, Natchez, and Charleston—free black communities managed to flourish relatively unmolested by whites and with some economic stability. Most southern free blacks, however, lived in abject poverty, under conditions even worse than those of blacks in the North. Yet, great as were the hardships of freedom, blacks usually preferred them to slavery.

Slave Resistance

Slaveowners, and many white Americans after emancipation, liked to argue that the slaves were generally content, "happy with their lot." That may have been true in some cases. But it is clear that the vast majority of southern blacks were not content with being slaves, that they yearned for freedom even though most realized there was little they could do to se-cure it. Evidence for that conclusion can be found, if nowhere else, in the reaction of slaves when emancipation finally came. Virtually all reacted to freedom with great joy; relatively few chose to remain in the service of the whites who had owned them before the Civil War.

Rather than contented acceptance, the dominant response of blacks to slavery was a complex one: a combination of adaptation and resistance. At the extremes, slavery could produce two very different reactions, each of which served as the basis for a powerful stereotype in white society. One extreme was what became known as the "Sambo"—the shuffling, grinning, head-scratching, deferential slave who acted out the role that he recog-nized the white world expected of him. More often than not, the "Sambo" pattern of behavior was a charade, a facade assumed in the presence of whites. The other extreme was the slave rebel—the African American who could not bring himself or herself to either acceptance or accommodation but remained forever rebellious.

Actual slave revolts were extremely rare, but the knowledge that they were possible struck terror into the hearts of white southerners everywhere. In 1800, Gabriel Prosser gathered 1,000 rebellious slaves outside Richmond; but two Africans gave the plot away, and the Virginia militia stymied the up-rising before it could begin. Prosser and thirty-five others were executed. In 1822, the Charleston free black Denmark Vesey and his followers—rumored to total 9,000—made preparations for revolt; but again word leaked out, and suppression and retribution followed. On a summer night in 1831, Nat Turner, a slave preacher, led a band of African Americans armed with guns and axes from house to house in Southampton County, Virginia. They killed sixty white men, women, and children before being overpowered by state and federal troops. More than a hundred blacks were executed in the after-math. Nat Turner's was the only actual slave insurrection in the nineteenth-century South, but fear of slave conspiracies and renewed violence pervaded the section as long as slavery lasted.

For the most part, however, resistance to slavery took other, less dras-tic forms. Some blacks attempted to resist by running away. A small num-ber managed to escape to the North or to Canada, especially after sympa-thetic whites and free blacks began organizing the so-called underground railroad to assist them in flight. But the odds against a successful escape, particularly from the Deep South, were very high. The hazards of distance and the slaves' ignorance of geography were serious obstacles. So were the white "slave patrols," which stopped wandering blacks on sight through-out the South demanding to see travel permits. Despite all the obstacles to

HARRIET TUBMAN WITH ESCAPED SLAVES Harriet Tubman (c. 1820–1913) was born into slavery in Maryland. In 1849, when her master died, she escaped to Philadelphia to avoid being sold out of state. Over the next ten years, she assisted first members of her own family and then up to 300 other slaves to escape from Maryland to freedom. During the Civil War, she served alternately as a nurse and as a spy for Union forces in South Carolina. She is shown here, on the left, with some of the slaves she helped to free.

success, however, blacks continued to run away from their masters in large numbers. Some did so repeatedly, undeterred by the whippings and other penalties inflicted on them when captured.

But perhaps the most important method of resistance was simply a pattern of everyday behavior by which blacks defied their masters. That whites so often considered blacks to be lazy and shiftless suggests one means of resistance: refusal to work hard. Some slaves stole from their masters or from neighboring whites. Some performed isolated acts of sabotage: losing or breaking tools (southern planters gradually began to buy unusually heavy hoes because so many of the lighter ones got broken) or performing tasks improperly. In extreme cases, blacks might make themselves useless by cutting off their fingers or even committing suicide. Or, despite the terrible consequences, a few turned on their masters and killed them. The extremes, however, were rare. For the most part, blacks resisted by building subtle methods of rebellion into their normal patterns of behavior.

THE CULTURE OF SLAVERY

Resistance was only part of the slave response to slavery. Another was an elaborate process of adaptation—a process that did not imply contentment with bondage but a recognition that there was no realistic alternative. One of the ways blacks adapted was by developing their own, separate culture, one that enabled them to sustain a sense of racial pride and unity.

Slave Religion

A separate slave religion was not supposed to exist. Almost all African Americans were Christians by the early nineteenth century. Some had converted voluntarily and some after coercion from their masters and Protestant missionaries who evangelized among them. Masters expected their slaves to worship under the supervision of white ministers. Indeed, autonomous black churches were banned by law, and many slaves became members of the same denominations as their owners—usually Baptist or Methodist.

Nevertheless, blacks throughout the South developed their own version of Christianity, at times incorporating into it such practices as voodoo or other polytheistic religious traditions of Africa. Or they simply bent religion to the special circumstances of bondage. Natural leaders emerging within the slave community rose to the rank of preacher.

African-American religion was more emotional than its white counterpart and reflected the influence of African customs and practices. Slave prayer meetings routinely involved fervent chanting, spontaneous exclamations from the congregation, and ecstatic conversion experiences. Black religion was also more joyful and affirming than that of many white denominations. And above all, African-American religion emphasized the dream of freedom and deliverance. In their prayers and songs and sermons, black Christians talked and sang of the day when the Lord would "call us home," "deliver us to freedom," "take us to the Promised Land." And while their white masters generally chose to interpret such language merely as the expression of hopes for life after death, many blacks themselves used the images of Christian salvation to express their own dream of freedom in the present world. Christian images, and biblical injunctions, were central to Gabriel Prosser, Denmark Vesey, Nat Turner, and others who planned or engaged in open resistance to slavery.

D E B A T I N G   T H E   P A S T

The Character of Slavery

N O ISSUE IN American history has produced a richer literature or a more spirited debate than the nature of plantation slavery. The debate began even before the Civil War, when abolitionists strove to expose slavery to the world as a brutal, dehumanizing institution, while Southern defenders of slavery tried to depict it as a benevolent, paternalistic system. That same debate continued for a time after the Civil War; but by the late nineteenth century, with white Americans eager for sectional conciliation, most Northern and Southern chroniclers of slavery began to accept a romanticized and unthreatening picture of the Old South and its peculiar institution.

The first major scholarly examination of slavery was fully within this romantic tradition. Ulrich B. Phillips's *American Negro Slavery* (1918) portrayed slavery as an essentially benign institution in which kindly masters looked after submissive, childlike, and generally contented African Americans. Phillips's apologia for slavery remained the authoritative work on the subject for nearly thirty years.

In the 1940s, as concern about racial injustice increasingly engaged the attention of white Americans, challenges to Phillips began to emerge. In 1941, for example, Melville J. Herskovits challenged Phillips's contention that black Americans retained little of their African cultural inheritance. In 1943, Herbert Aptheker published a chronicle of slave revolts as a way of challenging Phillips's claim that blacks were submissive and content.

A somewhat different challenge to Phillips emerged in the 1950s from historians who emphasized the brutality of the institution. Kenneth Stampp's *The Peculiar Institution* (1956) and, even more powerfully, Stanley Elkins's *Slavery* (1959) described a labor system that did serious physical and psychological damage to its victims. Stampp and Elkins portrayed slavery as something like a prison, in which men and women had virtually no space to develop their own social and cultural lives. Elkins compared the system to Nazi concentration camps during World War II and likened the childlike "Sambo" personality of slavery to the tragic distortions of character produced by the Holocaust.

In the early 1970s, an explosion of new scholarship on slavery shifted the emphasis away from the damage the system inflicted on African Americans and toward the striking success of the slaves themselves in building a culture of their own despite their enslavement. John Blassingame in 1973, echoing Herskovits's claims of thirty years earlier, argued that "the most remarkable aspect of the whole process of enslavement is the extent to which the American-born slaves were able to retain their ancestors' culture." Herbert Gutman, in *The Black Family in Slavery and Freedom* (1976), challenged the prevailing belief that slavery had weakened and even destroyed the African-American family. On the contrary, he argued, the black family survived slavery with impressive strength, although with some significant differences from the prevailing form of the white family. Eugene Genovese's *Roll, Jordan, Roll* (1974) revealed how African Americans manipulated the paternalist assumptions that lay at the heart of slavery to build a large cultural space of their own, within the system, where they could develop their own family life, social traditions, and religious patterns. That same year, Robert Fogel and Stanley Engerman published their controversial *Time on the Cross,* a highly quantitative study that supported some of the claims of Gutman and Genovese about black achievement but that went much further in portraying slavery as a successful and reasonably humane (if ultimately immoral) system. Slave workers, they argued, were better treated and lived in greater comfort than most Northern industrial workers of the same era. Their conclusions produced a storm of criticism.

Some of the most important recent scholarship on slavery extends the notion of slave autonomy to discussions of African-American women. Elizabeth Fox-Genovese's *Within the Plantation Household* (1988) examined the lives of both white and black women on the plantation. Rejecting the claims of some feminist historians that black and white women shared a common female identity born of their shared subordination to men, she portrayed slave women as defined by their dual roles as members of the plantation work force and anchors of the black family. Slave women, she argued, professed loyalty to their mistresses when forced to serve them as domestics; but their real loyalty remained to their own communities and families.

In cities and towns in the South, some African Americans had their own churches, where free blacks occasionally worshiped alongside slaves. In the countryside, however, slaves usually attended the same churches as their masters. Seating in such churches was usually segregated. Blacks sat in the rear or in balconies. They held their own services later, often in secret, usually at night.

Language and Music

In many areas, slaves retained a language of their own, sometimes incorporating African speech patterns into English. Having arrived in America speaking many different African languages, the first generations of slaves had as much difficulty communicating with one another as they did with white people. To overcome these barriers, they learned a simple, common language (known to linguists as "pidgin"). It retained some African words, but it drew primarily, if selectively, from English. And while slave language grew more sophisticated as blacks spent more time in America—and as new generations grew up never having known African tongues—some features of this early pidgin survived in black speech for many generations.

Music was especially important in slave society. In some ways, it was almost as important to African Americans as language. Again, the African heritage was an important influence. African music relied heavily on rhythm, and so did black music in America. Africans thought of music as an accompaniment to dance, and so did blacks in America. The banjo, an instrument original to Africa, became important to slave music. But most important were voices and song.

Field workers often used songs to pass the time in the fields; since they sang them in the presence of the whites, they usually attached relatively innocuous words to them. But African Americans also created more emotionally rich and politically challenging music in the relative privacy of their religious services. It was there that the tradition of the spiritual emerged in the early nineteenth century. Through the spiritual, Africans in America not only expressed their religious faith, but also lamented their bondage and expressed continuing hope for freedom. Similar sentiments surfaced throughout slave religion.

Slave songs were rarely written down and often seemed entirely spontaneous; but much slave music was really derived from African and Caribbean traditions passed on through generations. Performers also improvised variations on other songs they had heard. Slaves sang whether or not there were musical instruments to accompany them, but they often created instruments

THE OLD PLANTATION This painting, by an unidentified folk artist of the early nineteenth century, suggests the importance of music in the lives of plantation slaves in America. The banjo, which the black musician at right is playing, was originally an African instrument.

for themselves out of whatever materials were at hand. When the setting permitted it, African Americans danced to their music—dances very different from and much more spontaneous than the formal steps that nineteenth-century whites generally learned. They also used music to accompany another of their important cultural traditions: storytelling.

The Slave Family

The slave family was the other crucial institution of black culture in the South. Like religion, it suffered from legal restrictions—most notably the lack of legal marriage. Nevertheless, what we now call the "nuclear family" consistently emerged as the dominant kinship model among African Americans.

Such families did not always operate according to white customs. Black women generally began bearing children at younger ages than most whites, often as early as age fourteen or fifteen. Slave communities did not condemn premarital pregnancy in the way white society did, and black couples would often begin living together before marrying. It was customary, however, for couples to marry—in a ceremony involving formal vows—soon after conceiving a child. Many marriages occurred between slaves living on neighboring plantations. Husbands and wives sometimes visited each other with the permission of their masters, but often such visits had to be in secret, at night. Family ties were generally no less strong than those of whites, and many slave marriages lasted through long lifetimes.

When marriages did not survive, it was often because of circumstances over which blacks had no control. Up to a third of all black families were broken apart by the slave trade; an average slave might expect during a lifetime to see ten or more relatives sold. That accounted for some of the other distinctive characteristics of the black family. Extended kinship networks—which grew to include not only spouses and their children but aunts, uncles, grandparents, even distant cousins—were strong and important, and often helped compensate for the breakup of nuclear families. A slave forced suddenly to move to a new area, far from his or her family, might create fictional kinship ties and become "adopted" by a family in the new community. Even so, the impulse to maintain contact with a spouse and children remained strong long after the breakup of a family. One of the most frequent causes of flight from the plantation was a slave's desire to find a husband, wife, or child who had been sent elsewhere.

However much blacks resented their lack of freedom, they often found it difficult to maintain an entirely hostile attitude toward their owners. They depended on whites for the material means of existence—food, clothing, and shelter—and they relied on them as well for security and protection. There was, in short, a paternal relationship between slave and master—sometimes harsh, sometimes kindly, but always important. That paternalism, in fact, became (even if not always consciously) a vital instrument of white control. By creating a sense of mutual dependence, whites helped reduce resistance to an institution that, in essence, served only the interests of the ruling race.

CONCLUSION

While the North was creating a complex and rapidly developing commercial-industrial economy, the South was expanding its agrarian economy without making many fundamental changes in its character. Great migrations took many southern whites, and even more African-American slaves, into new agricultural areas in the Deep South, where they created a booming "cotton kingdom" that raised crops for export around the world. The cotton economy created many great fortunes, and some modest ones. It also entrenched the planter class as the dominant force within southern society—both as owners of vast numbers of slaves and as patrons, creditors, landlords, and marketers for the large number of poor whites who lived on the edge of the planter world.

The differences between the North and the South were a result of differences in natural resources, differences in social structure, differences in climate, and differences in culture. Above all, they were the result of the existence within the South of an unfree labor system that prevented the kind of social fluidity that an industrializing society usually requires.

FOR FURTHER REFERENCE

Suggested Readings

Frederick Douglass's *Narrative of the Life of Frederick Douglass*, first published in 1845, is an American classic. Peter Kolchin, *American Slavery, 1619–1877* (1993) is the most recent synthesis of the history of slavery in the United States from the settlement of Virginia through Reconstruction. James Oakes, *Slavery and Freedom* (1990) provides an overview of southern politics and society in the antebellum period. Eugene Genovese, *Roll, Jordan, Roll: The World the Slaves Made* (1974) argues that masters and slaves forged a system of mutual obligations within a fundamentally coercive social system. Genovese's *The Political Economy of Slavery* (1965) argues that slavery blocked southern economic development. Robert Fogel and Stanley Engerman, *Time on the Cross*, 2 vols. (1974) is a controversial quantitative study of slavery. Herbert Gutman, *The Black Family in Slavery and Freedom* (1976) is a sweeping and important history. Elizabeth Fox-Genovese, *Within the Plantation Household* (1988) argues against the idea that black and white women shared a community of interests on southern plantations. Charles Joyner, *Down by the Riverside: A South Carolina Slave Community* (1984) is an excellent study of slavery in a single community. Bertram Wyatt-Brown, *Southern Honor: Ethics and Behavior in the Old South* (1982) argues that concepts of honor lay at the core of southern white identity in the antebellum period. Suzanne Lebsock, *The Free Women of Petersburg: Status and Culture in a Southern Town* (1984) is an excellent local study of southern white women, and Anne Firor Scott, *The Southern Lady* (1970) is a pioneering general study. Steven Hahn, *The Roots of Southern Populism: Yeomen Farmers and the Transformation of the Georgia Upcountry, 1850–1890* (1983) argues that white farmers in upcountry regions of the antebellum South maintained economically self-sufficient communities on the periphery of the market.

Films

(The best source for information on how to find these and other films is *Bowker's Complete Video Directory*—3 volumes.) *The Antebellum South* (1987) is a brief introduction to the economic and political consequences of the rise of the cotton economy. *The Plantation South* portrays the development of the plantation system in antebellum southern society. *The African American Experience: 1500–1864* covers the role and contributions of black Americans from the earliest presence of Africans on American soil. See also *Black Americans of Achievement, No. 24: A History of Slavery in America* (1994). *African American Gender Roles* (1994) examines the gender patterns established in the slave community. *A Slave's Story: Running a Thousand Miles to Freedom* (1972) is based on the story of fugitive slaves William and Ellen Craft. *Virginia Plantations: Mount Vernon, Monticello & Other Great Houses of Old Virginia* (1986) is an introduction to the planter class through their architecture.

Internet Resources

Internet websites containing historical material relevant to the subjects discussed in this chapter can be reached through the McGraw-Hill history site at www.mhhe.com/socscience/history/usa/link/linktop.htm.

CHAPTER TWELVE

Antebellum Culture and Reform

The Romatic Impulse ~ Remaking Society
The Crusade Against Slavery

T HE UNITED STATES in the mid-nineteenth century was growing rapidly in geographical extent, in the size and diversity of its population, and in the dimensions and complexity of its economy. And like any people faced with such rapid and fundamental change, Americans reacted with ambiguity. On one hand, they were excited by the new possibilities that economic growth was providing. On the other hand, they were painfully aware of the dislocations that it was creating: the challenges to traditional values and institutions, the social injustice and instability, the uncertainty about the future.

One result of these conflicting attitudes was the emergence of movements to "reform" the nation. Such movements were highly diverse, but most reflected one of two basic impulses, and at times elements of both. Some rested on an optimistic faith in human nature, a belief that within every individual resided a spirit that was basically good and that society should attempt to unleash. This assumption—which produced in both Europe and America a movement known as romanticism—stood in marked contrast to the traditional Calvinist assumption that human desires and instincts were sinful and needed to be repressed.

A second impulse was a desire for order and control. With their society changing so rapidly, with their traditional values and institutions being challenged and eroded, many Americans yearned above all for a restoration of stability and discipline to their nation. Often, this impulse embodied a conservative nostalgia for better, simpler times. But it also inspired efforts to create new institutions of social control, suited to the realities of the new age.

TIME LINE

1821	1826	1830	1831
New York constructs first penitentiary	Cooper's *The Last of the Mohicans*	Joseph Smith publishes the Book of Mormon	The *Liberator* begins publication

1833	1837	1840	1841	1845
American Antislavery Society founded	Horace Mann secretary of Massachusetts Board of Education	Liberty Party formed	Brook Farm founded	Frederick Douglass's autobiography

1848	1850	1851	1852	1854	1855
Women's rights convention at Seneca Falls, N.Y.	Hawthorne's *The Scarlet Letter*	Melville's *Moby Dick*	Beecher Stowe's *Uncle Tom's Cabin*	Thoreau's *Walden*	Whitman's *Leaves of Grass*
Oneida Community founded					

Reform efforts took many forms and could be found in every part of the nation. By the end of the 1840s, however, one issue—slavery—had come to overshadow all others. And one group of reformers—the abolitionists—had become the most influential of all. At that point, the reform impulse became another wedge between the North and the South.

THE ROMANTIC IMPULSE

"In the four quarters of the globe," wrote the English wit Sydney Smith in 1820, "who reads an American book? or goes to an American play? or looks at an American picture or statue?" The answer, he assumed, was obvious: no one.

American intellectuals were painfully aware of the low regard in which Europeans held their culture, and they tried in the middle decades of the nineteenth century to create an American artistic life that would express their own nation's special virtues. At the same time, many of the nation's cultural leaders were striving for another kind of liberation, which was—

ironically—largely an import from Europe: the spirit of romanticism. In literature, in philosophy, in art, even in politics and economics, American intellectuals were committing themselves to the liberation of the human spirit.

Nationalism and Romanticism in American Painting

When Sydney Smith asked in 1820 who looked at an American painting, he was expressing the almost universal belief among European artists that they—and they alone—stood at the center of the world of art. But in the United States, a great many people were, in fact, looking at American paintings in the antebellum era—and they were doing so not because the paintings introduced them to the great traditions of Europe, but because they believed Americans were creating important new artistic traditions of their own.

The most important and popular American paintings of the first half of the nineteenth century set out to evoke the wonder of the American landscape. American painters sought to capture the undiluted power of nature by portraying some of the nation's most spectacular and undeveloped areas. The first great school of American painters emerged in New York. Frederic Church, Thomas Cole, Thomas Doughty, and Asher Durand—who were, along with others, known as the Hudson River School—painted the spectacular vistas of the rugged and still largely untamed Hudson Valley. Like Emerson and Thoreau, whom many of the painters read and admired, they considered nature—far more than civilization—the best source of wisdom and fulfillment. In portraying the Hudson Valley, they seemed to announce that in America, unlike in Europe, "wild nature" still existed; and that America, therefore, was a nation of greater promise than the played-out lands of the Old World. And yet there was also a sense of nostalgia in many of the Hudson River paintings, an effort to preserve and cherish a kind of nature that many Americans feared was fast disappearing.

In later years, some of the Hudson River painters traveled further west, in search of even more profound spiritual experiences in an even more rugged and spectacular natural world. Their enormous canvases of great natural wonders—the Yosemite Valley, Yellowstone, the Rocky Mountains—touched a passionate chord among the public. Some of the most famous of their paintings—particularly the works of Albert Bierstadt and Thomas Moran—traveled around the country attracting enormous crowds.

KINDRED SPIRITS Thomas Cole was one of the early leaders of the Hudson River School of artists in New York, and he is shown here, in a painting by Asher Durand, standing in the wilderness of the Hudson Valley with the great New York poet and editor William Cullen Bryant, a hero of mid-nineteenth century intellectual life. Durand, who succeeded Cole as a leader of the Hudson Valley School, painted this scene not long after Cole's death. It was inspired by a moving eulogy Bryant had given at Cole's funeral, and Durand concluded that the two men were "kindred spirits" in their reverence for nature. Durand himself once wrote that "art must be a vision of God through nature."

An American Literature

The effort to create a distinctively American literature, which Washington Irving and others had begun in the first decades of the century, made considerable progress in the 1820s through the work of the first great American novelist: James Fenimore Cooper. What most distinguished his work was its evocation of the American West. Cooper had a lifelong fascination with the human relationship to nature and with the challenges (and dangers) of America's expansion westward. His most important novels—among them *The Last of the Mohicans* (1826) and *The Deerslayer* (1841)—explored the experience of rugged white frontiersmen with Indians, pioneers, violence, and the law. Cooper not only celebrated the American spirit and landscape; he also evoked the ideal of the independent individual with a natural inner goodness—an ideal that many Americans feared was in jeopardy in the expanding, industrializing world of the East.

Another later group of American writers displayed more clearly the appeal of romanticism to the nation's artists and intellectuals. In 1855, Walt Whitman published his first book of poems, *Leaves of Grass*, and established himself as one of the nation's most important writers. His poems celebrated democracy, the liberation of the individual spirit, and the pleasures of the flesh. Whitman helped liberate verse from traditional, restrictive conventions; he also expressed a yearning for emotional and physical release and personal fulfillment—a yearning perhaps rooted in part in his own experience as a homosexual living in a society profoundly intolerant of unconventional sexuality.

Less exuberant was Herman Melville, perhaps the greatest American writer of his era. The most important of his novels was *Moby Dick*, published in 1851—the story of Ahab, the powerful, driven captain of a whaling vessel, who was obsessed with his search for Moby Dick, the great white whale that had once maimed him. It was a story of courage and of the strength of human will. But it was also a tragedy of pride and revenge, and an uncomfortable metaphor for the harsh, individualistic, achievement-driven culture of nineteenth-century America.

Literature in the Antebellum South

Similarly bleak were the works of the southern writer Edgar Allan Poe, who produced stories and poems that were primarily sad and macabre. His first book, *Tamerlane and Other Poems* (1827), received little recognition. But later works, including his most famous poem, "The Raven" (1845), established him as a major, if controversial, literary figure. Poe evoked images of individuals rising above the narrow confines of intellect and exploring the deeper world of the spirit and the emotions. Yet that world, he seemed to say, contained much pain and horror. Other American writers were contemptuous of Poe's work and his message, but he was ultimately to have a profound effect on European poets such as Baudelaire.

Poe, however, was something of an exception in the world of southern literature. The South experienced a literary flowering of its own in the mid-nineteenth century, and it produced writers and artists who were, like their northern counterparts, concerned with defining the nature of American society and of the American nation. But white southerners tended to produce very different images of what that society was and should be.

Southern novelists of the 1830s (among them Beverly Tucker, William Alexander Caruthers, and John Pendleton Kennedy), some of them writers of great talent, many of them residents of Richmond, produced historical romances or romantic eulogies of the plantation system of the upper South. In the 1840s, the southern literary capital moved to Charleston, home of the most distinguished of the region's men of letters: William Gilmore Simms. For a time, his work expressed a broad nationalism that transcended his regional background; but by the 1840s he too had become a strong defender of southern institutions—especially slavery—against the encroachments of the North. There was, he believed, a unique quality to southern life that it was the duty of intellectuals to defend.

One group of southern writers, however, produced works that were more broadly American and less committed to a glorification of the peculiarities of southern life. These were writers from the fringes of plantation society, who depicted the world of the backwoods rural areas. Augustus B. Longstreet, Joseph G. Baldwin, Johnson J. Hooper, and others focused not on aristocratic "cavaliers," but on ordinary people and poor whites. Instead of romanticizing their subjects, they were deliberately and sometimes painfully realistic. And they seasoned their sketches with a robust, vulgar humor that was new to American literature. These southern realists established a tradition of American regional humor that was ultimately to find its most powerful voice in Mark Twain.

The Transcendentalists

One of the outstanding expressions of the romantic impulse in America came from a group of New England writers and philosophers known as the transcendentalists. Borrowing heavily from German and English writers and philosophers, the transcendentalists embraced a theory of the individual that rested on a distinction between what they called "reason" and "understanding"—words they used in ways that seem unfamiliar, even strange, to modern ears. Reason, as they defined it, had little to do with rationality. It was, rather, the individual's innate capacity to grasp beauty and truth by giving full expression to the instincts and emotions; and as such it was the highest human faculty. Understanding, by contrast, was the use of intellect in the narrow, artificial ways imposed by society; it involved the repression of instinct and the victory of externally imposed learning. Every person's goal, therefore, should be liberation from "understanding" and, instead, the cultivation of "reason." Each individual should strive to "transcend" the limits of the intellect and allow the emotions, the "soul," to create an "original relation to the Universe."

Transcendentalist philosophy emerged first in America among a small group of intellectuals centered in Concord, Massachusetts, and led by Ralph Waldo Emerson. A Unitarian minister in his youth, Emerson left the clergy in 1832 to devote himself to writing, teaching, and lecturing. In "Nature" (1836), Emerson wrote that in the quest for self-fulfillment, individuals should work for a communion with the natural world: "in the woods, we return to reason and faith. . . . Standing on the bare ground,—my head bathed by the blithe air, and uplifted into infinite space,—all mean egotism vanishes. . . . I am part and particle of God." In other essays, he was even more explicit in advocating a commitment of the individual to the full exploration of inner capacities. "Nothing is at last sacred," he wrote in "Self-Reliance" (1841), "but the integrity of your own mind."

Almost as influential as Emerson was another Concord transcendentalist, Henry David Thoreau. Thoreau went even further than his friend Emerson in repudiating the repressive forces of society, which produced, he said, "lives of quiet desperation." Each individual should work for self-realization by resisting pressures to conform to society's expectations and responding instead to his or her own instincts. Thoreau's own effort to free himself—immortalized in *Walden* (1854)—led him to build a small cabin in the Concord woods on the edge of Walden Pond, where he lived alone for two years as simply as he could, attempting to liberate himself from repressive convention and from what he considered society's excessive interest in material comforts. Thoreau's rejection of what he considered the artificial constraints of society extended to his relationship with government. In his 1849 essay "Resistance to Civil Government," he argued that a government that required an individual to violate his or her own morality had no legitimate authority. The proper response was "civil disobedience," or "passive resistance"—a public refusal to obey unjust laws.

Visions of Utopia

Although transcendentalism was at its heart an individualistic philosophy, it helped spawn one of the most famous of all nineteenth-century experiments in communal living: Brook Farm. The dream of the Boston transcendentalist George Ripley, Brook Farm was established in 1841 as an experimental community in West Roxbury, Massachusetts. There, according to Ripley, individuals would gather to create a new society that would permit every member to have full opportunity for self-realization. All residents would share equally in the labor of the community so that all could share in the leisure as well, which was essential for cultivation of the self. (Ripley was one of the first Americans to attribute positive connotations to the idea of leisure; most of his contemporaries equated it with laziness and sloth.) The tension between the ideal of individual freedom and the demands of a communal society took their toll on Brook Farm. Many residents became disenchanted and left. When a fire destroyed the central building of the community in 1847, the experiment dissolved.

Among the original residents of Brook Farm was the writer Nathaniel Hawthorne, who expressed his disillusionment with the experiment and, to some extent, with transcendentalism in a series of novels voicing some of the same concerns that his contemporary Herman Melville was articulating. In *The Blithedale Romance* (1852), he wrote scathingly of Brook Farm itself. In other novels—most notably *The Scarlet Letter* (1850) and *The House of the Seven Gables* (1851)—he wrote equally passionately about the price individuals pay for cutting themselves off from society. Egotism, he claimed (in an indirect challenge to the transcendentalist faith in the self), was the "serpent" that lay at the heart of human misery.

The failure of Brook Farm did not, however, prevent the formation of other experimental communities. The Scottish industrialist and philanthropist Robert Owen founded an experimental community in Indiana in 1825, which he named New Harmony. It was to be a "Village of Cooperation," in which every resident worked and lived in total equality. The community was an economic failure, but the vision that had inspired it continued to enchant some Americans. Dozens of other "Owenite" experiments began in other locations in the ensuing years.

PLAN FOR THE COLONY AT NEW HARMONY The English reformer Robert Owen came to America in the 1820s to create an experimental community in which to test his own theories of cooperative living. This architect's drawing reveals the grandiose plans Owen and his followers had for the colony, which was in Indiana on the banks of the Wabash River on the site of an earlier social experiment by German idealists. In this plan, which was never constructed, the architecture reflects the sense of order and rationality Owen hoped to bring to the community. The plan was designed "to form a new combination of circumstances, capable of producing permanently greater physical, moral, and intellectual advantages . . . than have ever yet been realized in any age or country."

Redefining Gender Roles

Many of the new utopian communities (and many of the new social philosophies on which they rested) were centrally concerned with the relationship between men and women. Some experimented with a radical redefinition of gender roles.

Such a redefinition was central to one of the most enduring of the utopian colonies of the nineteenth century: the Oneida Community, established in 1848 in upstate New York by John Humphrey Noyes. The Oneida "Perfectionists," as residents of the community called themselves, rejected traditional notions of family and marriage. All residents, Noyes declared, were "married" to all other residents; there were to be no permanent conjugal ties. But Oneida was not, as horrified critics often claimed, an experiment in unrestrained "free love." It was a place where the community carefully monitored sexual behavior; where women were protected from unwanted childbearing; and where children were raised communally, often seeing little of their own parents. The Oneidans took pride in what they considered their liberation of women from the demands of male "lust" and from the traditional bonds of family.

The Shakers, too, made a redefinition of traditional gender roles central to their society. Founded by "Mother" Ann Lee in the 1770s, the society of the Shakers survived into the twentieth century. (A tiny remnant is left today.) But the Shakers attracted a particularly large following in the mid-nineteenth century and established more than twenty communities throughout the Northeast and Northwest in the 1840s. They derived their name from a unique religious ritual—a sort of dance, in which members of a congregation would "shake" themselves free of sin while performing a loud chant and an ecstatic dance.

The most distinctive feature of Shakerism, however, was its commitment to complete celibacy—which meant, of course, that no one could be born into Shakerism; all Shakers had to choose the faith voluntarily. Shakerism attracted about 6,000 members in the 1840s, more women than men. They lived in communities where contacts between men and women were strictly limited, and they endorsed the idea of sexual equality. Within Shaker society, women exercised the most power. Shakerism, one observer wrote in the 1840s, was a refuge from the "perversions of marriage" and "the gross abuses which drag it down."

The Shakers were not, however, motivated only by a desire to escape the burdens of traditional gender roles. They were trying as well to create a society separated and protected from the chaos and disorder that they believed had come to characterize American life as a whole. In that, they were much like other dissenting religious sects and other utopian communities of their time.

The Mormons

Perhaps the most important effort to create a new and more ordered society in America was that of the Church of Jesus Christ of Latter-day Saints, whose members are known as Mormons. Mormonism began in upstate New York as a result of the efforts of Joseph Smith, an energetic but economically unsuccessful man, who had spent most of his twenty-four years moving restlessly through New England and the Northeast. Then, in 1830, he published a remarkable document—the Book of Mormon—which he claimed was a translation of a set of golden tablets he had found in the hills of New York after a revelation by an angel of God. The Book of Mormon told the story of an ancient civilization in America, whose now vanished kingdom could become a model for a new holy community in the United States.

Gathering a small group of believers around him, Smith began in 1831 to seek a sanctuary for his new community of "saints," an effort that would continue, unhappily, for more than twenty years. Time and again, the Mormons attempted to establish their "New Jerusalem." Time and again, they met with persecution from surrounding communities suspicious of their radical religious doctrines—which included polygamy (the right of men to take several wives), a rigid form of social organization, and an intense secrecy that gave rise to wild rumors among their critics of conspiracy and depravity.

Driven from their original settlements in Independence, Missouri, and Kirtland, Ohio, the Mormons founded Nauvoo, Illinois, which in the early 1840s became an imposing and economically successful community. In 1844, however, Joseph Smith was arrested, charged with treason (for conspiring against the government to win foreign support for a new Mormon colony in the Southwest), and imprisoned in nearby Carthage, Illinois. There an angry mob attacked the jail, forced Smith from his cell, and shot and killed him. The Mormons then abandoned Nauvoo and, under the leadership of Smith's successor, Brigham Young, traveled across the desert—a society of 12,000 people, one of the largest group migrations in American history—and established a new settlement in Utah, the present Salt Lake City. There, at last, the Mormons were able to create a permanent settlement.

Like other experiments in social organization of the era, Mormonism reflected a belief in human perfectibility. God had once been a man, the church taught; and thus every man or woman could aspire to become, in effect, a god—as Joseph Smith had done. But the Mormons did not celebrate individual liberty. Instead, they created a highly organized, centrally directed, almost militarized social structure as a refuge against the disorder and uncertainty of the secular world. They placed particular emphasis on the structure of the family. The original Mormons were, for the most part, men and women who felt displaced in their rapidly changing society—economically marginal people left behind by the material growth and social progress of their era. In the new religion, they found security and order.

REMAKING SOCIETY

The reform impulse also helped create new movements to remake mainstream society—movements in which, to a striking degree, women formed both the rank and file and the leadership. By the 1830s, such movements had taken the form of organized reform societies.

Revivalism, Morality, and Order

The philosophy of reform arose in part from the optimistic vision of those such as the transcendentalists who preached the divinity of the individual. But another, and in many respects more important, source was Protestant revivalism—the movement that had begun with the Second Great Awakening early in the century and had, by the 1820s, evolved into a powerful force for social reform.

The New Light evangelicals—having rejected the Calvinist idea of predestination—embraced the optimistic belief that every individual was capable of salvation through his or her own efforts. Partly as a result, revivalism soon became not only a means of personal salvation but an effort to reform the larger society. In particular, revivalism produced a crusade against personal immorality. "The church," said Charles Grandison Finney, the leading revivalist of his time, "must take right ground on the subject of Temperance, the Moral Reform, and all the subjects of practical morality which come up for decision from time to time."

Evangelical Protestantism added major strength to one of the most influential reform movements of the era: the crusade against drunkenness. No social vice, temperance advocates argued, was more responsible for crime, disorder, and poverty than the excessive use of alcohol. Women, who were particularly active in the temperance movement, complained that men spent money their families needed on alcohol and that drunken husbands often beat and abused their wives. Temperance also appealed to those who were alarmed by immigration; drunkenness, many nativists believed, was responsible for violence and disorder in immigrant communities and temperance was a way to discipline them. By 1840, temperance had become a major national movement, with powerful organizations and more than a million followers who had signed a formal pledge to forgo hard liquor.

Health, Science, and Phrenology

For some Americans, the search for individual and social perfection led to an interest in new theories of health and knowledge. Threats to public health were critical to the sense of insecurity that underlay many reform movements, especially after the terrible cholera epidemics of the 1830s and 1840s. Cholera is a severe bacterial infection of the intestines, usually a result of consuming contaminated food or water. In the nineteenth century, before the emergence of the germ theory of disease (which eventually helped with prevention) and long before the discovery of antibiotics (which made possible a cure), fewer than half of those who contracted the

THE DRUNKARD'S PROGRESS This 1846 lithograph by Nathaniel Currier shows what temperance advocates argued was the inevitable consequence of alcohol consumption. Beginning with an apparently innocent "glass with a friend," the young man rises step by step to the summit of drunken revelry, then declines to desperation and suicide while his abandoned wife and child grieve.

disease normally survived. Thousands of people died of cholera during its occasional outbreaks, and in certain cities—New Orleans in 1833 and St. Louis in 1849—the effects were truly catastrophic. Nearly a quarter of the population of New Orleans died in the 1833 epidemic. Many municipalities, pressured by reformers, established city health boards to try to find solutions to the problems of epidemics. But the medical profession of the time, unaware of the nature of bacterial infections, had no answers, and the boards therefore found little to do.

Instead, many Americans turned to nonscientific theories for improving health. Affluent men and, especially, women flocked to health spas for the celebrated "water cure" (known to modern scientists as hydrotherapy), which purported to improve health through immersing people in hot or cold baths or wrapping them in wet sheets. Although the water cure in fact delivered few of the benefits its promoters promised, it did have some therapeutic value; some forms of hydrotherapy are still in use today. Other people adopted new dietary theories. Sylvester Graham, a Connecticut-born Presbyterian minister and committed reformer, won many followers with his prescriptions for eating fruits, vegetables, and bread made from coarsely ground flour—a prescription not unlike some dietary theories today—instead of meat. (The "Graham cracker" is made from a kind of flour named for him.) Graham accompanied his dietary prescriptions with moral warnings about the evils of excess and luxury.

Perhaps strangest of all to modern sensibilities was the widespread belief in the new "science" of phrenology, which appeared first in Germany and became popular in the United States beginning in the 1830s through the efforts of Orson and Lorenzo Fowler, publishers of the *Phrenology Almanac.*

PHRENOLOGY This lithograph illustrates some of the ideas of the popular "science" of phrenology in the 1830s. Drawing from the ideas of the German writer Johann Gaspar Spurzheim, American phrenologists promoted the belief that a person's character and talents could be understood by the formation of his or her skull—that the brain was, in fact, a cluster of autonomous organs, each controlling some aspect of human thought or behavior. In this diagram, the areas of the brain that supposedly control "identity," "acquisitiveness," "secretiveness," "marvellousness," and "hope" are clearly identified. The theory has no scientific basis.

Phrenologists argued that the shape of an individual's skull was an important indicator of his or her character and intelligence. They made elaborate measurements of bumps and indentations to calculate the size (and, they claimed, the strength) of different areas of the brain. For a time, phrenology seemed to many Americans an important vehicle for improving society. It provided a way of measuring an individual's fitness for various positions in life and seemed to promise an end to the arbitrary process by which people matched their talents to occupations and responsibilities. The theory is now universally believed to have no scientific value at all.

Medical Science

In an age of rapid technological and scientific advances, the science of medicine sometimes seemed to lag behind. In part, that was because of the greater difficulty of experimentation in medicine, which required human subjects as compared to other areas of science and technology that relied on inanimate objects. In part, it was because of the character of the medical profession, which—in the absence of any significant regulation—attracted many poorly-educated people and many quacks, in addition to trained physicians. Efforts to regulate the profession were beaten back in the 1830s and 1840s by those who considered the licensing of physicians to be a form of undemocratic monopoly. The prestige of the profession, therefore, remained low, and it was for many people a career of last resort.

The biggest problem facing American medicine, however, was the absence of basic knowledge about disease. The great medical achievement of the eighteenth century—the development of a vaccination against smallpox by Edward Jenner—came from no broad theory of infection, but from a brilliant adaptation of folk practices among country people. The development of anesthetics came not from medical doctors at first, but from a New England dentist, William Morton, who was looking for ways to help his patients endure the extraction of teeth. Beginning in 1844, Morton began experimenting with using sulphuric ether. John Warren, a Boston surgeon, soon began using ether to sedate surgical patients. Even these advances met with stiff resistance from traditional physicians, some of whom continued to believe that all medical knowledge derived from timeless truths and ancient scholars and who mistrusted innovation and experimentation. Others rejected scientific advances because they became convinced of the power of new, unorthodox, and untested "medical" techniques popularized by entrepreneurs, many of them charlatans.

In the absence of any broad acceptance of scientific methods and ex-perimental practice in medicine, it was very difficult for even the most tal-ented doctors to make progress in treating disease. Indeed, almost no one had any idea at all how diseases were transmitted. Even so, halting progress toward the discovery of the germ theory did occur in antebellum America. In 1843, the Boston essayist, poet, and physician Oliver Wendell Holmes published his findings from a study of large numbers of cases of "puerperal fever" (septicemia in children) and concluded that the disease could be transmitted from one person to another. This discovery of conta-gion met with a storm of criticism, but was later vindicated by the clinical success of the Hungarian physician Ignaz Semmelweis, who noticed that the infection seemed to be spread by medical students who had been working with corpses. Once he began requiring students to wash their hands and disinfect their instruments, the infections virtually disappeared.

Education

One of the most important reform movements of the mid-nineteenth cen-tury was the effort to produce a system of universal public education. As of 1830, no state had such a system, although some—such as Massachusetts—were supporting limited versions. Soon after that, however, interest in pub-lic education began growing rapidly.

The greatest of the educational reformers was Horace Mann, the first secretary of the Massachusetts Board of Education, which was established in 1837. To Mann and his followers, education was the only way to "coun-terwork this tendency to the domination of capital and the servility of labor." It was also the only way to protect democracy, for an educated electorate was essential to the workings of a free political system. Mann reorganized the Massachusetts school system, lengthened the academic year (to six months), doubled teachers' salaries (although he did not elimi-nate the large disparities between the salaries of male and female teach-ers), broadened the curriculum, and introduced new methods of profes-sional training for teachers. Other states followed similar courses: building new schools, creating teachers' colleges, and offering many children access to education for the first time. By the 1850s, the principle (although not yet the reality) of tax-supported elementary schools was established in every state.

Yet the quality of public education continued to vary widely. In some places—Massachusetts, for example—educators were generally capable men and women, often highly trained, who had an emerging sense of themselves as career professionals. In other areas, however, teachers were often barely literate, and funding for education was severely limited. In much of the West, where the population was highly dispersed, many children had no access to schools at all. In the South, all African Americans were barred from education (although approximately 10 percent of them managed to achieve literacy anyway), and only about a third of all white children of school age were actually enrolled in schools in 1860. In the North, 72 percent were enrolled, but even there, many students attended classes only briefly and casually.

The interest in education also was visible in the growing movement to educate American Indians in the antebellum period. Some reformers, even many who considered black people inferior and unredeemable, believed that Indians could be "civilized" if only they could be taught the ways of the white world. Efforts by missionaries and others to educate Indians and encourage them to assimilate were particularly prominent in such areas of the Far West as Oregon, where substantial numbers of whites were beginning to settle in the 1840s and where conflicts with the natives had not yet become acute. Nevertheless, the great majority of Native Americans remained outside the reach of educational reform, either by choice or by circumstance, or both.

Despite limitations and inequities, the achievements of the school reformers were impressive. By the beginning of the Civil War, the United States had one of the highest literacy rates of any nation of the world: 94 percent of the population of the North, 83 percent of the white population (and 58 percent of the total population) of the South.

Rehabilitation

The belief in the potential of the individual also sparked the creation of new institutions to help the disabled: institutions that formed part of a great network of charitable activities known as the Benevolent Empire. Among them was the Perkins School for the Blind in Boston, the first such school in America. Nothing better exemplified the romantic spirit of the era than the belief of those who founded Perkins that even society's supposedly most disadvantaged members—unsighted and otherwise handicapped people—could be helped to discover their own inner strength and wisdom.

More typical of educational reform, however, were efforts to use schools to impose a set of social values on children—values that reformers and others believed were appropriate for their new, industrializing society.

These values included thrift, order, discipline, punctuality, and respect for authority. Horace Mann, for example, spoke of the role of public schools in extending democracy and expanding individual opportunity. But he spoke, too, of their role in creating social order: "The unrestrained passions of men are not only homicidal, but suicidal. . . . Train up a child in the way he should go, and when he is old he will not depart from it."

Similar impulses produced another powerful movement of reform: the creation of "asylums" for criminals and the mentally ill. In advocating prison and hospital reform, Americans were reacting against one of society's most glaring ills: antiquated jails and mental institutions whose inmates lived in almost inhuman conditions. Beginning in the 1820s, many states built new penitentiaries and mental asylums. New York built the first penitentiary at Auburn in 1821. In Massachusetts, the reformer Dorothea Dix began a national movement for new methods of treating the mentally ill.

But the creation of asylums for social deviants was not simply an effort to curb the abuses of the old system. It was also an attempt to reform and rehabilitate the inmates. New forms of prison discipline were designed to rid criminals of the "laxness" that had presumably led them astray. Solitary confinement and the imposition of silence on work crews (both instituted in Pennsylvania and New York in the 1820s) were meant to give prisoners opportunities to meditate on their wrongdoings and develop "penitence" (hence the name "penitentiary").

Some of the same impulses that produced asylums underlay the emergence in the 1840s and 1850s of a new "reform" approach to the problems of Native Americans: the idea of the reservation. For several decades, the dominant thrust of the United States' policy toward the Indians in areas of white settlement had been relocation. The principal motive behind relocation was simple: getting the tribes out of the way of white civilization. But among some whites there had also been another, if secondary, intent: to move the Indians to a place where they would be protected from whites and allowed to develop to a point at which assimilation might be possible.

It was a small step from the idea of relocation to the idea of the reservation, the notion of creating an enclosed region in which Indians would live in isolation from white society. Just as prisons, asylums, and orphanages would provide society with an opportunity to train and uplift misfits and unfortunates within white society, so the reservations might provide a way to undertake what one official called "the great work of regenerating the Indian race."

The Rise of Feminism

Many of the women who became involved in reform movements in the 1820s and 1830s came to resent the social and legal restrictions that limited their participation. Out of their concerns emerged the first American feminist movement. Sarah and Angelina Grimké, sisters born in South Carolina who had become active and outspoken abolitionists, ignored attacks by men who claimed that their activism was inappropriate to their gender. "Men and women were created equal," they argued. "They are both moral and accountable beings, and whatever is right for man to do, is right for women to do." Other reformers—Catharine Beecher, Harriet Beecher Stowe (her sister), Lucretia Mott, Elizabeth Cady Stanton, and Dorothea Dix—similarly pressed at the boundaries of "acceptable" female behavior, chafing at the restrictions placed on women by men.

In 1840, American female delegates arrived at a world antislavery convention in London, only to be turned away by the men who controlled the proceedings. Angered at the rejection, several of the delegates—notably Lucretia Mott and Elizabeth Cady Stanton—became convinced that their first duty as reformers should now be to elevate the status of women. Over the next several years, Mott, Stanton, and others began drawing pointed parallels between the plight of women and the plight of slaves; and in 1848, in Seneca Falls, New York, they organized a convention to discuss the question of women's rights. Out of the meeting came the "Declaration of Sentiments and Resolutions" (patterned on the Declaration of Independence), which stated that "all men and women are created equal," that women no less than men are endowed with certain inalienable rights. In demanding the right to vote, they launched a movement for woman suffrage that would survive until the battle was finally won in 1920. The Seneca Falls document was at least equally important for its rejection of the whole notion that men and women should be assigned separate "spheres" in society.

Many of the women involved in these feminist efforts were Quakers. Quakerism had long embraced the ideal of sexual equality and had tolerated, indeed encouraged, the emergence of women as preachers and community leaders. Of the women who drafted the Declaration of Sentiments, all but Elizabeth Cady Stanton were Quakers. Stanton, joined two years later by Susan B. Anthony, led the movement to implement the Seneca Falls resolutions in the 1850s and beyond. Together, they ultimately transformed it into a powerful force for change.

Feminists benefited greatly from their association with other reform movements, most notably abolitionism, but they also suffered as a result. The demands of women were usually assigned—even by some women themselves—a secondary position to what many considered the far greater issue of the rights of slaves.

THE CRUSADE AGAINST SLAVERY

The antislavery movement was not new to the mid-nineteenth century. But only in 1830 did it begin to gather the force that would ultimately enable it to overshadow virtually all other efforts at social reform.

Early Opposition to Slavery

In the early years of the nineteenth century, those who opposed slavery were, for the most part, a calm and genteel lot, expressing moral disapproval but doing little else. To the extent that there was an organized anti-slavery movement, it centered on the concept of colonization—the effort to resettle American blacks in Africa or the Caribbean. In 1817, a group of prominent white Virginians organized the American Colonization Society (ACS), which tried to challenge slavery without challenging property rights or southern sensibilities. The ACS proposed a gradual freeing of slaves, with masters receiving compensation. The liberated blacks would then be transported out of the country and helped to establish a new society of their own. The ACS received some funding from private donors, some from Congress, some from the legislatures of Virginia and Maryland. And it arranged to have several groups of blacks transported out of the United States, some of them to the west coast of Africa, where in 1830 they established the nation of Liberia. (In 1846, Liberia became an independent black republic, with its capital, Monrovia, named for the American president who had presided over the initial settlement.)

But the ACS was in the end a negligible force. Neither private nor public funding was nearly enough to carry out the vast projects its supporters envisioned. There were far too many blacks in America in the nineteenth century to be transported to Africa by any conceivable program. And the ACS met resistance, in any case, from blacks themselves, many of whom were now three or more generations removed from Africa and, despite their loathing of slavery, had no wish to emigrate.

Garrison and Abolitionism

In 1830, with slavery spreading rapidly in the South and the antislavery movement seemingly on the verge of collapse, a new figure emerged to transform it: William Lloyd Garrison. Born in Massachusetts in 1805, Garrison was in the 1820s an assistant to the New Jersey Quaker Benjamin Lundy, who published the leading antislavery newspaper of the time. Garrison grew impatient with his employer's moderate tone and mild proposals for reform. In 1831, therefore, he returned to Boston to found his own weekly newspaper, the *Liberator*.

Garrison's philosophy was so simple that it was genuinely revolutionary. Opponents of slavery, he said, should not talk, as earlier reformers had done, about the evil influence of slavery on white society; they should talk about the damage the system did to blacks. And they should, therefore, reject "gradualism" and demand the immediate, unconditional, universal abolition of slavery and the extension to blacks of all the rights of American citizenship. Garrison wrote in a relentless, uncompromising tone. "I am aware," he wrote in the very first issue of the *Liberator*, "that many object to the severity of my language; but is there not cause for severity? I will be as harsh as truth, and as uncompromising as justice. . . . I am in earnest—I will not equivocate—I will not excuse—I will not retreat a single inch—and I will be heard."

Garrison soon attracted a large group of followers throughout the North, enough to enable him to found the New England Antislavery Society in 1832 and a year later, after a convention in Philadelphia, the American Antislavery Society. By 1835, there were more than 400 local societies; by 1838, there were 1,350, with more than 250,000 members.

Abolitionists were a part of the larger spirit of reform of their era. Like other reformers, they were calling for an unleashing of the individual human spirit, the elimination of artificial social barriers to fulfillment. Who, after all, needed help in realizing individual potential more than enslaved men and women?

Black Abolitionists

Abolitionism had a particular appeal to the free black population of the North, which in 1850 numbered about 250,000, mostly concentrated in cities. These free blacks lived in conditions of poverty and oppression at times worse than those of their slave counterparts in the South. For all their problems, however, northern blacks were fiercely proud of their freedom and sensitive to the plight of those members of their race who remained in bondage; and they were aware that their own position in society would remain precarious as long as slavery existed. Many in the 1830s came to support Garrison. But they also rallied to leaders of their own.

The greatest of the black abolitionists was Frederick Douglass, one of the most electrifying orators of his time. Born a slave in Maryland, Douglass escaped to Massachusetts in 1838, became an outspoken leader of antislavery sentiment, and spent two years lecturing in England, where members of that country's vigorous antislavery movement lionized him. On his return to the United States in 1847, Douglass purchased his freedom from his Maryland owner and founded an antislavery newspaper, the *North Star*, in Rochester, New York. He achieved wide renown as well for his autobiography, *Narrative of the Life of Frederick Douglass* (1845), in which he presented a damning picture of slavery. Douglass demanded not only freedom but full social and economic equality.

FREDERICK DOUGLASS Frederick Douglass was the most prominent African American of the nineteenth century. Born in Maryland to an unknown white father and a slave mother, he escaped from slavery into the North in 1838. He quickly became a leader in the abolitionist movement.

Anti-Abolitionism

The rise of abolitionism was a powerful force, but it provoked a powerful opposition as well. Almost all white southerners, of course, were bitterly hostile to the movement. But even in the North, abolitionists were a small, dissenting minority whom most whites viewed as dangerous radicals. Some feared that abolitionism would produce a destructive war between the sections. Others feared that it would lead to a great influx of free blacks into the North.

The result of such fears was an escalating wave of violence directed toward abolitionists in the 1830s. A mob in Philadelphia attacked the abolitionist headquarters there in 1834, burned it to the ground, and began a bloody race riot. Another mob seized Garrison on the streets of Boston in 1835 and threatened to hang him. He was saved from death only by being locked in jail. Elijah Lovejoy, the editor of an abolitionist newspaper in Alton, Illinois, was victimized repeatedly by mob violence and finally killed when he tried to defend his press from attack.

That so many men and women continued to embrace abolitionism in the face of such vicious opposition from within their own communities suggests that abolitionists were not people who made their political commitments lightly or casually. They were strong-willed, passionate crusaders who displayed not only enormous courage and moral strength but at times a fervency that many of their contemporaries (even some who shared their dislike of slavery) found deeply disturbing. The mobs were only the most violent expression of a hostility to abolitionism that many, perhaps most, other white Americans shared.

Abolitionism Divided

By the mid-1830s, the abolitionist crusade had begun to experience serious internal strains and divisions. One reason was the violence of the anti-abolitionists, which persuaded some members of the movement that a more moderate approach was necessary. Another reason was the growing radicalism of William Lloyd Garrison, who shocked even many of his own allies (including Frederick Douglass) by attacking not only slavery but the government itself. The Constitution, he said, was "a covenant with death and an agreement with hell." The nation's churches, he claimed, were bulwarks of slavery. In 1840, Garrison precipitated a formal division within the American Antislavery Society by insisting that women, who had always been central to the organization's work, be permitted to participate in the movement on terms of full equality. He continued after 1840 to arouse controversy with new and even more radical stands: an extreme pacifism that rejected even defensive wars; opposition to all forms of coercion—not just slavery, but prisons and asylums; and finally, in 1843, a call for northern disunion from the South. The nation could, he suggested, purge itself of the sin of slavery by expelling the slave states from the Union.

From 1840 on, therefore, abolitionism moved in many channels and spoke with many different voices. The Garrisonians, with their radical and uncompromising moral stance, remained influential. But others operated in more moderate ways, arguing that abolition could be accomplished only as the result of a long, patient, peaceful struggle— "immediate abolition gradually accomplished," as they called it. They appealed to the conscience of the slaveholders, attempting to convince them that their institution was sinful. When that produced no results, they turned to political action, seeking to induce the northern states and the federal government to aid the cause. They joined the Garrisonians in helping runaway slaves find refuge in the North or in Canada through what became known as the underground railroad (although their efforts were never as highly organized as the name suggests). After the Supreme Court (in *Prigg* v. *Pennsylvania*, 1842) ruled that states need not aid in enforcing the 1793 law requiring the return of fugitive slaves to their owners, abolitionists won passage in several northern states of "personal liberty laws," which forbade state officials to assist in the capture and return of runaways. The antislavery societies also petitioned Congress to abolish slavery in places where the federal government had jurisdiction—in the territories and in the District of Columbia—and to prohibit the interstate slave trade.

Antislavery sentiment underlay the formation in 1840 of the Liberty Party, which ran Kentucky antislavery leader James G. Birney for president. But this party and its successors never campaigned for outright abolition (an illustration of the important fact that "antislavery" and "abolitionism" were not always the same thing). They stood instead for "free soil," for keeping slavery out of the territories. Some free-soilers were concerned about the welfare of blacks; others were people who cared nothing about slavery but simply wanted to keep the West a country for whites. Garrison dismissed free-soilism as "white-manism." But the free-soil position would ultimately do what abolitionism never could: attract the support of large numbers, even a majority, of the white population of the North.

The frustrations of political abolitionism drove some critics of slavery to embrace more drastic measures. A few began to advocate violence; it was a group of prominent abolitionists in New England, for example, who funneled money and arms to John Brown for his bloody uprisings in Kansas and Virginia. Others attempted to arouse public anger through propaganda. The most powerful of all abolitionist propaganda was Harriet Beecher Stowe's novel *Uncle Tom's Cabin*, published as a book in 1852. It rocked the nation. It sold more than 300,000 copies within a year of publication and was later issued again and again, becoming one of the most remarkable best-sellers in American history. It succeeded in bringing the message of abolitionism to an enormous new audience—not only those who read the book but those who watched dramatizations of its story by countless theater companies across the nation. Reviled throughout the South, Stowe became a hero to many in the North. And in both regions, her novel helped inflame sectional tensions to a new level of passion. Few books in American history have had so great an impact on the course of public events.

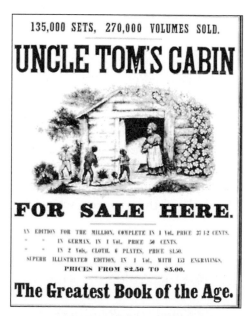

UNCLE TOM'S CABIN This poster (advertising, among other things, a German edition of Harriet Beecher Stowe's novel) did not exaggerate when it described *Uncle Tom's Cabin* as "The Greatest Book of the Age." There were, to be sure, greater literary accomplishments; but no American book of the nineteenth century had so profound a political impact.

Even divided, therefore, abolitionism remained a powerful influence on the life of the nation. Only a relatively small number of people before the Civil War ever accepted the abolitionist position that slavery must be entirely eliminated in a single stroke. But the crusade that Garrison had launched, and that thousands of committed men and women kept alive for three decades, was a constant, visible reminder of how deeply the institution of slavery was dividing America.

CONCLUSION

The rapidly changing society of antebellum America intensified cultural nationalism and encouraged interest in a wide range of reforms. Writers, artists, intellectuals, and others drew heavily from new European notions of personal liberation and fulfillment—a set of ideas often known as romanticism. But they also strove to create a truly American cultrure, unbeholden to European models. The literary and artistic life of the nation expressed the rising interest in personal liberation—in giving individuals the freedom to explore their own souls and to find in nature a full expression of their divinity. It also called attention to some of the nation's glaring social problems.

Reformers, too, made use of the romantic belief in the divinity of the individual. They flocked to religious revivals, worked on behalf of such "moral" reforms as temperance, supported education, and articulated some of the first statements of modern feminism. Above all, in the North, they rallied against slavery. Out of this growing antislavery movement emerged a new and powerful phenomenon: abolitionism, which rejected moderate reform and insisted on nothing less than immediate emancipation of slaves. The abolitionist movement galvanized much of the North. It also contributed greatly to the growing schism between North and South.

FOR FURTHER REFERENCE

Suggested Readings

Ronald G. Walters, *American Reformers, 1815–1860* (1978) is a good overview of antebellum reform. David Reynolds, *Walt Whitman's America* (1995) is both a cultural biography of Whitman and an evocation of the society Whitman celebrated. Van Wyck Brooks, *The Flowering of New England: 1815–1865* (1936) is a classic study. Ann Douglas, *The Femi-*

nization of American Culture (1977) is a pioneering work in the history of gender and culture. Leo Marx, *The Machine in the Garden* (1964) is an influential study of ideas about technology in the era of industrialization. Paul Johnson, *A Shopkeeper's Millennium: Society and Revivals in Rochester, New York, 1815–1837* (1978) links revivalism in the "Burnt-Over District" to changing patterns of work and social control. Jon Butler, *Awash in a Sea of Faith: Christianizing the American People* (1990) is an important study of revivalism. Nancy F. Cott, *The Bonds of Womanhood: "Woman's Sphere" in New England, 1780–1835* (1977) argues that nineteenth century feminism emerged from the separation of home and work in the early nineteenth century. James Brewer Stewart, *Holy Warriors* (1976) is a good summary of the trajectory of abolitionism from the American Revolution through emancipation. Ronald G. Walters, *The Antislavery Appeal: American Abolitionists After 1830* (1976) emphasizes the religious motivations of antebellum abolitionism.

Films

(The best source for information on how to find these and other films is *Bowker's Complete Video Directory*—3 volumes.) *The American Story, No. 9: Social Reform* (1985) documents attempts by reformers to eliminate the disruptive effects of industrialization and to abolish slavery. *Walt Whitman: Poet for a New Age* (1971) reveals Whitman's faith in democracy, as well as his mystical ideas about life and death, personality, and love. *Thoreau's Walden* re-creates the two-year period when Henry David Thoreau lived alone at Walden Pond. *The Second Great Awakening* (1994) illuminates the resurgence of religious reform in the early nineteenth century. *Reforming the Republic* weaves together the urges for religious revivalism and reform in antebellum America. *The Abolitionists* (1987) discusses abolitionists such as Frederick Douglass and William Lloyd Garrison. *Frederick Douglass—An American Life* (1985) explores the life and times of one of the most famous fugitive slaves and black abolitionists. *Rebel Hearts* (1995) is a lively portrait of Sarah and Angelina Grimké, two important white women abolitionists. *Black Americans of Achievement, No. 8: Sojourner Truth*, and *Black Americans of Achievement, No. 9: Harriet Tubman* explore the lives of two very important black women abolitionists.

Internet Resources

Internet websites containing historical material relevant to the subjects discussed in this chapter can be reached through the McGraw-Hill history site at www.mhhe.com/socscience/history/usa/link/linktop.htm.

CHAPTER THIRTEEN

The Impending Crisis

Looking Westward ～ *Expansion and War*
The Sectional Debate ～ *The Crisis of the 1850s*

NTIL THE 1840S, the tensions between North and South remained relatively contained. Had no new sectional issues arisen,
it is possible that the two sections might have resolved their differences
peaceably over time. But new issues did arise, centered around the expansion of slavery. From the North came the strident and increasingly powerful abolitionist movement. From the South came a newly militant defense
of slavery and the way of life it supported. And from the West, more significantly, came a series of controversies that would ultimately tear the
fragile Union apart.

LOOKING WESTWARD

More than a million square miles of new territory came under the control
of the United States during the 1840s—the greatest wave of expansion
since the Louisiana Purchase nearly forty years before. By the end of the
decade, the nation possessed all the territory of the present-day United
States except Alaska, Hawaii, and a few relatively small areas acquired
later through border adjustments. Many factors accounted for this great
new wave of expansion, but one of the most important was an ideology
known as "Manifest Destiny."

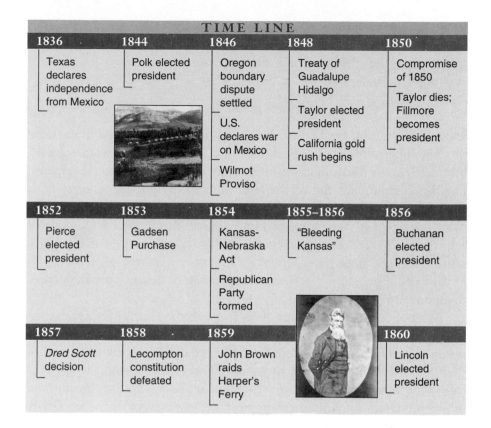

TIME LINE				
1836	**1844**	**1846**	**1848**	**1850**
Texas declares independence from Mexico	Polk elected president	Oregon boundary dispute settled U.S. declares war on Mexico Wilmot Proviso	Treaty of Guadalupe Hidalgo Taylor elected president California gold rush begins	Compromise of 1850 Taylor dies; Fillmore becomes president
1852	**1853**	**1854**	**1855–1856**	**1856**
Pierce elected president	Gadsen Purchase	Kansas-Nebraska Act Republican Party formed	"Bleeding Kansas"	Buchanan elected president
1857	**1858**	**1859**		**1860**
Dred Scott decision	Lecompton constitution defeated	John Brown raids Harper's Ferry		Lincoln elected president

Manifest Destiny

Manifest Destiny reflected both the burgeoning pride that characterized American nationalism in the mid-nineteenth century and the idealistic vision of social perfection that fueled so much of the reform energy of the time. It rested on the idea that America was destined—by God and by history—to expand its boundaries over a vast area.

By the 1840s, the idea of Manifest Destiny had spread throughout the nation, publicized by the new "penny press," which made newspapers available to a far greater proportion of the population than ever before, and fanned by the rhetoric of nationalist politicians. Some advocates of Manifest Destiny had relatively limited territorial goals; others envisioned a vast new "empire of liberty" that would include Canada, Mexico, Caribbean and Pacific islands, and ultimately, a few dreamed, much of the rest of the world. Henry Clay and others warned that territorial expansion would reopen the painful controversy over slavery. Their voices, however, could not compete with the enthusiasm over expansion in the 1840s, which began with the issues of Texas and Oregon.

Americans in Texas

Twice in the 1820s, the United States had offered to purchase Texas from the Republic of Mexico, only to meet with indignant Mexican refusals. But in 1824, the Mexican government launched an ill-advised experiment. Hoping to strengthen the economy of the sparsely-populated territory, it enacted a colonization law offering cheap land and a four-year exemption from taxes to any American willing to move into Texas. Thousands of Americans flocked into the region, the great majority of them white southerners and their slaves, intent on establishing cotton plantations. By 1830, there were about 7,000 Americans living in Texas, more than twice the number of Mexicans there.

Most of the settlers came to Texas through the efforts of American intermediaries, who received sizable land grants from Mexico in return for promising to bring new residents into the region. The most successful of them was Stephen F. Austin, a young immigrant from Missouri who established the first legal American settlement in Texas in 1822. Austin and others recruited many American immigrants to Texas; in the process, they created centers of power in the region that competed with the Mexican government. In 1830, after an unsuccessful effort by its own American *impresario* to establish Texas as an independent nation, the Mexcian government barred any further American immigration into the region. But Americans kept flowing into Texas anyway. By 1835 over 30,000 Americans, white and black, had settled there.

Friction between the American settlers and the Mexican government was already growing in the mid-1830s when instability in Mexico itself drove General Antonio López de Santa Anna to seize power as a dictator and create a new, more autocratic regime. He increased the powers of the national government at the expense of the state governments, a measure that Texans from the United States assumed Santa Anna was aiming specifically at them. Sporadic fighting between Americans and Mexicans in Texas began in 1835, and in 1836, the American settlers defiantly proclaimed their independence from Mexico.

Santa Anna led a large army into Texas, where the American settlers were divided into several squabbling factions. Mexican forces annihilated an American garrison at the Alamo mission in San Antonio after a famous, if futile, defense by a group of Texas "patriots" that included, among others, the renowned frontiersman and former Tennessee congressman Davy Crockett. Another garrison at Goliad suffered substantially the same fate when the Mexicans executed most of the force after it had surrendered. By the end of 1836, the rebellion appeared to have collapsed.

But General Sam Houston managed to keep a small force together. And on April 21, 1836, at the Battle of San Jacinto (near the present-day city of Houston), he defeated the Mexican army and took Santa Anna prisoner. Santa Anna, under pressure from his captors, signed a treaty giving Texas independence.

A number of Mexican residents of Texas (*Tejanos*) had fought with the Americans in the revolution. But soon after Texas won its independence, their positions grew difficult. The Americans did not trust them, feared that they were agents of the Mexican government, and in effect drove many of them out of the new republic. Most of those who stayed had to settle for a politically and economically subordinate status within the fledgling republic.

One of the first acts of the new president of Texas, Sam Houston, was to send a delegation to Washington with an offer to join the Union. But President Jackson, fearing that adding a large new slave state to the Union would increase sectional tensions, blocked annexation and even delayed recognizing the new republic until 1837. Presidents Martin Van Buren and William Henry Harrison also avoided the issue during their terms of office.

Spurned by the United States, Texas cast out on its own. England and France, concerned about the growing power of the United States, saw Texas as a possible check on its growth and began forging ties with the new republic. At that point, President Tyler persuaded Texas to apply for statehood again in 1844. But Secretary of State Calhoun presented an annexation treaty to Congress as if its only purpose were to extend slavery, and northern senators defeated it. The Texas question quickly became the central issue in the election of 1844.

Oregon

Control of what was known as Oregon country, in the Pacific Northwest, was another major political issue in the 1840s. Its half-million square miles included the present states of Oregon, Washington, and Idaho, parts of Montana and Wyoming, and half of British Columbia. Both Britain and the United States claimed sovereignty in the region. Unable to resolve their conflicting claims diplomatically, they agreed in an 1818 treaty to

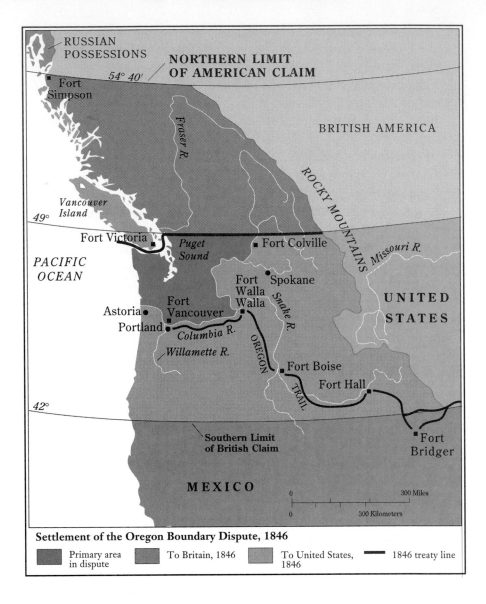

RUSSIAN POSSESSIONS

54° 40'

NORTHERN LIMIT OF AMERICAN CLAIM

Fort Simpson

Fraser R.

BRITISH AMERICA

ROCKY MOUNTAINS

Vancouver Island

49°

Fort Victoria

Puget Sound

Fort Colville

Missouri R.

PACIFIC OCEAN

Fort Walla Walla

Spokane

Snake R.

Astoria

Fort Vancouver

UNITED STATES

Portland

Columbia R.

OREGON

Willamette R.

TRAIL

Fort Boise

Fort Hall

42°

Southern Limit of British Claim

Fort Bridger

MEXICO

0   300 Miles

0   300 Kilometers

Settlement of the Oregon Boundary Dispute, 1846

Primary area in dispute | To Britain, 1846 | To United States, 1846 | 1846 treaty line

allow citizens of each country equal access to the territory. This arrange-
ment, known as "joint occupation," continued for twenty years.

In fact, at the time of the treaty neither Britain nor the United States
had established much of a presence in Oregon country. White settlement
in the region consisted largely of American and Canadian fur traders, and
the most significant white settlements were scattered fur trading posts, the

largest of which was John Jacob Astor's Astoria. But American interest in Oregon grew substantially in the 1820s and 1830s.

By the mid-1840s, white Americans substantially outnumbered the British in Oregon. They had also devastated much of the Indian population, in part through a measles epidemic that spread through the Cayuse. American settlements had spread up and down the Pacific coast, and the new settlers (along with advocates of Manifest Destiny in the East) were urging the United States government to take possession of the disputed Oregon Territory.

The Westward Migration

The migrations into Texas and Oregon were part of a larger movement that took hundreds of thousands of white and black Americans into the far western regions of the continent between 1840 and 1860. Southerners flocked mainly to Texas. But the largest number of migrants came from the Old Northwest (today's Midwest)—white men and women, and a few blacks, who undertook arduous journeys in search of new opportunities. Most traveled in family groups, until the early 1850s, when the great California gold rush attracted many single men (See pp. 379–380). Most were relatively young people. Few were wealthy, but many were relatively prosperous. Poor people who could not afford the trip on their own usually had to join other families or groups as laborers—men as farm or ranch hands, women as domestic servants, teachers, or, in some cases, prostitutes. Groups heading for areas where mining or lumbering was the principal economic activity consisted mostly of men. Those heading for farming regions traveled mainly as families.

Most migrants—about 300,000 between 1840 and 1860—traveled west along the great overland trails. They generally gathered in one of several major depots in Iowa and Missouri (Independence, St. Joseph, or Council Bluffs), joined a wagon train led by hired guides, and set off with their belongings piled in covered wagons, livestock trailing behind. The major route west was the 2,000-mile Oregon Trail, which stretched from Independence across the Great Plains and through the South Pass of the Rocky Mountains. From there, migrants moved north into Oregon or south (along the California trail) to the northern California coast. Other migrations moved along the Santa Fe Trail, southwest from Independence into New Mexico.

However they traveled, overland migrants faced an arduous journey—although the death rate for travelers was only slightly higher than the rate for the American population as a whole. Most journeys lasted five or six

Western Trails, to 1860

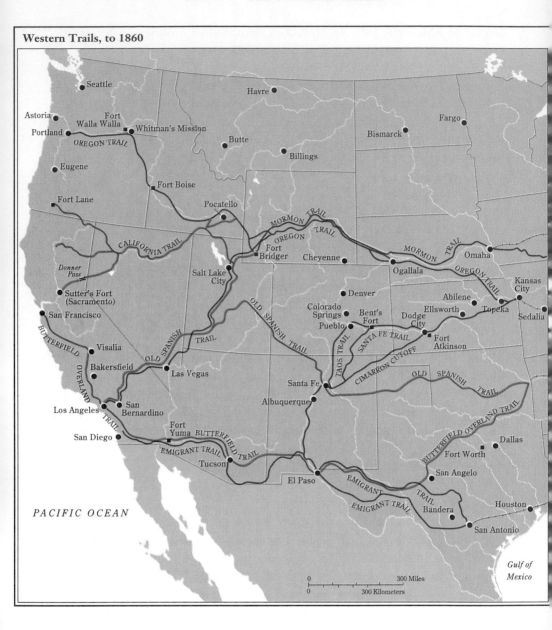

Seattle

Havre

Astoria
Portland
Fort
Walla Walla
Whitman's Mission
OREGON TRAIL
Eugene

Fargo

Bismarck

Butte

Billings

Fort Boise

Fort Lane

Pocatello

CALIFORNIA TRAIL

MORMON TRAIL
OREGON TRAIL

Fort
Bridger
Cheyenne

MORMON TRAIL
OREGON TRAIL
Omaha

Donner
Pass

Salt Lake
City

Ogallala

Kansas
City

Sutter's Fort
(Sacramento)

Denver

Colorado
Springs
Bent's
Fort

Abilene
Ellsworth
Dodge
City

Topeka
Sedalia

San Francisco

Pueblo

Fort
Atkinson

BUTTERFIELD

Visalia

OLD SPANISH TRAIL

TAOS TRAIL

SANTA FE TRAIL

CIMARRON CUTOFF

OLD

SPANISH

TRAIL

OVERLAND

Bakersfield

OLD SPANISH TRAIL

Las Vegas

Santa Fe

Albuquerque

BUTTERFIELD OVERLAND TRAIL

Los Angeles
San
Bernardino

TRAIL

Fort
Yuma

San Diego

EMIGRANT TRAIL
BUTTERFIELD TRAIL

Tucson

Dallas

Fort Worth
San Angelo

El Paso

EMIGRANT
TRAIL

Bandera

Houston

PACIFIC OCEAN

EMIGRANT TRAIL

San Antonio

Gulf of
Mexico

0   300 Miles

0   300 Kilometers

months (from May to November), and there was always pressure to get through the Rockies before the snows began, often not an easy task given the very slow pace of most wagon trains (about fifteen miles a day). There was also the danger of disease; many groups were decimated by cholera. Almost everyone, male or female, walked the great majority of the time, to

CROSSING THE PLAINS A long wagon train carries migrants across the Plains toward Montana in 1866. This photograph gives some indication of the rugged condition of even some of the most well-traveled trails.

lighten the load for the horses drawing the wagons. The women, who did the cooking and washing at the end of the day, generally worked harder than the men, who usually rested when the caravan halted.

Only a few expeditions experienced Indian attacks. In the twenty years before the Civil War, fewer than 400 migrants (slightly more than one-tenth of 1 percent) died in conflicts with the tribes. In fact, Indians were usually more helpful than dangerous to the white migrants. They often served as guides, and they traded horses, clothing, and fresh food with the travelers.

Despite the traditional image of westward migrants as rugged individualists, most travelers found the journey a very communal experience. That was partly because many expeditions consisted of groups of friends, neighbors, or relatives who had decided to pull up stakes and move west together. And it was partly because of the intensity of the journey: many weeks of difficult travel with no other human contact except, occasionally, with Indians. It was a rare expedition in which there were not some internal conflicts before the trip was over; but those who made the journey successfully generally learned the value of cooperation.

EXPANSION AND WAR

The growing number of white Americans in the lands west of the Mississippi put great pressure on the government in Washington to annex Texas, Oregon, and other territory. And in the 1840s, these expansionist pressures helped push the United States into a war that—however dubious its origins—became a triumph for the advocates of Manifest Destiny.

The Democrats and Expansion

In preparing for the election of 1844, the two leading candidates—Henry Clay and the Democrat and former president Martin Van Buren—both tried to avoid taking a stand on the controversial issue of the annexation of Texas. Sentiment for expansion was mild within the Whig Party, and Clay had no difficulty securing the nomination despite his noncommittal position. But many southern Democrats supported annexation, and the party passed over Van Buren to nominate a strong supporter of annexation, the previously unheralded James K. Polk.

Polk was not as obscure as his Whig critics claimed. He had represented Tennessee in the House of Representatives for fourteen years, four of them as Speaker, and had subsequently served as governor. But by 1844, he had been out of public office—and for the most part out of the public mind—for three years. What made his victory possible was his support for the position, expressed in the Democratic platform, "that the re-occupation of Oregon and the re-annexation of Texas at the earliest practicable period are great American measures." By combining the Oregon and Texas questions, the Democrats hoped to appeal to both northern and southern expansionists. Polk carried the election by 170 electoral votes to 105, although his popular majority was less than 40,000.

Polk entered office with a clear set of goals and with plans for attaining them. John Tyler accomplished the first of Polk's goals for him in the last days of his own presidency. Interpreting the election returns as a mandate for the annexation of Texas, the outgoing president won congressional approval for it in February 1845. That December, Texas became a state.

Polk himself resolved the Oregon question. The British minister in Washington brusquely rejected a compromise Polk offered that would establish the United States–Canadian border at the 49th parallel; he did not even refer the proposal to London. Incensed, Polk again asserted the American claim to all of Oregon. There was loose talk of war on both sides of the Atlantic—talk that in the United States often took the form of the bellicose slogan "Fifty-four forty or fight!" (a reference to where the Americans hoped to draw the northern boundary of their part of Oregon). But neither country really wanted war. Finally, the British government accepted Polk's original proposal to divide the territory at the 49th parallel. On June 15, 1846, the Senate approved a treaty that fixed the boundary at the 49th parallel, where it remains today.

The Southwest and California

One of the reasons the Senate and the president had agreed so readily to the British offer to settle the Oregon question was that new tensions were emerging in the Southwest—tensions that ultimately led to a war with Mexico. As soon as the United States admitted Texas to statehood in 1845, the Mexican government broke diplomatic relations with Washington. Mexican-American relations grew still worse when a dispute developed over the boundary between Texas and Mexico. Texans claimed the Rio Grande as their western and southern border, a claim that would have added much of what is now New Mexico to Texas. Mexico, although still not conceding the loss of Texas, argued nevertheless that the border had always been the Nueces River, to the north of the Rio Grande. Polk accepted the Texas claim, and in the summer of 1845 he sent a small army under General Zachary Taylor to Texas to protect it against a possible Mexican invasion.

Part of the area in dispute was New Mexico, whose Spanish and Indian residents lived in a multiracial society that had by the 1840s endured for nearly a century and a half. In the 1820s, the Mexican government had invited American traders into the region (just as it invited American settlers into Texas), hoping to speed development of the province. And New Mexico, like Texas, soon began to become more American than Mexican. A flourishing commerce soon developed between Santa Fe and Independence, Missouri.

Americans were also increasing their interest in an even more distant province of Mexico: California. In this vast region lived members of several western Indian tribes and perhaps 7,000 Mexicans, mostly descendants of Spanish colonists. Gradually, however, white Americans began to arrive: first maritime traders and captains of Pacific whaling ships, who stopped to barter goods or buy supplies; then merchants, who established stores, imported merchandise, and developed a profitable trade with the Mexicans and Indians; and finally pioneering farmers, who entered California from the east, by land, and settled in the Sacramento Valley. Some of these new settlers began to dream of bringing California into the United States.

President Polk soon came to share their dream and committed himself to acquiring both New Mexico and California for the United States. At the same time that he dispatched the troops under Taylor to Texas, he sent secret instructions to the commander of the Pacific naval squadron to seize the California ports if Mexico declared war. Representatives of the president quietly informed Americans in California that the United States would respond sympathetically to a revolt against Mexican authority there.

The Mexican War

Having appeared to prepare for war, Polk turned to diplomacy and dispatched a special minister, John Slidell, to try to buy off the Mexicans. But Mexican leaders rejected Slidell's offer to purchase the disputed territories. On January 13, 1846, as soon as he heard the news, Polk ordered Taylor's army in Texas to move across the Nueces River, where it had been stationed, to the Rio Grande. For months, the Mexicans refused to fight. But finally, according to disputed American accounts, some Mexican troops crossed the Rio Grande and attacked a unit of American soldiers. Polk now told Congress: "War exists by the act of Mexico herself." On May 13, 1846, Congress declared war by votes of 40 to 2 in the Senate and 174 to 14 in the House.

The war had many opponents in the United States. Whig critics charged from the beginning (and not without some justification) that Polk had deliberately maneuvered the country into the conflict and had staged the border incident that had precipitated the declaration. Many argued that the hostilities with Mexico were draining resources and attention away from the more important issue of the Pacific Northwest; and when the United States finally reached its agreement with Britain on the Oregon question, opponents claimed that Polk had settled for less than he should have because he was preoccupied with Mexico. Opposition intensified as the war continued and as the public became aware of the casualties and expense.

American forces did well against the Mexicans, but victory did not come as quickly as Polk had hoped. The president ordered Taylor to cross the Rio Grande, seize parts of northeastern Mexico, beginning with the city of Monterrey, and then march on to Mexico City itself. Taylor captured Monterrey in September 1846, but he let the Mexican garrison evacuate without pursuit. Polk now began to fear that Taylor lacked the tactical skill for the planned advance against Mexico City. He also feared that, if successful, Taylor would become a powerful political rival (as, in fact, he did).

San Francisco
(Yerba Buena)

Sutter's Fort

Sonoma
Bear Flag Revolt
June 14, 1845

Monterey

Santa Barbara

Los Angeles

San Gabriel
Jan. 8, 1847

San Pasqual
Dec. 6, 1846

San Diego

Gila R.

Tucson

El Paso

Sacramento River
Feb. 28, 1847

Chihuahua

STOCKTON 1846

SLOAT 1846

Gulf of California

PACIFIC OCEAN

Colorado R.

Pueblo

Bent's
Fort

KEARNY 1846

MO.

Fort Leavenworth

UNITED STATES

Arkansas R.

Mexican Revolt
Feb. 3, 1847

Taos

Santa Fe

Las Vegas

Albuquerque

Valverde
Dec. 12, 1846

**DISPUTED
AREA**

Red R.

ARK.

Sabine R.

El Brazito
Dec. 25, 1846

KEARNY 1846

DONIPHAN
1847

Rio Grande

TEXAS

Austin

San Antonio

San Jacinto

Goliad

LA.

Corpus Christi

Laredo

Monclava

Monterrey
Sept. 1846

Mier

WOOL 1846

MEXICO

TAYLOR
1846

SCOTT 1846

Fort Brown

Matamoros

*Gulf of
Mexico*

Buena Vista
Feb. 22–23, 1847

Victoria

Mazatlán

San Luis Potosí

SANTA ANNA
1847

Tampico

SCOTT 1847

Cerro Gordo
April 17–18, 1847

Mexico City
Sept. 13–14, 1847

Puebla

Vera Cruz

Capture of Mexico City
September 1847

Lake Texcoco

Guadalupe
Hidalgo

Mexico City occupied
Sept. 14

Chapultepec
Sept. 13

San Angel

Churubusco
Aug. 20

San Antonio

TAYLOR 1847

*Lake
Chalco*

Buena Vista

*Lake
Vochimilco*

Padierna
Aug.18

San
Gregorio

Ayocingo

0   10 Miles

0   10 Kilometers

The Mexican War, 1846–1848

TROOP MOVEMENTS

⬅ American forces

⬅ Mexican forces

BATTLES

✶ American victory

✶ Mexican victory

0   400 Miles

0   400 Kilometers

In the meantime, Polk ordered other offensives against New Mexico and California. In the summer of 1846, a small army under Colonel Stephen W. Kearny captured Santa Fe with no opposition. Then Kearny proceeded to California, where he joined a conflict already in progress that was being staged jointly by American settlers, a well-armed exploring party led by John C. Frémont, and the American navy: the so-called Bear Flag Revolution. Kearny brought the disparate American forces together under his command, and by the autumn of 1846 he had completed the conquest of California.

The United States now controlled the two territories for which it had gone to war. But Mexico still refused to concede defeat. At this point, Polk and General Winfield Scott, the commanding general of the army and its finest soldier, launched a bold new campaign. Scott assembled an army at Tampico, which the navy transported down the Mexican coast to Veracruz. With an army that never numbered more than 14,000, Scott advanced 260 miles along the Mexican National Highway toward Mexico City, kept American casualties low, and never lost a battle before finally seizing the Mexican capital. A new Mexican government took power and announced its willingness to negotiate a peace treaty.

President Polk was now growing thoroughly unclear about his objectives. He continued to encourage those who demanded that the United States annex much of Mexico itself. At the same time, concerned about the approaching presidential election, he was growing anxious to get the war finished quickly. Polk had sent a special presidential envoy, Nicholas Trist, to negotiate a settlement. On February 2, 1848, he reached agreement with the new Mexican government on the Treaty of Guadalupe Hidalgo, by which Mexico agreed to cede California and New Mexico to the United States and acknowledge the Rio Grande as the boundary of Texas. In return, the United States promised to assume any financial claims its new citizens had against Mexico and to pay the Mexicans $15 million. Trist had obtained most of Polk's original demands, but he had not satisfied the new, more expansive dreams of acquiring additional territory in Mexico itself. Polk angrily claimed that Trist had violated his instructions, but he soon realized that he had no choice but to accept the treaty to silence a bitter battle growing between ardent expansionists demanding the annexation of "All Mexico!" and antislavery leaders charging that the expansionists were conspiring to extend slavery to new realms. The president submitted the Trist treaty to the Senate, which approved it by a vote of 38 to 14. The war was over, and America had gained a vast new territory. But it had also acquired a new set of troubling and divisive issues.

STEVEN KEARNY IN SANTA FE Colonel Stephen Kearny led a small U.S. military party to Santa Fe in 1846 and seized the town without opposition. In this 1909 drawing (which the artist Kenneth Chapman acknowledged was not entirely accurate), Kearny raises the American Flag over the "old palace" in Santa Fe. The image appeared on a U.S. postage stamp in 1946.

THE SECTIONAL DEBATE

James Polk tried to be a president whose policies transcended sectional divisions. But conciliating the sections was becoming an ever more difficult task, and Polk gradually earned the enmity of northerners and westerners alike, who believed his policies (and particularly his enthusiasm for territorial expansion in the Southwest) favored the South at their expense.

Slavery and the Territories

In August 1846, while the Mexican War was still in progress, Polk asked Congress to appropriate $2 million for purchasing peace with Mexico. Representative David Wilmot of Pennsylvania, an antislavery Democrat, introduced an amendment to the appropriation bill prohibiting slavery in any territory acquired from Mexico. The so-called Wilmot Proviso passed

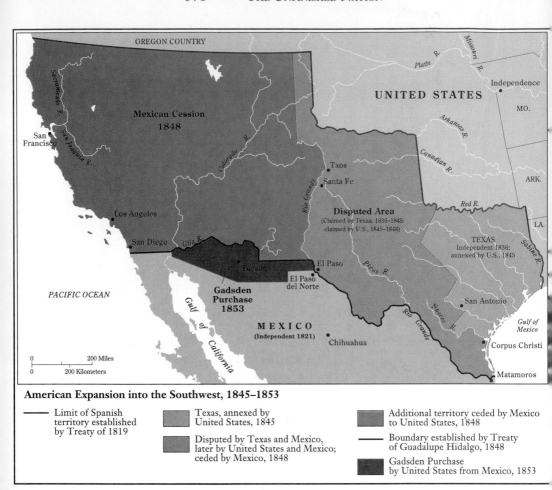

American Expansion into the Southwest, 1845–1853

— Limit of Spanish territory established by Treaty of 1819

Texas, annexed by United States, 1845

Disputed by Texas and Mexico, later by United States and Mexico; ceded by Mexico, 1848

Additional territory ceded by Mexico to United States, 1848

— Boundary established by Treaty of Guadalupe Hidalgo, 1848

Gadsden Purchase by United States from Mexico, 1853

the House but failed in the Senate. It would be called up, debated, and voted on repeatedly for years. Southern militants, in the meantime, contended that all Americans had equal rights in the new territories, including the right to move their slaves (which they considered property) into them.

As the sectional debate intensified, President Polk supported a proposal to extend the Missouri Compromise line through the new territories to the Pacific coast, banning slavery north of the line and permitting it south of the line. Others supported a plan, originally known as "squatter sovereignty" and later by the more dignified phrase "popular sovereignty," which would allow the people of each territory (acting through their legislature) to decide the status of slavery there. The debate over these various proposals dragged on for many months, and the issue remained unresolved when Polk left office in 1849.

The presidential campaign of 1848 dampened the controversy for a time as both Democrats and Whigs tried to avoid the slavery question. When Polk, in poor health, declined to run again, the Democrats nominated Lewis Cass of Michigan, a dull, aging party regular. The Whigs nominated General Zachary Taylor of Louisiana, hero of the Mexican War but a man with no political experience whatsoever. Opponents of slavery found the choice of candidates unsatisfying, and out of their discontent emerged the new Free-Soil Party, which drew from the existing Liberty Party and the antislavery wings of the Whig and Democratic Parties and which endorsed the Wilmot Proviso. Its candidate was former president Martin Van Buren.

Taylor won a narrow victory. But while Van Buren failed to carry a single state, he polled an impressive 291,000 votes (10 percent of the total), and the Free-Soilers elected ten members to Congress. The emergence of the Free-Soil Party as an important political force, like the emergence of the Know-Nothing and Liberty Parties before it, signaled the inability of the existing parties to contain the political passions slavery was creating. It was an important part of a process that would lead to the collapse of the second party system in the 1850s.

The California Gold Rush

By the time Taylor took office, the pressure to resolve the question of slavery in the far western territories had become more urgent as a result of dramatic events in California. In January 1848, a foreman working in a sawmill owned by John Sutter (one of California's leading ranchers) found traces of gold in the foothills of the Sierra Nevada. Within months, news of the discovery had spread throughout the nation and much of the world. Almost immediately, hundreds of thousands of people began flocking to California in a frantic search for gold. The non-Indian population of the territory increased nearly twentyfold in only four years.

The atmosphere in California at the peak of the gold rush was one of almost crazed excitement and greed. Most migrants to the Far West prepared carefully before making the journey. But the California migrants (known as "Forty-niners") threw caution to the winds. They abandoned farms, jobs, homes, families; they piled onto ships and flooded the overland trails—many carrying only what they could pack on their backs. The overwhelming majority of the Forty-niners (perhaps 95 percent) were men, and the society they created on their arrival in California was unusually fluid and volatile because of the almost total absence of women, children, or families.

The gold rush also attracted some of the first Chinese migrants to the western United States. News of the discoveries created great excitement in China, particularly in impoverished areas, where letters home from Chinese already in California and reports from American visitors spread the word. It was, of course, extremely difficult for a poor Chinese peasant to get to America; but many young, adventurous people (mostly men) decided to go anyway—in the belief that they could quickly become rich and then return to China. Emigration brokers loaned many migrants money for passage to California, which the migrants were to pay off out of their earnings there. The Chinese in California were free laborers and merchants, looking for gold or, more often, hoping to profit from other economic opportunities the gold boom was creating.

The gold rush was producing a serious labor shortage in California, as many male workers left their jobs and flocked to the gold fields. That created opportunities for many people who needed work (including Chinese immigrants). It also led to a frenzied exploitation of Indians that resembled slavery in all but name. A new state law permitted the arrest of "loitering" or orphaned Indians and their assignment to a term of "indentured" labor.

The gold rush was of critical importance to the growth of California, but not for the reasons most of the migrants hoped. There was substantial gold in the hills of the Sierra Nevada, and many people got rich from it. But only a tiny fraction of the Forty-niners ever found gold, or even managed to stake a claim to land on which they could look for gold. Some disappointed migrants returned home after a while. But many stayed in California and swelled both the agricultural and urban populations of the territory. By 1856, for example, San Francisco—whose population had been 1,000 before the gold rush (and at one point declined to about 100 as people left for the mines)—was the home of over 50,000 people. By the early 1850s, California, which had always had a diverse population, had become even more heterogeneous. The gold rush had attracted not just white Americans but Europeans, Chinese, South Americans, Mexicans, free blacks, and slaves who accompanied southern migrants. Conflicts over gold intersected with racial and ethnic tensions to make the territory an unusually turbulent place. The gold rush, therefore, became another factor putting pressure on the United States to resolve the status of the territories—and of slavery within them.

Rising Sectional Tensions

Zachary Taylor believed statehood could become the solution to the issue of slavery in the territories. As long as the new lands remained territories, the federal government was responsible for deciding the fate of slavery within them. But once they became states, he thought, their own governments would be able to settle the slavery question. At Taylor's urging, California quickly adopted a constitution that prohibited slavery, and in December 1849 Taylor asked Congress to admit California as a free state. New Mexico, he added, should also be granted statehood as soon as it was ready and should, like California, be permitted to decide for itself what it wanted to do about slavery.

Congress balked, in part because of several other controversies concerning slavery that were complicating the debate. One was the effort of antislavery forces to abolish slavery in the District of Columbia, a movement bitterly resisted by southerners. Another was the emergence of personal liberty laws in northern states, which barred courts and police officers from helping to return runaway slaves to their owners. In response, southerners demanded a stringent law that would require northern states to return fugitive slaves to their owners. But the biggest obstacle to the president's program was the white South's fear that two new free states would be added to the northern majority. The number of free and slave states was equal in 1849—fifteen each. But the admission of California would upset the balance; and New Mexico, Oregon, and Utah might upset it further, leaving the South in a minority in the Senate, as it already was in the House.

Tempers were now rising to dangerous levels. Even many otherwise moderate southern leaders were beginning to talk about secession from the Union. In the North, every state legislature but one adopted a resolution demanding the prohibition of slavery in the territories.

The Compromise of 1850

Faced with this mounting crisis, moderates and unionists spent the winter of 1849–1850 trying to frame a great compromise. The aging Henry Clay, who was spearheading the effort, believed that no compromise could last unless it settled all the issues in dispute between the sections. As a result, he took several measures that had been proposed separately, combined them into a single piece of legislation, and presented it to the Senate on January 29, 1850. Among the bill's provisions were the admission of California as a free state; the formation of territorial governments in the rest of the lands acquired from Mexico, without restrictions on slavery; the abolition of the slave trade, but not slavery itself, in the District of Columbia; and a new and more effective fugitive slave law. These resolutions launched a debate that raged for seven months—both in Congress and throughout the nation. The debate occurred in two phases, the differences between which revealed much about how American politics was changing in the 1850s.

In the first phase of the debate, the dominant voices in Congress were those of old men—national leaders who still remembered Jefferson, Adams, and other founders—who argued for or against the compromise on the basis of broad ideals. Clay himself, seventy-three years old in 1850, appealed to shared national sentiments of nationalism. Early in March, another of the older leaders—John C. Calhoun, sixty-eight years old and so ill that he had to sit grimly in his seat while a colleague read his speech for

Slave and Free Territories According to the Compromise of 1850

Free states and territories

Slave states and territories

Decision left to territories

42.7% Slaves as percentage of total population

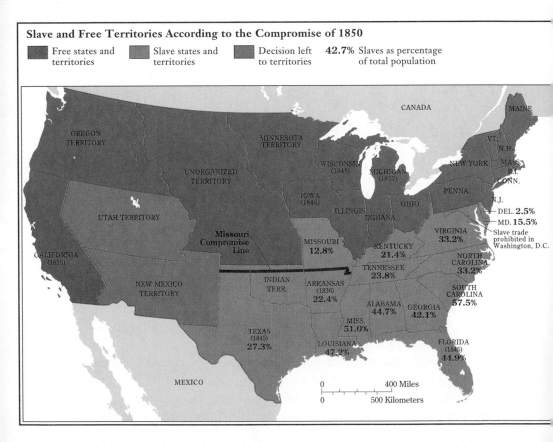

him—joined the debate. He insisted that the North grant the South equal rights in the territories, that it agree to observe the laws concerning fugitive slaves, that it cease attacking slavery, and that it amend the Constitution to create dual presidents, one from the North and one from the South, each with a veto. Calhoun was making radical demands that had no chance of passage. But like Clay, he was offering what he considered a comprehensive, permanent solution to the sectional problem that would, he believed, save the Union. After Calhoun came the third of the elder statesmen, sixty-eight-year-old Daniel Webster, one of the great orators of his time. Still nourishing presidential ambitions, he delivered an eloquent address in the Senate, trying to rally northern moderates to support Clay's compromise.

But in July, after six months of this impassioned, nationalistic debate, Congress defeated the Clay proposal. And with that, the controversy moved into its second phase, in which a very different cast of characters predominated. Clay, ill and tired, left Washington to spend the summer resting in the mountains. Calhoun had died even before the vote in July. And Webster accepted a new appointment as secretary of state, thus removing himself from the Senate and from the debate.

In place of these leaders, a new, younger group now emerged. One spokesman was William H. Seward, forty-nine years old, of New York, a wily political operator who staunchly opposed the proposed compromise. The ideals of Union were to him less important than the issue of eliminating slavery. Another was Jefferson Davis of Mississippi, forty-two years old, a representative of the new, cotton South. To him, the slavery issue was less one of principles and ideals than one of economic self-interest. Most important of all, there was Stephen A. Douglas, a thirty-seven-year-old Democratic senator from Illinois. A westerner from a rapidly growing state, he was an open spokesman for the economic needs of his section—and especially for the construction of railroads. His was a career devoted not to any broad national goals but frankly to sectional gain and personal self-promotion.

The new leaders of the Senate were able, as the old leaders had not been, to produce a compromise. One spur to the compromise was the disappearance of the most powerful obstacle to it: the president. Zachary Taylor had been adamant that only after California and possibly New Mexico were admitted as states could other measures be discussed. But on July 9, 1850, Taylor suddenly died—the victim of a violent stomach disorder. He was succeeded by Millard Fillmore of New York—a dull, handsome, dignified man who understood the political importance of flexibility. He supported the compromise and used his powers of persuasion to swing northern Whigs into line.

The new leaders also benefited from their own pragmatic tactics. Douglas's first step, after the departure of Clay, was to break up the "omnibus bill" that Clay had envisioned as a great, comprehensive solution to the sectional crisis and to introduce instead a series of separate measures to be voted on one by one. Thus representatives of different sections could support those elements of the compromise they liked and oppose those they did not. Douglas also gained support with complicated backroom deals linking the compromise to such nonideological matters as the sale of government bonds and the construction of railroads. As a result of his efforts, by mid-September Congress had enacted and the president had signed all the components of the compromise.

The Compromise of 1850, unlike the Missouri Compromise thirty years before, was not a product of widespread agreement on common national ideals. It was, rather, a victory of self-interest. Still, members of Congress hailed the measure as a triumph of statesmanship; and Millard Fillmore, signing it, called it a just settlement of the sectional problem, "in its character final and irrevocable."

THE CRISES OF THE 1850S

For a few years after the Compromise of 1850, the sectional conflict seemed briefly to be forgotten amid booming prosperity and growth. But the tensions between North and South remained, and the crisis continued to smolder until—in 1854—it once more burst into the open.

The Uneasy Truce

Both major parties endorsed the Compromise of 1850 in 1852, and both nominated presidential candidates unidentified with sectional passions. The Democrats chose the obscure New Hampshire politician Franklin Pierce and the Whigs the military hero General Winfield Scott, a man of entirely unknown political views. But the sectional question was a divisive influence in the election anyway, and the Whigs were the principal victims. They suffered massive defections from antislavery members angered by the party's evasiveness on the issue. Many of them flocked to the Free-Soil Party, whose antislavery presidential candidate, John P. Hale, repudiated the Compromise of 1850. The divisions among the Whigs helped produce a victory for the Democrats in 1852.

Franklin Pierce, a charming, amiable man of no particular distinction, attempted to maintain party—and national—harmony by avoiding divisive issues, and particularly by avoiding the issue of slavery. But it was an impossible task. Northern opposition to the Fugitive Slave Act intensified quickly after 1850, when southerners began appearing occasionally in northern states to pursue people they claimed were fugitives. Mobs formed in some northern cities to prevent enforcement of the law, and several northern states also passed their own laws barring the deportation of fugitive slaves. White southerners watched with growing anger and alarm as the one element of the Compromise of 1850 that they had considered a victory seemed to become meaningless as a result of northern defiance.

"Young America"

One of the ways Franklin Pierce hoped to dampen sectional controversy was through his support of a movement in the Democratic Party known as "Young America." Its adherents saw the expansion of American democracy throughout the world as a way to divert attention from the controversies over slavery. The great liberal and nationalist revolutions of 1848 in Europe stirred them to dream of a republican Europe with governments based on the model of the United States. They dreamed as well of expanding American commerce in the Pacific and acquiring new territories in the Western Hemisphere.

But efforts to extend the nation's domain could not avoid becoming entangled with the sectional crisis. Pierce had been pursuing unsuccessful diplomatic attempts to buy Cuba from Spain (efforts begun in 1848 by Polk). In 1854, however, a group of his envoys sent him a private document from Ostend, Belgium, making the case for seizing Cuba by force. When the Ostend Manifesto, as it became known, was leaked to the public, it enraged many antislavery northerners, who charged the administration with conspiring to bring a new slave state into the Union.

The South, for its part, opposed all efforts to acquire new territory that would not support a slave system. The kingdom of Hawaii agreed to join the United States in 1854, but the treaty died in the Senate because it contained a clause prohibiting slavery in the islands. A powerful movement to annex Canada to the United States—a movement that had the support of many Canadians eager for access to American markets—similarly foundered, at least in part because of slavery.

Slavery, Railroads, and the West

What fully revived the sectional crisis, however, was the same issue that had produced it in the first place: slavery in the territories. By the 1850s, the line of substantial white settlement had moved beyond the boundaries of Missouri, Iowa, and what is now Minnesota into a great expanse of plains, which many white Americans had once believed was unfit for cultivation. Now it was becoming apparent that large sections of this region were, in fact, suitable for farming. In the states of the Old Northwest, therefore, prospective settlers urged the government to open the area to them, provide territorial governments, and—despite the solemn assurance the United States had earlier given the Indians of the sanctity of their reservations—dislodge the tribes located there so as to make room for white settlers. There was relatively little opposition from any segment of white society to this proposed violation of Indian rights. But the interest in further settlement raised two issues that did prove highly divisive and that gradually became entwined with each other: railroads and slavery.

As the nation expanded westward, the problem of communication between the older states and the areas west of the Mississippi River became more and more critical. As a result, broad support began to emerge for building a transcontinental railroad. The problem was where to place it— and in particular, where to locate the railroad's eastern terminus, where the line could connect with the existing rail network east of the Mississippi. Northerners favored Chicago, the rapidly growing capital of the free states of the Northwest. Southerners supported St. Louis, Memphis, or New Orleans—all located in slave states. The transcontinental railroad, in other words, had become part of the struggle between the North and the South.

Pierce's secretary of war, Jefferson Davis of Mississippi, removed one obstacle to a southern route. Surveys indicated that a railroad with a southern terminus would have to pass through an area in Mexican territory. But in 1853 Davis sent James Gadsden, a southern railroad builder, to Mexico, where he persuaded the Mexican government to accept $10 million in exchange for a strip of land that today comprises part of Arizona and New Mexico. The so-called Gadsden Purchase only accentuated the sectional rivalry.

The Kansas-Nebraska Controversy

As a senator from Illinois, a resident of Chicago, and the acknowledged leader of northwestern Democrats, Stephen A. Douglas naturally wanted the transcontinental railroad for his own city and section. He also realized the strength of the principal argument against the northern route west of the Mississippi: that it would run mostly through country with a substantial Indian population. As a result, he introduced a bill in January 1854 to organize (and thus open to white settlement) a huge new territory, known as Nebraska, west of Iowa and Missouri.

Douglas knew the South would oppose his bill because it would prepare the way for a new free state; the proposed territory was in the area of the Louisiana Purchase north of the Missouri Compromise line (36°30′) and hence closed to slavery. In an effort to make the measure acceptable to southerners, Douglas inserted a provision that the status of slavery in the territory would be determined by the territorial legislature—that is, according to "popular sovereignty." In theory, the region could choose to open itself to slavery (although few believed it actually would). When southern Democrats demanded more, Douglas agreed to an additional clause explicitly repealing the Missouri Compromise. He also agreed to divide the area into two territories—Nebraska and Kansas—instead of one. The new, second territory (Kansas) was more likely to become a slave state. In its final form the measure was known as the Kansas-Nebraska Act. President Pierce supported the bill, and after a strenuous debate, it became law in May 1854 with the unanimous support of the South and the partial support of northern Democrats.

No piece of legislation in American history produced so many immediate, sweeping, and ominous consequences. It divided and destroyed the Whig Party, which disappeared almost entirely by 1856. It divided the northern Democrats (many of whom were appalled at the repeal of the Missouri Compromise, which they considered an almost sacred part of the fabric of the Union) and drove many of them from the party. Most important of all, it spurred the creation of a new party that was frankly sectional in composition and creed. People in both major parties who opposed Douglas's bill began to call themselves Anti-Nebraska Democrats and Anti-Nebraska Whigs. In 1854, they formed a new organization and named it the Republican Party. It instantly became a major force in American politics. In the elections of that year, the Republicans won enough seats in Congress to permit them, in combination with allies among the Know-Nothings, to organize the House of Representatives.

"Bleeding Kansas"

Events in Kansas itself in the next two years increased the political turmoil in the North. White settlers from both the North and the South began moving into the territory almost immediately after the passage of the Kansas-Nebraska Act. In the spring of 1855, elections were held for a territorial legislature. There were only about 1,500 legal voters in Kansas by then, but thousands of Missourians, some traveling in armed bands into Kansas, swelled the vote to over 6,000. The result was that pro-slavery forces elected a majority to the legislature, which immediately legalized slavery. Outraged free-staters elected their own delegates to a constitutional convention, which met at Topeka and adopted a constitution excluding slavery. They then chose their own governor and legislature and petitioned Congress for statehood. President Pierce denounced them as traitors and threw the full support of the federal government behind the pro-slavery territorial legislature. A few months later a pro-slavery federal marshal assembled a large posse, consisting mostly of Missourians, to arrest the free-state leaders, who had set up their headquarters in Lawrence. The posse sacked the town, burned the "governor's" house, and destroyed several printing presses. Retribution came quickly.

Among the most fervent abolitionists in Kansas was John Brown, a grim, fiercely committed zealot who considered himself an instrument of God's will to destroy slavery. He had moved to Kansas with his sons so that they could fight to make it a free state. After the events in Lawrence, he gathered six followers (including four of his sons) and in one night murdered five pro-slavery settlers, leaving their mutilated bodies to discourage other supporters of slavery from entering Kansas. This terrible episode, known as the Pottawatomie Massacre, led to more civil strife in Kansas—irregular, guerrilla warfare conducted by armed bands, some of them more interested in land claims or loot than in ideologies. Northerners and southerners alike came to believe that the events in Kansas illustrated (and were caused by) the aggressive designs of the other section. "Bleeding Kansas" became a symbol of the sectional controversy.

Another symbol soon appeared, in the United States Senate. In May 1856, Charles Sumner of Massachusetts—a militant and passionately doctrinaire opponent of slavery—rose to give a speech entitled "The Crime Against Kansas." In it, he gave particular attention to Senator Andrew P. Butler of South Carolina, an outspoken defender of slavery. The South Carolinian was, Sumner claimed, the "Don Quixote" of slavery, having "chosen a mistress . . . who, though ugly to others, is always lovely to

"BLEEDING KANSAS" The battle over the fate of slavery in Kansas was one of the most turbulent events of the 1850s. This 1855 poster invites antislavery forces to a meeting to protest the actions of the "bogus" pro-slavery territorial legislature, which had passed laws that, among other things, made it illegal to speak or write against slavery. "Squatter sovereignty" was another term for "popular sovereignty," the doctrine that gave residents of a prospective state the power to decide the fate of slavery there.

him, though polluted in the sight of the world, is chaste in his sight . . . the harlot slavery."

The pointedly sexual references and the general viciousness of the speech enraged Butler's nephew, Preston Brooks, a member of the House of Representatives from South Carolina. Several days after the speech, Brooks approached Sumner at his desk in the Senate chamber during a recess, raised a heavy cane, and began beating him repeatedly on the head and shoulders. Sumner, trapped in his chair, rose in agony with such strength that he tore the desk from the bolts holding it to the floor. Then he collapsed, bleeding and unconscious. So severe were his injuries that he was unable to return to the Senate for four years. Throughout the North, he became a hero—a martyr to the barbarism of the South. In the South, Preston Brooks became a hero, too. Censured by the House, he resigned his seat, returned to South Carolina, and stood successfully for reelection.

The Free-Soil Ideology

What had happened to produce such deep hostility between the two sections? In part, the tensions were reflections of the two sections' differing economic and territorial interests. But they were also reflections of a hardening of ideas in both North and South. As the nation expanded and political power grew more dispersed, each section became concerned with ensuring that its vision of America's future would be the dominant one.

In the North, assumptions about the proper structure of society came to center on the belief in "free soil" and "free labor." Although abolitionists generated some support for their argument that slavery was a moral evil and must be eliminated, most white northerners came to believe that the existence of slavery was dangerous not because of what it did to blacks but because of what it threatened to do to whites. At the heart of American democracy, they argued, was the right of all citizens to own property, to control their own labor, and to have access to opportunities for advancement.

According to this vision, the South was the antithesis of democracy—a closed, static society, in which slavery preserved an entrenched aristocracy and in which common whites had no opportunity to improve themselves. While the North was growing and prospering, the South was stagnating, rejecting the values of individualism and progress. The South was, northern free-laborites further maintained, engaged in a conspiracy to extend slavery throughout the nation and thus to destroy the openness of northern capitalism and replace it with the closed, aristocratic system of the South. The only solution to this "slave power conspiracy" was to fight the spread of slavery and extend the nation's democratic (i.e., free-labor) ideals to all sections of the country.

This ideology, which lay at the heart of the new Republican Party, also strengthened the commitment of Republicans to the Union. Since the idea of continued growth and progress was central to the free-labor vision, the prospect of dismemberment of the nation—a diminution of America's size and economic power—was unthinkable.

The Pro-Slavery Argument

In the South, in the meantime, a very different ideology—entirely incompatible with the free-labor ideology—was emerging out of a rapid hardening of position among southern whites on the issue of slavery. It was a result of many things: the Nat Turner uprising in 1831, which terrified southern whites and made them more determined than ever to make slavery secure; the expansion of the cotton economy into the Deep South, which made slavery unprecedentedly lucrative; and the growth of the Garrisonian abolitionist movement, with its strident attacks on southern society. The popularity of Harriet Beecher Stowe's *Uncle Tom's Cabin* was perhaps the most glaring evidence of the success of those attacks, but other abolitionist writings had been antagonizing white southerners for years.

In response to these pressures, a number of white southerners produced a new intellectual defense of slavery. Professor Thomas R. Dew of the College of William and Mary helped begin that effort in 1832. Twenty years later, apologists for slavery summarized their views in an anthology that gave their ideology its name: *The Pro-Slavery Argument.* John C. Calhoun stated the essence of the case in 1837: Southerners should stop apologizing for slavery as a necessary evil and defend it as "a good—a positive good." It was good for the slaves, the southern apologists argued, because they enjoyed better conditions than industrial workers in the North. Slavery was good for southern society as a whole because it was the only way the two races could live together in peace. It was good for the entire country because the southern economy, based on slavery, was the key to the prosperity of the nation.

Above all, southern apologists argued, slavery was good because it served as the basis for the southern way of life—a way of life superior to any other in the United States, perhaps in the world. White southerners looking at the North saw a spirit of greed, debauchery, and destructiveness. "The masses of the North are venal, corrupt, covetous, mean and selfish," wrote one southerner. Others wrote with horror of the factory system and the crowded, pestilential cities filled with unruly immigrants. But the South, they believed, was a stable, orderly society, operating at a slow and human pace. It was free from the feuds between capital and labor plaguing the North. It protected the welfare of its workers. And it allowed the aristocracy to enjoy a refined and accomplished cultural life. It was, in short, an ideal social order in which all elements of the population were secure and content.

The defense of slavery rested, too, on increasingly elaborate arguments about the biological inferiority of African Americans, who were, white Southerners claimed, inherently unfit to take care of themselves, let alone exercise the rights of citizenship. And just as abolitionist arguments drew strength from Protestant theology in the North, the pro-slavery defense mobilized the Protestant clergy in the South to give the institution a religious and biblical justification.

Buchanan and Depression

In this unpromising climate, the presidential campaign of 1856 began. Democratic Party leaders wanted a candidate who, unlike President Pierce, was not closely associated with the explosive question of "Bleeding Kansas." They chose James Buchanan of Pennsylvania, a reliable party stalwart who as minister to England had been safely out of the country during the recent controversies. The Republicans, participating in their first presidential contest, denounced the Kansas-Nebraska Act and the expansion of slavery but also endorsed a Whiggish program of internal improvements, thus combining the idealism of antislavery with the economic aspirations of the North. As eager as the Democrats to present a safe candidate, the Republicans nominated John C. Frémont, who had made a national reputation as an explorer of the Far West and who had no political record. The Native American, or Know-Nothing, Party was beginning to break apart, but it nominated former president Millard Fillmore, who also received the endorsement of a sad remnant of the Whig Party.

After a heated, even frenzied campaign, Buchanan won a narrow victory over Frémont and Fillmore. A slight shift of votes in Pennsylvania and Illinois would have elected the Republican candidate. Particularly ominous was that Frémont had attracted virtually no votes at all in the South while outpolling all other candidates in the North. At the time of his inauguration, Buchanan was, at age sixty-five, the oldest president, except for William Henry Harrison, ever to have taken office. Whether because of age and physical infirmities or because of a more fundamental weakness of character, he became a painfully timid and indecisive president at a critical moment in history.

In the year Buchanan took office, a financial panic struck the country, followed by a depression that lasted several years. In the North, the depression strengthened the Republican Party because distressed manufacturers, workers, and farmers came to believe that the hard times were the result of the unsound policies of southern-controlled Democratic administrations. They expressed their frustrations by moving into an alliance with antislavery elements and thus into the Republican Party.

The Dred Scott *Decision*

On March 6, 1857, the Supreme Court of the United States projected itself into the sectional controversy with one of the most controversial and notorious decisions in its history—its ruling in the case of *Dred Scott* v. *Sandford*, handed down two days after Buchanan was inaugurated. Dred Scott was a Missouri slave, once owned by an army surgeon who had taken Scott with him into Illinois and Wisconsin, where slavery was forbidden. In 1846, after the surgeon died, Scott sued his master's widow for freedom on the grounds that his residence in free territory had liberated him from slavery. The claim was well grounded in Missouri law, and in 1850 the circuit court in which Scott filed the suit declared him free. By now, John Sanford, the brother of the surgeon's widow, was claiming ownership of Scott, and he appealed the circuit court ruling to the state supreme court, which reversed the earlier decision. When Scott appealed to the federal courts, Sanford's attorneys claimed that Scott had no standing to sue because he was not a citizen, but private property.

The Supreme Court (which misspelled Sanford's name in its decision) was so divided that it was unable to issue a single ruling on the case. The thrust of the various rulings, however, was a stunning defeat for the antislavery movement. Chief Justice Roger Taney, who wrote one of the majority opinions, declared that Scott could not bring a suit in the federal courts because he was not a citizen. Blacks had no claim to citizenship, Taney argued, and in fact virtually no rights at all under the Constitution. Slaves were property, and the Fifth Amendment prohibited Congress from taking property without "due process of law." Consequently, Taney concluded, Congress possessed no authority to pass a law depriving persons of

394 ~ THE UNFINISHED NATION

their slave property in the territories. The Missouri Compromise, therefore, had always been unconstitutional.

The ruling did nothing to challenge the right of an individual state to prohibit slavery within its borders, but the statement that the federal government was powerless to act on the issue was a drastic and startling one. Few judicial opinions have ever created as much controversy. Southern whites were elated: the highest tribunal in the land had sanctioned parts of the most extreme southern argument. In the North, the decision produced widespread dismay. Republicans threatened that when they won control of the national government, they would reverse the decision—by "packing" the Court with new members.

Deadlock over Kansas

President Buchanan timidly endorsed the *Dred Scott* decision. At the same time, he tried to resolve the controversy over Kansas by supporting its admission to the Union as a slave state. In response, the pro-slavery territorial legislature called an election for delegates to a constitutional convention. The free-state residents refused to participate, claiming that the legislature had discriminated against them in drawing district lines. As a result, the pro-slavery forces won control of the convention, which met in 1857 at Lecompton, framed a constitution legalizing slavery, and refused to give voters a chance to reject it. When an election for a new territorial legislature was called, the antislavery groups turned out to vote and won a majority. The new legislature promptly submitted the Lecompton constitution to the voters, who rejected it by more than 10,000 votes.

Both sides had resorted to fraud and violence, but it was clear nevertheless that a majority of the people of Kansas opposed slavery. Buchanan, however, pressured Congress to admit Kansas under the Lecompton constitution. Stephen A. Douglas and other western Democrats refused to support the president's proposal, which died in the House of Representatives. Finally, in April 1858, Congress approved a compromise: The Lecompton constitution would be submitted to the voters of Kansas again. If it was approved, Kansas would be admitted to the Union; if it was rejected, statehood would be postponed. Again, Kansas voters decisively rejected the Lecompton constitution. Not until the closing months of Buchanan's administration in 1861, after several southern states had already withdrawn from the Union, did Kansas enter the Union—as a free state.

The Emergence of Lincoln

Given the gravity of the sectional crisis, the congressional elections of 1858 took on a special importance. Of particular note was the United States Senate election in Illinois, which pitted Stephen A. Douglas, the most prominent northern Democrat, against Abraham Lincoln, who was largely unknown outside Illinois but who quickly emerged as one of the most skillful politicians in the Republican Party.

Lincoln was a successful lawyer who had long been involved in state politics. He had served several terms in the Illinois legislature and one undistinguished term in Congress. But he was not a national figure like Douglas, and so he tried to increase his visibility by engaging Douglas in a series of debates. The Lincoln-Douglas debates attracted enormous crowds and received wide attention. By the time they ended, Lincoln's increasingly eloquent and passionate attacks on slavery had made him nationally prominent.

At the heart of the debates was a basic difference on the issue of slavery. Douglas appeared to have no moral position on the issue and, Lincoln claimed, did not care whether slavery was "voted up, or voted down." Lincoln's opposition to slavery was more fundamental. If the nation could accept that blacks were not entitled to basic human rights, he argued, then it could accept that other groups—immigrant laborers, for example—could be deprived of rights, too. And if slavery were to extend into the western territories, he argued, opportunities for poor white laborers to better their lots there would be lost. The nation's future, he argued (reflecting the central idea of the Republican Party), rested on the spread of free labor.

Lincoln believed slavery was morally wrong, but he was not an abolitionist. That was in part because he could not envision an easy alternative to slavery in the areas where it already existed. He shared the prevailing view among northern whites that the black race was not prepared (and perhaps never would be) to live on equal terms with whites. He and his party would "arrest the further spread" of slavery—that is, prevent its expansion into the territories; they would not directly challenge it where it already existed, but would trust that the institution would gradually die out there of its own accord.

Douglas's position satisfied his followers sufficiently to win him reelection to the Senate, but it aroused little enthusiasm and did nothing to enhance his national political ambitions. Lincoln, by contrast, lost the election but emerged with a growing following both in and beyond the state. And outside Illinois, the elections went heavily against the Democrats, who lost ground in almost every northern state. The party retained control of the Senate but lost its majority in the House, with the result that the congressional sessions of 1858 and 1859 were bitterly deadlocked.

John Brown's Raid

The battles in Congress, however, were almost entirely overshadowed by a spectacular event that enraged and horrified the entire South and greatly hastened the rush toward disunion. In the fall of 1859, John Brown, the antislavery zealot whose bloody actions in Kansas had inflamed the crisis there, staged an even more dramatic episode, this time in the South itself. With private encouragement and financial aid from some prominent eastern abolitionists, he made elaborate plans to seize a mountain fortress in Virginia from which, he believed, he could foment a slave insurrection in the South. On October 16, he and a group of eighteen followers attacked and seized control of a United States arsenal in Harpers Ferry, Virginia. But the slave uprising Brown hoped to inspire did not occur, and he quickly found himself besieged in the arsenal by citizens, local militia companies, and before long United States troops under the command of Robert E. Lee. After ten of his men were killed, Brown surrendered. He was promptly tried in a Virginia court for treason against the state, found guilty, and sentenced to death. He and six of his followers were hanged.

JOHN BROWN Even in this formal photographic portrait (taken in 1859, the last year of his life), John Brown coveys the fierce sense of righteousness that fueled his extraordinary activities in the fight against slavery.

No other single event did more than the Harpers Ferry raid to convince white southerners that they could not live safely in the Union. John Brown's raid, many southerners believed (incorrectly) had the support of the Republican Party, and it suggested to them that the North was now committed to producing a slave insurrection.

The Election of Lincoln

The presidential election of 1860 had the most momentous consequences of any in American history. It was also among the most complex.

The Democratic Party was torn apart by a battle between southerners, who demanded a strong endorsement of slavery, and westerners, who supported the idea of popular sovereignty. The party convention met in April in Charleston, South Carolina. When the convention endorsed popular sovereignty, delegates from eight states in the lower South walked out. The remaining delegates could not agree on a presidential candidate and finally adjourned after agreeing to meet again in Baltimore in June. The decimated convention at Baltimore nominated Stephen Douglas for president. In the meantime, disenchanted southern Democrats met in Richmond and nominated John C. Breckinridge of Kentucky. Later, a group of conservative ex-Whigs met in Baltimore to form the Constitutional Union Party, with John Bell of Tennessee as their presidential candidate. They endorsed the Union and remained silent on slavery.

The Republican leaders, in the meantime, were trying to broaden their appeal so as to attract every major interest group in the North that feared the South was blocking its economic aspirations. The platform endorsed such traditional Whig measures as a high tariff, internal improvements, a homestead bill, and a Pacific railroad to be built with federal financial assistance. It supported the right of each state to decide the status of slavery within its borders. But it also insisted that neither Congress nor territorial legislatures could legalize slavery in the territories. The Republican convention chose Abraham Lincoln as the party's presidential nominee. Lincoln was appealing because of his growing reputation for eloquence, because of his firm but moderate position on slavery, and because his relative obscurity ensured that he would have none of the drawbacks of other, more prominent (and therefore more controversial) Republicans. He was a representative of the West, a considerable asset in a race against Douglas.

In the November election, Lincoln won the presidency with a majority of the electoral votes but only about two-fifths of the fragmented popular vote. The Republicans, moreover, failed to win a majority in Congress. Even

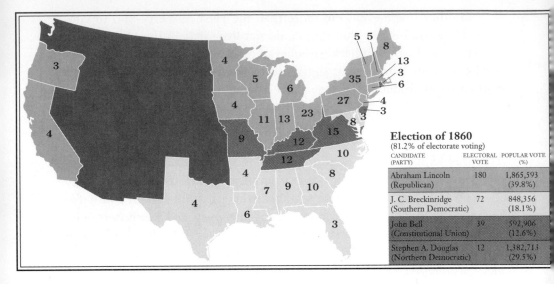

Election of 1860
(81.2% of electorate voting)

CANDIDATE (PARTY)	ELECTORAL VOTE	POPULAR VOTE (%)
Abraham Lincoln (Republican)	180	1,865,593 (39.8%)
J. C. Breckinridge (Southern Democratic)	72	848,356 (18.1%)
John Bell (Constitutional Union)	39	592,906 (12.6%)
Stephen A. Douglas (Northern Democratic)	12	1,382,713 (29.5%)

so, the election of Lincoln became the final signal to many white southerners that their position in the Union was hopeless. And within a few weeks of Lincoln's victory, the process of disunion began—a process that would quickly lead to a prolonged and bloody war between two groups of Americans, each heir to more than a century of struggling toward nationhood, each now convinced that it shared no common ground with the other.

CONCLUSION

In the decades following the War of 1812, a vigorous sense of nationalism pervaded much of American life, helping to smooth over the growing differences among the very different societies emerging in the regions of the United States. During the 1850s, however, the forces that had worked to hold the nation together in the past fell victim to new and much more divisive pressures that were working to split the nation apart.

Driving the sectional tensions of the 1850s was a battle over national policy toward the western territories, which were clamoring to become states of the Union—and over the place of slavery within them. Should slavery be permitted in the new states? And who should decide whether to permit it or not? There were strenuous efforts to craft compromises and solutions to this dilemma: the Compromise of 1850, the Kansas–Nebraska Act of 1854, and others. But despite these efforts, positions on slavery continued to harden in both the North and South until ultimately each region came to consider the other its enemy. Bitter battles in the territory of Kansas over whether to permit slavery there; growing agitation by abolitionists in the North and pro-slavery advocates in the South; the Supreme Court's controversial *Dred Scott* decision in 1857; the popularity of *Uncle Tom's Cabin* throughout the decade; and the emergence of a new political party—the Republican party—openly and centrally opposed to slavery: all worked to destroy the hopes for compromise and push the South toward secession.

In 1860, all pretense of common sentiment collapsed when no political party presented a presidential candidate capable of attracting national support. The Republicans nominated Abraham Lincoln of Illinois, a little-known politician recognized for his eloquent condemnations of slavery in a Senate race two years earlier. The Democratic party split apart, with its northern and southern wings each nominating different candidates. A third party, devoted to the Constitution and the Union, forlornly nominated a candidate of its own who found almost no constituency at all. Lincoln won the election easily, but with less than forty percent of the vote. And almost immediately after his victory, the states of the South began preparing to secede from the Union.

FOR FURTHER REFERENCE

Suggested Readings

David Potter, *The Impending Crisis* (1976) is an excellent summary of the decisive decade of the 1850s. Allan Nevins, *The Ordeal of the Union*, 2 vols. (1947), and *The Emergence of Lincoln*, 2 vols. (1950) comprise a classic narrative history of the coming of the Civil War. Anders Stephanson, *Manifest Destiny* (1995) briefly traces the origins of American expansion ideology. John M. Faragher, *Women and Men on the Overland Trail* (1979) is a good social history of the westward migration. David M. Pletcher, *The Diplomacy of Annexation: Texas, Oregon, and the Mexican War* (1973) is the standard work on war and diplomacy in the 1840s. William W. Freehling, *The Road to Disunion. Vol. 1: Secessionists at Bay, 1776–1854* (1990) explores the successful containment of sectionalism prior to the 1850s. Eric Foner, *Free Soil, Free Labor, Free Men* (1970) traces the emergence of the Republican Party. Michael Holt, *The Political Crisis of the 1850s* (1978) challenges Foner by emphasizing ethnic and religious alignment in northern politics. David Donald, *Charles Sumner and the Coming of the Civil War* (1960) is a superb biography of one of the most powerful and controversial figures in the early Republican party. Don E. Fehrenbacher, *The Dred Scott Case* (1978) explains the Supreme Court's most infamous decision.

Films

(The best source for information on how to find these and other films is *Bowker's Complete Video Directory*—3 volumes.) *The American Story, No. 10: Manifest Destiny* (1985) traces American industrial growth and commercial expansion through the Taylor, Fillmore, and Polk presidencies. *Manifest Destiny* examines the implications of this concept for war and diplomacy in the United States. *Texas & the Mexican Cession* (1990) brings to life the days of Davy Crockett and Sam Houston. *Uncle Tom's Cabin* (1987) is a recent adaptation of Harriet Beecher Stowe's influential and controversial novel. *The Background of the Civil War* (1981) introduces the differences between North and South that eventually led to war. *The Civil War: Union at Risk* (1989) presents the pre-Civil War differences between North and South and argues that the war was fought over Constitutional interpretation. *Abraham Lincoln: A New Birth of Freedom* (1992) features commentators from Mario Cuomo to Ted Koppel. *The Lincoln-Douglas Debates: The House Divides* (1989) examines the two barnstorming politicians' pivotal debates over the status of slavery in the western territories.

Internet Resources

Internet websites containing historical material relevant to the subjects discussed in this chapter can be reached through the McGraw-Hill history site at www.mhhe.com/socscience/history/usa/link/linktop.htm.

CHAPTER FOURTEEN

The Civil War

The Secession Crisis ∼ *The Mobilization of the North*
The Mobilization of the South ∼ *Strategy and Diplomacy*
Campaigns and Battles

B Y THE END of 1860, the cords that had once bound the Union together seemed to have snapped. The almost mystical veneration of
the Constitution and the romantic vision of America's great national destiny
had now taken very different forms in the North and the South. The relatively stable second party system had collapsed, replaced by a new one that
accentuated rather than muted regional controversy. The federal government
was no longer the remote, unthreatening presence it once had been; the need
to resolve the status of the territories had made it necessary for Washington
to deal directly with sectional issues. The election of 1860 brought these tensions to a head and precipitated the most terrible war in the nation's history.

THE SECESSION CRISIS

Almost as soon as the news of Abraham Lincoln's election reached the
South, the militant leaders of the region began to demand an end to the
Union. Within weeks, the process of secession had begun.

The Withdrawal of the South

South Carolina, long the hotbed of southern separatism, seceded first, on De-
cember 20, 1860. By the time Lincoln took office, six other southern states—
Mississippi (January 9, 1861), Florida (January 10), Alabama (January 11),
Georgia (January 19), Louisiana (January 26), and Texas (February 1)—had

TIME LINE

1861	1862	1863
Confederate States of America formed	Battles of Shiloh, Antietam, Bull Run	Emancipation Proclamation
Davis president of Confederacy	Confederacy enacts military draft	Battle of Gettysburg
Conflict at Fort Sumter		Vicksburg surrenders
First Battle of Bull Run		New York City antidraft riots
		Union enacts military draft

1864	1865
Battle of the Wilderness	Lee surrenders to Grant
Sherman's March to the Sea	13th Amendment
Lincoln reelected	

withdrawn from the Union. In February 1861, representatives of the seven seceded states met at Montgomery, Alabama, and formed a new nation—the Confederate States of America. President James Buchanan told Congress in December 1860 that no state had the right to secede from the Union but that the federal government had no authority to stop a state if it did.

The seceding states immediately seized the federal property—forts, arsenals, government offices—within their boundaries. But they did not at first have sufficient military power to seize two fortified offshore military installations: Fort Sumter, on an island in the harbor of Charleston, South Carolina, garrisoned by a small force under Major Robert Anderson; and Fort Pickens, in the harbor of Pensacola, Florida. Buchanan, timid though he was on most matters, refused to yield Fort Sumter when South Carolina demanded it. Instead, in January 1861, he ordered an unarmed merchant ship to proceed to Fort Sumter with additional troops and supplies. Confederate guns turned it back. Still, neither section was yet ready to concede that war had begun. And in Washington, efforts began once more to forge a compromise.

The Failure of Compromise

Gradually, the compromise efforts came together around a proposal first submitted by Senator John J. Crittenden of Kentucky and known as the Crittenden Compromise. The heart of the plan was a proposal to reestablish the Missouri Compromise line and extend it westward, so that it would

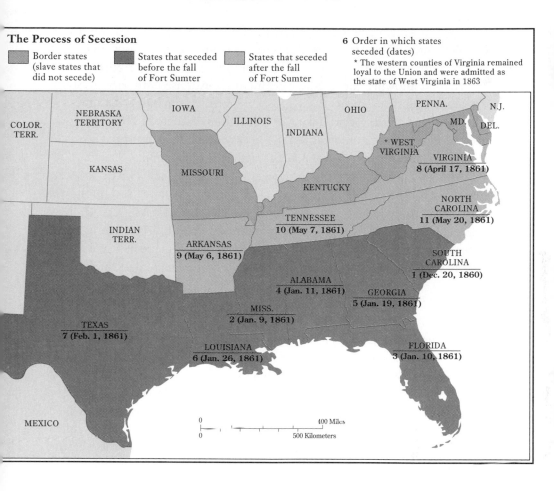

The Process of Secession

Border states
(slave states that
did not secede)

States that seceded
before the fall
of Fort Sumter

States that seceded
after the fall
of Fort Sumter

6 Order in which states
seceded (dates)
* The western counties of Virginia remained
loyal to the Union and were admitted as
the state of West Virginia in 1863

COLOR.
TERR.

NEBRASKA
TERRITORY

IOWA

ILLINOIS

INDIANA

OHIO

PENNA.

N.J.

MD.

DEL.

* WEST
VIRGINIA

VIRGINIA
8 (April 17, 1861)

KANSAS

MISSOURI

KENTUCKY

NORTH
CAROLINA
11 (May 20, 1861)

INDIAN
TERR.

ARKANSAS
9 (May 6, 1861)

TENNESSEE
10 (May 7, 1861)

SOUTH
CAROLINA
1 (Dec. 20, 1860)

ALABAMA
4 (Jan. 11, 1861)

GEORGIA
5 (Jan. 19, 1861)

TEXAS
7 (Feb. 1, 1861)

MISS.
2 (Jan. 9, 1861)

LOUISIANA
6 (Jan. 26, 1861)

FLORIDA
3 (Jan. 10, 1861)

MEXICO

0   400 Miles
0   500 Kilometers

divide all the present and future territory of the United States: slavery would be prohibited north of the line and permitted south of it. Southerners in the Senate seemed willing to accept the plan. But the compromise would have required the Republicans to abandon their most fundamental position—that slavery not be allowed to expand—and they rejected it.

And so nothing had been resolved when Abraham Lincoln arrived in Washington for his inauguration—entering the city in disguise on a night train to avoid assassination as he passed through the slave state of Maryland. In his inaugural address, Lincoln insisted acts of force or violence to support secession were insurrectionary and that the government would "hold, occupy, and possess" federal property in the seceded states—a clear reference to Fort Sumter.

But Union forces at Fort Sumter were running short of supplies; unless they received fresh provisions, they would have to evacuate the fort.

So Lincoln sent a relief expedition to the fort and informed the South Carolina authorities that he would send no troops or munitions unless the supply ships met with resistance. But the new Confederate government, rather than allowing the U.S. government to exercise authority in South Carolina, ordered General P. G. T. Beauregard, commander of Confederate forces at Charleston, to take the fort. When Anderson refused to give up, the Confederates bombarded it for two days, April 12–13, 1861. On April 14, Anderson surrendered. The Civil War had begun.

Almost immediately, Lincoln began mobilizing the North for war. Equally promptly, four more slave states seceded from the Union and joined the Confederacy: Virginia (April 17, 1861), Arkansas (May 6), Tennessee (May 7), and North Carolina (May 20). The four remaining slave states, Maryland, Delaware, Kentucky, and Missouri—under heavy political and even military pressure from Washington—remained in the Union.

The Opposing Sides

All the important material advantages for waging war lay with the North. Its population was more than twice as large as that of the South. It had an advanced industrial system and was able by 1862 to manufacture almost all its own war materials. The South had almost no industry at all.

In addition, the North had a much better transportation system than did the South, and in particular more and better railroads: twice as much trackage and a much better integrated system of lines. During the war, the already inferior Confederate railroad system steadily deteriorated and by the beginning of 1864 had almost collapsed.

But the South had advantages as well. The Southern armies were, for the most part, fighting a defensive war on familiar land with local support. The Northern armies, on the other hand, were fighting mostly within the South amid hostile local populations; they had to maintain long lines of communication and had access only to the South's own inadequate transportation system. The commitment of the white population of the South to the war was, with limited exceptions, clear and firm. In the North, opinion about the war was more divided, and support for it remained shaky until very near the end. A major Southern victory at any one of several crucial moments might have proved decisive by breaking the North's will to continue the struggle. Finally, the dependence of the English and French textile industries on American cotton inclined many leaders in those countries to favor the Confederacy; and Southerners hoped, with some reason, that one or both might intervene on their behalf.

THE MOBILIZATION OF THE NORTH

In the North, the war produced considerable discord, frustration, and suffering. But it also produced prosperity and economic growth by giving a major stimulus to both industry and agriculture. With the South now gone from Congress, the Republican Party had almost unchallenged supremacy. During the war, it enacted an aggressively nationalistic program to promote economic development.

Economic Nationalism

Two acts of 1862 assisted the rapid development of the West. The Homestead Act permitted any citizen or prospective citizen to purchase 160 acres of public land for a small fee after living on it for five years. The Morrill Act transferred substantial public acreage to the state governments, which could now sell the land and use the proceeds to finance public education. This act led to the creation of many new state colleges and universities, the so-called land-grant institutions. Congress also passed a series of tariff bills that by the end of the war had raised duties to the highest level in the nation's history—a great boon to domestic industries eager for protection from foreign competition, but a hardship for many farmers and other consumers.

Congress also moved to spur completion of a transcontinental railroad. It created two new federally chartered corporations: the Union Pacific Railroad Company, which was to build westward from Omaha, and the Central Pacific, which was to build eastward from California. The two projects were to meet in the middle and complete the link. The government provided free public lands and generous loans to the companies.

The National Bank Acts of 1863–1864 created a new national banking system. Existing or newly formed banks could join the system if they had enough capital and were willing to invest one-third of it in government securities. In return, they could issue United States Treasury notes as currency. The new system eliminated much (although not all) of the chaos and uncertainty in the nation's currency and created a uniform system of national bank notes.

More difficult than promoting economic growth was financing the war itself. The government tried to do so in three ways: levying taxes, issuing paper currency, and borrowing. Congress levied new taxes on almost all goods and services; and in 1861 the government levied an income

The Causes of the Civil War

A| BRAHAM LINCOLN, in his 1865 inaugural address, looked back at the beginning of the terrible war that was now nearing its end and said, "All knew [that slavery] was somehow the cause of the war." Few historians dispute that. But disagreement has been sharp over whether slavery was the only, or even the principal cause of the war, and on such other questions as whether or not the war was inevitable.

The debate began even before the war itself. In 1858, Senator William H. Seward of New York took note of the two competing explanations of the sectional tensions that were then inflaming the nation. On one side, he said, stood those who believed the conflicts to be "accidental, unnecessary, the work of interested or fanatical agitators." Opposing them stood those (among them Seward himself) who believed there to be "an irrepressible conflict between opposing and enduring forces." Without realizing it, Seward had identified a division of opinion that would survive among historians for more than a century.

The "irrepressible-conflict" argument dominated historical discussion of the war from the 1860s to the 1920s. War was inevitable, some historians claimed, because there was no room for compromise on the central issue of slavery. Others de-emphasized slavery and pointed to the economic differences between the agrarian South and the industrializing North. Charles and Mary Beard, for example, wrote in 1927 of the "inherent antagonisms" between the interests of planters and those of industrialists.

Each group was seeking to control the federal government to promote its own economic interests. Still others cited social and cultural differences between the two sections as the source of an irrepressible conflict. Slavery, the historian Allan Nevins argued, was only one factor in the cultural divergence that was making residents of the North and South "separate peoples." There were fundamental differences in "assumptions, tastes, and cultural aim" that made it virtually impossible for the two societies to live together in peace.

More recent proponents of irrepressible-conflict arguments similarly emphasize culture and ideology but define the concerns of the North and the South in different terms. Eric Foner, writing in 1970, argued that the moral concerns of abolitionists and the economic concerns of industrialists were less important in explaining Northern hostility to the South than was the broad-based "free-labor" ideology of the region. Northerners opposed slavery because they feared it might spread into their own region and threaten the position of free white laborers, hence their insistence that it not be allowed to expand into the West.

Other historians have argued that the war was not inevitable, beginning with a group of scholars in the 1920s known as the revisionists. James G. Randall and Avery Craven were the two leading proponents of the view that the differences between the North and the South were not so great as to require a war, that only a "blundering generation" of leaders caused the conflict. Michael Holt revived the revisionist argument in a 1978 book, in which he too emphasized the partisan ambitions of politicians who used sectional rivalries to advance their own aims. But Holt also helped introduce another element to the debate. He was, along with Paul Kleppner, Joel Silbey, and William Gienapp, one of the creators of an "ethnocultural" interpretation of the war, which emphasizes that the collapse of the party system—which was central to the coming of the conflict—was a result less of the debate over slavery than of such ethnocultural issues as temperance and nativism. These scholars would not entirely dispute Lincoln's claim that slavery was "somehow the cause of the war." But they do challenge the arguments of Eric Foner and others that the "free-labor ideal" of the North—and the challenge slavery and its possible expansion into the territories posed to that ideal—was the principal reason for the conflict.

tax for the first time, with rates that eventually rose to 10 percent on incomes above $5,000. But taxation raised only a small proportion of the funds necessary for financing the war, and strong popular resistance prevented the government from raising the rates.

At least equally controversial was the printing of paper currency, or "greenbacks." The new currency was backed not by gold or silver but simply by the good faith and credit of the government (much like today's currency). The value of the greenbacks fluctuated according to the fortunes of the Northern armies. Early in 1864, with the war effort bogged down, a greenback dollar was worth only 39 percent of a gold dollar. Even at the close of the war, with confidence high, it was worth only 67 percent of a gold dollar. The government used greenbacks sparingly.

By far the largest source of financing for the war, therefore, was loans. The Treasury persuaded ordinary citizens to buy over $400 million worth of bonds—the first example of mass financing of a war in American history. But public bond purchases constituted only a small part of the government's borrowing, which in the end totaled $2.6 billion, most of it from banks and large financial interests.

Raising the Union Armies

Over 2 million men served in the Union military forces during the Civil War. But at the beginning of 1861, the regular army of the United States consisted of only 16,000 troops, many of them stationed in the West to protect white settlers from Indians. So the Union, like the Confederacy, had to raise its army mostly from scratch. Lincoln called for an increase of 23,000 in the regular army, but the bulk of the fighting, he knew, would have to be done by volunteers in state militias. When Congress convened in July 1861, it authorized enlisting 500,000 volunteers for three-year (as opposed to the customary three-month) terms.

This voluntary system of recruitment produced adequate forces only briefly, during the first flush of enthusiasm for the war. By March 1863, Congress was forced to pass a national draft law. Virtually all young adult males were eligible to be drafted, although a man could escape service by hiring someone to go in his place or by paying the government a fee of $300. Only about 46,000 men were ever actually conscripted, but the draft greatly increased voluntary enlistments.

To many who were accustomed to a remote and inactive national government, conscription was strange and threatening. Opposition to the law was widespread, particularly among laborers, immigrants, and Democrats opposed to the war. Occasionally it erupted into violence. Demonstrators against the draft rioted in New York City for four days in July 1863. Over 100 people died. The rioters lynched several African Americans (whom many opponents of the war blamed for the conflict) and burned down black homes, businesses, and even an orphanage. It was the bloodiest riot in American history. Only the arrival of federal troops halted the violence.

Wartime Leadership and Politics

When Abraham Lincoln arrived in Washington early in 1861, many Republicans considered him a minor politician from the prairie who would be easily controlled by the real leaders of his party. The new president understood his own (and his party's) weaknesses, and he assembled a cabinet representing every faction of the Republican Party and every segment of Northern opinion—men of exceptional prestige, influence, and in some cases arrogance, several of whom believed that they, not Lincoln, should be president. But Lincoln was a man of great self-confidence, and he was not cowed by the distinguished figures around him. He moved boldly to use the war powers of the presidency, blithely ignoring inconvenient parts of the Constitution because, he said, it would be foolish to lose the whole by being afraid to disregard a part.

He sent troops into battle without asking Congress for a declaration of war, arguing that the conflict was a domestic insurrection and that no congressional authorization was necessary. He increased the size of the regular army without receiving legislative authority to do so. He unilaterally proclaimed a naval blockade of the South.

Lincoln's greatest political problem was the widespread popular opposition to the war, mobilized by those in the Democratic Party who were known as Peace Democrats (or, by their enemies, "Copperheads"). Lincoln used extraordinary methods to suppress them. He ordered military arrests of civilian dissenters and suspended the right of habeas corpus (the right of an arrested person to receive a speedy trial). At first, Lincoln used these methods only in sensitive areas such as the border states; but in 1862, he proclaimed that all persons who discouraged enlistments or engaged in disloyal practices were subject to martial law. In all, more than 13,000 persons were arrested and imprisoned for varying periods.

By the time of the presidential election of 1864, the North was in political turmoil. The Republicans had suffered heavy losses in 1862, and in response leaders of the party tried to create a broad coalition of all the groups that supported the war. They called the new organization the Union Party, but it was, in reality, little more than the Republican Party and a small faction of War Democrats. The Union Party nominated Lincoln for another term as president and Andrew Johnson of Tennessee, a War Democrat who had opposed his state's decision to secede, for the vice presidency.

The Democrats nominated George B. McClellan, a celebrated former Union general who had been relieved of his command by Lincoln, and adopted a platform denouncing the war and calling for a truce. McClellan repudiated that demand, but the Democrats were clearly the peace party in the campaign, trying to profit from growing war weariness and from the Union's discouraging military position in the summer of 1864. For a time, Lincoln's prospects for reelection seemed doubtful.

At this crucial moment, however, several Northern military victories, particularly the capture of Atlanta, Georgia, early in September, rejuvenated Northern morale and boosted Republican prospects. Lincoln won reelection comfortably, with 212 electoral votes to McClellan's 21. But Lincoln's lead in the popular vote was a more modest 10 percent.

The Politics of Emancipation

Despite their surface unity in supporting the war and their general agreement on most economic matters, the Republicans disagreed sharply with one another on the issue of slavery. Radicals—led in Congress by such men as Representative Thaddeus Stevens of Pennsylvania and Senators Charles Sumner of Massachusetts and Benjamin Wade of Ohio—wanted to use the war to abolish slavery immediately and completely. Conservatives favored a more cautious policy—in part so as to placate the border slave states that remained, precariously, within the Union. In the beginning, at least, the president seemed to share that caution.

Nevertheless, momentum began to gather behind Emancipation early in the war. In 1861, Congress passed the Confiscation Act, which declared that all slaves used for "insurrectionary" purposes (that is, in support of the Confederate military effort) would be considered freed. Subsequent laws in the spring of 1862 abolished slavery in the District of Columbia and in the western territories and provided for the compensation of owners. In July 1862, Radicals pushed through Congress the second Confiscation Act, which declared free the slaves of persons supporting the insurrection (whether or not the slaves themselves were doing so) and authorized the president to employ African Americans, including freed slaves, as soldiers.

As the war progressed, many in the North seemed slowly to accept emancipation as a central war aim; nothing less, they believed, would justify the enormous sacrifices the struggle had required. As a result, the Radicals gained increasing influence within the Republican Party—a development that did not go unnoticed by the president, who decided to seize the leadership of the rising antislavery sentiment himself.

On September 22, 1862, after the Union victory at the Battle of Antietam, the president announced his intention to use his war powers to issue an executive order freeing all slaves in the Confederacy. And on January 1, 1863, he formally signed the Emancipation Proclamation, which declared forever free the slaves inside the Confederacy. The proclamation did not apply to the border slave states, which had never seceded from the Union; nor did it affect those parts of the Confederacy already under Union control (Tennessee, western Virginia, and southern Louisiana). It applied, in short, only to slaves over which the Union had no control and thus had few immediate results. But the document was of great importance because it clearly and irrevocably established that the war was being fought not only to preserve the Union but also to eliminate slavery. Eventually, as federal armies occupied much of the South, the proclamation became a practical reality and led directly to the freeing of thousands of slaves. About 186,000 of them served in the Union forces.

Even in areas not directly affected by the proclamation, the antislavery impulse gained strength. By the end of the war, two Union slave states (Maryland and Missouri) and three Confederate states occupied by Union forces (Tennessee, Arkansas, and Louisiana) had abolished slavery. In 1865, finally, Congress approved and the states ratified the Thirteenth Amendment, which abolished slavery as an institution in all parts of the United States, not just the areas covered by the Emancipation Proclamation. After more than two centuries, legalized slavery finally ceased to exist in the United States.

African Americans and the Union Cause

About 186,000 emancipated blacks served as soldiers, sailors, and laborers for the Union forces, joining a significant number of free blacks from the North. The services of African Americans to the Union military were significant in many ways, not least because of the substantial obstacles many blacks had to surmount in order to enlist.

In the first months of the war, blacks were largely excluded from the military. A few black regiments eventually took shape in some of the Union-occupied areas of the Confederacy, largely because they were a ready source of manpower in these defeated regions. But once Lincoln issued the Emancipation Proclamation, black enlistment increased rapidly and the Union military began actively to recruit African-American soldiers and sailors in both the North and, where possible, the South.

Some of these men were organized into fighting units, of which the best known was probably the Fifty-fourth Massachusetts infantry which (like most black regiments) had a white commander: Robert Gould Shaw, a member of an aristocratic Boston family. Shaw and more than half his regiment died during a battle near Charleston, South Carolina, in the summer of 1863.

Most black soldiers, however, were assigned menial tasks behind the lines such as digging trenches and transporting water. Even though many fewer blacks than whites died in combat, the African-American mortality rate was actually higher than the rate for white soldiers because so many black soldiers died of disease from working long, arduous hours in unsanitary conditions. Conditions for blacks and whites were unequal in other ways as well. Black soldiers were paid a third less than were white soldiers (until Congress changed the law in mid-1864). Black fighting men captured by the Confederates were, unlike white prisoners, not returned to the North in exchange for Southern soldiers being returned to the South. They were sent back to their masters (if they were escaped slaves) or often executed. In 1864, Confederate soldiers killed over 260 black Union soldiers after capturing them in Tennessee.

AFRICAN-AMERICAN TROOPS Although most of the black soldiers who enlisted in the Union army during the Civil War performed noncombat jobs behind the lines, there were also black combat regiments—members of one of which are pictured here—that fought with great success and valor in critical battles.

The War and Economic Development

The Civil War did not, as some historians used to claim, transform the North from an agrarian to an industrial society. Industrialization was already far advanced when the war began, and in some areas, the war actually retarded growth by diverting labor and resources to military purposes.

On the whole, however, the war sped the economic development of the North. That was in part a result of the political dominance of the Republican Party and its promotion of nationalistic economic legislation. But it was also because the war itself required the expansion of certain sectors of the economy. Coal production increased by nearly 20 percent during the war. Railroad facilities improved—mainly through the adoption of a standard gauge (track width) on new lines. The loss of farm labor to the military forced many farmers to increase the mechanization of agriculture.

The war was a difficult experience for many American workers. Industrial laborers suffered a substantial loss of purchasing power, as prices in the North rose by more than 80 percent during the war while wages rose only about 40 percent. Wages remained low because liberalized immigration laws permitted a flood of new workers to enter the labor market and because the increasing mechanization of production eliminated the jobs of many skilled workers. One result was a substantial increase in union membership in some industries and the creation of several national unions for coal miners, railroad engineers, and others—organizations bitterly opposed and rigorously suppressed by employers.

Women, Nursing, and the War

The war thrust women into new and often unfamiliar roles. They took over positions vacated by men as teachers, salesclerks, office workers, and mill and factory hands. Above all, women entered nursing, a field previously dominated by men. The United States Sanitary Commission, an organization of civilian volunteers led by Dorothea Dix, mobilized large numbers of female nurses to serve in field hospitals. By the end of the war, women were the dominant force in nursing; by the end of the century, nursing had become an almost entirely female profession.

Female nurses encountered considerable resistance from male doctors, many of whom considered women too weak for medical work and many of whom thought it inappropriate for women to be taking care of male strangers. The Sanitary Commission countered such arguments by presenting nursing in domestic terms: as a profession that made use of the same maternal, nurturing roles women played as wives and mothers.

THE U.S. SANITARY COMMISSION Mathew Brady took this photograph of female nurses and Union soldiers standing before an infirmary at Brandy Station, Virginia, near Petersburg, in 1864. The infirmary was run by the U.S. Sanitary Commission, the government-supported nursing corps that became indispensable to the medical care of wounded soldiers during the Civil War.

Some women, especially those who had been committed to feminist causes earlier, came to see the war as an opportunity to win support for their own goals. Elizabeth Cady Stanton and Susan B. Anthony, who together founded the National Woman's Loyal League in 1863, worked simultaneously for the abolition of slavery and the awarding of suffrage to women.

THE MOBILIZATION OF THE SOUTH

Early in February 1861, representatives of the seven states that had seceded from the Union met at Montgomery, Alabama, to create a new Southern nation. When Virginia seceded several months later, the leaders of the Confederacy moved to Richmond—one of the few Southern cities large enough to house a government.

There were, of course, important differences between the new Confederate nation and the nation it had left. But there were also important similarities between the Union and the Confederacy, which became particularly clear as the two sides mobilized for war.

Confederate Government

The Confederate constitution was almost identical to the Constitution of the United States, with several significant exceptions. It explicitly acknowledged the sovereignty of the individual states (although not the right of secession). And it specifically sanctioned slavery and made its abolition (even by one of the states) practically impossible.

The constitutional convention at Montgomery named a provisional president and vice president: Jefferson Davis of Mississippi and Alexander H. Stephens of Georgia. They were later elected by the general public, without opposition, for six-year terms. Davis had been a moderate secessionist before the war. Stephens had argued against secession. The Confederate government, like the Union government, was dominated throughout the war by men of the political center.

Davis was an unsuccessful president. He was a reasonably able administrator, and encountered little interference from the generally tame members of his unstable cabinet. He served, in effect, as his own secretary of war. But he rarely provided genuinely national leadership. He spent too much time on routine items, and unlike Lincoln, he displayed a punctiliousness about legal and constitutional requirements inappropriate to the needs of a new nation at war. One shrewd Confederate official wrote: "All the revolutionary vigor is with the enemy. . . . With us timidity—hair splitting."

There were no formal political parties in the Confederacy, but its congressional and popular politics were badly divided nevertheless. Some white Southerners (and most blacks who were aware of the course of events) opposed secession and war altogether. Most white Southerners supported the war, but as in the North many were openly critical of the government and the military, particularly as the tide of battle turned against the South and the Confederate economy decayed.

States' rights had become such a cult among many white Southerners that they resisted virtually all efforts to exert national authority, even those necessary to win the war. States' rights enthusiasts restricted Davis's ability to impose martial law and suspend habeas corpus. They obstructed conscription. Governors such as Joseph Brown of Georgia and Zebulon M. Vance of North Carolina tried at times to keep their own troops apart from the Confederate forces and insisted on hoarding surplus supplies for their own state militias. But the national government was not impotent. It experimented, successfully for a time, with a "food draft," which permitted soldiers to feed themselves by seizing crops from farms in their path. The government impressed slaves, often over the objections of their owners, to work as laborers on military projects. The Confederacy seized control of the railroads and shipping; it imposed regulations on industry; it limited corporate profits. States' rights sentiment was a significant handicap, but the South nevertheless took dramatic steps in the direction of centralization—becoming in the process increasingly like the region whose institutions it was fighting to escape.

Money and Manpower

Financing the Confederate war effort was a monumental and ultimately impossible task. The Confederate congress tried at first to requisition funds from the individual states; but the states were as reluctant to tax their citizens as the congress was and usually failed to comply. In 1863, therefore, the congress enacted an income tax. But taxation produced only about 1 percent of the government's total income. Borrowing was not much more successful. The Confederate government issued bonds in such vast amounts that the public lost faith in them and stopped buying them, and efforts to borrow money in Europe using cotton as collateral fared no better.

As a result, the Confederacy had to pay for the war through the least stable, most destructive form of financing: paper currency, which it began issuing in 1861. By 1864, the Confederacy had issued the staggering total of $1.5 billion in paper money, more than three times what the Union had produced. The result was a disastrous inflation—a 9,000 percent increase in prices in the course of the war (in contrast to 80 percent in the North)—with devastating effects on Confederate morale.

Like the United States, the Confederacy first raised armies by calling for volunteers. And as in the North, by the end of 1861 voluntary enlistments were declining. In April 1862, therefore, the congress enacted the Conscription Act, which subjected all white males between the ages of eighteen and thirty-five to military service for three years. As in the North, a draftee could avoid service if he furnished a substitute. But since the price of substitutes was high, the provision aroused such opposition from poorer whites that it was repealed in 1863. Even more controversial were other provisions of the draft, especially the exemption of one white man on each plantation with twenty or more slaves.

Even so, conscription worked for a time, in part because enthusiasm for the war was intense and widespread among white men in most of the South. At the end of 1862, about 500,000 soldiers were in the Confederate army. That number did not include the many slave men and women recruited by the military to perform such services as cooking, laundry, and

CONFEDERATE VOLUNTEERS Smiling and apparently confident, young Southern soldiers pose for a photograph in 1861, shortly before the First Battle of Bull Run. The Civil War was one of the first military conflicts extensively chronicled by photographers.

manual labor, hence freeing additional white manpower for fighting. Small numbers of slaves and free blacks enlisted, apparently voluntarily, in the Confederate army, and a few participated in combat.

After 1862, however, conscription began producing fewer men, and by 1864 the Confederate government faced a critical manpower shortage. The nation was suffering from intense war weariness, and many had concluded that defeat was inevitable. Nothing could attract or retain an adequate army any longer. In 1864–1865, there were 100,000 desertions. In a frantic final attempt to raise men, the congress authorized the conscription of 300,000 slaves, but the war ended before the government could attempt this incongruous experiment.

Economic and Social Effects of the War

The war had a devastating effect on the South's economy. It cut off Southern planters and producers from markets in the North, and a Union blockade of Confederate ports made the sale of cotton overseas much more difficult. The war robbed those farms and industries that did not have large slave populations of a male work force. In the North, production of all goods increased during the war; in the South, it declined by more than a third. Above all, the fighting itself—almost all of which occurred inside the Confederacy—wreaked havoc on the Southern landscape, destroying farmland, towns, cities, and railroads.

As the war continued, the shortages, the inflation, and the carnage created increasing instability in Southern society. There were major food riots (some led by women) in cities in Georgia, North Carolina, and Alabama in 1863, as well as a large and violent demonstration in Richmond. Resistance to conscription, food impressment, and taxation increased throughout the Confederacy, as did hoarding and black-market commerce.

The war forced many women (and some men) to question the prevailing assumption of their society that females were not suited for the public sphere, since so many women had to perform untraditional, nondomestic tasks during the conflict. The war also decimated the male population and created a major gender imbalance in the region. After the war, women outnumbered men in most Southern states by significant margins. The result was a large number of unmarried or widowed women who, both during and after the war, had no choice but to find employment.

Even before emancipation, the war had far-reaching effects on the lives of slaves. Confederate leaders were more terrified of slave revolts during the war than they had been in peacetime, and they enforced slave codes with particular severity. Even so, many slaves—especially those near the front—escaped their masters and crossed Union lines.

STRATEGY AND DIPLOMACY

The social and economic circumstances of the North and the South helped shape the outcome of the war. But much rested on the military and diplomatic strategies that the two sides employed.

The Commanders

The most important Union military commander was Abraham Lincoln, whose previous military experience consisted only of brief service in his state militia. Lincoln made many mistakes, but he was on the whole a successful commander in chief because he realized that numbers and resources were on his side and because he knew how to exploit the North's material advantages. He realized, too, that the proper objective of his armies was the destruction of the Confederate armies and not the occupation of Southern territory. It was fortunate for the North that Lincoln had a good grasp of strategy, because many of his generals did not. The problem of finding adequate commanders for the troops in the field plagued him throughout the first three years of the war.

From 1861 to 1864, Lincoln tried time and again to find a chief of staff capable of orchestrating the Union war effort. He turned first to General Winfield Scott, the aging hero of the Mexican War. But Scott was unprepared for the magnitude of the new conflict and soon retired. Lincoln then appointed the young George B. McClellan, who was the commander of the Union forces in the East, the Army of the Potomac; but the proud, arrogant McClellan had a wholly inadequate grasp of strategy and in any case returned to the field in March 1862. For most of the rest of the year, Lincoln had no chief of staff at all. And when he eventually appointed General Henry W. Halleck to the post, he found him an ineffectual strategist who left all substantive decision making to the president or the generals in the field. Not until March 1864 did Lincoln finally find a general he trusted to command the war effort: Ulysses S. Grant, who shared Lincoln's belief in unremitting combat and in making enemy armies and resources, not enemy territory, the target of military efforts.

Lincoln's handling of the war effort faced constant scrutiny from the Committee on the Conduct of the War, a joint investigative committee of the two houses of Congress and the most powerful voice the legislative branch has ever had in formulating war policies. Established in December 1861 and chaired by Senator Benjamin E. Wade of Ohio, it complained constantly of the inadequate ruthlessness of Northern generals, which Radicals on the committee attributed (largely inaccurately) to a secret sympathy among the officers for slavery. The committee's efforts often seriously interfered with the conduct of the war.

Southern military leadership centered on President Davis, who unlike Lincoln was a trained professional soldier but who, also unlike Lincoln, failed ever to create an effective central command system. Early in 1862, Davis named General Robert E. Lee as his principal military adviser. But in fact, Davis had no intention of sharing control of strategy with anyone. After a few months, Lee left Richmond to command forces in the field, and for the next two years Davis planned strategy alone. In February 1864, he named General Braxton Bragg as a military adviser, but Bragg never provided much more than technical advice.

At lower levels of command, men of markedly similar backgrounds controlled the war in both the North and the South. Many of the professional officers on both sides were graduates of the United States Military Academy at West Point and the United States Naval Academy at Annapolis and thus had been trained in similar ways. Amateur officers played an important role in both armies as commanders of volunteer regiments. In both North and South, such men were usually economic or social leaders in their communities who appointed themselves officers and rounded up troops to lead. Sometimes this system produced officers of real ability; more often it did not.

The Role of Sea Power

The Union had an overwhelming advantage in naval power, and it gave its navy two important roles in the war. One was enforcing a blockade of the Southern coast. The other was assisting the Union armies in field operations.

The blockade of the South, which began in the first weeks of the war, kept most oceangoing ships out of Confederate ports, but for a time small blockade runners continued to slip through. Gradually, however, federal forces tightened the blockade by seizing the ports themselves. The last important port in Confederate hands—Wilmington, North Carolina—fell to the Union early in 1865.

The Confederates made a bold attempt to break the blockade with an ironclad warship, constructed by plating with iron a former United States frigate, the *Merrimac*, which the Union navy had scuttled in Norfolk harbor when Virginia seceded. On March 8, 1862, the refitted *Merrimac*, renamed the *Virginia*, left Norfolk to attack a blockading squadron of wooden ships at nearby Hampton Roads. It destroyed two of the ships and scattered the rest. But the Union government had already built ironclads of its own. And one of them, the *Monitor*, arrived off the coast of Virginia only a few hours after the *Virginia's* dramatic foray. The next day, it met the *Virginia* in the first battle ever between ironclad ships. Neither vessel was able to sink the other, but the *Monitor* put an end to the Virginia's raids and preserved the blockade.

The Union navy was particularly important in the western theater of the war—the vast region between the Appalachian Mountains and the Mississippi River—where the major rivers were navigable by large vessels. The navy transported supplies and troops and joined in attacking Confederate strong points. The South had no significant navy of its own and could defend against the Union gunboats only with ineffective fixed land fortifications.

Europe and the Disunited States

Judah P. Benjamin, the Confederate secretary of state for most of the war, was an intelligent but undynamic man who attended mostly to routine administrative tasks. William Seward, his counterpart in Washington, gradually became one of the outstanding American secretaries of state. He had invaluable assistance from Charles Francis Adams, the American minister to London, who had inherited the considerable diplomatic talents of his father, John Quincy Adams, and his grandfather, John Adams. The gap between the diplomatic skills of the Union and the Confederacy proved to be a decisive factor in the war.

At the beginning of the conflict, the sympathies of the ruling classes of England and France, the two nations whose support was most crucial to both sides, lay largely with the Confederacy. That was partly because the two nations imported much Southern cotton; but it was also because they were eager to weaken the United States, an increasingly powerful rival to them in world commerce. But France was unwilling to take sides in the conflict unless England did so first. And in England, the government was reluctant to act because there was powerful popular support for the Union—particularly from the large and influential English antislavery movement. After Lincoln issued the Emancipation Proclamation, antislavery groups worked particularly avidly for the Union. Southern leaders hoped to counter the strength of the British antislavery forces by arguing that access to Southern cotton was vital to the English and French textile industries, an approach known as "King Cotton diplomacy." But English manufacturers had a surplus of both raw cotton and finished goods on hand in 1861 and could withstand a temporary loss of access to American cotton. Later, as the supply of cotton began to diminish, both England and France managed to keep at least some of their mills open by importing cotton from Egypt, India, and other sources. Equally important, even the 500,000 English textile workers thrown out of jobs as a result of mill closings continued to support the North. In the end, therefore, no European nation offered diplomatic recognition to the Confederacy or intervened in the war. No nation wanted to antagonize the United States unless the Confederacy seemed likely to win, and the South never came close enough to victory to convince its potential allies to support it.

Even so, there was considerable tension, and on occasion near hostilities, between the United States and Britain. The Union government was angry when Great Britain, France, and other nations declared themselves neutral early in the war, thus implying that the two sides to the conflict had equal stature. Washington was insisting that the conflict was simply a domestic insurrection, not a war between two legitimate governments.

A more serious crisis, the so-called *Trent* affair, began in late 1861. Two Confederate diplomats, James M. Mason and John Slidell, had slipped through the then-ineffective Union blockade to Havana, Cuba, where they boarded an English steamer, the *Trent*, for England. Waiting in Cuban waters was the American frigate *San Jacinto*, commanded by the impetuous Charles Wilkes. Acting without authorization, Wilkes stopped the British vessel, arrested the diplomats, and carried them in triumph to Boston. The British government demanded the release of the prisoners, reparations, and an apology. Lincoln and Seward, aware that Wilkes had violated maritime law and unwilling to risk war with England, eventually released the diplomats with an indirect apology.

A second diplomatic crisis produced problems that lasted for years. Unable to construct large ships itself, the Confederacy bought six ships, known as commerce destroyers, from British shipyards. The best known of them were the *Alabama*, the *Florida*, and the *Shenandoah*. The United States protested that this sale of military equipment to a belligerent violated the laws of neutrality, and the protests became the basis, after the war, of a prolonged battle over damage claims (known as the *Alabama* claims) by the United States against Great Britain.

CAMPAIGNS AND BATTLES

In the absence of direct intervention by the European powers, the two contestants in North America were left to resolve the conflict between themselves. They did so in four long years of bloody combat that produced more carnage than any other war in American history, before or since. More than 618,000 Americans died in the course of the Civil War, far more than the 115,000 who perished in World War I or the 318,000 who died in World War II—more, indeed, than died in all other American wars prior to Vietnam combined. There were nearly 2,000 deaths for every 100,000 of population during the Civil War. In World War I, the comparable figure was only 109; in World War II, 241.

The Technology of War

Much of what happened on the battlefield in the Civil War was a result of new technologies that transformed the nature of combat. The Civil War has often been called the first "modern" war and the first "total" war. Such descriptions are imprecise and debatable. But it is certainly true that the great conflict between the North and the South was unlike any war fought before it. It is also clearly true that it suggested a great deal about what warfare would be like in the future.

The most obvious change in the character of warfare in the 1860s was the nature of the armaments that both sides used in battle. Among the most important was the introduction of repeating weapons. Samuel Colt had patented a repeating pistol (the revolver) in 1835, but more important for military purposes was the repeating rifle, introduced in 1860 by Oliver Winchester. Two years later, Richard Gatling perfected the revolving machine gun (although it was little used during the Civil War). Also important were greatly improved cannons and artillery, a result of advances in iron and steel technology of the previous decades.

These devastating advances in the effectiveness of arms and artillery changed the way soldiers in the field fought. It was now impossibly deadly to fight battles as they had been fought for centuries, with lines of infantry soldiers standing erect in the field firing volleys at their opponents until one side withdrew. Fighting in that way now produced almost inconceivable slaughter, and soldiers quickly learned that the proper position for combat was staying low to the ground and behind cover. For the first time in the history of organized warfare, therefore, infantry did not fight in formation, and the battlefield became a more chaotic place. Gradually, the deadliness of the new weapons encouraged armies on both sides to spend a great deal of time building elaborate fortifications and trenches to protect themselves from enemy fire. The sieges of Vicksburg and Petersburg, the defense of Richmond, and many other military events all produced the construction of vast fortifications around the cities and around the attacking armies. (They became the predecessors to the great network of trenches that became so central a part of World War I.)

Other weapons technologies were less central to the fighting of the war, but important nevertheless. There was sporadic use of the relatively new technology of hot-air balloons, employed intermittently to provide a view of enemy formations in the field. (During one battle, a Union balloonist took a telegraph line aloft with him in his balloon and tapped out messages about troop movements to the commanders below.) Iron-clad ships such as the *Merrimac* (or *Virginia*) and the *Monitor* suggested the dramatic changes that would soon overtake naval warfare, but did not have a great impact on the fighting of the Civil War. Torpedoes and submarine technology also made a fleeting appearance in the 1860s, showing the way to future innovations in warfare but not playing a major role in the Civil War.

Critical to the conduct of the war, however, were two other rela-tively new technologies: the railroad and the telegraph. The railroad was particularly important in a war in which millions of soldiers were being mobilized and transferred to the front, and in which a single field army could number as many as 250,000 men. Transporting such enor-mous numbers of soldiers, and the supplies necessary to sustain them, by land or by horse and wagon would have been almost impossible. Railroads made it possible for these large armies to be assembled and moved from place to place. However, they also limited the mobility of the armies. Railroad lines and stations are, of course, in fixed positions. Commanders, therefore, were forced to organize their campaigns at least in part around the location of the railroads rather than on the basis of the best topography or most direct land route to a destination. The dependence on the rails—and the resulting necessity of concentrating huge numbers of men in a few places—also encouraged commanders to prefer great battles with large armies rather than smaller engagements with fewer troops.

The impact of the telegraph on the war was limited both by the scarcity of qualified telegraph operators and by the difficulty of bringing telegraph wires into the fields where battles were being fought. Things improved somewhat after the new U.S. Military Telegraph Corps, headed by Thomas Scott and Andrew Carnegie, trained and employed over 1,200 operators. Gradually, too, both the Union and Confederate armies learned to string telegraph wires along the routes of their troops (who, once they were off the railroads, generally moved slowly, on foot or horseback), so that field commanders were able to stay in close touch with one another during battles. Both the North and the South sent spies behind enemy lines who tried to tap the telegraph lines of their op-ponents and send important information back about troop movements and formations.

The Opening Clashes, 1861

The Union and the Confederacy fought their first major battle of the war in northern Virginia. A Union army of over 30,000 men under the command of General Irvin McDowell was stationed just outside Washington. About thirty miles away, at Manassas, was a slightly smaller Confederate army under P. G. T. Beauregard. If the Northern army could destroy the Southern one, Union leaders believed, the war might end at once. In mid-July, McDowell marched his inexperienced troops toward Manassas. Beauregard moved his troops behind Bull Run, a small stream north of Manassas, and called for reinforcements, which reached him the day before the battle. The two armies were now approximately the same size.

On July 21, in the First Battle of Bull Run, or First Battle of Manassas, McDowell almost succeeded in dispersing the Confederate forces. But the Southerners managed to stop a last strong Union assault and then began a savage counterattack. The Union troops, exhausted after hours of hot, hard fighting, suddenly panicked. They broke ranks and retreated chaotically. McDowell was unable to reorganize them, and he had to order a retreat to Washington—a disorderly withdrawal complicated by the presence along the route of many civilians, who had ridden down from the capital, picnic baskets in hand, to watch the battle from nearby hills. The Confederates, as disorganized by victory as the Union forces were by defeat, did not pursue. The battle was a severe blow to Union morale and to the president's confidence in his officers.

Elsewhere, Union forces achieved some small but significant victories in 1861. Nathaniel Lyon, who commanded a small regular army force in St. Louis, moved his troops into southern Missouri to face secessionists trying to lead the state out of the Union. On August 10, at the Battle of Wilson's Creek, he was defeated and killed—but not before he had seriously weakened the striking power of the Confederates. Union forces were subsequently able to hold most of the state.

Meanwhile, a Union force under George B. McClellan moved east from Ohio into western Virginia. By the end of 1861, it had "liberated" the antisecession mountain people of the region, who created their own state government loyal to the Union; the state was admitted to the Union as West Virginia in 1863.

The Western Theater, 1862

After the battle at Bull Run, military operations in the East settled into a long and frustrating stalemate. The first decisive operations in 1862 occurred, therefore, in the western theater. Here the Union forces were trying to seize control of the southern part of the Mississippi River; this would divide the Confederacy and give the North easy transportation into the heart of the South. Northern soldiers advanced on the southern Mississippi from both the north and south, moving down the river from Kentucky and up from the Gulf of Mexico toward New Orleans.

In April, a Union squadron of ironclads and wooden vessels commanded by David G. Farragut gathered in the Gulf of Mexico, then smashed past weak Confederate forts near the mouth of the Mississippi, and from there sailed up to New Orleans. The city was virtually defenseless because the Confederate high command had expected the attack to come from the north. The surrender of New Orleans on April 25, 1862, was the first major Union victory and an important turning point in the war. From then on, the mouth of the Mississippi was closed to Confederate trade, and the South's largest city and most important banking center was in Union hands.

Farther north in the western theater, Confederate troops under the command of Albert Sidney Johnston were stretched out in a long defensive line around two forts in Tennessee, Fort Henry and Fort Donelson, on the Tennessee and Cumberland Rivers respectively. Early in 1862, Ulysses S. Grant attacked Fort Henry, whose defenders, awed by the ironclad riverboats accompanying the Union army, surrendered with almost no resistance on February 6. Grant then moved both his naval and ground forces to Fort Donelson, where the Confederates put up a stronger fight but finally, on February 16, had to surrender. Grant thus gained control of river communications and forced Confederate troops out of Kentucky and half of Tennessee.

With about 40,000 men, Grant now advanced south along the Tennessee River to seize control of vital Confederate railroad lines. At Shiloh, Tennessee, he met a force almost equal to his own, commanded by Albert Sidney Johnston and P. G. T. Beauregard. The result was the Battle of Shiloh, April 6–7. In the first day's fighting (during which Johnston was killed), the Southerners drove Grant back to the river. But the next day, reinforced by 25,000 fresh troops, Grant recovered the lost ground and forced Beauregard to withdraw. After the narrow Union victory at Shiloh, Northern forces occupied Corinth, Mississippi, the hub of several important railroads, and took control of the Mississippi River as far south as Memphis.

The War in the West, 1861–1863

TROOP MOVEMENTS
← Union forces
← Confederate forces

BATTLES
✳ Union victories
✳ Confederate victories

▲▲▲▲ Siege line

Under Union control, January 1, 1862

Union gains

Map labels

KANSAS

MISSOURI

ILLINOIS

INDIANA

St. Louis

Mississippi River

Louisville

Lexington

BUELL

KIRBY SMITH

KENTUCKY

Ohio River

BRAGG

Perryville
Oct. 8, 1862

BRAGG

Cairo

Fort Donelson
June 3, 1864

ROSECRANS

BUELL

Cumberland River

Wilson's Creek
April 10, 1861

Island No. 10
April 8, 1862

GRANT

Fort Henry
Feb. 6, 1862

Nashville

Murfreesboro
Dec. 31, 1862–
Jan. 2, 1863

Knoxville

Pea Ridge

SHERMAN

BUELL

Arkansas River

ARKANSAS

Memphis
June 6, 1862

Shiloh
April 6–7, 1862

TENNESSEE

BUELL

INDIAN
TERRITORY

GRANT

Corinth

GRANT

Tennessee River

BRAGG

Chattanooga

Little Rock

BEAUREGARD

SHERMAN

BRAGG

Atlanta

MISSISSIPPI

ALABAMA

GA.

BRAGG

Red River

Mississippi River

Vicksburg
bombarded
June 1862

Jackson

Montgomery

FARRAGUT

BRAGG

BRAGG

TEXAS

LOUISIANA

Baton Rouge

Mobile

Pensacola

FLORIDA

New Orleans
Captured April 25, 1862

FARRAGUT

0   100 Miles
0   100 kilometers

Braxton Bragg, now in command of the Confederate army in the West, gathered his forces at Chattanooga, in eastern Tennessee, where he faced a Union army (commanded first by Don Carlos Buell and then by William S. Rosecrans) trying to capture Chattanooga. The two armies maneuvered for advantage inconclusively in northern Tennessee and southern Kentucky for several months until they finally met, on December 31–January 2, in the Battle of Murfreesboro, or Stone's River. Bragg was forced to withdraw to the South in defeat.

By the end of 1862, therefore, Union forces had made considerable progress in the West. But the major conflict remained in the East, and the North was having much less success there.

The Virginia Front, 1862

George B. McClellan, commander of the Army of the Potomac and the most controversial general of the war, was a superb trainer of men; but he often seemed reluctant to commit his troops to battle. During the winter of 1861–1862, McClellan concentrated on training his army of 150,000 men near Washington. Finally, he designed a spring campaign to capture the Confederate capital at Richmond. But instead of heading overland directly toward Richmond, McClellan chose a complicated route that he thought would circumvent the Confederate defenses. The navy would carry his troops down the Potomac to a peninsula east of Richmond, between the York and James Rivers; the army would approach the city from there. The combined operations became known as the Peninsular campaign.

McClellan set off with 100,000 men, reluctantly leaving 30,000 members of his army behind, under General Irvin McDowell, to protect Washington. McClellan eventually persuaded Lincoln to send him the additional men. But before the president could do so, a Confederate army under Thomas J. ("Stonewall") Jackson staged a rapid march north through the Shenandoah Valley, as if preparing to cross the Potomac and attack Washington. Lincoln postponed sending reinforecments to McClellan, retaining McDowell's corps to head off Jackson. In the Valley campaign of May 4–June 9, 1862, Jackson defeated two separate Union forces and slipped away before McDowell could catch him.

Meanwhile, McClellan was battling Confederate troops under Joseph E. Johnston outside Richmond in the two-day Battle of Fair Oaks, or Seven Pines (May 31–June 1), and holding his ground. Johnston, badly wounded, was replaced by Robert E. Lee, who then recalled Stonewall Jackson from the Shenandoah Valley. With a combined force of 85,000 to

The Virginia Theater, 1861–1863

TROOP MOVEMENTS

Union forces

Confederate forces

BATTLES

★ Union victories

★ Confederate victories

★ Inconclusive

face McClellan's 100,000, Lee launched a new offensive, known as the Battle of the Seven Days (June 25–July 1), in an effort to cut McClellan off from his base on the York River. But McClellan fought his way across the peninsula and set up a new base on the James. There, with naval support, the Army of the Potomac was safe.

McClellan was now only twenty-five miles from Richmond and in a good position to renew the campaign. But despite continuing pressure from Lincoln, he did not advance. Instead of replacing McClellan with a more aggressive commander, as many were urging him to do, the president finally ordered the army to move back to northern Virginia and join a smaller force under John Pope. The president hoped to begin a new offensive against Richmond on the direct overland route that he himself had always preferred. As the Army of the Potomac left the peninsula by water, Lee moved north with the Army of Northern Virginia to strike Pope before McClellan could join him. Pope was as rash as McClellan was cautious, and he attacked the approaching Confederates without waiting for the arrival of all of McClellan's troops. In the Second Battle of Bull Run, or Manassas (August 29–30), Lee threw back the assault and routed Pope's army, which fled to Washington. With hopes for an overland campaign against Richmond now in disarray, Lincoln removed Pope from command and put McClellan back in charge of all the federal forces in the region.

Lee soon went on the offensive again, heading north through western Maryland, and McClellan moved out to meet him. McClellan had the good luck to get a copy of Lee's orders, which revealed that a part of the Confederate army, under Stonewall Jackson, had separated from the rest to attack Harpers Ferry. But instead of attacking quickly before the Confederates could recombine, McClellan stalled and gave Lee time to pull most of his forces together behind Antietam Creek, near the town of Sharpsburg. There, on September 17, in the bloodiest engagement of the war, McClellan's 87,000-man army repeatedly attacked Lee's force of 50,000, with staggering casualties on both sides. In all, 6,000 men were killed, 17,000 wounded. Late in the day, just as the Confederate line seemed ready to break, the last of Jackson's troops arrived from Harpers Ferry to reinforce it. McClellan might have broken through with one more assault. Instead, he allowed Lee to retreat into Virginia. Technically, Antietam was a Union victory; but in reality, McClellan had squandered an opportunity to destroy much of the Confederate army. In November, Lincoln finally removed McClellan from command for good.

McClellan's replacement, Ambrose E. Burnside, was a short-lived mediocrity. He tried to move toward Richmond by crossing the Rappahannock River at Fredericksburg, the strongest defensive point on the river. There, on December 13, he launched a series of attacks against Lee, all of them bloody, all of them hopeless. After losing a large part of his army, he withdrew to the north bank of the Rappahannock. He was relieved at his own request. The year 1862 ended, therefore, with a series of frustrations for the Union.

SKIRMISH AT ANTIETAM The American public followed the course of the Civil War through newspaper reports and, at times, through published drawings of the battlefields by traveling artists who sketched important events for publication. Photographers chronicled the war as well. But cameras in the 1860s could not easily capture action scenes, and very few newspapers or magazines were technologically equipped to publish photographs. So drawings such as this one by A. R. Waud—of a Brooklyn, New York, regiment fighting Southern calavry at the battle of Antietam—were much in demand.

1863: Year of Decision

At the beginning of 1863, General Joseph Hooker was commanding the still-formidable Army of the Potomac, whose 120,000 troops remained north of the Rappahannock, opposite Fredericksburg. Taking part of his army, Hooker crossed the river above Fredericksburg and moved toward the town and Lee's army. But at the last minute, he drew back to a defensive position in a desolate area of brush and scrub trees known as the Wilderness. Lee had only half as many men as Hooker had, but he boldly divided his forces for a dual assault on the Union army. In the Battle of Chancellorsville, May 1–5, Stonewall Jackson attacked the Union right and Lee himself charged the front. Hooker barely managed to escape with his army. Lee had frustrated Union objectives, but he had not destroyed the Union army. And his ablest officer, Jackson, was fatally wounded in the course of the battle.

While the Union forces were suffering repeated frustrations in the East, they were winning some important victories in the West. In the spring of 1863, Ulysses S. Grant was driving at Vicksburg, Mississippi, one of the Confederacy's two remaining strongholds on the southern Mississippi River. Vicksburg was well protected on land and had good artillery coverage of the river itself. But in May, Grant boldly moved men and supplies—over land and by water—to an area south of the city, where the terrain was reasonably good. He then attacked Vicksburg from the rear. Six weeks later, on July 4, Vicksburg—whose residents were by then literally starving as a result of the prolonged siege—surrendered. At almost the same time, the other Confederate strong point on the river, Port Hudson, Louisiana, also surrendered to a Union force that had moved north from New Orleans. The Union had achieved one of its basic military aims: control of the whole length of the Mississippi. The Confederacy was split in two, with Louisiana, Arkansas, and Texas cut off from the other seceded states. The victories on the Mississippi were one of the great turning points of the war.

During an early stage of the siege of Vicksburg, Lee proposed an invasion of Pennsylvania, which would, he argued, divert Union troops north and remove the pressure on the lower Mississippi. Further, he argued, if he could win a major victory on Northern soil, England and France might come to the Confederacy's aid. The war-weary North might even quit the war before Vicksburg fell.

In June 1863, Lee moved up the Shenandoah Valley into Maryland and then entered Pennsylvania. The Union Army of the Potomac, commanded first by Hooker and then (after June 28) by George C. Meade, moved north, too, paralleling the Confederates' movement and staying between Lee and Washington. The two armies finally encountered one another at the small town of Gettysburg, Pennsylvania. There, on July 1–3, 1863, they fought the most celebrated battle of the war.

Meade's army established a strong, well-protected position on the hills south of the town. The confident and combative Lee attacked, even though his army of 75,000 was outnumbered by Meade's 90,000. His first assault on the Union forces on Cemetery Ridge failed. A day later, he ordered a second, larger effort. In what is remembered as Pickett's Charge, a force of 15,000 Confederate soldiers advanced for almost a mile across open country while being swept by Union fire. Only about 5,000 made it up the ridge, and this remnant finally had to surrender or retreat. By now, Lee had lost nearly a third of his army. On July 4, the same day as the surrender of Vicksburg, he withdrew from Gettysburg. The retreat was another major turning point in the war. Never again were the weakened Confederate forces able seriously to threaten Northern territory.

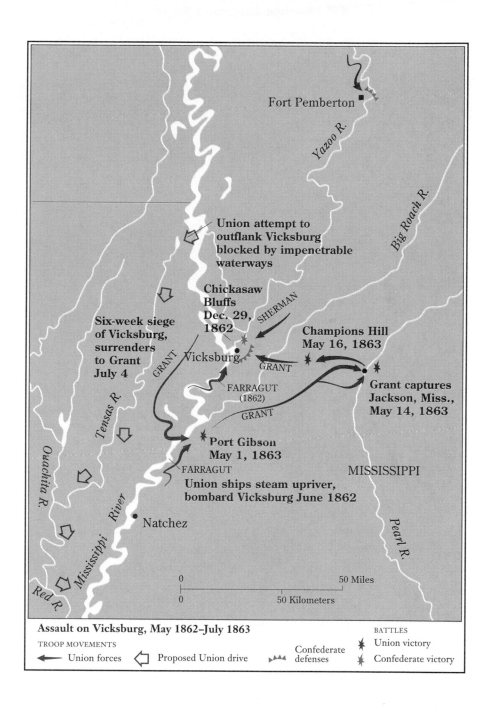

Fort Pemberton

Yazoo R.

Big Roach R.

Union attempt to outflank Vicksburg blocked by impenetrable waterways

Chickasaw Bluffs Dec. 29, 1862

SHERMAN

Six-week siege of Vicksburg, surrenders to Grant July 4

Champions Hill May 16, 1863

GRANT

Vicksburg

GRANT

Grant captures Jackson, Miss., May 14, 1863

FARRAGUT (1862)

GRANT

Tensas R.

Port Gibson May 1, 1863

FARRAGUT

MISSISSIPPI

Union ships steam upriver, bombard Vicksburg June 1862

Ouachita R.

Mississippi River

• Natchez

Pearl R.

Red R.

0		50 Miles
0	50 Kilometers	

Assault on Vicksburg, May 1862–July 1863

TROOP MOVEMENTS

⬅ Union forces   ⬜ Proposed Union drive   ▸▴▴ Confederate defenses

BATTLES

✳ Union victory

✳ Confederate victory

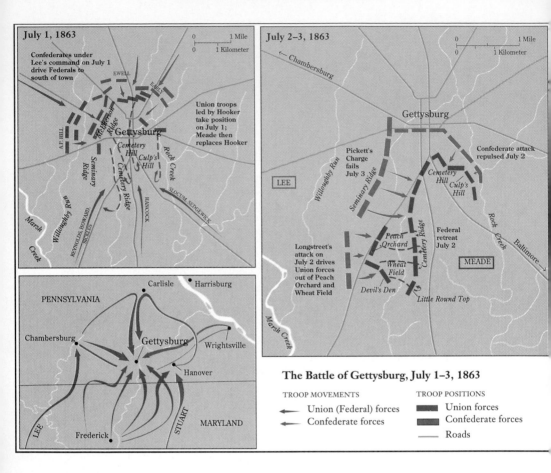

The Battle of Gettysburg, July 1–3, 1863

Before the end of the year, there was another important turning point, this one in Tennessee. After occupying Chattanooga on September 9, Union forces under William Rosecrans began an unwise pursuit of Bragg's retreating Confederate forces. The two armies engaged in western Georgia, in the Battle of Chickamauga (September 19–20), one of the few battles in which the Confederates enjoyed a numerical superiority (70,000 to 56,000). Union forces could not break the Confederate lines and retreated back to Chattanooga.

Bragg now began a siege of Chattanooga itself, seizing the heights nearby and cutting off fresh supplies to the Union forces. Grant came to the rescue. In the Battle of Chattanooga (November 23–25), the reinforced Union army drove the Confederates back into Georgia. Northern troops then occupied most of eastern Tennessee. Union forces had now achieved a second important objective: control of the Tennessee River. Four of the eleven Confederate states were now effectively cut off from the rest of the Southern nation.

ULYSSES S. GRANT One observer said of Grant (photographed here during the Wilderness campaign of 1864): "He habitually wears an expression as if he had determined to drive his head through a brick wall, and was about to do it." It was an apt metaphor for Grant's military philosophy, which relied on constant, unrelenting assault.

The Last Stage, 1864–1865

By the beginning of 1864, Ulysses S. Grant had become general in chief of all the Union armies. Grant was not a subtle, strategic or tactical general; he simply believed in using the North's great advantage in troops and material resources to overwhelm the South. He was not afraid to absorb massive casualties as long as he was inflicting similar or greater casualties on his opponents.

Grant planned two great offensives for 1864. In Virginia, the Army of the Potomac would advance toward Richmond and force Lee into a decisive battle. In Georgia, the western army, under William T. Sherman, would advance east toward Atlanta and destroy the remaining Confederate force, now under the command of Joseph E. Johnston.

The northern campaign began when the Army of the Potomac, 115,000 strong, plunged into the rough, wooded Wilderness area of northwestern Virginia in pursuit of Lee's 75,000-man army. After avoiding an engagement for several weeks, Lee turned Grant back in the Battle of the Wilderness (May 5–7), but without stopping to rest or reorganize, Grant resumed his march toward Richmond and met Lee again in the bloody, five-day Battle of Spotsylvania Court House, in which 12,000 Union troops and a large, but unknown, number of Confederates fell. Grant kept moving, but victory continued to elude him. Lee kept his army between Grant and the Confederate capital and on June 1–3 repulsed the Union forces again, just northeast of Richmond, at Cold Harbor. The month-long Wilderness campaign had cost Grant 55,000 men (killed, wounded, or captured) and had cost Lee 31,000. Richmond still had not fallen.

Grant now changed his strategy. He moved his army east of Richmond, bypassing the capital altogether, and headed south toward the railroad center at Petersburg. If he could seize Petersburg, he could cut off the capital's communications with the rest of the Confederacy. But Petersburg had strong defenses; and once Lee came to the city's relief, the assault became a prolonged siege, which lasted nine months.

In Georgia, meanwhile, Sherman was facing less ferocious resistance. With 90,000 men, he confronted Confederate forces of 60,000 under Johnston, who was unwilling to risk a direct engagement. As Sherman advanced, Johnston tried to delay him by maneuvering. The two armies fought only one real battle—Kennesaw Mountain, northwest of Atlanta, on June 27— where Johnston scored an impressive victory. Even so, he was unable to stop the Union advance toward Atlanta. Sherman took the city on September 2 and burned it. News of the victory electrified the North and helped unite the previously divided Republican Party behind President Lincoln.

Hood now tried unsuccessfully to draw Sherman out of Atlanta by moving back up through Tennessee and threatening an invasion of the North. Sherman sent Union troops to reinforce Nashville. In the Battle of Nashville on December 15–16, 1864, Northern forces practically destroyed what was left of Hood's army.

Meanwhile, Sherman had left Atlanta to begin his soon-to-be-famous "March to the Sea." Living off the land, destroying supplies it could not use, his army cut a sixty-mile-wide swath of desolation across Georgia. "War is all hell," Sherman had once said. By that he meant not that war is terrible, and to be avoided, but that it should be made as horrible and costly as possible for the opponent. He sought not only to deprive the Confederate army of war materials and railroad communications but also to break the will of the Southern people by burning towns and plantations along his route. By December 20, he had reached Savannah, which surrendered two days later. Early in 1865, Sherman continued his destructive march, moving northward through South Carolina. He was virtually unopposed until he was well inside North Carolina, where a small force under Johnston could do no more than cause a brief delay.

In April 1865, Grant's Army of the Potomac—still engaged in the prolonged siege at Petersburg—finally captured a vital railroad junction south-

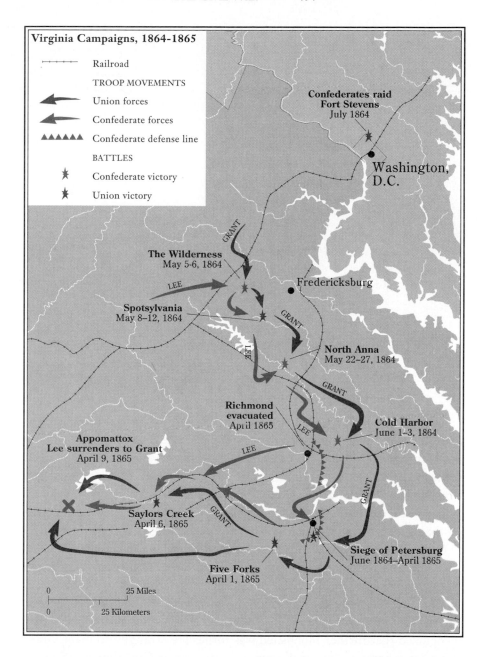

Virginia Campaigns, 1864-1865

┈┼┼┈	Railroad
	TROOP MOVEMENTS
←	Union forces
←	Confederate forces
▲▲▲▲▲	Confederate defense line
	BATTLES
✳	Confederate victory
✴	Union victory

Confederates raid
Fort Stevens
July 1864

Washington,
D.C.

GRANT

The Wilderness
May 5-6, 1864

Fredericksburg

LEE

Spotsylvania
May 8–12, 1864

GRANT

LEE

North Anna
May 22–27, 1864

GRANT

Richmond
evacuated
April 1865

LEE

Cold Harbor
June 1–3, 1864

Appomattox
Lee surrenders to Grant
April 9, 1865

LEE

GRANT

GRANT

Saylors Creek
April 6, 1865

Siege of Petersburg
June 1864–April 1865

Five Forks
April 1, 1865

0   25 Miles

0   25 Kilometers

west of the town. Without rail access to the South, cut off from other Confederate forces, plagued by heavy casualties and massive desertions, Lee informed the Confederate government that he could no longer defend Richmond. Within hours, Jefferson Davis, his cabinet, and as much of the white population as could find transportation fled along with Lee's soldiers. That

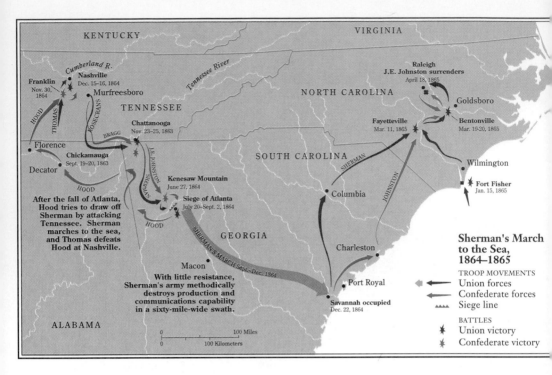

KENTUCKY
VIRGINIA
Cumberland R.
Tennessee River
Franklin
Nov. 30, 1864
Nashville
Dec. 15–16, 1864
Murfreesboro
Raleigh
J.E. Johnston surrenders
April 18, 1865
NORTH CAROLINA
Goldsboro
TENNESSEE
Chattanooga
Nov. 23–25, 1863
Fayetteville
Mar. 11, 1865
Bentonville
Mar. 19-20, 1865
Florence
Chickamauga
Sept. 19–20, 1863
SOUTH CAROLINA
Wilmington
Decator
Fort Fisher
Jan. 15, 1865
Kenesaw Mountain
June 27, 1864
Columbia
After the fall of Atlanta,
Hood tries to draw off
Sherman by attacking
Tennessee. Sherman
marches to the sea,
and Thomas defeats
Hood at Nashville.
Siege of Atlanta
July 20–Sept. 2, 1864
GEORGIA
Charleston
Macon
With little resistance,
Sherman's army methodically
destroys production and
communications capability
in a sixty-mile-wide swath.
Port Royal
Savannah occupied
Dec. 22, 1864
ALABAMA

**Sherman's March
to the Sea,
1864–1865**

TROOP MOVEMENTS
Union forces
Confederate forces
Siege line

BATTLES
Union victory
Confederate victory

0   100 Miles
0   100 Kilometers

night, mobs roamed the city, setting devastating fires. And the next morning, Northern forces (led by an African-American infantry brigade) entered the Confederate capital. With them was Abraham Lincoln, who walked through the streets of the burned-out city surrounded by black men and women cheering him as the "Messiah" and "Father Abraham." In one particularly stirring moment, the president turned to a former slave kneeling on the street before him and said: "Don't kneel to me. . . . You must kneel to God only, and thank Him for the liberty you will enjoy hereafter."

With the remnant of his army, now about 25,000 men, Lee began moving west in the forlorn hope of finding a way around the Union forces so that he could move south and link up with Johnston in North Carolina. But the Union army pursued him and blocked his escape route. Lee finally recognized that further bloodshed was futile. He arranged to meet Grant at a private home in the small town of Appomattox Courthouse, Virginia, where on April 9 he surrendered what was left of his forces. Nine days later, near Durham, North Carolina, Johnston surrendered to Sherman.

The long war was now effectively over. Jefferson Davis was finally captured in Georgia. A few Southern diehards continued to fight, but even their resistance collapsed before long. And well before the last shot was fired, the difficult process of reuniting the shattered nation had begun.

CONCLUSION

The American Civil War began with high hopes and high ideals on both sides. In the North and the South alike, thousands of men enthusiastically enlisted in local regiments and went off to war. Four years later, over 600,000 of them were dead and many more maimed and traumatized for life. A fight for "principles" and "ideals"—a fight few people had thought would last more than a few months—had become one of the longest wars, and by far the bloodiest war, in American history, before or since.

During the first two years of fighting, the Confederate forces seemed to have all the advantages. They were fighting on their own soil. Their troops seemed more committed to the cause than those of the North. Their commanders were exceptionally talented, while Union forces were, for a time, erratically led. Gradually, however, the Union's advantages began to assert themselves. The North had a stabler political system led by one of the greatest leaders in the nation's history (as opposed to the Confederacy's untested government led by a relatively weak president). It had a much larger population, a far more developed industrial economy, superior financial institutions, and a better railroad system. By the middle of 1863, the tide of the war had shifted; over the next two years, Union forces gradually wore down the Confederate armies before finally triumphing in 1865.

The war strengthened the North's economy, giving a spur to industry and railroad development. It greatly weakened the South's, by destroying millions of dollars of property and depleting the region's young male population. Southerners had gone to war in part because of their fears of growing northern dominance. The war itself, ironically, confirmed and strengthened that dominance. There was no doubt by 1865 that the future of the United States lay in the growth of industry and commerce, which would occur for many years primarily outside the South.

But most of all, the Civil War was a victory for the millions of African-American slaves, over whose plight the conflict had largely begun in the first place. The war produced Abraham Lincoln's epochal Emancipation Proclamation and, later, the Thirteenth Amendment to the Constitution, which abolished slavery altogether. It also encouraged hundreds of thousands of slaves literally to free themselves, to desert their masters and seek refuge behind Union lines—at times to fight in the Union armies. The future of the freed slaves was not to be an easy one, but three and a half million people who had once lived in bondage emerged from the war as free men and women.

FOR FURTHER REFERENCE

Suggested Readings

James McPherson, *Battle Cry of Freedom* (1988) is the standard text on the Civil War. Shelby Foote, *The Civil War: A Narrative*, 3 vols. (1958–1974) is an elegant and powerful military history of the war. Allan Nevins, *The War for the Union*, 4 vols. (1959–1971) and Bruce Catton, *This Hallowed Ground* (1956) are among many other powerful and popular general histories of the Civil War. David Donald, *Lincoln* (1995) is the best modern biography of Abraham Lincoln. James M. McPherson, *Abraham Lincoln and the Second American Revolution* (1990) offers provocative reflections on the life and significance of Lincoln. Douglas Southall Freeman, *Robert E. Lee*, 4 vols. (1934–1935) and William McFeely, *Grant* (1981) are the leading biographies of the two most important Civil War generals. Iver Bernstein, *The New York City Draft Riots* (1990) is a good study of one of the most dramatic nonmilitary events in the North during the Civil War. Emory Thomas, *The Confederate Nation* (1979) is a fine one-volume history of the Confederacy. Drew Gilpin Faust, *Mothers of Invention: Women of the Slaveholding South in the American Civil War* (1996), and C. Vann Woodward, ed., *Mary Chesnut's Civil War* (1982) are important sources for understanding the role and experiences of women in the Confederacy. Ira Berlin, et al., eds., *Free at Last: A Documentary History of Slavery, Freedom and the Civil War* (1992) is a superb compilation of primary sources from slaves and slaveowners relating to the demise of slavery during the Civil War years. Ira Berlin, et al., *Slaves No More: Three Essays on Emancipation and the Civil War* (1992), the companion volume to the documents in *Free at Last*, argues that slaves and freedmen played an active role in destroying slavery and redefining freedom. Catherine Clinton and Nina Silber, *Divided Houses* (1992) is a collection of essays demonstrating the importance of gender in the history of the Civil War.

Films

(The best source for information on how to find these and other films is *Bowker's Complete Video Directory*—3 volumes.) *The Civil War* (1989) is Ken Burns's award-winning, nine-volume epic documentary. *Civil War Journal*, hosted by Danny Glover, focuses on the private stories within the great conflict. *The American Story, No. 11: The Eve of Conflict, No. 12: The Blue and the Grey*, and *No. 13: The Road to Appomattox* (1985) explore the Civil War from Lincoln's election to the end of the war. *Civil War Legends* (1989) includes biographies of Robert E. Lee, Stonewall Jackson, Ulysses S. Grant, and Abraham Lincoln. *The Civil War: Anguish of Emancipation* (1972) reenacts the events confronting Abraham Lincoln as he prepared to issue the Emancipation Proclamation. *The Fifty-Fourth Massachusetts*, from the Arts & Entertainment Network Civil War Series, illuminates the history of Massachusetts's famous regiment of African-American soldiers. *Clara Barton* (1995) traces the life of a woman who became a nurse during the Civil War and was instrumental in establishing the American Red Cross.

Internet Resources

Internet websites containing historical material relevant to the subjects discussed in this chapter can be reached through the McGraw-Hill history site at www.mhhe.com/socscience/history/usa/link/linktop.htm.

CHAPTER FIFTEEN

Reconstruction and the New South

The Problems of Peacemaking ∼ *Radical Reconstruction*

The South in Reconstruction ∼ *The Grant Administration*

The Abandonment of Reconstruction ∼ *The New South*

EW PERIODS IN the history of the United States have produced as much bitterness or created such enduring controversy as the era of Reconstruction—the years following the Civil War during which Americans attempted to reunite their shattered nation. To many white Southerners, Reconstruction was a vicious and destructive experience—a period when vindictive Northerners inflicted humiliation and revenge on the prostrate South. Northern defenders of Reconstruction, in contrast, argued that their policies were the only way to prevent unrepentant Confederates from restoring Southern society to what it had been before the war; without forceful federal intervention, there would be no way to forestall the reemergence of a backward aristocracy and the continued subjugation of former slaves.

To most African Americans at the time, and to many people of all races since, Reconstruction was notable for other reasons. Neither a vicious tyranny, as white Southerners charged, nor a thoroughgoing reform, as many Northerners claimed, it was, rather, a small but important first step in the effort to secure civil rights and economic power for the former slaves. Reconstruction did not provide African Americans with either the legal protections or the material resources to assure them anything like real equality. For the remainder of the nineteenth century, and through much of the twentieth, most black men and women who continued to live in what came to be known as the New South had little power to resist their oppression.

TIME LINE

1863	1864	1865	1866	1867
Lincoln announces Reconstruction plan	Lincoln vetoes Wade-Davis bill	Lincoln assassinated; Johnson becomes president	Republicans gain in congressional elections	Congressional Reconstruction begins
		Freedmen's Bureau established		
		Joint Committee on Reconstruction established		

1868	1869	1872	1873	1875
Grant elected president	Congress passes 15th Amendment	Grant reelected	Panic and depression	"Whiskey ring" scandal
Johnson impeached and acquitted				

1877	1883	1890s	1895	1896
Hayes wins disputed election	Supreme Court upholds segregation	Jim Crow laws in South	Atlanta Compromise	*Plessy* v. *Ferguson*
Compromise of 1877 ends Reconstruction				

And yet for all its shortcomings, Reconstruction did help African Americans create some new institutions and some important legal precedents that helped them survive and that ultimately, well into the twentieth century, became the basis of later efforts to win freedom and equality.

THE PROBLEMS OF PEACEMAKING

In 1865, when it became clear that the war was almost over, no one in Washington was certain about what to do. Abraham Lincoln could not negotiate a treaty with the defeated government; he continued to insist that the Confederate government had no legal right to exist. Yet neither could he simply readmit the Southern states into the Union as if nothing had happened.

The Aftermath of War and Emancipation

The South after the Civil War was a desolate place. Towns had been gutted, plantations burned, fields neglected, bridges and railroads destroyed. Many white Southerners—stripped of their slaves through emancipation and stripped of the capital they had invested in now worthless Confederate bonds and currency—had almost no personal property. More than 258,000 Confederate soldiers had died in the war, and thousands more returned home wounded or sick. Many families had to rebuild their lives without the help of adult males. Some white Southerners faced starvation and homelessness.

If conditions were bad for Southern whites, they were far worse for Southern blacks—the 4 million men and women now emerging from

CHARLESTON, 1865 Not until 1864 did substantial fighting and destruction begin to take place in the urban South. But in the last year of the war, several major cities (and many towns and smaller communities) experienced devastation at the hands of the Northern armies—among them Richmond, Atlanta, and (as seen here) Charleston.

bondage. As soon as the war ended, hundreds of thousands of them—young and old, many of them ill and feeble—left the plantations in search of a new life in freedom. But most had nowhere to go, and few had any possessions except the clothes they wore.

Competing Notions of Freedom

Despite the disarray of Southern society, almost everyone faced the future with some very clear aspirations. For blacks and whites alike, Reconstruction became a struggle to define the meaning of freedom. But the former slaves and the defeated whites had very different conceptions of what freedom meant.

For African Americans, freedom meant above all an end to slavery. But it also meant acquiring rights and protections that would enable them to live as free people, just as whites did. Some blacks believed the only way to secure freedom was to have the government take land away from white people, who owned virtually all of it, and give it to black people, who owned virtually none. Others asked only for legal equality, confident that they could advance successfully in American society once the formal obstacles to their advancement disappeared. But whatever their particular demands, virtually all former slaves were united in their desire for independence from white control. Throughout the post-Civil War South, African Americans separated themselves from white institutions—pulling out of white-controlled churches and establishing their own, creating clubs and societies for their own people, and in some cases starting their own schools.

For most white Southerners, freedom meant something very different. It meant the ability to control their own destinies without interference from the North or the federal government. And in the immediate aftermath of the war, they attempted to exercise this version of freedom by trying to restore their society to its antebellum form. When these white Southerners fought for what they considered freedom, they were fighting above all to preserve local and regional autonomy and white supremacy.

In the immediate aftermath of the war, the federal government's contribution to solving the question of the future of the South was modest. Federal troops remained in the South to preserve order and protect the freedmen. And in March 1865, Congress established the Freedmen's Bureau, an agency of the army directed by General Oliver O. Howard. The Freedmen's Bureau distributed food to millions of former slaves. It established schools, staffed by missionaries and teachers who had been sent to

A MONUMENT TO THE CONFEDERATE DEAD This monument in the town square of Greenwood, South Carolina, was typical of many such memorials erected all across the South in the aftermath of the Civil War. They served to commemorate the soldiers who had died in the struggle, but also to remind white Southerners of what was by the 1870s already widely known and romanticized as the "Lost Cause."

the South by Freedmen's Aid Societies and other private and church groups in the North. It made a modest effort to settle blacks on lands of their own. (The bureau also offered considerable assistance to poor whites, many of whom were similarly destitute and homeless after the war.) But the Freedmen's Bureau was not a permanent solution. It had authority to operate for only one year, and it was, in any case, far too small to deal effectively with the enormous problems facing Southern society. By the time the war ended, other proposals for reconstructing the defeated South were emerging.

Plans for Reconstruction

Control of Reconstruction remained in the hands of the Republicans, who had substantial majorities in both houses of Congress and who were divided in their approach to the issue. Conservatives within the party insisted that the South accept the abolition of slavery, but they proposed few other conditions for the readmission of the seceded states. The Radicals, led by Representative Thaddeus Stevens of Pennsylvania and Senator Charles Sumner of Massachusetts, urged a much harsher course, including disfranchising large numbers of Southern whites, protecting black civil rights, and confiscating the property of wealthy white Southerners who had aided the Confederacy and distributing the land among the freedmen. There was also a group of Republican Moderates, who rejected the most stringent demands of the Radicals but supported extracting at least some concessions from the South on black rights.

President Lincoln's sympathies lay with the Moderates and Conservatives of his party. He favored a lenient Reconstruction policy, and he believed that Southern Unionists (mostly former Whigs) could become the nucleus of new, loyal state governments in the South. Lincoln announced his Reconstruction plan in December 1863, more than a year before the war ended. It offered a general amnesty to white Southerners—other than high officials of the Confederacy—who would pledge an oath of loyalty to the government and accept the elimination of slavery. When 10 percent of a state's total number of voters in 1860 took the oath, those loyal voters could set up a state government. Lincoln also proposed extending suffrage to those African Americans who were educated, owned property, and had served in the Union army. Three Southern states—Louisiana, Arkansas, and Tennessee, all under Union occupation—reestablished loyal governments under the Lincoln formula in 1864.

The Radical Republicans were outraged at the mildness of Lincoln's program and refused to admit representatives from the three "reconstructed" states to Congress. In July 1864, they pushed their own plan through Congress in the form of the Wade-Davis Bill. It called for the

ABRAHAM LINCOLN Lincoln was the subject of many photographic portraits, of which this one, by Mathew Brady, is among the most famous.

president to appoint a provisional governor for each conquered state. When a majority (not Lincoln's 10 percent) of the white males of a state pledged their allegiance to the Union, the governor could summon a state constitutional convention, whose delegates were to be elected by voters who had never borne arms against the United States (again, a major departure from Lincoln's plan). The new state constitutions would be required to abolish slavery, disfranchise Confederate civil and military leaders, and repudiate debts accumulated by the state governments during the war. Only then would Congress readmit the states to the Union. Like the president's proposal, the Wade-Davis Bill left the question of political rights for blacks up to the states.

Congress passed the bill a few days before it adjourned in 1864, and Lincoln disposed of it with a pocket veto. His action enraged the Radical leaders, and the pragmatic Lincoln realized he would have to accept at least some of the Radical demands. In the first weeks of 1865, he began to move toward a new approach to Reconstruction.

The Death of Lincoln

What plan he might have produced no one can say. On the night of April 14, 1865, Lincoln and his wife attended a play at Ford's Theater in Washington. As they sat in the presidential box, John Wilkes Booth, an actor fervently committed to the Southern cause, entered the box from the rear and shot Lincoln in the head. Early the next morning, the president died.

The circumstances of Lincoln's death earned him immediate martyrdom. They also produced something close to hysteria throughout the North, especially because it quickly became clear that Booth had been the leader of a conspiracy. One of his associates shot and wounded Secretary of State William Seward on the night of the assassination, and another abandoned at the last moment a scheme to murder Vice President Andrew Johnson. Booth himself escaped on horseback into the Maryland countryside, where, on April 26, he was cornered by Union troops and shot to death in a blazing barn. Eight other people were convicted by a military tribunal of participating in the conspiracy (at least two of them on the basis of virtually no evidence). Four were hanged.

To many Northerners, however, the murder of the president seemed evidence of an even greater conspiracy—one masterminded and directed by the unrepentant leaders of the defeated South. Militant Republicans exploited such suspicions relentlessly in the ensuing months, ensuring that Lincoln's death would help doom his plans for a relatively easy peace.

Johnson and "Restoration"

Leadership of the Moderates and Conservatives fell to Lincoln's successor, Andrew Johnson of Tennessee, who was not well suited, either by circumstance or personality, for the task. A Democrat until he had joined the Union ticket with Lincoln in 1864, he became president at a time of growing partisan passions. Johnson himself was an intemperate and tactless man, filled with resentments and insecurities.

Johnson revealed his plan for Reconstruction—or "Restoration," as he preferred to call it—soon after he took office, and he implemented it during the summer of 1865 when Congress was in recess. Like Lincoln, he offered some form of amnesty to Southerners who would take an oath of allegiance. In most other respects, however, his plan resembled the Wade-Davis Bill. The president appointed a provisional governor in each state and charged him with inviting qualified voters to elect delegates to a constitutional convention. In order to win readmission to Congress, a state had to revoke its ordinance of secession, abolish slavery and ratify the Thirteenth Amendment, and repudiate Confederate and state war debts.

By the end of 1865, all the seceded states had formed new governments—some under Lincoln's plan, some under Johnson's—and awaited congressional approval of them. But Radicals in Congress vowed not to recognize the Johnson governments, just as they had previously refused to recognize the Lincoln regimes, for, by now, Northern opinion had become more hostile toward the South than it had been a year earlier when Congress had passed the Wade-Davis Bill. Delegates to the Southern conventions had angered much of the North by their apparent reluctance to abolish slavery and by their refusal to grant suffrage to any blacks. Southern states had also seemed to defy the North by electing prominent Confederate leaders to represent them in Congress, among them Alexander H. Stephens, former vice president of the Confederacy, who was selected as a United States senator from Georgia.

RADICAL RECONSTRUCTION

Reconstruction under Johnson's plan—often known as "presidential Reconstruction"—continued only until Congress reconvened in December 1865. At that point, Congress refused to seat the representatives of the "restored" states and created a new Joint Committee on Reconstruction to frame a Reconstruction policy of its own. The period of "congressional" or "Radical" Reconstruction had begun.

The Black Codes

Meanwhile, events in the South were driving Northern opinion in even more radical directions. Throughout the South in 1865 and early 1866, state legislatures were enacting sets of laws known as the Black Codes, designed to give whites substantial control over the former slaves. The codes authorized local officials to apprehend unemployed blacks, fine them for vagrancy, and hire them out to private employers to satisfy the fine. Some of the codes forbade blacks to own or lease farms or to take any jobs other than as plantation workers or domestic servants.

Reconstruction

D EBATE OVER THE nature of Reconstruction has been unusually intense, not only among historians but among much of the larger
public as well. Indeed, few issues in American history have raised such
deep and enduring passions.

Beginning in the late nineteenth century and continuing well into the
twentieth, a relatively uniform and highly critical view of Reconstruction
prevailed among historians—a reflection of a broad consensus among
white Americans about the inferiority of blacks and of a yearning in both
the North and the South for sectional reconciliation. William A. Dunning's *Reconstruction, Political and Economic* (1907) was the principal scholarly expression of this prevailing view. Dunning portrayed Reconstruction
as a corrupt and oppressive outrage imposed on a prostrate South by a
vindictive group of Northern Republican Radicals. Unscrupulous carpetbaggers flooded the South and plundered the region. Ignorant African
Americans were thrust into political offices for which they were unfit. Reconstruction governments were awash in corruption and compiled enormous levels of debt. The Dunning interpretation dominated several generations of historical scholarship. It also helped shape such popular images
of Reconstruction as those in the novel and film *Gone with the Wind*.

Among historians, at least, the Dunning interpretation gradually lost
credibility in the face of a series of challenges. W. E. B. Du Bois, the great
African-American scholar, offered one of the first alternative views in
Black Reconstruction (1935). To Du Bois, Reconstruction was an effort by
freed blacks (and their white allies) to create a more democratic society in
the South, and it was responsible for many valuable social innovations. In

the early 1960s, John Hope Franklin and Kenneth Stampp, building on a generation of work by other scholars, published new histories of Reconstruction that also radically revised the Dunning interpretation. Reconstruction, they argued, was a genuine, if flawed, effort to solve the problem of race in the South. The Reconstruction governments were not perfect, but they were bold experiments in interracial politics. Congressional Radicals were not saints, but they were genuinely concerned with protecting the rights of former slaves. Reconstruction had brought important, if temporary, progress to the South and had created no more corruption there than governments were creating in the North at the same time. What was tragic about Reconstruction, the revisionists claimed, was not what it did to Southern whites but what it failed to do for Southern blacks. It was, in the end, too weak and too short-lived to guarantee African Americans genuine equality.

In more recent years, some historians have begun to question the assessment of the first revisionists that, in the end, Reconstruction accomplished relatively little. Leon Litwack argued in *Been in the Storm So Long* (1979) that former slaves used the protections Reconstruction offered them to carve out a certain level of independence for themselves within Southern society: strengthening churches, reuniting families, and resisting the efforts of white planters to revive the gang labor system.

Eric Foner's *Reconstruction: America's Unfinished Revolution* (1988) also emphasized how far African Americans moved toward freedom and independence in a short time, how much of lasting value they were able to accomplish despite imposing obstacles, and how important they were in shaping the execution of Reconstruction policies. Reconstruction, he argues, "can only be judged a failure" as an effort to secure "blacks' rights as citizens and free laborers." But it "closed off even more oppressive alternatives. . . . The post-Reconstruction labor system embodied neither a return to the closely supervised gang labor of antebellum days, nor the complete dispossession and immobilization of the black labor force and coercive apprenticeship systems envisioned by white Southerners in 1865 and 1866. Nor were blacks, as in twentieth-century South Africa, barred from citizenship, herded into labor reserves, or prohibited by law from moving from one part of the country to another. . . . The doors of economic opportunity that had opened could never be completely closed."

Congress first responded to the Black Codes by passing an act extending the life of the Freedmen's Bureau and widening its powers so that it could nullify work agreements forced on freedmen under the Black Codes. Then, in April 1866, Congress passed the first Civil Rights Act, which declared blacks to be citizens of the United States and gave the federal government power to intervene in state affairs to protect the rights of citizens. Johnson vetoed both bills, but Congress overrode him on each of them.

The Fourteenth Amendment

In April 1866, the Joint Committee on Reconstruction proposed a new amendment to the Constitution, which Congress approved in early summer and sent to the states for ratification. Eventually, it became one of the most important of all the provisions in the Constitution.

The Fourteenth Amendment offered the first constitutional definition of American citizenship. Everyone born in the United States, and everyone naturalized, was automatically a citizen and entitled to all the "privileges and immunities" guaranteed by the Constitution, including equal protection of the laws by both the state and national governments. There could be no other requirements for citizenship. The amendment also imposed penalties—reduction of representation in Congress and in the electoral college—on states that denied suffrage to any adult male inhabitants. (The wording reflected the prevailing view in Congress and elsewhere that the franchise was properly restricted to men.) Finally, it prohibited former members of Congress or other former federal officials who had aided the Confederacy from holding any state or federal office unless two-thirds of Congress voted to pardon them.

Congressional Radicals offered to readmit to the Union any state whose legislature ratified the Fourteenth Amendment. Only Tennessee did so. All the other former Confederate states, along with Delaware and Kentucky, refused, leaving the amendment temporarily without the necessary approval of three-fourths of the states.

But by now, the Radicals were growing more confident and determined. Bloody race riots in New Orleans and other Southern cities—riots in which African Americans were the principal victims—were among the events that strengthened their hand. In the 1866 congressional elections, Johnson actively campaigned for Conservative candidates, but he did his own cause more harm than good with his intemperate speeches. The voters returned an overwhelming majority of Republicans, most of them Radicals, to Congress. In the Senate, there were now 42 Republicans to 11 Democrats; in the

House, 143 Republicans to 49 Democrats. (The South remained largely un-represented in both chambers.) Congressional Republicans were now strong enough to enact a plan of their own even over the president's objections.

The Congressional Plan

The Radicals passed three Reconstruction bills early in 1867 and overrode Johnson's vetoes of all of them. These bills finally established, nearly two years after the end of the war, a coherent plan for Reconstruction.

A CELEBRATION OF RECONSTRUCTION The celebrated cartoonist Thomas Nast—best known for his savage caricatures of machine politicians in New York's Tammany Hall—drew this celebratory, and optimistic, image of Reconstruction not long after the end of the Civil War: a classical goddess restoring the former Confederate states to their rightful place within a symbolic fasces that represented union. In fact, the Reconstruction process proved much more difficult than this hopeful image suggested.

Under the congressional plan, Tennessee, which had ratified the Fourteenth Amendment, was promptly readmitted. But Congress rejected the Lincoln-Johnson governments of the other ten Confederate states and, instead, combined those states into five military districts. A military commander governed each district and had orders to register qualified voters (defined as all adult black males and those white males who had not participated in the rebellion). Once registered, voters would elect conventions to prepare new state constitutions, which had to include provisions for black suffrage. Once voters ratified the new constitutions, they could elect state governments. Congress had to approve a state's constitution, and the state legislature had to ratify the Fourteenth Amendment. Once that happened, and once enough states ratified the amendment to make it part of the Constitution, then the former Confederate states could be restored to the Union.

By 1868, seven of the ten former Confederate states (Arkansas, North Carolina, South Carolina, Louisiana, Alabama, Georgia, and Florida) had fulfilled these conditions (including ratification of the Fourteenth Amendment, which now became part of the Constitution) and were readmitted to the Union. Conservative whites held up the return of Virginia and Texas until 1869 and Mississippi until 1870. By then, Congress had added an additional requirement for readmission—ratification of another constitutional amendment, the Fifteenth, which forbade the states and the federal government to deny suffrage to any citizen on account of "race, color, or previous condition of servitude."

To stop the president from interfering with their plans, the congressional Radicals passed two remarkable laws of dubious constitutionality in 1867. One, the Tenure of Office Act, forbade the president to remove civil officials, including members of his own cabinet, without the consent of the Senate. The principal purpose of the law was to protect the job of Secretary of War Edwin M. Stanton, who was cooperating with the Radicals. The other law, the Command of the Army Act, prohibited the president from issuing military orders except through the commanding general of the army (General Grant), who could not be relieved or assigned elsewhere without the consent of the Senate.

The congressional Radicals also took action to stop the Supreme Court from interfering with their plans. In 1866, the Court had declared in the case of *Ex parte Milligan* that military tribunals were unconstitutional in places where civil courts were functioning, a decision that seemed to threaten the system of military government the Radicals were planning for the South. Radicals in Congress immediately proposed several bills that would require two-thirds of the justices to support any decision overruling a law of Congress, would deny the Court jurisdiction in Reconstruction cases, would reduce its membership to three, and would even abolish it. The justices apparently took notice. Over the next two years, the Court refused to accept jurisdiction in any cases involving Reconstruction (and the congressional bills concerning the Court never passed).

The Impeachment of the President

President Johnson had long since ceased to be a serious obstacle to the passage of Radical legislation, but he was still the official charged with administering the Reconstruction programs. As such, the Radicals believed, he remained a serious impediment to their plans. Early in 1867, they began looking for a way to impeach him and remove him from office. A search for grounds for impeachment began. Republicans found them, they believed, when Johnson dismissed Secretary of War Stanton despite Congress's refusal to agree, thus deliberately violating the Tenure of Office Act in hopes of testing the law before the courts. Elated Radicals in the House quickly impeached the president and sent the case to the Senate for trial.

The trial before the Senate lasted throughout April and May 1868. The Radicals put heavy pressure on all the Republican senators, but the Moderates (who were losing faith in the Radical program) vacillated. On the first three charges to come to a vote, seven Republicans joined the Democrats and independents to support acquittal. The vote was 35 to 19, one short of the constitutionally required two-thirds majority. After that, the Radicals dropped the impeachment effort.

THE SOUTH IN RECONSTRUCTION

Reconstruction may not have accomplished what its framers intended or what its defenders had hoped. But it did have profound effects on the South.

The Reconstruction Governments

Critics labeled Southern white Republicans with the derogatory terms "scalawags" and "carpetbaggers." Many of the "scalawags" were former Whigs who had never felt comfortable in the Democratic Party or farmers who lived in remote areas where there had been little or no slavery; most of these Republicans hoped the party's program of internal improvements would help end their economic isolation. The "carpetbaggers" were white men from the North, most of them veterans of the Union army who looked on the South as a new frontier, more promising than the West. They had settled there at war's end as hopeful planters, businessmen, or professionals.

The most numerous Republicans in the South were the black freedmen, most of whom had no previous experience in politics and tried, therefore, to build institutions through which they could learn to exercise their power. In several states, African-American voters held their own conventions to chart their future course. Freedmen had created their own churches after emancipation, withdrawing from the white-dominated congregations they had been compelled to attend under slavery. This religious independence also helped give them unity and self-confidence.

African Americans played a significant role in the politics of the Reconstruction South. They served as delegates to the constitutional conventions. They held public offices of practically every kind. Between 1869 and 1901, twenty blacks served in the United States House of Representatives, two in the Senate. They served, too, in state legislatures and in various other state offices. Southern whites complained loudly about "Negro rule" during Reconstruction, but no such thing ever actually existed in any of the states. In the South as a whole, the percentage of black officeholders was always far lower than the percentage of blacks in the population.

The record of the Reconstruction governments is mixed. Critics at the time and later denounced them for corruption and financial extravagance, and there is some truth to both charges. But the corruption in the South, real as it was, was hardly unique to the Reconstruction governments. Corruption had been rife in some antebellum and Confederate governments, and it was at least as rampant in the Northern states. And the large state expenditures of the Reconstruction years were huge only in comparison with the meager budgets of the antebellum era. They repre-

AFTER SLAVERY Although most freed slaves remained agricultural laborers after Emancipation, a considerable number moved off the land in search of new occupations and new homes. For many, that meant living for some time without stable employment or a permanent home. This photograph from the late 1860s shows a group of former slaves at a county almshouse in the South.

sented an effort to provide the South with desperately needed services that antebellum governments had never offered: public education, public works programs, poor relief, and other costly new commitments.

Education

Perhaps the most important of the accomplishments of the Reconstruction governments was a dramatic improvement in Southern education— an improvement that benefited both whites and blacks. In the first years of Reconstruction, much of the impetus for educational reform in the South came from outside groups—from the Freedmen's Bureau, from Northern private philanthropic organizations, from the many Northern white women who traveled to the South to teach in freedmen's schools— and from African Americans themselves. Over the opposition of many

Southern whites, who feared that education would give blacks "false no-tions of equality," these reformers established a large network of schools for former slaves—4,000 schools by 1870, staffed by 9,000 teachers (half of them black), teaching 200,000 students (about 12 percent of the total school-age population of the freedmen). In the 1870s, Reconstruction governments began to build a comprehensive public school system in the South. By 1876, more than half of all white children and about 40 per-cent of all black children were attending schools in the South (although almost all such schools were racially segregated). Several black "acade-mies," offering more advanced education, also began operating. Gradu-ally, these academies grew into an important network of black colleges and universities.

Landownership and Tenancy

The most ambitious goal of the Freedmen's Bureau, and of some Re-publican Radicals in Congress, was to reform landownership in the South. The effort failed. By June 1865, the bureau had settled nearly 10,000 black families on their own land—most of it drawn from aban-doned plantations in areas occupied by the Union armies. By the end of that year, however, Southern plantation owners were returning and de-manding the restoration of their property. President Johnson supported their demands, and the government eventually returned most of the confiscated lands to their original white owners. Congress never had much stomach for the idea of land redistribution, and the experiment quickly died.

Even so, the distribution of landownership in the South changed con-siderably in the postwar years. Among whites, there was a striking decline in landownership, from 80 percent before the war to 67 percent by the end of Reconstruction. Some whites lost their land because of unpaid debt or increased taxes; some left the marginal lands they had owned to move to more fertile areas, where they rented. Among blacks, during the same period, the proportion who owned land rose from virtually none to more than 20 percent.

Still, most blacks, and a growing minority of whites, did not own their own land during Reconstruction, and some who acquired land in the 1860s had lost it by the 1890s. Instead, they worked for others in one form or another. Many black agricultural laborers—perhaps 25 percent of the total—simply worked for wages. Most, however, became tenants of white landowners—that is, they worked their own plots of land and paid their landlords either a fixed rent or a share of their crop (hence the term "sharecropping"). The new system represented a repudiation by blacks of the gang-labor system of the antebellum plantation, in which slaves had lived and worked together under the direction of a master. As tenants and sharecroppers, blacks enjoyed at least a physical independence from their landlords and had the sense of working their own land, even if in most cases they could never hope to buy it. But tenantry also benefited landlords in some ways, relieving them of the cost of purchasing slaves and of responsibility for the physical well-being of their workers.

Incomes and Credit

In some respects, the postwar years were a period of remarkable economic progress for African Americans in the South. The per capita income of blacks (when the material benefits of slavery are counted as income) rose 46 percent between 1857 and 1879, while the per capita income of whites declined 35 percent. This represented one of the most significant redistributions of income in American history. African Americans were also able to work less than they had under slavery. Women and children were less likely to labor in the fields, and adult men tended to work shorter days. In all, the black labor force worked about one-third fewer hours during Reconstruction than it had been compelled to work under slavery—a reduction that brought the working schedule of blacks roughly into accord with that of white farm laborers.

But other developments were limiting these gains. While black share of profits was increasing, the total profits of Southern agriculture were declining—a result of the dislocations of the war and a reduction in the world market for cotton. Nor did the income redistribution of the postwar years lift many blacks out of poverty. Black per capita income rose from about one-quarter of white per capita income (which was itself low) to about one-half in the first few years after the war. After this initial increase, however, it rose hardly at all.

Blacks and poor whites alike often found themselves virtually imprisoned by the crop-lien system. Few of the traditional institutions of credit in the South—the "factors" and banks—returned after the war. In their stead emerged a new system of credit, centered in large part on local country stores—some of them owned by planters, others owned by independent merchants. Blacks and whites, landowners and tenants—all depended on these stores for such necessities as food, clothing, seed, and farm implements. And since farmers did not have the same steady cash flow as other workers, customers usually had to rely on credit from these merchants in order to purchase what they needed. Most local stores had no competition (and went to great lengths to ensure that things stayed that way). As a result, they were able to set interest rates as high as 50 or 60 percent. Farmers had to give the merchants a lien (or claim) on their crops as collateral for the loans (thus the term "crop-lien system," generally used to describe Southern farming in this period). Farmers who suffered a few bad years in a row, as many did, could become trapped in a cycle of debt from which they could never escape.

One effect of this burdensome credit system was that some blacks who had acquired land during the early years of Reconstruction gradually lost it as they fell into debt. So, to a lesser extent, did white small landowners. Another was that Southern farmers became almost wholly dependent on cash crops—and most of all on cotton—because only such marketable commodities seemed to offer any possibility of escape from debt. The relentless planting of cotton contributed to an exhaustion of the soil. The crop-lien system, in other words, was not only helping to impoverish small farmers; it was also contributing to a general decline in the Southern agricultural economy.

The African-American Family in Freedom

One of the most striking features of the black response to Reconstruction was the effort to build or rebuild family structures. A major reason for the rapid departure of so many blacks from plantations was the desire to find lost relatives and reunite families. Thousands of African Americans wandered through the South looking for husbands, wives, children, or other relatives from whom they had been separated. Former slaves rushed to have their marriages, previously without legal standing, sanctified by church and law.

Within the black family, the definition of male and female roles quickly came to resemble that within white families. Many women and children ceased working in the fields. Such work, they believed, was a badge of slavery. Instead, many women restricted themselves largely to domestic tasks—cooking, cleaning, gardening, raising children, attending

AFRICAN-AMERICAN WORK AFTER SLAVERY Black men and women engaged in a wide range of economic activities in the aftermath of slavery. But discrimination by white Southerners and the former slaves' own lack of education limited most of them to relatively menial jobs. Many black women (including this former slave) earned money for their families by working as "washer women," doing laundry for white people

to the needs of their husbands. Still, economic necessity often compelled black women to engage in income-producing activities: working as domestic servants, taking in laundry, or helping their husbands in the fields. By the end of Reconstruction, half of all black women over the age of sixteen were working for wages.

THE GRANT ADMINISTRATION

Exhausted by the political turmoil of the Johnson administration, American voters in 1868 yearned for a strong, stable figure to guide them through the troubled years of Reconstruction. They turned trustingly to General Ulysses S. Grant, the hero of the war and, by 1868, a revered national idol.

The Soldier President

Grant could have had the nomination of either party in 1868. But believing that Republican Reconstruction policies were more popular in the North, he accepted the Republican nomination. The Democrats nominated former governor Horatio Seymour of New York. The campaign was a bitter one, and Grant's triumph was surprisingly narrow. Without the 500,000 new black Republican voters in the South, he would have had a minority of the popular vote.

Grant entered the White House with no political experience, and his performance was clumsy and ineffectual from the start. Except for Hamilton Fish, whom Grant appointed secretary of state and who served for eight years with great distinction, most members of the cabinet were ill-equipped for their tasks. Grant relied chiefly, and increasingly, on established party leaders—the group most ardently devoted to patronage, and his administration used the spoils system even more blatantly than most of its predecessors, embittering reform-minded members of his party. Grant also alienated the many Northerners who were growing disillusioned with the Radical Reconstruction policies, which the president continued to support. Some Republicans suspected, correctly, that there was also corruption in the Grant administration itself.

By the end of Grant's first term, therefore, members of a substantial faction of the party—who referred to themselves as Liberal Republicans—had come to oppose what they called "Grantism." In 1872, hoping to prevent Grant's reelection, they bolted the party and nominated their own presidential candidate: Horace Greeley, veteran editor and publisher of the *New York Tribune*. The Democrats, somewhat reluctantly, named Greeley their candidate as well, hoping that the alliance with the Liberals would enable them to defeat Grant. But the effort was in vain. Grant won a substantial victory, polling 286 electoral votes to Greeley's 66, and nearly 56 percent of the popular total.

The Grant Scandals

During the 1872 campaign, the first of a series of political scandals came to light that would plague Grant and the Republicans for the next eight years. It involved the French-owned Crédit Mobilier construction company, which had helped build the Union Pacific Railroad. The heads of Crédit Mobilier had used their positions as Union Pacific stockholders to steer large fraudulent contracts to their construction company, thus bilking the Union Pacific (and the federal government, which provided large subsidies to the railroad) of millions. To prevent investigations, the directors had given Crédit Mobilier stock to key members of Congress. But in 1872, Congress did conduct an investigation, which revealed that some highly placed Republicans—including Schuyler Colfax, now Grant's vice president—had accepted stock.

One dreary episode followed another in Grant's second term. Benjamin H. Bristow, Grant's third Treasury secretary, discovered that some of his officials and a group of distillers operating as a "whiskey ring" were cheating the government out of taxes by filing false reports. Then a House investigation revealed that William W. Belknap, secretary of war, had accepted bribes to retain an Indian-post trader in office (the so-called Indian ring). Other, lesser scandals added to the growing impression that "Grantism" had brought rampant corruption to government.

The Greenback Question

Compounding Grant's, and the nation's, problems was a financial crisis, known as the Panic of 1873. It began with the failure of a leading investment banking firm, Jay Cooke and Company, which had invested too heavily in postwar railroad building. There had been panics before—in 1819, 1837, and 1857—but this was the worst one yet. The depression it produced lasted four years.

Debtors now pressured the government to redeem federal war bonds with greenbacks, paper currency of the sort printed during the Civil War, which would increase the amount of money in circulation. But Grant and most Republicans wanted a "sound" currency—based solidly on gold reserves—which would favor the interests of banks and other creditors. There was approximately $356 million in paper currency issued during the Civil War that was still in circulation. In 1873, the Treasury issued more in response to the panic. But in 1875, Republican leaders in Congress, in an effort to crush the greenback movement for good, passed the Specie Resumption Act. It provided that after January 1, 1879, the greenback dollars, whose value constantly fluctuated, would be redeemed by the government and replaced with new certificates, firmly pegged to the price of gold. The law satisfied creditors, who had worried that debts would be repaid in paper currency of uncertain value. But "resumption" made things more difficult for debtors, because the gold-based money supply could not easily expand.

In 1875, the "greenbackers," as the inflationists were called, formed their own political organization: the National Greenback Party. It was active in the next three presidential elections, but it failed to gain widespread support. It did, however, keep the money issue alive. The question of the proper composition of the currency was to remain one of the most controversial and enduring issues in late-nineteenth-century American politics.

Republican Diplomacy

The Johnson and Grant administrations achieved their greatest successes in foreign affairs. The accomplishments were the work not of the presidents themselves, who displayed little aptitude for diplomacy, but of two outstanding secretaries of state: William H. Seward, who had served Lincoln and who remained in office until 1869; and Hamilton Fish, who served throughout the two terms of the Grant administration.

An ardent expansionist, Seward acted with as much daring as the demands of Reconstruction politics and the Republican hatred of President Johnson would permit. Seward accepted a Russian offer to sell Alaska to the United States for $7.2 million, despite criticism from many who considered Alaska a frozen wasteland and derided it as "Seward's Folly." In 1867, Seward also engineered the American annexation of the tiny Midway Islands, west of Hawaii.

Hamilton Fish's first major challenge was resolving the longstanding controversy with England over the American claims that it had violated neutrality laws during the Civil War by permitting English shipyards to build ships (among them the *Alabama*) for the Confederacy. American demands that England pay for the damage these vessels had caused became known as the "*Alabama* claims." In 1871, after a number of failed efforts, Fish forged an agreement, the Treaty of Washington, which provided for international arbitration and in which Britain expressed regret for the escape of the *Alabama* from England.

THE ABANDONMENT OF RECONSTRUCTION

As the North grew increasingly preoccupied with its own political and economic problems, interest in Reconstruction began to wane. By the time Grant left office, Democrats had taken back (or, as white Southerners liked to put it, "redeemed") seven of the governments of the former Confederate states. For three other states—South Carolina, Louisiana, and Florida—the end of Reconstruction had to wait for the withdrawal of the last federal troops in 1877, a withdrawal that was the result of a long process of political bargaining and compromise at the national level.

The Southern States "Redeemed"

In the states where whites constituted a majority—the states of the upper South—overthrowing Republican control was relatively simple. By 1872, all but a handful of Southern whites had regained suffrage. Now a clear majority, they needed only to organize and elect their candidates.

In other states, where blacks were a majority or where the populations of the two races were almost equal, whites used intimidation and violence to undermine the Reconstruction regimes. Secret societies—the Ku Klux Klan, the Knights of the White Camellia, and others—used terrorism to frighten or physically bar blacks from voting or otherwise exercising citizenship. Paramilitary organizations –the Red Shirts and White Leagues—armed themselves to "police" elections and worked to force all white males to join the Democratic Party and to exclude all blacks from meaningful political activity. Strongest of all, however, was the simple weapon of economic pressure. Some planters refused to rent land to Republican blacks; storekeepers refused to extend them credit; employers refused to give them work.

The Republican Congress responded to this wave of repression with the Enforcement Acts of 1870 and 1871 (better know as the Ku Klux Klan Acts), which prohibited states from discriminating against voters on the basis of race and gave the national government the authority to supersede state courts and prosecute crimes by individuals under federal law—the first time the federal government had ever asserted that right. The laws also authorized the president to use federal troops to protect civil rights—a provision President Grant used in 1871 in nine counties of South Carolina. The Enforcement Acts, although seldom used, discouraged Klan violence, which declined by 1872.

Waning Northern Commitment

But this Northern commitment to civil rights in the South did not last very long. Southern blacks were gradually losing the support of many of their former advocates in the North. After the adoption of the Fifteenth Amendment in 1870, some reformers convinced themselves that their long campaign on behalf of black people was now over, that with the vote blacks ought to be able to take care of themselves. Former Radical leaders such as Charles Sumner and Horace Greeley now began calling themselves Liberals, cooperating with the Democrats, and denouncing what they viewed as black-and-carpetbag misgovernment. Within the South itself, many white Republicans now moved into the Democratic Party.

The Panic of 1873 further undermined support for Reconstruction. In the congressional elections of 1874, the Democrats won control of the House of Representatives for the first time since 1861. Grant took note of the changing temper of the North and reduced the use of military force to prop up the Republican regimes in the South.

By the end of 1876, only three states were left in the hands of the Republicans—South Carolina, Louisiana, and Florida. In the state elections that year, Democrats (after using terrorist tactics) claimed victory in all three. But the Republicans claimed victory as well and were able to remain in office because of the presence of federal troops. If the troops were to be withdrawn, the last of the Republican regimes would fall.

The Compromise of 1877

Grant had hoped to run for another term in 1876, but most Republican leaders—shaken by recent Democratic successes, afraid of the scandals with which Grant was associated, and worried about the president's failing health—resisted. Instead, they settled on Rutherford B. Hayes, a former Union army officer and congressman, three-time governor of Ohio, and a champion of civil service reform. The Democrats united behind Samuel J. Tilden, the reform governor of New York, who had been instrumental in overthrowing the corrupt Tweed Ring of New York City's Tammany Hall.

Although the campaign was a bitter one, there were few differences of principle between the candidates. The November election produced an apparent Democratic victory. Tilden carried the South and several large Northern states, and his popular margin over Hayes was nearly 300,000

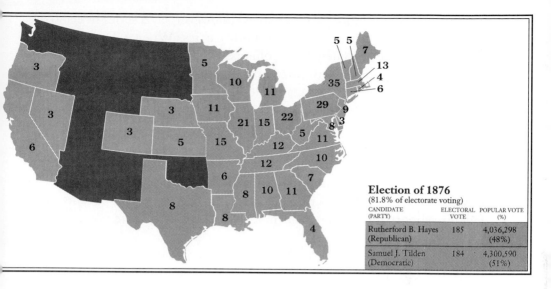

Election of 1876
(81.8% of electorate voting)

CANDIDATE (PARTY)	ELECTORAL VOTE	POPULAR VOTE (%)
Rutherford B. Hayes (Republican)	185	4,036,298 (48%)
Samuel J. Tilden (Democratic)	184	4,300,590 (51%)

votes. But disputed returns from Louisiana, South Carolina, Florida, and Oregon, whose electoral votes totaled 20, threw the election in doubt. Tilden had undisputed claim to 184 electoral votes, only one short of the majority. But Hayes could still win if he managed to receive all 20 disputed votes.

The Constitution had established no method to determine the validity of disputed returns. The decision clearly lay with Congress, but it was not clear with which house or through what method. (The Senate was Republican, and the House was Democratic.) Members of each party naturally supported a solution that would yield them the victory. Finally, late in January 1877, Congress tried to break the deadlock by creating a special electoral commission composed of five senators, five representatives, and five justices of the Supreme Court. The congressional delegation would consist of five Republicans and five Democrats. The Court delegation would include two Republicans, two Democrats, and the only independent, Justice David Davis. But when the Illinois legislature elected Davis to the United States Senate, the justice resigned from the commission. His seat went instead to a Republican justice. The commission voted along straight party lines, 8 to 7, awarding every disputed vote to Hayes. Congress accepted the verdict on March 2. Two days later, Hayes was inaugurated.

Behind the resolution of the deadlock, however, lay a series of elaborate compromises among leaders of both parties. When a Democratic filibuster threatened to derail the commission's report, Republican Senate leaders met secretly with Southern Democratic leaders to work out terms by which the Democrats would support Hayes. As the price of their cooperation, the Southern Democrats (among them some former Whigs) exacted several pledges from the Republicans: the appointment of at least one Southerner to the Hayes cabinet, control of federal patronage in their areas, generous internal improvements, federal aid for the Texas and Pacific Railroad, and withdrawal of the troops. Many powerful Southern Democrats believed that Republican programs of federal support for business and industry would help their region develop economically.

In his inaugural address, Hayes announced that the South's most pressing need was the restoration of "wise, honest, and peaceful local self-government," and he soon withdrew the troops and let white Democrats take over the remaining southern state governments. That produced charges that he was paying off the South for acquiescing in his election and strengthened the widespread characterization of him as "His Fraudulency." But the election had already created such bitterness that not even Hayes's promise to serve only one term could mollify his critics.

The president and his party hoped to build up a "new Republican" organization in the South drawn from Whiggish conservative white groups and committed to modest support for black rights. But all such efforts failed. Although many white Southern leaders sympathized with Republican economic policies, resentment of Reconstruction was so deep that supporting the party was politically impossible. The "solid" Democratic South, which would survive until the mid-twentieth century, was taking shape.

The Legacy of Reconstruction

Reconstruction made important contributions to the efforts of former slaves to achieve dignity and equality in American life. There was a significant redistribution of income, from which blacks benefited. There was a more limited but not unimportant redistribution of landownership, which enabled some former slaves to acquire property. Perhaps most important, there was a large, and largely successful, effort by

African Americans themselves to carve out a society and culture of their own within the American South, to create or strengthen their own institutions, and to convince themselves that they were, indeed, no longer slaves.

In addition, Reconstruction was not as disastrous an experience for Southern white elites as most believed at the time. Within little more than a decade after the end of a devastating war, the white South had regained control of its own institutions and, to a great extent, restored its traditional ruling class to power. Former Confederate leaders received no severe punishments. The federal government imposed no drastic economic reforms on the region, and indeed few lasting political changes of any kind other than the abolition of slavery. Not many conquered peoples have fared as well.

But Reconstruction was also notable for its limitations. For in those years the United States failed in its first serious effort to resolve its oldest and deepest social problem—the problem of race. What was more, the experience so disappointed, disillusioned, and embittered white Americans that it would be nearly a century before they would try again in any serious way to end racism.

Given the odds confronting them, however, African Americans had reason for considerable pride in the gains they were able to make during Reconstruction. And future generations could be grateful for two great charters of freedom—the Fourteenth and Fifteenth Amendments to the Constitution—which, although widely ignored at the time, would one day serve as the basis for a "Second Reconstruction" that would renew the drive to bring freedom to all Americans.

THE NEW SOUTH

The agreement between southern Democrats and northern Republicans that helped settle the disputed election of 1876 was supposed to be the first step toward developing a stable, permanent Republican Party in the South. In that respect, at least, it failed. In the years following the end of Reconstruction, white southerners established the Democratic Party as the only viable political organization for the region's whites. Even so, the South did change in the years after Reconstruction in some of the ways the framers of the Compromise of 1877 had hoped.

"IS THIS A REPUBLICAN FORM OF GOVERNMENT?" The New York artist and cartoonist Thomas Nast marked the end of Reconstruction in 1876 with this biting cartoon in *Harper's Weekly*, expressing his dismay at what he considered the nation's betrayal of the former slaves, who still had not received adequate guarantees of their rights. The caption of the carton continued: "Is *this* protecting life, liberty, or property? Is *this* equal protection of the laws?"

The "Redeemers"

Many white southerners rejoiced at the restoration of what they liked to call "home rule" after the last of the Reconstruction regimes fell in 1877. But in reality, political power in the region was soon more restricted than at any time since the Civil War. Once again, the South fell under the control of a powerful, conservative oligarchy, whose members were known variously as the "Redeemers" or the "Bourbons."

In some places, this post-Reconstruction ruling class was much the same as the ruling class of the antebellum period. In Alabama, for example, the old planter elite—despite challenges from new merchant and industrial forces—retained much of its former power and continued largely to dominate the state for decades. In other areas, however, the Redeemers constituted a genuinely new ruling class. They were merchants, industrialists, railroad developers, and financiers. Some of them were former planters, some of them northern immigrants who had been absorbed into the region's life, some of them ambitious, upwardly mobile white southerners from the region's lower social tiers. They combined a commitment to "home rule" and social conservatism with a commitment to economic development.

The various Bourbon governments of the New South behaved in many respects quite similarly. Virtually all the new Democratic regimes lowered taxes, reduced spending, and drastically diminished state services. One state after another eliminated or reduced its support for public school systems.

Industrialization and the "New South"

Many white southern leaders in the post-Reconstruction era hoped to see their region become the home of a vigorous industrial economy, a "New South." Henry Grady, editor of the *Atlanta Constitution*, and other New South advocates seldom challenged white supremacy, but they did advocate other important changes in southern values. Above all, they promoted the virtues of thrift, industry, and progress—qualities that prewar southerners had often denounced in northern society.

Southern industry did expand dramatically in the years after Reconstruction. Most visible was the growth in textile manufacturing, which increased ninefold in the last twenty years of the century. In the past, southern planters had usually shipped their cotton out of the region to manufacturers in the North or in Europe. Now textile factories appeared in the South itself—many of them drawn to the region from New England by the abundance of water power, the ready supply of cheap labor, the low taxes, and the accommodating conservative governments. The tobacco-processing industry, similarly, established an important foothold in the region. In the lower South, and particularly in Birmingham, Alabama, the iron (and, later, steel) industry grew rapidly. By 1890, the southern iron and steel industry represented nearly a fifth of the nation's total capacity.

Railroad development also increased substantially in the post-Reconstruction years—at a rate far greater than that of the nation at large.

Between 1880 and 1890, trackage in the South more than doubled. And in 1886, the South changed the gauge (width) of its trackage to correspond with the standards of the North. No longer would it be necessary for cargoes heading into the South to be transferred from one train to another at the borders of the region.

Yet southern industry developed within strict limits, and its effects on the region were never even remotely comparable to the effects of industrialization on the North. The southern share of national manufacturing doubled in the last twenty years of the century, but it was still only 10 percent of the total. The region's per capita income increased 21 percent in the same period, but average income in the South was still only 40 percent of that in the North; in 1860 it had been more than 60 percent. And even in those industries where development had been most rapid—textiles, iron, railroads—much of the capital had come from, and many of the profits thus flowed to, the North.

The growth of industry in the South required the region to recruit a substantial industrial work force for the first time. From the beginning, a high percentage of the factory workers (and an especially high percentage of textile workers) were women. Heavy male casualties in the Civil War had helped create a large population of unmarried women who desperately needed employment. Factories also hired entire families, many of whom moved into towns from failed farms. Hours were long (often as much as twelve hours a day), and wages were far below the northern equivalent; indeed, one of the greatest attractions of the South to industrialists was that employers were able to pay workers there as little as one-half what northern workers received. Life in most mill towns was rigidly controlled by the owners and managers of the factories. They rigorously suppressed attempts at protest or union organization. Company stores sold goods to workers at inflated prices and issued credit at exorbitant rates (much like country stores in agrarian areas), and mill owners ensured that no competing merchants were able to establish themselves in the community.

Some industries, such as textiles, offered virtually no opportunities to African-American workers. Others—tobacco, iron, and lumber, for example—did provide some employment for blacks, usually the most menial and lowest-paid positions. Some mill towns, therefore, were places where the black and white cultures came into close contact. This juxtaposition of cultures inhibited the growth of racial harmony and increased the determination of white leaders to take additional measures to protect white supremacy.

Tenants and Sharecroppers

Despite significant growth in southern industry, the region remained primarily agrarian. The most important economic reality in the post-Reconstruction South, therefore, was the impoverished state of agriculture. The 1870s and 1880s saw an acceleration of the process that had begun in the immediate postwar years: the imposition of systems of tenantry and debt peonage on much of the region; the reliance on a few cash crops rather than on a diversified agricultural system; and increasing absentee ownership of valuable farmlands. During Reconstruction, perhaps a third or more of the farmers in the South were tenants; by 1900 the figure had increased to 70 percent.

Tenantry, which now dominated Southern agriculture, took several forms. Farmers who owned tools, equipment, and farm animals—or who had the money to buy them—usually paid an annual cash rent for their land. But many farmers (including most black ones) had no money or equipment at all. Landlords would supply them with land, a crude house, a few tools, seed, and sometimes a mule. In return, the farmers would promise the landlord a large share of the annual crop. After paying their landlords and their local furnishing merchants (who were often the same people), these "sharecroppers" seldom had anything left to sell on their own.

African Americans and the New South

The "New South creed" was not the property of whites alone. Many African Americans were attracted to the vision of progress and self-improvement as well. Some blacks succeeded in elevating themselves into a distinct middle class—even if one far less prosperous than the white middle class. These were former slaves (and, as the decades passed, their offspring) who managed to acquire property, establish small businesses, or enter professions. This rising group of African Americans believed strongly that education was vital to the future of their people, and they expanded the network of black colleges and institutes that had taken root during Reconstruction into an important educational system.

TUSKEGEE INSTITUTE, 1881 From these modest beginnings, Booker T. Washington's Tuskegee Institute in Alabama became the preeminent academy offering technical and industrial training to black men. It deliberately de-emphasized the traditional liberal arts curricula of most colleges. Washington considered such training less important than developing practical skills.

The chief spokesman for this commitment to education, and for a time the most prominent spokesman for black people as a whole, was Booker T. Washington, founder and president of the Tuskegee Institute in Alabama. Born into slavery, Washington had worked his way out of poverty after acquiring an education (at Virginia's Hampton Institute). He urged other blacks to follow the same road to self-improvement.

Washington's message was both cautious and hopeful. African Americans should attend school, learn skills, and establish a solid footing in agriculture and the trades. Industrial, not classical, education should be their goal. Blacks should, moreover, refine their speech, improve their dress, and adopt habits of thrift and personal cleanliness; they should, in short, adopt the standards of the white middle class. Only thus, he claimed, could they win the respect of the white population, the prerequisite for any larger social gains.

In a famous speech in Georgia in 1895, Washington outlined a controversial philosophy of race relations that became widely known as the Atlanta Compromise. Blacks, he said, should forgo agitating for political rights and concentrate on self-improvement and preparation for equality. If blacks were ever to win the rights and privileges of citizenship, they must first show that they were "prepared for the exercise of these privileges." Washington offered a powerful challenge to those whites who wanted to discourage African Americans from acquiring an education or winning any economic gains. But his message was also intended to assure whites that blacks would not challenge the system of segregation, which southern governments were in the process of creating.

The Birth of Jim Crow

Few white southerners had ever accepted the idea of racial equality. That the former slaves acquired any legal and political rights at all after emancipation was in large part the result of their own efforts and critical federal support. That outside support all but vanished after 1877, when federal troops withdrew and the Supreme Court stripped the Fourteenth and Fifteenth Amendments of much of their significance. In the so-called civil rights cases of 1883, the Court ruled that the Fourteenth Amendment prohibited state governments from discriminating against people because of race but did not restrict private organizations or individuals from doing so. Thus railroads, hotels, theaters, and the like could legally practice segregation.

Eventually, the Court also validated state legislation that institutionalized the separation of the races. In *Plessy v. Ferguson* (1896), a case involving a Louisiana law that required separate seating arrangements for the races on railroads, the Court held that separate accommodations did not deprive blacks of equal rights if the accommodations were equal, a decision that survived for years as part of the legal basis of segregated schools. In *Cumming v. County Board of Education* (1899), the Court ruled that communities could establish schools for whites only, even if there were no comparable schools for blacks.

Even before these decisions, white southerners were working to separate the races to the greatest extent possible. They were particularly determined to strip African Americans of the right to vote. In some states, disfranchisement had begun almost as soon as Reconstruction ended. But in other areas, black voting continued for some time after Reconstruction—largely because conservative whites believed they could control the black electorate and use it to beat back the attempts of poor white farmers to take control of the Democratic Party.

In the 1890s, however, franchise restrictions became much more rigid. During those years, some small white farmers began to demand complete black disfranchisement—because they objected to the black vote being used against them by the Bourbons. At the same time, many members of the conservative elite began to fear that poor whites might unite politically with poor blacks to challenge them. They too began to support further franchise restrictions.

In devising laws to disfranchise black males (black females, like white women, had never voted), the southern states had to find ways to evade the Fifteenth Amendment, which prohibited states from denying anyone the right to vote because of race. Two devices emerged before 1900 to accomplish this goal. One was the poll tax or some form of property qualification; few blacks were prosperous enough to meet such requirements. Another was the "literacy" or "understanding" test, which required voters to demonstrate an ability to read and to interpret the Constitution. Even those African Americans who could read had a hard time passing the difficult test white officials gave them. The laws affected poor white voters as well as blacks. By the late 1890s, the black vote had decreased by 62 percent, the white vote by 26 percent. The Supreme Court proved as compliant in upholding the disfranchising laws as it was in dealing with the civil rights cases.

Laws restricting the franchise and segregating schools were only part of a network of state and local statutes—known as the Jim Crow laws—that by the first years of the twentieth century had institutionalized an elaborate system of segregation reaching into almost every area of southern life. Blacks and whites could not ride together in the same railroad cars, sit in the same waiting rooms, use the same washrooms, eat in the same restaurants, or sit in the same theaters. Blacks had no access to many public parks, beaches, or picnic areas; they could not be patients in many hospitals. Much of the new legal structure did no more than confirm what had already been widespread social practice in the South since well before the end of Reconstruction. But the Jim Crow laws also stripped blacks of many of the modest social, economic, and political gains they had made in the more fluid atmosphere of the late nineteenth century.

More than legal efforts were involved in this process. The 1890s witnessed a dramatic increase in white violence against blacks, which, along with the Jim Crow laws, served to inhibit black agitation for equal rights. The worst such violence—lynching of blacks by white mobs, either because the victims were accused of crimes or because they had seemed somehow to violate their proper station—reached appalling levels. In the nation as a whole in the 1890s, there was an average of 187 lynchings each year, more than 80 percent of them in the South. The vast majority of victims were black. Those involved in lynchings often saw their actions as a legitimate form of law enforcement, and some victims of lynchings had in fact committed crimes. But lynchings were also a means by which whites controlled the black population through terror and intimidation.

The rise of lynchings shocked the conscience of many white Americans in a way that other forms of racial injustice did not. In 1892 Ida B. Wells, a committed black journalist, launched what became an international antilynching movement with a series of impassioned articles after the lynching of three of her friends in Memphis, Tennessee, her home. The movement gradually gathered strength in the first years of the twentieth century, attracting substantial support from whites in both the North and South (particularly from white women). Its goal was a federal antilynching law, which would allow the national government to do what state and local governments in the South were generally unwilling to do: punish those responsible for lynchings.

But the substantial southern white opposition to lynchings stood as an exception to the general white support for suppression of African Americans. Indeed, just as in the antebellum period, the shared commitment to white supremacy helped dilute class animosities between poorer whites and the Bourbon oligarchies. Economic issues tended to play a secondary role to race in southern politics, distracting people from the glaring social inequalities that afflicted blacks and whites alike. The commitment to white supremacy, in short, was a burden for poor whites as well as for blacks.

CONCLUSION

Reconstruction, long remembered by many whites as a vindictive outrage or a tragic failure, was a profoundly important moment in American history. Despite the bitter political battles in Washington and throughout the South, culminating in the unsuccessful effort to remove President Andrew

Johnson from office, the most important result of the effort to reunite the nation after its long and bloody war was a reshaping of the lives of ordinary people in all regions of the nation.

In the North, Reconstruction solidified the power of the Republican Party and ensured that public policy would support the continued growth of an advanced industrial economy. The rapid expansion of the northern economy continued and accelerated, drawing more and more of its residents into a burgeoning commercial world.

In the South, Reconstruction did more than simply bring slavery to an end. It fundamentally rearranged the relationship between the region's white and black citizens. Only for a while did Reconstruction permit African Americans to participate actively and effectively in southern politics. After a few years of widespread black voting and significant black officeholding, the forces of white supremacy forced most African Americans to the margins of the southern political world, where they would mostly remain until the 1960s.

In other ways, the lives of southern blacks changed dramatically. Overwhelmingly, they left the plantations. Some sought work in towns and cities. Some left the region altogether. But the great majority began farming on small farms of their own—not as landowners, except in rare cases, but as tenants and sharecroppers on land owned by whites. The result was a form of economic bondage, driven by debt, only scarcely less oppressive than the legal bondage of slavery. Within this system, however, African Americans managed to carve out a much larger sphere of social and cultural activity than they had ever been able to create under slavery. Black churches proliferated in great numbers. African-American schools emerged in some communities, and black colleges began to operate in the region. Some former slaves owned businesses and flourished. In southern cities and towns, a fledgling black middle class began to emerge.

The system of tenantry, which emerged in the course of Reconstruction, continued after its end to dominate the southern economy. Strenuous efforts by "New South" advocates to advance industry and commerce in the region produced significant results in a few areas. But the South on the whole remained what it had always been: an overwhelmingly rural society with a sharply defined class structure. It was also a region with a deep commitment among its white citizens to the subordination of African Americans—a commitment solidified in the 1890s and the early twentieth century when white southerners erected an elaborate legal system of segregation (the "Jim Crow" laws). The promise of the great Reconstruction amendments to the Constitution—the Fourteenth and Fifteenth—remained largely unfulfilled in the South as the century drew to its close.

FOR FURTHER REFERENCE

Suggested Readings

Eric Foner, *Reconstruction: America's Unfinished Revolution, 1863–1877* (1988), the most important modern synthesis of Reconstruction scholarship, emphasizes the radicalism of Reconstruction and the agency of freedpeople in the process of political and economic renovation. Eric McKitrick, *Andrew Johnson and Reconstruction* (1960) is a classic study of the national political battles over Reconstruction. Leon Litwack, *Been in the Storm So Long: The Aftermath of Slavery* (1979) is an excellent examination of the immediate consequences of emancipation. Thomas Holt, *Black over White: Negro Political Leadership in South Carolina During Reconstruction* (1977) examines Reconstruction in the state where black political power reached its apex. Jacqueline Jones, *Soldiers of Light and Love: Northern Teachers and Georgia Blacks, 1865–1873* (1980) is a study of the interaction between northern white women and freedpeople. C. Vann Woodward, *Origins of the New South* (1951), still the leading work on the history of the South after Reconstruction after forty years, argues that a rising middle class defined the economic and political transformation of the New South. Jonathan Wiener, *Social Origins of the New South: Alabama, 1860–1885* (1978) offers an alternative view of the origins of the New South. Edward Ayers, *The Promise of the New South* (1992) offers a rich portrait of social and cultural life in the New South. Steven Hahn, *The Roots of Southern Populism: Yeoman Farmers and the Transformation of the Georgia Upcountry* (1983) argues that southern farmers experienced an erosion of autonomy in the years after the Civil War, and their increasing discontent with market relations helped produce the populist revolt of the 1890s. Roger L. Ransom and Richard Sutch, *One Kind of Freedom: The Economic Consequences of Emancipation* (1977) explores the emergence of the crop-lien system. C. Vann Woodward, *The Strange Career of Jim Crow* (rev. 1974) claims that segregation emerged only gradually across the South after Reconstruction. The "Woodward Thesis" has been challenged by, among others, Joel Williamson, *After Slavery: The Negro in South Carolina During Reconstruction* (1965); John W. Cell, *The Highest Stage of White Supremacy: The Origins of Segregation in South Africa and the American South* (1982); and Howard N. Rabinowitz, *Race Relations in the Urban South, 1865–1890* (1978). J. Morgan Kousser, *The Shaping of Southern Politics: Suffrage Restriction and the Establishment of the One-Party South, 1880–1910* (1974) is an important quantitative study of the effects of disfranchisement.

Films

(The best source for information on how to find these and other films is *Bowker's Complete Video Directory*—3 volumes.) *The American Story, No. 14: Reconstruction* and *No. 14: Rebuilding the Union* (1985) detail the effects of Lincoln's assassination and the course of Reconstruction under the Grant Administration. *Reconstructing the South*, featuring Eric Foner, highlights the difficult social, political, and economic adjustments of the postwar era. *Reconstruction & Segregation 1870–1910* (1996) follows race relations from the assassination of Lincoln through the rise of the Ku Klux Klan and the imposition of Jim Crow. *The Civil War: Promise of Reconstruction* (1972) focuses on the Port Royal "experiment" in South Carolina.

Internet Resources

Internet websites containing historical material relevant to the subjects discussed in this chapter can be reached through the McGraw-Hill history site at www.mhhe.com/socscience/history/usa/link/linktop.htm.

APPENDIXES

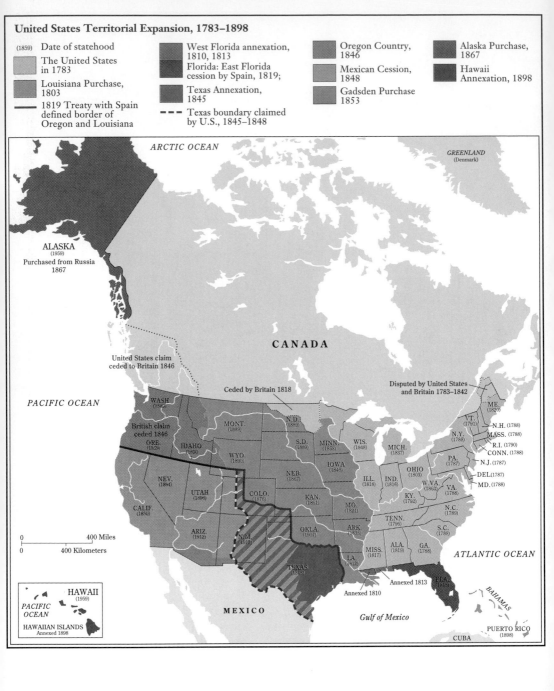

United States Territorial Expansion, 1783–1898

(1859) Date of statehood

The United States in 1783

Louisiana Purchase, 1803

1819 Treaty with Spain defined border of Oregon and Louisiana

West Florida annexation, 1810, 1813

Florida: East Florida cession by Spain, 1819;

Texas Annexation, 1845

Texas boundary claimed by U.S., 1845–1848

Oregon Country, 1846

Mexican Cession, 1848

Gadsden Purchase 1853

Alaska Purchase, 1867

Hawaii Annexation, 1898

ARCTIC OCEAN

GREENLAND
(Denmark)

ALASKA
(1959)
Purchased from Russia
1867

CANADA

United States claim
ceded to Britain 1846

Ceded by Britain 1818

Disputed by United States
and Britain 1783–1842

PACIFIC OCEAN

WASH.
(1889)

British claim
ceded 1846

ORE.
(1859)

IDAHO
(1890)

MONT.
(1889)

N.D.
(1889)

WIS.
(1848)

MICH.
(1837)

VT.
(1791)

ME.
(1820)

N.H. (1788)

MASS. (1788)

R.I. (1790)

N.Y.
(1788)

CONN. (1788)

N.J. (1787)

PA.
(1787)

DEL (1787)

MD. (1788)

S.D.
(1889)

MINN.
(1858)

IOWA
(1846)

OHIO
(1803)

IND.
(1816)

ILL.
(1818)

W.VA.
(1863)

VA.
(1788)

WYO.
(1890)

NEV.
(1864)

UTAH
(1896)

NEB.
(1867)

KY.
(1792)

COLO.
(1876)

KAN.
(1861)

MO.
(1821)

TENN.
(1796)

N.C.
(1789)

CALIF.
(1850)

ARIZ.
(1912)

N.M.
(1912)

OKLA.
(1907)

ARK.
(1836)

S.C.
(1788)

MISS.
(1817)

ALA.
(1819)

GA.
(1788)

TEXAS
(1845)

LA.
(1812)

ATLANTIC OCEAN

FLA.
(1845)

BAHAMAS

Annexed 1813

Annexed 1810

MEXICO

Gulf of Mexico

PUERTO RICO
(1898)

CUBA

0   400 Miles

0   400 Kilometers

HAWAII
(1959)

PACIFIC
OCEAN

HAWAIIAN ISLANDS
Annexed 1898

Documents and Tables

THE DECLARATION OF INDEPENDENCE

In Congress, July 4, 1776,

THE UNANIMOUS DECLARATION OF THE THIRTEEN UNITED STATES OF AMERICA

When, in the course of human events, it becomes necessary for one people to dissolve the political bands which have connected them with another, and to assume, among the powers of the earth, the separate and equal station to which the laws of nature and of nature's God entitle them, a decent respect to the opinions of mankind requires that they should declare the causes which impel them to the separation.

    We hold these truths to be self-evident, that all men are created equal; that they are endowed by their Creator with certain unalienable rights; that among these, are life, liberty, and the pursuit of happiness. That, to secure these rights, governments are instituted among men, deriving their just powers from the consent of the governed; that, whenever any form of government becomes destructive of these ends, it is the right of the people to alter or to abolish it, and to institute a new government, laying its foundation on such principles, and organizing its powers in such form, as to them shall seem most likely to effect their safety and happiness. Prudence, indeed, will dictate that governments long established, should not be changed for light and transient causes; and, accordingly, all experience hath shown, that mankind are more disposed to suffer, while evils are sufferable, than to right themselves by abolishing the forms to which they are accustomed. But, when a long train of abuses and usurpations, pursuing invariably the same object, evinces a design to reduce them under absolute despotism, it is their right, it is their duty, to throw off such government and to provide new guards for their future security. Such has been the patient sufferance of these colonies, and such is now the necessity which constrains them to alter their former systems of government. The history of the present King of Great Britain is a history of repeated injuries and usurpations, all having, in direct object, the establishment of an absolute tyranny over these States. To prove this, let facts be submitted to a candid world:

He has refused his assent to laws the most wholesome and necessary for the public good.

He has forbidden his governors to pass laws of immediate and pressing importance, unless suspended in their operation till his assent should be obtained; and, when so suspended, he has utterly neglected to attend to them.

He has refused to pass other laws for the accommodation of large districts of people, unless those people would relinquish the right of representation in the legislature; a right inestimable to them, and formidable to tyrants only.

He has called together legislative bodies at places unusual, uncomfortable, and distant from the depository of their public records, for the sole purpose of fatiguing them into compliance with his measures.

He has dissolved representative houses repeatedly for opposing, with manly firmness, his invasions on the rights of the people.

He has refused, for a long time after such dissolutions, to cause others to be elected; whereby the legislative powers, incapable of annihilation, have returned to the people at large for their exercise; the state remaining, in the meantime, exposed to all the danger of invasion from without, and convulsions within.

He has endeavored to prevent the population of these States; for that purpose, obstructing the laws for naturalization of foreigners, refusing to pass others to encourage their migration hither, and raising the conditions of new appropriations of lands.

He has obstructed the administration of justice, by refusing his assent to laws for establishing judiciary powers.

He has made judges dependent on his will alone, for the tenure of their offices, and the amount and payment of their salaries.

He has erected a multitude of new offices, and sent hither swarms of officers to harass our people, and eat out their substance.

He has kept among us, in time of peace, standing armies, without the consent of our legislatures.

He has affected to render the military independent of, and superior to, the civil power.

He has combined, with others, to subject us to a jurisdiction foreign to our Constitution, and unacknowledged by our laws; giving his assent to their acts of pretended legislation:

For quartering large bodies of armed troops among us:

For protecting them by a mock trial, from punishment, for any murders which they should commit on the inhabitants of these States:

For cutting off our trade with all parts of the world:

For imposing taxes on us without our consent:

For depriving us, in many cases, of the benefit of trial by jury:

For transporting us beyond seas to be tried for pretended offences:

For abolishing the free system of English laws in a neighboring province, establishing therein an arbitrary government, and enlarging its boundaries, so as to render it at once an example and fit instrument for introducing the same absolute rule into these colonies:

For taking away our charters, abolishing our most valuable laws, and altering, fundamentally, the powers of our governments:

For suspending our own legislatures, and declaring themselves invested with power to legislate for us in all cases whatsoever.

He has abdicated government here, by declaring us out of his protection, and waging war against us.

He has plundered our seas, ravaged our coasts, burnt our towns, and destroyed the lives of our people.

He is, at this time, transporting large armies of foreign mercenaries to complete the works of death, desolation, and tyranny, already begun, with circumstances of cruelty and perfidy scarcely paralleled in the most barbarous ages, and totally unworthy the head of a civilized nation.

He has constrained our fellow citizens, taken captive on the high seas, to bear arms against their country, to become the executioners of their friends, and brethren, or to fall themselves by their hands.

He has excited domestic insurrections amongst us, and has endeavored to bring on the inhabitants of our frontiers, the merciless Indian savages, whose known rule of warfare is an undistinguished destruction of all ages, sexes, and conditions.

In every stage of these oppressions, we have petitioned for redress, in the most humble terms; our repeated petitions have been answered only by repeated injury. A prince, whose character is thus marked by every act which may define a tyrant, is unfit to be the ruler of a free people.

Nor have we been wanting in attention to our British brethren. We have warned them, from time to time, of attempts made by their legislature to extend an unwarrantable jurisdiction over us. We have reminded them of the circumstances of our emigration and settlement here. We have appealed to their native justice and magnanimity, and we have conjured them, by the ties of our common kindred, to disavow these usurpations, which would inevitably interrupt our connections and correspondence. They, too, have been deaf to the voice of justice and consanguinity. We must, therefore, acquiesce in the necessity which denounces our separation, and hold them as we hold the rest of mankind, enemies in war, in peace, friends.

We, therefore, the representatives of the United States of America, in general Congress assembled, appealing to the Supreme Judge of the world for the rectitude of our intentions, do, in the name, and by the authority of the good people of these colonies, solemnly publish and declare, that these united colonies are, and of right ought to be, free and independent states: that they are absolved from all allegiance to the British Crown, and that all political connection between them and the state of Great Britain is, and ought to be, totally dissolved; and that, as free and independent states, they have full power to levy war, conclude peace, contract alliances, establish commerce, and to do all other acts and things which independent states may of right do. And, for the support of this declaration, with a firm reliance on the protection of Divine Providence, we mutually pledge to each other our lives, our fortunes, and our sacred honor.

The foregoing Declaration was, by order of Congress, engrossed, and signed by the following members:

John Hancock

New Hampshire	*Massachusetts Bay*	*Rhode Island*
Josiah Bartlett	Samuel Adams	Stephen Hopkins
William Whipple	John Adams	William Ellery
Matthew Thornton	Robert Treat Paine	
	Elbridge Gerry	

Connecticut
Roger Sherman
Samuel Huntington
William Williams
Oliver Wolcott

New York
William Floyd
Philip Livingston
Francis Lewis
Lewis Morris

New Jersey
Richard Stockton
John Witherspoon
Francis Hopkinson
John Hart
Abraham Clark

Pennsylvania
Robert Morris
Benjamin Rush
Benjamin Franklin
John Morton
George Clymer
James Smith
George Taylor
James Wilson
George Ross

Delaware
Caesar Rodney
George Read
Thomas M'Kean

Maryland
Samuel Chase
William Paca
Thomas Stone
Charles Carroll,
    of Carrollton

Virginia
George Wythe
Richard Henry Lee
Thomas Jefferson
Benjamin Harrison
Thomas Nelson, Jr.
Francis Lightfoot Lee
Carter Braxton

North Carolina
William Hooper
Joseph Hewes
John Penn

South Carolina
Edward Rutledge
Thomas Heyward, Jr.
Thomas Lynch, Jr.
Arthur Middleton

Georgia
Button Gwinnett
Lyman Hall
George Walton

Resolved, That copies of the Declaration be sent to the several assemblies, conventions, and committees, or councils of safety, and to the several commanding officers of the continental troops; that it be proclaimed in each of the United States, at the head of the army.

THE CONSTITUTION
OF THE UNITED STATES[1]

We the People of the United States, in Order to form a more perfect Union, establish Justice, insure domestic Tranquility, provide for the common defence, promote the general Welfare, and secure the Blessings of Liberty to ourselves and our Posterity, do ordain and establish this CONSTITUTION for the United States of America.

Article I

Section 1.
All legislative Powers herein granted shall be vested in a Congress of the United States, which shall consist of a Senate and House of Representatives.

Section 2.
The House of Representatives shall be composed of Members chosen every second Year by the People of the several States, and the Electors in each State shall have the Qualifications requisite for Electors of the most numerous Branch of the State Legislature.

No Person shall be a Representative who shall not have attained to the Age of twenty-five Years, and been seven Years a Citizen of the United States, and who shall not, when elected, be an Inhabitant of that State in which he shall be chosen.

[Representatives and direct Taxes[2] shall be apportioned among the several States which may be included within this Union, according to their respective Numbers, which shall be determined by adding to the whole Number of free Persons, including those bound to Service for a Term of Years, and excluding Indians not taxed, three fifths of all other Persons.][3] The actual Enumeration shall be made within three Years after the first Meeting of the Congress of the United States, and within every subsequent Term of ten Years, in such Manner as they shall by Law direct. The Number of Representatives shall not exceed one for every thirty Thousand, but each State shall have at Least one Representative; and until such enumeration shall be made, the State of New Hampshire shall be entitled to chuse three, Massachusetts eight, Rhode-Island and Providence Plantations one, Connecticut five, New York six, New Jersey four, Pennsylvania eight, Delaware one,

---

[1] This version, which follows the original Constitution in capitalization and spelling, was published by the United States Department of the Interior, Office of Education, in 1935.
[2] Altered by the Sixteenth Amendment.
[3] Negated by the Fourteenth Amendment.

Maryland six, Virginia ten, North Carolina five, South Carolina five, and Georgia three.

When vacancies happen in the Representation from any State, the Executive Authority thereof shall issue Writs of Election to fill such Vacancies.

The House of Representatives shall chuse their Speaker and other Officers; and shall have the sole Power of Impeachment.

Section 3.

The Senate of the United States shall be composed of two Senators from each State, chosen by the Legislature thereof, for six Years; and each Senator shall have one Vote.

Immediately after they shall be assembled in Consequence of the first Election, they shall be divided as equally as may be into three Classes. The Seats of the Senators of the first Class shall be vacated at the Expiration of the second Year, of the second Class at the Expiration of the fourth Year, and of the third Class at the Expiration of the sixth Year, so that one-third may be chosen every second Year; and if Vacancies happen by Resignation, or otherwise, during the Recess of the Legislature of any State, the Executive thereof may make temporary Appointments until the next Meeting of the Legislature, which shall then fill such Vacancies.

No Person shall be a Senator who shall not have attained to the Age of thirty Years, and been nine Years a Citizen of the United States, and who shall not, when elected, be an Inhabitant of that State for which he shall be chosen.

The Vice President of the United States shall be President of the Senate, but shall have no vote, unless they be equally divided.

The Senate shall chuse their other Officers, and also a President pro tempore, in the absence of the Vice President, or when he shall exercise the Office of President of the United States.

The Senate shall have the sole Power to try all Impeachments. When sitting for that purpose they shall be on Oath or Affirmation. When the President of the United States is tried, the Chief Justice shall preside: And no person shall be convicted without the Concurrence of two thirds of the Members present.

Judgment in Cases of Impeachment shall not extend further than to removal from Office, and disqualification to hold and enjoy any Office of honor, Trust, or Profit under the United States: but the Party convicted shall nevertheless be liable and subject to Indictment, Trial, Judgment, and Punishment, according to Law.

Section 4.

The Times, Places and Manner of holding Elections for Senators and Representatives, shall be prescribed in each State by the Legislature thereof; but the Congress may at any time by Law make or alter such Regulations, except as to the Places of Chusing Senators.

The Congress shall assemble at least once in every Year, and such Meeting shall be on the first Monday in December, unless they shall by Law appoint a different Day.

Section 5.

Each House shall be the Judge of the Elections, Returns and Qualifications of its own Members, and a Majority of each shall constitute a Quorum to do Business; but a smaller number may adjourn from day to day, and may be authorized to compel the Attendance of absent Members, in such Manner, and under such Penalties, as each House may provide.

Each House may determine the Rules of its Proceedings, punish its Members for disorderly Behaviour, and, with the Concurrence of two thirds, expel a Member.

Each House shall keep a Journal of its Proceedings, and from time to time publish the same, excepting such Parts as may in their Judgment require Secrecy; and the Yeas and Nays of the Members of either House on any question shall, at the Desire of one fifth of those Present, be entered on the Journal.

Neither House, during the Session of Congress, shall, without the Consent of the other, adjourn for more than three days, nor to any other Place than that in which the two Houses shall be sitting.

Section 6.

The Senators and Representatives shall receive a Compensation for their Services, to be ascertained by Law, and paid out of the Treasury of the United States. They shall in all Cases, except Treason, Felony, and Breach of the Peace, be privileged from Arrest during their Attendance at the Session of their respective Houses, and in going to and returning from the same; and for any Speech or Debate in either House, they shall not be questioned in any other Place.

No Senator or Representative shall, during the Time for which he was elected, be appointed to any civil Office under the Authority of the United States, which shall have been created, or the Emoluments whereof shall have been increased, during such time; and no Person holding any Office under the United States shall be a Member of either House during his continuance in Office.

Section 7.

All Bills for raising Revenue shall originate in the House of Representatives; but the Senate may propose or concur with Amendments as on other bills.

Every Bill which shall have passed the House of Representatives and the Senate, shall, before it become a Law, be presented to the President of the United States; If he approve he shall sign it, but if not he shall return it, with his Objections, to that House in which it shall have originated, who shall enter the Objections at large on their Journal, and proceed to reconsider it. If after such Reconsideration two thirds of that House shall agree to pass the bill, it shall be sent, together with the objections, to the other House, by which it shall likewise be reconsidered, and if approved by two thirds of that House, it shall become a Law. But in all such Cases the Votes of both Houses shall be determined by Yeas and Nays, and the Names of the Persons voting for and against the Bill shall be entered on the Journal of each House respectively. If any Bill shall not be returned by the President within ten Days (Sundays excepted) after it shall have been presented to him, the Same shall be a Law, in like Manner as if he had signed it, unless the Congress by their Adjournment prevent its Return, in which Case it shall not be a Law.

Every Order, Resolution, or Vote to which the Concurrence of the Senate and House of Representatives may be necessary (except on a question of Adjournment) shall be presented to the President of the United States; and before the Same shall take Effect, shall be approved by him, or being disapproved by him, shall be repassed by two thirds of the Senate and House of Representatives, according to the Rules and Limitations prescribed in the Case of a Bill.

Section 8.

The Congress shall have Power To lay and collect Taxes, Duties, Imposts and Excises, to pay the Debts and provide for the common Defence and general Welfare of the United States; but all Duties, Imposts and Excises shall be uniform throughout the United States;

To borrow money on the credit of the United States;

To regulate Commerce with foreign Nations, and among the several States, and with the Indian Tribes;

To establish an uniform rule of Naturalization, and uniform Laws on the subject of Bankruptcies throughout the United States;

To coin Money, regulate the Value thereof, and of foreign Coin, and fix the Standard of Weights and Measures;

To provide for the Punishment of counterfeiting the Securities and current Coin of the United States;

To establish Post Offices and post Roads;

To promote the Progress of Science and useful Arts, by securing for limited Times to Authors and Inventors the exclusive Right to their respective Writings and Discoveries;

To constitute Tribunals inferior to the Supreme Court;

To define and punish Piracies and Felonies committed on the high Seas, and Offenses against the Law of Nations;

To declare War, grant Letters of Marque and Reprisal, and make Rules concerning Captures on Land and Water;

To raise and support Armies, but no Appropriation of Money to that Use shall be for a longer Term than two Years;

To provide and maintain a Navy;

To make Rules for the Government and Regulation of the land and naval forces;

To provide for calling forth the Militia to execute the Laws of the Union, suppress Insurrections and repel Invasions;

To provide for organizing, arming, and disciplining the Militia, and for governing such Part of them as may be employed in the Service of the United States, reserving to the States respectively, the Appointment of the Officers, and the Authority of training the Militia according to the discipline prescribed by Congress;

To exercise exclusive Legislation in all Cases whatsoever, over such District (not exceeding ten Miles square) as may, by Cession of particular States, and the acceptance of Congress, become the Seat of the Government of the United States, and to exercise like Authority over all Places purchased by the Consent of the Legislature of the State in which the Same shall be, for the Erection of Forts, Magazines, Arsenals, Dock-yards, and other needful Buildings;—And

To make all Laws which shall be necessary and proper for carrying into Execution the foregoing Powers, and all other Powers vested by this Constitution in the Government of the United States, or in any Department or Officer thereof.

Section 9.

The Migration or Importation of such Persons as any of the States now existing shall think proper to admit, shall not be prohibited by the Congress prior to the Year one thousand eight hundred and eight, but a tax or duty may be imposed on such Importation, not exceeding ten dollars for each Person.

The privilege of the Writ of Habeas Corpus shall not be suspended, unless when in Cases of Rebellion or Invasion the public Safety may require it.

No bill of Attainder or ex post facto Law shall be passed.

No capitation, or other direct, Tax shall be laid unless in Proportion to the Census or Enumeration herein before directed to be taken.

No Tax or Duty shall be laid on Articles exported from any State.

No Preference shall be given by any Regulation of Commerce or Revenue to the Ports of one State over those of another: nor shall Vessels bound to, or from, one State, be obliged to enter, clear, or pay Duties in another.

No Money shall be drawn from the Treasury, but in Consequence of Appropriations made by Law; and a regular Statement and Account of the Receipts and Expenditures of all public Money shall be published from time to time.

No Title of Nobility shall be granted by the United States: And no Person holding any Office of Profit or Trust under them, shall, without the Consent of the Congress, accept of any present, Emolument, Office, or Title, of any kind whatever, from any King, Prince, or foreign State.

Section 10.

No State shall enter into any Treaty, Alliance, or Confederation; grant Letters of Marque and Reprisal; coin Money; emit Bills of Credit; make any Thing but gold and silver Coin a Tender in Payment of Debts; pass any Bill of Attainder, ex post facto Law, or Law impairing the Obligation of Contracts, or grant any Title of Nobility.

No State shall, without the Consent of the Congress, lay any Imposts or Duties on Imports or Exports, except what may be absolutely necessary for executing its inspection Laws; and the net Produce of all Duties and Imposts, laid by any State on Imports or Exports, shall be for the use of the Treasury of the United States; and all such Laws shall be subject to the Revision and Control of the Congress.

No state shall, without the Consent of Congress, lay any duty of Tonnage, keep Troops, or Ships of War in time of Peace, enter into any Agreement or Compact with another State, or with a foreign Power, or engage in War, unless actually invaded, or in such imminent Danger as will not admit of delay.

Article II

Section 1.

The executive Power shall be vested in a President of the United States of America. He shall hold his Office during the Term of four years, and, together with the Vice President, chosen for the same Term, be elected, as follows:

Each State shall appoint, in such Manner as the Legislature thereof may direct, a Number of Electors, equal to the whole Number of Senators and Representatives to which the State may be entitled in the Congress: but no Senator or Representative, or Person holding an Office of Trust or Profit under the United States, shall be appointed an Elector.

[The Electors shall meet in their respective States, and vote by Ballot for two persons, of whom one at least shall not be an Inhabitant of the same State with themselves. And they shall make a List of all the Persons voted for, and of the Number of Votes for each; which List they shall sign and certify, and transmit sealed to the Seat of the Government of the United States, directed to the President of the Senate. The President of the Senate shall, in the Presence of the Senate and House of Representatives, open all the Certificates, and the Votes shall then be counted. The Person having the greatest Number of Votes shall be the President, if such Number be a Majority of the whole Number of Electors appointed; and if there be more than one who have such Majority, and have an equal Number of Votes, then the House of Representatives shall immediately chuse by Ballot one of them for President; and if no Person have a Majority, then from the five highest on the List the said House shall in like Manner chuse the President. But in chusing the President, the Votes shall be taken by States, the Representation from each State having one Vote; a quorum for this Purpose shall consist of a Member or Members from two-thirds of the States, and a Majority of all the States shall be necessary to a Choice. In every Case, after the Choice of the President, the Person having the greatest Number of Votes of the Electors shall be the Vice President. But if there should remain two or more who have equal votes, the Senate shall chuse from them by Ballot the Vice President.][4]

The Congress may determine the Time of chusing the Electors, and the Day on which they shall give their Votes; which Day shall be the same throughout the United States.

No person except a natural-born Citizen, or a Citizen of the United States, at the time of the Adoption of this Constitution, shall be eligible to the Office of President; neither shall any Person be eligible to that Office who shall not have attained to the Age of thirty-five years, and been fourteen Years a Resident within the United States.

In Case of the Removal of the President from Office, or of his Death, Resignation, or Inability to discharge the Powers and Duties of the said Office, the same

[4] Revised by the Twelfth Amendment.

shall devolve on the Vice President, and the Congress may by Law provide for the Case of Removal, Death, Resignation, or Inability, both of the President and Vice President, declaring what Officer shall then act as President, and such Officer shall act accordingly, until the disability be removed, or a President shall be elected.

The President shall, at stated Times, receive for his Services a Compensation, which shall neither be increased nor diminished during the Period for which he shall have been elected, and he shall not receive within that Period any other Emolument from the United States, or any of them.

Before he enter on the execution of his Office, he shall take the following Oath or Affirmation:—"I do solemnly swear (or affirm) that I will faithfully execute the Office of President of the United States, and will, to the best of my Ability, preserve, protect, and defend the Constitution of the United States."

Section 2.

The President shall be Commander in Chief of the Army and Navy of the United States, and of the Militia of the several States, when called into the actual Service of the United States; he may require the Opinion, in writing, of the principal Officer in each of the executive Departments, upon any subject relating to the Duties of their respective Offices, and he shall have Power to Grant Reprieves and Pardons for Offenses against the United States, except in Cases of Impeachment.

He shall have Power, by and with the Advice and Consent of the Senate, to make Treaties, provided two-thirds of the Senators present concur; and he shall nominate, and by and with the Advice and Consent of the Senate, shall appoint Ambassadors, other public Ministers and Consuls, Judges of the supreme Court, and all other Officers of the United States, whose Appointments are not herein otherwise provided for, and which shall be established by Law: but the Congress may by Law vest the Appointment of such inferior Officers, as they think proper, in the President alone, in the Courts of Law, or in the Heads of Departments.

The President shall have Power to fill up all Vacancies that may happen during the Recess of the Senate, by granting Commissions which shall expire at the End of their next Session.

Section 3.

He shall from time to time give to the Congress Information of the State of the Union, and recommend to their Consideration such Measures as he shall judge necessary and expedient; he may, on extraordinary occasions, convene both Houses, or either of them, and in Case of Disagreement between them, with respect to the Time of Adjournment, he may adjourn them to such Time as he shall think proper; he shall receive Ambassadors and other public Ministers; he shall take care that the Laws be faithfully executed, and shall Commission all the Officers of the United States.

Section 4.

The President, Vice President and all civil Officers of the United States, shall be removed from Office on Impeachment for, and Conviction of, Treason, Bribery, or other high Crimes and Misdemeanors.

Article III

Section 1.

The judicial Power of the United States, shall be vested in one supreme Court, and in such inferior Courts as the Congress may from time to time ordain and establish. The Judges, both of the supreme and inferior Courts, shall hold their Offices during good Behaviour, and shall, at stated Times, receive for their Services, a Compensation, which shall not be diminished during their Continuance in Office.

Section 2.

The judicial Power shall extend to all Cases, in Law and Equity, arising under this Constitution, the Laws of the United States, and Treaties made, or which shall be made, under their Authority;—to all Cases affecting ambassadors, other public ministers and consuls;—to all cases of admiralty and maritime Jurisdiction;—to Controversies to which the United States shall be a Party;—to Controversies between two or more States;—between a State and Citizens of another State;[5]—between Citizens of different States—between Citizens of the same State claiming Lands under Grants of different States, and between a State, or the Citizens thereof, and foreign States, Citizens, or Subjects.

In all Cases affecting Ambassadors, other public Ministers and Consuls, and those in which a State shall be Party, the supreme Court shall have original Jurisdiction. In all the other Cases before mentioned, the supreme Court shall have appellate Jurisdiction, both as to Law and Fact, with such Exceptions, and under such Regulations as the Congress shall make.

The trial of all Crimes, except in Cases of Impeachment, shall be by Jury; and such Trial shall be held in the State where the said Crimes shall have been committed; but when not committed within any State, the Trial shall be at such Place or Places as the Congress may by Law have directed.

Section 3.

Treason against the United States, shall consist only in levying War against them, or in adhering to their Enemies, giving them Aid and Comfort. No Person shall be convicted of Treason unless on the Testimony of two Witnesses to the same overt Act, or on Confession in open Court.

The Congress shall have power to declare the Punishment of Treason, but no Attainder of Treason shall work Corruption of Blood, or Forfeiture except during the Life of the Person attained.

---

[5] Qualified by the Eleventh Amendment.

Article IV

Section 1.

Full Faith and Credit shall be given in each State to the public Acts, Records, and judicial Proceedings of every other State. And the Congress may by general Laws prescribe the Manner in which such Acts, Records and Proceedings shall be proved, and the Effect thereof.

Section 2.

The Citizens of each State shall be entitled to all Privileges and Immunities of Citizens in the several States.

A Person charged in any State with Treason, Felony, or other Crime, who shall flee from Justice, and be found in another State, shall on demand of the executive Authority of the State from which he fled, be delivered up, to be removed to the State having Jurisdiction of the crime.

No Person held to Service or Labour in one State, under the Laws thereof, escaping into another, shall, in Consequence of any Law or Regulation therein, be discharged from such Service or Labour, but shall be delivered up on Claim of the Party to whom such Service or Labour may be due.

Section 3.

New States may be admitted by the Congress into this Union; but no new State shall be formed or erected within the Jurisdiction of any other State; nor any State be formed by the Junction of two or more States, or parts of States, without the Consent of the Legislatures of the States concerned as well as of the Congress.

The Congress shall have Power to dispose of and make all needful Rules and Regulations respecting the Territory or other Property belonging to the United States; and nothing in this Constitution shall be so construed as to Prejudice any Claims of the United States, or of any particular State.

Section 4.

The United States shall guarantee to every State in this Union a Republican Form of Government, and shall protect each of them against Invasion; and on Application of the Legislature, or of the Executive (when the Legislature cannot be convened) against domestic Violence.

Article V

The Congress, whenever two-thirds of both Houses shall deem it necessary, shall propose Amendments to this Constitution, or, on the Application of the Legislatures of two-thirds of the several States, shall call a Convention for proposing Amendments, which, in either Case, shall be valid to all Intents and Purposes, as part of this Constitution, when ratified by the Legislatures of three-fourths of the several States, or by Conventions in three-fourths thereof, as the one or the other Mode of Ratification may be proposed by the Congress; Provided that no Amendment which may be made prior to the Year One thousand eight hundred and eight shall in any Manner affect the first and fourth Clauses in the Ninth Section of the first Article; and that no State, without its Consent, shall be deprived of its equal Suffrage in the Senate.

Article VI

All Debts contracted and Engagements entered into, before the Adoption of this Constitution, shall be as valid against the United States under this Constitution, as under the Confederation.

This Constitution, and the Laws of the United States which shall be made in Pursuance thereof; and all Treaties made, or which shall be made, under the Authority of the United States, shall be the supreme Law of the Land; and the Judges in every State shall be bound thereby, any Thing in the Constitution or Laws of any State to the Contrary notwithstanding.

The Senators and Representatives before mentioned, and the Members of the several State Legislatures, and all executive and judicial Officers, both of the United States and of the several States, shall be bound by Oath or Affirmation to support this Constitution; but no religious Tests shall ever be required as a qualification to any Office or public Trust under the United States.

Article VII

The Ratification of the Conventions of nine States shall be sufficient for the Establishment of this Constitution between the States so ratifying the same.

Done in Convention by the Unanimous Consent of the States present the Seventeenth Day of September in the Year of our Lord one thousand seven hundred and Eighty seven, and of the Independence of the United States of America the Twelfth. In Witness whereof We have hereunto subscribed our Names.[6]

George Washington
President and deputy from Virginia

New Hampshire	*Pennsylvania*	*Virginia*
John Langdon	Benjamin Franklin	John Blair
Nicholas Gilman	Thomas Mifflin	James Madison, Jr.
	Robert Morris	
Massachusetts	George Clymer	*North Carolina*
Nathaniel Gorham	Thomas FitzSimons	William Blount
Rufus King	Jared Ingersoll	Richard Dobbs
	James Wilson	Spaight
	Gouverneur Morris	Hugh Williamson

[6] These are the full names of the signers, which in some cases are not the signatures on the document.

Connecticut
William Samuel Johnson
Roger Sherman

New York
Alexander Hamilton

New Jersey
William Livingston
David Brearley
William Paterson
Jonathan Dayton

Delaware
George Read
Gunning Bedford, Jr.
John Dickinson
Richard Bassett
Jacob Broom

Maryland
James McHenry
Daniel of
   St. Thomas Jenifer
Daniel Carroll

South Carolina
John Rutledge
Charles Cotesworth
   Pinckney
Charles Pinckney
Pierce Butler

Georgia
William Few
Abraham Baldwin

Articles in Addition to, and Amendment of, the Constitution of the United States of America, Proposed by Congress, and Ratified by the Legislatures of the Several States, Pursuant to the Fifth Article of the Original Constitution.[7]

[Article I]

Congress shall make no law respecting an establishment of religion, or prohibiting the free exercise thereof; or abridging the freedom of speech, or of the press; or the right of the people peaceably to assemble, and to petition the Government for a redress of grievances.

[Article II]

A well regulated Militia, being necessary to the security of a free State, the right of the people to keep and bear Arms shall not be infringed.

[Article III]

No Soldier shall, in time of peace, be quartered in any house, without the consent of the Owner, nor in time of war, but in a manner to be prescribed by law.

[Article IV]

The right of the people to be secure in their persons, houses, papers, and effects, against unreasonable searches and seizures, shall not be violated, and no Warrants shall issue, but upon probable cause, supported by Oath or affirmation, and particularly describing the place to be searched, and the persons or things to be seized.

[7] This heading appears only in the joint resolution submitting the first ten amendments.

[Article V]

No person shall be held to answer for a capital or otherwise infamous crime, unless on a presentment or indictment of a Grand Jury, except in cases arising in the land or naval forces, or in the Militia, when in actual service in time of War or public danger; nor shall any person be subject for the same offence to be twice put in jeopardy of life or limb; nor shall be compelled in any criminal case to be a witness against himself, nor be deprived of life, liberty, or property, without due process of law; nor shall private property be taken for public use, without just compensation.

[Article VI]

In all criminal prosecutions, the accused shall enjoy the right to a speedy and public trial, by an impartial jury of the State and district wherein the crime shall have been committed, which district shall have been previously ascertained by law, and to be informed of the nature and cause of the accusation; to be confronted with the witnesses against him; to have compulsory process for obtaining witnesses in his favour, and to have the Assistance of Counsel for his defense.

[Article VII]

In suits at common law, where the value in controversy shall exceed twenty dollars, the right of trial by jury shall be preserved, and no fact tried by a jury, shall be otherwise reexamined in any Court of the United States, than according to the rules of the common law.

[Article VIII]

Excessive bail shall not be required, nor excessive fines imposed, nor cruel and unusual punishments inflicted.

[Article IX]

The enumeration of the Constitution, of certain rights, shall not be construed to deny or disparage others retained by the people.

[Article X]

The powers not delegated to the United States by the Constitution, nor prohibited by it to the States, are reserved to the States respectively, or to the people.
[Amendments I–X, in force 1791.]

[Article XI][8]

The Judicial power of the United States shall not be construed to extend to any suit in law or equity, commenced or prosecuted against one of the United States by Citizens of another State, or by Citizens or Subjects of any Foreign State.

[Article XII][9]

The Electors shall meet in their respective States and vote by ballot for President and Vice-President, one of whom, at least, shall not be an inhabitant of the same State with themselves; they shall name in their ballots the person voted for as President, and in distinct ballots the person voted for as Vice-President, and they shall make distinct lists of all persons voted for as President, and of all persons voted for as Vice-President, and of the number of votes for each, which lists they shall sign and certify, and transmit sealed to the seat of the government of the United States, directed to the President of the Senate;—The President of the Senate shall, in the presence of the Senate and House of Representatives, open all the certificates and the votes shall then be counted;—The person having the greatest number of votes for President, shall be the President, if such number be a majority of the whole number of Electors appointed; and if no person have such majority, then from the persons having the highest numbers not exceeding three on the list of those voted for as President, the House of Representatives shall choose immediately, by ballot, the President. But in choosing the President, the votes shall be taken by states, the representation from each state having one vote; a quorum for this purpose shall consist of a member or members from two-thirds of the states, and a majority of all the states shall be necessary to a choice. And if the House of Representatives shall not choose a President whenever the right of choice shall devolve upon them, before the fourth day of March next following, then the Vice-President shall act as President, as in the case of the death or other constitutional disability of the President.—The person having the greatest number of votes as Vice-President, shall be the Vice-President, if such number be a majority of the whole number of Electors appointed, and if no person have a majority, then from the two highest numbers on the list, the Senate shall choose the Vice-President; a quorum for the purpose shall consist of two-thirds of the whole number of Senators, and a majority of the whole number shall be necessary to a choice. But no person constitutionally ineligible to the office of President shall be eligible to that of Vice-President of the United States.

[8] Adopted in 1798.
[9] Adopted in 1804.

[Article XIII][10]

Section 1.
Neither slavery nor involuntary servitude, except as a punishment for crime whereof the party shall have been duly convicted, shall exist within the United States, or any place subject to their jurisdiction.

Section 2.
Congress shall have power to enforce this article by appropriate legislation.

[Article XIV][11]

Section 1.
All persons born or naturalized in the United States, and subject to the jurisdiction thereof, are citizens of the United States and of the State wherein they reside. No State shall make or enforce any law which shall abridge the privileges or immunities of citizens of the United States; nor shall any State deprive any person of life, liberty, or property, without due process of law; nor deny to any person within its jurisdiction the equal protection of the laws.

Section 2.
Representatives shall be apportioned among the several States according to their respective numbers, counting the whole number of persons in each State, excluding Indians not taxed. But when the right to vote at any election for the choice of electors for President and Vice-President of the United States, Representatives in Congress, the Executive and Judicial officers of a State, or the members of the Legislature thereof, is denied to any of the male inhabitants of such State, being twenty-one years of age, and citizens of the United States, or in any way abridged, except for participation in rebellion, or other crime, the basis of representation therein shall be reduced in the proportion which the number of such male citizens shall bear to the whole number of male citizens twenty-one years of age in such State.

Section 3.
No person shall be a Senator or Representative in Congress, or elector of President and Vice-President, or hold any office, civil or military, under the United States, or under any State, who, having previously taken an oath, as a member of Congress, or as an officer of the United States, or as a member of any State legislature, or as

[10] Adopted in 1865.
[11] Adopted in 1868.

an executive or judicial officer of any State, to support the Constitution of the United States, shall have engaged in insurrection or rebellion against the same, or given aid or comfort to the enemies thereof. But Congress may by a vote of two-thirds of each House, remove such disability.

Section 4.
The validity of the public debt of the United States, authorized by law, including debts incurred for payment of pensions and bounties for services in suppressing insurrection or rebellion, shall not be questioned. But neither the United States nor any State shall assume or pay any debts or obligation incurred in aid of insurrection or rebellion against the United States, or any claim for the loss or emancipation of any slave; but all such debts, obligations, and claims shall be held illegal and void.

Section 5.
The Congress shall have the power to enforce, by appropriate legislation, the provisions of this article.

[Article XV][12]

Section 1.
The right of citizens of the United States to vote shall not be denied or abridged by the United States or by any State on account of race, color, or previous condition of servitude—

Section 2.
The Congress shall have power to enforce this article by appropriate legislation.

[Article XVI][13]

The Congress shall have power to lay and collect taxes on incomes, from whatever source derived, without apportionment among the several States, and without regard to any census or enumeration.

[Article XVII][14]

The Senate of the United States shall be composed of two Senators from each State, elected by the people thereof, for six years; and each Senator shall have one vote. The electors in each State shall have the qualifications requisite for electors of the most numerous branch of the State legislatures.

---

[12] Adopted in 1870.
[13] Adopted in 1913.
[14] Adopted in 1913.

When vacancies happen in the representation of any State in the Senate, the executive authority of such State shall issue writs of election to fill such vacancies: *Provided,* That the legislature of any State may empower the executive thereof to make temporary appointments until the people fill the vacancies by election as the legislature may direct.

This amendment shall not be so construed as to affect the election or term of any Senator chosen before it becomes valid as part of the Constitution.

[Article XVIII][15]

Section 1.
After one year from the ratification of this article the manufacture, sale, or transportation of intoxicating liquors within, the importation thereof into, or the exportation thereof from the United States and all territory subject to the jurisdiction thereof for beverage purposes is hereby prohibited.

Section 2.
The Congress and the several States shall have concurrent power to enforce this article by appropriate legislation.

Section 3.
This article shall be inoperative unless it shall have been ratified as an amendment to the Constitution by the legislatures of the several States, as provided in the Constitution, within seven years from the date of the submission hereof to the States by the Congress.

[Article XIX][16]

The right of citizens of the United States to vote shall not be denied or abridged by the United States or by any State on account of sex.

Congress shall have power to enforce this article by appropriate legislation.

[Article XX][17]

Section 1.
The terms of the President and Vice-President shall end at noon on the 20th day of January, and the terms of Senators and Representatives at noon on the 3d day of January, of the years in which such terms would have ended if this article had not been ratified; and the terms of their successors shall then begin.

[15] Adopted in 1918.
[16] Adopted in 1920.
[17] Adopted in 1933.

Section 2.
The Congress shall assemble at least once in every year, and such meeting shall begin at noon on the 3d day of January, unless they shall by law appoint a different day.

Section 3.
If, at the time fixed for the beginning of the term of the President, the President elect shall have died, the Vice-President elect shall become President. If a President shall not have been chosen before the time fixed for the beginning of his term or if the President elect shall have failed to qualify, then the Vice-President elect shall act as President until a President shall have qualified; and the Congress may by law provide for the case wherein neither a President elect nor a Vice-President elect shall have qualified, declaring who shall then act as President, or the manner in which one who is to act shall be selected, and such person shall act accordingly until a President or Vice-President shall have qualified.

Section 4.
The Congress may by law provide for the case of the death of any of the persons from whom the House of Representatives may choose a President whenever the right of choice shall have devolved upon them, and for the case of the death of any of the persons from whom the Senate may choose a Vice-President whenever the right of choice shall have devolved upon them.

Section 5.
Sections 1 and 2 shall take effect on the 15th day of October following the ratification of this article.

Section 6.
This article shall be inoperative unless it shall have been ratified as an amendment to the Constitution by the legislatures of three-fourths of the several States within seven years from the date of its submission.

[Article XXI][18]

Section 1.
The eighteenth article of amendment to the Constitution of the United States is hereby repealed.

Section 2.
The transportation or importation into any State, Territory, or possession of the United States for delivery or use therein of intoxicating liquors, in violation of the laws thereof, is hereby prohibited.

[18] Adopted in 1933.

Section 3.

This article shall be inoperative unless it shall have been ratified as an amendment to the Constitution by conventions in the several States, as provided in the Constitution, within seven years from the date of the submission hereof to the States by the Congress.

[Article XXII][19]

No person shall be elected to the office of the President more than twice, and no person who has held the office of President, or acted as President, for more than two years of a term to which some other person was elected President shall be elected to the office of the President more than once.

But this Article shall not apply to any person holding the office of President when this Article was proposed by the Congress, and shall not prevent any person who may be holding the office of President, or acting as President, during the term within which this Article becomes operative from holding the office of President or acting as President during the remainder of such term.

This article shall be inoperative unless it shall have been ratified as an amendment to the Constitution by the legislatures of three-fourths of the several states within seven years from the date of its submission to the states by the Congress.

[Article XXIII][20]

Section 1.

The District constituting the seat of Government of the United States shall appoint in such manner as the Congress may direct:

A number of electors of President and Vice-President equal to the whole number of Senators and Representatives in Congress to which the District would be entitled if it were a State, but in no event more than the least populous State; they shall be in addition to those appointed by the States, but they shall be considered, for the purposes of the election of President and Vice-President, to be electors appointed by a State; and they shall meet in the District and perform such duties as provided by the twelfth article of amendment.

Section 2.

The Congress shall have power to enforce this article by appropriate legislation.

[19] Adopted in 1961.
[20] Adopted in 1961.

[Article XXIV][21]

Section 1.
The right of citizens of the United States to vote in any primary or other election for President or Vice President, for electors for President or Vice President, or for Senator or Representative in Congress, shall not be denied or abridged by the United States or any state by reason of failure to pay any poll tax or other tax.

Section 2.
The Congress shall have the power to enforce this article by appropriate legislation.

[Article XXV][22]

Section 1.
In case of the removal of the President from office or of his death or resignation, the Vice President shall become President.

Section 2.
Whenever there is a vacancy in the office of the Vice President, the President shall nominate a Vice President who shall take office upon confirmation by a majority vote of both Houses of Congress.

Section 3.
Whenever the President transmits to the President Pro Tempore of the Senate and the Speaker of the House of Representatives his written declaration that he is unable to discharge the powers and duties of his office, and until he transmits to them a written declaration to the contrary, such powers and duties shall be discharged by the Vice President as Acting President.

Section 4.
Whenever the Vice President and a majority of either the principal officers of the executive departments or of such other body as Congress may by law provide, transmit to the President Pro Tempore of the Senate and the Speaker of the House of Representatives their written declaration that the President is unable to discharge the powers and duties of his office, the Vice President shall immediately assume the powers and duties of the office as Acting President.

Thereafter, when the President transmits to the President Pro Tempore of the Senate and the Speaker of the House of Representatives his written declaration that no inability exists, he shall resume the powers and duties of his office unless the Vice President and a majority of either the principal officers of the executive departments or of such other body as Congress may by law provide, transmit within four days to

[21] Adopted in 1964.
[22] Adopted in 1967.

the President Pro Tempore of the Senate and the Speaker of the House of Representatives their written declaration that the President is unable to discharge the powers and duties of his office. Thereupon Congress shall decide the issue, assembling within forty-eight hours for that purpose if not in session. If the Congress, within twenty-one days after receipt of the latter written declaration, or, if Congress is not in session, within twenty-one days after Congress is required to assemble, determines by two-thirds vote of both Houses that the President is unable to discharge the powers and duties of his office, the Vice President shall continue to discharge the same as Acting President; otherwise, the President shall resume the powers and duties of his office.

[Article XXVI][23]

Section 1.
The right of citizens of the United States, who are eighteen years of age or older, to vote shall not be denied or abridged by the United States or by any State on account of age.

Section 2.
The Congress shall have power to enforce this article by appropriate legislation.

[Article XXVII][24]

No law varying the compensation for the services of the Senators and Representatives shall take effect until an election of Representatives shall have intervened.

[23] Adopted in 1971.
[24] Adopted in 1992.

PRESIDENTIAL ELECTIONS

Year	Candidates	Parties	Popular Vote	Percentage of Popular Vote	Electoral Vote	Percentage of Voter Participation
1789	**GEORGE WASHINGTON (Va.)***				69	
	John Adams				34	
	Others				35	
1792	**GEORGE WASHINGTON (Va.)**				132	
	John Adams				77	
	George Clinton				50	
	Others				5	
1796	**JOHN ADAMS (Mass.)**	Federalist			71	
	Thomas Jefferson	Democratic-Republican			68	
	Thomas Pinckney	Federalist			59	
	Aaron Burr	Dem.-Rep.			30	
	Others				48	
1800	**THOMAS JEFFERSON (Va.)**	Dem.-Rep.			73	
	Aaron Burr	Dem.-Rep.			73	
	John Adams	Federalist			65	
	C. C. Pinckney	Federalist			64	
	John Jay	Federalist			1	
1804	**THOMAS JEFFERSON (Va.)**	Dem.-Rep.			162	
	C. C. Pinckney	Federalist			14	

Year	Candidate	Party	Popular Vote	% of Popular Vote	Electoral Vote	% Voter Participation
1808	JAMES MADISON (Va.)	Dem.-Rep.			122	
	C. C. Pinckney	Federalist			47	
	George Clinton	Dem.-Rep.			6	
1812	JAMES MADISON (Va.)	Dem.-Rep.			128	
	De Witt Clinton	Federalist			89	
1816	JAMES MONROE (Va.)	Dem.-Rep.			183	
	Rufus King	Federalist			34	
1820	JAMES MONROE (Va.)	Dem.-Rep.			231	
	John Quincy Adams	Dem.-Rep.			1	
1824	JOHN Q. ADAMS (Mass.)	Dem.-Rep.	108,740	30.5	84	26.9
	Andrew Jackson	Dem.-Rep.	153,544	43.1	99	
	William H. Crawford	Dem.-Rep.	46,618	13.1	41	
	Henry Clay	Dem.-Rep.	47,136	13.2	37	
1828	ANDREW JACKSON (Tenn.)	Democratic	647,286	56.0	178	57.6
	John Quincy Adams	National Republican	508,064	44.0	83	
1832	ANDREW JACKSON (Tenn.)	Democratic	687,502	55.0	219	55.4
	Henry Clay	National Republican	530,189	42.4	49	
	John Floyd	Independent			11	
	William Wirt	Anti-Mason	33,108	2.6	7	
1836	MARTIN VAN BUREN (N.Y.)	Democratic	765,483	50.9	170	57.8
	W. H. Harrison	Whig			73	
	Hugh L. White	Whig	739,795	49.1	26	
	Daniel Webster	Whig			14	
	W. P. Magnum	Independent			11	

* State of residence at time of election.

(continued)

Year	Candidates	Parties	Popular Vote	Percentage of Popular Vote	Electoral Vote	Percentage of Voter Participation
1840	**WILLIAM H. HARRISON (Ohio)**	Whig	1,274,624	53.1	234	80.2
	Martin Van Buren	Democratic	1,127,781	46.9	60	
	J. G. Birney	Liberty	7,069		—	
1844	**JAMES K. POLK (Tenn.)**	Democratic	1,338,464	49.6	170	78.9
	Henry Clay	Whig	1,300,097	48.1	105	
	J. G. Birney	Liberty	62,300	2.3	—	
1848	**ZACHARY TAYLOR (La.)**	Whig	1,360,967	47.4	163	72.7
	Lewis Cass	Democratic	1,222,342	42.5	127	
	Martin Van Buren	Free-Soil	291,263	10.1	—	
1852	**FRANKLIN PIERCE (N.H.)**	Democratic	1,601,117	50.9	254	69.6
	Winfield Scott	Whig	1,385,453	44.1	42	
	John P. Hale	Free-Soil	155,825	5.0	—	
1856	**JAMES BUCHANAN (Pa.)**	Democratic	1,832,955	45.3	174	78.9
	John C. Frémont	Republican	1,339,932	33.1	114	
	Millard Fillmore	American	871,731	21.6	8	
1860	**ABRAHAM LINCOLN (Ill.)**	Republican	1,865,593	39.8	180	81.2
	Stephen A. Douglas	Democratic	1,382,713	29.5	12	
	John C. Breckinridge	Democratic	848,356	18.1	72	
	John Bell	Union	592,906	12.6	39	
1864	**ABRAHAM LINCOLN (Ill.)**	Republican	2,213,655	55.0	212	73.8
	George B. McClellan	Democratic	1,805,237	45.0	21	

Year	Candidate	Party	Popular Vote	%	Electoral Vote	% Turnout
1868	**ULYSSES S. GRANT (Ill.)**	Republican	3,012,833	52.7	214	78.1
	Horatio Seymour	Democratic	2,703,249	47.3	80	
1872	**ULYSSES S. GRANT (Ill.)**	Republican	3,597,132	55.6	286	71.3
	Horace Greeley	Democratic; Liberal Republican	2,834,125	43.9	66	
1876	**RUTHERFORD B. HAYES (Ohio)**	Republican	4,036,298	48.0	185	81.8
	Samuel J. Tilden	Democratic	4,300,590	51.0	184	
1880	**JAMES A. GARFIELD (Ohio)**	Republican	4,454,416	48.5	214	79.4
	Winfield S. Hancock	Democratic	4,444,952	48.1	155	
1884	**GROVER CLEVELAND (N.Y.)**	Democratic	4,874,986	48.5	219	77.5
	James G. Blaine	Republican	4,851,981	48.2	182	
1888	**BENJAMIN HARRISON (Ind.)**	Republican	5,439,853	47.9	233	79.3
	Grover Cleveland	Democratic	5,540,309	48.6	168	
1892	**GROVER CLEVELAND (N.Y.)**	Democratic	5,556,918	46.1	277	74.7
	Benjamin Harrison	Republican	5,176,108	43.0	145	
	James B. Weaver	People's	1,041,028	8.5	22	
1896	**WILLIAM McKINLEY (Ohio)**	Republican	7,104,779	51.1	271	79.3
	William J. Bryan	Democratic-People's	6,502,925	47.7	176	
1900	**WILLIAM McKINLEY (Ohio)**	Republican	7,207,923	51.7	292	73.2
	William J. Bryan	Dem.-Populist	6,358,133	45.5	155	
1904	**THEODORE ROOSEVELT (N.Y.)**	Republican	7,623,486	57.9	336	65.2
	Alton B. Parker	Democratic	5,077,911	37.6	140	
	Eugene V. Debs	Socialist	402,283	3.0	—	

(continued)

PRESIDENTIAL ELECTIONS (*cont.*)

Year	Candidates	Parties	Popular Vote	Percentage of Popular Vote	Electoral Vote	Percentage of Voter Participation
1908	**WILLIAM H. TAFT (Ohio)**	Republican	7,678,908	51.6	321	65.4
	William J. Bryan	Democratic	6,409,104	43.1	162	
	Eugene V. Debs	Socialist	420,793	2.8	—	
1912	**WOODROW WILSON (N.J.)**	Democratic	6,293,454	41.9	435	58.8
	Theodore Roosevelt	Progressive	4,119,538	27.4	88	
	William H. Taft	Republican	3,484,980	23.2	8	
	Eugene V. Debs	Socialist	900,672	6.0	—	
1916	**WOODROW WILSON (N.J.)**	Democratic	9,129,606	49.4	277	61.6
	Charles E. Hughes	Republican	8,538,221	46.2	254	
	A. L. Benson	Socialist	585,113	3.2	—	
1920	**WARREN G. HARDING (Ohio)**	Republican	16,152,200	60.4	404	49.2
	James M. Cox	Democratic	9,147,353	34.2	127	
	Eugene V. Debs	Socialist	919,799	3.4	—	
1924	**CALVIN COOLIDGE (Mass.)**	Republican	15,725,016	54.0	382	48.9
	John W. Davis	Democratic	8,386,503	28.8	136	
	Robert M. LaFollette	Progressive	4,822,856	16.6	13	
1928	**HERBERT HOOVER (Calif.)**	Republican	21,391,381	58.2	444	56.9
	Alfred E. Smith	Democratic	15,016,443	40.9	87	
	Norman Thomas	Socialist	267,835	0.7	—	
1932	**FRANKLIN D. ROOSEVELT (N.Y.)**	Democratic	22,821,857	57.4	472	56.9
	Herbert Hoover	Republican	15,761,841	39.7	59	
	Norman Thomas	Socialist	881,951	2.2	—	

Year	Candidate	Party	Popular Vote	%	Electoral Vote	Turnout %
1936	**FRANKLIN D. ROOSEVELT (N.Y.)**	Democratic	27,751,597	60.8	523	61.0
	Alfred M. Landon	Republican	16,679,583	36.5	8	
	William Lemke	Union	882,479	1.9	—	
1940	**FRANKLIN D. ROOSEVELT (N.Y.)**	Democratic	27,244,160	54.8	449	62.5
	Wendell L. Willkie	Republican	22,305,198	44.8	82	
1944	**FRANKLIN D. ROOSEVELT (N.Y.)**	Democratic	25,602,504	53.5	432	55.9
	Thomas E. Dewey	Republican	22,006,285	46.0	99	
1948	**HARRY S. TRUMAN (Mo.)**	Democratic	24,105,695	49.5	304	53.0
	Thomas E. Dewey	Republican	21,969,170	45.1	189	
	J. Strom Thurmond	State-Rights Democratic	1,169,021	2.4	38	
	Henry A. Wallace	Progressive	1,156,103	2.4	—	
1952	**DWIGHT D. EISENHOWER (N.Y.)**	Republican	33,936,252	55.1	442	63.3
	Adlai E. Stevenson	Democratic	27,314,992	44.4	89	
1956	**DWIGHT D. EISENHOWER (N.Y.)**	Republican	35,575,420	57.6	457	60.6
	Adlai E. Stevenson	Democratic	26,033,066	42.1	73	
	Other	—			1	
1960	**JOHN F. KENNEDY (Mass.)**	Democratic	34,227,096	49.9	303	62.8
	Richard M. Nixon	Republican	34,108,546	49.6	219	
	Other	—			15	
1964	**LYNDON B. JOHNSON (Tex.)**	Democratic	43,126,506	61.1	486	61.7
	Barry M. Goldwater	Republican	27,176,799	38.5	52	
1968	**RICHARD M. NIXON (N.Y.)**	Republican	31,770,237	43.4	301	60.6
	Hubert H. Humphrey	Democratic	31,270,533	42.7	191	
	George Wallace	American Independent	9,906,141	13.5	46	

(continued)

PRESIDENTIAL ELECTIONS (*cont.*)

Year	Candidates	Parties	Popular Vote	Percentage of Popular Vote	Electoral Vote	Percentage of Voter Participation
1972	**RICHARD M. NIXON (N.Y.)**	Republican	47,169,911	60.7	520	55.2
	George S. McGovern	Democratic	29,170,383	37.5	17	
	Other	—	—		1	
1976	**JIMMY CARTER (Ga.)**	Democratic	40,828,587	50.0	297	53.5
	Gerald R. Ford	Republican	39,147,613	47.9	241	
	Other	—	1,575,459	2.1	—	
1980	**RONALD REAGAN (Calif.)**	Republican	43,901,812	50.7	489	52.6
	Jimmy Carter	Democratic	35,483,820	41.0	49	
	John B. Anderson	Independent	5,719,722	6.6	—	
	Ed Clark	Libertarian	921,188	1.1	—	
1984	**RONALD REAGAN (Calif.)**	Republican	54,455,075	59.0	525	53.3
	Walter Mondale	Democratic	37,577,185	41.0	13	
1988	**GEORGE BUSH (Tex.)**	Republican	47,946,422	54.0	426	50.2
	Michael S. Dukakis	Democratic	41,016,429	46.0	112	
1992	**WILLIAM J. CLINTON (Ark.)**	Democratic	43,728,375	43.0	370	55.0
	George Bush	Republican	38,167,416	38.0	168	
	Ross Perot	Independent	19,237,247	19.0	0	
1996	**WILLIAM J. CLINTON (Ark.)**	Democratic	47,401,185	49.3	379	49.0
	Robert Dole	Republican	39,197,469	40.7	159	
	Ross Perot	Reform	8,085,294	8.4	—	

POPULATION OF THE UNITED STATES, 1790–1998

Year	Population	Percent Increase	Population per Square Mile	Percent Urban/ Rural	Percent White/ Nonwhite	Median Age
1790	3,929,214		4.5	5.1/94.9	80.7/19.3	NA
1800	5,308,483	35.1	6.1	6.1/93.9	81.1/18.9	NA
1810	7,239,881	36.4	4.3	7.3/92.7	81.0/19.0	NA
1820	9,638,453	33.1	5.5	7.2/92.8	81.6/18.4	16.7
1830	12,866,020	33.5	7.4	8.8/91.2	81.9/18.1	17.2
1840	17,069,453	32.7	9.8	10.8/89.2	83.2/16.8	17.8
1850	23,191,876	35.9	7.9	15.3/84.7	84.3/15.7	18.9
1860	31,443,321	35.6	10.6	19.8/80.2	85.6/14.4	19.4
1870	39,818,449	26.6	13.4	25.7/74.3	86.2/13.8	20.2
1880	50,155,783	26.0	16.9	28.2/71.8	86.5/13.5	20.9
1890	62,947,714	25.5	21.2	35.1/64.9	87.5/12.5	22.0
1900	75,994,575	20.7	25.6	39.6/60.4	87.9/12.1	22.9
1910	91,972,266	21.0	31.0	45.6/54.4	88.9/11.1	24.1
1920	105,710,620	14.9	35.6	51.2/48.8	89.7/10.3	25.3
1930	122,775,046	16.1	41.2	56.1/43.9	89.8/10.2	26.4
1940	131,669,275	7.2	44.2	56.5/43.5	89.8/10.2	29.0
1950	150,697,361	14.5	50.7	64.0/36.0	89.5/10.5	30.2
1960	179,323,175	18.5	50.6	69.9/30.1	88.6/11.4	29.5
1970	203,302,031	13.4	57.4	73.5/26.5	87.6/12.4	28.0
1980	226,545,805	11.4	64.0	73.7/26.3	86.0/14.0	30.0
1990	248,709,873	9.9	70.3	77.5/22.5	80.3/19.7	32.9
1998	270,312,000	8.6	76	80/20	82.6/17.4	35.3

NA = Not available.

Employment, 1870–1998

Year	Number of Workers (in millions)	Male/Female Employment Ratio	Percentage of Workers in Unions
1870	12.5	85/15	—
1880	17.4	85/15	—
1890	23.3	83/17	—
1900	29.1	82/18	3
1910	38.2	79/21	6
1920	41.6	79/21	12
1930	48.8	78/22	7
1940	53.0	76/24	27
1950	59.6	72/28	25
1960	69.9	68/32	26
1970	82.1	63/37	25
1980	108.5	58/42	23
1985	108.9	57/43	19
1988	114.9	55/45	17
1990	124.8	54/46	16
1998	137.7	54/46	13.9

PRODUCTION, TRADE, AND FEDERAL SPENDING/DEBT, 1790–1998

Year	Gross National Product (GNP) (in billions $)	Balance of Trade (in millions $)	Federal Budget (in billions $)	Federal Surplus/Deficit (in billions $)	Federal Debt (in billions $)
1790	—	−3	.004	+.00015	.076
1800	—	−20	.011	+.0006	.083
1810	—	−18	.008	+.0012	.053
1820	—	−4	.018	−.0004	.091
1830	—	−3	.015	+.100	.049
1840	—	+25	.024	−.005	.004
1850	—	−26	.040	+.004	.064
1860	—	−38	.063	−.01	.065
1870	7.4	−11	.310	+.10	2.4
1880	11.2	+92	.268	+.07	2.1
1890	13.1	+87	.318	+.09	1.2
1900	18.7	+569	.521	+.05	1.2
1910	35.3	+273	.694	−.02	1.1
1920	91.5	+2,880	6.357	+.3	24.3
1930	90.7	+513	3.320	+.7	16.3
1940	100.0	−3,403	9.6	−2.7	43.0
1950	286.5	+1,691	43.1	−2.2	257.4
1960	506.5	+4,556	92.2	+.3	286.3
1970	992.7	+2,511	196.6	+2.8	371.0
1980	2,631.7	+24,088	579.6	−59.5	914.3
1990	5,465.1	−100,997.1	1,251.8	−220.3	3,223.3
1998	8,509.0	−231,000	1,653.0	69.0	5,479.0

Illustration Credits

Chapter 13, page 365(left): © The New-York Historical Society; **p. 365(right):** Library of Congress; **p. 371,** © The New-York Historical Society; **p. 377:** Museum of New Mexico; **p. 389:** Corbis-Bettmann; **p. 396:** Library of Congress.

Chapter 14, page 402(left): Cook Collection, Valentine Museum; **pp. 402(right), 412:** Library of Congress; **p. 414:** Corbis-Bettmann; **p. 417:** Cook Collection, Valentine Museum; **p. 431:** Corbis-Bettmann; **p. 435,** Library of Congress.

Chapter 15, page 442(left): Library of Congress; **p. 442(middle):** Corbis-Bettmann; **p. 442(right):** North Wind Picture Archives; **p. 443:** Library of Congress; **p. 445:** The Museum of the Confederacy, Richmond, Virginia; **p. 447,** Library of Congress; **p. 453:** North Wind Picture Archives; **p. 457:** Corbis-Bettmann; **p. 461:** Historic New Orleans Collection; **p. 470:** The Newberry Library, Chicago, Illinois; **p. 474:** Corbis-Bettmann.

Index

Note: Page numbers followed by the letter *i* refer to illustrations and by the letter *m* to maps.

Abolitionism: African-Americans and, 357–58; and divisions in movement, 359–62; early opposition to slavery, 356; free-soil ideology and, 390–91; Garrison and, 357; Great Britain and, 421–22; historical debate on character of slavery, 330; impact of, 362; Kansas controversy and, 388, 399; Lincoln and, 395; raid on Harpers Ferry and John Brown, 396–97; role of women, 355, 356. *See also* Antiabolitionism

Acadia, 98

"Act Concerning Religion" (1649), 36

Adams, Abigail, 139–40

Adams, Charles Francis, 421

Adams, John: American Revolution and, 123, 124, 136; Continental Congress and diplomacy, 146; election of 1800 and, 175–76, 177; as president, 173, 174; as vice president, 164

Adams, John Quincy: election of 1824 and, 237, 238; election of 1828 and, 239; Monroe Doctrine and, 236; peace settlement after War of 1812, 214–15; as president, 228–29, 238–39; as secretary of state, 228

Adams, Samuel, 111, 117, 118, 123, 152, 162

Adams-Onís Treaty of 1819, 229

Africa: African-American language and music, 332; circumnavigation of, 9; slavery in Americas and, 17–18; trade with American colonies, 76, 77. *See also* Slave trade

African-Americans: American Revolution and, 138, 153; Civil War and, 411–12, 438; colonization movement and emigration to Liberia, 356; concepts of freedom in post-Civil War South, 444–46; conscription riots in 1863 and violence against, 409; education and, 88, 182, 353, 457–58; 473–75; family and, 460–61; industrialization in New South and, 472–73; population growth in 1820s and 1830s, 273; Reconstruction and, 441–42, 450–51, 456–61, 468–69, 478; revivalism and, 187; slavery and development of society and culture, 322, 329, 332–34. *See also* Free Blacks; Slavery

Agriculture: in Africa, 17; Industrial Revolution and labor supply, 290–91; Native Americans and, 3, 4, 16, 34–35, 46; northern colonies and, 74; North in antebellum period, 303–8; plain folk of antebellum South and subsistence, 319–21; profitability of in South, 316, 459–60; sharecropping in South, 459, 473. *See also* Cotton industry; Land ownership; Rural life; *specific crops*

Alabama: secession of, 401–2; slave population, 312, *313m;* statehood and, 224

Alabama (ship), 422, 464

Alamo (Texas, 1836), 366–67

Alaska, 1, 464

Albany Plan, 96

Albany Regency, 246

Algonquin tribes, 3–4, 5

Alien and Sedition Acts (1798–1799), 174–75

Almanacs, 86, *87i*

Altamaha River (Georgia), 55

American Antislavery Society, 357, 359–60

American Colonization Society (ACS), 356

American Fur Company, 225

American Museum, 303

American Party, 277

American Revolution: cooperation among colonies and beginning of, 116–20; events leading up to, 107–16; historical debate on origins of, 126–27; importance of, 152–53; national governments and, 144–52; preparations for war, 122–25; society and, 137–41; state governments and, 141–44; war for independence, 128–37

American System, 237, 263

Amherst, Jeffrey, 101

Ancestor worship, 18

Anderson, Robert, 402, 404

Andros, Sir Edmund, 56, 57

Anglican Church, 137. *See also* Church of England

Anthony, Susan B., 355, 414

Anti-abolitionism, 359. *See also* Pro-slavery argument

Antietam, Battle of (1862), 411, 430, *431i*

Antifederalists, 162–63

Antilynching movement, 477

Anti-Mason Party, 262

Antinomian heresy, 46

Apaches, 15

Apologists, for slavery, 391

Appomattox Courthouse, Lee's surrender at, 438

Aptheker, Herbert, 330

Aristocracy, and planter class of antebellum South, 317–18, 320

Arizona, 386

Ark (ship), 36

Arkansas, 404

Army. *See* Confederate Army; Continental Army; Union Army

Arnold, Benedict, 129, 132, 134

Aroostook War (1838), 269
Art, nationalism and romanticism in painting, 339. *See also* Culture
Articles of Confederation (1777), 125, 144, 146, 147–49
Artisan tradition, and factory system, 292–94
Ashburton, Lord, 269
Ashley, Andrew and William, 225
Assimilation policy, and Native Americans, 207
Astor, John Jacob, 225, 369
Astor Place Opera House, 302
Asylums, and reform movements, 354
Atlanta, Georgia, 436
Atlanta Compromise (1895), 475
Attucks, Crispus, 110
Austin, Stephen F., 366
Automatic reaper, 306
Aztecs, 2, 11–13

Bacon, Nathaniel, 37–38
Bacon's Rebellion, 36–38, 61
Bagley, Sarah, 291
Bailyn, Bernard, 127
Balboa, Vasco de, 11
Baldwin, Joseph G., 342
Baltimore, Lord, 35, 36, 57, 58
Baltimore and Ohio Railroad, 280–81
Banjo, 332
Bank of the United States, 167, 219, 230, 233, 258–61, 265
Banks and banking: currency crisis after War of 1812, 219; Federalists and establishment of national, 166, 167; plantation economy of antebellum South, 315. *See also* Bank of the United States
Bank War (1830s), 258–61
Baptist Church, 83, 138, 186
Barbados, 40, 51. *See also* West Indies
Barbary states, 196
Barn raisings, 307
Barnum, P. T., 303
Barron, James, 205
Baseball, 303
Beans, 35, 46
Beard, Charles and Mary, 406–7
Bear Flag Revolution (1846), 376
Beauregard, Gen. P. G. T., 404, 425, 426
Becker, Carl, 126
Becknell, William, 224
Beecher, Catharine, 355
Belknap, William W., 463
Bell, John, 397
Benevolent Empire, 353
Benjamin, Judah P., 421
Benson, Lee, 249
Bering Strait, land bridge, 1
Berkeley, Sir John, 52
Berkeley, Sir William, 36–38
Bermuda, 38
Biddle, Nicholas, 258, 259, 260
Bierstadt, Albert, 339
Bill of Rights, 164, 171
Biological exchanges, between Native Americans and Europeans 15–17, 34–35
Birney, James G., 360

Birth rate: Industrial Revolution and decline in, 300; population growth in 1820s and 1830s, 273; population of Colonial America, 62–63; white women in antebellum South and, 319. *See also* Population
Black Belt, 224
Blackburn, Robin, 69
Black Codes, 449, 452–55
Black Death (bubonic plague), 8, 15
Black Hawk (Sauk chief), 254
Black Hawk War (1831–1832), 254
Blair, Francis P., 251
Blassingame, John, 331
Blithedale Romance, The (Hawthorne, 1852), 344
Blockade, of South during Civil War, 420
Bolívar, Simón, 238
Bonds, and financing of Civil War, 408
Book of Mormon, 346
Booth, John Wilkes, 448
Boston, Massachusetts: American Revolution, 108, 109–11, 116; founding of, 44; population of, 82, 275
Boston Massacre, 109–11
Boston tea party, 116
Bourbons, and New South, 470, 471, 476
Bradford, William, 43
Brady, Matthew, *414i*, *447i*
Bragg, Gen. Braxton, 419, 427, 434
Brant, Joseph and Mary, 132
Brazil, 11, 14, 18
Breckinridge, John C., 397
Bristow, Benjamin H., 463
Brokers, and plantation economy, 315
Brook Farm, 344
Brooks, Preston, 390
Brown, Charles Brockden, 185
Brown, John, 361, 388, 396–97
Brown, Joseph, 415
Brown, Moses, 189
Brown, Robert E., 127
Bryant, William Cullen, *340i*
Buchanan, James, 392–93, 394, 402
Bucktails, 246
Buell, Don Carlos, 428
Bull Run: First Battle of (1861), 425; Second Battle of (1862), 430
Bunker Hill, Battle of (1775), 129
Bureaucracy, and patronage system, 52
Burgoyne, John, 131–32
Burnside, Ambrose E., 430
Burr, Aaron, 176–77, 202–3
Burr Conspiracy, 202–3
Business: corporate organization, 289; expansion of 1820–1840, 285. *See also* Commerce; Industry; Manufacturing; Trade
Butler, Andrew P., 388, 390

Cabot, John, 19
Cahokia (Missouri), 3
Calhoun, John C.: Compromise of 1850 and, 382–83; government financing of transportation and, 221; nullification crisis and, 250, 252, 253; pro-slavery argument and, 391; as secretary of state, 268; as secretary of war, 228; Texas and, 367; War of 1812 and, 209; Whig Party and, 263

California: gold rush, 369, 379–80; Mexican-American War and, 376; statehood and, 381; westward migration and American settlement of, 369, 373–74
Calvert family, 35–36. *See also* Baltimore, Lord
Calvin, John, 20
Calvinism, 20, 83
Camp followers, and American Revolution, 139
Camp meetings, and revivalism, 186, *187i*
Canada: American Revolution and, 129–30; annexation movements in U.S., 208–9, 385–86; Oregon boundary dispute and, 368–69, 372–73; rebellion against colonial government in 1837, 269; War of 1812 and Rush-Bagot agreement of 1817, 215. *See also* Newfoundland; Nova Scotia; Quebec
Canals, 277–79
Canoe, 35
Cape Cod, Massachusetts, 42
Cape of Good Hope, 9
Caribbean: European colonialism in, 11, 38–41; slave trade and, 41, 67, 77. *See also* Cuba; Haiti; West Indies
Carnegie, Andrew, 424
Caroline (ship), 269
Carpetbaggers, 456
Carteret, Sir George, 52
Caruthers, William Alexander, 342
Case, Jerome I., 306
Cass, Lewis, 379
Cast-iron stove, 297–98
Catholic Church: American Revolution and, 138; in Colonial America, 83–84; immigrants from Scotland and, 71; Jesuit missionaries, 97; Maryland colonies and, 36, 57–58, 83–84; political parties in 1830s and 1840s, 262–63; Protestant Reformation and, 20; Spanish settlement in New World, 14. *See also* Religion
Catlin, George, 6
Cavaliers, and English Civil War, 49
Cayuga tribe. *See* Iroquois Confederacy
Central America, early civilizations of, 2–3. *See also* Latin America
Central Pacific Railroad, 405
Central Park (New York), 295
Chancellorsville, Battle of (1863), 431
Chandler, William, *183i*
Chapman, Kenneth, *377i*
Charles I, King of England, 43, 49
Charles II, King of England, 49, 50, 51, 53
Charles River (Massachusetts), 44
Charles River Bridge v. Warren Bridge (1837), 260–61
Charleston, South Carolina: Civil War and, 436, *443i*; founding of, 50; population of, 82
Charter of Liberties (1701), 54
Chattanoga, Battle of (1863), 434
"Checks and balances," and Constitution, 160–61
Cherokee Nation v. Georgia (1832), 255
Cherokee tribe: American Revolution and, 138; Proclamation of 1763 and, 104; removal of from Georgia, 238, 255; Trail of Tears, 255; western land claims and, 149; *Worcester v. Georgia* decision, 235. *See also* Native Americans

Chesapeake colonies: early years of, 28–38; slavery and, 67; women and families in, 64–65. *See also* Maryland; Mid-Atlantic region; Virginia
Chesapeake (ship), 205
Chicago, Illinois, 281, 304
Chickamauga, Battle of (1863), 434
Chickasaw tribe, 149, 255
Children: African societies and, 18; educational reform and social values, 353–54; mortality rates in Chesapeake colonies and, 62; Native Americans and, 5; slavery and, 70, 79. *See also* Family
China: California gold rush and immigration from, 380; Tyler administration relations with, 269
Choctaw tribe, 149, 255
Cholera, 348–49
Church, Frederic, 339
Church of England, 21, 83. *See also* Anglican Church
Church of Jesus Christ of Latter-day Saints, 346–47
Circumnavigation, of globe (1519–1922), 11
Circus, 303
Cities: industrialization and growth of, 192–93; leisure in antebellum period, 302; Native American civilizations and, 2; population growth in 1840s and 1850s, 275–76; populations of colonial, 82; slavery in antebellum South, 325. *See also* Urban life
Citizenship, and Fourteenth Amendment, 452
Civil disobedience, and Thoreau, 344
Civil rights, and New South, 475–76. *See also* Voting rights
Civil Rights Act (1866), 452
Civil War, American: campaigns and battles of, 422–38; class system of antebellum South, 320; diplomacy and, 421–22; historical debate on causes of, 406–7; legacy of, 439; military strategy and, 418–22; mobilization of North, 405, 408–14; mobilization of South, 414–18; negotiation of peace following, 442–49; secession crisis and, 401–4; status of North and South at beginning of, 404; status of South at end of, 443–44
Clark, George Rogers, 134, 200
Clark, William, 200–201
Class, socioeconomic: Carolina colonies and, 50; cities in colonial period and, 82; education in antebellum South and, 320; English system of and colonization, 60–61, 78; poverty in antebellum South and, 321; Quakers and, 53; rise of middle class, 297–99; social mobility in antebellum period, 296–97. *See also* Aristocracy; Middle class; Working class
Clay, Henry: Bank of United States and, 259; Compromise of 1850 and, 381, 382, 383; election of 1824 and, 237–38; election of 1844 and, 372; Missouri Compromise and, 231, 232; nullification crisis and, 253; on territorial expansion, 365–66; War of 1812 and, 209, 214–15; Whig Party and, 263
Clermont (steamship), 192, 222

Climate, and industrial development in antebellum South, 316
Clinton, De Witt, 246, 278
Clinton, Sir Henry, 134, 136
Clipper ships, 289
Coal, 287
Coercive Acts (1774), 116
Cohens v. Virginia (1821), 233
Cole, Thomas, 339, *340i*
Colfax, Schuyler, 463
Colleges and universities: in antebellum South, 320; in Colonial America, 88–89; cultural nationalism and, 182; Morrill act and land-grant, 405; women and, 300
Collings, Samuel, *90i*
Colonial America: characteristics of North and South, 58, 92; cooperation and beginnings of American Revolution, 116–20; economy of, 71, 73–77; imperialism after 1763, 102–106; intellectual life of, 83–91; loosening of ties with England, 94–96; population of, 60–67, 70–71; precursors of revolt, 107–16; Quaker colonies, 52–54; Restoration colonies, 49–55; society of, 78–82. *See also* American Revolution; Chesapeake; Government, colonial; New England; *specific states*
Colonization: Africa and Free Blacks, 356; Dutch, 22; English, 19–22, 27, 38–41, 49–58; French, 22; Spanish, 13–14. *See also* Colonial America; England; Spain
Colt, Samuel, 423
Columbian Centinel (newspaper), 228
Columbia University, 88
Columbus, Christopher, 7, 9, 11, 15, 38
Command of the Army Act (1867), 454
Commerce: in Colonial America, 76–77; England and early colonization efforts, 19; European voyages of discovery and, 8–9; government regulation of interstate, 234; Industrial Revolution and, 285–89; Native Americans and English colonies, 46; War of 1812 and, 204. *See also* Trade
Committee on the Conduct of the War, 419
Committees of correspondence, 111, 117
Common, and Puritan village, 80
Common law, and women, 140
Common Sense (Paine, 1776), 123–24
Commonwealth, and Massachusetts Puritans, 44
Commonwealth v. Hunt (1842), 294
Communications, and Industrial Revolution, 283–85. *See also* Newspapers; Telegraph
Compromise of 1850, 381–84
Compromise of 1877, 466–68
Conciliatory Propositions (1775), 118
Concord, Massachusetts, 118–20
Confederate Army, 408, 416–17, *445i*
Confederate States of America, 402, 415–16
Confederation: adoption and adaptation of Constitution, 161–64; Constitutional Convention and, 155–61; diplomacy and, 146–47; economy of, 150–52; establishment of, 144, 146; Native Americans and, 149–50; Old Northwest and, 147–49. *See also* Continental Congress
Confiscation Act (1861), 410
Congregational Church, 83, 138

Connecticut, 45, 142
Conquistadores, 13, 16
Conscription, and Civil War, 408–9, 416–17
Constitution, U.S.: adoption and adaptation of, 161–64; Confederate States of America and, 415; Confederation Congress and Constitutional Convention, 155–61; election of 1876 and, 467; importance of, 177–78; text of, A10–A20. *See also specific amendments*
Constitutional Union Party, 397
Constitutions, of states, 142–43, 394, 447
Continental Army, 125
Continental Congress: Articles of Confederation, 144; defining war aims, 123; establishment of, 117–18. *See also* Confederation
Continental System, 204
Contract theory, 124
Coode, John, 57–58
Cooper, Anthony Ashley, 50
Cooper, James Fenimore, 340
Cooper, Peter, *280i*
Copperheads, 409
Corinth, Mississippi, 426
Corn, 16, 34, 35
Cornwallis, Lord, 134, 136
Corporations, 285, 289
Corrupt bargain (1824), 237–38
Cortés, Hernando, 11, 13
Cotton gin, 189–91
Cotton industry: economy of antebellum South, 310–17; industrialization and, 189–91; slavery and, 190, 312–14, *322i*. *See also* Textile industry
Coureurs de bois, 22
Courts. *See* Supreme Court
Covenant, and Puritan community, 79
Cowpens, Battle of (1781), 134
Craven, Avery, 407
Crawford, William H., 237–38
Crédit Mobilier scandal, 463
Creek tribe, 210, 212, 238, 255
Creole (ship), 269
Creoles, 97
Crittenden, John J., 402
Crittenden Compromise (1861), 402–3
Crockett, Davy, 367
Cromwell, Oliver, 49
Crop-lien system, 459–60
Crosby, Alfred, 7
Cuba: Columbus and, 9; Monroe Doctrine and, 236; Ostend Manifesto and, 385; Spanish settlement of, 38
Cult of Domesticity, 300–301
Cultural nationalism: rise of in early nineteenth century, 180–88; society of antebellum period and, 362
Culture: biological exchanges between Native Americans and Europeans, 15–17; Civil War and, 407; cultural nationalism and, 180–88, 362; industrialization and, 308; public leisure and, 302; slavery and, 41, 79, 322, 329, 332–34; taverns and American Revolution, 113–14. *See also* Art; Intellectual life; Literature; Music; Popular culture
Cummings v. County Board of Education (1899), 475

Currency: Civil War and paper, 408, 416; Grant administration and greenback question, 463–64; Jackson administration and "specie circular," 265
Currency Act of 1764, 106
Currier, Nathaniel, *349i*
Customs houses, 109

Dale, Sir Thomas, 33
Dame schools, 88
Dance, and African-Americans, 333
Dare, Virginia, 24
Dartmouth College v. Woodward (1819), 232–33
Daughters of Liberty, 115
Davis, David, 467
Davis, Jefferson, 383, 386, 415, 419, 437, 438
Dawes, William, 119
Death rate: Jamestown colony and, 30; plantation system of antebellum South and, 78; population of Colonial America and, 62; slavery in Caribbean and, 40; slavery in South and, 324; westward migration and, 369. *See also* Mortality; Population
De Bow, James B. D., 315, *316i*
De Bow's Commercial Review, 315, *316i*
DeBry, Theodore, *24i*
Declaration of Independence, 124–25, 141, A5–A9
"Declaration of Sentiments and Resolutions," (1848), 355
Declaratory Act (1766), 108
Deep South, 224, 312
Deere, John, 305
Deerslayer, The (Cooper, 1841), 341
Degas, Edgar, *314i*
Delaware, 54, 162
De La Warr, Lord, 30, 31
Democracy: historical debate on Jacksonian, 248–49, 270; South and free-soil ideology, 390–91
Democratic Party: Civil War and, 409, 410; emergence of, 246; Hayes administration and, 468; Jackson administration and, 261–64; Lincoln and election of 1860, 397–98; New South and, 469, 476; Young America movement and, 385–86
Democratic Republicans, 239
Demographics. *See* Population
Denevan, William M., 7
Depressions: antebellum of 1857, 393; postrevolutionary period (1784–1787), 150–52. *See also* Panics
Deism, 185
Dew, Thomas R., 391
Dias, Bartholomeu, 9
Dickinson, John, 123
Diet: of middle class in antebellum period, 298–99; poverty in antebellum South and, 321; slavery and, 324
Diplomacy: Adams administration and, 238; American Revolution and, 146–47; Civil War and, 421–22; Johnson and Grant administrations, 464; post-revolutionary policy of neutrality, 171–72; Tyler administration and Whig Party, 269–70. *See also* Foreign policy
Discovery (ship), 28

Disease, epidemic: Black Death and population of Europe, 8, 15; early English colonies and, 29, 30; medical science and understanding of, 351; Native American population and European contact, 7, 13, 15, 25; Native American population of Oregon and, 369; reform movements and cholera, 348–49; vaccination in colonial period and, 89
District of Columbia. *See* Washington, D.C.
Divorce, 140
Dix, Dorothea, 354, 355, 413
Dobyns, Henry, 7
Domesticity, cult of, 300–301
Domestic service: African-American women in post-Civil War South, 461; indentured servitude and, 61; slavery and, 79, 324–25; working-class women and, 301
Dominion of New England, 56, 57
Dorr, Thomas L., 244–45
Dorr Rebellion (1842), 245
Doughty, Thomas, 339
Douglas, Stephen A.: Compromise of 1850 and, 383, 384; debates with Lincoln, 395; Kansas-Nebraska Controversy and, 387, 394
Douglass, Frederick, 358
Dove (ship), 36
Draft. *See* Conscription
Dragging Canoe (Cherokee chief), 138
Drake, Sir Francis, 23–24
Dred Scott decision (1857), 393–94, 399
Du Bois, W. E. B., 450–51
Dunning, William A., 450
Duran Codex, *13i*
Durand, Asher, 339, *340i*
Dutch Reformed Church, 83
Dutch West India Company, 22, 52

East, and images of West, 226
East India Company, 115–16
East Jersey, 52
Eaton, John H., 251
Economics: American Revolution and, 126, 127, 140–41; Civil War and development in North, 413, 439; Civil War and impact on South, 417–18; Civil War and nationalism, 405, 408; Colonial America and, 71, 73–77; cotton and antebellum South, 310–17; depression after American Revolution, 150–52; Industrial Revolution and, 308; production, trade, and national debt from 1790 to 1996, A39; railroads and, 282–83; War of 1812 and postwar boom, 218–21. *See also* Currency; Depressions; Financing; National debt; Panics; Taxation
Edict of Nantes, 70
Education: African-Americans and, 88, 182, 353, 457–58, 473–75; in antebellum South, 319, 320; Colonial America, 88–89; cultural nationalism, 181–82; Native Americans and, 88, 182, 353; reform movements and, 352–53; women and, 182, 319. *See also* Colleges and universities
Edwards, Jonathan, 85, 89
Eighteenth Amendment, of Constitution, A25

Eighth Amendment, of Constitution, A21
Elections, presidential: of 1789, 163–64, A30; of 1792, 169, A30; of 1796, 173; of 1800, 175–77, A30; of 1804, 195, A30; of 1808, 205–6, A31; of 1812, A31; of 1816, 227, A31; of 1820, 228, A31; of 1824, 237–38, 245, A31; of 1828, 239, 245, A31; of 1832, A31; of 1836, 263–64, A31; of 1840, 266, A32; of 1844, 372–73, A32; of 1848, 379, A32; of 1852, 384–85, A32; of 1856, 392–93, A32; of 1860, 397–98, A32; of 1864, 409–10, A32; of 1868, 462, A33; of 1872, 462, A33; of 1876, 466–67, A33; of 1880, A33; of 1884, A33; of 1888, A33; of 1892, A33; of 1896, A33; of 1900, A33; of 1904, A33; of 1908, A34; of 1912, A34; of 1916, A34; of 1920, A34; of 1924, A34; of 1928, A34; of 1932, A34; of 1936, A35; of 1940, A35; of 1944, A35; of 1948, A35; of 1952, A35; of 1956, A35; of 1960, A35; of 1964, A35; of 1968, A35; of 1972, A36; of 1976, A36; of 1980, A36; of 1984, A36; of 1988, A36; of 1992, A36; of 1996, A36. See also Political parties; Politics
Electoral college, 245
Electricity, 89, 90i
Eleventh Amendment, of Constitution, A22
Elizabeth I, Queen of England, 21, 23
Elkins, Stanley, 330–31
Emancipation Proclamation (1863), 411, 421, 439, 443–44
Embargo, and War of 1812, 205–6
Emerson, Ralph Waldo, 343
Encomiendas, 14
Energy, and industrialization, 287
Enforcement Acts of 1870 and 1871, 465
Engerman, Stanley, 331
England: birth rate in seventeenth century, 62; Caribbean colonies of, 38–41; development of colonial empire, 55–57; early exploration and colonization, 19–22, 23–25; factors shaping character of colonies, 27; Glorious Revolution and, 57–58; Restoration and colonies of, 49–55; trade with American colonies, 76, 77. See also Colonial America; Great Britain
English Reformation, 20–21
Enlightenment, and Colonial America: government and, 85; intellectual life and, 83, 85–86; medicine and, 64; science and, 89
Epidemics. See Disease, epidemic
Era of Good Feelings, 226–30, 240
Erie Canal, 275, 278–79
Eriksson, Leif, 8
Eskimos, 3
Essex Junto, 202
Ethnicity, political parties and social divisions in 1830s and 1840s, 262–63. See also Immigration
Ethnocultural interpretation, of Civil War, 407
Europe: American Civil War and, 421–22; Black Death and population of, 8, 15; colonial expansion in Caribbean, 38, 39m; sources of immigration to colonies, 70–71, 72m; trade with American colonies, 76, 77; transatlantic telegraph cable and, 284; voyages of discovery and early colonization of New World, 8–25. See also specific countries

Evans, Oliver, 191
Expansionism: Democrats and, 372–73; Great Migration and, 222–23; Jefferson administration and, 198–203; Manifest Destiny and, 365–66; Mexican-American War and, 374–76; Oregon and, 367–69; overland trails and wagon trains, 369–71; Southwest and California, 373–74, 378m; Texas and, 366–67; U.S. from 1783 to 1898, A4m; War of 1812 and, 203–15. See also Migrations; West
Ex parte Milligan (1866), 454–55

Factory: artisan tradition and, 292–94; beginnings of industrialism, 189; Industrial Revolution and emergence of, 286. See also Industry; Manufacturing
Factory Girls Association, 291
Fair Oaks, Battle of (1862), 428
Fallen Timbers, Battle of (1794), 150
Family: African-Americans and Reconstruction, 460–61; in Colonial America, 64–65; Industrial Revolution and, 299–300; slavery and, 79, 324, 333–34. See also Children; Women
Farms and farming. See Agriculture; Rural life
Farragut, David G., 426
Federalists: Constitution and, 161–63; disagreements about nature of new government, 165–69; downfall of, 172–77; end of, 228; War of 1812 and secession movement in New England, 214
Fell, Margaret, 52
Female Labor Reform Association, 291
Feminism: interpretations of history and, 331; reform movements and rise of, 355–56. See also Women's rights movement
Feminist historians, 331
Ferdinand of Aragon, King of Spain, 9
Fifteenth Amendment, of Constitution, 454, 466, 475, 476, A24
Fifth Amendment, of Constitution, A21
"Fifty-four forty or fight!" 372
Fifty-fourth Massachusetts infantry, 412
Fillmore, Millard, 383, 384, 392
Financing: of American Revolution, 125; of Civil War in North, 408; of Civil War in South, 416. See also National debt; Taxation
Finney, Charles Grandison, 348
First Amendment, of Constitution, A20
Fish, Hamilton, 462, 464
Fishing: Native Americans and, 4i, 35; New England industry, 43, 75
Fitch, John, 191
Fitzhugh, George, 318
Five civilized tribes, 254–55
Fletcher v. Peck (1810), 232
Flintlock rifle, 47, 48
Florida: Adams-Onís Treaty and Spanish cessation of, 228–29; boundaries of and treaties with Spain, 147; secession of, 401–2; Spanish settlements and English colonization of Georgia, 54; War of 1812 and, 209
Florida (ship), 422
Fogel, Robert, 331
Foner, Eric, 407, 451

Food. *See* Diet
Foreign policy: Jefferson administration and, 198; Latin America and Monroe Doctrine, 235–36. *See also* Diplomacy
Forrest, Edwin, 302
Fort Donelson (Tennessee), 426
Fort Duquesne, 101
Fort Henry (Tennessee), 426
Fort Necessity, 99
Fort Pickens (Pensacola, Florida), 402
Fort Sumter (Charleston, South Carolina), 402, 403–4
Forty-niners, 379–80
Forty-Ninth parallel, 372–73
"Founding Fathers," 157
Fourteenth Amendment, of Constitution, 452, 475, A23-A24
Fourth Amendment, of Constitution, A20
Fourth of July, 301
Fowler, Orson and Lorenzo, 350–51
Fox, George, 52, 53
Fox-Genovese, Elizabeth, 331
Fox tribe, 254
France: American Civil War and, 404, 421, 422; American Revolution and, 132–33; early colonization and, 22; French Revolution, 169; Great Britain and war in 1790s, 171–72; Iroquois Confederacy and, 97–98; Louisiana Purchase and, 198–200; quasi war with in 1790s, 173–74; Seven Years' War and struggle for control of North America, 98–99
Franklin, Benjamin: Albany Plan and, 96; almanacs and, 86; American Revolution and, 132, 133, 136; Constitutional Convention and, 157, 159, 161; Declaration of Independence and, 124; University of Pennsylvania and, 89
Franklin, John Hope, 451
Free blacks: abolitionism and, 357–58; communities of in cities of antebellum period, 296, 326; in southern cities of prerevolutionary period, 79; voting rights and, 245. *See also* African-Americans
Freedmen's Bureau, 444–46, 452
Freedom, concepts of in post-Civil War South, 444–46
Free love, and Oneida Community, 345–46
Freemasonry, 262
Free soil movement, 360, 390–91
Free-Soil Party, 379, 384
Fremont, John C., 376, 392
French and Indian War (1754–1763), 99–102, 120
French Revolution, 169
Fugitive Slave Act, 385
Fulton, Robert, 191–92, 222, 234
Fundamental Articles of New Haven (1639), 45
Fundamental Constitution for Carolina (1669), 50
Fundamental Orders of Connecticut (1634), 45
Fur trade: in Far West, 224–26; French colonization and, 22; northern colonies and, 43, 75; Virginia colonies and, 37

Gadsden, James, 386
Gadsden Purchase (1853), 386
Gage, Gen. Thomas, 118–19

Galen, 63
Gallatin, Albert, 196, 214–15
Gama, Vasco de, 9
Garrison, William Lloyd, 357, 359
Gates, Gen. Horatio, 132, 134
Gatling, Richard, 423
Gender roles, and Utopian communities, 345–46. *See also* Women
Genovese, Eugene, 331
Geography: exploration of West and, 200–202, 226; mobility of antebellum population, 223, 296–97; voyages of Columbus and, 9, 11
George I, King of England, 95
George II, King of England, 55, 95
George III, King of England, 103
Georgia: Civil War and, 436; founding of, 54–55; ratification of Constitution by, 162; removal of Native Americans from, 238; rice production and, 71, 73; secession of, 401–2; state government of, 142
Germany, 70–71, 276
Gettysburg, Battle of (1863), 432, *434m*
Ghana, kingdom of, 17
Ghent, Treaty of (1815), 215
Gibbons, Thomas, 234
Gibbons v. Ogden (1824), 234
Gienapp, William, 407
Gilbert, Sir Humphrey, 23
Glorious Revolution (1688), 57–58
Godspeed (ship), 28
Gold rush, 369, 379–80
Goliad (Texas, 1836), 367
Gone with the Wind (novel and film), 450
Goodyear, Charles, 287
Government
—colonial: British imperialism after 1763 and, 102–6; of Carolina colonies, 50; of Connecticut, 45; Dominion of New England and, 56, 57; English colony of New York, 52; Enlightenment and, 85; French and Indian War, 101; of Georgia, 55; Glorious Revolutions and reorganizations of, 57–58; loosening of ties with England, 94–96; of Maryland, 57–58; of New Jersey, 52; of Pennsylvania, 54; Plymouth Plantation and, 43; revolutionary ideology and, 111–13; of Rhode Island, 45–46; Stamp Act crisis and, 107–8; Townshend Program and, 108–9; tradition of self-government and, 91; of Virginia, 33, 36–38
—Confederate States of America, 415–16
—federal: American Revolution and establishment of national, 144–52; Constitutional Convention and framing of, 155–61; contract theory and, 124; downfall of Federalists, 172–77; economic growth after War of 1812, 219–20; Federalists and Republicans and disagreement about nature of, 165–69; Jackson and concept of union, 250–53; Marshall Court and, 234; national sovereignty and, 169–72; regulation of interstate commerce by, 234. *See also* Politics
—states: American Revolution and, 141–44; constitutions of, 142–43, 394, 447; Reconstruction in South and, 456–57. *See also specific states*

Grady, Henry, 471
Graham, Sylvester, 349–50
Grant, Gen. Ulysses C.: Civil War and, 419, 426, 432, 435–38; election of 1868 and, 462; Reconstruction and administration of, 462–64, 466
Grasse, Admiral de, 136
Great Awakening, 84–85
Great Britain: *Alabama* claims, 464; American Civil War and, 404, 421–22; American Revolution and, 123, 128–37, 146; France and war in 1790s, 171–72; imperialism after 1763, 102–6; impressment and Navy of, 204–5; loosening of ties with colonies, 94–96; Native Americans and, 206–7; Oregon boundary dispute and, 367–69, 372–73; railroads and, 280; Seven Years' War and control of North America, 96–102; War of 1812 and, 210–15. *See also* England
Great Compromise, and Constitutional Convention, 159
Great Lakes: canal system and, 279; steam-powered shipping on, 221; urban growth in upper Midwest, 275; War of 1812 and, 210, 215
Great Migration, 222–23
Great Plains: Native American cultures of, 3; railroads and white settlement of, 386
Great Triumvirate, 263
Greeley, Horace, 462, 466
Greenbacks, 408, 463–64
Greene, Nathanael, 134, 136
Greenville, Treaty of (1795), 150
Grenville, George, 103
Grenville, Sir Richard, 23
Grid system, 147, *148m*, 149
Grimké, Sarah and Angelina, 355
Griswold, Roger, 175, *176i*
Gross National Product, from 1790 to 1996, A39
Guadalupe Hidalgo, Treaty of (1848), 376
Guilford Court House, Battle of (1781), 134, 136
Guinea, Upper, 17
Gutman, Herbert, 331

Haiti, 238. *See also* Hispaniola
Hale, John P., 384
Halleck, Gen. Henry W., 419
Hamilton, Alexander: Burr conspiracy and, 202; Confederation Congress and, 150–51; Constitutional Convention and, 156, 157; diplomacy and policy of neutrality, 172; Federalists and, 162, 165–66, 177; as secretary of treasury, 164; and Washington as president, 169
Hamilton, Andrew, 91
Hammond, Bray, 249
Hancock, John, 118
Handlin, Oscar and Mary, 68, 69
Handsome Lake (Iroquois prophet), 187–88
Harpers Ferry, John Brown's raid on, 396–97
Harrison, William Henry, 206–7, 208, 210, 264, 266–68, 367
Harrison Land Law (1800), 207
Hartford, Connecticut, 45

Hartford Convention (1814), 214
Harvard University, 88
Hasenclever, Peter, 74–75
Hawaii, annexation of, 385
Hawley, Nathan, *298i*
Hawthorne, Nathaniel, 344
Hayes, Rutherford B., 466–67, 468
Hayne, Robert Y., 251–52
Headright system, 32, 36, 50
Health, and reform movements of antebellum period, 348–51. *See also* Death rates; Disease, epidemic; Medicine; Mortality; Public health
Hemmings, Sally, 176
Henry, Patrick, 107, 162
Henry the Navigator, Prince of Portugal, 9
Henry VII, King of England, 19
Henry VIII, King of England, 20–21
Herskovits, Melville J., 330
"Hill people," of antebellum South, 320
Hispaniola, 9, 15, 38. *See also* Haiti
History and historians, subjects of debate: causes of Civil War, 406–7; character of slavery, 330–31; Jacksonian democracy, 248–49; nature of Reconstruction, 450–51; origins of American Revolution, 126–27; origins of slavery, 68–69; population of Native Americans before European contact, 6–7
Hoe, Richard, 284
Hofstadter, Richard, 248–49
Holidays, and leisure in antebellum period, 301
Holmes, Oliver Wendell, 352
Homeopathic medicine, 64
Homer, Winslow, *290i*
Homestead Act (1862), 405
Hood, Gen. John B., 436
Hooker, Gen. Joseph, 431, 432
Hooker, Thomas, 45
Hooper, Johnson J., 342
Horses and horse racing, 16, 193
Horseshoe Bend, Battle of (1814), 212
Hot-air balloons, 423–24
Household servants. *See* Domestic service
House of Burgesses (Virginia), 33, 37
House of Delegates (Maryland), 36
House of Seven Gables, The (Hawthorne, 1851), 344
Housing: early plantations and, 78; middle class in antebellum period and, 299; slavery and, 78, 324
Houston, Gen. Sam, 367
Howard, Gen. Oliver O., 444
Howe, Elias, 288
Howe, Gen. William, 130–31
Hudson, Henry, 22
Hudson River, English exploration of, 22
Hudson River School, of painting, 339
Huguenots, 20, 70
Humoralism, theory of, 63
Hunting: migration of early peoples to Americas, 1; Native Americans and English colonies, 35. *See also* Fur trade
Hutchinson, Anne, 43, 46
Hutchinson, Thomas, 108, 137
Hydrotherapy, 349

Iceboxes, 299
Ideology: abolitionism and free-soil, 390–91; American Revolution and, 111–13, 126–27; Civil War and, 407
Illinois, 224, 347
Illinois tribe, 234–35
Immigration: California gold rush and Chinese, 380; changing sources of European to colonies, 70–71, 72m; labor and, 289, 292; nativism and, 276–77; population growth in 1830s, 274–76; prejudice against Irish, 296; slave trade and Africans, 17–18; Texas and, 366; Virginia colonies and headright system, 32. See also Migrations
Impeachment, of Andrew Johnson, 455
Imperialism, British empire and Colonial America, 102–6
Impressment, and British navy, 204–5
Incas, 2–3, 12m, 13
Income: African-Americans and Reconstruction, 459–60; per capita in New South, 472
Income tax, 408, 416
Indentured servants, 33, 61–62, 64
India, 9
Indiana, 224
Indiana Territory, 207
Indian Intercourse Act (1834), 255
Indian ring scandal, 463
Indian Territory, 255, 256
Industrialism: agriculture and, 305; beginnings of in early-nineteenth century, 188–93; in New South, 471–73. See also Industrial Revolution; Industry
Industrial Revolution: changes in demographics and, 272–77; commerce and, 285–89; communication and, 283–85; economy and, 308; labor and, 289–94; society and, 295–303; transportation and, 277–83. See also Industrialism
Industry: in Colonial America, 74–75, 82; economy of antebellum South and, 314–15; Industrial Revolution and, 285–89. See also Industrialism
Inflation, and Civil War in South, 416
Intellectual life: in antebellum period, 339–47; in Colonial America, 83–91. See also Culture
"Intolerable Acts" (1774), 116, 117
Inventions, and Industrial Revolution, 287–88
Ireland: English colonization of, 21–22, 27; immigration to Colonial America from, 71; immigration from in 1830–1860, 275, 276, 292, 296
Iron Act of 1750, 75
Ironworks, 74–75, 314–15. See also Steel industry
Iroquois Confederacy: American Revolution and, 132, 138, 139; colonies and treaty with, 96; France and, 97–98; French and Indian War and, 102; Handsome Lake and revivalism, 187–88; in precontact period, 4, 5; western lands and, 149. See also Native Americans
"Irrepressible-conflict" argument, and debate on causes of Civil War, 406–7

Irving, Washington, 185, 340
Isabel of Castile, Queen of Spain, 9
Islam, 17, 18

Jackson, Andrew: Bank of United States and, 258–61; election of 1824 and, 237, 238; Florida and, 228; historical debate on democracy and, 248–49; inauguration of, 242, 244i; influence of on government and democracy, 270; Native Americans and, 210, 212, 253, 255; nullification crisis and, 252–53; paper currency and, 265; as president, 239–40, 246–47, 250–53; Texas and, 367; Van Buren and, 251; War of 1812 and, 213
Jackson, Rachel, 239, 244i
Jackson, Thomas J. (Stonewall), 428, 431
Jamaica, 40. See also West Indies
James I, King of England, 21, 25, 28, 34, 43
James II, King of England, 51–52, 56, 57
Jameson, J. Franklin, 126
Jamestown, Virginia: establishment of, 22, 23, 28–31; Native American agricultural technology and survival of, 34
Jay, John, 136, 162, 172
Jay Cooke and Company, 463
Jefferson, Thomas: contributions of, 215, 216; Declaration of Independence and, 124; election of 1800 and, 175–77; and expansion of national domain, 198–203; Native Americans and, 139, 207; Northwest Ordinance and, 147; as president, 193–98; on religious toleration, 143; Republicans and, 169; as secretary of state, 164; slavery and, 144, 218; as vice president, 173; War of 1812 and, 205
Jenner, Edward, 351
Jesuit missionaries, 97
Jim Crow laws, 475–77
Johnson, Andrew: Democratic Party and Civil War, 410; impeachment of, 455, 477; Reconstruction and, 448–49, 452, 458
Johnson v. McIntosh (1823), 234–35
Johnston, Albert Sidney, 426
Johnston, Joseph E., 428, 435, 436
Joint occupation, and Oregon boundary dispute, 368
Jordan, Winthrop, 68–69
Journalism, and technological advancements in 1840s, 284–85. See also Magazines; Newspapers
Judiciary Act of 1801, 177, 197

Kansas, slavery and sectional conflict, 387, 388–90, 394
Kansas-Nebraska Controversy, 387
Kearny, Col. Stephen W., 376, 377i
Keckley, Elizabeth, 326
Kendall, Amos, 242, 251
Kennedy, John Pendleton, 342
Kennesaw Mountain, Battle of (1863), 436
Kentucky, 171
Kerber, Linda, 127
Key, Francis Scott, 212
King, Rufus, 227
King George's War (1744–1748), 98
King Philip's War (1675–1676), 47–49

King's Mountain, Battle of (1780), 134
King William's War (1689–1697), 98
Kinship networks, and slavery, 334
Kitchen Cabinet, 251
Kleppner, Paul, 407
Knights of the White Camellia, 465
Know-Nothings, 277, 387, 392
Knox, Gen. Henry, 164
Kroeber, Alfred, 6–7
Ku Klux Klan, 465

Labor: California gold rush and shortage of, 380; Industrial Revolution and, 289–94; mutual aid system in Old Northwest and shortage of, 223; origins of slavery in colonial period, 17, 33, 38, 40, 62, 66; post-Reconstruction system in South, 451, 458–59; slavery and cities of antebellum South, 325; slave system and white women in antebellum South, 319, 325; tobacco economy of early Chesapeake and, 32; U.S. work force, 1870–1994, A38; women in New South and, 472. See also Unions and unionization; Work
Lafayette, Marquis de, 136
Lancaster Pike, 192, 221
Land grant colleges, 405
Land ownership: and conflicts with Native Americans in New England colonies, 47; as incentive for English colonization, 19; inheritance and subdivision in colonial New England, 80; speculators and speculation in Old Northwest, 149, 230, 264–65; tenant farmers in post-Civil War South, 458–59
Languages: African-Americans and, 332; Algonquin group of, 3–4; Spanish Empire and dialects, 16
Last of the Mohicans, The (Cooper, 1826), 341
Latin America, nationalist revolutions and Monroe Doctrine, 235–36. See also Central America; South America
Law: concepts of in Colonial America, 90–91; Jim Crow laws in New South, 475–77; legal rights of women, 140. See also Slave codes; Supreme Court
Leaves of Grass (Whitman, 1855), 341
Lectures, as entertainment in antebellum period, 303
Lee, "Mother" Ann, 346
Lee, Richard Henry, 123
Lee, Robert E., 396, 419, 428–29, 431, 432, 435, 437, 438
Leisler, Jacob, 57
Leisure, and society in antebellum period, 301–3
L'Enfant, Pierre, 193–94
Leopard (ship), 205
Lesser Antilles, 39m
Lewis, Meriwether, 200–201
Lexington, Massachusetts, 119–20
Liberator (newspaper), 357
Liberia, 356
Liberty Party, 360
Life expectancy: in Colonial America, 62, 64; slavery and, 324. See also Death rates; Mortality

Lincoln, Abraham: African-Americans and, 438; assassination of, 448; on economy of Old Northwest, 307; election of 1860 and, 397–98; emergence of as political figure, 395; Fort Sumter and, 403–4; leadership and politics of Civil War, 409–10; Reconstruction plan of, 446; sectional conflicts and election of, 399; strategy of Civil War and, 418–19; terms of peace after Civil War and, 442
Literacy: in antebellum period, 353; in Colonial America, 86–87; and voting rights in New South, 476
Literature: of antebellum South, 341–42; cultural nationalism and, 184–85; romanticism and nationalism in antebellum period, 340–41; women in antebellum period and, 301, 302. See also Magazines; Newspapers; Poetry
Little Turtle (Miami chief), 150
Litwack, Leon, 451
Livingston, Robert R., 191–92, 199, 234
Locke, John, 50, 111, 124, 175
Log cabin, election of 1840 and image of, 266–68
London Company, 28–30, 43
Long, Stephen H., 226
Longstreet, Augustus B., 342
Lords of Trade, 56
Louisbourg, Nova Scotia, 98, 101
Louisiana, 401–2, 432. See also New Orleans
Louisiana Purchase, 198–200, 201m
Lovejoy, Elijah, 359
Lowell, Francis Cabot, 220
Lowell system, 291
Loyalists, and American Revolution, 137–38
Lundy, Benjamin, 357
Luther, Martin, 20
Lynching, in New South, 477
Lyon, Mary, 300
Lyon, Matthew, 175, 176i
Lyon, Nathaniel, 425

McClellan, Gen. George B., 410, 419, 425, 428–30
McCormick, Cyrus H., 306
McCulloch v. Maryland (1819), 233–34
McDowell, Gen. Irvin, 425, 428
Machine tools, 286–87
McIntosh, William, 238
McNeill, William, 7
Macon's Bill No. 2 (1810), 206
Macready, Charles, 302
Madison, James: Bill of Rights and, 164; Confederation Congress and taxation, 151; Constitutional Convention and, 156, 157, 159, 160; Federalists and, 162; Marbury v. Madison and, 197; national debt and, 167; as president, 205–6, 221; Republicans and, 169; War of 1812 and, 205, 209
Magazines, of antebellum period: economy of South and, 315; women's literature and, 301. See also Newspapers
Magellan, Ferdinand, 11
Maine: Aroostook War and, 269; settlement of, 46; statehood and, 231–32
Maize. See Corn

Malaria, 28, 30, 73
Mali, empire of, 17, 18
Manifest Destiny, 365–66
Mann, Horace, 352, 354
Manufacturing: government promotion of after War of 1812, 219–20; growth from 1840 to 1860, 286; interchangeability of parts and, 191, 287; in New South, 472. *See also* Factory; Industry
Marbury, William, 197
Marbury v. Madison (1803), 197
"March to the Sea," 436, *438m*
Marcy, William L., 247
Marion, Francis, 134
Marriage: African-Americans and Reconstruction, 460; indentured servants in Chesapeake colonies and, 64; New England colonies and, 65; slavery and, 78–79, 333–34. *See also* Divorce; Family; Women
Marshall, John, 197–98, 203, 232–34, 243
Martial law, and Civil War, 409
Mary, Queen of England, 21, 57
Maryland: Catholic Church and, 36, 57–58, 83–84; early colonies of, 35–36; Glorious Revolution and, 57–58
Mason, James M., 422
Masons, and Society of Freemasons, 262
Massachusetts: American Revolution and, 116, 118–20; Dominion of New England, 56, 57; education and, 88, 182, 352–53; ironworks in colonial, 74; Massachusetts Bay experiment, 43–44; mental hospitals and, 354; Shays' Rebellion and, 151–52; state government of, 143; tavern culture and, 114; textile industry in, *220i*. *See also* Boston; New England
Matchlock rifle, 47, 48
Mather, Cotton, 89
Matrilineality, of African and Native American societies, 17–18
Mayas, 2–3, 15
Mayflower (ship), 42
Mayflower Compact, 43
Meade, George C., 432
Medicine: advances in antebellum period, 351–52; in Colonial America, 63–64, 89; cultural nationalism and, 183–84. *See also* Health; Public health
Melodrama, 302
Melville, Herman, 341, 344
Memorials, to Confederate dead in South, *445i*
Mennonites, 71
Mental hospitals, 354
Mercantilism, 19–20
Mercenaries, and American Revolution, 123
Merrimac (ship), 420, 424
Mestizos, 16
Metacomet (King Philip), 47
Methodist Church, 186
Mexican-Americans, and independence movement in Texas, 367
Mexican-American War (1846–1848), 374–76
Mexico: early civilizations of, 2–3; Gadsden Purchase and, 386; independence from Spain in 1821, 224; Mexican-American War and, 374–76; Texas and, 366, 376. *See also* Mexico City

Mexico City, 2, 374, *375m*
Meyers, Marvin, 249
Meynell, Lt. Francis, *66i*
Miami tribe, 150
Mid-Atlantic region, and American Revolution, 130–32. *See also* Chesapeake colonies
Middle class: Reconstruction and African-American, 478; society of antebellum period and rise of, 297–99; women and, 301. *See also* Class, socioeconomic
Middle passage, and slave trade, 67
"Midnight appointments," 177
Midway Islands, annexation of, 464
Midwest, and population growth from 1840 to 1860, 275. *See also* Northwest, Old; *specific states*
Midwives, 63, 64, 184
Migrations: of early peoples to Americas, 1; westward in antebellum period, 369–71. *See also* Great migration; Immigration
Military: American Revolution and, *117i*, 125; Civil War and strategy, 418–22; Civil War and technology of war, 423–24; French and Indian War and, *100i*, 101; Grant's philosophy of, *435i*; Jefferson administration and, 196; Quartering Act of 1765, 108–109; and settlement of Georgia, 54
Military districts, and Reconstruction, 454
Miller, Alfred Jacob, *247i*
Minstrel shows, 302
Minutemen, 118–20
Mississippi: Civil War and, 426; secession of, 401–2; slave population of, 312, *313m*; statehood and, 224. *See also* Vicksburg
Mississippi River: Civil War and, 426, 432; railroads and, 281; steam-powered shipping on, 221. *See also* New Orleans
Missouri, 231–32
Missouri Compromise (1819), 230–32, 378, 387
Mobility: rural life and westward movement in early-nineteenth century, 223; social in antebellum period, 296–97
Moby Dick (Melville, 1851), 341
Mohawk and Hudson Railroad, 281
Mohawk tribe, 47, 97. *See also* Iroquois Confederacy
Monitor (ship), 420, 424
Monroe, James, 199, 205, 227–28
Monroe Doctrine, 235–36
Montcalm, Marquis de, 101
Montesquieu, Baron de, 160
Montezuma, 11
Montgomery, Gen. Richard, 129
Montreal, Quebec, 22
Mooney, James, 6
Moore's Creek Bridge, Battle of (1776), 129
Morality, and reform movements, 348. *See also* Values
Moran, Thomas, 339
Moravians, 71
Morgan, Edmund, 69, 127
Morgan, William, 262
Mormons, 346–47
Morrill Act (1865), 405
Morris, Robert, 150–51

Morse, Samuel F. B., 283–84
Morse Code, 283
Mortality: Civil War and, 412, 422; Plymouth colony and, 43; population growth in 1820s and 1830s and, 273; Puritan settlements and, 44. *See also* Death rate; Population
Morton, William, 351
Mott, Lucretia, 355
Mountain men, 225–26
Mt. Holyoke College, 300
Murfreesboro, Battle of (1862), 428
Murray, Judith Sargent, 140, 182
Music, and African-Americans, 332–33
Muskogean tribes, 4, 5
Mutiny Act of 1765, 104, 108–9

Napoleon Bonaparte, 174, 199, 204, 212
Narragansett tribe, 45, 48–49
Narrative of the Life of Frederick Douglass (Douglas, 1845), 358
Nash, Gary, 127
Nashville, Battle of (1864), 436
Nast, Thomas, *453i, 470i*
National Bank Acts (1863–1864), 405
National debt: Federalists and, 166, 167; Jefferson administration and, 196; trade and gross national product from 1790 to 1996, A39. *See also* Financing
National Greenback Party, 464
Nationalism: Civil War and economic, 405, 408; Compromise of 1850 and, 382; cultural nationalism of early nineteenth century, 180–88; Manifest Destiny and, 365–66; Marshall Court and, 232–35; Missouri Compromise and, 230–32; Monroe Doctrine and, 235–36; popular culture and, 240; sectionalist conflicts of 1850s and, 398; voyages of discovery and European, 8–9
National Road, 221
National Trades' Union, 294
National Women's Loyal League, 414
Native American Party, 276
Native Americans: agriculture of, 3, 4, 34–35, 46, 304–5; American Revolution and, 138–39; biological and cultural exchanges with Europeans, 15–17; British empire after 1763 and relations with, 103–4, 206–7; California gold rush and, 380; Columbus and, 9; Constitution and sovereignty, 171; early civilizations of, 2–5, 25; early English colonies in Virginia and, 33–34, 37, 38; education and, 88, 182, 353; empires of at European contact, *10m, 12m;* French and Indian War and, 102; French relations with, 22, 97; Great Plains and white settlement, 386; New England colonies and, 43, 46–49; Oregon territory and, 369; population before European contact, 1, 2, 6–7, 25; Quaker colonies and, 53–54; reform movements and, 354; removal of from Southeast, 238, 253–58; reservations and, 354; revivalism and, 187–88; subsistence patterns of, *5m;* Supreme Court and, 234–35; War of 1812 and, 210, 212, 215; western lands and, 149–50; westward migrations and wagon trains, 371. *See also* Cherokee tribe; Disease, epidemic; Iroquois Confederacy; *specific tribes*

Nativism, and immigration, 276–77
Nature: Hudson River School of painting and, 339; Native American religions and, 4
"Nature" (Emerson, 1836), 343
Nauvoo, Illinois, 347
Navajos, 15
Navigation Acts (1660–1673), 56, 77
Navy, U.S.: Civil War and, 420, 422, 424; creation of Department of, 174. *See also* Impressment
Nebraska, and Kansas-Nebraska Controversy, 387
Neolin (Native American prophet), 188
Netherlands: Caribbean colonies and war with Spain, 38, 40; early colonization by, 22; English Separatists in, 42; New Amsterdam colony, 22, 51–52
Nevins, Allan, 407
New Amsterdam, 22, 51–52
New England: American Revolution and, 128–30; Burr conspiracy and secessionism, 202; Dominion of, 56, 57; early years of, 41–49; population in seventeenth century, 62; Shays' Rebellion and, 151–52; slavery in, 144; society of colonial, 79–82; Transcendentalists and, 342; triangular trade and, 77; War of 1812 and revolt of, 214; women and families in colonial period, 65. *See also* Massachusetts
New England Antislavery Society, 357
Newfoundland, 23, 98
New Hampshire: Massachusetts Bay Company and, 44; ratification of Constitution by, 162; as separate crown colony, 46, 56
New Harmony (Indiana), 344, *345i*
New Haven, Connecticut, 45
New Jersey: English settlement of, 52; ironworks in colonial period, 75; ratification of Constitution by, 162; women and voting rights, 140
New Jersey Plan, 158
New Left historians, 127
New Light revivalists, 85, 348
New Mexico: Americans and trade, 224, 373; Gadsden Purchase and, 386; Mexican-American War and, 376; Spanish empire and, 14–15; westward migration of Americans to, 373
New Netherland, 22
New Orleans: cholera epidemics in, 349; Civil War and, 426; cotton exchange of, *314i;* as French colony, 97; Jefferson administration and Louisiana Purchase, 198–99, 200; Reconstruction and race riots, 452; War of 1812 and Battle of, 213. *See also* Louisiana
Newport, Rhode Island, 82
Newspapers: abolitionism and, 357, 358; in Colonial America, 87; penny press and, 266–67, 365; rotary press and, 284–85. *See also* Journalism; Magazines
New York: American Revolution and, 131–32; canals and, 278–79; Dutch colonization of, 22, 51–52; English colonies in, 52, 57; mental hospitals and, 354; Oneida Community and, 345–46; population of colonial, 82; ratification of

Constitution by, 162; state politics in
1830s, 246; Tammany Society and, 176.
See also New York City
New York City: Central Park, 295; Jewish
community in colonial period, 84; population
growth in 1830s, 275. *See also* New York
New York Herald (newspaper), 285
New York *Sun* (newspaper), 266–67, 285
Nicholson, Capt. Francis, 57
Nicolls, Richard, 51
Nineteenth Amendment, of Constitution, A25
Ninth Amendment, of Constitution, A21
Non-Intercourse Act (1809), 206
North: agriculture in antebellum period,
303–8; American Revolution and, *129m;*
character of colonies, 58, 92; character of
compared to South in antebellum period,
334, 335; economy in colonial period,
74–75; free-soil ideology and, 390–91
—Civil War: mobilization of, 405, 408–14;
status at beginning of, 404
North, Lord, 109, 115, 118, 132
North, Simeon, 287
North America: early civilizations of, 3–5, 25;
Native American population before
European contact, 6, 7; northern outposts of
Spanish empire in, 14–15, 25; Seven Years'
War and struggle for control of, 96–102
North Carolina: Civil War and, 436;
ratification of Constitution by, 163;
Regulators and, 106; Restoration colonies
of, 50–51; Roanoke colony and, 23–24;
Scottish immigrants to, 71; secession of,
404; statehood and, 171
North Star (newspaper), 358
Northwest, Old: agriculture in antebellum
period, 304–7; American Revolution and
claims of states to, *145m;* Articles of
Confederation and, 147–49; national
sovereignty and, 170–71; Native Americans
and, 149–50; settlement of after War of
1812, 223; transportation routes and
settlement of, 279; westward migration
from, 369. *See also* Midwest; West
Northwest Ordinance of 1784, 147, *148m,* 149
Nova Scotia, 98, 101
Noyes, John Humphrey, 345–46
Nullification crisis, 250, 252–53
Nursing, and Civil War, 413–14

Oberlin College, 300
Ogden, Aaron, 234
Oglethorpe, Gen. James, 54–55
Ohio, 221
Ohio and Scioto Companies, 149
Ohio Valley, and French and Indian War,
98–102. *See also* Northwest, Old
Oklahoma, 255
"Old Light" traditionalists, and revivalism, 85
Onate, Don Juan de, 14
O'Neal, Peggy, 251
Oneida Community (New York), 345–46
Oneida tribe. *See* Iroquois Confederacy
Onís, Luis de, 228, 229
Onondaga tribe. *See* Iroquois Confederacy
Opechancanough (Powhatan), 33
Oral history, and Native Americans, 6. *See
also* Storytelling

"Orders in council," 204
Oregon: Canada and boundary dispute,
372–73; Spanish voyages of discovery, 11;
westward expansion and migration,
367–69
Oregon Trail, 369, *370m*
Osceola (Seminole chief), 256
Ostend Manifesto (1854), 385
Otis, James, 107
Ottawa tribe, 103
Overseers, and slavery, 323–24
Owen, Robert, 344, *345i*

Pacific Northwest, and Native American
cultures, 3. *See also* Oregon
Pacific Ocean, and Spanish voyages of
discovery, 11
Pacific Telegraph, 284
Pacifism, and abolitionism, 360
Paine, Thomas, 123–24
Painting, nationalism and romanticism in
American, 339
Pakenham, Sir Edward, 213
Palatinate, 70
Panama, Isthmus of, 11
Panics: of 1819, 230; of 1837, 264–65; of
1873, 466. *See also* Depressions
Paramilitary organizations, in post-
Reconstruction South, 465
Parliament, English: American Revolution
and, 116, 118; Charles I and dissolution of,
43, 49; Colonial America and, 95–96, 112
Patents, and inventions, 287–88
Paternalism, and slavery, 334
Paterson, William, 158
Patronage system, and Jackson
administration, 247
Patroons, and Dutch colonies, 52
Paxton Boys, 106
Peace Democrats, 409
Peace of Paris (1763), 101
Peale, Rembrandt, *194i*
"Peculiar institution," of slavery in
antebellum South, 321–28
Penn, William, 53
Pennsylvania: Civil War and, 432; German
immigration to, 71; Quaker colonies and,
52–54; slavery and, 144; state government
of, 142, 143; voting rights in 1830s, 245;
Whiskey Rebellion and, 170–71. *See also*
Philadelphia
Pennsylvania Dutch, 71
Penny press, 266–67, 285, 365
Pequot War (1637), 47, 48
Perkins School for the Blind (Boston), 353
Perry, Oliver Hazard, 210
"Personal liberty laws," 360
Peru, 2
Pessen, Edward, 249
Petersburg, Virginia, siege of, 423, 436–38
Philadelphia: American Revolution and, 131;
founding of, 53; population of colonial, 82;
population growth from 1840 to 1860, 275
Philip II, King of Spain, 23
Philippines, 11
Phillips, Ulrich B., 330
Philosophy, and Transcendentalism, 342–44
Photography, and Civil War, *417i*

Phrenology, 350–51
Pickens, Andrew, 134
Pidgin language, 332
Pierce, Franklin, 384–85, 387
Pike, Zebulon, 201–202, 226
Pilgrims. *See* Plymouth; Separatists
Pinakeshaw tribe, 234–35
Pinckney, Charles Cotesworth, 173, 195, 206
Pinckney, Thomas, 172
Pinckney's Treaty (1795), 172, 199
Pitcairn, Major Thomas, 120
Pitcher, Molly, 139
Pitt, William, 99, 100, 108
Pizarro, Francisco, 13
Plain folk, of antebellum South, 319–21
Plantations: early Virginia and tobacco cultivation, 31; Old Southwest and system of, 224; slavery in South and, 78–79, 323–24; white society of antebellum South and, 317–18, 319, 320–21
Plattsburgh, Battle of (1814), 212
Plessy v. Ferguson (1896), 475
Plows, 305
Plymouth, Massachusetts, 25, 41–43, 44
Pocahontas, 33
Poe, Edgar Allan, 341
Poetry, of antebellum South, 341. *See also* Literature
Political parties: Constitution and, 168–69; end of first system of, 227–28; legitimization of in 1830s, 245–46; revival of after 1816, 236–40; second party system and Jackson administration, 261–64. *See also* Democratic Party; Politics; Republican Party
Politics: American Revolution and, 152; in Colonial America, 90–91; emancipation and Civil War, 410–11; Grant administration and scandals, 463; Jacksonian era and rise of mass, 242–47; leadership and Civil War, 409–10; repression and Alien and Sedition Acts, 174–75; Van Buren administration and, 264–70. *See also* Elections, presidential; Government, federal; Political parties
Polk, James K.: Mexican-American War and, 374–76; sectionalism and territories, 378; westward expansion and, 372, 373, 374
Poll tax, 476
Polo, Marco, 8
Pontiac (Ottawa chief), 103
Poor Richard's Almanac (Franklin), 86
Pope, John, 430
Pope (Pueblo religious leader), 14
Popular culture, and nationalism, 240. *See also* Culture
Popular sovereignty, 378, 387, *389i*
Population: of Americas before European contact, 1, 2, 6–7, 25; of Cahokia, 3; California in 1850s, 380; of Colonial America, 60–67, 70–71; distribution of in 1996, *A2–A3m*; growth of European in fifteenth century, 8, 19; industrialization and growth of urban, 192; Industrial Revolution and changes in, 272–77; Native Americans and European diseases, 15, 25, 369; of New York in 1685, 52; slavery in antebellum South, 312, *313m*, 324; Spanish colonization of New Mexico and, 15; of

U.S., 1790–1996, A37; of Virginia colonies, 37; Westward expansion and increase in, 222–23
Port Hudson, Louisiana, 432
Port Royal (Carolinas), 50
Portugal, 9, 11, 18, 25
Pottawatomie Massacre (Kansas, 1855), 388
Poverty: in cities of colonial period, 82; in cities of 1850s, 295–96; class system of antebellum South and, 321; and motives for English colonization, 20; technological progress in colonial period and, 75–76
Powhatan Indians, 33–34
Predestination, doctrine of, 20, 53, 185
Presbyterian Church, 83, 138, 185–86
Presidency. *See* Elections, presidential; *specific presidents*
Preston, Capt. Thomas, 110
Prigg v. Pennsylvania (1842), 360
Primogeniture, English system of, 80
Princeton University, 88
Printing press, 86–87
Prisons: founding of Georgia and, 54–55; reform movements and, 354
Proclamation of 1763, 103–4
Progressive historians, 126, 248
Propaganda, and abolitionism, 361
Property rights: Supreme Court and Native Americans, 235; voting and, 142. *See also* Land ownership
Pro-slavery argument, 391–92. *See also* Anti-abolitionism
Prosser, Gabriel, 187, 327, 329
Protestant Reformation, 20
Public health, and growth of population in 1820s and 1830s, 273. *See also* Disease, epidemic; Health; Medicine
Publick Occurrences (newspaper), 87
Pueblos, 5, 14–15
Puerto Rico, 38
Puritans: Massachusetts Bay colony and, 43–44; Protestant Reformation and, 20, 21; society of colonial New England and, 79–82, 84; women and families, 65
Put-In Bay, Battle of (1813), 210

Quakers: American Revolution and, 137; education and, 88; English colonies and, 52–54; feminism and, 355; slavery and abolitionism, 144
Quebec, 22, 97, 101
Quebec Act (1774), 116
Queen Anne's War (1701–1713), 54, 98

Racism: class system of antebellum South, 321; Jim Crow laws, 475–77; legacy of Reconstruction and, 469; and origins of slavery, 68–69; pro-slavery argument and, 392
Railroads: Civil War and technology of war, 424; industrialization in New South and, 471–72; Industrial Revolution and early, 280–83; in North and South at start of Civil War, 404, 405; settlement of West and, 386; telegraph and, 284
Raleigh, Sir Walter, 23, 24
Ranchos, 14
Randall, James G., 407

Randolph, Edmund, 157, 164, 172
Randolph, John, 326
"Raven, The" (Poe, 1845), 341
Reconstruction: abandonment of, 465–69;
    education of African-Americans, 457–58;
    Grant administration and, 462–64;
    historical debate on nature of, 450–51;
    income and credits of African-Americans,
    459–60; Johnson and, 448–49; land
    ownership and tenant farmers, 458–59;
    legacy of, 441, 468–69, 477–79; plans for,
    446–47; Radical, 449, 452; state
    governments in South, 456–57
Redeemers, and New South, 470–71
Red Shirts, 465
Reform movements: characteristics of, 337;
    society and, 347–56, 362. See also
    Abolitionism
Regulators, 106
Rehabilitation, and reform movements, 353–54
Religion: African societies and, 18; cultural
    nationalism and, 185–88; Great Awakening
    and, 84–85; Jesuit missionaries, 97; in
    Maryland colonies, 36; Massachusetts Bay
    experiment and, 43–44, 46; Mormons,
    346–47; Native Americans and, 2, 4;
    patterns of in Colonial America, 83–84;
    political parties in 1830s and 1840s and,
    262–63; rural life and, 307; Shakers, 346;
    slavery and, 41, 79, 143, 329, 332; state
    constitutions and, 143; toleration in
    Colonial America, 36, 50, 83. See also
    Catholic Church; Islam; Protestant
    Reformation; Puritans
Remini, Robert V., 249
Removal, of Native Americans from
    Southeast, 253–58
Rendezvous, and fur trade in Far West, 225i
"Report on Manufactures" (Hamilton,
    1791), 166
Representation: American Revolution and,
    112–13; Constitutional Convention and, 158
Repression, Alien and Sedition Acts, 174–75
Republican Party: Civil War and, 411;
    depression of 1857 and, 393; diplomacy
    during Johnson and Grant administrations,
    464; emergence of, 236–37, 387; free-soil
    ideology and, 391; Hayes administration
    and, 468; Lincoln and election of 1860,
    397–98, 399; Reconstruction and, 446
Republicans and republicanism: and creation
    of state governments, 141–42;
    disagreements about nature of federal
    government, 165, 168–69; election of 1800
    and, 175–77
Reservations, and Native Americans, 354
Resistance: American Revolution and,
    113–14; Civil War in South and, 418; labor
    movement and, 294; slavery and, 41, 79,
    326–28
"Resistance to Civil Government" (Thoreau,
    1849), 343–44
Restoration, and English colonies, 49–55
Revere, Paul, 110i, 111, 119
Revisionist historians, 407, 451
Revivalism: cultural nationalism and, 185–88;
    reform movements of antebellum period
    and, 348

Revolutions, liberal and nationalist in Europe,
    385. See also American Revolution; French
    Revolution; Slave revolts
Rhode Island: Constitutional Convention
    and, 142; founding of, 45–46; Jews in
    colonial period, 84; King Philip's War and,
    48–49; statehood and, 171; voting rights in,
    244–45. See also New England
Rice, cultivation of in South, 51, 67, 71,
    73, 311
Richmond, Virginia, siege of, 423, 428, 429–30
Rifles, flintlock and matchlock, 47, 48
Riots: anti-abolitionism and, 359; British
    military and New York City, 100;
    conscription and Civil War in North, 409;
    food and Civil War in South, 418; Radical
    Reconstruction in South and, 452. See also
    Boston Massacre
Ripley, George, 344
Roads, and government funding for
    construction, 192, 221. See also
    Transportation; Turnpikes
Roanoke colony (Virginia), 23–24, 27
Rochambeau, Count de, 136
Rockingham, Marquis of, 108
Rocky Mountain Fur Company, 225, 226
Rogin, Michael, 249
Rolfe, John, 31, 33
Roman Catholics. See Catholic Church
Romanticism: antebellum culture and, 339;
    nationalism in American painting and, 339;
    reform movements and, 337
Rosecrans, William S., 428, 434
Roundheads, and English Civil War, 49
Royal African Company, 67
Royal Society of London, 89
Rubber industry, 287–88
Rum, and triangular trade, 77
Rural life: agriculture in antebellum North
    and, 307–8; geographic mobility in
    nineteenth century, 223; leisure in
    antebellum period and, 302; and white
    women in antebellum South, 318–19
Rush, Benjamin, 183, 184
Rush-Bagot agreement (1817), 215
Russia: purchase of Alaska from, 464;
    railroads and, 283; Siberia and Bering land
    bridge, 1

Sabotage, and resistance to slavery, 328
Sacajawea, 200–201
St. Augustine, Florida, 14, 25
St. Kitts, 40
St. Leger, Col. Barry, 131, 132
St. Louis, Missouri, 349
St. Mary's, Maryland, 36
Salem, Massachusetts, 81
Salt Lake City, Utah, 347
"Sambo" image, and resistance to slavery,
    327, 331
Sanford, John, 393
San Francisco, California, 380
San Ildefonso, Treaty of (1800), 198
San Jacinto, Battle of (1836), 367
Santa Anna, Gen. Antonio López de, 366–67
Santa Fe, New Mexico, 14, 377i
Santa Fe Trail, 224, 369, 370m
Saratoga, Battle of (1777), 132

Sauk tribe, 254
Savannah River (Georgia), 55
Saxton, Alexander, 249
Scalawags, 456
Scarlet Letter, The (Hawthorne, 1851), 344
Schlesinger, Arthur M., 126, 248
Science: in Colonial America, 89; cultural
  nationalism and, 183–84. *See also* Medicine;
  Technology
Scotch-Irish immigrants, 71
Scotland, 71
Scott, Dred, 393–94
Scott, Gen. Winfield, 255, 376, 384, 419
Scott, Thomas, 424
Scrooby, England, 41, 42
Secession: Civil War and, 401–4; War of 1812
  and discussion of in New England, 214
Second Amendment, of Constitution, A20
Second Battle of Bull Run (1862), 430
Second Great Awakening, 185–87
Sectionalism: crises of mid- to late-1850s,
  384–98; debate on territories and
  statehood in 1850s, 377–84; importance of
  controversies in 1850s, 398–99; Missouri
  Compromise and, 230–32. *See also*
  Nationalism
Sedition Act (1798), 174–75
Segregation, in New South, 476
Seigneuries, 22, 97
"Self-Reliance" (Emerson, 1841), 343
Seminole tribe, 228–29, 255–57
Seminole War, 229, 256
Semmelweis, Ignaz, 352
Seneca Falls Women's Convention (New
  York), 355
Seneca tribe. *See* Iroquois Confederacy
"Separation of powers," and Constitution,
  160–61
Separatists, 21, 41–43
Seven Days, Battle of the (1862), 429
Seventeenth Amendment, of Constitution,
  A24–A25
Seventh Amendment, of Constitution, A21
Seven Years' War, 96–102
Seward, William H., 383, 406, 421, 448, 464
Sewing machines, 288
Sexual abuse, and slavery, 325
Seymour, Horatio, 462
Shakers, 346
Shakespeare, William, 302
Sharecropping, 459, 473
Shattuch, Job, *151i*
Shaw, Robert Gould, 412
Shawnee tribe, 207–209
Shays, Daniel, 151–52
Shays' Rebellion, 151–52, 161
Shelburne, Lord, 136
Shenandoah (ship), 422
Sherman, William T., 435, 436, *438m*
Shiloh, Battle of (1862), 426
Shipbuilding: in Colonial America, 74; trade
  in 1840s and 1850s and, 289. *See also* Navy
Siberia, and Bering Strait land bridge, 1
Sierra Nevada, 380
Silbey, Joel, 407

Simms, William Gilmore, 342
Singer, Isaac, 288
Sixteenth Amendment, of Constitution, A24
Sixth Amendment, of Constitution, A21
Slater, Samuel, 189
Slater's Mill, *189i*
Slave codes, 70, 323, 418
Slave revolts: in American South, 79, 187,
  326, 327, 329, 391; in Caribbean, 40; Civil
  War in South and, 418; Nat Turner's, 326,
  327, 329, 391
Slavery: African societies and, 17–18;
  beginnings of in Colonial America, 33,
  66–67, 70; in Caribbean colonies, 40–41;
  Civil War and politics of emancipation,
  410–11, 439; Compromise of 1850 and,
  381–84; Confederate Army and, 416–17;
  Constitutional Convention and, 159;
  cotton production in antebellum South
  and, 190, 312–14; culture and, 329,
  332–34; and debate on causes of Civil War,
  406, 407; *Dred Scott* decision and, 393–94;
  historical debate on character of, 330–31;
  historical debate on origins of, 68–69;
  Kansas-Nebraska Controversy and, 387,
  394; Lincoln-Douglas debates and, 395;
  Missouri Compromise and, 230–32; as
  "peculiar institution" in antebellum South,
  321–28; percentage of southern whites
  owning, 317; plantation system in South
  and, 51, 78–79; political turmoil in Kansas
  and, 388–90, 394; population growth and,
  273; pro-slavery argument in South,
  391–92; sectionalism and territories,
  377–79, 386, 388–90, 394; Spanish empire
  and Native Americans, 16–17; state
  constitutions and, 143; white women in
  antebellum South and, 319. *See also*
  Abolitionism; Emancipation Proclamation;
  Slave codes; Slave revolts; Slave trade
Slave trade: Caribbean and, 41, 67, 77; *Creole*
  mutiny and, 269; end of, 273, 382; middle
  passage and, *66i*, 67; Portuguese and, 18.
  See also Slavery
Slidell, John, 374, 422
Smallpox, 13, 43, 89
Smith, Capt. John, 30, 33, 34, 35, 41, 43
Smith, Joseph, 346–47
Smith, Sydney, 338, 339
Smuggling, and American Revolution, 109
Social mobility, in antebellum period, 296–97
Society: American Revolution and, 127,
  137–41, 153; Civil War and South, 417–18;
  Colonial America and, 78–82; in early
  years of nineteenth century, 215–16; of
  European settlers in Caribbean, 41;
  Industrial Revolution and, 295–303;
  multiracial in West, 257; railroads and,
  281–82; reform movements in antebellum
  period and, 347–56, 362; slavery and
  development of African-American, 322;
  sub-Saharan Africa and, 17–18; white in
  antebellum South, 317–21
Society of Friends. *See* Quakers
Sons of Liberty, 108

South: American Revolution and, 133–36; beginnings of slavery in colonial, 67; character of colonies, 58, 92; character of compared to antebellum North, 334–35; cotton production in, 189–90, 310–17; economy of antebellum and, 310–17; economy of colonial and, 71, 73; education and, 319, 320, 353; free-soil ideology and, 390–91; literature of antebellum period in, 341–42; "peculiar institution" of slavery, 321–28; plantation system and slavery, 78–79; pro-slavery argument and, 391–92; urban growth from 1840 to 1860, 275; voting rights in 1830s and, 245; white society in antebellum period and, 317–21
—Civil War: mobilization of, 414–18; secession crisis and, 401–404; status of at beginning, 404; status of at end, 443–44
—New: African-Americans and education, 473–75; Democratic Party and, 469; industrialization and, 471–73; Redeemers and, 470–71; tenant farmers and sharecroppers, 473
—Reconstruction: abandonment of, 465–69; education of African-Americans, 457–58; Grant administration and, 462–64; incomes and credit of African-Americans, 459–60; Johnson and, 448–49; legacy of, 468–69, 477–79; plans for, 446–47l; postwar concepts of freedom, 444–46; Radical, 449, 452; state governments and, 456–57
South America: early civilizations and, 2, 25; Spanish colonial empire and, 14, 25. See also Brazil; Latin America
South Carolina: Civil War and, 436; nullification doctrine and, 250, 252; Restoration colonies of, 50–51; rice production and, 71, 73; secession of, 401–2; slavery and, 67, 70. See also Charleston, South Carolina
Southwest: and expansionism in antebellum period, 373–74, 378m; and Spanish empire, 14 See also California; New Mexico; Texas
Sovereignty: American Revolution and, 113; Constitutional Convention and, 160; federal government and establishment of national, 169–72; Supreme Court and Native Americans, 235
Spain: Caribbean colonies and, 38–40; Cuba and, 385; empire in New World, 11, 12m, 25; Florida and, 54, 147, 228, 229; Latin American revolutions and Monroe Doctrine, 236; northern outposts of empire, 14–15; Pinckney's Treaty of 1795, 172; U.S. treaty with in 1786, 147; voyages of discovery and, 9, 11
Spanish Armada, 23
Specie Resumption Act (1875), 464
Species circular, 265
Spiritual music, 332
Spoils system, 247
Sporting events, 302–3. See also Horses and horse racing
Spotsylvania Court House, Battle of, 435–36
Spurzheim, Johann, 350i

Squatter sovereignty, 389i
Stamp Act (1765), 87, 106, 107
Stampp, Kenneth, 330, 451
Standish, Miles, 47
Stanton, Edwin M., 454, 455
Stanton, Elizabeth Cady, 355, 414
"Star-Spangled Banner, The," 212
Starving time, and Jamestown, 31
States: American Revolution and governments of, 141–44; claims of to western lands, 145m; Cohen v. Virginia and rights of, 233; Compromise of 1850 and slavery, 382m; Confederate government and rights of, 415, 416; Constitutional Congress and representation, 158; constitutions of, 142–43, 394, 447; Missouri Compromise and, 230–32; voting reforms in 1830s and, 244–45. See also specific states
Steam power: industrialism and, 191; railroads and, 280
Steamships, 191–92, 221, 222i
Steel industry, 471. See also Ironworks
Stephens, Alexander H., 415, 449
Steuben, Baron von, 125
Stevens, John, 280
Stevens, Thaddeus, 410, 446
Stono Rebellion (1739), 79
Story, Joseph, 242–43
Storytelling, and African-Americans, 333
Stowe, Harriet Beecher, 355, 361, 391
Stuyvesant, Peter, 51
Submarines, 424
Subsistence farming, and plain folk of antebellum South, 319
Subtreasury system, 265
Sugar Act of 1764, 104, 106, 108
Sugar plantations, 18, 40, 77, 311
Suicide, and resistance to slavery, 328
Sullivan, Gen. John, 132
Sumner, Charles, 388, 390, 410, 446
Sumter, Thomas, 134
Supreme Court: abolitionism and, 360; civil rights in New South and, 475, 476; Constitution and, 164; Dred Scott decision and, 393–94; Jackson administration and, 260; Jefferson administration and, 197–198; Marshall as Chief Justice of, 232–34; Native Americans and, 234–35, 255; Reconstruction and, 454–55
Supreme Order of the Star-Spangled Banner, 276–77
Susan Constant (ship), 28
Sutter, John, 379

Talleyrand, Prince, 173
Tallmadge, James, Jr., 230–31
Tamerlane and Other Poems (Poe, 1827), 341
Tammany Society, 176
Taney, Roger B., 259, 260, 393–94
Tariffs: Adams administration and, 238–39; Federalists and, 166, 168; nullification crisis and, 250; protectionism after War of 1812, 220
Taverns, and revolutionary culture, 113–14

Taxation: British empire and American colonies, 104, 106; Civil War and income tax, 408, 416; Continental Congress and war debt, 151–52; Federalists and, 166, 168; Jefferson administration and, 195–96; Whiskey Rebellion and, 170–71

Taylor, Zachary: Compromise of 1850 and, 383; election of 1848 and, 379; Mexican-American War and, 373, 374; slavery and sectionalism, 381

Tea Act of 1773, 115–16

Technology: in Colonial America, 75–76, 86–87; industrialism and, 188–91; Industrial Revolution and advances in, 286–88; Native Americans and agricultural, 34–35; of war, 47, 48, 423–24

Tecumseh (Shawnee chief), 206, 208–9, 215

Tejanos, 367

Telegraph, 283–84, 424

Temperance movement, *349i*

Tenant farmers, and agriculture in South, 458–59, 473

Tennessee: Civil War and, 426, 428, 434; Fourteenth Amendment and, 452, 454; secession of, 404; statehood and, 171, 452

Tenochtitlán, 2, 13. *See also* Mexico City

Tenskwatawa (Shawnee prophet), 207–208

Tenth Amendment, of Constitution, A22

Tenure of Office Act (1867), 454, 455

Texas: Adams-Onís Treaty of 1819 and, 229; secession of, 401–402; settlement of Americans in, 366–67, 372; statehood and, 373. *See also* Mexican-American War

Textile industry: Civil War and diplomatic relations with England and France, 404, 421–22; economy of antebellum South and, 315; emergence of factory system and, 286; growth of after War of 1812, 219–20; labor supply and, 290–91; in New South, 471. *See also* Cotton industry

Thames, Battle of (1813), 210

Thanksgiving, 43

Theater, and society in antebellum period, 302

Theocracy, and Puritan colonies, 44

Third Amendment, of Constitution, A20–A21

Thirteenth Amendment, of Constitution, 411, 439, A23

Thomas, Jesse B., 232

Thoreau, Henry David, 343–44

Threshers, 306

Tilden, 466–67

Timber industry, 305

Timbuktu, 17

Tippecanoe, Battle of (1811), 208

Tobacco: industrialization in New South, 471; slavery and plantation system, 78, 312; southern economy in colonial period, 71, 73; Virginia colonies and, 31–32

Toleware, *293i*

Toll roads, 192

Torpedoes, 424

Town meeting, 80

Towns, in colonial New England, 79–82

Townshend, Charles, 108–9

Townships, and grid system, 147, *148m*, 149

Trade: African societies and, 17; American

Revolution and, 141; California and maritime, 373; China and, 269; cotton in antebellum period, 312; economy of antebellum South and, 314–15; English regulation of colonial, 56, 104, 106; production and gross national product, 1790–1996, A39; Spanish routes in Caribbean, *39m*. *See also* Commerce; Fur Trade; Slave trade

Trafalgar, Battle of (1805), 204

Trail of Tears (1830–1838), 255

Transatlantic cable, and telegraph, 284

Transcendentalists, 342–44

Transcontinental railroad, 386, 405

Transportation: and economic growth after War of 1812, 221; economy of antebellum South and, 315; industrialization and innovations in, 191–92; Industrial Revolution and, 277–83; North and South at start of Civil War, 404. *See also* Railroads

Trent affair (1861), 422

Triangular trade, 76–77

Tripoli, 196

Trist, Nicholas, 376

Tubman, Harriet, *328i*

Tucker, Beverly, 342

Turner, Frederick Jackson, 248

Turner, Nat, 326, 327, 329, 391

Turnpikes, 192, 221

Tuskegee Institute, 474

Twain, Mark, 342

Twelfth Amendment, to Constitution, 173, 237, A22–A23

Twentieth Amendment, of Constitution, A25–A26

Twenty-eighth Amendment, of Constitution, A28

Twenty-fifth Amendment, of Constitution, A28–A29

Twenty-first Amendment, of Constitution, A26–A27

Twenty-fourth Amendment, of Constitution, A28

Twenty-second Amendment, of Constitution, A27

Twenty-seventh Amendment, of Constitution, A29

Twenty-sixth Amendment, of Constitution, A29

Twenty-third Amendment, of Constitution, A27

Tyler, John, 268, 367, 372

Uncle Tom's Cabin (Stowe, 1852), 361, 391, 399

Underground railroad, 327

Union Army, 408–9, 411–12

Union Pacific Railroad Company, 405

Union Party, 409–10

Unions and unionization: artisan traditions and origins of, 294; Civil War and, 413

Unitarianism and universalism, 185

United States: distribution of population in 1996, *A2 – A3m*; employment statistics, 1870–1994, A38; population from 1790 to 1996, A37; territorial expansion, 1783–1898, *A4m*

United States Military Academy (West Point), 196
United States Military Telegraph Corps, 424
United States Sanitary Commission, 413, *414i*
Universities. *See* Colleges and universities
University of Pennsylvania, 89, 183
Urban life: immigration and population growth in 1840s and 1850s, 275–76; poverty and wealth, 295–96. *See also* Cities
Utah, 347
Utopian movements, 344–46
Utrecht, Treaty of (1713), 98

Valley campaign of 1862, 428
Values: educational reform and, 353–54; industrial development in antebellum South and, 316; planter class of antebellum South and, 318. *See also* Morality
Van Buren, Martin: election of 1836 and, 263–64; election of 1844 and, 372; election of 1848 and, 379; nullification controversy and, 250–51; as president, 265; state politics in New York and, 246; Texas and, 367
Vance, Zebulon M., 415
Vergennes, Count de, 132, 133, 136
Verger, Jean Baptist de, *128i*
Vesey, Denmark, 327, 329
Vespucci, Amerigo, 11
Vicksburg, Mississippi, siege of, 423, 432, *433m*
Vikings, 8
Virginia: Bacon's Rebellion and, 36–38; Civil War and, 428–30, *437m*; early English settlements in, 23, 28–35; government of during Civil War, 414; ratification of Constitution by, 162; religious toleration and, 143; secession of, 404. *See also* Jamestown
Virginia and Kentucky Resolutions, 175
Virginia Company, 30, 32, 34, 42
Virginia Dynasty, and presidency, 227
Virginia Plan, 157–59, 160
Virginia Resolves (1765), 107
Voodoo, 329
Voting rights: civil rights in New South and, 475–76; Fourteenth Amendment and African-Americans, 452, 454; Jackson era and expansion of, 243–45; property requirements and, 142; women and, 140. *See also* Civil rights

Wabash River, Battle of (1791), 150
Wade, Benjamin E., 410, 419
Wade-Davis Bill (1864), 446–47
Wagon trains, 369–71
Walden (Thoreau, 1854), 343
Waltham system, 291
Wampanoag tribe, 47
Wang Hya, Treaty of (1844), 269
War, technology of: Civil War and, 423–24; Pequot and King Philip's Wars and, 47–49
War Hawks, 209
War of 1812, 203–15
Warren, John, 351

Washington, Booker T., 474–75
Washington, George: American Revolution and, 125, 130, 131, 136; Constitutional Convention and, 157; death of, 184; French and Indian War and, 99; on political parties, 168; as president, 163–64, 165, 169; slavery and, 144
Washington, Treaty of (1871), 464
Washington D.C.: building of, 193–95; debate on location of national capital, 167; First Battle of Bull Run and, 425; inauguration of Monroe and, *227i*; slavery in, 381, 410; War of 1812 and burning of capital, 212, *213i*
"Water cure," and health spas, 349
Wayne, Gen. Anthony, 150
Wealth, Industrial Revolution and distribution of, 295
Webster, Daniel: Bank of United States and, 234, 259; Compromise of 1850 and, 383; *Dartmouth College v. Woodward* and, 232; election of 1836 and, 264; nullification controversy and debate with Haynes, 252; Tyler administration and, 268; War of 1812 and, 214; Whig Party and, 263
Webster, Noah, 184
Webster-Ashburton Treaty (1842), 269
Wells, Ida B., 477
Wesley, John and Charles, 85
West: East and images of, 226; expansionism and migration in antebellum period, 364–71; fur trade in Far West, 224–26; Jefferson administration and exploration of, 200–202; literature and, 340–41; multiracial societies of, 257; Native Americans cultures of Far West, 3; population movement after War of 1812, 222–24; railroads and settlement of, 386. *See also* Northwest; Southwest
Western theater, of Civil War: military operations in 1862, 426–28; Union Navy and, 420
Western Union Telegraph Company, 284
West Indies: and commerce with American colonies, 76, 77; English colonies in, 38–41; Seven Years' War and, 99; slave trade and, 67. *See also* Caribbean
West Jersey, 52
West Virginia, and statehood, 425
Wheelwright, John, 46
Whig Party: diplomacy and, 269–70; election of 1840 and, 267–68; emergence of, 246; Jackson administration and, 261–64; Kansas-Nebraska Controversy and, 387; Tyler administration and, 268
Whirling Thunder (Sauk tribe), *254i*
Whiskey Rebellion (1794), 170–71
Whiskey ring scandal, 463
White, Hugh Lawson, 264
White, John, *4i*, 24
Whitefield, George, 85
White Leagues, 465
Whitman, Walt, 341
Whitney, Eli, 189–91, 287
Wilderness, Battle of (1863), 431, 435
Wilentz, Sean, 249

Wilkes, Charles, 422
Wilkie, William, *298i*
Wilkinson, Gen. James, 200, 202, 203
William and Mary College, 88
William of Orange, King of England, 57
Williams, Roger, 45–46, 83
Wilmot, David, 377
Wilmot Proviso (1846), 377–78, 379
Wilson's Creek, Battle of (1861), 425
Winchester, Oliver, 423
Winthrop, John, 44
Witchcraft, 80–82
Wolfe, James, 101
Women: African societies and, 18; African-
American family and, 460–61; American
Revolution and, 115, 116, 139–40; Civil
War and, 413–14, 418; in Colonial America,
33, 63, 64–65; cult of domesticity and,
300–301; education for, 182, 319; feminism,
355–56; fur trade in Far West and, 225; as
indentured servants, 61, 64; labor and textile
industry, *290i*, 291–92; labor in New South
and, 472; literacy rates in colonies, 86;
middle class and, 297, 301; midwifery and
medicine, 184; Native Americans and, 5;
Quakers and, 53; reform movements and,
347; religious revivalism and, 186; rural life
and, 307–8; Shaker society, 346; slavery and,
324, 325, 333–34; unions and, 294;

westward migration and, 370, 371; white
society in antebellum South, 318–19, 325;
witchcraft accusations and, 82. *See also*
Gender roles; Women's rights movement
Women's rights movement: American
Revolution and, 139–40; rise of feminism
in antebellum period, 355–56. *See also*
Voting rights
Wood, Gordon, 127
Wood, Peter, 69
Woodland cultures, 3
Wool trade, 19, 20
Worcester v. Georgia (1832), 235, 255
Work, and Industrial Revolution, 289–94. *See
also* Labor; Unions and unionization
Working class: and social mobility in
antebellum period, 296; women and
employment, 301. *See also* Class,
socioeconomic

XYZ Affair, 173–74

Yale University, 88
Yorktown, British surrender at (1781), 136
Young, Brigham, 347
Young America, and Democratic Party,
385–86

Zenger, John Peter, 91

THE
UNFINISHED
NATION

A CONCISE
HISTORY OF
THE AMERICAN
PEOPLE

ALAN BRINKLEY

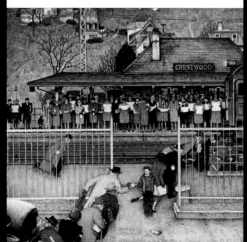

16,000–14,000 B.C.
- Asians migrate to North America

1492
- Columbus discovers America

1502
- African slaves arrive in Spanish America

1518–1530
- Smallpox ravages Indians

1608
- French establish Quebec

1609
- Spanish found Santa Fe

1619
- First African workers in Virginia

1620
- Pilgrims found Plymouth Colony

1624
- Dutch settle Manhattan

1630
- Puritans establish Massachusetts Bay Colony

1634
- Maryland founded

1636
- Roger Williams founds Rhode Island

1637
- Pequot War

1663
- Carolina chartered

1664
- English capture New Netherlands

1675
- King Phillip's War

1676
- Bacon's Rebellion

1681
- Pennsylvania chartered

1692
- Salem witchcraft trials

1732
- Georgia chartered

1734
- Great Awakening begins

1754
- Beginning of French and Indian War

1756
- Seven Years' War begins

1763
- Peace of Paris
- Proclamation of 1763

1764
- Sugar Act

1765
- Stamp Act

1767
- Townshend Duties

1770
- Boston Massacre
- Most Townshend Duties repealed

1773
- Tea Act, Boston Tea Party

1774
- First Continental Congress in Philadelphia

1775
- Battles of Lexington and Concord
- American Revolution begins
- Second Continental Congress
- Washington commands American forces

1776
- Paine's *Common Sense*
- Declaration of Independence

1777
- Articles of Confederation adopted
- British defeat at Saratoga

1781
- Articles of Confederation ratified
- Cornwallis surrenders at Yorktown

1783
- Treaty of Paris

1786
- Shays's Rebellion

1787
- Northwest Ordinance
- Constitutional Convention; Constitution adopted

1787–1788
- States ratify Constitution

1789
- Washington becomes first president
- Bill of Rights adopted
- French Revolution

1791
- First Bank of U.S. chartered

1793
- Eli Whitney invents cotton gin

1796
- John Adams elected president

1797
- Alien and Sedition Acts

1800
- Jefferson elected president
- U.S. capital moves to Washington

1801
- Marshall chief justice of Supreme Court

1803
- Louisiana Purchase
- *Marbury* v. *Madison*

1804–1806
- Lewis and Clark expedition

1807
- Embargo

1808
- Madison elected president
- Slave importation banned

1812
- U.S. d[e]... war on [Great] Britain

1814
- Hartfo[rd] Conven[tion]
- Treaty [of] Ghent

1815
- Battle [of New] Orleans
- U.S. ta[kes] wester[n land] from Ind[ians]

1816
- Secon[d Bank] of U.S.
- Monro[e] elected preside[nt]

1817–1[8]
- Erie C[anal] constru[cted]

1820
- Misso[uri] Compro[mise]

1822
- Denm[ark] Vesey's conspira[cy]

1823
- Monro[e] Doctrine

1824
- John [Q.] Adams [elected] preside[nt]

1828
- Jacks[on] elected preside[nt]

TIME LINE

oviet
ession

War II

a First
ee

ase

attacks
rbor
ters
ar II

of

se
ns

founded

vade
dy

velt
man
s
t
ny
rs
ops
ombs
hima,
ki

rs
nd

ices
Nations

1947
- Truman Doctrine
- Marshall Plan proposed
- Levittown construction begins

1948
- Berlin blockade
- Hiss case begins

1949
- NATO established
- Soviet Union explodes A-bomb

1950
- Korean War begins
- McCarthy's anticommunism campaign begins

1952
- Eisenhower elected president

1953
- Korean War ends

1954
- *Brown* v. *Board of Education*
- Army-McCarthy hearings

1955
- Montgomery bus boycott

1957
- *Sputnik* launched
- Little Rock desegregation crisis

1959
- Castro seizes power in Cuba

1960
- U-2 incident
- Kennedy elected president

1961
- First American in space
- Freedom rides
- Bay of Pigs
- Berlin Wall erected

1962
- Cuban missile crisis

1963
- March on Washington
- Kennedy assassinated; Johnson becomes president

1964
- Johnson launches war on poverty
- Civil Rights Act
- Gulf of Tonkin resolution

1965
- Malcolm X assassinated
- Voting Rights Act
- U.S. troops in Vietnam

1966
- National Organization for Women founded

1968
- Tet offensive
- Martin Luther King, Jr. assassinated
- Robert Kennedy assassinated
- Nixon elected president

1969
- Americans land on moon

1970
- Cambodian incursion

1972
- Nixon visits China
- SALT I
- Watergate burglary

1973
- U.S. withdraws from Vietnam
- Arab oil embargo
- Supreme Court decides *Roe* v. *Wade*

1974
- Nixon resigns; Ford becomes president
- Ford pardons Nixon

1976
- Carter elected president

1977
- Apple introduces first personal computer

1978-1979
- Camp David accords
- American hostages in Iran
- Soviet Union invades Afghanistan
- U.S. and China restore relations

1980
- Reagan elected president

1981
- American hostages in Iran released
- AIDS first reported in U.S.

1986
- Iran-contra scandal revealed

1988
- Bush elected president

1989
- Berlin Wall dismantled
- Communist regimes collapse

1991
- Collapse of Soviet regime
- Persian Gulf War

1992
- Los Angeles race riots
- Clinton elected president

1995
- O. J. Simpson trial

1998
- Clinton impeached by House

1999
- Clinton aquitted by Senate

Seattle
Olympia
WASHINGTON
CASCADE MTS.
Portland
Salem
OREGON
Columbia R.

Great Falls
Helena
MONTANA
Missouri R.
ROCKY MOUNTAINS

NORTH

IDAHO
Boise
Snake R.

WYOMING
BLACK HILLS
Pierre

SOUTH

Sacramento R.
Sacramento
SIERRA NEVADA
San Francisco
San Joaquin R.

Carson City
NEVADA

Great Salt L.
Salt Lake City
UTAH

Cheyenne

NEBR

Denver
COLORADO

L. W

CALIFORNIA
Las Vegas
Colorado R.

Los Angeles
San Diego

ARIZONA
Phoenix

Santa Fe
Albuquerque

NEW MEXICO

Arkansas R.

PACIFIC OCEAN

MEXICO

Rio Grande

TEX

HAWAII
Kauai
Niihau
Oahu
Honolulu
Molokai
Lanai
Maui
Kaho'olawe
Hawaii
0   75   150 Miles
0   75   150 Kilometers
PACIFIC OCEAN

SOVIET UNION
Bering Strait

ARCTIC OCEAN
BROOKS RANGE
Yukon R.
ALASKA

CANADA

ALASKA RANGE
Anchorage

BERING SEA

0   200   400 Miles
0   200   400 Kilometers

Juneau

MAINE

★Augusta

NEW
HAMPSHIRE
•Portland

Concord
★ •Manchester

•Boston
MASSACHUSETTS
Providence

★ RHODE
Hartford ISLAND
CONNECTICUT

w York
ark
on

Y

RE

YLAND

*ATLANTIC
OCEAN*

Land Elevation

Feet		Meters
10,000		3,000
7,000		2,000
3,000		1,000
700		200
Level) 0		0 (Sea Level)
ea Level		Below Sea Level

150   300 Miles
150   300 Kilometers

AHAMAS

For more helpful study tools, visit

our Online Learning Center at

www.mhhe.com/unfinishednation

YOU'LL FIND

materials to help you review

chapter content

interactive maps with exercises

quizzes for every chapter

links to interesting history sites,

organized by chapter and much

more!